Christianizing Homer

Christianizing Homer

The Odyssey, Plato, and
The Acts of Andrew

Dennis Ronald MacDonald

New York   Oxford
OXFORD UNIVERSITY PRESS
1994

Oxford University Press

Oxford   New York   Toronto
Delhi   Bombay   Calcutta   Madras   Karachi
Kuala Lumpur   Singapore   Hong Kong   Tokyo
Nairobi   Dar es Salaam   Cape Town
Melbourne   Auckland   Madrid

and associated companies in
Berlin   Ibadan

Published by Oxford University Press, Inc.
200 Madison Avenue, New York, New York 10016

Oxford is a registered trademark of Oxford University Press, Inc.

Library of Congress Cataloging-in-Publication Data
MacDonald, Dennis Ronald, 1948–
Christianizing Homer : the Odyssey, Plato, and the Acts of Andrew
Dennis Ronald MacDonald.
p.   cm.   Includes bibliographical references and index.
ISBN 0-19-508722-4
1. Acts of Andrew—Criticism, interpretation, etc.
2. Homer. Odyssey.
3. Plato—Influence.
4. Socrates—Influence.
5. Mythology, Greek—Controversial literature.
6. Apologetics—Early church, ca. 30–600.
I. Title.
BS2880.A372M34   1994
229'.92—dc20   93-5653

2 4 6 8 9 7 5 3 1

Printed in the United States of America
on acid-free paper

For Katya and Julian

Such wondrous, fine, fantastic tales
Of dragons, gypsies, queens, and whales
And treasure isles, and distant shores
Where smugglers rowed with muffled oars,
And pirates wearing purple pants,
And sailing ships and elephants,
And cannibals crouching 'round the pot,
Stirring away at something hot.
(It smells so good, what can it be?
Good gracious, it's Penelope.)
. . . .
Oh, books, what books they used to know,
Those children living long ago!

Song of the Oompa-Loompas, in Roald Dahl,
Charlie and the Chocolate Factory

Preface

Thanks to a grant from the National Endowment for the Humanities and another from the Association of Theological Schools, I spent much of the summer of 1983 at the Folklore Institute of Indiana University, Bloomington, looking for evidence of folklore lurking behind *The Acts of Andrew*. My first book, *The Legend and the Apostle: The Battle for Paul in Story and Canon*, argued that *The Acts of Paul* took much of its content from legends told by ascetic Christians, especially by women, in second-century Asia Minor. I had hoped that a similar analysis of the textual remains of *The Acts of Andrew* might disclose an oral tradition about the apostle Andrew. I brought to Bloomington photocopies of the best texts then available and attempted to identify in them possible oral traditions. The longer I worked at this task, the more I became convinced that, unlike *The Acts of Paul*, *The Acts of Andrew* was a purely literary composition with no access to traditions about Andrew apart from the sparse information available in the New Testament.

Why, then, I asked myself, did the author compose this huge work, the longest of the apocryphal Acts? More important, where did the author derive his narrative inspiration for these amazing tales, many of which have no obvious analogies in contemporary Jewish or Christian literature? These questions plagued me and remained unanswered for much of my time at the institute. The evening before I was to return to Colorado, I treated myself to a long walk when—*eureka!*—it suddenly occurred to me that many of the stories were strangely reminiscent of Homer's *Odyssey*. If the author wrote the *Acts* as a Christian *Odyssey*, it might account for its length, its interests in the sea, shipwrecks, pirates, cannibals, demons, and the very selection of Andrew as the Christian hero. After all, Andrew was an erstwhile fisherman whose name meant 'manliness' (ἀνδρεία). The next morning, as soon as the university bookstore opened, I bought a copy of Fitzgerald's translation of *The Odyssey*, and, unknown to the highway patrols of five states, I read the entire epic while driving home. The edges of the paperback folded back into the steering wheel so that I had only to turn the pages and yo-yo my eyes a few inches between text and road. That single, bumpy reading of Homer convinced me that the author of *The Acts of Andrew* had indeed tried to Christianize *The Odyssey*.

In 1983 no reliable text of *The Acts of Andrew* existed, so my first task was to collect, edit, and translate the available manuscript evidence. Two years and three hundred pages later I learned that Jean-Marc Prieur was preparing an edition of the *Acts* for Series Apocryphorum of Corpus Christianorum. Our subsequent correspondence revealed that, despite nearly identical reconstructions of some sections, he and I differed radically in others. He published his edition in 1989; mine appeared in 1990. Since then, I have devoted most of my research to the present volume, in which I attempt to articulate the insight that first enthralled me a decade ago.

This study argues for a consistent reading of the text against Homer and, to a lesser degree, Euripides and Plato, but this focus cannot account for all of its content. *The Acts of Andrew* is a marvelously rich document whose treasures for understanding Christian Platonism, asceticism, apologetics, and poetics have scarcely been mined. For this reason, I strongly encourage readers to keep a copy of my edition handy for reference, so that they can both gain a fuller appreciation of the text and test my reading against their own.

This project would have been impossible without the generous support of the Iliff School of Theology. I hesitate to name individuals who contributed to this research lest I overlook someone, but a few people require special thanks. Over the years I have been blessed with several student assistants who brought their considerable talents and efforts to bear on this book. Rebecca Kantor, Linda Seracuse, David Gould, Beth Mae Emerich, Yoseop Ra, and Larry Altepeter proofread, typed, searched through bibliographies, and filled out a small tree's worth of interlibrary loan request forms, freeing me from necessary drudgery so that I could dally with the texts. In the final stages of my work, Richard I. Pervo carefully read the manuscript and provided many valuable suggestions; the endnotes are much the richer for his erudition. As always, my wife, Diane, endured my obsessions with good humor, patience, and feigned interest. Most of all I must thank my children, Katya and Julian, for not overly resenting my frequent absences when following my Muse. To them I dedicate this book, less out of paternal guilt than out of hope that they, like the author of *The Acts of Andrew*, will learn to transmythologize their world through the myth we Christians call the Gospel.

Denver, Col.   D.R.M.
July 1993

Contents

Abbreviations

AAA	*Acta apostolorum apocrypha* (Lipsius and Bonnet)
AAMt	*The Acts of Andrew and Matthias in the City of the Cannibals* (MacDonald, *Acts of Andrew,* 70–169)
ACS	*American Classical Studies*
AJ	*The Acts of John* (Junod and Kaestli, *Acta Iohannis,* 160–315)
AJPr	*The Acts of John by Prochorus* (Zahn, *Acta Joannis,* 1–252)
ANF	The Ante-Nicene Fathers
ANRW	*Aufstieg und Niedergang der römischen Welt*
APe	*The Acts of Peter* (*AAA* 1:45–103)
APeA	*The Acts of Peter and Andrew* (*AAA* 2.1:117–27)
APh	*The Acts of Philip* (*AAA* 2.2:1–98)
ApocPe	*The Apocalypse of Peter*
ATh	*The Acts of Thomas* (*AAA* 2.2:99–291)
AV	*Actus Vercellenses* (a Latin translation of *The Acts of Peter, AAA* 1:45–103)
AXP	*The Acts of Xanthippe and Polyxena* (James, *Apocrypha anecdota* 2.3:58–85)
BZNW	Beihefte zur Zeitschrift für die neutestamentliche Wissenschaft
CA	Christian Apocrypha
CCSA	Corpus Christianorum. Series Apocryphorum
CCSL	Corpus Christianorum. Series Latina
CF	*Classical Folia*
CSEL	Corpus scriptorum ecclesiasticorum latinorum
DACL	*Dictionnaire d'archéologie chrétienne et de liturgie*
DHGE	*Dictionnaire d'histoire et de géographie ecclésiastique*
DOS	Dumbarton Oaks Studies
DRund	*Deutsche Rundschau*
DS	*Dictionnaire de spiritualité*
E	Epiphanius the Monk, *The Life of Andrew* (*PG* 120:216–60)
ET	English translation
ÉtClass	*Les Études classiques*
Eth	Ethiopic version of *The Apocalypse of Peter*
FC	Fathers of the Church
FF	*Forschungen und Fortschritte*
FRLANT	Forschungen zur Religion und Literatur des Alten und Neuen Testaments
G&R	*Greece and Rome*

GE	Gregory of Tours, epitome of *The Acts of Andrew* (Bonnet, *Liber de miraculis*, 821–46, and Prieur, *Acta Andreae*, 555–631)
GrOrthTR	*Greek Orthodox Theological Review*
GRR	Graeco-Roman Religion
Hermes	Hermes. Zeitschrift für klassische Philologie
HSCP	*Harvard Studies in Classical Philology*
HTR	*Harvard Theological Review*
JAC	*Jahrbuch für Antike und Christentum*
JTS	*Journal of Theological Studies*
L	*Laudatio* (Bonnet, *Acta Andreae*, 3–44)
LIMC	*Lexicon iconographicum mythologiae classicae*
LSJ	Liddell-Scott-Jones, *Greek-English Lexicon*
LXX	Septuagint
M	*Martyrium prius* (Prieur, *Acta Andreae*, 675–703)
MLR	*Modern Language Review*
MMt	*The Martyrdom of Matthew* (AAA 2.1:217–62)
NHL	*Nag Hammadi Library* (Robinson, 2d edition)
NovT	*Novum Testamentum*
NovTSup	Novum Testamentum, Supplements
NPNF	Nicene and Post-Nicene Fathers
NTAbh	Neutestamentliche Abhandlungen
NTApoc	*New Testament Apocrypha* (Hennecke and Schneemelcher)
P	*Paris graecus 1313* (unpublished manuscript of the *AAMt*)
PCU 1	*Papyrus Coptic Utrecht 1* (Prieur, *Acta Andreae*, 656–71)
PG	*Patrologia Graeca* (J. P. Migne)
PL	*Patrologia Latina* (J. P. Migne)
PO	*Patrologia orientalis*
PTA	Papyrologische Texte und Abhandlungen
P-W	Pauly-Wissowa, *Real-Encyclopädie der classischen Altertumswissenschaft*
RAC	*Reallexikon für Antike und Christentum*
RDM	*Revue des deux mondes*
REA	*Revue des études anciennes*
RivAC	*Rivista di archeologia cristiana*
RevScRel	*Revue des sciences religieuses*
RHR	*Revue de l'histoire des religions*
RMP	*Rheinisches Museum für Philologie*
RPL	*Revue philosophique de Louvain*
RTHP	Recueil de travaux d'histoire et de philologie
SBLDS	Society of Biblical Literature Dissertation Series
StudWR	Studies in Women and Religion
TDNT	*Theological Dictionary of the New Testament* (Kittel)

TT	Texts and Translations
TU	Texte und Untersuchungen zur Geschichte der altchristlichen Literatur
VC	*Vigiliae christianae*
ZPE	*Zeitschrift für Papyrologie und Epigraphik*
ZKT	*Zeitschrift für katholische Theologie*
ZNW	*Zeitschrift für die neutestamentliche Wissenschaft*

Christianizing Homer

Introduction

Late in the sixth century, Georgius Florentius Gregorius, bishop of Tours, claimed to have discovered an important manuscript: "I have found a book of miracles of the holy apostle Andrew," wrote Gregory,

> which some dub apocryphal because of its excessive verbosity. It seemed advantageous to abstract from it and summarize only the wonders, disregarding whatever would breed disgust, and to enclose the marvelous miracles in one small volume that might ingratiate its readers and deflect the criticism of its detractors.[1]

Indeed, in orthodox references to *The Acts of Andrew* the verdict was nearly uniform: apocryphal and outrageous. More objectionable than its prolixity or even its content was its popularity among groups labeled heretic: Manichaeans, Encratites, Apostolics, Priscillianists, and certain Origenists.[2] As a result of this orthodox rejection, the *Acts* fell into disuse and textual disrepair. After the ninth century no one seems to have had access to the work as a whole.

Gregory's editing reduced the *Acts* drastically. He deleted most speeches and entire episodes, often skewed the itinerary, and purged nearly every trace of its original sexual asceticism, nonviolence, and Platonism. Nevertheless, his *Liber de miraculis* now is the most valuable extant witness to the architecture of *The Acts of Andrew* as a whole. Beginning with Andrew sailing off to rescue Matthias from cannibals and ending, more than thirty episodes later, with a radically abbreviated account of Andrew's death, Gregory's epitome provides the most reliable evidence concerning the extent and sequence of the original *Acts*.

Fortunately, Gregory's *Liber de miraculis* is not the only survivor. A more expansive version of the first story he epitomized still exists, now known as *The Acts of Andrew and Matthias in the City of the Cannibals*. It survives not only in Greek but also in translations into Latin, Syriac, Coptic, Ethiopic, Armenian, Slavonic, and even Anglo-Saxon.[3] Several citations, an extensive Coptic fragment, and three Byzantine Andrean "Lives" allow one to improve on Gregory at several points.[4] Furthermore, several recensions exist of Andrew's passion, or martyrdom, the most important of which have been published recently in two editions prepared independently by Jean-Marc Prieur and me.[5] Even though the text remains incomplete, these new editions attest to an enormous ancient book. Modern readers, like Gregory's, may object to the book merely "because of its excessive verbosity."

On the basis of these textual reconstructions, scholars now set the date of *The*

Acts of Andrew at the end of the second century or early in the third.[6] Its similarities with *The Acts of John* and the writings of Clement of Alexandria suggest that it most likely derived from Grecophone Egypt, probably Alexandria.[7]

The book purports to narrate the missionary career and martyrdom of Andrew, one of Jesus' twelve disciples, who is nearly invisible in writings composed prior to *The Acts of Andrew*. Luke's Acts mentions him only once, in a list of apostles (1:13). From the Synoptic Gospels one learns that he and his brother Peter were fishermen from Capernaum whom Jesus called to fish for humans (Mark 1:16–18 and Matt. 4:18–20). Mark, not followed by Matthew or Luke, claims that Andrew, along with Peter, James, and John, heard Jesus predict the destruction of the temple (13:3).

Although the Gospel of John gives somewhat more attention to Andrew, he remains little more than a shadow. The Fourth Gospel portrays him as a follower of John the Baptist who turned instead to Jesus and later brought his brother Peter to him (1:35–42). Andrew also informed Jesus about the boy with the expandable lunch (6:8–9) and about Greeks who wanted to see him (12:22). Although he often appears in Mark and John as the apostle fourth in prominence after Peter, James, and John, Andrew never enjoyed commensurate popularity in later tradition. He does appear occasionally in several early apocrypha,[8] but his depiction adds little to the information provided by the New Testament.[9] Somehow one must explain why this relatively obscure apostle dominated the longest of the apocryphal Acts.

The curious setting for Andrew's execution also requires explaining. Other apocryphal Acts follow tradition in locating the deaths of Peter and Paul in Rome (*The Acts of Peter* and *The Acts of Paul*),[10] John's death in Ephesus (*The Acts of John*),[11] and Thomas's in India (*The Acts of Thomas*).[12] *The Acts of Andrew*, however, situates Andrew's death in Patras, for which there exists absolutely no corroboration from the early church.[13] Undaunted by the absence of external evidence, one scholar supposed that the author was an Achaean who expanded on a local legend of the apostle's death there.[14] Another thought that "in that city, the cult of a local Saint with the same or a similar name had inspired a patriotic intellectual to identify him with the Apostle, and to supply what was wanting—a description of his martyrdom."[15] But Achaea is the one place in the Roman Empire almost certainly *not* home to the author. No Achaean would have made Patras the provincial capital, with its own resident proconsul and praetorium. Achaea's provincial capital was Corinth.[16] Furthermore, not until centuries later does one find evidence of Christians in Patras. If the author did not live in Achaea and if Patras was not a traditional location for Andrew's ministry, why did the *Acts* place his death at this unlikely site?

These peculiarities—a Brobdingnagian novel about a Lilliputian apostle dying in an implausible location—appear in all reconstructions of the *Acts*. Mine contains more. All other editions, including Prieur's, omit *The Acts of Andrew and Matthias in the City of the Cannibals*. I include it, as did Gregory's *Liber de miraculis* and every other ancient recasting of *The Acts of Andrew* attesting to the apostle's adventures prior to his martyrdom.[17] As a result, my edition sends Andrew from Achaea by ship in order to rescue Matthias from cannibals, and many episodes later he returns to Achaea to preach and die. This looping itinerary, beginning and ending in Achaea, is unique among the apocryphal Acts, each of which sends its hero more or less directly to the region of his martyrdom.

In this volume I will argue that one best accounts for these and many other peculiarities by viewing *The Acts of Andrew* as a Christianizing of Homer, especially of *The Odyssey*. The author selected Andrew as the protagonist because the Gospels had equipped him better than any of the Twelve to be an evangelizing Odysseus. He was a former fisherman who brought Greeks to Jesus, and his very name derived from the Greek word for courage (Ἀνδρέας/ ἀνδρεία).[18] Andrew left Achaea to rescue Matthias and eventually returned there because the author wished his readers to recognize similarities with Odysseus's departure from Achaea to rescue Helen from Troy and his eventful νόστος, or 'homecoming', to Ithaca.[19]

Like Odysseus, Andrew endures storms, enters the netherworld, and escapes demons, cannibals, and monsters. One also finds parallel characterizations of Penelope, Telemachus, Circe, Calypso, Menelaus, Helen, and Nestor, along with many other characters from Greek mythology, including Oedipus, Heracles, Zeus, Hera, Apollo, Ares, Artemis, Agamemnon, Dionysus, Orestes, Hephaestus, Actaeon, Orpheus, Atalanta, Tiresias, Hector, Sarpedon, Philoctetes, Patroclus, and Achilles. A Roman proconsul orders Andrew crucified next to the sea and bound to his cross like Odysseus tied to the mast of his ship. Patras is his final destination because it is the Achaean city closest to Ithaca.[20] Odyssean pretensions could also account for its herculean prolixity.

This hypothesis by no means accounts for all aspects of *The Acts of Andrew*. Andrew is not only a baptized Odysseus but also a baptized Socrates: initiate in divination and maieutics (interrogative midwifery); expert in helping his listeners remember the true nature of the soul. At the end of the *Acts* the apostle is eager for death and lectures his closest friends concerning the soul. Nor is *The Odyssey* the only anterior text informing the *Acts*. One finds parallels to biblical texts, especially Jonah and the Gospel of Matthew. The genre and much of the content apparently derive from an imitation of *The Acts of Peter*.[21] One also finds striking parallels with *The Iliad*, the plays of Euripides, and especially the dialogues of Plato. In fact, Andrew's martyrdom unmistakably imitates Plato's construal of the death of Socrates in the *Phaedo*. Even when one takes into account the author's use of multiple sources, the resemblances with *The Odyssey* cannot be dismissed as faint echoes, as casual, accidental, or cosmetic allusions. They are sufficiently strong, numerous, and tendentious to compel the reader to consider the book a transformative rewriting of the epic.

This hypothesis at first might seem incredible. No Christian author mentioned Homer until Justin Martyr (mid-second century),[22] and Justin, like the other apologists, referred to the bard primarily to lambaste his gods for their adulteries, murders, and thefts.[23] Christian texts that betray the most obvious Homeric literary influence were composed in epic hexameters, were more invested in *The Iliad* than in *The Odyssey*, and imitated Homer not in order to transform him but simply to ornament Christian content,[24] just as Jewish poets had beautified biblical content centuries earlier.[25]

It would be naive, however, to deduce that Homer could not also have influenced early Christian prose. The Homeric epics were the basic texts of Greek education. To quote Hegel: "Homer is that element in which the Greek world lived, like a human in air."[26] Quintilian's simile for Homer was not the air but the sea, "the source of every stream and river; for he has given us a model and an inspiration for every department of eloquence."[27] In addition to poetry, the ancient rhetorician had in mind historical writings as well, which "may be regarded as a kind of prose poem."[28]

Although *The Iliad*, too, had its debtors,[29] it was *The Odyssey* that became, according to Gérard Genette, "the favorite target of hypertextual writing."[30] (By "hypertextual" Genette means any imitation or transformation of an anterior hypotext.) Odysseus's poem was imitated,[31] provided narrative for linking it back to *The Iliad*,[32] supplemented with various conclusions to Odysseus's life,[33] parodied,[34] burlesqued,[35] dramatized,[36] prosified,[37] commented on,[38] abridged,[39] and transformed to serve a wide assortment of un-Homeric values.[40] By the end of the third century B.C.E. it had been translated into Latin.[41]

Particularly relevant to *The Acts of Andrew* is the strong influence *The Odyssey* exerted on the ancient historical novel, "the epic of the Hellenistic period, fulfilling the functions of epic in a new age, and assuming some of its techniques."[42] One might go so far as to say that *The Odyssey* itself "is simply the first novel of love, travel, and adventure in Greek."[43] Many of its themes may be found in later novels in which lovers, like Odysseus and Penelope, become separated from each other—far from home, victims of shipwrecks, pirates, lechers, and other scoundrels—until they fight their way back to their native land and into each other's arms. Evidence of Odyssean influence is apparent in novels by Chariton, Iambulus, Antonius Diogenes, Philostratus, Achilles Tatius, Heliodorus, and especially Petronius, Lucian, and Apuleius.[44]

Scholars long have recognized that the apocryphal Acts of the apostles contain striking technical, topical, and thematic similarities to ancient novels. They are so similar, in fact, that perhaps one should consider them exemplars of the same genre.[45] In a derivative sense, one could claim that all apocryphal Acts are indebted to *The Odyssey*.

The relationship of *The Acts of Andrew* to *The Odyssey*, however, is not remote, analogical, or generic; rather, it is strategically transformative, an example of what Genette calls hypertextual transvaluation ("la transvalorisation"). Transvaluing occurs when characters in the hypertext (viz. the derivative text) acquire roles and attributes derived from a system of values not found in the hypotext (the targeted text).[46] This strategy succeeds not simply when new values find narrative expression in lieu of the old ones but when readers recognize that these new values represent an intentional devaluing ("la dévalorisation") of those in the hypotext. A transvaluating text, therefore, must advertise its hypertextuality, if ever so subtly. James Joyce did so by entitling his book *Ulysses*. Lucian of Samosata warned readers at the outset of his *True History* that he would attempt to outdo Homer by lying about fabulous adventures. Petronius announced the hypertextuality of *The Satyricon* by using Odyssean names (e.g., Circe and Menelaus), mimetic type-scenes, and outright analogies ("just as Odysseus. . ."). According to Apuleius, Homer, "that divine inventor of ancient poetry among the Greeks, desiring to portray a hero of highest intelligence, was quite right to sing of a man who acquired the highest excellence by visiting many cities and learning to know various peoples."[47] With these words, the first-person-singular narrator identifies himself and his tribulations with Odysseus; other such allusions abound.

The preferred hypertextual indicators in *The Acts of Andrew* are proper nouns, especially of dramatis personae. In some cases a name may point directly to its classical antecedent: Myrmidonia designates the city of Homer's Myrmidons. At other times the author plays with similarities between two names (Nicolaus ≅ Menelaus),[48] or with ironic associations (Antiphanes ['inconspicuous' or 'unsung'] ≅ Heracles). In most cases, however, a name designates a dominant attribute of its mythological counterpart (e.g., Carpianus ['fruitful'] ≅ Zeus; Callistus ['most-beautiful'] ≅ Ganymedes; Adimantus ['fearless'] ≅ Sarpedon; Leontius ['lionlike'] ≅ Achilles; Philopater ['father-lover'] ≅ Orestes; Alcman ≅ Heracles [son of Alcmene]; Anthimus ['flowery'] ≅ Orpheus; Lesbius ['goblet'] ≅ Dionysus; Calliope ['sweet-singer'] ≅ Circe, and so on). Such onomastic playfulness corresponds with the use of names as signs of *sensus plenior* in Homeric allegories (e.g., Uranus = heaven [οὐρανός]; Zeus = life [ζῆν]; Hera = air [ἀήρ]; Demeter = earth [γη‾μητηρ]; Pluto = wealth [πλούτειν]).[49]

The investment of *The Acts of Andrew* in proper nouns partially compensates for its present textual disrepair. Gregory, the only witnesses to the content of much of the *Acts*, seems to have recorded names precisely as he had seen them in the Latin translation he epitomized; thus, one can confidently restore the original Greek name and from it speculate concerning its mythological target. For this reason, Gregory's names usually supply his most reliable hypertextual clues.

Geographical associations (e.g., Macedonia/Mount Olympus and Patras/Ithaca) and common themes (e.g., shipwrecks, a visit to the netherworld, cannibals) raise additional suspicions of Odyssean hypertextuality. By the end of the story, when Andrew is strapped to his cross at the edge of the sea, ancient readers should have decoded the "mystery" of the cross by recognizing its similarities with Odysseus's mast. By veiling its deeper meanings, albeit thinly, the *Acts* once again resembles *The Odyssey*, inasmuch as ancient intellectuals read it as an adventure story offering allegorical treasures for those wise and diligent enough to find them.[50]

The veiling of the hypertextuality of the *Acts* appears more opaque to modern eyes. Few readers today are able to view the narrative through the powerful interpretive lenses that had been ground and polished for centuries by Stoics, Pythagoreans, and Platonists. People living in the second and third centuries simply read *The Odyssey* differently. Odysseus was not merely Homer's protagonist but also a character in poetic comedy, in caustic tragedy, and in philosophical rejection, allegorization, or ethical appropriation. In addition to being Homer's queen of Ithaca, Penelope was the paragon of sexual purity. Circe came to represent reincarnation, Poseidon water and the material world, Calypso the temptations of beauty, comfort, and immortality. Only by reading through these ancient lenses can one now fully appreciate the author's transformative accomplishment. For this reason it will be necessary throughout this volume to compare the *Acts* not merely with *The Odyssey* per se but also with its subsequent interpretations.

The author's primary means of transvaluing the epic was countercharacterization: nonviolence replaces heroic violence; poverty replaces fabulous wealth; celibacy replaces adventurous sex. Although the author employed various strategies of countercharacterization, each emerged from a coherent philosophical orientation. Like other Platonists of late antiquity, the author believed that the soul, through ignorance, had fallen from the realm of being into the realm of becoming (γένεσις), and therefore was alienated from—and even forgetful of—its true kindred. To be saved from this condition one must liberate the soul from its material captivity through intellectual self-discovery and self-denial. Long before *The Acts of Andrew,* Platonists had viewed Odysseus as a cipher for the soul adrift in the ocean of matter, bedeviled by monsters, beautiful temptresses, and shipwrecks, yet resolutely headed for its heavenly home and kindred. Christian Platonists, including the author of the *Acts,* saw in Odysseus's mast a resemblance to Christ's cross, by which he returned to his heavenly *patria*. According to *The Acts of Andrew,* the journey of the soul back to its true homeland required a total rejection of sexual intercourse and violence. What need has the soul of alien bodily delights? What good is self-defense if the goal of salvation is disembodiment? "What does it profit someone to gain the whole world and lose one's soul?"

The author's most immediate allies in this attack on Homeric epic were Christian apologists, especially Justin Martyr and Clement of Alexandria, who never tired of ridiculing Greek gods for their feuds, their madness, their violence, and their violations of boys and other men's wives. But the ultimate cause of all such *nausea mythologica* was Plato's Socrates, whose objections to Homer populate dozens of notes in this volume. Socrates vilified the immorality of Homer's gods and heroes and, in fact, banished the poet from his utopia. Later philosophers and Christian intellectuals repeated Socrates' complaints (see chapter 1), and many of these criticisms correspond exactly to the transvaluative ambitions of Andrew's *Acts.*

One may, of course, read *The Acts of Andrew* profitably without appealing to *The Odyssey.* As Genette expressed it, "Every hypertext . . . can . . . be read for its own sake and carries its own signification, which is both autonomous and, to a degree, sufficient. But sufficient does not mean exhaustive."[51] So, for example, one might read Joyce's *Ulysses* without reference to Homer, but doing so would rob the text of its playful hypertextuality. So, too, with *The Acts of Andrew*: to ignore its transvaluation of *The Odyssey* would be to deprive it of its dialectical power. "The hypertext always wins," says Genette, "even if this gain be judged . . . in the negative, by the perception that it is hypertextual."[52] The task of this volume is to show that *The Acts of Andrew* is indeed a hypertextual transvaluation of *The Odyssey* and to suggest what the recognition of this literary strategy might contribute to its interpretation.

Studies attempting to describe the influence of literary classics on later compositions seldom sail altogether unscathed past the Sirens of Overinterpretation, Fabrication, and Speculation. If this study ever reaches its destination, it may do so with loose timbers, the result of the temptation to collect too many direct allusions between the hypertext and its prototype. *The Odyssey* exerted an enormous influence on nearly all genres of ancient narrative; therefore, some parallels between it and *The Acts of Andrew* may be nothing more than residual, negligible traces of Homeric radiation. Other parallels may derive simply from the conventions of everyday language or from rhetorical topoi. In other words, many of the similarities identified in this book may be unconvincing, especially when viewed atomistically. I have relegated the weakest parallels into the notes, but some may pop up in the main argument. Even the most suspicious reader, however, should find the evidence sufficiently numerous and compelling to forgive my occasional—perhaps inevitable—succumbing to the Sirens that inhabit the island of Influenceomania.

This book will test the generosity of those accustomed to reading early Christian texts in light of Judaism and the New Testament. One often and rightly will identify dependence of *The Acts of Andrew* on the Bible and postbiblical Jewish writings. Specialists will find resonances with other apocryphal Acts, Christian apologists, and especially the works of Clement of Alexandria. These texts do indeed supply important information concerning the religious perspectives of the *Acts* insofar as its author was a Christian, but Jewish and Christian literary tradition alone cannot account for those aspects of *The Acts of Andrew* that make it most exceptional. Jewish and Christian writings provided the author with arrows for his theological bow, but he was hunting epos and mythos. If the hypothesis in this book is correct, *The Acts of Andrew* might suggest a new hermeneutic for reading other early Christian texts.[53]

Furthermore, if *The Acts of Andrew* indeed Christianized Homer, it also enriches one's understanding of the reception of Homeric epic in the empire as a whole. Its redefinitions of Homeric mythology are more extensive than that of the *Quaestiones Homericae* by Heraclitus, more patently interpretive than *De vita et poesi Homeri* by Ps.-Plutarch, and more hypertextually transvaluative than *The Aeneid* of Virgil, *The True Story* of Lucian, *The Satyricon* of Petronius, or *Metamorphoses* of Apuleius. The author of the *Acts* has thus provided modern readers with an intricate, imaginative, sophisticated, and fascinating glimpse into the intellectual life of the period in this recasting of Homeric mythology, this Christian Odyssey.

Before looking at *The Acts of Andrew* immediately, I examine in chapter 1 how pagans and Christians alike attempted to limit the moral damage that Homer's epics inflicted on their readers, especially on young readers. Only by placing the *Acts* in the context of these controversies over Homer can one fully appreciate its transvaluative ambitions.

Notes

1. Maximilian Bonnet, ed, "Gregorii episcopi turonensis liber de miraculis beati Andreae apostoli," in *Gregorii episcopi turonensis miracula et opera minora*, ed. Bruno Krusch, Monumenta Germaniae historica. Scriptores rerum Merovingicarum 1,2 (Hanover: Hahn, 1885), 826.

2. Eusebius *Historia ecclesiastica* 3.25.6, Philaster *Diversarum hereseon liber* 61 (*CSEL* 38), Turibius *Epistula ad Idacium et Ceponium* 5 (*PL* 54.694C), Innocent I *Epistle to Exuperius* (Wurm), Evodius of Uzala *De fide contra Manichaeos* 38 (*CSEL* 25), the *Decretum Gelasianum* (TU 38.4:49–52), Timothy of Constantinople *De receptione haereticorum* (*PG* 86.21), Epiphanius *Panarion* 47.1, 61.l, and 63.2, the anonymous treatise *Ad Iustinum Manichaeum* (*PL* 8.999–1010), and Photius *Bibliotheca* codex 114.

3. See Dennis R. MacDonald, *The Acts of Andrew and The Acts of Andrew and Matthias in the City of the Cannibals,* TT 33, CA 1 (Atlanta: Scholars Press, 1990), 63–169.

4. Ibid., 181–317.

5. Prieur, *Acta Andreae,* CCSA 5 and 6 (Turnhout: Brepols, 1989); MacDonald, *Acts of Andrew.*

6. *The Acts of Andrew* imitated *The Acts of Peter* and *The Acts of John,* both of which were written sometime before the end of the second century. Andrew's *Acts* in turn influenced *The Acts of Thomas,* which was written no later than the end of the third century. (It also informed several later Acts, in particular *The Acts of Philip, The Acts of John by Prochorus,* and probably *The Acts of Xanthippe and Polyxena.*) According to Eusebius, in Origen's no longer extant commentaries on Genesis the great exegete stated that

> Thomas, as tradition relates, obtained by lot Parthia, Andrew Scythia, John Asia (and he stayed there and died in Ephesus), but Peter seems to have preached to the Jews of the Dispersion in Pontus and Galatia and Bithynia, Cappadocia, and Asia, and at the end he came to Rome and was crucified head downwards, for so he had demanded to suffer. What need be said of Paul, who fulfilled the gospel of Christ from Jerusalem to Illyria and afterward was martyred in Rome under Nero? (*Historia ecclesiastica* 3.1)

Origen mentions here the same five apostles who star in their own apocryphal Acts, and his information about them seems uncannily consistent with these Acts (though see Eric Junod's cautions in "Origène, Eusèbe et la tradition sur la répartition des champs de mission des apôtres [Eusèbe, *HE* III,1,1–3]," in *Les Actes apocryphes des apôtres. Christianisme et monde païen*, ed. François Bovon, Publications de la Faculté de Théologie de l'Université de Genève 4 [Geneva: Labor et Fides, 1981], 233–48). *The Acts of Thomas, The Acts of Andrew*, and perhaps *The Acts of John* began with the apostolic real estate lottery: Thomas drew India (bordering Origen's Parthia), John went to Asia, where he died, and Andrew drew Achaea but quickly left in order to rescue Matthias from cannibals. Origen seems to have taken Andrew's mission among the cannibals as evidence of the evangelization of notoriously savage Scythia. *The Acts of Peter* narrates Peter's death on an inverted cross; *The Acts of Paul* has that apostle lose his head in Rome under Nero. Origen wrote his Genesis commentaries while still in Alexandria, prior to leaving for Caesarea in 231/232, so one probably should date *The Acts of Andrew* sometime prior to 225, time enough for this information to have become "tradition."

7. MacDonald, *Acts of Andrew*, 55–59, and Prieur, *Acta Andreae*, 413–16. For a discussion of authorship see chapter 8, 287–89.

8. *The Gospel of the Ebionites* (Epiphanius *Panarion* 30.13), *Gospel of Peter* 14 (60), *Epistula Apostolorum* 2, and *Pistis Sophia* 96 and 136. *The Muratorian Fragment* says Andrew received a vision that John would write his Gospel.

9. For discussions of Andrean traditions in the early church, see the following: Joseph Flamion, *Les Actes apocryphes de l'apôtre André. Les Actes d'André et de Mathias, de Pierre et d'André et les textes apparentés*, RTHP 33 (Louvain: Bureaux de Recueil, 1911); N. Trempela, Ὁ ἀπόστολος Ἀνδρέας. βίος, δράσις καὶ μαρτύριον αὐτοῦ ἐν Πάτραις (Patras, 1956); Peter Megill Peterson, *Andrew, Brother of Simon Peter: His History and His Legends*, NovTSup 1 (Leiden: E. J. Brill, 1958); and Francis Dvornik, *The Idea of Apostolicity in Byzantium and the Legend of the Apostle Andrew*, DOS 4 (Cambridge: Harvard University Press, 1958).

10. Peter: 1 Peter 5:13 and Papias in Eusebius *Historia ecclesiastica* 2.15.2; cf. *1 Clement* 5; Paul: Acts 28, 2 Timothy, *1 Clement* 5.

11. Polycrates of Ephesus in Eusebius *Historia ecclesiastica* 3.31.3; cf. Irenaeus *Adversus haereses* 3.1.1 and Clement of Alexandria *Quis dives salvetur* 42.

12. See Albrecht Dihle, "Neues zur Thomas-Tradition," *JAC* 6 (1963): 54–70.

13. Clement of Alexandria preserves a quotation from the Gnostic teacher Heracleon stating that some of the apostles gave witness to their faith in speech alone, without martyrdom. He explicitly mentions in this category "Matthew, Philip, Thomas, Levi, and many others" (*Stromateis* 4.9.71.3). This statement might suggest that he knew of the martyrdoms of other apostles, including that of Andrew. But even if Heracleon did know of a traditional account of Andrew's death, it remains true that no document prior to *The Acts of Andrew* points to Patras as the location of his execution.

14. Flamion, *Actes d'André*, 264–68.

15. Dvornik, *Apostolicity*, 220.

16. According to Edmund Groag, the highest administrative officer in Patras was an

occasional curator, whom it shared with Athens (*Die römischen Reichsbeamten von Achaia bis auf Diokletian*, Akademie der Wissenschaft in Wien, Schriften der Balkankommission, Antiquarische Abteilung 9 [Vienna: Hölder-Pichler-Tempsky, 1939], 179). See the excellent discussion in Prieur, *Acta Andreae*, 72–80.

17. Detailed arguments appear in MacDonald, *Acts of Andrew*, 3–47. See also Conclusion, 316–18.

18. On Odysseus's ἀνδρεία see Ps.-Plutarch *De vita et poesi Homeri* 4 and 141. It is curious but perhaps irrelevant to note that the first line of *The Odyssey* begins ἄνδρα μοι, ἔννεπε, μοῦσα, πολύτροπον, "Tell me, O Muse, of the man (ἄνδρα) of the many turns." Virgil, imitating the opening of *The Odyssey*, begins *The Aeneid Arma virumque cano*, "Of arms and the man I sing." The first line of John Milton's *Paradise Lost* tells "Of man's disobedience."

19. The *nostoi* of Greek warriors from the Trojan War was a favorite topic of Greek mythology. Many Achaeans were lost at sea (viz. Odysseus's crew and Locrian Ajax), Agamemnon returned to a treacherous wife, while some others spent the rest of their days in wealth and renown (viz. Nestor and Menelaus). Homer's magnificent treatment of Odysseus's return—with its storms, cannibals, monsters, witches, visit with the dead, and return to an estate in near ruin—made it antiquity's most notorious *nostos*.

20. Notice also that it allows wordplay on the Homeric formula ἐς πατρίδα γαῖαν, "to the ancestral land."

21. See Flamion, *Actes d'André*, 132–89 passim, and Dvornik, *Apostolicity*, 220–21. The *Acts* also seems to rely on *The Acts of John* with which it shares philosophical vocabulary and distinctive rhetorical conventions (Prieur, *Acta Andreae*, 385–403).

22. In his treatment of Homer in early Christianity, Günther Glockmann claimed that

das Neue Testament weder eine Äusserung über Homer noch eine bewusste oder unbewusste Benutzung der homerischen Dichtung enthält. Die Untersuchung der übrigen urchristlichen Literatur führte zu dem gleichen Ergebnis. Es konnten also auch in den älteren der neutestamentlichen Apokryphen, in den Schriften der Apostolischen Väter sowie in den ersten Dokumenten der Apologetik des 2. Jahrhunderts . . . , keine Spuren des Dichters gefunden werden. (*Homer in der frühchristlichen Literatur bis Justinus*, TU 105 [Berlin: Akademie-Verlag, 1968], 57–58)

This assessment is shared by Nicole Zeegers-Vander Vorst, *Les Citations des poètes grecs chez les apologistes chrétiens du IIe siècle*, RTHP 4.47 (Louvain: Bibliothèque de l'Université, 1972), 21.

23. See, for example: Justin Martyr *First Apology* 21–23, 25, 44, and 54 and *Second Apology* 10, Athenagoras *Legatio* 21 and 29, Theophilus of Antioch *Ad Autolycum* 2.8 and 3.3, Aristides of Athens *Apology* 8–9 and 13, Ps.-Justin *Cohortatio ad gentiles* 5, Tatian *Oratio ad graecos* 21, Clement of Alexandria *Protrepticus* 2.24, 27, 28, 31, and 32, 3.37–38, 4.43 and 49, and 52–53, Irenaeus *Adversus haereses* 1.12, Tertullian *Ad nationes* 2.7, and *De idololatria* 10, and Minucius Felix *Octavius* 22.

24. See chapter 1.

25. E.g., Theodotus *On the Jews* and Philo Epicus *On Jerusalem* (Eusebius *Praeparatio*

evangelica 9.17–20, 22–24, and 35–38). An obscure medieval note states that a certain "Sosates, the Jewish Homer, flourished in Alexandria" sometime between 142 and 51 B.C.E. (Shaye J. D. Cohen, "Sosates the Jewish Homer," *HTR* 74 [1981]: 391–96).

26. "Homer ist das Element, in dem die griechische Welt lebt wie der Mensch in der Luft" (*Vorlesungen über die Philosophie der Weltgeschichte*, ed. Georg Lasson [Leipzig: F. Meiner, 1923], 5.529).

27. *Institutio oratoria* 10.1.4. When possible, all citations from classical literature conform with those in the Loeb Classical Library. Translations from other sources are so indicated unless they are my own. A list of translations used appears at the beginning of the bibliography.

28. Ibid., 10.1.31; cf. Strabo *Geography* 1.2.6. Homer himself was considered a historian (see Richard Claverhouse Jebb, *Homer: An Introduction to the "Iliad" and the "Odyssey,"* 5th ed. [Boston: Ginn, 1894], 84–85). On Homer and Greek historiography, see Hermann Strasburger, *Homer und die Geschichtsschreibung*, Sitzungsberichte der Heidelberger Akademie der Wissenschaften, Philosophisch-historische Klasse (Heidelberg: C. Winter, 1972).

29. Most obviously the poems of the Epic Cycle: *Thebais, Epigoni, Cypria Aethiopis, Little Iliad, Iliu Persis,* and *The Titanomachia* of Eumelus or Arctinus of Miletus. Latin poetic imitations include Ennius's *Annales* and Virgil's *Aeneid. The Iliad* was supplemented by *The Posthomerica* of Quintus Smyrnaeus; parodied in *The Batrachyomachia* (or *The War of the Frogs*), in *The Gigantomachia* of Hegemon, and in *Le Roi des Mirmidons* by Viard Zacharias (1966); refuted in *The Anthomerus* of Ptolemy "Chennus" of Alexandria; translated into Latin by Gnaeus Martius and Lucius Licinius Crassus; digested into Latin verse by Silius Italicus, *The Latin Iliad,* and into prose by the *Excidium Trojae* (see also the *Compendium Historiae Troianae-Romanae*); prosified and "corrected" in the Trojan novels of "Dictys" and "Dares" (these works, in turn, were prosified into English by Joseph of Exeter [mid-1180s] and into French by Benoît de Sainte-Maure [ca. 1160]); and transvalued in Shakespeare's *Troilus and Cressida* (1609) and in Jean Giraudoux's *La Guerre de Troie n'aura pas lieu* (1935). A survey of these later rewritings of *The Iliad* appears in Howard Clarke's *Homer's Readers: A Historical Introduction to the "Iliad" and the "Odyssey"* (Newark: University of Delaware Press, 1980), 20–59. See also: John A. Scott, *Homer and His Influence* (Boston: Marshall Jones, 1925); William Cranston Lawton, *The Successors of Homer* (New York: Cooper Square, 1969 [reprint of the 1898 edition]); and Martin Mueller, *The Iliad* (London: George Allen and Unwin, 1984), especially "The Life of the *Iliad*," 177–93. Perhaps the most curious example of rewriting *The Iliad* is that of Lucius Septimius Nestor, a contemporary of the author of *The Acts of Andrew.* Both *The Iliad* and *The Odyssey* consist of twenty-four books, each designated by a different letter of the Greek alphabet. Nestor's version of each book of *The Iliad* lacked the letter by which it was designated.

30. *Palimpsestes. La Littérature au second degré* (Paris: Éditions du Seuil, 1982), 201.

31. Among many such imitations are Apollonius's *Argonautica*, three *Nostoi* (one attributed to Homer or to Hagias of Troezen, another by Stesichorus, and a third by Anticleides), Virgil's *Aeneid*, and Ovid's *Metamorphoses*. J. D. Ellsworth shows that

Ovid imitated *The Odyssey* directly, not just through the intermediary of *The Aeneid* ("Ovid's 'Odyssey,' *Met.* 13.623–14.608," *Mnemosyne* 41 [1988]: 333–40). Apollonius's work, in turn, inspired the "Orphic Argonautica" and at least two Latin imitations, one that survives by Valerius Flaccus and one that does not by Varro Atacinus. Fragments also survive of other epics on Odyssean themes. See Roger A. Pack, *The Greek and Latin Literary Texts from Greco-Roman Egypt*, 2d edition (Ann Arbor: University of Michigan Press, 1965), nos. 1831, 1838, 1843, and 1844.

32. Quintus Smyrnaeus *Posthomerica*.

33. *The Telegonia*, sometimes assigned to Eugammon of Cyrene, and Nikos Kazantzakis, *The Odyssey: A Modern Sequel* (ET 1958).

34. *The Margites* and Lucian's *True Story*.

35. Hugues de Picou's *L'Odyssée d'Homère* (1650), and Pierre Marivaux's *Télémaque travesti* (1736).

36. Claudio Monteverdi's *Il ritorno d'Ulisse in patria* (1641).

37. The Trojan novel of Ps.-Dictys. Plato himself prosified the beginning of *The Iliad* in order to tell a Homeric tale without the taint of poetry (*Republic* 3.393c–394b).

38. E.g., Eustathius.

39. Mary Lamb's *Adventures of Ulysses* (1808).

40. François Fénelon's *Aventures de Télémaque* (1699), Louis Aragon's *Aventures de Télémaque* (1922), James Joyce's *Ulysses* (1922), and Jean Giono's *Naissance de l'Odyssée* (1930).

41. Livius Andronicus. According to Dio Chrysostom (d. ca. 112 C.E.), Homer's poetry had also been translated into Indian languages, but the source of this information was hearsay (*Discourse* 53).

42. Tomas Hägg, *The Novel in Antiquity* (Berkeley: University of California Press, 1983), 111. Hägg notes:

> Chariton ends his novel by letting Chaereas and his father-in-law retell the main plot in some detail, just as Odysseus recounts his adventures to Penelope in the twenty-third book of *The Odyssey*. In Achilles Tatius's novel [ca. 200 C.E.] the hero himself is responsible for narrating the whole story—the literary prototype of the first-person narrative is of course Odysseus' account to the Phaeacians of his fantastic adventures among the Lotus-Eaters and Cyclopes. Heliodorus absolutely excels in imitation of Homer. The *in-medias-res* technique is consciously adopted, and developed with ingenuity. (110; cf. 54)

43. Ibid., 110. Graham Anderson writes:

> The most suitable starting-point for scholarship on the novel is still Epic. It has long been recognised that *The Odyssey* was particularly influential in our extant example; and *The Odyssey* rather than *The Iliad* offers outlets for humour which the novelists themselves were able to reproduce. A long action of travel and separation has plenty of scope for entertaining falsehood. (*Eros Sophistes: Ancient Novelists at Play*, ACS 9 [Chico: Scholars Press, 1982], 2)

Ben Edwin Perry, who called *The Odyssey* a "romance epic," even claimed that "Romance and epic are basically the same genre" (*The Ancient Romances: A Literary-Historical Account of Their Origins* [Berkeley: University of California Press, 1967], 45). B. P. Reardon writes: "Homère est le père non seulement des sophistes mais aussi des romanciers" (*Courants littéraires grecs des IIe et IIIe siècles après J.-C.*, Annales littéraires de l'Université de Nantes 5 [Paris: Belles Lettres, 1971], 320; cf. 319–32, 344, and 387). See especially Massimo Fusillo, "Textual Patterns and Narrative Situations in the Greek Novel," in *Groningen Colloquia on the Novel*, ed. H. Hofmann (Groningen: Egbert Forsten, 1988), 1.17–31.

44. For a more detailed description of these texts and their reliance on Homer, see Conclusion, 311–14.

45. Ernst von Dobschütz was the first to describe the novelistic properties of the apocryphal Acts ("Der Roman in der altchristlichen Literatur," *DRund* 111 [1902]: 87–106). For refinements of this relationship see: Ludwig Radermacher, *Hippolytus und Thekla. Studien zur Geschichte von Legende und Kultus,* Kaiserliche Akademie der Wissenschaften in Wien, Philosophisch-historische Klasse, Sitzungsberichte 182,3 (Vienna: Alfred Hölder, 1916); Karl Kerenyi, *Die griechisch-orientalische Romanliteratur in religionsgeschichtlicher Beleuchtung* (Darmstadt: Wissenschaftliche Buchgesellschaft, 1962; reprint of 1927 edition); Rosa Söder, *Die apokryphen Apostelgeschichten und die romanhafte Literatur der Antike*, Würzburger Studien zur Altertumswissenschaft 3 (Darmstadt: Wissenschaftliche Buchgesellschaft, 1969; reprint of 1932 edition); and Philipp Vielhauer, "Apokryphe Apostelgeschichten," in *Geschichte der urchristliche Literatur* (Berlin: Walter de Gruyter, 1975), 693–718. Jean-Daniel Kaestli summarizes and judiciously assesses this scholarship in "Les Principales Orientations de la recherche sur les Actes apocryphes des apôtres" (Bovon, *Actes apocryphes,* 49–67). See also: Hägg, *Novel in Antiquity*, 154–68; Virginia Burrus, *Chastity as Autonomy: Women in the Stories of Apocryphal Acts*, StudWR 23 (Lewiston: Edwin Mellen, 1987), 7–30; and Richard I. Pervo, *Profit with Delight: The Literary Genre of the Acts of the Apostles* (Philadelphia: Fortress Press, 1987), esp. 86–138.

46. *Palimpsestes,* 418–19; cf. 393.

47. *Metamorphoses* 9.13, referring to the opening lines of *The Odyssey*.

48. The symbol ≈ designates an approximate equivalent between the items so linked; this is preferable to a simple equal sign (=), which would equate the two items. The author of the *Acts* apparently did not want to make his characters the same as their mythological counterparts but to transform them.

49. For discussions of etymology in Homeric allegories, see David Dawson, *Allegorical Readers and Cultural Revision in Ancient Alexandria* (Berkeley: University of California Press, 1992), 24–38. Homer himself engaged in onomastic wordplay (see *Odyssey* 1.60–62, 18.6–7 and 73, 19.406–9, and 24.304–6). For a discussion of significant names in ancient novels, see Conclusion, 311–13.

50. See Félix Buffière, *Les Mythes d'Homère et la pensée grecque*, Collection Budé (Paris: Belles Lettres, 1956), 37–38. On the importance of allegory for Alexandrian Jews, Gnostics, and Christians, see Dawson, *Allegorical Readers*, passim.

51. *Palimpsestes*, 450.

52. Ibid., 451.

53. In a future work I will argue that many of the literary features distinctive of the Gospel of Mark ultimately derived from the poetics of Homeric epic: an uncomprehending band of followers, murderous rivals, walking on water, stilling the storm, fighting demons, visiting the dead, and traveling in secrecy. Like Homer's Odysseus, Mark's Jesus is a noble hero who "suffers many things" at the hands of his enemies—both mortal and supernatural—but who, in the end, emerges victorious. Other scholars have seen evidence of Homeric vocabulary and topoi in the Acts of the Apostles, especially the shipwreck in chapter 27; see, e.g., Frederick Fyvie Bruce, *Commentary on the Book of Acts*, New International Commentary on the New Testament (Grand Rapids: Eerdmans, 1954), 498.

1

Homer in the Early Church

"This poet," Plato said of Homer, "educated Greece,"[1] a statement that would hold true for nearly two millennia. Greek youngsters learned their ΑΒΓs from lists of Homeric names; one of the first sentences they wrote was "Homer was not a man but a god"; and among their first reading assignments was a selection of verse from *The Odyssey*.[2] Among papyri that survive from the early empire are scraps of lines from *The Iliad* and *The Odyssey* copied as a writing exercise,[3] a school manual quoting from *The Odyssey* and containing an elegy celebrating a temple in Homer's honor,[4] an epitome of Books 3 and 5 of *The Odyssey*,[5] and student essays on Homeric themes, such as the preparations for the Trojan War,[6] events of the war after the death of Achilles,[7] and the sufferings of Philoctetes.[8] A first-century C.E. interpreter of Homer put it this way:

> From the earliest age, children beginning their studies are nursed on Homer's teaching. One might say that while we were still in swathing bands we sucked from his epics as from fresh milk. He assists the beginner and later the adult in his prime. In no stage of life, from boyhood to old age, do we ever cease to drink from him.[9]

Homer's status in Greek education can also be illustrated by the sheer bulk of surviving Homeric texts. One catalogue of manuscripts from Greco-Roman Egypt lists 604 of the poet κατ᾽ ἐξοχήν, and another 73 contain Homeric scholia, anthologies, or commentaries. Compare these combined 677 Homeric fragments with only 83 from Demosthenes, 77 from Euripides, 72 from Hesiod, and 42 from Plato.[10] "If a Greek owned any books—that is, papyrus rolls—he was almost as likely to own the *Iliad* and *Odyssey* as anything from the rest of Greek literature."[11] Plato's Protagoras obviously was not alone in thinking that "the most important aspect of a man's education is facility with epic poetry."[12]

Nowhere was Homer's pedagogical influence more deeply felt than in his shaping of the Greek moral climate through the characterization of his heroes.[13] Socrates, according to Plato, knew that "by adorning countless deeds of the ancients [poetry] educates later generations."[14] Homer's warriors were paradigms of proper conduct, heroes of a golden age when manly honor ruled supreme, exemplars of excellence, nobility, prudence, and courage. Greek aristocrats demonstrated savoir faire by reciting apposite Homeric lines;

17

Alexander the Great kept a copy of Homer's poems nearby less for strategic than
for social engagements. The great Roman rhetor Quintilian (first century C.E.)
stated that

> uninformed minds which are liable to be all the more deeply impressed by
> what they learn in their days of childish ignorance, must learn not merely what
> is eloquent; it is even more important that they should study what is morally
> excellent.
>
> It is therefore an admirable practice which now prevails, to begin by
> reading Homer and Vergil. . . . [T]he boy will read them more than once. . . .
> [L]et his mind be lifted by the sublimity of heroic verse, inspired by the
> greatness of its theme and imbued with the loftiest sentiments.[15]

And Strabo wrote:

> The ancients assert . . . that poetry is a kind of elementary philosophy, which,
> taking us in our very boyhood, introduces us to the art of life and instructs us,
> with pleasure to ourselves, in character, emotions, and actions. . . . That is the
> reason why in Greece the various states educate the young, at the very
> beginning of their education, by means of [Homeric] poetry; not for the mere
> sake of entertainment, of course, but for the sake of moral discipline.[16]

"My father was anxious to see me develop into a good man," said a contemporary
of Plato, "and as a means to this end he compelled me to memorize all of Homer;
and so even now I can repeat the whole *Iliad* and the *Odyssey* by heart."[17]
Ironically, Plato and many others after him attacked Homer precisely at this point,
precisely over the content of his moral instruction, the character of the ἀνὴρ
ἀγαθός.[18]

Plato's Socrates claimed that the epics undermined manliness (ἀνδρεία) by
depicting the terrors of the netherworld, the weeping of Achilles at the death of
Patroclus, and the servile pleadings of Priam.[19] Worse than Homer's heroes were
his Olympians, who battled each other,[20] appeared to mortals in various guises
and lied,[21] lamented,[22] laughed,[23] and lusted.[24] Socrates exiled Homer from his
republic for having persuaded the young "that the gods are the begetters of
evil."[25] "Neither will we allow teachers to use him for the education of the young
if our guardians are to be god-fearing."[26] Not even moralizing allegories could
redeem the epics for Plato, for "the young are not able to distinguish what is and
what is not allegory, but whatever opinions are taken into the mind at that age are
wont to prove indelible and unalterable."[27] Plato sometimes manufactured his
own Homeric hypertexts as strategic improvements on epos. The most famous
example is the myth of Er in *Republic* Book 10, where he has Socrates narrate a
tour of the netherworld intended to supplant Odysseus's *nekyia*: "It is not, let me
tell you, . . . the tale to Alcinous told."[28]

Other philosophers, however, changed Homer's poison into wine by adding
large quantities of allegory. Moral criticisms of the epics were justified when

applied to surface meanings, but at a deeper level, so it was said, the divine poet was the supreme theologian. Homer had hidden in myth the very philosophical truths Plato and others articulated discursively. As one prude put it: "If nothing is allegory, everything is blasphemy."[29] Physical philosophers saw in Homer's gods the elements of the cosmos: Artemis was the moon, Apollo the sun, Hera air, Poseidon water, Hephaestus fire, Zeus ether, or life. The myths, therefore, became allegories of the relationships and combinations of these physical entities.[30] Stoics and others took Olympians and heroes to be hypostasized human traits, so Athena represented wisdom, Ares violence, Aphrodite love, Achilles petulance, Circe desire, Nestor prudence, Zeus power, Penelope chastity, and Telemachus *pietas*.[31] Neoplatonists and Neopythagoreans viewed the epics as mystical treatises on the soul. The cave of the nymphs, where Odysseus hid his Phaeacian wealth, was a cipher for the world and was made to correspond with Plato's cosmology.[32] Odysseus himself stood for the soul, cast about in the world, enduring hardships until it reached its immaterial Ithaca. Circe's transformation of Odysseus's crew spoke of Platonic reincarnation; the Sirens' song was the Pythagorean harmony of the spheres; Calypso's island called to mind the allurements of the world.[33]

A twelfth-century archbishop of Thessalonica named Eustathius, Homer's finest Christian exegete, looked back on ancient intellectual accomplishments and indebted them all to Homeric epic:

> Of all the men one could mention who labored at astronomy, or science, or ethics, or profane literature generally, not one passed by Homer's tent without a welcome. All lodged with him, some to spend the rest of their lives being fed from his table, others to fulfill a need and to borrow something useful from him for their own argument. . . . The philosophers are concerned with Homer . . . so are the orators; the scholars have no other way to their goal but through him. . . .[34]

> You may object that his poetry is heavy with myth, and that for this reason he risks banishment from our admiration. I answer . . . Homer's myths are not there for fun. They are shadows, or veils, of noble thoughts. . . . He weaves his poetry with myths to attract the multitude. The trick is to use their surface appearance as a bait and charm for men who are frightened of the subtleties of philosophy, until he traps them in the net. Then he will give them a taste of truth's sweetness, and set them free to go their ways as wise men, and to hunt for it in other places.[35]

Such allegorizing not only protected Homer from Plato's attacks but also promoted him to the pagan equivalent of Moses, the supreme revealor of the divine mind. "If Homer be a god," says an ancient epigram, "let him be honored as a god, but if he be not a god, let him be considered a god."[36]

Unlike Archbishop Eustathius, earlier Christians disdained such allegories that sought to justify heavenly misdeeds by strip-mining the epics for philosophical ore beneath noxious topsoil.[37] The sins of Homer's gods were revelations of their true diabolical essence. When Greek-speaking Christians read their Psalters they heard David warning them that "all the gods of the gentiles are demons (δαιμόνια), but the Lord made the heavens."[38] When they read Homer, they found him saying the same thing, for he, too, dubbed his deities "demons (δαίμονες)."[39] Homer's δαίμων simply meant "divinity," without pejorative connotation, but by the early empire the word had acquired progressively dreadful associations, becoming synonymous with malevolent power.[40] This semantic drift provided early Christians with ammunition for attacking the poet. For example, Clement of Alexandria was quick to point out to his pagan readers that Homer called his gods demons.[41] When discussing Greek poetry, Justin Martyr wrote: "[W]e not only assert that the *daimones* who commit such acts are not actually gods but are [indeed] wicked and unholy demons (δαίμονας)."[42] Therefore, one should not be astonished to read of them deflowering virgins and young boys,[43] killing their fathers,[44] and fomenting "murders, wars, adulteries, debaucheries, and all wickedness."[45]

Many Christians therefore forbade the reading of epic poetry altogether. A Syrian of the third century suggested that such poems be tossed to the flames so that "they may not persuade the still tender age of boys that Jupiter himself, the chief of the gods, was a parricide towards his parents, incestuous towards his sisters and his daughters, and even impure towards boys."[46] A contemporary wrote:

> [I]t behoves the young not to be satisfied with those corrupting lessons, and those who are in their prime should carefully avoid listening to the mythologies of the Greeks. For lessons about their gods are much worse than ignorance. . . . Truly, such fables of theirs, and spectacles, and books, ought to be shunned.[47]

A Syrian church order proscribed the reading of "all books of the heathen" because they "turn away from the faith them that are young."[48]

Such absolute bannings were exceptional. To be sure, rhetorical vituperations against the epics were commonplace, such as Augustine's congratulating Plato for not stomaching "insults offered to the gods," and for banning the poets from his utopia lest "the minds of the citizens be tarnished and depraved by poetic fictions."[49] But Augustine could not keep Homer out of his City of God any better than Plato had been able to keep him out of his Republic. Homer took refuge in the school where his epics persisted as cultural inevitabilities. There were no Christian schools for basic literary instruction in antiquity,[50] so all educated Christians once ruminated over their Homer beside pagan schoolmates. Since there was no avoiding Homer, the Church decided to tame him.

Some theologians employed Homer to support their own religious claims, not with philosophical allegories but with scriptural analogies. They had learned from Jews to argue that Homer had plagiarized Moses, so that occasionally even Homer spoke the truth.[51] Put baldly: when Moses and Homer differed, Homer erred; when they agreed, Homer shoplifted.

Perhaps no one more clearly expressed this two-tiered Homeric hermeneutic than the second-century apologist Theophilus of Antioch. On the one hand, Homer's Muses were demons. "This is clearly proved by the fact that up to the present day those who are possessed by demons are sometimes exorcized in the name of the real God, and the deceiving spirits themselves confess that they are the demons who were also at work at the time of the poets."[52] However, he is quick to add that "sometimes some poets, becoming sober in soul and departing from the demons, made statements in agreement with those of the prophets in order to bear witness to themselves and to all men concerning the rule of God and the judgement and the other matters they discussed."[53]

Justin, too, denounced Homer for having spoken under "the influence of the wicked demons, to deceive and lead astray the human race,"[54] but whenever Homer spoke about the immortality of the soul or eternal punishment, he betrayed his dependence on Moses and the prophets.[55] Clement of Alexandria repeated the nearly universal Christian objections to the comportment of Homer's gods: murder,[56] adultery,[57] and pederasty.[58] Such behavior demonstrates that the Greek gods were not gods at all but wicked demons.[59] On the other hand, whenever Homer happened to speak the truth, his Muses had read their Moses: "[E]very poetic Muse . . . filched from barbarian [i.e., Hebrew] philosophy the notions of penalties after death and punishment by fire."[60] This dependence on Jewish scriptures explains why, "strange as it may seem, even though Homer foisted human passions onto the gods, he seems to have understood the divine."[61]

So Christians continued reading epic poetry. In fact, so many teachers and grammarians themselves belonged to the new faith that by the end of the second century they had become a problem for purists. Tertullian conceded that it was counterproductive for youths to "repudiate secular studies without which divine studies cannot be pursued," but he did repudiate schoolmasters and professors of literature. While it is possible for a wary student to be exposed to poison without drinking it, a teacher *eo ipso* endorses it.[62] The *Canones Hippolyti* was only slightly more lenient: grammarians who knew no other trade might continue to teach young boys, providing they warned their pupils that the gods of the pagans were *daemones*.[63]

In the fourth century, the emperor Julian banned Christians from teaching the poets. The vigorous objections to this legislation[64]—not just by Christians but also by the proud pagan Ammianus Marcellinus[65]—leave little doubt that this ruling affected many scholars, such as Victorinus of Rome and Prohaeresius of Athens.[66] Had there been only a few Christian Homeric scholars, Julian hardly would have bothered to legislate against them. The emperor was convinced that these "Galileans" could not transmit the values of paganism articulated in Homer and Hesiod unless they honestly ascribed to those values themselves.[67] The problem was not that Christians knew no Homer but that they knew him too well—on their own ethical terms.[68] Julian reportedly applied a popular proverb to his cause by lamenting, "'We are shot with arrows feathered from our own wings,' for they make war against us armed from our own books."[69]

Two letters, one by Plutarch (a pagan) and one by Basil (a Christian) illustrate how morally sensitive men of the age taught young boys to read Homeric epic, sorting out the good from the bad, like the bee that "discovers amid the most pungent flowers and the roughest thorns the smoothest and most palatable honey." This quotation is from Plutarch, who lost sleep worrying about the Homeric lessons of his young son, Soclarus. To his friend Marcus Sedatus, himself the father of a young lad, Plutarch wrote: "Let us keep a very close watch over [the boys], in the firm belief that they require oversight in their reading even more than in the streets."[70] "Many the lies the poets tell," ran the proverb, but, Plutarch insisted, the answer is not to ban poetry altogether:[71]

> Shall we then stop the ears of the young, as those of the Ithacans were stopped, with a hard and unyielding wax, and force them to put to sea . . . , and avoid poetry and steer their course clear of it; or rather shall we set them against some upright standard of reason and there bind them fast, guiding and guarding their judgement, that it may not be carried away from the course by pleasure towards that which will do them hurt?[72]

For Plutarch, this Odyssean mast consisted of an a priori suspicion of poetry— "keeping clearly in mind the prevaricating sorcery of the poetic craft"[73]—along with an inculcation of philosophically based criteria for sorting out the noble from the base, vice from virtue.

Basil, writing to his nephews concerning how to read pagan literature, hit upon the same solution, though without having read his *Odyssey* as carefully. Whenever the boys come upon seamy or steamy passages they should flee the Sirens' songs, "stuffing up their ears no less than Odysseus did."[74] Basil acknowledged, however, that not everything in Greek authors was harmful, so the boys must keep on their guard to reject the venal and emulate the virtuous. In fact, Basil once heard the rhetorician Libanius demonstrate that "Homer's entire poetic enterprise was in praise of virtue and how everything said by him led to this end."[75] Thus Odysseus was not ashamed to stand naked before Nausicaa insofar as he was "bedecked with virtue instead of clothes."[76] Even though Odysseus arrived among the fabulously wealthy Phaeacians entirely stripped of possessions, they "one and all admired and envied the hero, and none of the Phaeacians at the moment would have desired anything else more than to become Odysseus, and that too just saved from shipwreck."[77] According to Basil's literary authority, Homer's message in *The Odyssey* was this: "You must give heed unto virtue, O men, which swims forth even with a man who has suffered shipwreck, and, on his coming naked to land, will render him more honoured than the happy Phaeacians."[78]

Plutarch, Libanius, and Basil were not unique in their advice. Most philosophically oriented educators during the first centuries of the common era probably shared their desire to establish criteria for helping young people combine epics and ethics. Nor were these intellectuals alone in appealing to

Odysseus as a model of moral ideals. For them, and for many of their contemporaries, the puritanical Odysseus of moral allegory was a sanitizing hermeneutic for reading *The Odyssey* itself.

This high esteem for Odysseus's character may astonish readers familiar with Homer's depiction of him. To be sure, Homer's Odysseus is courageous, mighty, clever, adaptable, wise,[79] chivalrous at court, consummate in oratory, and devoted to his father, mother, wife, and son. But he also enjoys extended affairs with Circe and Calypso, savagely slaughters the suitors, and lies unabashedly whenever it serves his ends. Because of his complex and ambiguous treatment in epic, Odysseus's morality, more than that of any other character in ancient literature, became the object of intense scrutiny.[80] Athenian dramatists, especially Sophocles and Euripides, enlarged on Odysseus's lying, adding to it his despicable treatment of Palamedes, Philoctetes, and Astyanax. Ancient Victorians caviled his occasional gluttony and frequent nakedness. Virgil and many Latin authors after him traced Roman ancestry back to the Trojans and therefore relished bashing him as a slick, merciless opportunist.

For the most part, however, writers of the Hellenistic and Imperial periods considered Odysseus among the noblest of the Achaeans. To Cynics he was an exemplar of the self-sufficient, unconventional individual, inured to privation and pain, a king in rags, willing to sacrifice his own comfort for the common good, preferring "wise Penelope" to the beautiful and immortal Calypso.[81] Stoics saw in his intelligence, courage, adaptability, and endurance sufficient reason to elevate him to the model σοφός and *The Odyssey* to "a kind of Stoic *Pilgrim's Progress*."[82] Seneca wrote: "[W]e Stoics have declared that these [viz. Odysseus and Heracles] were wise men, because they were unconquered by struggles, were despisers of pleasure, and victors over all terror."[83] A Homeric allegorist named Heraclitus (first century C.E.) claimed that Odysseus was "an instrument of every virtue."[84] He allegorized the Lotus-eaters to represent pleasure; the Cyclops (Κύκλωψ) stood for "that which atrophies (ὑποκλωπῶν) the intelligence"; the *nekyia* (visit to the netherworld) was the sage's refusal to leave anything unexplored; the Sirens were the raconteurs of events from all time; Charybdis was insatiability; Scylla impudence; the cattle of the sun dietary restraint; and on and on.[85] To rhetoricians Odysseus was the eloquent wandering philosopher, "the wisest and best of the Greeks."[86] Pythagoreans and later Platonists, however, viewed him as a cipher for the soul, bounced about in a sea of matter, bedeviled by temptations and monsters, longing to return to its immaterial, noumenal home.[87]

Early Christian philosophers, debtors to the Stoa and the Academy, likewise found in Odysseus a champion of virtue.[88] The first Christian now known to have discussed Homer systematically was Justin Martyr, who, with typical Platonic disdain, blasted the poet for the immorality of his Olympians, but when he appealed to the epics sympathetically, he always, without exception, had in mind not *The Iliad* but *The Odyssey*.[89] Clement of Alexandria, writing at about the same time as the author of *The Acts of Andrew* and probably from the same city, frequently appealed to Odysseus as a hero of the moral life. For example, he faulted antiintellectual Christians who so feared Greek music that they "stop up their ears with ignorance," like Odysseus's shipmates and unlike Odysseus himself, who dared to hear the song of the Sirens.[90] In order to recognize the futility of their ways, Greeks would do well to ask themselves, as Odysseus did on returning to Ithaca, "Whither this wealth do I bear; my journey, where doth it lead me?"[91] *The Odyssey* in general served Clement as a treasure of tropes.[92] Christ shines on all peoples, so that "no one is a Cimmerian," those Homeric denizens of total darkness;[93] the appetitive part of the soul is as polymorphic as Proteus;[94] the truth is like Ithaca, "'rough' at first but a 'goodly rearer of youth'";[95] the bathing practices of Penelope and Telemachus symbolize baptism;[96] and Christ is a "tender father" like the one for whom Telemachus pined.[97] Clement, like many Christians before and after him, including the author of *The Acts of Andrew*, saw in Odysseus tied to his mast a metaphor of Christ nailed to his cross.[98]

One also can detect positive Homeric influence on early Christian poetry. Already in the second-century poets ripped lines out of the epics and pasted them into collages, or centones. Irenaeus preserves a cento that Valentinian Gnostics seem to have assembled: six lines from *The Iliad* and four from *The Odyssey* scrambled into an apparently Gnostic allegory of Christ's descent into the world.[99] Tertullian, too, when refuting Gnostics, mentions *Homerocentones,* "who stick into one piece, patchwork fashion, works of their own from the likes of Homer, out of many scraps put together from this passage and from that."[100] A curious inscription from Phrygia says that a certain Zosimos served as a local oracle and made his predictions with "spiritual writings and Homeric verses."[101] Zosimos apparently knew his Bible and Homer well enough to patch quotations together into oracular utterances. The inscription itself displays archaic Homeric style.

The golden age of Christian poetry occurred in the late fourth and early fifth centuries, after Julian had banned Christians from teaching pagan poets. Though inoculated against Homer's morally flawed Olympians, these authors were by no means immune to his beguiling art.[102] Apollinarius of Laodicea, the son of a grammarian,

> employed his great learning and ingenuity in the production of a heroic epic on the antiquities of the Hebrews to the reign of Saul, as a substitute for the poems of Homer. He divided this work into twenty-four parts, to each of which he appended the name of one of the letters of the Greek alphabet, according to their number and order. He also wrote comedies in imitation of Menander, tragedies resembling those of Euripides, and odes on the model of Pindar. In short, he produced, within a very brief space of time, a set of works which in manner, expression, character and arrangement are well approved as similar to the Greek literatures.[103]

Gregory of Nazianzus wrote several poems in hexameters, including an autobiography that "could be described as a series of variations on Homeric language and techniques," motivated in part by a desire to provide "some sort of poetic literature, possibly for schools."[104]   An anonymous Christian poet who imitated the verse of Nonnos of Panopolis (the author of the fifth-century *Dionysiaca,* the longest of all Greek epics) rewrote the Gospel of John in hexameters.[105] The empress Eudocia, daughter of a teacher of rhetoric and wife of Theodosius II, whiled away her banishment in Jerusalem by composing epic hexameters on Christians themes, including paraphrases of the Octateuch (viz. the Pentateuch, Joshua, Judges, and Ruth), of Zechariah, and of Daniel, homerocentones on the life of Christ, and versified accounts of the martyrdoms of Cyprian and Justina.[106] Later in the fifth century a Christian Neoplatonist named Musaeus wrote a hexametric allegory of the soul's ascent to the divine. Musaeus's protagonists, Hero and Leander, play roles derived from Homer's Nausicaa and Odysseus.[107]

But it is a recently discovered manuscript of an otherwise unknown work that reveals most about the hypertextual ambitions of *The Acts of Andrew.* The unearthing of papyri at Dishna, Egypt, in 1952 brought to light "the oldest now known specimen of [original] Christian hexametric poetry,"[108] dated to the late third century. *Bodmer Papyrus 29* contains most of a work entitled *The Vision of Dorotheus,* who calls himself "son of Quintus the poet."[109] This Quintus almost certainly was Quintus Smyrnaeus, author of *The Posthomerica,* an epic poem bridging the gap between *The Iliad* and *The Odyssey,* between the mourning for Hector and the Achaean *nostoi.* Quintus's son Dorotheus very well may be the late third-century Dorotheus of Antioch whom Eusebius called a "learned man," well acquainted "especially with Greek elementary education and liberal arts," and a eunuch from birth.[110]

Its 343 lines of dactylic hexameters and archaic Homeric vocabulary leave little doubt that Dorotheus advanced the poem as a Homeric hypertext.[111] It describes the young eunuch's vision of the heavenly palace where he was commanded to guard a gate. Because of his cowardly failure to perform his duty, he was severely punished and asked: "Do you desire to take upon you the graceful strength and the rank of the heroes that are standing before the palace?"[112] When he said yes, Gabriel invited him to select a new name to symbolize his intention. He selected Andrew because he needed ἀνδρεία, 'courage':

> But I made the choice as before when still among the people on earth,
> —but then I had vehemently disavowed—what I wanted: to be Andrew.
> So they called me Andrew, and forthwith Jesus prayed
> on my behalf to the Most High, the renowned Father of the blessed ones,
> that he might now confer upon me faith and courage (ἀνδρείαν).
> And to give me my fearless name in his mercy
> he took the divine water of the Most High from a well and poured it out.
> When my limbs were baptized they all leapt up high.

> The long men, high as heaven, looked at me in astonishment
> seeing the wondrous giant, the strong man (that I was)
> . . . of all, and I had been made of unbreakable courage.
>
> .   .   .   .
> For Christ the Lord had created joy and youthfulness
> . . . for his servant; and he called him Andrew.[113]

In spite of "Andrew's" immense size, strength, and courage, he is commanded never to use violence:

>   [Y]ou may not . . .
> of yourself beat with your hands; but neither, if another comes
> first with brutal force upon you, must you turn around and run away
> like a child. . . .
> .   .   .   .
> But most of all you must give way in order that your strength remains firm.[114]

"Andrew" agrees to absorb violence and not to indulge in it (the text here is lacunose):

>   But I answered: ". . .
> in order that I may endure the . . . blows of men.[115]
> That I may not be the first to throw . . . one here, another there (?)
> Having beaten off with my (?) hands . . .
> may I ward off gently, whenever . . .
> having received blows. . . ."[116]

Thus Dorotheus, the author of the earliest of all Christian hexametric poems, imitates Homer and renames himself Andrew in order to transvalue ἀνδρεία as the courageous absorption of violence. It is quite possible that this Dorotheus is the same Dorotheus whom Eusebius knew to be a "highly honored" member of Diocletian's court who, in the end, possessed ἀνδρεία sufficient to prefer his Lord to his life.[117]

It is impossible to know if Dorotheus had read *The Acts of Andrew*, which had been written nearly a century earlier; there seem to be no additional verbal or thematic agreements with it. In any case, the only two texts of the first three centuries focused on the apostle Andrew are transvaluative Homeric hypertexts, and both redefine ἀνδρεία.

In sum, Homer's status in the Church ranged from pariah to Brahman. He was banished and embraced, excoriated and adduced, repudiated and imitated. In general, however, early Christians viewed his poems as unfortunate inevitabilities, a view shared by the author of *The Acts of Andrew*, who demonstrated his oscillating outrage and respect by transvaluing *The Odyssey*. Like his contemporaries, the author of the *Acts* understood Homer's gods to be demons; the demons Andrew opposes play the roles of Olympians: they blind their victims, strike them with madness, or seduce, strangle, and mutilate them. Andrew's God inevitably undoes their harm though exorcisms, healings, and raisings from the dead. Odysseus's lying, violence, and sexual appetite characterize Andrew's opponents, especially his executioner Aegeates. The apostle himself embodies Odysseus's courage, eloquence, fearless determination, and desire to return to his homeland, the realm of the divine. Apparently the author thought that Andrew—the fisherman who brought Greeks to Jesus and whose name meant manliness—might embody Odysseus's virtues without his carousing, cunning, and carnage. The first story in the *Acts* sends the apostle to a land far from his allotted Achaea, to the land of ferocious Myrmidons, Achilles' wild warriors in *The Iliad.*

Notes

1. *Republic* 10.606e.

2. H.-I. Marrou, *A History of Education in Antiquity,* trans. George Lamb (New York: Sheed and Ward, 1956), 162. See also Werner Jaeger, "Homer the Educator," in *Paideia: The Ideals of Greek Culture,* 2d edition, trans. Gilbert Highet (New York: Oxford University Press, 1945), 1.35–56; and Buffière, *Mythes d'Homère,* 10–11.

3. Pack, *Literary Texts,* no. 2707.

4. Ibid., no. 2642.

5. Ibid., no. 1208.

6. Ibid., nos. 2453, 2644, and 2650.

7. Ibid., no. 2457.

8. Ibid., nos. 2454, 2455, and 2723. See also nos. 2651, 2724, 2725, and 2731.

9. Heraclitus *Quaestiones Homericae* 1.5–6; cf. 76.3–5.

10. Pack, *Literary Texts.*

11. M. I. Finley, *The World of Odysseus,* 2d edition (New York: Penguin Books, 1978), 21.

12. *Protagoras* 339a.

13. See Marrou, *Education,* 10.

14. *Phaedrus* 245a. The heroes of *The Iliad* and *The Odyssey* frequently were identified with particular virtues. Heraclitus writes: "wise (φρόνιμος) Odysseus, manly (ἀνδρεῖος) Ajax, chaste (σώφρων) Penelope, consistently just Nestor, faithful-to-father Telemachus, loyal-to-friends Achilles" (*Quaestiones Homericae* 78). Cf. Maximus of Tyre 32.5 (Hobein) and Ps.-Plutarch *De vita et poesi Homeri* 185: Telemachus = honor, Agamemnon and Menelaus = intelligence and fidelity, Penelope = love of her husband, and especially chastity (σωφροσύνη). In *The Odyssey* itself, Orestes serves as a model for

the education of Telemachus.

15. *Institutio oratoria* 1.8.4–5.

16. *Geography* 1.2.3; cf. 1.2.17 and esp. 1.2.8:

For in dealing with a crowd of women, at least, or with any promiscuous mob, a philosopher cannot influence them by reason or exhort them to reverence, piety and faith; nay, there is need of religious fear also, and this cannot be aroused without myths and marvels. . . . But the founders of states gave their sanction to these things as bugbears wherewith to scare the simple-minded. Now since this is the nature of mythology, and since it has come to have its place in the social and civil scheme of life as well as in the history of actual facts, the ancients clung to their system of education for children and applied it up to the age of maturity; and by means of poetry they believed that they could satisfactorily discipline every period of life.

17. Xenophon *Symposium* 3.5; cf. 4.6. See also Plato's *Ion.*

18. Even prior to P'ato, Xenophanes of Colophon attacked Homer and Hesiod for their immoral depictions of gods and heroes. Plato wrote that: "there is from old a quarrel between philosophy and poetry" (*Republic* 10.607b).

19. *Republic* 3.386a–388b.

20. Ibid., 2.378b.

21. Ibid., 2.371a and 383a.

22. Ibid., 3.388c.

23. Ibid., 3.389a.

24. Ibid., 3.390b–c.

25. Ibid., 3.391d.

26. Ibid., 2.383c.

27. Ibid., 2.378d.

28. Ibid., 10.614b. For a more appreciative assessment of Homer, see 10.595b–c.

29. Heraclitus *Quaestiones Homericae* 1.1.

30. Buffière, *Mythes d'Homère,* 79–248.

31. Ibid., 249–391. See Strabo *Geography* 1.2.6–8.

32. Porphyry *De antro nympharum.*

33. Buffière, *Mythes d'Homère,* 392–520. See also Armand Delatte, *Études sur la littérature pythagoricienne* (Paris: Édouard Champion, 1915), 109–36, and Stefan Weinstock, "Die platonische Homerkritik und ihre Nachwirkung," *Philologus* 82, n.s. 36 (1927): 121–53.

34. Cf. Plato *Republic* 10.598d–e: "[H]ave we not next to sanitize tragedy and its leader Homer, since some people tell us that these poets know all the arts and all things human pertaining to virtue and vice, and all things divine."

35. From the introduction of Eustathius's commentary on *The Iliad,* trans. C. J. Herington, in "Homer, A Byzantine Perspective," *Arion* 8 (1969): 433–34. Robert Browning provides a masterful overview of "The Byzantines and Homer" in *Homer's Ancient Readers: The Hermeneutics of Greek Epic's Earliest Exegetes,* Magie Classical Publications, ed. Robert Lamberton and John J. Keaney (Princeton: Princeton University

Press, 1992), 134–48.

36. *Palatine Anthology* 16.301.

37. For examples of Christian allergies to allegory see: Tatian *Oratio ad graecos* 21 and 33, Eusebius *Praeparatio evangelica* 2.7 and 3.2, Gregory of Nazianzus *Oratio contra Iulianum* 1.118 (*PG* 35.657A–B), Augustine *De civitate Dei* 2.7, and especially *Ps.-Clementine Recognitions* 10.33–42. The most important recent works on the Christian reception of Homer are: Wilhelm Krause, *Die Stellung der frühchristlichen Autoren zur heidnischen Literatur* (Vienna: Herder, 1958); Glockmann, *Homer*, Zeegers-Vander Vorst, *Citations des poètes*; Jean Pépin, *Mythe et allégorie: Les Origines grecques et les contestations judéo-chrétiennes*, 2d edition (Paris: Études augustiniennes, 1976); and Arthur J. Droge, *Homer or Moses? Early Christian Interpretations of the History of Culture*, Hermeneutische Untersuchungen zur Theologie 26 (Tübingen: J. C. B. Mohr [Siebeck], 1989).

38. Ps. 95:5 (LXX 96:5). This verse was cited by Justin (*First Apology* 41 and *Dialogue with Trypho* 73), by Theophilus (*Ad Autolycum* 1.10), by Clement of Alexandria (*Protrepticus* 4.62.4), and by Origen (*Contra Celsum* 7.65).

39. Examples abound. Often Homer used δαίμων to designate hostile deities (e.g., *Iliad* 1.222, 3.420, 5.438, 459, and 884, 6.115, 7.291, 377, and 396, 9.600, 11.480 and 792, 15.418 and 468, 16.705 and 786, 17.98 and 104, 19.188, 20.447 and 493, 21.18, 93, and 227, and 23.595; *Odyssey* 4.275, 5.421, 6.172, 10.64, 11.61, 12.295, 14.386, 16.64 and 194, 18.256, 19.10, 129, 201, and 512, and 24.149).

40. See Werner Foerster, "Δαίμων, δαιμόνιον," *TDNT* 2.1–20, and John E. Rexine, "Daimon in Classical Greek Literature," *GrOrthTR* 30 (1985): 335–61. Even pagan authors at times associated Homer's gods with demons, though usually without the same pejorative meanings given them by Christians; see Buffière, *Mythes d'Homère*, 521–40, who discusses δαίμων in Plutarch and Maximus of Tyre.

41. *Protrepticus* 4.55.4–5, quoting *Iliad* 1.222: μετὰ δαίμονας ἄλλους.

42. Justin *First Apology* 5. See also *First Apology* 9 and *Second Apology* 5, and Athenagoras *Legatio* 23–27.

43. Justin *First Apology* 5 and 21.

44. Ibid., 21.

45. Justin *Second Apology* 5. Cf. Tatian *Oratio ad graecos* 8–9, *Ps.-Clementine Recognitions* 10.38, Tertullian *Ad Scapulam* 2, Origen *Contra Celsum* 7.69, and Eusebius *Praeparatio evangelica* 4.17. According to *The Acts of Andrew and Matthias*, quite possibly derived from *The Acts of Andrew*, pagan "priests themselves who conduct worship in the temple purify themselves for fear of the demons" (14).

46. *Ps.-Clementine Recognitions* 10.38 (ANF 8.202); see also 10.28 and 42.

47. Ibid., 4.19 (ANF 8.255).

48. *Didascalia Apostolorum* 2 (Connolly, 12). See also John Chrysostom's concerns expressed in *Homily 21 on Ephesians* 6 (*PG* 62.150).

49. *De civitate Dei* 2.14. Cf. Tertullian *Ad nationes* 2.7, Justin *Second Apology* 10, Ps.-Justin *Cohortatio ad gentiles* 5, Minucius Felix *Octavius* 22, Origen *Contra Celsum* 4.36 (which might be a later gloss), Athanasius *Contra gentes* 15–16, and Eusebius

Praeparatio evangelica 2.7. See also Josephus *Contra Apionem* 2.256–57.

50. Marrou, *Education,* 317–18.

51. Justin Martyr *First Apology* 23 and 54–60, Julius Africanus (in Eusebius *Praeparatio evangelica* 10.10), Julius Cassianus (Clement of Alexandria *Stromateis* 1.21), Tatian *Oratio ad graecos* 31 and 36–38, and Origen *Contra Celsum* 4.11–12 and 21. See Droge, *Homer or Moses?,* passim.

52. Theophilus of Antioch *Ad Autolycum* 2.8 (Grant, 39). For similar criticisms of Homer's diabolical inspirations see *Ps.-Clementine Homilies* 6.17 and 18 (the poets told "crooked riddles and . . . filthy stories, . . . as if impelled by an evil spirit" [ANF 8.265–66]). Homily 4.12 goes further: "Greek culture is in its entirety a most malicious concoction of the evil spirit" (*NTApoc* 2.559); cf. *Sibylline Oracles* 3.419–33 and Aristides *Apologia* 13.4.

53. *Ad Autolycum* 2.8 (Grant); cf. Lucian *Zeus Catechized* 2.

54. *First Apology* 54.

55. Ibid., 1.44.

56. *Protrepticus* 2.24; cf. Aristides *Apologia* 8, Theophilus *Ad Autolycum* 3.3, Justin *First Apology* 25, Athenagoras *Legatio* 21 and 29, and Irenaeus *Adversus haereses* 1.12.

57. *Protrepticus* 2.27, 28, and 31, and 4.52–53; cf. Aristides *Apologia* 8–9, Justin *First Apology* 21 and 25, Athenagoras *Legatio* 21, and Tatian *Oratio ad graecos* 21.

58. *Protrepticus* 2.31 and 4.43; cf. Theophilus *Ad Autolycum* 1.9, Justin *First Apology* 21 and 25, and Ps.-Justin *Cohortatio ad gentiles* 2.

59. *Protrepticus* 3.37–38; 4.49, 52, and 54; cf. Justin *First Apology* 21 and 23.

60. *Stromateis* 5.14.90.4.

61. Ibid., 5.14.116.4. See P. Camelot, "Les Idées de Clément d'Alexandrie sur l'utilisation des sciences et de la littérature profane," *RevScRel* 21 (1931): 38–66.

62. *De idololatria* 10. Similarly, Eusebius says of Origen: "[C]onsidering that the teaching of letters was not consonant with training in the divine studies, without more ado he broke off the task of teaching letters . . . he disposed of all the volumes of ancient literature which formerly he so fondly cherished" (*Historia ecclesiastica* 6.3.8–9; but see 6.15 and 18–19).

63. *Canones Hippolyti* 69.

64. Augustine *De civitate Dei* 18.52, Socrates *Historia ecclesiastica* 3.12, Rufinus *Historia ecclesiastica* 10.33, and Sozomen *Historia ecclesiastica* 5.18.1.

65. *History* 22.10.7 and 25.4.19.

66. Augustine *Confessions* 8.5 and Jerome *Chronicle,* s.v. year 363.

67. Julian *Epistles* 422a–c.

68. "By explicitly barring Christians from teaching, and so from interpreting, Homer, he [Julian] implicitly conceded the power of the interpretive community to shape the meaning of the poems. For him, a Christian Homer was worse than no Homer at all" (Robert Lamberton, *Homer the Theologian: Neoplatonist Allegorical Reading and the Growth of the Epic Tradition,* Transformation of the Classical Heritage 9 [Berkeley: University of California Press, 1986], 138).

69. Theodoret *Historia ecclesiastica* 3.4.

70. *How the Young Man Should Study Poetry* 15a. Lucian jests: "When I was a boy, when I read in Homer and Hesiod about wars and quarrels . . . amours and assaults and abductions and lawsuits and banishing fathers and marrying sisters, I thought that all these things were right" (*Menippus* 3).

71. *How the Young Man Should Study Poetry* 19e–f.

72. Ibid., 15d. The image of Odysseus at the mast and his crew with clogged ears was a philosophical topos (e.g., Lucian *Nigrinus* 19, *Charon* 21, *The Dance* 3, and *Essays in Portraiture* 14).

73. *How the Young Man Should Study Poetry* 16d.

74. *To Young Men, on How They Might Derive Benefit from Greek Literature* 4.2.

75. Ibid., 5.6.

76. Ibid. Ernest L. Fortin provides a helpful analysis in "Christianity and Hellenism in Basil the Great's Address *Ad Adulescentes*," in *Neoplatonism and Early Christian Thought*, ed. H. J. Blumenthal and R. A. Marcus (London: Variorum Publications, 1981), 189–203. See also Fernand Boulenger, *Saint Basil. Aux Jeunes Gens sur la manière de tirer profit des lettres helléniques* (Paris: Belles Lettres, 1935), 16–23.

77. *To Young Men, on How They Might Derive Benefit from Greek Literature* 5.7–8.

78. Ibid., 5.8.

79. *Iliad* 10.247 (Diomedes): "wise above all is he in understanding."

80. "The archetypal Ulysses, then, offered a wider foundation for later development than any other figure of Greek mythology, thanks to Homer's far-reaching conception of his character and exploits" (William Bedell Stanford, *The Ulysses Theme: A Study in the Adaptability of a Traditional Hero*, 2d edition [Oxford: Blackwell, 1963], 7).

81. Ibid., 97–100. See also Buffière, *Mythes d'Homère*, 372–74; and Pépin, *Mythe et allégorie*, 105–9, and "The Platonic and Christian Ulysses," in *Neoplatonism and Christian Thought*, International Society for Neoplatonic Studies, ed. Dominic J. O'Meara, (Albany: State University of New York, 1982), 3–5. Ragnar Höistad discusses the Cynic Odysseus in detail in *Cynic Hero and Cynic King: Studies in the Cynic Conception of Man* (Uppsala: Carl Bloms Boktryckeri A.–B., 1948), 94–102 and 196.

82. Pépin, *Mythe et allégorie*, 121; cf. Epictetus *Dissertationes* (Arrian) 3.24.12–14 and 26.33–35, and Porphyry *Quaestionum Homericarum ad Odysseam* 2.4, 69.17, and 100.9. See also Buffière, *Mythes d'Homère*, 374–77.

83. *De constantia sapientis* 2.1.

84. *Quaestiones Homericae* 70.

85. See Buffière, *Mythes d'Homère*, 377–80, and Pépin, *Mythe et allégorie*, 159–67. Other moralizing examples, though avoiding allegory, appear in Seneca *Epistulae* 31.2 and 9, 88.7–8, and 123.12, and Horace *Epistulae* 1.2.17–31.

86. Aelius Aristides *Orationes* 46.39; cf. 2.88, 96, 415, and 417, 24.7, 28.26–29 and 47, and 42.14. See also Maximus of Tyre 21.6, 22.6, 28.2, 40.1, and esp. 32.5–9 (Hobein), Dio Chrysostom 9.9, Epictetus *Dissertationes* (Arrian) 2.24.26, Strabo *Geography* 1.2.4–5, and Lucian, *The Hall* 17 and *The Parasite* 10, where a character likewise calls Odysseus σοφώτατος τῶν ὅλων. Appreciation of Odysseus's oratory also is common among Latin rhetors (e.g., Cicero *Brutus* 40, Aulus Gellius *Attic Nights* 1.15.3 and 6.14.7). Quintilian

write of Homer that "when he seeks to express the supreme gift of eloquence possessed by Ulysses he gives a mighty voice and a vehemence of oratory equal to the snows of winter in the abundance and the vigour of its words. 'With him then,' he says, 'no mortal will contend, and men shall look upon him as on a god'" (*Institutio oratoria* 12.10.64–65; cf. 4.2.13 and 11.3.158). Quintilian here has in mind *Iliad* 3.221–23 and *Odyssey* 8.173. For fuller discussions of this aspect of Odysseus's *Rezeptionsgeschichte*, see Buffière, *Mythes d'Homère*, 365–69, and Jan Fredrik Kindstrand, *Homer in der zweiten Sophistik*, Acta Universitatis Upsaliensis, Studia Graeca Upsaliensia 7 (Uppsala: University of Uppsala, 1973).

87. E.g., Plotinus *Enneads* 1.6.8 and 5.9.1, Proclus *In Platonis Cratylum comm.* 158 (403d), and *In Platonis Parmenidem comm.* 5.1025: Ithaca stands for the "mystical port of the soul"; cf. Ps.-Plutarch *De vita et poesi Homeri* 126. Buffière says that among Neoplatonists *The Odyssey* is "le poème de l'âme exilée sur cette terre, loin de la patrie" (*Mythes d'Homère*, 395). See also Marcel Detienne, *Homère, Hésiode et Pythagore: Poésie et philosophie dans le pythagorisme ancien*, Collection Latomus 57 (Brussels-Berchem: Latomus, 1962), 52–60.

88. E.g., Fulgentius *Continentia* 151: "sapientissimus Ulixes."

89. As one authority on Justin has observed:

Was Justinus an Homer positiv einschätzt, findet er ohne Ausnahme in der Odyssee, vor allem in der Nekyia: Es sind die Schilderungen von Leben nach dem Tode. . . . Justins negative Wertung des Dichters bezieht sich dagegen auf den ganzen Homer, und sie trifft den Dichter der Ilias in noch grösserem Masse als den Dichter der Odyssee. (Glockmann, *Homer*, 194)

For example, Justin argued for the immortality of the soul by appealing to "the ditch in Homer and the descent of Odysseus to visit the dead" (*First Apology* 18; cf. 20), that is, Odysseus's soaking a ditch with sacrificial blood to attract the spirits of the dead and his subsequent observation of eternal torments, such as Sisyphus's endless mountain climbing and Tantalus's tantalization. Pythagoreans and Platonists also used the *nekyia* to argue for the immortality of the soul (Buffière, *Mythes d'Homère*, 399–404). Oskar Dreyer, however, rightly complains that Glockmann too quickly assumes that Justin's reference is to *The Odyssey* directly and not to uses of the *nekyia* by Platonists (*Göttingische gelehrte Anzeigen* 222 [1970]: 227–42, esp. 239). Even so, insofar as the concerns of this present study obtain also to the larger Odyssean legacy, Dreyer's caveat is irrelevant.

90. *Stromateis* 6.11.89.1.

91. *Protrepticus* 10.80, quoting *Odyssey* 13.203–4.

92. See Jean Daniélou, *A History of Early Christian Doctrine Before the Council of Nicaea*, vol. 2, *Gospel Message and Hellenistic Culture*, trans. J. A. Baker (Philadelphia: Westminster Press, 1973), 94–99.

93. *Protrepticus* 9.72; see *Odyssey* 11.13–16.

94. *Paidagogos* 3.1.

95. *Protrepticus* 10.85; see *Odyssey* 9.27.

96. *Stromateis* 4.22; see *Odyssey* 2.261, 4.750 and 760, and 17.48 and 58.

97. *Protrepticus* 9.68; see *Odyssey* 2.47.

98. *Protrepticus* 12.118.1–4. See chapter 7, 259–61.

99. *Adversus haereses* 1.9. See Daniélou, *History*, 2.85–89, and Robert L. Wilken, "The Homeric Cento in Irenaeus, *Adv. Haer.* 1,9,4," *VC* 21 (1967): 25–34. Irenaeus claims that by using such centones, Gnostics tricked the uneducated into thinking "that Homer composed the verses."

100. *De praescriptione haereticorum* 39 (ANF). A beautiful cento in the famous Palatine collection shows that Gnostics were not the only Christians to have written Homeric centones; its author was a Byzantine priest (*Anthologia graeca* 1.119). Most Christian centones come from the Latin-speaking world and were based on Virgil, not Homer (e.g., the cento of Proba [fourth century]). Michael Roberts demonstrates how these centones conform with the conventions of Homeric paraphrasing in ancient schools of rhetoric (*Biblical Epic and Rhetorical Paraphrase in Late Antiquity*, ARCA Classical and Medieval Texts, Papers and Monographs 16 [Liverpool: Francis Cairns, 1985]). Isolated Homeric lines appear as oaths or charms in Greek magical papyri (Betz, 260). The epics also served as a source for personal oracles. A list of 216 lines from *The Iliad* and *The Odyssey* gave cryptic advice to inquirers who chose among the lines with three rolls of a die or a knucklebone (ibid., 112–19).

101. Caroline H. E. Haspels, *Highlands of Phrygia: Sites and Monuments* (Princeton: Princeton University Press, 1971), 1.313–14, no. 40.

102. On learning literary skills from Homer see Jerome *Epistulae* 52.3.5–6, 58.5.2, and *Comm. on Amos* 1.2.

103. Sozomen *Historia ecclesiastica* 5.18 (NPNF).

104. Denis Molaise Meehan, *St. Gregory of Nazianzus. Three Poems*, FC 75 (Washington: Catholic University of America Press, 1986), 20–21.

105. *PG* 43.749–920.

106. See "Eudokia," P-W 6.1:906–12.

107. See Thomas Gelzer's introduction and edition in the Loeb Callimachus, 291–389. Latin-speaking Christians, too, wrote epic poems. See, for example, Juvencus (fourth century), whose recasting of the Gospels in 3,210 lines of dactylic hexameters was widely used as a textbook in medieval schools. Prudentius's *Psychomachia* (ca. 405) is an allegorical epic mimetic of *The Aeneid*.

108. A. H. M. Kessels and P. W. Van der Horst, "The Vision of Dorotheus (Pap. Bodmer 29)," *VC* 41 (1987): 314. The *editio princeps* was prepared by André Hurst, Olivier Reverdin, and Jean Rudhardt, *Papyrus Bodmer XXIX: Vision de Dorothéos* (Cologne: Fondation Martin Bodmer, 1984). E. Livrea provides an extended review with textual conjectures in *Gnomon* 58 (1986): 687–711.

109. According to the postscript; cf. line 300.

110. Eusebius *Historia ecclesiastica* 7.32.2–4.

111. "Le poème est composé d'hexamètres dactyliques souvent empruntés en tout ou en partie à Homère" (Hurst et al., *Papyrus Bodmer XXIX*, 39).

112. *Vision of Dorotheus* 215–16. All translations of this text come from Kessels and Van der Horst, "Vision," except when altered to reflect my own textual conjectures.

113. Ibid., 225–35 and 240–41.

114. Ibid., 254–57 and 261.

115. The translation of this line is my own, based on my reconstruction of the text, which reads: δ[   ]εσϙ[ ]πλ[   ]σιν[   ]ανδρων. I restore: δ[   ]εσϙ[ ]πλ[ήγα]σιν [τῶν] ἀνδρῶν.

116. *Vision of Dorotheus*, 277–82.

117. *Historia ecclesiastica* 8.1.4.

2

The Iliad

City of the Cannibals (Achilles' Myrmidons, *AAMt* 1a)

The Acts of Andrew and Matthias in the City of the Cannibals (*AAMt*), originally located at the beginning of *The Acts of Andrew*,[1] opens with the following scene: "At that time, all the apostles were gathered together at one place and divided the regions among themselves by casting lots, so that each would leave for his allotted share. The lot fell on Matthias to go to the region of the cannibals" (*AAMt* 1). Gregory's epitome begins similarly but adds that the lot fell on Andrew to go to Achaea,[2] and names the city of the cannibals Myrmidonia.[3] The word "Myrmidonia" certainly appeared in the original story. A Latin translation of the *AAMt*, earlier than any extant Greek text by at least two centuries, names the city Mermedonia,[4] and a Greek Andrean passion, like Gregory, sends Matthew (= Matthias) to "the city of Myrmenis."[5] Both Mermedonia and Myrmenis are variant spellings of Myrmidonia.

Ancient scribes never could agree concerning how best to spell it. The manuscripts of Gregory's *Liber de miraculis* read Myrmidonia, Mermidona, Mirmidona, Mirmidonia, Myrmidona, and Mirmydona.[6] Other related Latin documents read Myrmidon, Myrmidonensis, Mermedonia, Marmedonia, Marmadonia,[7] Medea,[8] Margundia,[9] and Mirdone.[10] Greek texts give the city name as Μυρμήνη,[11] Μυρμήνις,[12] Μύρνη,[13] Μυρμήκη or Σμυρμήνη,[14] and Σμύρνα.[15] The remarkable variety in the spellings of the name derives from its elusive location. Myrmidonia never existed, even though readers have tried to identify it with Sinope,[16] Athens,[17] Titaran,[18] Colchis,[19] Ethiopia,[20] or the Scythian port city of Myrmekion.[21]

The solution to the location of the city lies not in geographical speculations but in Homeric narrative; Myrmidonia is the mythological home of the Myrmidons, Achilles' savage troops.[22] Homer mentions Myrmidons only three times in *The Odyssey*,[23] but thirty-nine times explicitly in *The Iliad* and implicitly many more. They were ferocious warriors whose late involvement in the Trojan War swung the victory to the Greeks. Homer's favorite epithet for them is φιλοπτόλεμος, 'war-loving', and his characterizations of them border on cannibalism:

Achilles went to and fro throughout the huts and let harness in their armour all the Myrmidons, and they rushed forth like ravening wolves in whose hearts is fury unspeakable—wolves that have slain in the hills a great horned stag, and rend him, and the jaws of all are red with gore; and in a pack they go to lap with their slender tongues the surface of the black water from a dusky spring, belching forth the while blood and gore, the heart in their breasts unflinching, and their bellies gorged full; even in such wise the leaders and rulers of the Myrmidons sped forth round about the valiant squire of the swift-footed son of Aeacus. And among them all stood warlike Achilles, urging on both horses and men that bear the shield.[24]

Achilles himself wished he could sink his teeth into Hector's meat: "Would that in any wise wrath and fury might bid me carve thy flesh and myself eat it raw."[25] Thus Hecuba called him ὠμηστής, 'eater of raw flesh'.[26]

The *AAMt* similarly depicts the Myrmidons as barbarians:

[They] ate no bread and drank no water,[27] but ate human flesh and drank their blood. They would seize all who came to their city, dig out their eyes, make them drink a drug prepared by sorcery and magic. When forced by them to drink the drug, the victims' hearts became muddled and their minds deranged. Out of their minds and taken to prison, they would eat hay like cattle or sheep. (*AAMt* 1)[28]

Later in the *AAMt* two peculiar structures at Myrmidonia likewise might call to mind Homer's Myrmidons: "An earthen oven had been erected in the middle of the city, and next to it lay a large trough where they used to slay (ἐσφαγίαζον) people and their blood (αἷμα) would flow into the trough, whence they would draw up the blood (αἷμα) and drink it" (*AAMt* 22). In *The Iliad*, after the Myrmidonian warrior Patroclus fell to Hector's spear, Achilles offered lavish and bloody sacrifices: "Many sleek bulls bellowed about the knife, as they were slaughtered (σφαζόμενοι), many sheep and bleating goats, and many white-tusked swine, rich with fat, were stretched to singe over the flame of Hephaestus; and everywhere about the corpse the blood (αἷμα) ran so deep that one might dip cups therein."[29] Achilles then ordered the Greeks to gather wood to build a great pyre to consume the body of his friend. On the pyre he slew twelve young Trojans, an outrageously brutal act that earned Achilles the contempt of Plato's Socrates.[30] According to Homer, the Greeks

heaped up the wood, and made a pyre of an hundred feet this way and that. . . . And many goodly sheep and many sleek kine of shambling gait they flayed and dressed before the pyre: and from them all great-souled Achilles gathered the fat, and enfolded the dead therein from head to foot, and about him heaped the flayed bodies. And thereon he set two-handled jars of honey and oil, leaning them against the bier; and four horses with high-arched necks he cast swiftly upon the pyre, groaning aloud the while. Nine dogs had the prince, that fed beneath his table, and of these did Achilles cut the throats of twain, and cast them upon the pyre. And twelve valiant sons of the great-souled Trojans slew he with the bronze—and grim was the work he purposed in his heart—and thereto he set the iron might of fire, to range at large.[31]

But Homer's depiction of the Myrmidons only partially accounts for their traits in the *AAMt*, some of which refer rather to post-Homeric traditions that made them into ant-people.

The historical Myrmidons apparently assimilated with other Greek tribes even before Homer. In their place emerged two etymological myths that claimed they took their name and ferocity from μύρμηκες, 'ants'. According to the first, "Zeus, in the likeness of an ant (μύρμηκι) had intercourse with Eurymedusa . . . and begat Myrmidon,"[32] the grand ancestor of the tribe. According to the more ancient and popular myth, Aeacus, king of the island Aegina, pleaded with Zeus to repopulate his devastated island with citizens as numerous as the ants swarming a nearby oak. The god consented by transforming those very ants into humans, although they retained their former formic traits.[33] Homer's vivid portrayal and the μύρμηξ myth combined to provide the Myrmidons an enduring reputation for savagery. According to Lucian, they were "the most warlike of tribes."[34]

Even the Greek manuscripts of the *AAMt* that lack the word "Myrmidonia" depict the city as Antville. The oven (κλίβανος) in the center of town might remind the reader not only of the pyre of Patroclus but also of an anthill. One built such an oven by digging into the earth and packing mud and plaster into conical walls with an opening at the top. The social organization of the cannibals also reminds one of ants. They have no king, no proconsul, no magistrate, only "rulers," "superiors," "guards," "executioners," and "the young," who sail away in search of prey. In order to punish them, Andrew drowns them, a common method for killing ants. When the residents repent, Andrew calls off the flood, walks toward the middle of town, the waters receding before him, until he gets to the vat and the oven, where the earth opens and the abyss swallows the waters along with the most wicked of the cannibals—like ants plunged into their hole.

In other respects, Myrmidonia calls to mind the city of Troy. Like Troy, the city of the cannibals has a wall and a main gate and lies near the ocean. Such characteristics hold true, of course, for many ancient cities, but outside Myrmidonia, "along the road," was "a large fig tree (συκῆν μεγάλην)" (*AAMt* 21). Readers familiar with *The Iliad* might remember the wild fig tree just outside Troy's wall "along the wagon track."[35] Just as Odysseus and his comrades had sailed from Achaea in order to rescue Helen from Troy, Andrew will sail from Achaea to rescue Matthias from the city of the cannibals, who are no longer Trojans but rather Greek Myrmidons.

By depicting Greek heroes as cannibals, the author of the *Acts* waged an apologetic war, counterattacking charges of cannibalism that so preoccupied Christian intellectuals of the late second and early third centuries. Athenagoras met such accusations with the observation that it was not Christians but pagans who thronged to arenas, their eyes thirsty for gladiatorial blood.[36] The apologist Theophilus likewise insisted that whereas Christians abhorred the very thought of eating human flesh, the same could not be said of pagans:

> Zeno or Diogenes and Cleanthes . . . advocate cannibalism and the cooking and eating of fathers by their own children. . . . Diogenes . . . teaches that children should lead their own parents to the slaughter and eat them. And more—does not the historian Herodotus relate how Cambyses slew the children of Harpagus and after cooking them placed them before their father as food? Further, he tells the story that among the Indians fathers are eaten by their own children.[37]

Tertullian repeatedly addressed this matter, demonstrating not only the absurdity of the charges of cannibalism, but actually turning them against his accusers, citing human sacrifices to Saturn, Mercury, and Jupiter: "And they say that it was a custom among certain tribes of Scythians for every deceased member to be eaten by his relatives."[38]

Apparently the author of the *Acts*, like many of his contemporaries, was appalled at Homer's glorification of warfare—gouged eyes, severed limbs, smashed skulls, spilled guts, rolling heads, and the earth "black with blood." No Greek tribe was more savage than the Myrmidons, no hero less merciful than Achilles, their captain, and no portrayals of the gods more bloodthirsty than those in *The Iliad*. By transvaluing the epic, the author of the *Acts* not only promoted a vision of the Christian God who could throttle diabolical deities and pacify even "the most warlike of tribes," but also threw the charge of cannibalism back into the faces of their pagan critics. One source of inspiration for this counterattack was the book of Jonah. As was the case with the Hebrew prophet, God commands Andrew to preach to distant savages, but the apostle balks, goes to the shore, finds a boat, sails away,[39] converts his audience, rescues both humans and livestock from divine wrath, and suffers divine reproach for lack of compassion.[40]

On the other hand, the frame, plot, and characterization of the story derive primarily from *Odyssey* Book 10, where Odysseus rescues his comrades, whom Circe had transformed into beasts. Circe was de rigueur for Homeric hypertexts: she appears in *The Telegonia*, Apollonius's *Argonautica*,[41] Virgil's *Aeneid*,[42] Ovid's *Metamorphoses*,[43] and Petronius's *Satyricon*.[44] *AAMt* 1–2 describes the Myrmidons with imagery reminiscent of the witch of Aeaea: they, like Circe, turn their prey into animals with drugs and feed them fodder. This is how they treat Matthias when he arrives. Jesus appears to Andrew and dispatches him to Myrmidonia, and in chapters 18–21 the apostle, like Odysseus, restores the victims to their human condition. In the end, chapter 33, Andrew leaves Myrmidonia as Odysseus left Aeaea. Inserted between chapters 2 and 18 and between 21 and 33 are two sections derived from other sections of Homer's poems. The first section recasts episodes from *Odyssey* Books 2–15 (chapters 3–17), and the second recasts episodes from *The Iliad*. The general architecture then looks like this:

Odyssey		*AAMt*	
10.233–43	Circe drugs victims	1–2	Cannibals drug victims
	episodes from *Odyssey* 2–15	3–17	
10.277–395	Odysseus rescues crew	18–21	Andrew rescues Matthias
	episodes from *The Iliad*	22–32	
10.467–11.3	Odysseus sails	33	Andrew sails

To facilitate comparison, the points of similarity between the *AAMt* and Homeric epic appear in parallel columns. It will become obvious that the similarities pertain to motifs, themes, characterizations, and sequences, not to vocabulary, although Greek words and phrases do appear in parentheses when appropriate. Particularly striking similarities appear in **bold face**. Additional points of contact appear in the notes. Taken in isolation, some of these parallels may seem strained, but by the end of the chapter it will become clear that they repeatedly occur in the same order as in the epics, a phenomenon impossible to attribute to happenstance.

Abduction of Matthias (Circe the Cannibal, *AAMt* 1–2)

The Myrmidons as a tribe take on the role of Circe, the quondam cannibal. Homer suppressed her anthropophagy, but according to the ancient folktale she transformed Odysseus's crew into swine in order to provision her table.[45] When Odysseus's ships washed up on the island of Aeaea, the sailors discovered no trace of human habitation other than wisps of smoke in the distance. They cast lots to see which of two groups would go to investigate the origin of the smoke. Compare this scene with the apostolic land lottery in the *AAMt* (which also shares similarities with the casting of lots at the beginning of the book of Acts to select Matthias as Judas's replacement among the Twelve, Acts 1.23–26).

Odyssey 10.206–8
"Quickly then we
shook lots (κλήρους . . . πάλλομεν)
in a brazen helmet,
and **out leaped the lot** (κλῆρος)
of great-hearted Eurylochus.
So **he set out. . . ."**[46]

AAMt 1
[A]nd [they] divided the regions by
casting lots (βάλλοντες κλήρους),
so that each would leave for his
allotted share. **The lot fell** (κλῆρον)
on Matthias
to go to the city called <Myrmidonia>.

Odysseus's search party discovered a stone house surrounded by mysteriously docile wolves and lions. Inside sang a beautiful young woman. Disarmed by her charms, they entered and drank the drugged wine she offered. So did Matthias.

Odyssey 10.233–43
"She **brought them in** and made
them sit on chairs and seats,
and **made for them a potion** of

AAMt 2
So when Matthias **entered** the gate
of the city Myrmidonia,
the people of that city seized him

cheese and barley meal and yellow honey with Pramnian wine; but in the food she mixed baneful **drugs** (φάρμακα), that they might utterly forget their native land. Now when she had given them the potion and they **had drunk it off** (ἔκπιον), then she presently smote them with her wand, and **penned them in the sties.** And they had the heads, and voice, and bristles, and shape of swine,

but their minds (νοῦς) **remained unchanged** even as before. So they were penned there **weeping** (κλαίοντες), and before them Circe **flung mast and acorns, and the fruit of the cornel tree, to eat, such things as wallowing swine are wont to feed upon."**

and gouged out his eyes.

They made him **drink** the **drug** (φάρμακον) of their magical deceit . . . [Cf. *AAMt* 1: "When forced to drink (ἐκπότιζον) the **drug** (φάρμακον) . . ."] **led him off to the prison, and gave him grass to eat.** He ate nothing, **for his heart was not muddled and his mind** (νοῦς) **not deranged** when he took their **drug** (φάρμακον), but he prayed to God **weeping** (κλαίων). . . .

[Cf. *AAMt* 1: "[T]hey would eat hay like cattle or sheep."]

Both *The Odyssey* and the *AAMt* tell of strangers entering mysterious locations where cannibals used magical potions to transform their victims into animals. In both, drugged and incarcerated victims weep and nourish themselves on food fit only for beasts. Furthermore, the parallels cited above appear in the same order.

Jesus Consoles Matthias (Athena the Comforter, *AAMt* 3)

Chapters 3–17 temporarily switch from dependence on the Circe story to other narratives strewn throughout Books 2–15 of *The Odyssey*; parallels with Circe will reappear in chapter 18. I have subdivided chapters 3–17 into four units, each of which follows the Homeric order.

	Odyssey	*AAMt*
Jesus consoles Matthias	2.267–92	3
Voyage to Myrmidonia	2.292–418	4–7
	5.268–453	8–9
	8.550–9.11	10–11
Summoning the dead	10.490–11.376	12–15
Sleepy disembarkation	13.75–236	16–17

When Matthias complained to Jesus about his condition, his Lord appeared to him. Similarly, Telemachus, Odysseus's son, sat disconsolate in his own home while his mother's suitors partied raucously in his hall. The goddess Athena then appeared to him, promising to go with him, to provide a ship, and to take him to the palaces of Nestor and Menelaus.

Odyssey 2.267–92
So he spoke in **prayer** (εὐχόμενος) and Athene drew near to him in the likeness of Mentor, both in form and in **voice**; and she **spoke** (φωνήσασ᾽) ... "Telemachus, **neither hereafter shalt thou be a base man** ... So then shall this journey of thine be neither vain nor unfulfilled ... so true a friend of thy father's house am **I, who will equip for thee a swift ship, and myself go with thee** ... but I, going through the town, will quickly gather comrades to go."

AAMt 3
As Matthias was **praying** (προσευχομένου), a light shone in the prison, and a **voice** (φωνή) came out of the light **saying** ... "Brace yourself, our Matthias, and **do not be terrified,**

for **I will never abandon you. I will rescue you from every danger** ... for **I am with you** every hour and always. I will send Andrew to you, who will lead you out of this prison."

Having comforted the men with these speeches, the deities immediately departed.

These parallels raise an important issue of method that will arise repeatedly. One might quite reasonably attribute these and other parallels not to intertextual dependence but to shared type-scenes or, in the jargon of form criticism, to conventional compositional forms. Each of the two texts above is an epiphany, a widespread literary topos in which a deity appears to a mortal.[47] Even though such form-critical treatments of these passages are legitimate—indeed desirable, even necessary—they are unable, of themselves, adequately to explain the density of parallels lexical, thematic, and sequential between Homer and *The Acts of Andrew*. In isolated instances, a form-critical approach may suffice, but it cannot account for many of the more distinctive parallels.[48]

Voyage to Myrmidonia (Athena the Sailor, *AAMt* 4–11)

Twenty-seven days later, while Matthias languished in prison, "the Lord Jesus appeared in a city of Achaea, where Andrew was teaching and said to him, 'Arise, go with your disciples to the city called Myrmidonia, and bring Matthias out of that place, for in three days the citizenry will bring him out and slaughter him for their food'" (*AAMt* 4). The apostle was understandably reluctant, like Jonah, who tried to sail away from his mission to Nineveh. But even more relevant to a hypertextual reading of the *Acts* might be Odysseus's futile attempt to shirk his duty to rescue Helen from Troy by feigning madness.[49] Eventually, however, Andrew agreed to go when Jesus promised to provide a boat,[50] just as Athena had promised Telemachus.

Odyssey 2.292–94 and 386–87	*AAMt* 4 and 5
[Athena speaks:] "And **ships** there are full many in **sea**-girt Ithaca; . . . of these will I choose out for thee the one that is best."	[Jesus speaks:] "[Y]ou will find a **boat** on the shore that you and your disciples should board."
[Cf. *Odyssey* 1.319–20: So spake the goddess, flashing-eyed Athene, and departed, **flying upward as a bird**.]	**Having said this, the Savior . . .**
. . . [O]f Noemon, the glorious son of Phronius, she **asked a swift ship** and he promised it to her.	**went into the heavens**." . . . The Lord by his own power had **prepared the boat**.[51]

The next morning Andrew went to the shore and found a boat headed for Myrmidonia, but he failed to recognize Jesus disguised as the captain of the ship and two angels as his crew.[52] Telemachus sailed off to Pylos with Athena disguised as a mortal.

Odyssey 2.401	*AAMt* 5
[The goddess] **likened** herself to **Mentor** both in form and in voice.	He [Jesus] himself was in the boat **like a human captain**.

Compare the following excerpts concerning the embarkations of Telemachus and Andrew with their divine companions.

Odyssey 2.407–8 and 416–19	*AAMt* 5–7
[W]hen they had **come down** (κατ-ήλυθον) **to the ship and to the sea**, (ἐπὶ . . . θάλασσαν) they **found on the shore** their long-haired comrades.	Andrew and his disciples **went to the sea** (ἐπὶ τὴν θάλασσαν), and when he **descended** (κατελθών) to **the shore** he saw a small boat and seated in the boat **three men**.[53]
[O]n board the ship stepped (ἂν . . . βαῖν') Telemachus, and Athene went before him and **sat down in the stern of the ship**.	. . . Andrew and his disciples **boarded** (ἀνῆλθεν) **the boat**. After boarding, he **sat down by the sail of the boat**.[54]

The narration of the voyage in the *AAMt* begins with dependence on the famous shipwreck scene in *Odyssey* Book 5, where Odysseus sails from Calypso to the Phaeacians.

Odyssey 5.270–79	*AAMt* 8–9
[A]nd he **sat and guided his raft** skilfully (τεχνηέντως) with the **steering-oar** (πηδαλίῳ),	Jesus went and **sat at the rudder** (πηδάλιον) and **piloted the boat**. . . . [Andrew comforted his disciples by telling them how Jesus had stilled the storm. Then,] his disciples **fell asleep**
nor did **sleep** (ὕπνος) fall upon his eyelids. . . .	(εἰς ὕπνον). . . . [Andrew to Jesus:]

For seventeen days (ἑπτὰ δὲ καὶ δέκα) then he **sailed** (πλέεν) **over the sea, and on the eighteenth** (ὀκτωκαιδεκάτῃ). . .[55]

"Sir, show me your **sailing technique** (τέχνην). . . . **I sailed** (ἔπλευσα) **the seas sixteen times** (ἑξκαιδέκατον); this is my **seventeenth** (ἑπτακαιδέκατον), and I have never seen such **skill** (τέχνην). The ship actually responds as though it were on land. So, young man, show me your **technique** (τέχνην)."

Jesus tells Andrew that the apostle himself is the reason for the calm sea. Compare this with Zeus's stilling the storm for Odysseus.

Odyssey 5.451–53
[T]he god [Zeus] straightway stayed his stream, and **checked the waves** (κῦμα) and made a calm before him. (Cf. also 3:52)

AAMt 9
"[T]he sea knew that you were righteous and so it was still and **did not lift its waves** (κύματα) against the boat."

In the preceding parallels, both Odysseus and Jesus sit at the rudder and pilot their crafts with skill (τέχνη). In both columns one finds voyagers falling asleep (Andrew's disciples) or vigilantly staying awake (Odysseus), precise indications about how many times or how long the hero had sailed (Odysseus: 17/18 days; Andrew: 16/17 times), and gods calming the seas.

The sailing story Andrew told that put his disciples to sleep derived primarily from the Synoptic Gospels,[56] but the *AAMt* enhanced the adventure by describing the tempest with images similar to those Homer used to depict Odysseus's shipwreck:

Odyssey 5.313–17
[A] **great wave** (μέγα κῦμα) smote him **from on high** . . . but his **mast** (ἱστὸν) was broken in the midst by the fierce blast of tumultuous **winds** (ἀνέμων). (Cf. 365–67)

AAMt 8
"[A] **great wind** (ἀνέμου μεγάλου) arose, and the sea swelled, such that the **waves** (κύματα) **rose up and came down on** the **sail** (ἱστίῳ) of the boat."

Captain Jesus asked Andrew to explain why the Jews refused to believe in Jesus. Here the *Acts* borrows from Alcinous's questions to Odysseus, which initiated the hero's celebrated first-person narration of sea adventures in *Odyssey* Books 9–12.

Odyssey 8.550, 555, 564, and 572
"**Tell me** (εἴπ') the name by which they were wont to call thee in thy home. . . . **And tell me** (εἰπὲ δέ μοι) thy country. . . . [T]his story

AAMt 10–11
"**Tell me** (εἰπέ μοι) . . . why did the faithless Jews not believe in him. . . ?" "**Make it clear to me** (φανέρωσόν μοι) . . .

I once heard (ἄκουσα). . . . But come, now, **tell me this** (μοι τόδε εἰπὲ) and declare it truly."	for **we have heard** (ἠκούσαμεν). . . . What kind of miracles did he do privately? **Disclose them to me** (φανέρωσόν μοι)."

Andrew complained about the captain's pushy curiosity, but Jesus explained that he was fascinated by such stories. In Odysseus's response to Alcinous's string of questions, one finds another expression of the joy of listening:

Odyssey 9.5–11 "[T]here is no greater **fulfilment of delight** than when **joy** possess **a whole people**, and banqueters in a hall **listen** (ἀκουάζωνται) to a minstrel as they sit in order due, and by them tables **are laden** (πλήθωσι) **with bread and meat,** and the cup-bearer draws wine from the bowl and bears it round and pours it into the cups. This seems to my mind the fairest thing there is."[57]	*AAMt* 11 "[M]y soul **rejoices and exults—** and not only mine, but **every soul** that **hears** (ἀκούουσα) of his wonders." "O child," Andrew said, "the Lord will **fill** (πληρώσει) your soul with all **joy** **and every good thing.**"

The order of the parallels given for this unit can be broken down as follows:

	Odyssey	*AAMt*
Divinely supplied ships	2.292–94	3
	386–87	4
Goddess/god in disguise	401	5
Descending to the ships	407–8	5
Embarking	416–19	6–7
Skillful sailing	5.270–79	8–9
Storms at sea	313–17	8
Calm seas	451–53	9
Appeals for information	8.550, 555, 564, 572	10–11
Joys of listening	9.5–11	11

Summoning the Dead (*Nekyia, AAMt* 12–15)

Andrew's response to the inquiries of captain Jesus seems to have been inspired by Book 11 of *The Odyssey*, Odysseus's visit with the spirits in the netherworld, the famous *nekyia*. Jesus, so said Andrew, took his disciples, four Jewish high priests, and thirty others into a pagan temple that contained two sculpted sphinxes, which reminded Jesus of "the cherubim and seraphim in heaven" (*AAMt* 13). The sphinx, the cherub, and the seraph were all winged monsters with human faces. The seraph had six wings (Isa. 6:1–6); cherubim and sphinxes two wings and the bodies of lions or dogs. The cherub and the sphinx were the only sculpted objects shared by normative Hebrew and popular Greek religions.[58]

Jesus told the sphinx on the right side of the temple (cf. Ezek. 10:2–3) to leave its pedestal and refute the Jews. Immediately she jumped up, "acquired a human voice,"[59] and accused the high priests of blindness and of blinding others.[60] For this reason, pagan "temples will abolish your synagogues, so that they even become churches of the unique son of God" (*AAMt* 14).[61] After all, pagan "temples are more beautiful than your synagogue." This speech of the sphinx failed to budge the Jews, so Jesus sent the monster to summon Abraham, Isaac, and Jacob.[62] Jesus' command that she journey to fetch the dead functions like Circe's statement to Odysseus to conjure up the souls of the netherworld.

Odyssey 10.490–93	*AAMt* 15
"'[Y]ou must first complete another journey, and **come to the house of Hades** and dread Persephone, to seek soothsaying from the spirit of Theban Teiresias.'"	"Go and enter the land of the Canaanites, **go to the double cave** in the field of Mambre where lies the body of Abraham."

The sphinx did as she was told, but too many patriarchs revived. Odysseus had a similar problem.

Odyssey 11.36–37	*AAMt* 15
"Then there gathered from out of Erebus the spirits of those that are dead." (Cf. 11.42)	At once the twelve patriarchs came out of the tomb alive.

The sphinx told them she needed only Abraham, Isaac, and Jacob.

Odyssey 11.149–51	*AAMt* 15
[Tiresias to Odysseus:] "'[B]ut whomsoever thou refusest, he surely will **go back again.**' So saying the spirit of the prince, Teiresias, **went back into the house** of Hades."	"But as for you, **go and rest** until the time of resurrection." Hearing this, they **went into the tomb** and slept.

The three necessary patriarchs traveled with the sphinx, refuted the high priests, and returned to their tombs.[63] The sphinx returned to her pedestal.

Andrew feared that his long story might have bored his listener, just as Odysseus had worried that Alcinous would rather sleep than listen to his tales.

Odyssey 11.328–31	*AAMt* 15
"But **I cannot tell** or name all . . . that I saw, ere that immortal night would wane. Nay it is now time to sleep." (Cf. 12.450–53)	"He showed us many other mysteries, which, **should I narrate** to you, brother, you would not be able to endure them."

But neither Alcinous nor Jesus had had his fill of thrills.

Odyssey 11.362 and 374–76
Then again Alcinous **made answer
and said** . . . "Tell on, I pray thee,
the tale of these wondrous deeds.
Verily **I could abide** until bright
dawn, so thou wouldest be willing
to tell in the hall of these woes
of thine." (Cf. 11.377–84)[64]

AAMt 15
Jesus **answered and
said** to him,

"**I can endure** them,
for when the prudent hear useful
words, their hearts rejoice."

The parallels presented in this section again follow a common order:

	Odyssey	*AAMt*
Command to travel to		
the land of the dead	10.490–93	15
The dead gather	11.36–37	15
Sending the dead back	149–51	15
Tiresome tales	328–31	15
Avid listeners	362, 374–76	15

Sleepy Disembarkation (Odysseus's Arrival at Ithaca, *AAMt* 16–17)

Andrew's disembarkation on the Myrmidonian shore was modeled after Book 13 of *The Odyssey*, which recounts Odysseus's voyage back to Ithaca.

Odyssey 13.75–76 and 79–80
[Phaeacians] **laid him** [Odysseus]
down in silence. . . .
[S]weet **sleep** (ὕπνος) fell upon his
eyelids, an unawakening **sleep**. . . .

AAMt 16
Andrew, too, **lay his head**
on one of his disciples
and **fell asleep** (ἀφύπνωσεν).

Both heroes slept until the ships reached their destinations, where sailors deposited them on the shore.

Odyssey 13.116–25
Then they stepped forth from
the benched ship upon the land,
and first **they lifted** Odysseus out
of the hollow ship . . .
**and laid him down on the sand,
still overpowered by sleep**. . . .
**Then they themselves
returned home again**.[65]

AAMt 16–17
The angels did as Jesus commanded
them:
they **lifted** Andrew and his **sleeping**
disciples, raised them aloft,
and brought them outside the gate of
the city of the <Myrmidons>.
After **putting them down**, the angels
returned to Jesus, and then Jesus
and his angels **ascended into heaven**.

Both heroes awakened and were amazed to find themselves in strange surroundings.

Odyssey 13.187–97	*AAMt* 17
Odysseus **awoke** out of his sleep. . . .	Andrew **woke,**
So he sprang up and stood	**looked up**, and found himself sitting
and **looked** (εἴσιδε) **upon his**	on the ground (γῆν). When he **looked,**
native land (γαῖαν).	he saw (εἶδεν) **the gate of the city**
	<Myrmidonia>.[66]

When Andrew realized that the captain was Jesus in disguise, he asked his Lord to appear to him again, this time as himself; Jesus did so. When Odysseus awoke on shore, he did not know he was back at Ithaca until Athena appeared to him.

Odyssey 13.221–36	*AAMt* 18
And Athene **drew near him**	Jesus **came to him appearing like**
in the form of a young man. . . .	**a most beautiful small child.**
Odysseus was glad **at the sight**	When Andrew **saw him,** he fell to
of her, and came to meet her,	the earth, worshipped him,
and he spoke, "Friend . . .	**and said,** "Forgive me, Lord Jesus
to thee do I pray, **as to a god**	Christ, for on the sea I saw you **as a**
(ὥς τε θεῷ), and am come to thy	**human** (ὡς γὰρ ἄνθρωπον) and spoke
dear knees. . . . **What** (τίς) **land,**	with you. My Lord Jesus,
what (τίς) **people** is this?"	**what** (τί) sin had I committed. . . ?"
. . . Then the goddess, flashing-eyed	Jesus **answered Andrew.** . . .
Athene, **answered him.** . . .	

Both Odysseus and Andrew, thanks to miraculous assistance, arrived at their destinations with great speed, slept on board, were deposited asleep on shore, and awoke to revelations of their patron deities in the form of young men. Once again the parallels of this subunit follow the Homeric order:

	Odyssey	*AAMt*
Falling asleep on board	13.75–80	16
Disembarking asleep	116–25	16–17
Waking up on		
strange shores	187–97	17
Divine messengers	221–36	18

Andrew Rescues Matthias (Odysseus Rescues Crew, *AAMt* 18–21)

At this point in the *AAMt* the author returns to the Circe story. When Odysseus learned what Circe's drugs had done to his crew, he left his ship on the shore, and on his way to her hut he met Hermes disguised as a youth. This encounter appears in the left-hand column below, opposite a similar incident involving Andrew and Jesus. The column to the right repeats content from the preceding comparison, which pertained to Athena's appearance to Odysseus at Ithaca. The duplication is due to Homer's stock theme of a god appearing to mortals in disguise. It is possible that the author of the *Acts* noticed the similarities between the appearances of Athena in *Odyssey* Book 13 and of Hermes in Book 10, and used the scene as a means of returning to the Circe story at precisely the place where he had stopped following the tale in *AAMt* 2.

Odyssey 10.277–80	*AAMt* 18
"Hermes, of the golden wand, **met me** as I went toward the house, **in the likeness of a young man** with the first down upon his lip, in whom the charm of youth is fairest. He clasped my hand, **and spoke**, and addressed me."	Jesus **came to him** appearing like a most beautiful child and said, "Greetings, our Andrew."[67]

Both deities, Hermes and Jesus, instructed their heroes about impending peril and how to deal with it.

Odyssey 10.286–91	*AAMt* 18
"'Here, take this potent herb, **and go to the house of Circe. . . .** And **I will tell thee** all the baneful wiles of Circe. **She will mix thee a potion,** and cast drugs into the food; **but even so she shall not be able** (οὐδ᾽ . . . δυνήσεται) **to bewitch thee.'"**	"Now stand up **and go to Matthias in the city. . . .** For behold, **I show you**, Andrew, before you enter their city what you must suffer. **They will show you terrible insults,** contrive tortures. . . . **But they will not be able** (οὐ δύνανται) **to kill you."**

Hermes told Odysseus to rush upon Circe with his sword to threaten her with death. Jesus, on the other hand, instructed Andrew not to treat violence with violence, but to imitate Jesus' own sufferings. The *AAMt* clearly transvalues *The Odyssey* here by replacing the sword of the hypotext with nonviolent endurance.[68] The gods depart; the heroes continue walking in order to rescue their friends.

Odyssey 10.302–14	*AAMt* 18–19
"So saying . . . Hermes then **departed to high Olympus** through the wooded isle, and **I went on my way to the house** of Circe, and many things did my heart ponder as I went.	**After the Savior said these things, he ascended into the heavens.** Andrew rose up and **went to the city** with his disciples without anyone seeing him. They went to the prison,

So I stood at the gates (ἔστην δ᾽ εἰνὶ θύρῃσι) of the fair–tressed goddess. There I stood and called, and the goddess heard my voice. Straightway then she **came forth** (ἐξελθοῦσα),

and opened the bright **doors** (θύρας) and bade me in; and **I went** with her, my heart sore troubled. She **brought me in. . . .**"[70]

and Andrew saw seven guards **standing at the door of the prison** (ἐστῶτας . . . ἐπὶ τὴν θύραν) guarding it. He prayed silently, and the seven guards fell and died. When he **came to the door** (ἐλθὼν ἐπὶ τὴν θύραν) of the prison, Andrew marked it with the sign of the cross, **and the door** (ἡ θύρα) **opened** automatically.[69] On **entering** the prison with his disciples, he saw Matthias sitting, singing psalms by himself.[71]

Andrew asked Matthias why he was in prison in spite of Christ's great powers. Matthias reminded him that Jesus had told them: "I send you as sheep in the midst of wolves."[72] Like Odysseus, Andrew grieved over the beastlike condition of the drugged victims.[73]

After an extended speech,[74] Andrew healed the theriomorphs, just as Circe had.

Odyssey 10.391–95
"[A]nd she [Circe] went through the midst of them,

and anointed each man with another charm. Then from their limbs the bristles fell away . . . , and they **became men again.**"

AAMt 21
Andrew and Matthias rose up and prayed, and after the prayer, Andrew put his hands on the faces of the blind men in the prison, and immediately they received their sight. He also put his hand on their hearts, and their minds

regained human consciousness.[75]

The restored victims in each story expressed their gratitude.

The parallels for this subunit strictly follow the Homeric order:

	Odyssey	*AAMt*
Divine messengers	10.277–80	18
Warnings about ogres	286–91	18
Entering ogres' domain	302–14	19
Lamenting the victims	375–87	20
Healing the victims	391–95	21

Andrew told the erstwhile captives: "[G]o to the lower parts of the city, and you will find along the road a large fig tree. Sit under the fig tree and eat its fruit until I come to you." Troy also boasted a wild fig tree outside the walls next to a road.[76] Then Andrew ordered his disciples and Matthias to leave the city toward the east,[77] where a cloud would snatch them up and whisk them out of harm's way.[78] The apostle himself walked about in the city until he found a pillar supporting a copper statue, behind which he hid "in order to see what would happen."[79] What happened next derived from the events of the Trojan War.

Slaying the Children (Iphigenia and Orestes, *AAMt* 22–23)

When the Myrmidons discovered their dinners had fled, they agreed to eat the seven dead guards and brought them to their public furnace for butchering. Andrew prayed, and "the swords fell from the executioners' hands, and their hands became stone" (*AAMt* 22). They then held a lottery for their senior citizens. The seven whom they selected in the daily drawing they would execute to supply their oven. "One of those selected said to the attendants, 'I beg you! I have a small son. Take him, slaughter him in my place, and let me go.'" The authorities agreed.

> [A]nd the old man said to them, "In addition to my son I also have a daughter. Take and slaughter them, only let me go." He delivered up his children to the attendants for them to slaughter, and they dismissed him unharmed.

> As they went to the trough, the children wept together, and begged the attendants, "We beg you: do not kill us when we are so small, but let us reach full stature and then slaughter us." But the attendants did not listen to the children or have compassion on them, but brought them weeping and begging to the trough. (*AAMt* 23)

This old man is none other than Agamemnon, the Achaean general who sacrificed his own daughter Iphigenia at the altar of Artemis at Aulis in order to propitiate the goddess and thereby secure favorable sailing conditions for the Greek armada headed for Troy. Homer himself did not mention the story, but it did appear in the epic poem *Cypria*. Euripides immortalized the tale in his *Iphigenia at Aulis* and *Iphigenia in Tauris*.[80] The playwright depicted Agamemnon as a benighted pedicide who loved his daughter but valued valor more and felt himself a slave to fate, the tyrannous χρῆ. Clytemnestra, his wife and Iphigenia's mother, protested the murder and recommended that the Achaeans cast lots to see whose daughter should be put to death.[81] The chorus, Achilles, and even Menelaus encouraged the king of Mycenae to spare his daughter—all in vain. Not even his daughter's tender appeals and tears could soften his will. As the executioners dragged Iphigenia to the altar, she pleaded with them "[S]lay me not untimely! Sweet is light: / Constrain me not to see the nether gloom!"[82] Orestes, her infant brother, also mourned her early and tragic fate; Iphigenia cried to her father, "[B]y thy beard we pray thee, loved ones twain, / A nesting one, and a daughter grown."[83] Euripides depicted Orestes himself at an altar about to be slain by savages.[84] The two young people in the *AAMt*, too, came to the slaughtering trough "weeping and begging," appealing for mercy on their youth: "[D]o not kill us when we are so small."

Ancient authors denounced Agamemnon's unspeakable sacrifice and recognized its grave theological implications—a goddess who required human sacrifice![85] As one might imagine, Christian apologists would find the story useful for besmirching paganism. Arguing that Greek epics were nothing more than "monuments of madness and intemperance," one apologist cited this incident as his premier example: "For first they say that Agamemnon, abetting the extravagant lust of his brother [Menelaus], and his madness and unrestrained desire, readily gave even his daughter to be sacrificed, and troubled all Greece that he might rescue Helen, who had been ravished by the leprous shepherd."[86]

In the end, miracles saved both Euripides' Iphigenia and the children in the *AAMt*.[87] Having led Iphigenia to the bloody altar of Artemis,

> The priest took the knife, he spake the prayer,
> He scanned her throat for the fittest place to strike. . . .
>
> . . . .
>   [L]o, a sudden miracle!
> For each man plainly heard the blow strike home;
> But the maid—none knew whither she had
> Vanished.[88]

Artemis had substituted a deer for the girl whom she snatched up on a cloud and transported to distant, savage Tauris to serve as her priestess there.[89]

According to the *AAMt*, the Myrmidons brought the crying children to the slaying trough while Andrew prayed: "[L]isten to me, so that the executioners may not bring death on these children. Loosen the swords from the hands of the executioners" (23). Then one reads: "Immediately the swords were loosened and fell from the hands of the executioners like wax in fire." Andrew's prayer seems to have been inspired by the prayer of Chryses, the priest of Apollo, in Book 1 of *The Iliad*, whose daughter Agamemnon had stolen. Apollo sent a plague against the Greeks until they returned his daughter to Chryses. The priest then "joyfully took his dear child; but they made haste to set in array for the god the holy hecatomb around the well-built altar."[90] Compare Chryses' prayer with Andrew's.

Iliad 1.450–57	*AAMt* 23
Then Chryses **lifted up his hands,**	He **looked into heaven** weeping
and prayed aloud for them:	**and said,**
"Hear me, thou of the silver bow. . . .	"Lord Jesus Christ,
Even as aforetime thou didst hear	**just as you listened to me**
me when I prayed—to me thou	in the case of the dead guards and
didst do honour, **and didst mightily**	**did not**

smite the host of the Achaeans—
even so now (καὶ νῦν μοι) do thou
fulfil me this my desire ward thou
off now from the Danaans the
loathly pestilence."[91]

let them be devoured,
so now too (καὶ νῦν . . . μου),
listen to me,
so that the executioners may not
bring death on these children."

Both Apollo and Jesus granted the requests. Chryses, like the priest of
Artemis at Aulis, proceeded with the sacrifice: "[T]hey first drew back the
victims' heads, and cut their throats, and flayed them."[92] The Myrmidonian
executioners, on the other hand, were unable to slay the children with their melted
swords.

Devil's Advocate (Zeus's Lying Dream, *AAMt* 24)

The devil himself then appeared to advise the cannibals, and by so doing played
the role of Zeus's vicious dream to Agamemnon in *Iliad* Book 2. The king of
Olympus wanted to honor Achilles by showing the Achaeans the futility of their
efforts without the leader of the Myrmidons. To this end, he sent a dream, in the
form of the old man Nestor, urging Agamemnon to arms and promising victory,
even though Zeus knew the battle would "lay many low beside the ships of the
Achaeans."[93] Zeus lied. Greeks died.

Iliad 2.16–30
[Zeus's messenger] **went his way** to
Agamemnon. . .
in the likeness of the son of Neleus,
even Nestor, whom above all the
elders (γερόντων)[94] Agamemnon
held in honour. . . .
[T]he dream from heaven **spake,
saying** . . . [The dream reminds the
hero of the plight of the Achaeans.]
"**But now, hearken thou quickly
unto me.** . . . He biddeth thee arm
the long-haired Achaeans with all
speed, since now thou mayest take
the broad-wayed **city** (πόλιν) of the
Trojans."

AAMt 24
Then the devil **came**

looking like an old man (γέροντι)

and **began to speak** in the midst
of them all. . . . [The devil reminds
the Myrmidons of their plight.]
"**But if you wish to hear
me**, get up and search for a certain
stranger here residing in the **city** (πόλει)
named Andrew and kill him."

Once Agamemnon understood that Zeus had lied to him, he was outraged at the
deceit of the "cruel god."[95] Plato agreed with Agamemnon, and so did several
other protesters of "the sending of the dream by Zeus to Agamemnon."[96] Tatian
thought Zeus sent the dream because he wanted to annihilate all of humankind.[97]
Justin Martyr deduced from this tale that Zeus must be a demon insofar as he
wanted to "destroy so many Greeks" for the sake of petulant Achilles.[98] So, too,

in the *AAMt*, the devil plays the role of Zeus by appearing himself "like an old man" to urge the Myrmidons to kill Andrew. It is they, however, who will die because of this action.

Dragging the Apostle (Hector's Corpse, *AAMt* 25–28)

Andrew cursed the devil, the "warrior (πολεμιστής) against every creature,"[99] promising that Christ would humiliate him into the abyss.[100] The devil heard Andrew's curse, but could not see him.[101] The Myrmidons scoured the city unable to find the apostle until Andrew intentionally revealed himself. They then deliberated what torture would be most excruciating. Decapitation might be nice,[102] or an apostle-roast. "Then one of them whom the devil had entered and whose heart he had filled (πληρώσαντος), said to the crowd. . . ." The language used here is reminiscent of *Iliad* 17.210–12: "[A]nd there entered into him [Hector] Ares . . . and his limbs were filled (πλῆσθεν) with valour and with might."[103] But this character is not Hector but his enemy, the prince of the Myrmidons, Achilles himself.[104] The following columns demonstrate the similarities between Achilles and the unnamed Myrmidon possessed of the devil.

Iliad 22.395–402	*AAMt* 25
He spake, and **devised foul treatment** for the goodly Hector. [Achilles had said that he "would **drag Hector** hither	"Let us **invent the most heinous tortures** for him. Let us go, tie a rope around his neck, and **drag him** through all the boulevards and streets of the city each day until he dies. When he is dead, let us divide his body for all of
and give him (δώσειν) raw **unto the dogs to devour.**" (23.21)][105] The tendons of both his feet behind he pierced from heel to ankle and made fast therethrough thongs of oxhide, and **bound them** to his chariot. . . . And from Hector **as he was dragged** the dust rose up, and on either side his dark hair flowed outspread. (Cf. 22.463–65)	the citizens **and pass it out** (διαδῶμεν) **for their food.**" Hearing this, the crowds did as he had said to them. They **tied a rope** around his neck
	and dragged him through all the boulevards and streets of the city. As the blessed Andrew **was dragged**, his flesh stuck to the ground, and his blood flowed on the ground like water.[106]

The criticisms of Plato's Socrates against the Homeric epics included "the trailings of Hector's body around the grave of Patroclus."[107] An anonymous early Christian apologist also criticized Achilles for "dragging the corpse of Hector after death."[108] The author of the *AAMt* shared this disgust.

The cannibals tied Andrew's hands behind him,[109] threw him into prison, and brought him out again the next day for more dragging. Andrew prayed, expressing his willingness to die if need be, but pleaded that his Lord prevent the devil from mocking him (*AAMt* 26). Then the devil sneaked up behind him, like Apollo who sneaked up behind Patroclus to deliver him a crushing blow.

Iliad 16.791–92	*AAMt* 26
Apollo took his stand **behind** (ὄπισθεν) **him, and smote his back** and shoulders with the flat of his hand, and his eyes were made to whirl.	[T]he devil was walking **behind** (ὄπισθεν) **him**, saying to the crowds, **"Slap his mouth** to shut him up!"

The cannibals again threw the apostle into prison, where demons approached to heckle and jeer.[110] They were delighted to have in their clutches at last the one who had deprived them of their delicious sacrifices: "you who make our temples deserted houses, with the result that no sacrifices are offered in them, so that we might take our pleasure (τερφθῶμεν)" (*AAMt* 26). The word τέρπομαι ('take pleasure'), rare in early Christian literature, is standard Homeric fare, used at times to describe the gods at ease and enjoying the feasts mortals provided them.[111] Plato's Socrates and many other Greeks faulted Homer's gods for their hunger for hecatombs.[112] Christian apologists and the author of the *AAMt* joined their voices to Socrates'.[113]

The devil then commanded his demons to kill the apostle, but fear dissuaded them: "[W]hen they saw the seal on his forehead which the Lord had given him, they were afraid and were not able to approach him but fled (ἔφυγον)." When the devil asked them why they fled, they said it was because of the seal.[114] Too timid to kill the apostle, the demons continued their heckling. The devil, daring Andrew to deploy whatever powers he had at his disposal, uttered a taunt familiar to Homer's readers: "If you have some such power, use it."[115] The apostle retorted that he would indeed punish his diabolical hecklers, and when "the seven demons heard these things, they fled (ἔφυγον) with the devil." One consistent Christian objection to Greek gods was their flight from the scene of battle, an objection that may also lie behind the flight of the demons here in *AAMt*.[116]

Again the next morning, for a third day, the cannibals "fetched Andrew, tied a rope around his neck, and dragged him. Again his flesh stuck to the earth, and his blood flowed on the ground like water" (*AAMt* 28). During his horizontal tour of the city, the apostle complained to his Lord: "[W]here are your words which you spoke to us to strengthen us, telling us, "If you walk with me, you will not lose one hair from your head?" Therefore, Lord, look and see that my flesh and the hairs of my head stick to the ground'" (*AAMt* 28).[117] A voice then told him to look behind him, and when he did so, he "saw large fruit-bearing trees sprouting" where his flesh and hair had stuck to the pavement.

The parallels are transparent between this passage and the beginning of *Iliad* Book 24, which tells of Priam's dramatic rescue of Hector's body from Achilles:

Neither would he [Achilles] fail to mark the Dawn, as she shone over the sea and the sea-beaches, but would yoke beneath the car his swift horses, and bind

Hector behind the chariot to **drag him** withal; and when he had **haled him thrice about the barrow** of the dead son of Menoetius, he would rest again in his hut, but would leave Hector outstretched on his face in the dust. Howbeit **Apollo kept all defacement from his flesh**, pitying the warrior even in death, and with the golden aegis he covered him wholly, **that Achilles might not tear his body as he dragged him.** Thus Achilles in his fury did foul despite unto goodly Hector; but the blessed gods had pity of him as they beheld him.[118]

This is what Hermes told Priam about Hector's corpse:

[T]his is now the twelfth day that he lieth there, yet **his flesh decayeth not at all**, neither do worms consume it, such as devour men that be slain in fight. Truly **Achilles draggeth him ruthlessly about the barrow** of his dear comrade, so oft as sacred **Dawn appeareth, howbeit he marreth him not;** thou wouldst thyself marvel, wert thou to come and see how dewy-fresh he lieth, and is washen clean of blood, neither hath anywhere pollution; and all the wounds are closed wherewith he was stricken, for many there were that drave the bronze into his flesh. **In such wise do the blessed gods care for thy son.**[119]

Both Hector and Andrew, though dragged about early in the morning by Myrmidons—three times around the pyre of Patroclus and three days through city streets respectively—were protected by divine solicitude: the preservation of a hero's corpse and the sprouting of apostolic epidermis.

Fighting the Flood (Achilles and the Scamander, *AAMt* 29–32a)

Andrew's executioners returned him to prison,[120] where Jesus appeared and restored his health.[121] The apostle then ordered an alabaster statue to spew water from its mouth. The author of the *Acts* might have chosen any number of more natural sources for a propitious flood. The selection of an animated statue suggests some connection with a pagan divinity, and none would have been more appropriate than the river god Scamander/Xanthus, who flowed through the Trojan plain. Furious with Achilles for having glutted his waters with corpses, the River assumed anthropomorphic characteristics,[122] and for more than one hundred poetic lines battered the leader of the Myrmidons.[123] Compare the following passages:

Iliad 21.307, 311–15, and 234–40	*AAMt* 29
[The river god] **called** with a shout	He . . . **said**
to Simois [a river] . . . ,	to the pillar and the statue on it . . . ,
"[F]ill thy streams with	"[L]et the statue sitting on the pillar
water (ὕδατος) from thy springs,	spew from its mouth **water** (ὕδωρ) as
and arouse all **thy torrents** . . .	abundant **as a flood,**

that (ἵνα) we may check this fierce man that now prevaileth, and is minded to vie even with the gods." He **spake** . . . ; the River rushed upon him with **surging flood**, and roused all his springs tumultuously, and swept along the many dead that lay thick within his bed. . . . In terrible wise about Achilles **towered the tumultuous wave**.

so that (ἵνα) the residents of this city may be punished."

As soon as the blessed Andrew had **said** these things, the stone statue spewed from its mouth **a great quantity of water** as from a trench,

and the **water rose** on the earth. It was exceedingly brackish and consumed human flesh.

Iliad 21.346–48 and 255–56
. . . [B]ut Achilles, springing forth from the eddy, **hasted to fly** with swift feet over the plain, for he was seized with fear.
. . . [H]e swerved from beneath **the flood and fled** (φεῦγ') ever onward.

AAMt 30
When morning came, the men of the city saw what had happened and **began to flee** (φεύγειν), saying to themselves, "Woe to us, for now we die!"[124] The water killed their cattle and their children, **and they began to flee** (φεύγειν) the city.[125]

Andrew prevented the Myrmidons from escaping by asking Jesus to send the "archangel Michael in a fiery cloud and wall up this city so that if any should want to flee it they will not be able to pass through the fire" (*AAMt* 30).[126] So the waters continued to rise, just as in *The Iliad*:

Iliad 21.300–302, 306–7, and 324–27
[A]nd the whole plain was filled with a **flood of water**, and many goodly arms and corpses of youths slain in battle were floating there . . . and **raising himself on high** (ὑψόσ') he [the River] made the surge of his flood into a crest. He . . . rushed tumultuously up on Achilles, **raging on high** (ὑψόσε) and seething with foam and dead men. And the dark **flood** of the heaven-fed River rose **towering** above him.

AAMt 30
The water rose (ὑψώθη) to the necks of the men and was devouring them viciously.

The residents of Myrmidonia then decided to release Andrew from prison in order to stem the flood.[127]

Iliad 21.372–73 and 383–84
[The River told Hera to call off the fire of Hephaestus:] **"I will refrain**

AAMt 30
Then the blessed Andrew said to the alabaster statue, **"Now at last stop**

(ἀποπαύσομαι), if so thou biddest, and let him also refrain (παυέσθω)."

... But when the fury of Xanthus was quelled, the twain thereafter **ceased** (παυσάσθην).

(παῦσαι) spewing water from your mouth, for the time of rest (ἀναπαύσεως) has come. ...
[I]f the inhabitants of this city believe, I will build a church and place you in it, because you did this service to me."
The statue **ceased** (ἐπαύσατο) flowing and no longer emitted water.

The old man who sacrificed his children, the Andrean Agamemnon, pleaded for mercy:[128]

"I am amazed," said the holy Andrew to the old man, "that you can say, 'Have mercy on me,' when you did not have mercy on your own children but delivered them up in your place. Therefore I tell you, at that hour when the water recedes, you will go into the abyss, you and the fourteen executioners who killed people daily, and the lot of you will stay in Hades until I turn once again and raise you. So now, go into the abyss so that I may show these executioners the place of your murders and the place of peace, and to this old man the place of love and the surrender of his children. Now everyone follow me."

As the men of the city followed him, the water divided before the feet of the blessed Andrew until he came to the place of the trough where they used to slaughter people. Looking up into heaven, the blessed Andrew prayed before the entire crowd, and the earth opened and devoured the water along with the old man, and he and the executioners were carried down into the abyss. (*AAMt* 31)[129]

At this, the Myrmidons were terrified until Andrew reassured them:

"My little children, do not be afraid; for I will not let even them stay in Hades. They went there so that you should believe in our Lord Jesus Christ."

Then the blessed Andrew commanded all those who had died in the water to be brought to him, but they were unable to bring them because a great multitude had died, of men, women, children, and beasts.[130] Then Andrew prayed, and all revived.

Later, he drew up plans for a church and had the church built on the spot where the pillar in the prison had stood. (*AAMt* 31–32a)

Presumably, the reader is to assume that the church was built around the cooperative pagan statue.[131]

Jesus the Child (Hermes the Youth, *AAMt* 32b)

The conclusion of the *AAMt* recasts various scenes of Book 24 of *The Iliad*, where Priam fetches the body of Hector from merciless Achilles. Andrew told the Myrmidons he could not stay to teach them because he had to rejoin his disciples. The cannibals begged him to stay and shed tears like those shed in Troy over Hector's death.

Iliad 24.160–65
[Iris] came to the house of Priam, and found therein **clamour and wailing.** His **sons** (παῖδες) sat about their father within the court sullying their garments with tears, and in their midst was the old king, close-wrapped in his mantle; **and upon the old man's head** (κεφαλῇ) **and neck was filth in abundance,** which he had gathered in his hands as he grovelled on the earth.

AAMt 32b

And **the children** (τὰ παιδία) with the men **followed behind weeping and begging,**

and threw ashes on their heads (κεφαλάς).[132]

Iliad 24.218–19, 24, 322, and 327–31
[Hecabe, weeping, begged Priam not to leave Troy in quest of Hector's body, but the old man answered:] "Seek not to stay me that am fain to go . . . ; **thou shalt not persuade** (πείσεις) **me. . . . I will go forth. . . ."** Then the old man made haste. . . . [A]nd his kinsfolk all **followed wailing aloud. . . .** [B]ack then to Ilios turned **his sons** (παῖδες).

AAMt 32b

He was still **not persuaded** (ἐπείθετο) by them, but said, **"I will go** to my disciples, and later I will return to you." **He went on his way.**

Iliad 24.347–48 and 360–64
[Hermes left Olympus to accompany Priam into the Myrmidonian camp.] Then he went his way **in the likeness of a young man** that is a prince, with the first down upon his lip, in whom the charm of youth is fairest. . . . But of himself the Helper drew nigh, and took the old man's hand, and made question of him **saying,** "Whither, Father, dost thou thus guide horses and mules through the

AAMt 32b

The Lord Jesus descended, **becoming in appearance like a beautiful small child,**

and greeted Andrew, **saying,** "Andrew, why do you depart leaving them fruitless, immortal night when other mortals are sleeping? **Art thou untouched by fear** of the fury-breathing Achaeans?"

and **why do you have no compassion** on the children (παιδίοις) following after you and on the men who implore, 'Stay with us a few days'?"

Jesus then told the apostle to

> turn back, go into the city, and stay there seven days until I strengthen their souls in the faith. Then you may leave this city and you will go into the city of the barbarians, you and your disciples. After you enter that city and preach my gospel there, you may leave them and again come into this city and bring up all the men in the abyss. [133]

In the best texts of *The Acts of Andrew*, the apostle never goes to "the city of the barbarians" and never returns to rescue the Myrmidonian fifteen.

The parallels between *The Iliad* and *AAMt* 22–33 nearly follow the same order:

	Iliad	*AAMt*
Attempt to sacrifice	[the tale of Iphigenia]	22
Prayers and rescues	1.450–60	23
God/demon advises, disguised as old man	2.16–30	24
Heroes' bodies dragged	22.395–402	25–28
Fights against gods/demons	16.791–92 21.192–93	26–27
Gods protect bodies	24.12–23 and 413–22	28
Fighting the flood		
Floods summoned	21.307–15	29
Floods rise, people flee	234–56	29–30
Floods filled with dead	300–327	30
Floods cease	372–84	30–31
Gods appear as youths		
Weeping children	24.160–65	32
Decision to leave	218–24 and 322–31	33
Jesus/Hermes appears	347–48 and 360–64	33

Andrew Departs (Odysseus's Departure from Circe, *AAMt* 33)

The final Homeric parallels in the *AAMt* obtain once again to *Odyssey* Book 10, where Odysseus leaves Circe's island to sail to the netherworld.

Odyssey 10.467–72 and 11.1–3
"So there day after day for a full year we abode feasting

AAMt 33
He spent seven days there teaching and confirming them

on abundant flesh and sweet wine.
But when a year was gone . . . then
my trusty comrades called me forth,
and said, 'Strange man, bethink thee
now at last of thy native land.'"
. . . "But when we had come down
to the ship and to the sea, first of all
we drew the ship down to the bright
sea, and set the mast and the sail."

in the Lord Jesus Christ.
At the completion of seven days,
the time came for the blessed Andrew
to leave.

All the people of Myrmidonia were
gathered to him, young and old,
and sent him off.

The *AAMt* ends here, without Andrew fulfilling his promises to return. After
rejoining his disciples, he was supposed to preach in "the city of the barbarians"
and then return to Myrmidonia to raise from the abyss the old man and the
fourteen executioners (*AAMt* 32–33). I discuss these lost episodes in chapter 3.

The Order of the Parallels

An argument for the influence of one document on another ought not depend on
atomistic points of contact insofar as scattershot similarities may be due to
standard narrative topoi or, in the case of Homeric epic, to the influence of the
poet on Greek literature generally. But two characteristics of these parallels make
the case for hypertextuality nearly certain: density and parallel order. Every
major section of the *AAMt* betrays evidence of the epics, and these parallels for
the most part appear in the same order as in Homer, as has been seen in the
discussions of the various subunits.

Odysseus's encounter with Circe in *Odyssey* Book 10 provides the framework
into which the author inserts Odysseus's adventures and themes from the Trojan
War; each insertion retains the Homeric sequence. The only significant
exception in the sequences is the reversal of *Iliad* Books 22–23 with Book 21;
the reason is apparent: in Homer, Achilles battles the River prior to killing
Hector and dragging his corpse. The *AAMt*, however, uses the motif of the flood
as a means of punishing the Myrmidons for having dragged about Andrew's
body.

Odyssey		*AAMt*	
10.233–43	Circe drugs victims	1–2	Cannibals drug victims
Book 2	Athena's boat	3–7	Jesus' boat
Book 5	Odysseus at sea	8–9	Andrew at sea
Book 8	Alcinous's questions	10–11	Jesus' questions
Book 9	Alcinous's enjoyment of stories	11	Jesus' enjoyment of stories
Book 11	Visit to the netherworld	12–15	Visit of the patriarchs
Book 13	Odysseus sleeps on board	16–17	Andrew sleeps on board
10.277–395	Odysseus rescues crew	18–21	Andrew rescues Matthias
—	Slaying of Iphigenia	22	Slaying of children
Iliad 1	Chryses' prayer	23	Andrew's prayer
Book 2	Zeus's lying dream	24	Devil's advice

Books 22–24	Hector's body dragged	25–28	Andrew dragged
Book 21	Achilles fights the floods	29–31	Myrmidons fight the floods
Book 24	Hermes appears to Achilles	32	Jesus appears to Andrew
10.467–11.3	Odysseus sails	33	Andrew sails

The sequential agreement persists, for the most part, also among the small constituent themes of these larger narrative units. Parallels deviating from Homeric order appear in square brackets ([ ]).

City of the Cannibals (Achilles' Myrmidons)
Abduction of Matthias (Circe)

	Odyssey	*AAMt*
Casting lots	10.206–8	1
Magical drugs	233–43	2

Jesus Consoles Matthias (Athena the Comforter)

	2.267–92	3

Voyage to Myrmidonia (Athena the Sailor)

Divinely supplied ships	2.292–387	3–4
Goddess/god in disguise	401	5
Descending to the ships	407–8	5
Embarking	416–19	6–7
Skillful sailing	5.270–79	8–9
Storms at sea	313–17	8
Calm seas	451–53	9
Appeals for information	8.550, 555, 564, 572	10–11
Joys of listening	9.5–11	11

Summoning the Dead (*Nekyia*)

Command to travel to the land of the dead	10.490–93	15
The dead gather	11.36–37	15
Sending the dead back	149–51	15
Tiresome tales	328–31	15
Avid listeners	362, 374–76	15

Sleepy Disembarkation (Odysseus's Arrival at Ithaca)

Falling asleep on board	13.75–80	16
Disembarking asleep	116–25	16–17
Waking up on strange shores	187–97	17
Divine messengers	221–36	18

Andrew Rescues Matthias (Odysseus Rescues Crew)

Divine messengers	10.277–80	18
Warnings about ogres	286–91	18
Entering ogres' domain	302–14	19
Lamenting the victims	375–87	20
Healing the victims	391–95	21

Slaying the Children (Iphigenia and Orestes)

	Iliad	
Attempt to sacrifice	—	22
Prayers and rescues	1.450–60	23

Devil's Advocate (Zeus's Lying Dream)

	2.16–30	24

Dragging the Apostle (Hector's Corpse)

Heroes' bodies dragged	[22.395–402]	25–28
Fights against gods/demons	16.791–92, 21.192–93	26–27
Gods protect bodies	[24.12–23 and 413–22]	28

Fighting the Flood (Achilles and the Scamander)

Floods summoned	[21.307–15]	29
Floods rise, people flee	234–56	29–30
Floods filled with dead	300–327	30
Floods cease	372–84	30–31

Jesus the Child (Hermes the Youth)

Weeping children	24.160–65	32
Decision to leave	218–24 and 322–31	33
Jesus/Hermes appears	347–48 and 360–64	33

Andrew Departs (Odysseus's Departure from Circe)

	Odyssey	
	10.467–11.3	33

Even though the order is not identical, it is remarkably consistent and thus reinforces the argument that the author had before him at least partial copies of the Homeric epics.

Conclusion

The *AAMt* is a Christian *Iliad* in which Andrew reluctantly leaves Achaea to rescue Matthias from Myrmidonia, just as Odysseus begrudgingly left Ithaca to help rescue Helen from Troy. The narrative that follows the *AAMt* will correspond to Odysseus's *nostos* or 'return' to Ithaca against tremendous odds.

In addition to its contributions to the literary architecture of the *Acts* as a whole, the *AAMt* introduces its apologetic agenda. Like other Christian apologists, the author of this tale viewed *The Iliad* as a monument to human savagery and Olympian venality.[134] How ironic, then, that pagans should charge Christians with cannibalism! The author crafted his tale to incorporate stock Platonic and Christian objections to the epic: Achilles' ruthless murder of twelve Trojans on Patroclus's pyre,[135] Agamemnon's sacrifice of Iphigenia,[136] Zeus's murderous dream,[137] Achilles' dragging of Hector's corpse,[138] the gods fleeing mortals,[139] and their divine pettiness when forced to sacrifice their sacrifices.[140] The devil and his demons play the roles of the Homeric deities, especially Zeus, Ares, and Apollo, just as one might expect from apologetic denunciations of the gods as demons.

More remarkable is the depiction of Jesus in roles that Homer had given to Athena and Hermes. Just as Athena assisted Telemachus by sailing with him in disguise, Jesus does the same for Andrew. As Athena appeared to Odysseus after he awoke on his Ithacan shore, Jesus appears to Andrew when he awakes at

Myrmidonia. Jesus' appearance as a young child at the end of the *AAMt* imitates Hermes' appearance as a youth to Priam. Like Olympians who took sides between Greeks and Trojans, Jesus and the devil appear to their champions granting advice, inspiration, and strength. Andrew's characterization shifts from ersatz-Odysseus (who sails off to liberate drugged victims) to ersatz-Hector (dragged through the city for three days). Throughout *The Acts of Andrew*, Andrew's heroic identity shifts as necessary. In chapter 3 I explain what happened to Andrew's promised return to Myrmidonia to yank the old man and the executioners out of the pit.

Notes

1. See MacDonald, *Acts of Andrew*, 3–47. In the conclusion to this volume I argue that a primary reason for including the *AAMt* at the beginning of *The Acts of Andrew* is its contribution to the hypertextual strategies of the *Acts* as a whole (see 316–18).

2. Gregory's note concerning Andrew's allotment of Achaea probably appeared in the ancient *Acts*. *The Acts of Philip* almost certainly relies on a Greek text of *The Acts of Andrew* in which Andrew was allotted Achaea and Matthias a land of savages. According to the *Acts of Philip*, Act 3: "[B]rother Andrew went into Achaea and all of Thrace, and Thomas into India to violent flesheaters, and Matthew (= Matthias) to ruthless cavemen, for their nature is wild"; cf. Act 8. See MacDonald, *Acts of Andrew*, 38–41. Even the Greek manuscripts of the *AAMt* imply that Andrew had been allotted Achaea: "[T]he Lord Jesus appeared in a city of Achaea where Andrew was teaching" (*AAMt* 4).

3. Cf. Bonnet:

After the famous and glorious triumph of the ascension of the Lord, when the blessed apostles were dispersed throughout various regions to preach the word of God, the apostle Andrew began to proclaim the Lord Jesus Christ in the province of Achaea. But Matthew the apostle and evangelist proclaimed the word of salvation in the city of Myrmidonia. (*Liber de miraculis*, 826–27)

4. *Recensio Casantensis.* See Franz Blatt, *Die lateinischen Bearbeitungen der Acta Andreae et Matthiae apud Anthropophagos*, BZNW 12 (Giessen: Alfred Töpelmann, 1930), 6–7 and 141.

5. *Martyrium prius* (Prieur, *Acta Andreae*, 685).

6. Bonnet, *Liber de miraculis*, 826–27.

7. For references to these spellings see Kenneth R. Brooks, *Andreas and the Fates of the Apostles* (Oxford: Oxford University Press, 1961), xxix, and George Philip Krapp, *Andreas and the Fates of the Apostles* (Boston: Ginn, 1906), lxvi.

8. An eighth-century ms. of *The Martyrdom of Matthew (AAA* 2.1:218).

9. Jacobus a Voragine, *Legenda Aurea* (Graesse, 13).

10. The Old French *Vie Saint Andrier l'Apostle* (Alfred T. Baker, "The Passion of Saint Andrew," *MLR* 11 [1916]: 439).

11. An eleventh-century ms. of *The Martyrdom of Matthew* (see *AAA* 2.1:220) and Nicephorus Callistus *Ecclesiasticae historiae* 2.41.

12. A ninth-century ms. of *Martyrium prius (AAA* 2.1:47).

13. Most mss. of *The Martyrdom of Matthew (AAA* 2.1:220).

14. *Paris gr. 1313*, unpublished.

15. A tenth-century ms. of *The Martyrdom of Matthew (AAA* 2.1:227 and 262).

16. A monk named Theodosius wrote of his pilgrimage to Jerusalem, which also took him to Sinope,

> where the lord Andrew freed the evangelist, lord Matthew, from prison [at this point in the text several lines seem to be missing], for at that time Sinope was called Myrmidonia [a variant reads Mermidona]. Everyone who lived there devoured people for their food. The misery there is so great that they would sit in the street in order to snatch up travelers. (*De situ Terrae Sanctae* [CSEL 39.144])

See also *Narratio, Laudatio*, and two incipits to the Greek *AAMt (Paris gr. 881*, and *Escorial Y II, 4)*.

17. A twelfth-century Greek ms. of the *AAMt (AAA* 2.1:65).

18. The Ethiopic *Preaching of Saint Andrew and Saint Philemon Among the Kurds* (Budge, 2.137).

19. The Syriac text calls it the City of the Dogs, or 'Irka. The location of 'Irka is unknown, but Theodor Nöldeke noticed that a slight orthographic alteration of the Syriac word for dogs (*klbin*) makes it Colchians (*klkin*), residents of Colchis, a city on the eastern shore of the Black Sea (Richard Adelbert Lipsius, *Die apokryphen Apostelgeschichten und Apostellegenden* [Braunschweig: C. A. Schwetschke, 1883], 1.546–47). A catalogue of the fates of the apostles falsely attributed to Epiphanius of Cyprus likewise locates Andrew's ministry to savage Ethiopians at Sebastopolis Magna, the Roman name for Colchis (Schermann, 108–9); cf. *Narratio* 4b.

20. Flamion argues for Ethiopia as the original region of the cannibals (*Actes d'André*, 313–15). See also François N. Nau, *DHGE*, s.v. "Actes coptes." Ethiopians were commonly feared as savage barbarians (Athanasius *Apologia ad Constantium [PG* 25, col. 632] and Nestorius in Evagrius *Ecclesiastica historia* 1.7).

21. Alfred von Gutschmid, "Die Königsnamen in den apokryphen Apostelgeschichten. Ein Beitrag zur Kenntnis des geschichtlichen Romans," *RMP* n.s. 19 (1864): 161–83 and 380–401; reprinted in his *Kleine Schriften*, ed. Franz Rühl (Leipzig: B. G. Teubner, 1890), 332–94. Myrmekion was a city near Chersonesus Taurica, or the modern Crimean peninsula. See MacDonald, *Acts of Andrew*, 9–10.

22. The only occurrence of the word "Myrmidonia" outside of obvious dependence on *The Acts of Andrew* appears in a geographical catalogue compiled by the sixth-century C.E. ethnographer Stephen of Byzantium, who likewise identified Myrmidonia with

Myrmidons: "Myrmidonia: region of the Myrmidons." Stephen considered it to be the island Aegina (Meineke, 464). This remarkable fragment suggests that a text of the *AAMt* available to Stephen included the word "Myrmidonia." The word appears in no other connection in ancient literature. Furthermore, since Stephen's sources were predominantly Greek, it would seem likely that the text he knew also was Greek, viz. a Greek text related to *The Acts of Andrew* that contained the disputed word.

23. *Odyssey* 3.188, 4.9, and 11.495.

24. *Iliad* 16.155–67; cf. 200–209.

25. Ibid., 22.346–47. Homer frequently used cannibalistic hyperbole to express the ferocity of Achilles and other characters: "[H]is heart is set on cruelty, even as a lion that at the bidding of his great might and lordly spirit goeth forth against the flocks of men to win him a feast; even so hath Achilles lost all pity" (24.41–44; cf. 1.231 of Agamemnon, 4.34–36 of Hera, 20.77–78 of Achilles and Ares, and 24.212–13 of Hecuba). On Achilles' savagery see 1.146 and 177, and 22.312–13.

26. Ibid., 24.207.

27. Cf. *Iliad* 5.341–42.

28. *The Odyssey* is crowded with people-eaters. Polyphemus the Cyclops traps Odysseus and twelve of his crew in his cave: "Two of them at once he seized and dashed to the earth like puppies, and the brain flowed forth upon the ground and wetted the earth. Then he cut them limb from limb and made ready his supper, and ate them as a mountain-nurtured lion, leaving naught—ate the entrails, and the flesh, and the marrowy bones" (*Odyssey* 9.289–93). Later, the ogre ate four more Greeks (9.310–11). Only Odysseus's wiles robbed Polyphemus of more platters of *homo sapiens au point*. Odysseus claimed that when the crew put in at the port of the Laestrygonians, their king, Antiphates,

> seized one of my comrades and made ready his meal, but the other two sprang up and came in flight to the ships. Then he raised a cry throughout the city, and as they heard it the mighty Laestrygonians came thronging from all sides, a host past counting, not like men but like the Giants. They hurled at us from the cliffs with rocks huge as a man could lift, and at once there rose throughout the ships a dreadful din, alike from men that were dying and from ships that were being crushed. And spearing them like fishes they bore them home, a loathly meal. (*Odyssey* 10.116–24)

The Homeric character with the closest parallels to Andrew's Myrmidons is Circe the witch, who will be discussed shortly.

29. Ibid., 23.30–34.

30. E.g., Plato, *Republic* 3.391b–c.

31. *Iliad* 23.163–77.

32. Clement of Alexandria *Protrepticus* 2.34; see also *Ps.-Clementine Homilies* 5.13.

33. See "Myrmidones," P-W, and MacDonald, *Acts of Andrew*, 11–15, as well as "*The Acts of Andrew and Matthias* and *The Acts of Andrew*," and "Response," both in *Semeia 38: Apocryphal Acts of Apostles,* ed. Dennis R. MacDonald (Decatur: Scholars Press, 1986), 9–26 and 35–39.

34. *Icaromenippus* 19.

35. *Iliad* 22.145–46; cf. 6.433–34 and 11.167 and *Odyssey* 12.432.

36. *Legatio* 35.4.

37. *Ad Autolycum* 3.5 (Grant).

38. *Apology* 9.9 (FC); cf. *Apology* 2.5, 7.1, and 8.2–5 and *Adversus Marcionem* 1.1. Other early Christian treatments of cannibalism appear in Athenagoras *De resurrectione* 8.2–3, *The Martyrs of Lyons and Vienne* (*apud* Eusebius *Historia ecclesiastica* 5.1.14), Ps.-Justin *Ad graecos* 3, Minucius Felix *Octavius* 9 and 30, and especially Athanasius *Contra gentes* 25. Clement of Alexandria cites a story attributing unwitting cannibalism to Zeus (*Protrepticus* 2.36.5).

These charges of cannibalism and incest have generated extensive scholarly discussion; one essay worthy of special attention is Albert Henrichs's "Pagan Ritual and the Alleged Crimes of the Early Christians: A Reconsideration," in *Kyriakon: Festschrift Johannes Quasten*, 2 vols., ed. Patrick Granfield and Josef A. Jungmann (Münster: Aschendorff, 1970), 1.18–35. See also his selective bibliography (18, n. 1).

39. Jonah, of course, sailed away from the barbarians; Andrew sailed toward them.

40. See MacDonald, *Acts of Andrew*, 4–6.

41. *Argonautica* 4.557–752.

42. *Aeneid* 7.5–24.

43. *Metamorphoses* 14.

44. *Satyricon* 127–34. See also Lucian *True Story* 2.46 and the witch Meroe in Apuleius *Metamorphoses* 1.7–13.

45. There can be little doubt that prior to Homer, Circe was an ogre. Odyssean hypertexts make the witch of Aeaea increasingly respectable, as in *The Telegonia*, *The Argonautica*, and Ovid's *Metamorphoses*. In these works Circe is mysterious, quirky, and even dangerous, but not cannibalistic.

46. Warriors cast lots throughout *The Iliad* (e.g., 7.171–90, 23.351–57 and 861–62, and 24.400).

47. The episode in the *AAMt* conforms also to early Christian commissioning stories. See Benjamin J. Hubbard, *The Matthean Redaction of a Primitive Apostolic Commissioning: An Exegesis of Matthew 28:16–20*, SBLDS 19 (Missoula: Society of Biblical Literature, 1974).

48. For a more detailed treatment of method and criteria for determining intertextual dependence, see the conclusion, 302–16.

49. See Apollodorus *Epitome* 3.7, Cicero *De officiis* 3.26.97, Lucian *The Hall* 30, Philostratus *Heroicus* 11.2, and Hyginus *Fabulae* 95. Sophocles wrote a play about the ruse called *The Mad Odysseus*.

Andrew's reluctance also shares similarities with Tobias's complaints against going to Ecbatana in Tobit: "[H]ow can I obtain the money from him (πῶς δὲ δυνήσομαι αὐτὸ λαβεῖν παρ' αὐτοῦ), since he does not know (οὐ γινώσκει) me and I do not know (οὐ γινώσκω) him? . . . Also, I do not know the roads to Media, or how to get there (τὰς ὁδοὺς . . . οὐ γινώσκω τοῦ πορευθῆναι ἐκεῖ)" (5:1–20, recension B). Andrew: "I cannot travel there (οὐ δυνήσομαι φθάσαι) before the three-day limit, so send your angel quickly to get him out of there. [An angel accompanied Tobias to Ecbatana.] For you know (γινώσκεις), Lord, that I, too, am flesh and cannot go there quickly (οὐ δυνήσομαι . . . πορευθῆναι). I do not even know the route (οὐδὲ ἐπίσταμαι τὴν ὁδόν)" (*AAMt* 4); cf. Tobit 5:6: ἐπίσταμαι τὰς ὁδοὺς πάσας.

50. Jesus also emphasized his power over creation: "For if I were to command the horns of the winds (ἀνεμῶν), they would drive it [the city of the Myrmidons] here" (*AAMt* 4). This might call to mind the powers of Aeolus, the god of the winds, who lived on a floating island and who assisted Odysseus on his journey by providing him with a bag of winds (ἀνεμῶν) (*Odyssey* 10.1–27).

51. During negotiations for the fare, captain Jesus discovered that Andrew had no money because of his obligations to apostolic poverty. Jesus allowed the apostle to board anyway: "I prefer to bring about my boat you disciples of the one called Jesus rather than those who offer me gold and silver (χρυσίου καὶ ἀργυρίου)" (*AAMt* 6). When Telemachus provisioned his boat for the trip, he "went down to the high-roofed treasure-chamber of his father, a wide room where gold and bronze (χρυσὸς καὶ χαλκός) lay piled" (*Odyssey* 2.337–38). When the lad finally returns to Ithaca he brings with him Menelaus's "fairest and costliest" possession—a mixing bowl: "all of silver (ἀργύρεος) it is, and with gold (χρυσῷ) are the rims thereof gilded" (4.615–16). It is possible that the author of the *Acts* wished to contrast Telemachus's lavish wealth with Andrew's penury.

52. Cf. Clement of Alexandria *Protrepticus* 10.80: "Sail the sea, you who love sea-faring; but ever call upon the heavenly pilot."

53. Andrew's blessing of Jesus for granting him passage without fare is similar to Athena's blessing of Nestor. Athena says: "Hear me, Poseidon. . . . To Nestor first of all, and to his sons vouchsafe renown" (*Odyssey* 3.55–57). Andrew says: "May the Lord grant you glory and honor" (*AAMt* 6). Jesus ordered his crew to get bread for Andrew and his disciples; Telemachus brought barley meal for his voyage (*Odyssey* 2.355). Once they had set the sails, Telemachus's crew did not eat bread but "set forth bowls brim full of wine, and poured libations to the immortal gods" (2.431–32).

54. Even before the ship left shore, Andrew's disciples became seasick. Captain Jesus asked the apostle if his disciples would like "to return to land and wait for you until you finish your task and return to them again." Andrew turned to his disciples and asked them if they wished to return, to which they replied: "If we separate from you, we may become strangers to the good things that you provided us. We shall be with you now wherever you go" (*AAMt* 7). This exchange may have been inspired by the famous *peira* or 'test' Agamemnon gave to the Greeks in *Iliad* Book 2. After nine years of futile warfare, Apollo attacked the Greek camp with a devastating plague. The king decided to test his troops for their loyalty: "[L]et us flee with our ships to our dear native land; for no more is there hope that we shall take broad-wayed Troy" (*Iliad* 2.140–41). This invitation started a stampede for the ships, until Odysseus and Nestor convinced the host to turn their hearts and spears again toward Troy. The Achaeans then rallied to their king and promised never to abandon the battle until they had taken the spoils of the city. One might use the response of Andrew's disciples as a paraphrase of *Iliad* 2.166–454.

55. See also *Odyssey* 7.267–68, which is told in the first-person singular, as in *AAMt* 9: "[F]or seventeen (ἑπτὰ δὲ καὶ δέκα) days I sailed (πλέον) over the sea, and on the

eighteenth (ὀκτωκαιδεκάτη) appeared the shadowy mountains"; cf. *Odyssey* 24.63–65. Lucian parodied this peculiar formulation: "[W]e drove for seventy-nine days. On the eightieth . . ." (*True Story* 1.6; cf. 10).

56. Mark 4:35–41, Matt. 8:23–27, and Luke 8:22–25.

57. Plato's Socrates thought these lines entirely unbefitting "the wisest man" (*Republic* 2.390a–b).

58. Exod. 25:18–22, 26:1 and 31, and 37:6–9, 1 Kings 6:23–28, and 2 Chron 3:7–14. Homer does not mention sphinxes; the earliest Greek literary allusion appears in Hesiod *Theogony* 326–29.

59. Achilles' horse also had a human voice: "[T]he goddess, white-armed Hera, gave him speech" (*Iliad* 19.407). The mount then predicted Achilles' death, which would be caused by divine planning and fate. So, too, the sphinx predicts God's judgment on Jews.

60. Odysseus traveled to the netherworld in order to consult with Tiresias, the blind seer, who told the hero that his journey home would be perilous because he had blinded Polyphemus, Poseidon's son (*Odyssey* 11.100–103).

61. According to the sphinx, Jesus is Lord of the dead, not Minos.

Odyssey 11.568–71	*AAMt* 14
"There I saw Minos, the glorious son of Zeus, golden sceptre in hand, **giving judgment to the dead** (νέκυσσιν) from his seat, while they sat and stood about the king through the wide-gated house of Hades, **and asked of him judgment.**"	"He is **judge** of the living and **the dead** (νεκρῶν). He it is who prepares marvelous things for those who obey him, and **prepares punishment** (κόλασιν) for those who do not believe in him."

A major theme of the *nekyia*, of course, is the punishment of the wicked, like Tityus, Tantalus, and Sisyphus (*Odyssey* 11.576–600). Compare the conclusion of the sphinx's speech ("Having said this, the sphinx was silent [ἐσιώπησεν]"), with *Odyssey* 11.333: "So he [Odysseus] spoke, and they were all hushed in silence (σιωπῇ)."

Christian apologists repeatedly emphasized that God, not Minos or Rhadamanthus, will judge the dead. Athenagoras wrote: "Plato indeed said that Minos and Rhadamanthys would judge and punish (κολάσειν) evil men; we say no one, not a Minos or a Rhadamanthys or the father of them both [Zeus] will escape the judgement of God" (*Legatio* 12 [Schoedel]; cf. Plato *Gorgias* 523a–526d). Tatian agreed: "Our judges are not the mythical Minos and Rhadamanthys, before whose death no soul was ever judged. Our examiner is God the creator. . . . Someone says . . . that Minos and Rhadamanthys pronounce judgement on us, I that it is God himself" (*Oratio ad graecos* 6 and 25 [Whittaker]).

62. Cf. *The Testaments of the Twelve Patriarchs* (*Judah* 25 and *Benjamin* 10:4–8). The widespread association of the sphinx with death, apparent from her presence in Greek funerary art, made her an ideal choice for fetching the dead from the netherworld.

63. Cf. the departure of the spirits in *Odyssey* 11.150, 538–39, 563–64, and 627.

64. Apuleius may have parodied this passage (*Metamorphoses* 1.26).

65. This episode tested the credulity of many ancient interpreters, including Plutarch: "But some critics find fault also with the very act of putting him ashore, if this really was done while he was asleep, and assert that the Etruscans still preserve a tradition that Odysseus was naturally sleepy" (*How the Young Man Should Study Poetry* 27); cf. Aristotle *Poetics* 1460a–b.

66. Andrew woke his disciples and told them what had happened. They answered that while they slept, eagles descended and took them to heaven, where they saw marvelous things. Hearing this, Andrew rejoiced. Homer used eagles throughout his epics to reveal the divine will, to which mortals responded with mirth or dread. The appearance of an eagle in *Odyssey* Book 15 produced joy for Telemachus and Menelaus:

Odyssey 15.160–65	*AAMt* 17–18
[A] bird flew by on the right, an **eagle** (αἰετός), **bearing** (φέρων) in his talons a great, white goose . . .	"**Eagles** (αἰετοί) descended, carried away our souls, **brought us** to the heavenly paradise, and we saw great marvels . . . and they **brought** (ἤνεγκαν) our souls into our bodies."
and **they were glad** as they saw it, and **the hearts in the breasts of all were cheered**.	When Andrew heard this, **he was exuberant**. . . .

See also *Odyssey* 19.536–50, 20.242–46, and 24.53738 and *Iliad* 8.247–52, 12.200–209, 13.821–23, and esp. 24.315–21. For Homer the eagle was the "surest of omens among winged birds" (*Iliad* 8.247 and 24.315). According to post-Homeric tradition, Zeus himself took the form of an eagle to snatch up Ganymedes to be his lover "that he might dwell with the immortals," an act Christians loved to parade before their pagan neighbors (e.g., Justin Martyr *First Apology* 21 and 25, Tatian *Oratio ad graecos* 10, Clement of Alexandria *Protrepticus* 2.32, and Minucius Felix *Octavius* 24.7). Like Andrew's disciples, Ganymedes observed heavenly things, thanks to an eagle's wings. An eagle plays a crucial and unusual role again later in the *Acts* (Passion 53).

67. Jesus told Andrew that he had disguised himself not in order to punish the apostle for sin, but to demonstrate his power: "I can do anything (πάντα ποιῆσαι δυνατός εἰμι)" (*AAMt* 18). This claim resembles Hermes' statement that "the gods can do anything (θεοὶ δέ τε πάντα δύνανται)" (*Odyssey* 10.306), a line Christians enjoyed quoting (e.g., Ps.-Justin *De resurrectione* 5). See also Justin Martyr *First Apology* 18.5 and Hippolytus *Refutatio* on the use of this Homeric passage in the Simonian treatise *Apophasis Megale*.

68. It must be noted, however, that the apostle immediately slays the seven guards at Matthias's prison with a well-aimed prayer!

69. Cf. *Odyssey* 10.389: Circe "opened the doors of the sty (θύρας δ᾽ ἀνέῳξε συφειοῦ)"; *AAMt* 19: "the door opened (ἡ θύρα ἠνεῴχθη)." See also *Iliad* 24.442–46.

70. One might also profitably compare this entry scene with Priam's famous journey to the Myrmidonian ships to ransom the body of his son Hector from Achilles:

But when they were come to the walls and the trench that guarded the ships, even as the watchers were but now busying them about their supper, upon all of these the messenger Argeiphontes shed sleep and forthwith opened the gates, and thrust back the bars. . . . But when they were come to the hut of Peleus' son, the lofty hut which the Myrmidons had builded . . . then verily the helper Hermes opened the door for the old man. (*Iliad* 24.443–57)

71. Readers of the New Testament will hear in Matthias's solo an echo of the duet by Paul and Silas in the Philippian jail (Acts 16:25). It should also be noted, however, that Circe was a fine vocalist: "So they stood in the gateway of the fair-tressed goddess, and within they heard Circe singing with sweet voice" (*Odyssey* 10.220–21; cf. 227 and 255). It is also possible that the author of the *Acts* had in mind the famous scene in *The Iliad* where the embassy from Agamemnon went to the Myrmidonian camp begging Achilles to join the fight. They found the baritone in the middle of a ballad. Compare the two passages:

Iliad 9.185–96	*AAMt* 19
And they **came to the huts** and ships of the Myrmidons and they found him **delighting his soul with a clear-toned lyre**. . . . [A]nd he sang of the glorious deeds of warriors. . . . They took their stand before his face, and Achilles leaped up in amazement with the lyre in his hand, and **left the seat whereon he sat**, and in like manner Patroclus **when he beheld** (ἴδε) the men **uprose** (ἀνέστη). Then swift-footed Achilles **greeted the two** and said . . .	On **entering the prison** with his disciples, he saw Matthias **sitting, singing to himself**.
	When he saw (ἰδών) Andrew, Matthias **rose** (ἀνέστη), and they **greeted each other** with a holy kiss. Andrew **said** to Matthias . . .

72. Cf. Matt. 10:16 and Luke 10:3. Homer likened the Myrmidons to wolves in *Iliad* 16.155–67, cited earlier (cf. 16.352–55).

73. Cf. *Odyssey* 10.375–87 and *AAMt* 20.

74. Andrew launched into a long denunciation of the devil composed for the most part from Genesis: the expulsion of the first couple from paradise (Gen. 3:22–24), the altering of human diet from grains to meats (9:3–5), and the famous copulation of angels with mortals to produce monsters (6:1–4). Genesis, however, cannot explain everything in Andrew's speech, which states that these giants "devoured the people of the earth" (*AAMt* 20). One might simply attribute the giants' diet to the overriding theme of cannibalism in the *AAMt*, but one might also detect the presence of the gigantomachy, the primordial battle of the Gigantes in Greek mythology so abundantly represented in art. When the

Jewish philosopher Philo commented on Gen. 6:1–4, he felt obligated to point out that Moses' giants had nothing to do with Homer's. "Some may think that the Lawgiver is alluding to the myths of the poets about the giants (γιγάντων), but indeed myth-making is a thing most alien to him" (*On Giants* 58).

A look at the Greek version of Gen. 6:4 suggests how natural, even inevitable, this identification was. Instead of transliterating the Hebrew word נפלים 'Nephilim', the LXX reads γίγαντες 'giants'; rather than rendering נברים 'mighty men', with more natural Greek equivalents, the translator again preferred γίγαντες. The resultant text then might be translated: "There were giants on the earth in those days. . . . These were the primordial giants, men of renown"; cf. *Jubilees* 5:1. Furthermore, the giants of Genesis were offspring of "the sons [some texts read 'angels'] of God and the daughters of mortals" (6:4); the Gigantes of the Greeks were offspring of Uranus (heaven) and Ge (earth). Just as God destroyed the world with a flood to punish humans for wickedness, Zeus and the other gods (as well as Heracles) destroyed the Gigantes for hubris. The conflation of the two sets of giants, Jewish and Greek, lies behind *1 Enoch* 6–9, *2 Enoch* 18, *The Book of Giants*, *Jubilees* 5–7, and *Sibylline Oracles* 1.97–124 and 2.227–35. Among the giants' vices is anthropophagy: "And their flesh was devoured the one by the other and they drank blood" (*1 Enoch* 7:5); "[A]nd they began to eat one another" (*Jubilees* 5:2); and "Each one ate his fellow" (7:22).

In the episode immediately preceding the Circe story, Homer identified the Gigantes with Laestrygonian cannibals, whose chief, says Odysseus,

> seized one of my comrades and made ready his meal. . . . Then he raised a cry throughout the city, and as they heard it the mighty Laestrygonians came thronging from all sides, a host past counting, not like men but like the Giants. . . . And spearing them [Odysseus's comrades] like fishes they bore them home, a loathly meal. (*Odyssey* 10.116–24; cf. 7.59 and 206)

Andrew's assertion that the giants of Genesis "devoured the people of the earth" suggests that the author of the *AAMt* equated them with such Greek Gigantes. "Now you have come to this city as well," the apostle told the devil, "in order to make its residents eat humans and drink their blood, so that they too might end up accursed and destroyed."

75. Nebuchadnezzar, too, had a bout with beastly behavior (Daniel 4:31–35).

76. *Iliad* 22.145–46.

77. Cf. Troy's famous Scaean ('western') gates.

78. Several times in *The Iliad* the gods save warriors from certain death by sweeping them up in a cloud (e.g., 3.380–82, 20.321–29 and 443–44, and 21.597–98), but shortly it will be clear that the author had another hypertextual goal in mind for this unusual motif. See chapter 3, 78–80.

79. Cf. Jon. 4:5 LXX.

80. Aeschylus, too, wrote an *Iphigenia*, only one line of which survives, but he tells his version of the myth in *Agamemnon*.

81. Euripides *Iphigenia at Aulis* 1198–99.

82. Ibid., 1218–19.

83. Ibid., 1247–48; cf. 465 and *Iphigenia in Tauris* 852–54.

84. See chapter 3, 80–81.

85. Denunciations of Agamemnon's sacrifice permeate Euripides' two Iphigenia plays and probably dominated Aeschylus's *Iphigenia*. See also Horace *Satires* 2.3.199–207. Euripides refused to believe that this inhumanity was indeed the will of Artemis (*Iphigenia at Aulis* 378–91).

86. Ps.-Justin *Ad graecos* 1 (ANF).

87. Other versions of the myth say nothing of Iphigenia's rescue (viz. Aeschylus's *Agamemnon*).

88. Euripides *Iphigenia at Aulis* 1578–84; cf. *Iphigenia in Tauris* 26–31.

89. Compare this tale of Agamemnon and Iphigenia with that of Abraham and Isaac in Gen. 22:1–14. Ps.-Philo may well have been influenced by the Iphigenia story in retelling the sacrifice of Jephthah's daughter (39–40).

90. *Iliad* 1.445–47.

91. A prayer similar to this one appears in *Iliad* 16.236–41 on the lips of Achilles: "Aforetime verily thou didst hear my word, when I prayed: me thou didst honour, and didst mightily smite the host of the Achaeans; even so now also (καὶ νῦν μοι) fulfil thou for me this my desire. Myself verily will I abide in the gathering of the ships, but my comrade was I sending forth amid the host of the Myrmidons to war." See Ps.-Justin *Ad graecos* 1 concerning Agamemnon and Chryseis.

92. *Iliad* 1.459–60.

93. Ibid., 2.4.

94. Nestor was the Homeric old man par excellence: "Two generations of mortal men had he ere now seen pass away, who of old had been born and reared him in sacred Pylos, and he as king among the third" (*Iliad* 1.250–52). Frequently the poet designates him simply as "the old man" (e.g., 7.157–61, 8.146, and 14.136). Tatian makes a point of Nestor's longevity (*Oratio ad graecos* 32). On Nestor's age, see also Lucian *Essays in Portraiture Defended* 20.

95. *Iliad* 9.17–28.

96. *Republic* 2.383a; cf. Lucian *Zeus Rants* 40.

97. *Oratio ad graecos* 21; cf. Irenaeus *Adversus haereses* 1.12.

98. *First Apology* 25.

99. Homer three times repeated an identical formula, using the word πολεμιστής to refer to Ares (*Iliad* 5.289 and 20.78 and 267). The apologist Aristides was negatively impressed: "[T]hey call him a warrior (πολεμιστής)" (*Apology* 10.7), as was Clement of Alexandria (*Protrepticus* 2.36 and 5.64); cf. Theophilus *Ad Autolycum* 1.9 and Athenagoras *Legatio* 21.3.

100. There is nothing particularly suspicious about this threat to throw the devil into the abyss, but in light of the influence of *The Iliad* in this section of the *AAMt*, one should mention the celebrated passage concerning Zeus's threat to the other gods:

[O]r shall I take and hurl him [any contrary god or goddess] into murky Tartarus, far, far away, where is the deepest gulf beneath the earth, the gates whereof are of iron and the threshold of bronze, as far beneath Hades as heaven is above earth: then shall ye know how far the mightiest am I of all gods. Nay, come, make trial, ye gods, that ye all may know. Make ye fast from heaven a chain of gold, and lay ye hold thereof, all ye gods and all goddesses; yet could ye not drag to earth from out of heaven Zeus the counsellor most high, not though ye laboured sore. But whenso I were minded to draw of a ready heart, then with earth itself should I draw you and with sea withal; and the rope should I thereafter bind about a peak of Olympus and all those things should hang in space. By so much am I above gods and above men. (8.13–27)

If the author of the *Acts* had this passage in mind, Andrew would be calling Zeus's bluff: his God indeed is powerful enough to accept Zeus's challenge and to pull him off his throne. One early Christian apologist referred to this passage to show that Homer, in spite of his polytheism, believed in one supreme deity (Ps.-Justin *Cohortatio ad gentiles* 24); cf. Lucian *Zeus Catechized* 4, *Dialogues of the Gods* 1 (267–68), and *Zeus Rants* 14 and 45.

101. It was as though the apostle had been wearing the helmet of Hades that allowed one to see others without being seen. The origin of this tradition apparently was a forced etymology that attributed Hades to α-ιδ, 'the un-seen'. So Homer: Ἄϊδος ... μή ... ἴδοι (*Iliad* 5.845). See also Apollodorus *Library* 2.4.2, where Perseus used the helmet against Medusa and the Gorgons. According to Irenaeus, Hades' helmet played an important role in the "redemption" of Marcosian Gnostics, who wished to be rendered invisible to the evil powers (*Adversus haereses* 1.13.6). Behind Andrew's claim that the devil was blind might be *Iliad* 19.95–129, where Zeus was blinded for a time by Ate (esp. lines 95, 113, and 129). See also *Iliad* 20.318–52, where Poseidon blinds Achilles so that he cannot slay Aeneas.

102. See *Iliad* 17.126–27, where Hector wanted to cut off the head (κεφαλὴν τάμοι) of Patroclus and drag the corpse to the dogs. Cf. *AAMt* 25: ἄρωμεν ... κεφαλήν.

103. Cf. *Iliad* 13.60, of the Aiantes, and 17.573 of Menelaus.

104. Homer does not say that a god "filled" Achilles, but Athena and other deities repeatedly spurred him on in battle, as Ares had spurred on Hector. See *Iliad* 20.97–98 and 21.284–86 and 304.

105. Cf. *Iliad* 16.559–61.

106. Statements about Andrew's blood flowing on the ground like water appear four times in the *AAMt*, and similar phrases also appear often in *The Iliad*: "and the black earth flowed with blood" (15.715 and 20.494 [cf. 17.360–61]); "And the dark blood flowed forth and wetted the earth" (21.119). Compare *AAMt*: "And your blood will flow on the ground like water" (18); "and his blood flowed on the ground like water" (25); "and his blood flowed" (26); "and his blood flowed on the ground like water" (28).

107. *Republic* 3.391b–c.

108. Ps.-Justin *Cohortatio ad gentiles* 30 (ANF 1.286). In his attack on Christian allegorizing, Porphyry produced an allegory on Achilles slaying Hector as Christ subduing the devil. See G. Binder, "Eine Polemik des Porphyrios gegen die allegorische Auslegung des Alten Testaments durch die Christen," *ZPE* 3 (1968): 91–95.

109. *AAMt* 25: δήσαντες αὐτοῦ τὰς χεῖρας εἰς τὰ ὀπίσθια; *AAMt* 26: δήσαντες

αὐτοῦ τὰς χεῖρας ὄπισθεν. Cf. *Iliad* 21.30: δῆσε δ' ὀπίσσω χεῖρας, used of Achilles' tying up the twelve Trojan captives to be taken back to the Greek ships to await execution.

110. One widespread criticism of Homer's gods was their laughter. Especially controversial was *Iliad* 1.599–600, where the Olympians are sadistically amused at the lameness of Hephaestus: "And laughter unquenchable arose among the blessed gods, as they saw Hephaestus puffing through the palace." Plato thought this depiction of laughing gods was a lie (*Republic* 3.389a), and the apologist Tatian used the passage to ridicule pagan deities (*Oratio ad graecos* 8). For other examples of heavenly hysteria, see *Iliad* 15.101 and 21.389–90, 408, and 508 and *Odyssey* 8.326.

111. E.g., *Iliad* 1.457–74 describes in detail a sacrifice for Apollo and ends with the phrase "his heart was glad (τέρπετ')"; cf. 4.10, 5.760, 7.61, and 20.23. *Odyssey* 1.25–26 describes Poseidon visiting the Ethiopians "to receive a hecatomb of bulls and rams, and there he was taking his joy (ἐτέρπετο), sitting at the feast." Heracles, too, sat with the gods and enjoyed a good feast (11.603 [τέρπεται]; cf. 6.46 [τέρπονται μάκαρες θεοί]).

112. Socrates quoted *Iliad* 9.499–501 to point out just how petty the gods could be when sacrifices were involved: "The gods themselves are moved by prayers, / And men by sacrifice and soothing vows, / And incense and libation turn their wills / Praying, whene'er they have sinned and made transgression" (*Republic* 2.364d). Plato could have set his sights on any number of Homeric passages, such as *Iliad* 9.533–37. For other criticisms of gods seeking sacrifices, see Lucian *Prometheus* 16–18, *Zeus Rants* 13–22, *Icaromenippus* 27, and especially *On Sacrifices*.

113. E.g., Athenagoras *Legatio* 13, Clement of Alexandria *Protrepticus* 2.41.3, Tatian *Oratio ad graecos* 10, and Aristides *Apology* 13.

114. Cf. *Iliad* 18.202–27, where Athena bestows on the head of Achilles a gleam that routed the Trojans. See also the parody of this motif in *Odyssey* 18.353–55: "Not without the will of the gods has this man come to the palace of Odysseus; in any case there is a glare of torches from him—from his head, for there is no hair on it, no, not a trace." See also GE 26, where a character named Leontius, 'lionlike', represents Achilles and marvels at Andrew's glowing face.

115. *AAMt* 27: εἰ τί ἐστίν σοι δυνατόν, ποίησον. Achilles dared the river god to send the Scamander against him, "if so be he can avail thee aught (εἰ δύναταί τι χραισμεῖν)" (*Iliad* 21.192–93). Later, Achilles told Apollo, "I would avenge me on thee, had I but the power (εἴ μοι δύναμίς παρείη)" (22.20). Plato quoted this line to demonstrate the unacceptable hubris of Homeric heroes (*Republic* 3.391a).

116. When Tatian charged that a god "fled (φεύγων) from the battlefield and was wounded," he was thinking of *Iliad* 5.864–87, Diomedes' conquest of Ares (*Oratio ad graecos* 8). Theophilus, however, lodged the same complaint against *Iliad* Book 21, where Apollo "feared Achilles and fled (φεύγοντα)" (*Ad Autolycum* 1.9). Achilles chased the entire Trojan army, including Apollo disguised as Agenor, back into the city in a full-fledged rout (21.609 and 22.1). The god himself asked how it could be that a mortal would pursue him (22.8–10). Theophilus deduced from this flight that Apollo had fled because he was no god at all, a judgment shared by the *Apology* of Aristides (8.3). Clement of Alexandria cited *Iliad* 20.8–10 positively because Homer's Apollo states that

gods are immortal and cannot be overtaken by mortals (*Stromateis* 5.116.4–117.2).

117. Prior to this statement, Andrew said that Jesus "knows that human flesh is weak (γινώσκων . . . τὴν ἀνθρωπίνην σάρκα ἀσθενής ἐστιν)." Aelius Aristides said the same of Homer: ᾔδει γὰρ γῆς ἀνθρωπίνης φύσεως τὴν ἀσθένειαν (46.332d). Notice also the contrast with *Iliad* 22.213, where Apollo abandoned Hector in order for Achilles to fulfill Zeus's judgment against the Trojan champion.

118. *Iliad* 24.12–23. Cf. 22.165–66 and 250–51, where Achilles chases Hector around Troy three times, and 23.13, where Achaean chariots circle Patroclus's pyre three times.

119. Ibid., 24.413–22. Cf. 19.37–39 and esp. 23.185–87: "[T]he daughter of Zeus, Aphrodite, kept dogs from him by day alike and by night, and with oil anointed she him, rose-sweet, ambrosial, to the end that Achilles might not tear him as he dragged him."

120. The executioners said, "He will probably die during the night." Cf. *Iliad* 16.852–53, where the dying Patroclus tells Hector, "[T]hou shalt not thyself be long in life, but even now doth death stand hard by thee"; cf. 21.308–23.

121. Cf. *Iliad* 17.567–74 and 21.284–304.

122. E.g., *Iliad* 21.212–13.

123. Plato's Socrates criticized Homer for depicting Achilles' fight with the River; one ought never oppose a god (*Republic* 3.391b); cf. Ps.-Justin *Ad graecos* 1.

124. Cf. *Iliad* 21.272–83, where Achilles supposes that he will die in the flood.

125. This concern for the cattle might derive from Jon. 4:7, but it is worth noting that Apollo's devastation of the Achaean camp at the beginning of *The Iliad* began with innocent animals: "The mules he assailed first and the swift dogs, but thereafter on the men themselves he let fly his stinging arrows, and smote; and ever did the pyres of the dead burn thick" (*Iliad* 1.50–52).

126. This passage apparently derives from *Iliad* 21.327–82, where Hera asks Hephaestus to send fire to protect Achilles from the fury of the waters: "[D]o thou along the banks of Xanthus burn up his trees, and beset him about with fire" (337–38). Hephaestus complied, "and made ready wondrous-blazing fire. First on the plain was the fire kindled, and burned the dead . . . and all the plain was parched, and the bright water was stayed" (342–45); cf. Lucian *Dialogues of the Sea-Gods* 10 (316–18).

127. See *Iliad* 21.273–83, where Achilles cries out to Zeus for relief from the flood.

128. *AAMt* 31: ἐλέησόν με. Cf. *Iliad* 20.465 (Tros seeking mercy [ἐλεήσας] from Achilles), 21.74 (Lycaon seeking mercy [μ' ἐλέησον] from Achilles), 22.123 (Hector speaking of Achilles' lack of pity [μ' οὐκ ἐλεήσει]), 22.419–20 (Priam begging Achilles to have pity on his old age [ἐλεήσῃ γήρας]), and 24.503 (again Priam asking Achilles for mercy [ἐλέησον]).

129. Cf. *Iliad* 20.56–66.

130. See *Iliad* 21.218–20 and the river's complaint: "[F]ull are my lovely streams with death men, nor can I anywise avail to pour my waters forth into the bright sea, being choked with the dead."

131. This text may have inspired the sculpting of a statue at a shrine to Andrew in Sinope (E 220A–B).

132. See also Jon. 3:5–8.

133. *AAMt* 33. Jesus' rebuke of Andrew's lack of compassion might call to mind not only Jon. 4:9–11 but also *Iliad* 1.188–218 and 24.120–40, where Athena and then Thetis appear to Achilles urging him to restrain his wrath.

134. E.g., Tatian *Oratio ad graecos* 8, Ps.-Justin *Ad graecos* 1–2 and *Cohortatio ad gentiles* 2; cf. Plato *Republic* 2.378b–379e.

135. Plato *Republic* 3.391b–c.

136. Ps.-Justin *Cohortatio ad gentiles* 1.

137. Plato *Republic* 2.383a, Tatian *Oratio ad graecos* 21, and Justin Martyr *First Apology* 25.

138. Plato *Republic* 3.391b–c and Ps.-Justin *Cohortatio ad gentiles* 30.

139. Tatian *Oratio ad graecos* 8 and Theophilus *Ad Autolycum* 1.9.

140. Plato *Republic* 2.364d, Athenagoras *Legatio* 13, Clement of Alexandria *Protrepticus* 2.41.3, Tatian *Oratio ad graecos* 10, and Aristides *Apology* 13.

3

Nekyia

This chapter analyzes a section of *The Acts of Andrew* that no longer exists: it is missing in each of the most reliable manuscripts. Even so, three passages in the *AAMt* foreshadow events that were to have transpired after Andrew left Myrmidonia and that surely were narrated in the original.

• The apostle told the old, would-be pedicide (viz. the counter-Agamemnon),

[A]t the hour when the water recedes, you will go into the abyss, you and the fourteen executioners who killed people daily, and the lot of you will stay in Hades until I return once again and raise you. So now, go into the abyss so that I may show these executioners the place of your murder and the place of peace, and to this old man, the place of love and the surrender of his children. (*AAMt* 31)

• When the earth swallowed them, Andrew reassured the rest:

[D]o not be afraid; for I will not let even them stay in Hades. They went there so that you might believe in our Lord Jesus Christ. (*AAMt* 31)

• Andrew was about to leave Myrmidonia to rejoin his disciples when Jesus appeared to him telling him to return to the city for seven days:

Then you may leave this city and you will go into the city of the barbarians, you and your disciples. After you enter that city and preach my gospel there, you may leave them and again come to this city and bring up all the men in the abyss. (*AAMt* 33)

From these passages the reader should expect the following course of events. After leaving Myrmidonia, Andrew will sail off to rejoin his disciples (*AAMt* 21 and 33), and together they then will preach in "the city of the barbarians" (*AAMt* 33). Andrew and his disciples will return to Myrmidonia to raise the old man and the executioners out of Hades (*AAMt* 21, 31, and 33). Those rescued from the abyss then will narrate their visits to the "place of . . . murder" and "the sacrifice of . . . children" and to the "place" of peace and love; those who heard would

77

believe in Christ (*AAMt* 31). Then Andrew and his disciples will leave for other regions on their way back to Achaea, Andrew's allotted field of mission.

But Andrew does no such thing in the most trustworthy texts of the *AAMt*.[1] Ancient readers of the *AAMt* recognized its failure to live up to its narrative promises and attempted to resolve matters either by omitting the promises or by composing appropriate conclusions.[2]

Fortunately, the silence of the sources is not absolute. An unpublished fifteenth-century Greek manuscript (*Paris graecus 1313 = P*), which is full of misspellings, grammatical errors, and secondary additions, nevertheless relied on manuscripts derived from the ancient *Acts* that were more extensive than the *AAMt* as it now exists. For example, it retains a variant spelling of the word "Myrmidonia," and it ends anticipating an episode of Andrew in Amasia that dovetails perfectly with the second chapter of Gregory's epitome. More relevant to the present discussion, this manuscript sends Andrew from the region of the cannibals to rejoin his disciples and Matthias. Then they all return to Myrmidonia to raise the fifteen from the abyss. In this chapter, for the first time in any modern language, I am providing a translation of this important section of *Paris graecus 1313*.

Unfortunately, *P* does not supply all of the missing narrative and cannot be trusted uncritically when it does. For this reason one must compare *P* with later Andrean hagiographa and other apocryphal Acts that independently used *The Acts of Andrew* as a source: *The Acts of Thomas* (*ATh*), *The Acts of Philip* (*APh*), *The Acts of John by Prochorus* (*AJPr*), *The Acts of Peter and Andrew* (*APeA*), *The Martyrdom of Matthew* (*MMt*), and probably *The Acts of Xanthippe and Polyxena* (*AXP*).[3] Taken together, these apocrypha, *P*, and the suggestive anticipatory passages of the *AAMt* permit a reconstruction of what appeared in this missing section and suggest how the lost content contributed to the Homeric hypertextuality of the *Acts* as a whole.

Rendezvous at a Mountain

Andrew told the Myrmidons: "I am going to my disciples" (*AAMt* 31). Later Jesus told the apostle, "[Y]ou may leave this city and you will go into the city of the barbarians, you and your disciples" (33). In order to rejoin his disciples, Andrew probably sailed to "the mountain where Peter was teaching" (21), to which Andrew had sent them on a cloud.[4] Once he arrived, Andrew presumably would have told Peter, Matthias, and his disciples what had happened in Myrmidonia. A ninth-century Byzantine monk named Epiphanius composed his own life of Andrew, a mishmash of Anatolian legends and free recastings of various written sources, some of which derived ultimately from *The Acts of Andrew*. Epiphanius narrates a meeting of the apostolic brothers, Peter and Andrew, on a height outside Sinope, but his source of information in this case may have had nothing to do with *The Acts of Andrew*.[5] *The Acts of Peter and*

Andrew states that a "cloud of light snatched him [Andrew] up and deposited him on the mountain where Peter, Matthias, Alexander, and Rufus were sitting," and then the apostle told them what had happened in Myrmidonia.[6] Even though this passage shares several tantalizing readings with P,[7] it probably was inspired by *AAMt* 21 and not by a knowledge of texts that narrated Andrew's travels after he left Myrmidonia.

Our best source of information for this episode is P:

> The blessed apostle Andrew arrived at the place of the great rock where he found the apostle Matthew [= Matthias] and their disciples maintaining a fast. When Matthias saw the most blessed Andrew he was filled with joy and gladness, and said to him, "Narrate to us, servant of Christ, what the Lord did for you in the region of the cannibals." Andrew told them all in detail the tortures they inflicted.[8]

The manuscript continues for several lines with a play-by-play third-person narration of the apostle's ordeals among the cannibals.

> Then there was great rejoicing among the brethren, and after giving thanks, the blessed Andrew said, "Blessed Matthew, it is time for us now to go to Myrmeke [= Myrmidonia] just as our Lord Jesus Christ commanded, in order to revive those swallowed up by the abyss." Matthew said, "The will of the Lord be done." They left that place and began to make their way toward Myrmeke.[9]

Some of the statements here in P contradict the anticipatory information provided by the *AAMt*. Presumably, Peter, too, would have been at the mountain (*AAMt* 21),[10] although it is possible that in the original tale he had left by the time Andrew arrived. Second, there is nothing in the *AAMt* to suggest that Matthias was to accompany Andrew and his disciples back to the cannibals.[11] Third, before returning to Myrmidonia, Andrew and his followers were to go to "the city of the barbarians" in order to preach (*AAMt* 33), but they do not do so in P.[12] Prudence allows one to say only that in the ancient *Acts* Andrew rejoined his disciples and Matthias at a mountain and informed them of his experiences with the cannibals. To this extent at least, the anticipatory passages in the *AAMt* and the content of P agree—as do Epiphanius and *The Acts of Peter and Andrew*.

City of the Barbarians

No surviving text—not even P—narrates events in the city of the barbarians, but the cloud on which Andrew sent his disciples out of Myrmidonia may provide a clue concerning the identity of these savages. The preceding chapter described how the author of the *Acts* employed the Iphigenia tradition, especially Euripides' depiction of Artemis snatching the maiden away from the altar where she was to be slain and whisking her off to Tauris, the land of the barbarians. In return for her rescue, Iphigenia had to sacrifice to the goddess any Greek travelers unfortunate enough to be caught there, a theme once again reminiscent of the cannibals in *AAMt*. Iphigenia speaks:

> High raised was I, the sword in act to slay,—
> When Artemis stole me . . .
>   and through clear air
> Wafted me, in the Taurian land to dwell,
> Where a barbarian rules barbarians
> (ἀνάσσει βαρβάροισι βάρβαρος).[13]

Indeed, the Taurians were archetypical barbarians. Mixing hearsay and the prejudiced curiosity of a tourist, Herodotus described them as follows:

> [A]ll ship-wrecked men, and any Greeks whom they take in their sea-raiding, they sacrifice to the Virgin goddess as I will show: after the first rites of sacrifice, they smite the victim on the head with a club; according to some, they then throw down the body from the cliff whereon their temple stands, and place the head on a pole; others agree with this as to the head, but say that the body is buried, not thrown down from the cliff. This deity to whom they sacrifice is said by the Tauri themselves to be Agamemnon's daughter Iphigenia. As for the enemies whom they overcome, each man cuts off his enemy's head and carries it away to his house, where he places it on a tall pole and sets it standing high above the dwelling, above the smoke-vent for the most part. These heads, they say, are set aloft to guard the whole house. The Tauri live by plundering and war.[14]

In order to shame his pagan readers, Clement of Alexandria recalled Euripides' portrayal of these barbarians:

> The Taurian race, who dwell along the Taurian peninsula, whenever they capture strangers in their territory, that is to say, men who have been shipwrecked, sacrifice them on the spot to Tauric Artemis. These are your sacrifices which Euripides represents in tragedy upon the stage. . . . [S]uch sacrifice is murder and human butchery.[15]

The apologies of Athenagoras, Tertullian, Minucius Felix, Origen, and Athanasius likewise mention the Taurians' bad habit of slaying strangers.[16] Obviously an identification of "the city of the barbarians" with these Taurians would correspond with the apologetic interests of the *AAMt* as described in the preceding chapter. In order to counterpunch pagan accusations of cannibalism, the author of the *Acts* might have sent Andrew off to oppose the worship of bloodthirsty Artemis and to convert the barbarians.

In fact, later traditions about Andrew state that once, at a shrine to Artemis, he opposed demons looking for human sacrifices. Epiphanius the monk says that the following incident occurred in Nicea, in northeastern Anatolia:

[T]hey found a large rock along the road where there was a statue of Artemis and in which lived many spirits who used to cause apparitions and sought sacrificial victims. From the ninth hour to the third [viz. from three o'clock in the afternoon to nine o'clock the next morning], they permitted no one to pass along the road. Andrew came with his disciples and stayed there. The demons fled like crows, crying, "O power from Jesus the Galilean! His disciples pursue us everywhere!" Andrew ripped down the statue and set up a cross. The rock and the area were purified of demons. The region was quite appropriately named Nicea ['victory'].[17]

According to Euripides' *Iphigenia in Tauris*, Orestes went to barbarian Tauris and liberated Iphigenia, his sister, from her horrible task of preparing human sacrificial victims for Artemis. As they left, the two siblings took with them the statue of the goddess, thereby ending the practice. Andrew attained the same result by tearing the statue down. Unfortunately, there is no way of knowing for certain if such a passage ever appeared in the ancient *Acts*, let alone in the lost section about the city of the cannibals.[18]

Another witness to this missing story may be a passage in *The Acts of Philip*. Philip, Bartholomew, and Mariamne missionized the region of the Ophians, so named because they worshipped a monstrous snake (ὄφις), whom priests furnished with a diet of human blood drained from unfortunate travelers.[19] To avoid this involuntary and terminal blood donation, Philip plunged seven thousand of the Ophians into the abyss;[20] the passage clearly was patterned after the *AAMt*.[21] Later, Jesus raised everyone out of the pit, all but the idol of the viper and its complicitous proconsul.[22] Later I will suggest that this exhumation of the Ophians may attest to the promised but missing rescue of the Myrmidonian fifteen. Here one need only observe the correlation between Euripides' *Iphigenia in Tauris*, Epiphanius's story of Andrew and the statue of Artemis, and this account of Philip and the statue of the viper. In each case, barbarians or demons who served deities requiring human sacrifices (Artemis/Artemis/serpent) sought to capture strangers (Orestes/Andrew/Philip), only to have the stranger terminate the ritual homicides by stealing, dismantling, or engulfing the statue.

Raising the Myrmidons

Fortunately there exists firmer textual footing for reconstructing what happened when Andrew and entourage returned to Myrmidonia, presumably by ship, to rescue the fifteen from the abyss. *P* narrates Andrew's return as follows:

Before they got to the city, everyone en masse ran out to greet Andrew. After handing on to them many words of sagacity and knowledge, he said to the Lord, "Lord, it is your will, just as you commanded, that those in the abyss arise, because I was appointed by your goodness to me to return to bring them up. Command this to me a second time."

A voice came saying, "I permit it, Andrew, for I wish everyone to be saved." The blessed Andrew was with Matthias and the disciples when the command came.

A great crowd ran together to see what might happen next. Then Andrew said to the blessed Matthias and those with him, "Pray with me for those swallowed up in the abyss, so that the Lord even from there may perform his great deeds for them." He prayed for a long time.[23]

Beginning at this point, *P* parallels passages in *The Acts of Philip* and *The Acts of John by Prochorus*. In all three accounts, God rescues sinners who had been swallowed up by abysses.

P 160 (= *Acts of Andrew*)	APh 138	AJPr 35 (Zahn)
[Earlier: "I was appointed by your goodness to me to		
	[Jesus speaks to Philip:]	[John prays:]
return to **bring them up**	"I will **raise them up**	"**[R]aise them up**
(ἀναγαγεῖν αὐτούς). . . ."	(ἀναγάγω αὐτούς) so	(ἀνάστησον αὐτούς)
(God speaks:)	that those who see you	
"[F]or I wish everyone	**might believe in**	**to believe in**
to be saved."]	(πιστεύσωσιν) the	(πιστεύειν) you. . . ."
	glory of the one	
	who sent you. . . ."	
And while everyone		**And when John had**
was looking at Andrew,		**said these things,**
	[Jesus descends into	
all at once	the abyss.]	
there was a great	And behold,	again **there was a**
boiling up from the earth		**boiling**
(ἀναβρασμὸς ἐγένετο)		(βρασμὸς ἐγένετο)
and all the executioners	the entire crowd of those	and the eight hundred
and the old man **who**	**who**	men **who**
had been engulfed	**had been carried down**	**had been lying**
(καταποθέντες)	(κατενεχθέντων)	(κείμενοι)
boiled up	into the abyss **came up**	dead **came up**
(ἀνεβράσθησαν)	(ἀνέβησαν).	(ἀνέστησον).
and they lay down upon		
the ground (κείμενοι).		

A complete analysis of these parallels would derail the primary concerns of this chapter, but it should be noted that the *APh* and the *AJPr* only once agree with each other against *P* (πιστεύσωσιν and πιστεύειν), whereas each agrees independently with *P* several times. This pattern suggests that *P* indeed preserves readings from the ancient *Acts* which the two later Acts altered independently. One might schematize the relationship like this:

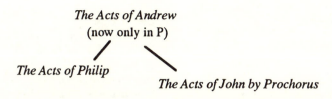

The Acts of Andrew
(now only in P)

The Acts of Philip

The Acts of John by Prochorus

P continues by telling how Andrew raised the Myrmidons back to life. At this point the text parallels a tale in *The Acts of Thomas* that will be crucial for reconstructing this missing section. According to *ATh* 51–58, a young man who had converted to celibacy slew his lover because she would not follow him in sexual renunciation. Thomas went to her and raised her back to life. Her resuscitation closely parallels the raising of the Myrmidons in *P* and leaves little doubt that at this point the author of *The Acts of Thomas* used *The Acts of Andrew* as a model.

P 160–61 (= *Acts of Andrew*)	*ATh* 53–54
[As the Myrmidon fifteen lay dead on the ground:]	[As the woman lay dead on the ground:]
Then Andrew spoke in a loud voice, **"Lord, you who** commanded that these people rise up, and **wish** (βουλόμενος) that they obtain salvation . . . ,	**The apostle** laid his hand on her and **began to say, "Jesus, you who** always appears to us, for you **wish** (βούλει) this. . . .
now **I ask you** (δέομαί σου) to command that the breath of life be granted to them,	**We ask** (δέομεθά σου) and entreat **you** that by your holy name,
through which they will be made alive and the multitude **of those present** become more **faithful** (τῶν παρεστώτων πιστότερα) and may proclaim your greatness."	by your power you raise up her who lies here, for glory and for the **faith of those present** (πίστιν τῶν παρεστώτων).
After praying, **he said** (εἶπε) to Matthew and Bishop Plato, **"Go to them** (προσέλθατε) yourselves and both of you **taking the hand** of each (καὶ λαβόμενοι ἀμφότεροι ἑκαστοῦ τῆς χειρός), **let us raise them up** (ἀνεγείρωμεν αὐτούς)."	After giving him the seal, **he said** (εἶπε) to the young man, **"Go off** (ἄπελθε) and **taking her hand** (καὶ λαβόμενος τῆς χειρός αὐτῆς), say to her: '. . . I am raising you (ἐγείρω σε).'"
The apostles along with bishop Plato **approached** them (προσεγγήσαντες), **calling upon** (ἐπικαλεσάμενοι)	The youth **approached** her (προσελθών) saying, "I believe in you,

the name of our **Lord** (κυρίου)
Jesus Christ.

                                      Christ Jesus."
[The youth asked Thomas to pray,]
"so that my **Lord** (κύριος)
on whom I call (ἐπικαλοῦμαι)
may come to my assistance."

[In Andrew's prayer earlier: [The lad took the girl's hand and said,]
"[C]ommand that the breath of **life**   "Come **Lord Jesus Christ,**
be **granted** to them (πνοὴν ζωῆς   **grant** to this girl **life** (ταύτῃ μὲν
αὐτοῖς παρασχεθῆναι) . . .   παράσχου τὴν ζωήν),
(and) the multitude of those present
become more   and to me the earnest
faithful (πιστότερα)."]   of your **faith** (πίστεως)."
[They] **raised** each of those   And immediately when he drew on her
who had erupted from the abyss.   hand, she **sprang up.**

The remarkable consistency and verbal resonances between these two episodes guarantee that P's version of the raising of the Myrmidons once appeared in *The Acts of Andrew*.[24] The relationship would look like this:

The Acts of Andrew
(now only in *P*)

|

The Acts of Thomas

Visit to the Netherworld

From the anticipatory passages in the *AAMt* one might have expected the Myrmidonian fifteen to have narrated what they had seen during their extended stay underground, where the executioners were to have seen "the place of . . . murder and the place of peace," and the old man "the place of love and the surrender of . . . children" (31). That is, one might have expected to read a tour of hell and heaven, such as one finds in many ancient texts—pagan, Jewish, and Christian. *P* preserves no such tour. Instead, when the Myrmidons emerged from the abyss, they gave thanks to Andrew's God for their rescue, saying only that while below they "expected the fire" and feared being "completely victimized by the devil":

> Immediately they all rose up and spoke with loud voices, "Glory be to you, who through your servant Andrew had mercy on us who were swallowed into the abyss and who had expected the fire. Glory to you, Jesus, who did not permit us to be completely victimized by the devil, but brought us to a knowledge of you." For a long time they gave thanks and proclaimed the God and Master of all.[25]

This final phrase, "For a long time they gave thanks and proclaimed the God and Master of all," suggests that the text of *The Acts of Andrew* originally provided the content of their proclamation.

The most promising witness to the missing speech of the revived Myrmidons appears in *The Acts of Thomas* on the lips of the woman whom Thomas brought back from the dead. Her reviving, already discussed, displays undeniable affinities with the reviving of the cannibals as recorded in *P*. Whereas the Myrmidons merely gave thanks for their rescue, the woman in the *ATh* narrated an elaborate tour, replete with fire, smoke, brimstone, and prisoners "being completely consumed (τελείως καταναλισκόμεναι),"[26] which may reflect the same reading in the ancient *Acts* that informed *P*: "completely victimized by the devil (τέλεον κερδεθῆναι)." The woman's speech also roughly corresponds with the anticipatory allusions in *AAMt* 31. When asked to describe what she had seen during her time dead, the woman said that she was led to a place (τόπος) full of chasms. In one chasm were fire and torture wheels, in another mire teeming with worms, in another smoke and brimstone with souls hanged by various offending body parts. In addition she witnessed "infants heaped one upon another and struggling with one another"; these are the children of parents who perverted sexual relations.[27] According to the *AAMt*, the old counter-Agamemnon was to see the "place (τόπος)" of the sacrifice of his children.

Thus, there is reason to suspect that the woman's speech in the *ATh* was based to some extent on a speech spoken by the Myrmidons on their return from Hades.[28] Furthermore, the woman's speech contains points of intertextual contact with two tours of hell that predate *The Acts of Andrew* and that may have inspired its vision of the netherworld. The beginning and ending of the woman's speech parallel the famous myth of Er in Book 10 of Plato's *Republic*;[29] the central section of the speech matches several of the torments of the wicked described in *The Apocalypse of Peter*.[30] The similarities are too close to ascribe to oral tradition or common literary topoi.[31] Although it is possible that the author of the *ATh* drew directly on Plato's *Republic* and Peter's Apocalypse, several considerations compel one to think that the parallels are indirect, that they already appeared in *The Acts of Andrew*.

- *The Apocalypse of Peter* (*ApocPe*), written sometime during the first half of the second century, enjoyed canonical status among Christians in Alexandria contemporary with the author of *The Acts of Andrew*.[32] Evidence for the *ApocPe* in Syria, the setting for the composition of the *ATh*, is less certain.[33]

- The anticipatory passages in the *AAMt* concerning what the Myrmidonian fifteen were to have seen in the abyss conforms with much of the content of the *ApocPe*. Peter first investigated the "place (τόπος)" of the blessed, full of flora and light. Then he saw "another place (τόπον)," "a place (τόπος) of punishment," where angels punished, among others, murderers and pedicides: a place of murder and the sacrifice of children.

- It is unnecessarily complex to assume that the author of the *ATh*, in order to describe the raising of the woman back to life, consulted *The Acts of Andrew*, then pulled out a copy of Plato's *Republic* for the frame of the tour of hell, and then borrowed from the *ApocPe* for the punishments. One can more easily imagine the author of *The Acts of Andrew* rewriting the myth of Er by replacing Plato's depiction of the netherworld with torments and rewards derived from the *ApocPe*.

- The *ATh* shows little interest in Plato, certainly nothing like the obsession of *The Acts of Andrew*. Therefore, if the parallels between the *ATh* and the myth of Er are literary (demonstrated later), it is likely that they appeared first in Andrew's *Acts*.

- Indeed, the author of *The Acts of Andrew* may have named the Myrmidonian bishop Plato as a hypertextual clue that the tour of hell and heaven is a Christian version of the Platonic story. Bishop Plato does not appear in the best texts of the *AAMt*, but *P* mentions him repeatedly, as in the scene of the raising of the Myrmidonian fifteen already discussed. Furthermore, some Latin and Anglo-Saxon translations of the *AAMt* claim that Andrew ordained a certain Plato after building a church and baptizing the neophytes.[34] *The Martyrdom of Matthew* sends Matthew/Matthias back to Myrne/Myrmidonia to plant, at the gate of the church, a rod that would sprout into a gigantic, fruit-bearing, honey-oozing tree from which the erstwhile cannibals would gather food compatible with their recent dedication to vegetarianism. They also would start wearing clothing and convert their huge roasting oven into a bakery. When Matthew/Matthias arrived, there to welcome him was none other than "Bishop Plato."[35] Thus, widespread evidence survives for this character in texts derived from *The Acts of Andrew*: the Latin and Anglo-Saxon manuscripts of the *AAMt*, *P*, and *The Martyrdom of Matthew*. But did he appear in the original?

I demoted Plato to a footnote in my edition of the *AAMt*, but I did so with great reluctance and perhaps wrongly. In addition to the textual evidence, there are internal reasons for including him. In the first place, Andrew's ordination of a bishop for the Myrmidons is altogether consistent with *The Acts of Andrew* generally; he ordained a certain Callistus to preside as bishop in Nicea.[36] Furthermore, one can understand how this character might have fallen out of the textual tradition: when the story stops at *AAMt* 33, Plato has no opportunity to help raise the Myrmidons from the abyss. Finally, the name Plato is so consistent with the apologetic strategies of *The Acts of Andrew* that if it did not appear there, it should have. The author repeatedly employed proper nouns as clues to his hypertextual aims (e.g., Andrew and Myrmidonia). He also appropriated several anti-Homeric criticisms of Plato's Socrates, such as his horror at Achilles' slaying the twelve Trojans at the funeral of Patroclus,[37] his disgust at Zeus's lying dream,[38] his objection to Achilles' dragging Hector's corpse behind his chariot,[39] and his contempt for gods bribed by sacrifices.[40] Andrew's speeches in the Passion (at the end of the *Acts*) offer undiluted Christian Platonism; indeed, the entire martyrdom is modeled after the execution of Socrates in Plato's *Phaedo*. The reference to Bishop Plato, therefore, may have signaled to the reader to view Andrew as a Christianized Socrates who transformed Homer's savage Myrmidons into residents befitting a moral republic. When the apostle, the new Socrates, left the cannibals, he bequeathed his charge to his aptly named successor.

One might visualize the intertextual connections among Plato's *Republic*, the *ApocPe*, *The Acts of Andrew*, and *The Acts of Thomas* like this:

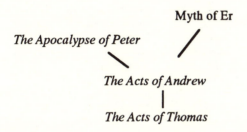

Myth of Er

The Apocalypse of Peter

The Acts of Andrew

The Acts of Thomas

Unfortunately, difficult textual problems impede any comparison of these texts. The text of *The Republic* is secure, but the *ApocPe* survives now in two deviating recensions, one represented by an Ethiopic translation and a few Greek witnesses, and one by a single Greek manuscript.[41] When citing evidence from Peter's Apocalypse, I will prefer the Greek (Akhmim) but cite the Ethiopic (Eth) when its readings are clearly superior. The tour of hell in the *ATh* likewise survives in two divergent recensions, one in Greek and another in Syriac. In my view, the Greek version is far more reliable and will serve as the basis for comparison, even though the Syriac has found patrons.[42]

According to the *ATh*, Thomas revived the dead woman and encouraged her to tell him what she had seen. Plato, similarly, tells of a young soldier, Er, the son of Armenius, who, "at the moment of his funeral, on the twelfth day, as he lay upon the pyre,[43] revived, and after coming to life related what . . . he had seen in the world beyond."[44] The *ApocPe* and many other tours of hell transport their tourists to the netherworld alive, but in the *ATh* and in the myth of Er—as well as in the missing tour from *The Acts of Andrew*—the tourists are those who had died and returned to life.

Republic 10.614b–c	*ATh* 55
"**He said** that when his soul exited it traveled with many others [Cf. 615e: "wild men of fiery **aspect** (ἰδεῖν) laid hold (διαλαβόντες) of them and took them away."[45]]	**She began to say,** "A man received (παρέλαβεν) me, hostile in appearance (τῇ ἰδέᾳ), entirely black, with clothing thoroughly soiled. [Cf. *ApocPe* 21 (Akhmim): "the punishing angels wore a garment

and that they **arrived at a certain**
supernatural **place at which**
there were two **chasms** in the earth
(καὶ ἀφικνεῖσθαι σφᾶς εἰς τόπον
τινὰ δαιμόνιον, ἐν ᾧ τῆς τε γῆς
δύ᾽ εἶναι χάσματα)."

darkened from the air"; cf. 30.]
He **brought me to a certain**
place at which
there were many **chasms**
(ἀπήγαγεν δέ με εἴς τινα τόπον
ἐν ᾧ
πολλὰ χάσματα ὑπῆρχεν)."

Er learned that he must observe everything carefully because he has been selected
to return to the living to tell what he has seen. So, too, with woman in the *ATh.*

Republic 10.614d
"[A]nd they commanded him to
hear and **to look** at everything
in the place (τόπῳ). He saw souls
coming out from **each chasm**
(καθ᾽ ἑκάτερον τὸ χάσμα)
of heaven and earth."

ATh 55
"And he kept forcing me
to look
into
each chasm
(εἰς ἕκαστον χάσμα)
and I saw in the **chasm** (χάσματι)
flaming fire."

Both Er and the woman saw people in great anguish.

Republic 10.614e–615a
"[T]hey told stories to each other,
the one group **lamenting and**
weeping when they remembered
how many and what types of tortures
they might have suffered and seen
during their journey under earth."

ATh 55
"There was a clamor there and lots of
lamentation,
but there was no one to redeem them."

The woman's speech will parallel Plato's *Republic* again later, but in order to
describe the torments of the wicked she borrows from the *ApocPe*. At first she
saw punishments of those guilty of sexual sins, punishments similar to those
afflicted on women who had procured abortions in Peter's Apocalypse.

ApocPe, Akhmim 26 (= Eth 8)
And near that place **I saw** (εἶδον)

another narrow place (τόπον)
in which the birthing blood and
discharge of the tortured ran down
and became like a lake.
Women sat there up to their necks
in birthing blood, and opposite them
many **children** sat, weeping, who
had been aborted. Rays of fire went
forth from them and struck the

ATh 55
"And then others were brought in their
place, and these souls similarly were
conducted to **another chasm.**

These souls are those who perverted
intercourse between a man and a woman.
And when I investigated, **I saw** (εἶδον)
infants heaped upon each other and as
they lay there, they wrestled with each

women in the eyes.
These were those
who conceived
out of wedlock and aborted.

other. He told me,
'**These are** their infants,
and for this reason they were
placed here to testify against them.'"

The Ethiopic version continues describing the place of pedicides. Allusions to the *ApocPe* in Clement of Alexandria and Methodius confirm that the following scene appeared in it:

> Other men and women are standing there naked, while their children stand here opposite them in the place of delight. There is a shout, and they groan and cry out to God concerning their parents: "It is they who have ignored and cursed and transgressed your commandment. They let us die, and (thereby) cursed the angel who molded us. They hung us up, and begrudged us light, though you gave it for all (people). . . ." Their children will be delivered to the angel Temelakos; but those who killed them will be punished forever, for this is what God has willed.[46]

It is quite possible that the old man in the *AAMt*, the counter-Agamemnon, was shown such sufferings.

The woman in the *ATh* next saw the punishment of adulterous women in a chasm full of filth (βόρβορον) and worms (σκώληκας), two standard props in the *ApocPe*.[47] Then she saw yet another chasm where people dangled from their tongues, hair, hands, or feet. The *ApocPe* likewise has victims hanging by their tongues, hair, and feet; no one hangs by their hands in Peter's Apocalypse. Punishments by hanging are common in tours of hell, but the shared wording in the following parallels and the same sequence of the anatomical culprits— tongues, hair, feet—argue for literary dependence.[48]

ApocPe, Akhmim 22–24	*ATh* 56
Some were there hanging by their tongues (ἐκ τῆς γλώσσης κρεμάμενοι). **These**	"I saw **some souls hanging by their tongues** (κρεμαμένης διὰ τῆς γλώττης). . . . **These souls hanged by the tongue** (κρεμασθεῖσαι διὰ τῆς γλώττης)
were those who blaspheme the way of righteousness. **And there were others,** women **hanging by their hair** (τῶν πλοκάμων ἐξηρτημέναι). . . . **These**	are slanderers, who speak false and despicable words without shame. . . . [O]thers [hanged] **by their hair** (διὰ τῶν πλοκάμων). . . . **The souls hanging from their hair** (διὰ τῶν τριχῶν κρεμάμενοι)
were women who were adorned for adultery. And those who had sex with them	are unabashed **women** who were not at all ashamed and went about in the world with their heads uncovered. . . . [O]thers

in the pollution of adultery were
hanging by their feet
(ἐκ τῶν ποδῶν [ἦσαν]
κ[ρεμάμενοι]) and had
their heads (κεφαλάς)
in the filth.

[hanged] **head downward by their feet**
(διὰ τῶν ποδῶν κατὰ κεφαλῆς)

smoky from smoke and brimstone. . . .
These **hanging upside down
by the feet** are those who run lightly
and gladly in the ways of wickedness
and in highways of disorder."

The uncompassionate rich suffer both in the *ApocPe* and in the *ATh*, although their punishments differ.

ApocPe, Akhmim 30 (= Eth 9)
In another place there were burning
pebbles sharper than swords or any
spit, and women and men wearing
filthy rags rolled upon them for
punishment. **These are** the rich
who trusted in their wealth and had
no compassion
on **orphans and widows**

and **disregarded
the command of God.**

ATh 56

"[O]thers [hanged] by their hands. . . .

These souls hanged by their hands **are**
those who stole and deprived others of
their goods, who never gave anything
to **the lowly**, never helped the afflicted,
but did this because they wanted
to take everything,
**paying no mind whatever
to justice or to law.**"

This ends the list of punishments told by the woman in the *ATh*, each of which corresponds to a section of the *ApocPe*. The scene that follows in the *ATh*, however, has no parallel in the *ApocPe*, but it does in Plato's myth of Er; in both stories, the incarcerated seek escape but are ruthlessly repelled.

Republic 10.615d–e
"'[W]hen we were near the mouth
[of a **chasm**] and about to issue
forth . . . , we suddenly **caught
sight of** him [Ardiaeus the tyrant]
and of others. . . .
And **when these supposed that at
last they were about to go up** and
out, the mouth would not receive
them, but it **bellowed** when anyone
of the incurably wicked or of those
who had not completed their
punishment tried to come up. And
thereupon,' he said, '**savage men**
of fiery aspect who stood by and

ATh 57
"Leading me off again,
he **showed me** an entirely dark **cave**,
exhaling great stench,
and many souls looked out,

wanting to take in some air,

and their **guards**

took note of the voice **laid hold
on them and bore them away.'"**   **would not let them look out."**

The woman's tour guide then told her how the prisoners rotated in and out, a motif that also appears in the myth of Er.

Er was not allowed to drink the oblivion-producing waters of Lethe; he had to return to the living at full capacity in order to tell what he had seen.[49] According to the *ATh*, the guards of Hades wanted to retain the woman, but her guide said he did not have the proper authorization to keep her there. He would have to return her.[50] In other words, both Plato and the author of the *ATh* described the conditions allowing Er and the woman to return to the living with their privileged information.

After the narrations of the visits to the netherworld, Socrates and Thomas both provide moralizing conclusions, encouraging their audiences to live righteously.

Republic 10.621c–d	*ATh* 58
"And it [the myth] will save us, if we **believe** it, . . . and **keep our soul unspotted** from the world.	"**Believe** therefore in Christ Jesus, and he . . . will **cleanse you** from all your bodily desires which remain on the earth. . . .
But if we are guided by me . . . we shall hold ever to the upward way and pursue **righteousness** with wisdom always and ever, **that we may be dear** to ourselves and **to the gods** both during our sojourn here and when we **receive our reward**, as the victors in the games go about to gather theirs."	**But walk rather in** faith and meekness and **holiness** and hope, in which God delights, **that ye may be his kinsmen, expecting from him the gifts** which only some few **receive**."[51]

On the basis of these comparisons, it would appear that the author of *The Acts of Andrew* imitated the myth of Er at the beginning and at the ending of the tour, but replaced Plato's description of the torments with those found in the *ApocPe*.

The *AAMt* anticipates two episodes that find no parallels in the woman's story in the *ATh*; they do, however, correspond with the myth of Er and the *ApocPe*: the Myrmidons plunged into the abyss were to see "the place of murder" and "the place of life." The woman saw no murderers punished,[52] no righteous rewarded. Er and Peter did.

In addition to tyrants and traitors, Er saw an assortment of murderers, such as "those responsible for many deaths," parricides, and suicides.[53] Peter also witnessed the torments of homicides: "And I observed murderers (φονεῖς) and their accomplices cast into a narrow place full of wicked reptiles and afflicted by those beasts, and thus writhing there in that torture."[54] Such a vision would conform with the anticipated episode in *AAMt* 31, "the place of . . . murder (φονεύσεως)."[55]

The Myrmidons were to observe a place of bliss. The woman in the *ATh* saw no such sight, but Er and Peter did. After viewing the place of torments, Er ascended to a place dominated by light, beauty, and cosmic harmony.[56] In the *ApocPe*, Jesus told the apostle how he intended to reward the just: "I will give them a good baptism in salvation from the Acherusian lake, which they say (is located) in the Elysian field."[57] Later in the Apocalypse one reads:

> And the Lord showed me a vast region outside this world, aglow with light, the air there gleaming with the rays of the sun, and the ground itself abloom with unfading flowers, full of spices and beautifully blossoming, unwithering plants heavy with magnificent fruit. . . . The inhabitants of that place (τόπου) wore garments of glimmering angels; their attire befitting their region. Angels walked among them there, and all the inhabitants had equal glory, praised the Lord God with one voice, and rejoiced in that place (τόπῳ).[58]

Finally, according to the myth of Er, souls are punished or rewarded for one thousand years, after which they reassemble for a casting of lots in order to select lives for the next round of reincarnations. Er observed one such lottery in which the winner, greedy for power, chose "the greatest tyranny" but "failed to observe that it involved the fate of eating his own children."[59] This calls to mind, of course, the old man in the *AAMt* (≈ Agamemnon) who sacrificed his offspring to his hungry, cannibalistic comrades.

Now at last one can summarize this attempt at reconstructing something of the missing tour of hell in *The Acts of Andrew*. The chart on page 93 identifies narrative elements attested in at least two potential witnesses to the content of the *Acts*. These witnesses may be grouped according to the following three units, which are arranged in order of descending reliability:

1. Manuscripts of *The Acts of Andrew* itself
   a. The anticipatory passages of the *AAMt*
   b. *P*
2. Correlations between the *ATh* and
   a. The myth of Er in Plato's *Republic* or
   b. The *ApocPe*
3. Other texts that seem dependent on *The Acts of Andrew*
   a. *The Acts of Philip*
   b. *The Acts of John by Prochorus*

The following diagram (which corresponds to the diagrams provided earlier in this chapter) suggests how these documents might be related to the missing tour of hell and heaven.

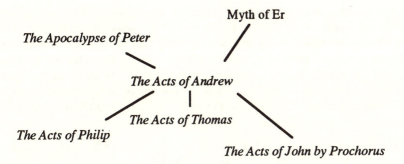

The following chart delineates narrative elements shared among these texts. Narrative elements expressed are designated by 'X'; elements anticipated but not expressed are designated by 'A'; elements transformed but nonetheless present are designated by 'T'.

Narrative Elements	AAMt	P	Plato	ApocPe	ATh	APh	AJPr
Andrew prayed		X					X
Myrmidons bubbled from the earth	X	X				X	X
Myrmidons lay dead on the ground		X					X
Andrew prayed for the dead to rise and for others to believe		X			X		
Andrew told Plato to raise the dead		X			X		
Andrew and Plato went to corpses		X			X		
"called on the Lord"		X			X		
the dead revived		X	X		X		
Myrmidons told what they saw		A		X	X		
a fearsome guide			T		X		
a place with many chasms			X		X		
forced to look into chasms with			X		X		
fire		X		X	X		
darkness				X	X		
filth				X	X		
worms				X	X		
punishments of pedicides	X		X	X	X		
punishments of murderers	X		X	X			
people hanged by their							
tongues (blasphemers/liars)				X	X		
hair (wanton women)				X	X		
hands (rich/robbers)				T	X		
feet (adulterers/wicked)				X	X		
people totally consumed		X			X		
victims tried to escape a							
cave or prison; rebuffed			X		X		
guards tried to retain visitors			T		X		
place of love and peace	X		X	X			
people who heard believe	A		X	T	X	X	X

Confirmation of the presence of such a tour in *The Acts of Andrew* comes from an obscure reference to an obscure fourth-century Manichaean intellectual. The ninth-century Byzantine patriarch and bibliophile Photius read a manuscript in twenty-three books written by a certain Agapius. Photius found the work utterly reprehensible, but his denunciation favored it with the only surviving evidence that it ever existed. From the little Photius says, it would appear that Agapius used a tour of heaven and hell from *The Acts of Andrew* and Plato to argue for reincarnation:

> He adduces arguments by relying on the so-called Acts of the twelve apostles, especially those of Andrew, maintaining that his thought is lifted from them. He also holds to metempsychosis. He sends off to God those who have achieved the zenith of virtue, consigns to fire and darkness those who achieved the nadir of wickedness, and brings down into bodies once more those who conducted their lives somewhere between these two extremes. He shamelessly employs martyrs and the lovers of Greek religion, especially Plato, to support his fight with God. [60]

The flow of Photius's argument suggests that Agapius discovered an articulation of this doctrine in Andrew's *Acts*, and insofar as no other section of the *Acts* seems a more likely candidate, Agapius probably referred to the missing tour, which told of "those who have achieved the zenith of virtue" enjoying "the place of life" and "those who achieved the nadir of wickedness" suffering in "fire and darkness." Testimonia from *The Manichaean Psalm-Book*, Philaster of Brescia, Augustine, Evodius of Uzala, the anonymous *Ad Iustinum Manichaeum*, and Timothy of Constantinople leave little doubt that *The Acts of Andrew* was indeed popular among Manichaeans. [61] The point to be made here is not that *The Acts of Andrew* itself promoted reincarnation, although that is possible, [62] but rather that it was an easy target for such an interpretation. Agapius's use of Plato to interpret *The Acts of Andrew* may have been suggested by the *Acts* itself—in the appearance of Bishop Plato and by the content of the missing tour.

If Manichaeans, like Agapius, did indeed use Andrew's raising of the Myrmidons to argue for reincarnation, it might explain why it disappeared except as a promise—why, for example, Gregory decided to delete it along with whatever else "would breed disgust." More than a century before Gregory, Turibius of Astorga had complained that Mani and his disciples "composed or interpolated" apocryphal books, especially *The Acts of Andrew*. [63] Turibius does not indicate what sections of the *Acts* he thought Mani added; much of it could be squeezed into a Manichaean mold without much pushing. More significant is his allowing a distinction between the original *Acts* and Manichaean interpolations, a distinction that could encourage scribes to excise the venal in order to preserve the virtuous. Such theological surgery was widespread. John of Thessalonica (late seventh century) speaks approvingly of his contemporaries and of authors long before him who redacted the apocryphal Acts in order to repair the damage done by heretical "additions." He explicitly mentions *The Acts of Andrew* along with those of Peter, Paul, and John.[64] Such statements as these by Turibius of Astorga and John of Thessalonica fuel the suspicion that the *AAMt*, Gregory, and the Byzantine "Lives" refused to narrate Andrew's return to raise the Myrmidons because of a common desire to rid the *Acts* of Manichaean prooftexts. Even *P*, the only witness sufficiently daring to depict Andrew raising the Myrmidons from the abyss, held back from narrating the tour of heaven and hell. Anti-Manichaeism accounts for the disappearance of much of the apocryphal Acts.[65]

If the author of *The Acts of Andrew* did indeed compose the missing tour to be a Christianized version of Plato's myth of Er, it might seem to militate against the hypothesis that he wrote the *Acts* in order to transvalue Homer. On the contrary, his dependence on Plato strengthens the case. Plato's Socrates advertised his tale about Er as a transvaluative hypertext based on Odysseus's journey to the netherworld: "It is not, let me tell you, . . . the tale to Alcinous told, . . . but the tale of a warrior bold."[66] The following précis highlights aspects of the Homeric story relevant to the myth of Er and its recasting in *The Acts of Andrew*.

Odysseus told his host, Alcinous, king of the Phaeacians, that he had sailed from Circe's island in order to consult with the blind seer Tiresias in the realm of Hades. When he arrived at the designated spot, Odysseus dug a pit (βόθρον), poured libations, and entreated the dead. "But when with vows and prayers I had made supplication to the tribes of the dead, I took the sheep and cut their throats over the pit, and the dark blood ran forth."[67] The souls of the dead then came to drink the blood.

Among the souls was the prophet Tiresias, who, though blind, mysteriously recognized the hero. After gulping his fill of hemoglobin, Tiresias told Odysseus how to get home and what would happen when he arrived. In order to die in peace, Odysseus learned, he must propitiate Poseidon by planting his oar so far inland that the residents would mistake the oar for a winnowing fan. He also saw his recently deceased mother, Anticleia, who told him to observe well things he saw happening in Hades, "that thou mayest hereafter tell them to thy wife."[68] He then observed several other women, including Jocasta (in Homer, Epicaste), the mother and unwitting wife of Oedipus, who slew herself on discovering her crime.

After the women came the men, including Agamemnon—slain by his own wife and her lover—and Achilles with his comrade, Patroclus.[69] In the ensuing conversation, Achilles uttered the immortal lines: "I should chose, so I might live on earth, to serve as the hireling of another, of some portionless man whose livelihood was but small, rather than be lord of all the dead that have perished."[70] Achilles asked about his Myrmidons and told of the Trojan "horse which Epeus made." Then came Telamonian Ajax, still furious at Odysseus for having won the contest for Achilles' armor.[71] "There then I saw Minos, the glorious son of Zeus, golden sceptre in hand, giving judgment to the dead from his seat."[72] Odysseus also witnessed the terrible punishments of Tityus, Tantalus, and Sisyphus, and spoke with Heracles before boarding ship again for Circe's island.

Plato's Socrates targeted the *nekyia* for particular contempt in Books 2 and 3 of *The Republic*. Homer's account failed to promote ἀνδρεία, 'courage', insofar as the poet depicted life after death as a state of terror and ignorance. Only Tiresias kept his wits.[73] The gods themselves recoiled at the sight of Hades, "horrible, noisome, dank."[74] Plato found particularly objectionable Achilles' statement that he would prefer the life of a slave on earth than to be king of the dead.[75] Furthermore, Homer's *nekyia* provided no rewards for the righteous. Tales of the afterlife, insisted Plato, ought somehow to praise it if they are to befit "the ears of boys and men who are destined to be free and to be more afraid of slavery than of death."[76]

At the end of *The Republic*, then, Plato told his story of Er not only to deter its readers from vice but to inspire them to virtue. In other words, he crafted a transvaluative Homeric hypertext. The wicked receive punishments as in Homer, but, in addition, the righteous enjoy bliss. One's fate in the beyond, whether accursed or blessed, depends on conduct here and now. After a thousand years of punishment or reward, all souls convene to choose their lot in their next reincarnations. Therefore, even sinners may ultimately enjoy delights if they learn from their errors and choose wisely for the future.

Plato never lets the reader lose sight of the fact that Er's tale is a transvalued Homeric *nekyia*. As in *Odyssey* Book 11, one finds the Telamonian Ajax still furious about Odysseus's besting him in the contest over Achilles' armor,[77] Agamemnon bemoaning his dysfunctional family,[78] and Epeus, the builder of the Trojan horse.[79] Odysseus himself figures prominently in Er's story:

> And it fell out that the soul of Odysseus drew the last lot of all and came to make its choice, and, from memory of its former toils having flung away ambition, went about for a long time in quest of the life of an ordinary citizen who minded his own business, and with difficulty found it lying in some corner disregarded by the others, and upon seeing it said that it would have done the same had it drawn the first lot, and chose it gladly.[80]

Plato transvalues Homer's *nekyia* again in *Gorgias* 523–26, where Socrates states that Rhadamanthus, Aeacus, and Minos preside as judges and send the wicked, most of whom are "despots and kings and potentates and public officials," off to "the greatest, sharpest, and most fearful sufferings."[81] As proof of the lofty status of those tormented, Plato cites the epic bard: "Homer also testifies to this, for he has represented kings and potentates as those who are punished everlastingly in the netherworld—Tantalus and Sisyphus and Tityus."[82] Homer also provided Socrates with proof of the supremacy of Minos's judgment, "as Odysseus in Homer tells how he saw him, 'holding a golden scepter, speaking dooms to the dead.'"[83]

The survivals of *The Acts of Andrew* indicate that, despite the parallels with the myth of Er, Plato was not the ultimate hypertextual target; it was Homer. The author of the *Acts* simply followed Plato's lead in rewriting Odysseus's visit to the dead.

- In chapter 2, I argued that the episode of the sphinx paralleled sections of the *nekyia*, especially her journey to summon the dead patriarchs for them to testify against the high priests (*AAMt* 15).[84]

- Andrew plunged the Myrmidons into the earth (and presumably brought them up again) at "the place of the trough where they used to slaughter people" (*AAMt* 31) and where they drank the blood (22). The text is curiously silent concerning the adjacent oven. This exclusive emphasis on the trough suggests hypertextual contact between it and Odysseus's bloody pit for luring the thirsty dead.

- The old man who sacrificed his children seems to be a counter-Agamemnon; Agamemnon appears in both *nekyiai* in *The Odyssey* (Books 11 and 24), and in other Greek visits to Hades.[85]

- The episodes that follow Andrew's exhumation of the Myrmidons (which I investigate in the next chapter) transvalue five characters whom Homer mentions in his *nekyia*: Tiresias (GE 2), Achilles and Patroclus (GE 3), and Jocasta and Oedipus (GE 4).

It therefore would appear that *The Acts of Andrew* once contained a vision of the netherworld that combined motifs and characters taken from *The Odyssey* with the philosophical concerns and narrative frame of the myth of Er and with the moral perspective and punishments of the *ApocPe*.

Plato was not the first, nor was the author of *The Acts of Andrew* the last, to rewrite Homer's *nekyia*; indeed, few episodes of ancient literature were more vulnerable to hypertextual activity.[86] Two ancient authors made particularly good use of Homer's *nekyia*, and both combined it with elements that appear in the myth of Er: Virgil and Lucian. Throughout Book 6 of *The Aeneid* Virgil displayed his dependence on the Homeric *nekyia*. Aeneas, like Odysseus, offered elaborate sacrifices to the gods and caught blood in bowls.[87] When he entered the netherworld, he witnessed Acheron, Phlegethon, Elysium, Lethe, Minos, Rhadamanthus, soldiers slain in the Trojan War, and the punishments of the wicked in Tartarus, including the giant Tityus. Aeneas's rendezvous with his father, Anchises, clearly was modeled after Odysseus's meeting with his mother, Anticleia.[88] The speech by Elpenor in *Odyssey* 11.51–80 inspired Palinurus's speech in *Aeneid* 6.337–83. Other Homeric allusions abound.[89]

In order to advance his own understanding of reincarnation, Virgil, the eclectic Epicurean, borrowed from Pythagorean-Platonic tradition.[90] The following passage has several points of contact with the myth of Er. Souls are

> schooled with penalties, and for olden sins pay punishment:[91] some are hung stretched out to the empty winds; from some the stain of guilt is washed away under swirling floods or burned out in fire. Each of us suffers his own spirit; then through wide Elysium are we sent, a few of us to abide in the joyous

fields; till lapse of days, when time's circle is complete. . . . All these, when they have rolled time's wheel through a thousand years,[92] the god summons in vast throng to the river of Lethe, in sooth that, reft of memory, they may revisit the vault above and conceive desire to return again to the body.[93]

Lucian, a contemporary of the author of *The Acts of Andrew*, adapted the *nekyia* of Menippus into his own humorous dialogue in which the protagonist, Menippus, tells a friend that he went to Hades to consult blind Tiresias "to find out from him in his capacity of prophet and sage what the best life was."[94] To succeed in his plan, Menippus sought out a Zoroastrian magician, who

> provided a boat, victims, mead, and everything else that we should need for the ritual. So we shipped all the stores, and at length ourselves
>
> "Gloomily hied us aboard, with great tears falling profusely."
>
> For a space we drifted along in the river, and then we sailed into the marsh and the lake in which the Euphrates loses itself. After crossing this, we came to a deserted, wooded, sunless place. There at last we landed with Mithrobarzanes leading the way; we dug a pit (βόθρον), we slaughtered the sheep, and we sprinkled their blood about it.[95]

Menippus then descended into a chasm and saw Acheron, Pyriphlegethon (the river of fire), Cerberus, Rhadamanthus, Minos, and the punishment of the wicked, including Sisyphus, Tantalus, and Tityus.[96] While he was there, the rulers of Hades passed a ruling concerning the rich to the effect that at the time of death their bodies would suffer in Hades, "but that their souls be sent back up into life and enter into donkeys until they shall have passed two hundred and fifty thousand years in the said condition, transmigrating from donkey to donkey, bearing burdens, and being driven by the poor."[97] Menippus then found Tiresias—"he is a blind little old gentleman, pale with a piping voice"—who told him that the best life of all is that of a commoner.[98] Like Virgil, Lucian obviously combined the Homeric *nekyia* with Pythagorean-Platonic versions of the hereafter, especially their doctrine of reincarnation.[99]

The netherworld also gets attention in Lucian's *True Story*. Even though the narrator faulted Homer's Odysseus for lying to Alcinous about his fabulous journeys, he had to admit that even "men who profess philosophy" told such tales, (viz. Plato in the myth of Er).[100] If the likes of Plato could lie about the netherworld, Lucian could too. Among his adventures was a visit to the Isle of the Blest, where Rhadamanthus reigned,[101] and where, "in the Elysian Fields," Homer and Odysseus led the grateful dead in the singing of *The Iliad* and *The Odyssey*.[102] Lucian saw many other famous people there, all except Plato: "[H]e was living in his imaginary city [the republic] under the constitution and the laws that he himself wrote."[103]

No attitude toward the Homeric and Platonic versions of the netherworld was more widespread than the attempt to harmonize them into a coherent presentation of philosophical truths. Ancients were convinced that, in spite of Plato's rejection of Homer, they basically agreed. Dionysius of Halicarnassus thought Plato had criticized Homer not because he disagreed philosophically, but because he was peeved that "it was through him [Homer] that every form of culture and finally philosophy itself, became a part of our lives."[104] Vindications of Homer against Plato also characterized several lost works.[105] The Neoplatonist Proclus devoted a major section of his commentary on *The Republic* to Plato's criticisms: *Plato's Statements in "The Republic" about Homer and Poetry*. Proclus then allegorized Homer platonically. Maximus of Tyre spoke for many ancients: "I trust in Homer; I believe in Plato."[106]

Among the most commonly cited points of agreement between the poet and the philosopher was the immortality of the soul. "The soul, for example, which he [Plato] conceives as deathless, and which at the dissolution of the body is separated from it, is so spoken of by Homer first. For Homer has said that the soul of Patroclus 'went down to the house of Hades, bewailing its doom, leaving manhood and youth.'"[107] Numenius, a contemporary of the author of the *Acts*, composed a commentary on the myth of Er in which he argued that its view of the soul was the same as that expressed in Homer's cave of the nymphs in *Odyssey* 13.102–12.[108] Later Platonists, including Plotinus, Porphyry, and Proclus, repeatedly conflated Homer's *nekyia* with Plato's myth of Er: "The use of the myths of Plato to explicate the myths of Homer and the idea that the two bodies of storytelling had like structures of meaning were perhaps the most important developments in the history of reading Homer in Platonic circles."[109]

Christian apologists, too, saw the Homeric *nekyia* through Platonic lenses, and witnessed both the poet and the philosopher arguing for the immortality of the soul in a manner congenial with Christian teaching. For example, Justin Martyr appealed to "Empedocles and Pythagoras, Plato and Socrates, Homer's ditch (βόθρος) and Odysseus's descent in order to investigate these matters."[110] Justin undoubtedly was thinking of *Odyssey* Book 11, which he interpreted by means of Plato's *Republic* and *Gorgias.*[111] An anonymous document transmitted together with the genuine works of Justin quoted extensively from the myth of Er. Plato properly understood the nature of the soul, claimed this Ps.-Justin, because he learned it from the prophets. Had he not feared "the Greeks," Plato would have acknowledged the barbarian source of his information; instead, he foisted them onto the lips of a dead Greek soldier.[112] The author continues: "Not only Plato, but Homer, too, learned [from the prophets] in Egypt and spoke about how Tityus was punished in like manner [as those in the story of Er]. For in his necromancy, Odysseus regales Alcinous like this: [quoting *Odyssey* 11.575–77]."[113] Clement of Alexandria claimed that "every poetic muse" (which would apply of course to Homer above all) "and Greek philosophy pilfered punishments after death and the torment of fire from barbarian philosophy. In the last book of *The Republic*, Plato speaks these very words. . . ." Clement then quotes several lines from the myth of Er concerning the savage guards of Hades.[114] Later in the same work Clement used this story (claiming Er was none other than Zoroaster!) to support

his understanding of the resurrection and the Sabbath.[115]   Origen also appealed to
the myth: "As the unbelievers mock at the resurrection of Jesus Christ, we will
quote Plato who says that Er the son of Armenius rose again from the funeral pyre
after twelve days and gave an account of his adventures in Hades."[116]   Hippolytus
also probably had the myth in mind when discussing the punishments of the
wicked, the rewards of the righteous, and reincarnation.[117]

Therefore, if the author of *The Acts of Andrew* did imitate the myth of Er in
order to improve on Homer's *nekyia*, he was by no means quixotic; indeed, he
participated in one of the most vibrant intellectual discourses of the second and
third centuries, one in which other Christian intellectuals also were engaged.

Departure from Myrmidonia for Amasia

Manuscript *P* alone states what happened as Andrew left Myrmidonia:

> Everyone in unison went to the church.   Then the blessed Andrew
> restrained the crowd with his hand and began to say, "Children, be strong, get
> control of yourselves, and keep what I have handed over to you, but here you
> have my fellow apostle Matthew to strengthen you in all the good things of our
> Lord Jesus Christ. I am going to my allotted place, but it will take me many
> days to get to them."
>
> Then he left the most blessed Matthew there and took off with his own
> disciples, while all the city ran together to send the blessed Andrew off again.
> He said to them, "My children, go off to <y>our father, my fellow apostle
> Matthew, and he will fulfill all your desires, for whatever you seek from God
> he will provide." With much grieving and groaning they returned. (161–62)

The Acts of Andrew probably contained some such scene, but one must be
suspicious about the role of Matthew/Matthias here. *P* says nothing concerning
Bishop Plato, who would have been the more likely character to guide the
Myrmidonian Church after Andrew's departure. *P* may demonstrate awareness
of later traditions that Matthew/Matthias was executed among savages and
substituted Matthew/Matthias for Plato accordingly,[118] but it is perhaps more
likely that the confusion derives from internal considerations. *P* sent Matthias
back to Myrmidonia, even though the *AAMt* suggests that the only ones to return
were Andrew and his disciples. Once Matthew/Matthias was in Myrmidonia, the
narrator had the problem of how best to dispose of him. One could either send
the apostle off to another region of mission, with or without Andrew, or make him
stay put. *P* chose the later. If the Myrmidonians had a resident apostle, what
further need had they of a mere bishop?

P ends like this: "Andrew went on his way with his disciples. When he
reached Amasia, he kept silent, glorifying the Father and the Son and the Holy
Spirit, in one Godhead, to whom is due glory and magnificence to the end of the

ages of the ages. Amen" (162). Surely the description here of Andrew's journey follows the ancient *Acts*. Only if the author of this passage had used a source could one account for the impossibly awkward transition between the narrative and the benediction: "When he reached Amasia, he kept silent, glorifying the Father. . . ." *P* gives no motivation for the apostle's entry into Amasia incognito and incommunicado, but Gregory's epitome does, as will become apparent in chapter 4.

Conclusion

Even though the most reliable texts of *The Acts of Andrew* fail to provide detailed information about the apostle's career after he left Myrmidonia and before he arrived in Amasia, it has been possible to piece together something of the missing episodes. Apparently Andrew left the city of the cannibals and went to his disciples on the mountain where he had sent them. There he told them of the conversion of the Myrmidons. Then he and his disciples went to the city of the barbarians, where the apostle perhaps neutralized a shrine devoted to human sacrifices—most likely an altar to Artemis Taurica. Like the conversion of the Myrmidons, the episode in the city of the barbarians probably sought to defend Christians against the charge of cannibalism. The deities who relished human blood were those of Greek temples, not the God of Christian churches. The reconstruction of these tales relies primarily on the anticipatory statements in the *AAMt* and on the unpublished Greek manuscript *P*.

Andrew and his disciples then returned to Myrmidonia, where he raised the Myrmidonian fifteen from the abyss—just as promised in the *AAMt* and as partially narrated in *P*. Once revived, those who had been in the abyss told of the torments of hell and the glories of heaven. One can restore much of the content of their speech by comparing *The Apocalypse of Peter* and Plato's myth of Er with *The Acts of Thomas* as well as with Agapius the Manichaean, *The Acts of Philip*, and *The Acts of John by Prochorus*. It would appear that the author composed this tour as an alternative to Homer's *nekyia*, Odysseus's visit to the netherworld. Like Plato's Socrates, the author replaced the hopelessness of Homer's Hades with a vision of an afterlife that not only disciplined the wicked but also compensated the righteous. Andrew then left the congregation in the care of Bishop Plato and traveled with his disciples back toward Achaea. First stop Amasia.

Notes

1. Gregory's epitome never sent the Myrmidons into Hades in the first place, so Andrew did not need to return to exhume them. He simply "left that place and went to his own region"; next stop Amasia.

2. One Greek manuscript (*Paris suppl. gr. 824*) and an Anglo-Saxon version of the *AAMt* removed Andrew's promises to exhume the Myrmidons. The Latin, Syriac, and Ethiopic versions say nothing about Andrew going to the barbarians. By clever omission, another Greek manuscript (*Palat. Vat. 4*) transformed the Myrmidons themselves into the barbarians Andrew was to evangelize, avoiding the need for his return. The Armenian version, a Latin poem based on the *AAMt* (*Recensio Vaticana*), and the Anglo-Saxon epic *Andreas* deleted the entire presaging passage of chapter 33.

Other texts work at the problem from the opposite end by supplying the foreshadowed but absent episodes. *The Acts of Peter and Andrew* picks up where the *AAMt* broke off, by sending Andrew on a cloud to his disciples (cf. *AAMt* 21). Then they go, as the *AAMt* had promised, to the city of the barbarians (*AAA* 2.1:117–18). In the Syriac and Ethiopic versions of the *AAMt*, Andrew raises the fifteen from the abyss before he leaves the city.

3. For an analysis of these intertextual connections see: Prieur, *Acta Andreae*, 385–403; and MacDonald *Acts of Andrew* 27–45.

4. According to *APeA* 1, Andrew, too, traveled there on a "cloud of light," but it is more likely that in the original story the apostle left as he had arrived, by ship. Two departure scenes, one in the *APh* and one in the *AXP*, seems to have been modeled after Andrew's departure in *AAMt* 33, and in both scenes travelers board ships (*APh*, Act 6 and *AXP* 39). *P* states that Andrew left the city (158), but does not indicate how he did so.

5. Epiphanius himself had visited Sinope, where the residents showed him venues related to the legend of St. Andrew, including a promontory where Peter and Andrew allegedly met (220A). Epiphanius (E) narrates their meeting *prior* to the cannibal story, not after it as in the *AAMt*. After freeing Matthias from prison, the two apostles meet again in E, this time to divide up the world, Peter to the west and Andrew to the east. This rendezvous also derives not from the *Acts* but from later traditions that claimed Andrew as the apostolic hero of the Byzantine empire. See Dvornik, *Apostolicity*, passim.

6. *APeA* 1 (*AAA* 2.1:117).

7. *P* 159: ἰδὼν δὲ ὁ Ματθαῖος τὸν μακαριώτατον Ἀνδρέαν, χαρᾶς καὶ εὐφροσύνης πλησθῆς; cf. *APeA* 1: ὁ δὲ ἰδὼν αὐτούς, ἠσπάσαντο αὐτὸν μετὰ πολλῆς χαρᾶς. Or again, *P* 159: ἐνεδείξαντο βασάνους . . . πῶς τὰς τρεῖς ἡμέρας ἔσυρον αὐτὸν πᾶσαν τὴν πόλιν, ὥστε . . . τὸ αἷμα . . . ἐν τῇ γῇ ῥυθῆναι; cf. *APeA* 1: πολλὰ κακά μοι ἐνέδειξαν . . . ἔσυραν γάρ με ἐν τῇ πλατείᾳ ἡμέρας τρεῖς, ὥστε τὸ αἷμα μου μολῦναι τὴν πλατεῖαν ὅλην. These parallels probably derived from a dependence on earlier sections of the *AAMt* and not on a missing rendezvous.

8. *P* 158–59.

9. Ibid., 159.

10. Cf. *APeA* 1.

11. Matthias/Matthew returns to Myrmidonia also in *The Martyrdom of Matthew*.

12. *The Acts of Peter and Andrew* places the apostles in the city of the barbarians, but the narrative telling of events there cannot have issued from the ancient *Acts*.

13. *Iphigenia in Tauris* 27–31. Although Euripides does not state explicitly that Artemis used a cloud to transport Iphigenia, it became the dominant interpretation. See Ovid *Ex Ponto* 3.2.61–64, Seneca *Octavia* 973–83, and Hyginus *Fab.* 98. Aeschylus and Sophocles both wrote plays entitled *Iphigenia*. For discussions of the development of the Iphigenia legend see Isaac Flagg, *Euripides. Iphigenia Among the Taurians* (Boston: Ginn, 1891), 7–15. Several Homeric characters also travel on clouds in *The Iliad* : Paris (3.380–82), Aeneas (20.321–29), Hector (20.443–44), and Agenor (21.597–98).

14. Herodotus 4.103; cf. Diodorus Siculus 4.44.7, Seneca *Octavia* 979–83, and Lucian *Toxaris* 2–6.

15. *Protrepticus* 3.42.3. Eusebius quoted this section of the *Protrepticus* extensively in his objections to alleged pagan savagery (*Praeparatio evangelica* 4.16 [157–58]).

16. Athenagoras *Legatio* 26.2, Tertullian *Apology* 9 (referring to Euripides' *Iphigenia in Tauris*), Minucius Felix *Octavius* 30, Origen *Contra Celsum* 5.27, and Athansius *Contra gentes* 25; cf. Tatian *Oratio ad graecos* 29.1 and Minucius Felix *Octavius* 6. Pagan authors, of course, also despised the sacrifices of Artemis (e.g., Lucian *Zeus Rants* 44 and *On Sacrifices* 13). Lucian has Apollo, Artemis's twin brother, state that the goddess herself was eager for Orestes and Pylades to rescue her from the Scythians insofar as it was they, not the goddess, who insisted on sacrificing Greeks (*Dialogues of the Gods* 3 [274]; cf. 18 [244]).

17. E 232B–C.

18. Notice, however, that Artemis appears later, in chapter 25 of Gregory's epitome. The *AJPr*, which recasts several stories from Andrew's *Acts*, repeatedly sends John against shrines of Artemis, but it is impossible to trace any of these stories back to *The Acts of Andrew* with confidence. At least one of them was inspired by the "Leucian" *Acts of John* (cf. *AJPr* 33–35 [Zahn] and *AJ* 38), even if indirectly (*pace* Eric Junod and Jean-Daniel Kaestli, *Acta Iohannis*, CCSA 1 and 2 [Turnhout: Brepols, 1983], 718–36). Both of these Johannine *Acts* concern themselves not with the nasty Artemis Taurica but with the Artemis Ephesiaca, who had no commerce with human sacrifice.

19. *APh* Act 15.123 and 131. This story may have been inspired by *Bel and the Dragon*, although this addition to the Book of Daniel argues that the dragon could not eat a thing: "[T]his thing is only clay inside and bronze outside, and it never ate or drank anything" (7).

20. *APh* Act 15.133.

21. See MacDonald, *Acts of Andrew*, 40–43.

22. *APh* Act 15.138.

23. The phrases "many words of sagacity and knowledge" and "prayed for a long time" may be all that is left of lengthy discourses.

24. Andrew had promised to raise the fifteen in *AAMt* 31, and similar scenes of raising multiple corpses appear in *AAMt* 32 and GE 24, where the apostle revived thirty-nine corpses of drowned sailors who had washed up on shore. Andrew himself raised the first

sailor by himself, but relied on associates to raise the other thirty-eight, just as in the passage in *P*. GE 24:

> The apostle again poured out prayer for each one of the others saying, "Lord Jesus, I ask that those who have been swept here by the sea also may rise again." Then he ordered each of the brothers to take a corpse and say, "Jesus Christ, the son of the living God revives you." When this was done, the thirty-eight were roused, and the spectators glorified God: "None is like you, O Lord."

25. *P* 160–61.

26. *ATh* 55–56.

27. Ibid., 55.

28. The author of *The Acts of Philip* also may have read a tour of hell in *The Acts of Andrew*. Those plunged into the abyss in *The Acts of Philip* pleaded for mercy, saying "[F]or now we see the judgments of those who did not confess the crucified. Behold, the cross enlightens us. Jesus Christ, appear to us, for all of us are descending into Hades alive and are being flogged, because we unjustly crucified your apostles" (*APh* 133). A recently published manuscript of the beginning of *The Acts of Philip* contains a heretofore unknown tour of hell (Bertrand Bouvier and François Bovon, "Actes de Philippe, I d'après un manuscrit inédit," in *Oecumenica et Patristica: Festschrift für Wilhelm Schneemelcher zum 75. Geburtstag*, ed. Damaskinos Papandreou et al. [Stuttgart: Kohlhammer, 1989]), 367–94. Several details in this tour point to Greek mythology and religion. Philip raises back to life a lad who had been a scrupulously faithful pagan; he had sacrificed to Ares, Apollo, Hermes, Artemis, Zeus, Athena, and even to Helios and Selene (1). In the netherworld he saw someone tortured with lead weights hanging from him (5; cf. Zeus's punishment of Hera in *Iliad* 15.18–21). He also saw the Hound of Hell, Cerberus, devouring a man and a woman who had maligned ecclesiastical leaders (9). Finally, the youth saw the refreshment of the righteous (14). No such vision of rewards appears in the *ATh*, but it surely did once in *The Acts of Andrew*. Although it is possible that this passage in the *APh* displays knowledge of Andrew's *Acts*, the parallels are closer to *The Apocalypse of Peter* and especially *The Acts of Thomas* 54–56. See also *The Acts of Peter*, a source used by *The Acts of Andrew*, in which a youth raised back to life states that while he was dead he saw Christ speaking with Peter (*AV* 28 [*AAA* 1.77]).

29. The myth of Er influenced other early Christian descriptions of the netherworld. See G. H. McCurdy, "Platonic Orphism in the Testament of Abraham," *JBL* 61 (1942): 213–26.

30. The *ApocPe* inspired several later apocalypses, including *The Apocalypse of Paul* and probably *Sibylline Oracles* 2.194–338.

31. Montague Rhodes James and Günther Bornkamm thought that the parallels between the two works derived from the dependence of the *ATh* directly on the *ApocPe* (James, *The Apocryphal New Testament* [Oxford: Oxford University Press, 1924], 390, n. 1; Bornkamm, *Mythos und Legende in der apokryphen Thomas-Akten*, FRLANT n.s. 31 [Göttingen: Vandenhoeck & Ruprecht, 1933], 46–48). Martha Himmelfarb has challenged this view on the grounds of minor differences between the punishments in the

two accounts (*Tours of Hell: An Apocalyptic Form in Jewish and Christian Literature* [Philadelphia: University of Pennsylvania Press, 1983], 132–33). She attributes the similarities to a common literary dependence on a now lost Jewish source.

Himmelfarb's primary thesis, in fact, is that Albrecht Dieterich was wrong in supposing that behind the tour of heaven and hell in the *ApocPe* lay an Orphic-Pythagorean tradition (*Nekyia: Beiträge zur Erklärung der neuentdeckten Petrusapokalypse*, 2d edition, annotated by R. Wünsch [Leipzig: B. G. Teubner, 1913]; reprint of 1893 edition). Instead, alleges Himmelfarb, the *ApocPe* relied on Jewish prototypes. Many of her objections are legitimate. Dieterich outstripped the evidence by insisting on the widespread influence of an Orphic "Descent into Hades" (Himmelfarb, *Tours of Hell*, 41–45). Furthermore, Dieterich did not have access to the Ethiopic version of the *ApocPe* (it was not published until 1910), and he slighted Jewish parallels. Himmelfarb is also convincing in her mapping of the interconnections of later Jewish and Christian tours.

The discussion that follows here—concerning the relationships among Plato's myth of Er, the *ApocPe*, and the *ATh* via the missing tour in *The Acts of Andrew*—does not necessarily call into question Himmelfarb's thesis concerning the indebtedness of the *ApocPe* to Jewish sources. On the other hand, this treatment does call into question Himmelfarb's framing of the matter as an "either . . . or"—either Greek or Jewish. Even though she frequently discusses Homer's *nekyia* and Plato's depictions of the netherworld (in *The Republic, Gorgias*, and *Phaedo*) she underestimates their influence on ancient Jewish and Christian literature. Furthermore, she does not do justice to the references to Acheron and the Elysian Fields in the "Rainer Fragment," which obviously point to the Greek world. See Erik Peterson, "Die Taufe im acherusischen See," *VC* 9 (1955): 1–20. Richard J. Bauckham provides an authoritative delineation of recent discussions of the *ApocPe* in "The Apocalypse of Peter: An Account of Research," *ANRW* 2.25.6.4712–50.

32. E.g., Clement of Alexandria *Eclogae propheticae* 41; cf. Methodius *Symposium* 2.6 and the Muratorian Canon. The surviving texts of the *ApocPe* all issue from northern Africa: the so-called Rainer Fragment (Vienna) and the Bodleian fragment (Oxford) from fourth- or fifth-century Egypt (perhaps both are fragments from the same text [Montague Rhodes James, "The Rainer Fragment of the Apocalypse of Peter," *JTS* 32 (1931): 278–79]), an eighth-century manuscript buried with a monk in Akhmim, Egypt, and the Ethiopic translation.

33. For an overview of testamonia to the *ApocPe*, see Dennis D. Buchholz, *Your Eyes Will Be Opened: A Study of the Greek (Ethiopic) Apocalypse of Peter*, SBLDS 97 (Atlanta: Scholars Press, 1988), 20–81.

34. *AAMt* 32. Bishop Plato came on the scene in *P* soon after Andrew first arrived in Myrmidonia.

35. *MMt* 6 (*AAA* 2.1:222).

36. GE 6. Epiphanius has the apostle ordaining bishops throughout his travels, but most of the ordinations seem to derive from traditions subsequent to the ancient *Acts*.

37. *Republic* 3.391b–c.

38. Ibid., 2.383a.

39. Ibid., 3.391b–c.

40. Ibid., 2.364d.

41. For a discussion of these texts and a translation of both recensions see Ch. Mauer and H. Duensing, *NTApoc* 2.663–83.

42. Most recently, Harold W. Attridge, "The Original Language of the Acts of Thomas," in *Of Scribes and Scrolls: Studies on the Hebrew Bible, Intertestamental Judaism, and Christian Origins*, College Theology Society Resources in Religion 5, Festschrift John Strugnell, ed. Harry W. Attridge et al., (Landham: University Press of America, 1990), 241–50 .

43. Compare the phrase ἐπὶ τῇ πυρᾷ κείμενος with *P*'s κείμενοι ἐπὶ τοῦ ἐδάφους.

44. *Republic* 10.614b.

45. Clement of Alexandria quoted this sentence and took these "wild men of fiery aspect" to be punishing angels (*Stromateis* 5.14.90.4–91.4).

46. Ethiopic *ApocPe* 8–9. I am grateful to Julian V. Hills for having provided me with a prototype of his translation of this text; I have modified it slightly. See Himmelfarb's excellent discussion of *temelouchos* (*Tours of Hell*, 101–3).

47. For βόρβορος see Akhmim 23, 24 (twice; for the punishment of adulterers, as in the *ATh*), and 31; σκώληξ appears in 25 and 27.

48. No two other tours of hell list the offending body parts in the same order. See Himmelfarb, *Tours of Hell*, 87–88.

49. *Republic* 10.621b.

50. *ATh* 57.

51. *NTApoc* 2.475. I cannot resist pointing out that this concluding speech by Thomas once uses the noun πολιτεία, 'public conduct', and once the verb πολιτεύω, 'behave': "Abolish your former demeanor and πολιτεία. . . . Conduct yourselves (πολιτεύσασθε) in the faith." The Greek title of *The Republic* is, of course, Πολιτεία. Cf. *Republic* 10.619c (from the myth of Er): "with well-ordered conduct (πολιτείᾳ) in a former life."

52. The sins punished are less severe than murder: fornicators, women who forsook husbands, slanderers, immodest women, robbers, and the greedy. This trend toward trivialization of sins, this lubrication of the slide toward perdition, characterizes the development of Christian tours of hell, to such a degree that in *The Apocalypse of Paul* the apostle can recount this incident:

> And I looked and saw others hanging over a channel of water and their tongues were very dry and much fruit was placed within their sight and they were not allowed to take of it; and I asked: Who are these, sir? And he said to me: They are those who broke their fast before the appointed hour; therefore they pay these penalties unceasingly. (*NTApoc* 2.783)

According to Himmelfarb, only two Christian tours punish murderers: the *ApocPe* and *The Apocalypse of Gorgorios* (*Tours of Hell*, 72–73).

The *MMt*, reliant in part on the *AAMt*, contains a passage that would have worked quite nicely had it appeared in *The Acts of Andrew*. Jesus appears to Matthew as a child, and the apostle says: "I know clearly that I saw you in paradise, while you were singing to a harp with the other infants who were slain in Bethlehem." Matthew then asks the Christ child about Herod. Jesus said: "He lives in Hades, and an unquenchable fire, undying Gehenna, punishing filth (βόρβορος), and a sleepless worm (σκώληξ) have been prepared for him because he slew three thousand infants in his desire to kill the baby Jesus" (*MMt* 3). Cf. *ATh* 56: "filth and worms (βόρβορον καὶ σκώληκας)."

53. *Republic* 10.615b–c .

54. *ApocPe*, Akhmim 25 (= Eth 7).

55. Cf. Lucian *Zeus Catechized* 18.

56. *Republic* 10.616b–617d.

57. "Rainer Fragment," based on the text of James, "Rainer Fragment," 271.

58. *ApocPe*, Akhmim 15–19.

59. *Republic* 10.619b–c.

60. *Bibliotheca* codex 179.

61. See the superb overview of these testimonia in Prieur, *Acta Andreae*, 100–111.

62. In favor of this possibility is Photius's charge that the lost *Hypotyposes* of Clement of Alexandria, who wrote from the same general location at about the same time as the author of *The Acts of Andrew*, taught "metempsychosis and many worlds prior to Adam" (*Bibliotheca* codex 109). Origen, too, may have believed in reincarnation (see Geddes MacGregor, *Reincarnation in Christianity: A New Vision of the Role of Rebirth in Christian Thought* [Wheaton: Theosophical Publishing House, 1978], 48–62).

63. *Epistula ad Idacium et Ceponium* 5: "libros omnes apocryphos vel compositos, vel infectos esse, manifestum est: specialiter autem Actus illos qui vocantur S. Andreae" (*PL* 54.694).

64. *Discourse on the Dormition of the Holy Virgin* (*PO* 19.377.8–10).

65. See Eric Junod and Jean-Daniel Kaestli, *L'Histoire des Actes apocryphes des apôtres du IIIᵉ au IXᵉ siècle: Le Cas des Actes de Jean*, Cahiers de la Revue de Théologie et de Philosophie 7 (Geneva, 1982), 50–86. On Manichaean uses of the apocryphal Acts, see Peter Nagel, "Die apokryphen Apostelakten des 2. und 3. Jahrhunderts in der manichäischen Literatur," in *Gnosis und Neues Testament*, ed. Karl-Wolfgang Tröger (Berlin: Evangelische Verlagsanstalt, 1973), 149–82, and Jean-Daniel Kaestli, "L'Utilisation des Actes apocryphes des apôtres dans le manichéisme," in *Gnosis and Gnosticism*, Nag Hammadi Studies 8, ed. Martin Krause (Leiden: E. J. Brill, 1977), 107–16.

66. *Republic* 10.614b.

67. *Odyssey* 11.34–36.

68. Ibid., 11.223–24.

69. Cf. *Odyssey* 24.76–77.

70. Ibid., 11.489–91.

71. Ibid., 11.543–46.

72. Ibid., 11.568–70.

73. *Republic* 3.386c–d.

74. Ibid., 3.386d.

75. Ibid., 3.386c, quoting *Odyssey* 11.489–91. See also 7.516d.

76. Ibid., 3.387b.

77. Cf. *Odyssey* 11.543–47 and *Republic* 10.620b.

78. Cf. *Odyssey* 11.387–461 and *Republic* 10.620b.

79. Cf. *Odyssey* 11.523 and *Republic* 10.620c.

80. *Republic* 10.620c–d. Lucian recognized Plato's hypertextual strategy. At the beginning of *True Story* I, the humorist defends his right to lie about his own visit to the dead by claiming the authority of Homer, Homeric imitators, and even "men who profess philosophy," viz. Plato (3–4).

81. *Gorgias* 525c.

82. Ibid., 525d–e.

83. Ibid., 526d–e. Socrates' reference at the end of the story to "an old wife's tale" many suggest he had in mind *Odyssey* 11.223–24, Anticleia's telling Odysseus to report to Penelope all that he saw in the netherworld; cf. Plutarch *How the Young Man Should Study Poetry* 16e–f.

84. Jesus, not Minos, was the judge of the dead (*AAMt* 14).

85. *Odyssey* 11.385–466 and 24.20–204, Virgil *Aeneid* 6.489, and Lucian *Dialogues of the Dead* 6 (413) and 23 (448–50); cf. Aeschylus *Agamemnon* 1525–29.

86. The lost epics *Minyas* and *Nostoi* narrated the terrors of Hades, probably in *nekyiai* (Pausanius 10.28.7; see George Leonard Huxley, *Greek Epic Poetry from Eumelos to Panyassis* [Cambridge: Harvard University Press, 1969], 165). In *The Frogs*, Aristophanes sent Dionysus and Heracles to the netherworld where among other things they saw the Acherusian lake, the river Lethe, "darkness and filth (σκότος καὶ βόρβορος)" (273), the punishments of "highwaymen, thieves, burglars, parricides" (772–74), and Aeschylus and Euripides competing for the role of Hades' poet laureate. In *The Argonautica* of Apollonius Rhodius, Jason called on the powers of the netherworld to help him gain the golden fleece, and, in order to get their attention, he followed Odysseus's recipe:

> he dug a pit (βόθρον) in the ground of a cubit's depth, and heaped the billets of wood, and over it cut the throat of the sheep, and duly placed the carcase above; and he kindled the logs placing fire beneath, and poured over them mingled libations, calling on Hecate Brimo to aid him in the contests. (3.1207–11; cf. *Odyssey* 11.23–50, esp. 25–26, 29, and 35–36)

Apollonius's contemporary, the comic playwright Menippus, composed a *Nekyia*, now lost, that ridiculed conventional attitudes toward the netherworld. *The Worlds Beyond the Thule* by Antonius Diogenes (ca. 100 C.E.) told how a woman had visited Hades and returned with her description (Photius *Bibliotheca* codex 166). In the novel by Heliodorus, a witch imitated Odysseus's bloody ritual for conjuring up the shades, and thereby revived her dead son long enough to learn from him how the heroine and hero would find their way home (*Aethiopica* 6). Heliodorus here obviously imitated Odysseus's consultation with Tiresias about his journey back to Ithaca. Apollonius of Tyana, the hero of Philostratus's novel (third century C.E.) conjured up Achilles' ghost with a mere invocation, without Odysseus's messy magic: "[I]t was not by digging a ditch (βόθρον) like Odysseus, nor by tempting the souls with the blood of sheep" (*The Life of Apollonius of Tyana* 4.15–16; cf. Apuleius *Metamorphoses* 2.28–30). *The Alexander Romance* (ca. 300 C.E.) narrated a visit to the dead facilitated by libations and resulting in a favorable prophecy (3.24). The Latin *Journal of the Trojan War,* falsely attributed to Dictys of Crete, paraphrased the *nekyia*: "Then they had gone to that place where, having performed the requisite rites, they learned of the future from the shades of the dead" (6.5 [Frazer]).

87. *Aeneid* 6.243–54.

88. Cf. *Aeneid* 6.679–702 and *Odyssey* 11.150–224.

89. For discussions of Virgil's dependence on Homer's *nekyia* see Henry W. Prescott, *The Development of Virgil's Art* (Chicago: University of Chicago Press, 1927), 359–410, and Raymond J. Clark, *Catabasis: Vergil and the Wisdom Tradition* (Amsterdam: B. R. Grüner, 1979).

90. For a discussion of Platonism in Book 6 of *The Aeneid* see Michael Murrin, *The Allegorical Epic: Essays in Its Rise and Decline* (Chicago: University of Chicago Press, 1980), 27–50. Virgil may have derived his Platonism not from Plato directly but from later philosophers. For Virgil's sources see Eduard Norden, *P. Vergilius Maro Aeneis Buch VI,* 8th edition (Darmstadt: Wissenschaftliche Buchgesellschaft, 1984), 3–48.

91. Cf. Plato *Republic* 10.615a: "For all the wrong they had ever done . . . they paid the penalty."

92. Ibid.: "It lasted a thousand years."

93. *Aeneid* 6.739–51; cf. 714–15. Plato *Republic* 10.621a: "[T]hey all journeyed to the Plain of Oblivion (Λήθης). . . . [A]nd there they camped at eventide by the river of Forgetfulness."

94. *Menippus* 1 and 6.

95. Ibid., 9; the quotation comes from *Odyssey* 11.5. Lucian ridiculed this rite by having Charon, the ferryman of Hades, and Hermes, the guide to the dead, trying to understand it. Charon says: "There are others also who . . . have dug trenches (βόθρον), and now they are burning up their fine dinners and pouring wine and mead, as far as one may judge, into the ditches." Hermes replies: "I don't know what good these are to men in Hades, ferryman; they are convinced, however, that the souls, allowed to come up from below, get their dinner as best they may by flitting about the smoke and steam and drink the mead out of the trench (βόθρου)." Charon says: "What, *they* eat and drink, when their skulls are dry as tinder?. . . What folly, the idiots!" (*Charon, or the Inspectors* 22). Cf. *Astrology* 24: "And when he [Odysseus] was come to the place whereunto Circe directed him, and had dug his pit (βόθρον) and slain his sheep, although many dead that were by, and amongst them his own mother, were fain to drink of the blood, he suffered none of them, not even his very mother, until he had wet the throstle of Tiresias." Apuleius wrote of a witch who performed "necromantic rituals in a ditch" (*Metamorphoses* 1.10).

96. *Menippus* 14 and 17.

97. Ibid., 20. This passage clearly is a parody of the myth of Er; Plato's Socrates himself states that some people would be reincarnated as animals (*Republic* 10.620a–d). See also *Phaedo* 81e: "[T]hose who have indulged in gluttony and violence and drunkenness, and have taken no pains to avoid them, are likely to pass into the bodies of asses and other beasts of that sort."

98. *Menippus* 21.

99. Such a combination appears elsewhere in his writings as well. In *The Lover of Lies*, for example, a character tells how he once paid a magician to summon the dead. "The man waited for the moon to wax, as it is then, for the most part, that such rites are performed; and after digging a pit (βόθρον) . . . the shades appeared" (14). A chasm opened up in the earth so that he could see "the River of Blazing Fire, and the Lake, and Cerberus, and the dead," including Socrates. Lucian apparently mentioned Socrates among the dead in order to refute Socratic-Platonic teaching on reincarnation.

Another character in *The Lover of Lies* likewise claimed to have been led "through a chasm to Hades," where he saw among other things Tantalus, Tityus, and Sisyphus. He came before Pluto for judgment, but prematurely: "His thread is not yet fully spun, so let him be off," said Pluto, "and bring me the blacksmith Demylus, for he is living beyond the spindle" (25). Lucian here is playing with "the spindle of Necessity" from the myth of Er (*Republic* 10.616c). See also the conflation of Homeric and Platonic elements in *On Funerals*.

100. *True Story* 1.3–4.

101. Ibid., 2.6.

102. Ibid., 2.15.

103. Ibid., 2.17. Lucian also saw the wicked punished: "a terrible odour greeted us as of asphalt, sulphur, pitch burning together, and a vile, unsufferable stench as if roasting human flesh. . . . [W]e heard the noise of scourges and the wailing of many men" (2.29).

For many ancients, however, visions of the netherworld were no laughing matter. Pythagoreans insisted that their master, "when he descended into Hades, . . . saw the soul of Hesiod bound fast to a brazen pillar and gibbering, and the soul of Homer hung on a tree with serpents writhing about it, this being their punishment for what they had said about the gods" (Hieronymus Rhodius *apud* Diogenes Laertius *Life of Pythagoras* 8.21). Orpheus allegedly visited the netherworld and recorded his observations in a celebrated *Catabasis* that mentioned Hermes "the conductor of Souls," Lake Acheron, "the punishments in Hades of the unrighteous, the Fields of the Righteous" (Diodorus Siculus 1.96.4–9; cf. Clement of Alexandria *Stromateis* 1.21.131.5).

Epicureans and others scorned such credulity. A famous inscription by Diogenes of Oenoanda praised Epicurus for having rescued him from Homeric horrors: "I have accepted what you say about death, and you have persuaded me to laugh at it. I have no fears on account of the Tityoses and Tantaluses whom some picture in Hades" (see the Loeb edition of Lucretius, 256–57). The Epicurean poet Lucretius demythologized Homer's hereafter like a modern existentialist:

[W]hatsoever things are fabled to exist in deep Acheron, these all exist for us in this life. There is no wretched Tantalus, as the story goes. . . .

No Tityos lying in Acheron is rummaged by winged creatures. . . . Tityos is here among us, the man who, as he lies in love, is torn by winged creatures and devoured by agonizing anguish or rent by anxieties through some other passion.

Sisyphus also appears in the life before our eyes, athirst to solicit from the people the lictor's rods and cruel axes. . . .

Cerberus also and the Furies and the withholding of light, and Tartarus belching horrible fires from his throat—these neither exist anywhere nor in truth can exist. (*De rerum natura* 3.978–81, 984, 992–96, and 1010–13)

Plutarch wrote a friend concerning the supervision of youths when reading Homer and singled out the dangers of the *nekyia*:

[T]he monstrous tales of visits to the shades and the descriptions, which in awful language create speeches and pictures of blazing rivers and hideous places and grim punishments, do not blind very many people to the fact that fable and falsehood in plenty have been mingled with them like poison in nourishing food. (*How the Young Man Should Study Poetry* 17b)

See also Plutarch's objections to Homer's netherworld in *Is "Live Unknown" a Wise Precept?* 1130e. When Plutarch wrote his own tour of the netherworld—in which he advocated reincarnation—he lifted his material not from Homer but from Plato (*Divine Vengeance* 563–68); cf. *On the Sign of Socrates* 589f–592e.

Apuleius, a philosopher and devotee of Isis, speaking through the voice of his protagonist Lucius, suggested that the secretive initiations to that religion consisted of a tour of the heights and depths:

I came to the boundary of death, and having trodden the threshold of Proserpina, I travelled through all the elements and returned. In the middle of the night I saw the sun flashing with bright light. I came face to face with the gods below and the gods above and paid reverence to them from close at hand. (*Metamorphoses* 11.23; cf. the *nekyia* of Psyche ['soul'] in 6.17–21)

104. *Epistula ad Pompeium* 1.12.

105. Dio Chrysostom wrote a four-volume work entitled *Against Plato in Defense of Homer* (see also his *Discourses* 53 and 55), Aelius of Sarapion *Was Plato Justified in Expelling Homer from the Republic?*, Telephus of Pergamon *On the Agreement of Homer and Plato*, Aristocles of Messene *Who Was Better, Homer or Plato?*, Ammonius the grammarian *What Plato Borrowed from Homer*, and Syrianus *In Defense of Homer Against Socrates in "The Republic."*

106. Maximus of Tyre 41.2 (475.13 Hobein).

107. Theopompus in Athenaeus *Deipnosophists* 507e, quoting *Iliad* 16.856.

108. Porphyry *De antro nympharum.* "Numenius's comparison and reconciliation of the views expressed by Homer and Plato on the fate of the souls became an established . . . part of many later Platonists' understanding both of Plato's myth of Er . . . and of Homer's fiction" (Lamberton, *Homer the Theologian*, 66; see also n. 64).

109. Porphyry *De antro nympharum* 37. See also 42, 100–103, 118–19, 182–85, and 230–32. The great Homeric scholar Eustathius agreed: "I do not think that any of the

ancient sages failed to taste of it [Homeric epic], least of all those who drew the waters of profane philosophy" (introduction to his commentary on *The Iliad*; trans. Herington, "Homer," 433). See also Weinstock, "Platonische Homerkritik," 121–53, esp. 145–53.

110. *First Apology* 18.

111. See Glockmann, *Homer*, 118–62, for an excellent discussion of this passage in Justin and its relationship to Platonic uses of Homer.

112. *Cohortatio ad gentiles* 27.

113. Ibid., 28. This passage seems to have been inspired by Justin's *First Apology* 44, in which Justin makes the same point about the dependence of "the philosophers and poets" on the prophets when they addressed matters concerning the immortality of the soul and punishments after death. Justin quotes from *Republic* 10.617e: "[T]o him who chooses belongs the guilt, but in God is no guilt." The same line is quoted in Clement of Alexandria *Paidagogos* 1.8.69.1 (cf. *Stromateis* 1.1.4.1, 2.16.75.3, 4.23.150.4, and 5.14.136.4), Hippolytus *Refutatio* 1.19.19 (Marcovich), and *Ps.-Clementine Homilies* 15.8. Behind the statement in Plato may lie *Odyssey* 1.32–33; cf. Lucian *On Salaried Posts in Great Houses* 42.

114. *Stromateis* 5.14.90.4–91.5; cf. 2.15.69.2.

115. Ibid., 5.14.103.2–4 and 106.2.

116. *Contra Celsum* 2.16 (Chadwick).

117. *Refutatio* 1.19.11–12 (Marcovich). The apologist Theophilus, too, seems to have been thinking of Homer and Plato: "[T]he poets and philosophers . . . spoke about justice and judgement and punishment" (*Ad Autolycum* 2.38 [Grant]). Theophilus then quotes, among other texts, from Homer's *nekyia* (*Odyssey* 11.222). See also *Praeparatio evangelica* 12.6, where Eusebius quotes extensively from the netherworld myth in Plato's *Gorgias* in order to argue for the immortality of the soul.

118. E.g., *The Martyrdom of Matthew, APh* Act 3 (32), and Ps.-Epiphanius s.v. Matthias.

4

Nostos

The next several stories narrate Andrew's return, or *nostos*, to Achaea. Unfortunately, these chapters survive almost exclusively in Gregory's epitome (GE), which in turn was based not on *The Acts of Andrew* directly but on a Latin translation. Gregory's surgery was brutal. He omitted nearly every speech and often tortured the story line in order to "summarize only the wonders." For example, he devoted only thirty-eight lines to the content treated thus far. Almost nothing remains of the speeches, including Andrew's long conversation with Captain Jesus. The residents of Myrmidonia are no longer cannibals, there is no reference to the old man and the fourteen executioners, Andrew never goes to the city of the barbarians, and he does not return to rescue people from the abyss. Apart from the retention of the word "Myrmidonia," Gregory's account contains nothing to suggest the slightest interest in Homer.

Elsewhere, too, few clues of Homeric hypertextuality escaped Gregory's heavy cleaver. Occasionally curious details alert the reader to search for some mythological background (an unusual characterization may call to mind a Greek deity), but the most reliable clues are the names that Gregory found already transliterated in his Latin translation. Because the author of the *Acts* invested significance in the names of dramatis personae, such as Andrew and Plato, and in the names of locations, such as Myrmidonia, the names surviving in Gregory's epitome provide precious and sometimes sole evidence concerning the Homeric antecedents of various episodes.

Andrew's journey from Myrmidonia takes him first to Amasia (GE 2–4), where the characters correspond to Tiresias, Achilles, Patroclus, Oedipus, and Jocasta, all of whom also appear in Homer's *nekyia*.[1] From Amasia the apostle travels along the northern shore of Anatolia through Sinope (5), Nicea (6), Nicomedia (7), and Byzantium (8) to Thrace (9–10). Along the way he encounters the likes of Nestor, Polycaste, and Actaeon. In Thrace he escapes from pirates and converts sailors who call to mind the Argonauts, especially the Thracian Orpheus. Chapters 11–20 pertain to Macedonia, especially to Philippi and Thessalonica. Andrew spends so much time in Macedonia because the author used this setting, so close to Mount Olympus, to recharacterize Greek deities. In fact, Greeks knew the mountain as Macedonian Olympus (Μακεδονικὸς Ὄλυμπος).[2] Mortals, too, find their counterparts in Macedonia (e.g., Menelaus, Melampus, Sarpedon, and Hector), but most of the characters here are transvalued gods, including Zeus, Hera, Hephaestus, Ares, Aphrodite, Heracles, and perhaps Apollo. GE 21 sends Andrew back to Achaea; his ministry there is the topic for chapter 5.

The Blind Savant (Tiresias, GE 2)

The ending of *P* narrates the same itinerary as the beginning of GE 2:

P	GE 2
[Andrew is in Myrmidonia.]	
"I am **going**	**Andrew left**
to my allotted place [Achaea]. . . ."	**that place** [Myrmidonia] and
Andrew went on his way	**went toward his own region** [Achaea].
with his disciples.	While he was walking **with his**
When he reached **Amasia,**	**disciples** . . . [in **Amasia**; see GE 3]
he kept silent.	

The curious reference in *P* to Andrew's silence is important for understanding the story that follows in Gregory. In spite of Andrew's arrival in Amasia incognito, a blind man was able, through supernatural powers, to recognize his identity: "[A] blind man approached him and said, 'Andrew, apostle of Christ, I know that you are able to restore my sight, but I do not want to receive it. Rather, I ask that you order those with you to give me money for adequate clothing and food'" (GE 2). The apostle recognized at once that this was no ordinary blind man. "'I know truly that this is not the voice of a human but of the devil, who does not allow that man to regain his sight.' Turning around, Andrew touched his eyes, and immediately he received light and glorified God."

The most famous blind savant of Greek mythology was Tiresias; both his blindness and his clairvoyance were the work of Olympians. As a youth, he saw two snakes copulating, killed the female, and immediately became female himself. After several years, a marriage, and a few children, she saw the same scene, this time killing the male, which made her male again. In order to settle their spat concerning which gender took more pleasure when making love, Zeus and Hera consulted Tiresias for his expert, bisexual opinion. When he answered that the pleasure of the female far exceeded the male's, Hera blinded him. To compensate him for his loss, Zeus granted him supernatural powers of prediction.[3] Tragedians made good use of his reliability as a forecaster in order to reveal the future.[4]

According to Homer, only Tiresias was able to keep his wits in Hades.[5] Indeed, when Odysseus arrived, Tiresias, like the blind man in GE 2, inexplicably recognized the identity of his visitor.

Odyssey 11.90–92	GE 2
"Then there **came up** the spirit of the Theban **Teiresias**, bearing his golden staff in his hand,	[A] **blind man approached** him
and he knew me and spoke to me: 'Son of Laertes, **sprung from Zeus,** Odysseus of many devices. . . .'"	**and said to him,** "Andrew, **apostle of Christ,** I know** that you are able to restore my sight."

Ancient readers of Homer recognized Tiresias's clairvoyance in this scene. One scholion on *Odyssey* 11.91 stated that Tiresias knew Odysseus "with his mind, not with his eyes, for he was blind." Another scholion noted: "[T]he knowledge of his intellect compensated for the defect of his eyes."[6]

The Acts of Andrew attributed both the man's blindness and his brilliance to a supernatural source, to "the devil, who does not allow that man to regain his sight." Unlike Hera who deprived Tiresias of his vision, Andrew's God restored vision to the blind. Clement of Alexandria also invited Tiresias to come to Christ, the healer of the blind:

> Come to me, old man, come thou too! Quit Thebes; fling away thy prophecy and Bacchic revelry and be led by the hand to truth. Behold, I give thee the wood of the cross to lean upon. Hasten, Tiresias, believe! Thou shalt have sight. Christ, by whom the eyes of the blind see again, shineth upon thee more brightly than the sun. Night shall fall from thee; fire shall fear thee; death shall depart from thee. Thou shalt see heaven, old man, though thou canst not see Thebes.[7]

Demetrius and His Slave (Achilles and Patroclus, GE 3)

Gregory next tells this tale:

> Demetrius, the leader of the community of Amaseans, had an Egyptian boy whom he cherished with unparalleled love. A fever overtook the boy, and he died. Later, when Demetrius heard of the signs the blessed apostle was performing, he came to him, fell at his feet with tears, and said, "I am sure that nothing is difficult for you, O servant of God. Behold, my boy, whom I cherish above all, is dead. I ask that you come to my house and restore him to me." (GE 3)

Demetrius and his slave were lovers. This is apparent not merely because the text emphasizes their intimacy—Demetrius "cherished him with unparalleled love"— but also because the boy is called an "Egyptian boy (*puer Aegyptius* = παῖς Αἰγύπτιος)," an expression that, in the late second century, would have called to mind Antinous, Hadrian's slave and lover. While accompanying the emperor to Egypt in the year 130, Antinous drowned in the Nile under suspicious circumstances. Devastated by the loss, Hadrian promoted his lover into a deity, founded an Egyptian city in his memory (Antinoöpolis), minted coins to the divine Antinous, built him a temple, and created numerous statues of him modeled after those of various Olympians.

Christian apologists enjoyed reminding their pagan readers of Antinous's deification. How capricious was Greek religion if a slave could win apotheosis solely for having been an imperial pet! For example, Clement of Alexandria mocked the new deity in Egypt, whom Hadrian had "loved as Zeus loved Ganymedes."[8] Athanasius wrote: "For when Hadrian was staying in Egypt, Antinous the servant of his lust died, and he decreed that he should be given a cult, for he loved the youth (παιδός) even after his death."[9]

But the author of *The Acts of Andrew* did not advance Demetrius as a new Hadrian nor his slave as Antinous; instead, they are Achilles and his servant Patroclus, two famous Greek lovers.[10] *The Acts of Andrew* apparently identified Amasia with the netherworld, home to the counter-Tiresias, so, when the author presents Demetrius as "the leader of the community of Amaseans (*primi civitatis Amaseorum*)," he seems to identify him with Achilles, "the ruler of the dead."[11] The very name Demetrius points down to the realm of Hades and Persephone, daughter of dark Demeter, "earth mother."[12]

In *The Iliad*, when Hector slew Patroclus, Achilles was beside himself with grief: "[A] black cloud of grief enwrapped Achilles, and with both hands he took the dark dust and strewed it over his head and defiled his fair face, and on his fragrant tunic the black ashes fell. And himself in the dust lay outstretched, mighty in his mightiness, and with his own hands he tore and marred his hair."[13] To show his love for his fallen ally, Achilles arranged for him antiquity's most extravagant and barbaric funeral. Achilles' sorrow became proverbial, and for Plato despicable.[14]

During his visit with the shades, Odysseus saw Achilles and Patroclus, still together after death.[15] In the second *nekyia* of *The Odyssey*, Achilles rejoiced when he learned that the ashes of his body had been mixed with those of Patroclus in a golden urn for eternal union.[16] Homer himself does not present the two men as lovers, merely as good friends. In fact, they long for the embraces of their maidservants, Briseis and Iphis. Even so, Achilles' extravagant funeral preparations and inconsolable grief at the death of his friend generated the notion, even prior to Plato, that their relationship was the pinnacle not only of friendship,[17] but also of male homoeroticism.[18]

Gregory completes the story of Demetrius and his slave: "After preaching at great length on matters pertaining to the salvation of the people, he turned to the bier and said, 'Lad, I tell you in the name of Jesus Christ, the Son of God, arise and stand up, healed.'[19] Immediately the Egyptian boy arose, and Andrew returned him to his master." Gregory almost certainly deleted a substantial speech prior to reviving the servant, "preaching at great length on matters pertaining to the salvation of the people." Presumably the content of this speech picked up issues generated from the story, so one might reasonably speculate that here Andrew denounced pederasty. Early Christians repeatedly caviled Homer's Olympians and heroes for homoerotic liaisons.[20]

To summarize, after healing a counter-Tiresias in Amasia Andrew encountered a counter-Achilles mourning the recent death of his beloved slave and lover, a counter-Patroclus. Andrew preached against pederasty, raised the lad back to life, and the two lovers presumably ceased their sexual encounters.

Sostratus and His Mother (Oedipus and Jocasta, GE 4)

The next story in Gregory's account begins:

> A Christian youth named Sostratus came secretly to the blessed Andrew and said, "My mother craved my beautiful looks and keeps pestering me to sleep with her. Because I curse this unspeakable act, I ran away. But she, crazed with venom, went to the proconsul in order to cast on me her own wrongdoing. I know that when accused I will make no defense, for I would rather relinquish my life than expose my mother's guilt. Now I admit this to you so that you might concede to pray to the Lord for me, lest I be deprived of this present life even though I am innocent."

Soldiers arrested the lad and brought him to the tribunal where his mother accused him of attempted incest. When the lad made no defense,

> the proconsul gave orders for the boy to be sewn into the leather bag (*culleum*) for parricides and thrown in the river. . . .

> But as the blessed apostle prayed, there was a great earthquake and frightful thunder. The proconsul fell from his seat, everyone sprawled on the ground. Lightning struck the boy's mother; she withered up and died. (GE 4)

Readers of the Bible will see here a Christian variant of the story of Joseph and Potiphar's wife,[21] which is itself a variant of an ancient folktale known in ancient Egypt as the "Tale of Two Brothers," and in the Greek world as either the tale of Bellerophon and Antia (or Stheneboea)[22] or the tale of Hippolytus and Phaedra.[23] In each case, a femme fatale, furious at her inability to seduce a virtuous young man, accuses him of lechery. In most cases, as here in *The Acts of Andrew*, the woman's plot comes to light and the man is vindicated.

There are, however, several details in Gregory's account suggesting that the author of the *Acts* used the folktale in order to rewrite the myth of Oedipus and Jocasta. According to the dominant form of the protean myth, Apollo warned Laius, king of Thebes, that if a son was born to him and his wife Jocasta, the lad would kill him. When a son indeed was born, Laius drove a spike through his feet and left him exposed to die. A shepherd happened upon the baby and delivered him to Polybus, king of Corinth, who named him 'Swell-foot' (οἰδέω, πούς) and raised him as his own son. When grown, Oedipus met his biological father and, unaware of his identity, killed him in an argument. The youth then arrived in Thebes, relieved the city of a plague imposed by a monstrous sphinx, and thus won the hand of Queen Jocasta, his mother. When the outrageous truth finally came to light, Jocasta strangled herself; Oedipus gouged out his eyes.[24]

Gregory's tale emphasizes the incestuous potential between Sostratus and his widowed mother,[25] which conforms with the Oedipus myth but not with the folktale tradition represented by Joseph and Potiphar's wife. Furthermore, the name Sostratus designates someone who had donated a σῶστρα, a gift given in thanksgiving for deliverance from danger. Both Oedipus ('swell-foot') and Sostratus, then, bear names derived from rescues from peril. The story takes place in Amasia, where the blind man, Demetrius, and the "Egyptian boy" correspond with Tiresias, Achilles, and Patroclus, each of whom Odysseus saw in the netherworld. Odysseus also saw Jocasta (Homer calls her Epicaste),

> who wrought a monstrous deed in ignorance of mind, in that she wedded her own son, and he, when he had slain his own father, wedded her, and straightway the gods made these things known among men. . . . [S]he went down to the house of Hades, the strong warder. She made fast a noose on high from a lofty beam, overpowered by her sorrow, but for him she left behind woes full many, even all that the Avengers of a mother bring to pass.[26]

The most striking hypertextual clue concerning the Oedipus myth pertains to the *culleum*. A *culleum* was a leather sack into which parricides were sewn and then thrown into water to drown. Although this form of execution was natively Roman,[27] imperial authorities employed it as well in the eastern provinces.[28] The *culleum* and the water into which it was thrown symbolize the womb that the parricide violated by killing a parent. By placing the criminal in the enclosed, immersible sack, the law implied it would have been better had the parricide never been born. Insofar as the lad in GE 4 had not been accused of murdering a parent but of attempted incest, death by *culleum* was altogether out of the ordinary and unexpected—unexpected, that is, if one fails to see in Sostratus the author's transvaluation of Oedipus.[29]

GE 4 and the Oedipus myth both tell of an only son of a widow who was accused, rightly or wrongly, of incest and parricide. In both tales there is a divine revelation concerning the actual state of affairs and the violent death of the mother. The differences between the two stories illustrate the transvaluative strategy of the *Acts* insofar as it contrasts Oedipus's innocent but outrageous incest and parricide with Sostratus's filial loyalty, which was so strong that he preferred death to exposing his mother's lust.

The author probably composed the tale as a counterattack on pagan accusations of Christian incest under the slur of Oedipal sex. Athenagoras addressed his apology against three accusations: atheism, cannibalism, and "Oedipal unions (Οἰδιποδείους μίξεις)."[30] Not content merely to deny the charges, Athenagoras took the offensive. If pagans were consistent, "they ought to hate . . . Zeus, who begat children by his mother, Rhea, and his daughter, Core, and had his own sister to wife."[31] Again later: "[T]hese adulterers and pederasts reproach men who abstain from intercourse or are satisfied with a single marriage, whereas they themselves live like fish. For they swallow up whatever comes their way."[32] Justin Martyr, too, in refuting charges of cannibalism and incest, argued that pagans were more guilty of these acts than were Christians.[33] In order to embarrass his pagan readers, an unknown apologist asked: "And what need one say about Oedipus's spikes [in his feet], or his slaying of Laius [his father], or his marriage to his mother?"[34] A letter narrating the execution of Christians in Gaul stated that local pagans "falsely accused us of Thyestean feasts [viz. cannibalism] and Oedipodean intercourse (Οἰδιποδείους μίξεις)."[35] Minucius Felix countered pagan accusations of Christian free sex by stating that it was pagans themselves who legitimated incest: "Your records and your tragedies, which you both read and hear with pleasure, glory in incests: thus also you worship gods who have intercourse with mothers, with daughters, with sisters."[36] If the author of the *Acts* did indeed compose the story of Sostratus and his mother in order to transvalue the Oedipus myth, he was merely expressing through narrative what his Christian contemporaries did through apologies: pagans, not Christians, are sexual deviants.

Gratinus and the Woman's Bath (Nestor and Polycaste, GE 5)

GE continues with this information:

> While being washed in a woman's bath, the son of Gratinus of Sinope was tortured senseless by a demon. Gratinus sent a letter to the proconsul asking that he prevail on Andrew to come to him. Gratinus himself was gravely ill with fever and his wife swollen with dropsy. At the proconsul's request, Andrew mounted a carriage and went to the city. (GE 5)

Apparently, Gratinus had sent a servant to Amasia with the letter requesting that Andrew ride his carriage back to Sinope. Insofar as this is the only place in *The Acts of Andrew* where the apostle travels by any means other than ships or sandals, the detail is striking and would seem to identify Gratinus (Γρατῖνος) with "Nestor Gerenios, tamer of horses (Γερήνιος ἱππότα Νέστωρ),"[37] "driver of chariots."[38] Insofar as the name Gratinus is not otherwise attested as a name,[39] the author seems to have concocted it in order to provide the character with a name sounding like Gerenios, 'of Gerenia'.[40]

When Odysseus's son, Telemachus, was at the palace in Pylos to consult with the old veteran of the Trojan War, antiquity's most notorious horseman, Nestor commanded his servants to tend to Telemachus:

> "[Y]oke for Telemachus horses with beautiful mane beneath the car that he may get forward on his journey."

So he spoke and quickly they yoked beneath the car the swift horses. . . .
[T]hen Telemachus mounted the beautiful car, and Peisistratus, son of Nestor,
a leader of men, mounted beside him, and took the reins in his hands. He
touched the horses with the whip to start them, and nothing loath the pair sped
on to the plain, and left the steep citadel of Pylos.[41]

Gratinus's horses and the resonance of his name and with the epithet Gerenios
are not the only adumbrations of Nestor. There is also the matter of the bath
labeled "Ladies," where Gratinus's son was smitten by a demon. Women
frequently bathe men in *The Odyssey*. For example, Laertes is bathed by a
maidservant,[42] and Telemachus by Menelaus's serving girls and by his own
maidservants.[43] Odysseus once asked permission to bathe himself, "for I am
ashamed to make me naked in the midst of fair-tressed maidens,"[44] but his
modesty did not prevent Helen, Calypso, Nausicaa and her ladies-in-waiting,
Circe, his own maidservant, Eurynome, and others from laying their soapy hands
on him.[45]

The closest parallel to the story in GE 5, however, pertains to Telemachus and
Polycaste, Nestor's daughter. Just before Odysseus's son left Pylos to consult
with Menelaus in Sparta, "the fair Polycaste, the youngest daughter of Nestor, son
of Neleus, bathed Telemachus. And when she had bathed him and anointed him
rightly with oil, and had cast about him a fair cloak and a tunic, forth from the
bath he came in form like unto the immortals."[46] This practice of women bathing
men was hospitable commonplace during the Greek archaic period, but it
scandalized later interpreters. One scholion on this passage stated dogmatically
that "Polycaste *caused* him to be washed, but did not wash him herself."[47]
Another claimed that "the daughter of Nestor did not bathe Telemachus nor Helen
Odysseus";[48] indeed, "virgins never bathed men."[49] If Polycaste did wash
Telemachus, it only proves that she was no virgin, "for we claim that washing is
no job for a virgin."[50] Other interpreters, however, thought that Polycaste was
both a virgin and a scrubber; Homer's line she "cast about him a fair cloak"
indicates that "while they were in the tub, they clothed themselves out of
shame."[51] More adventuresome readers, suspecting hanky-panky, took
Telemachus and Polycaste as lovers. As early as Hesiod, they were considered
parents to Persepolis,[52] and an oracle told the inquiring Emperor Hadrian that they
had parented Homer himself.[53]

Gratinus's son, too, was washed in a woman's bath, but he was punished for it
by demonic attack. Andrew exorcised the lad and then healed Gratinus's fever
and his wife's dropsy.[54] Once healed, Gratinus attempted to show his gratitude
by sending "lavish gifts to the holy apostle at the hands of his servants.
Afterwards he followed along with his wife, and they fell before him asking him
to receive their gifts. 'My dear friends,' he told them, 'I cannot accept these
things; rather, they are yours to expend for the poor.' He accepted nothing they
offered." Like Gratinus, Nestor was exceedingly wealthy and generous with gifts
to guests.[55] Telemachus took the gifts; Andrew refused.

Dog-Demons and the Dead Youth (Actaeon, GE 6–7)

Even though GE 6 and 7 take place in two different cities, Nicea and nearby Nicomedia, the two stories belong together. In GE 6 Andrew arrives in Nicea, "where there were seven demons lingering among the roadside tombs who stoned passersby in broad daylight and killed many." At the request of the residents, Andrew "ordered the demons to present themselves before all the people, but they came in the form of dogs." When the apostle commanded them to leave town, "the demons growled and vanished from the eyes of those present." Andrew baptized the residents "and installed Callistus as their bishop, a wise man who guarded blamelessly what he had received from the teacher."

Callistus (Κάλλιστος, 'most beautiful') is the only name appearing in this chapter or the next. If Callistus is a hypertextual clue, it probably refers to the beautiful Phrygian shepherd boy, Zeus's lover, "godlike Ganymedes that was born the fairest (κάλλιστος) of men; wherefore the gods caught him up on high to be cupbearer to Zeus by reason of his beauty (κάλλεος), that he might dwell with the immortals."[56] Both Ganymedes' Phrygia and Mount Ida were in northwest Anatolia, the general region of Callistus's Nicea.

Ancient Greeks frequently praised Ganymedes' superlative beauty,[57] and he figures prominently in a list of antiquity's loveliest lads.[58] Christian apologists, however, used the myth of Ganymedes to disparage Zeus's love life.[59] Our sources contain no evidence that *The Acts of Andrew* transvalued or in some other way referred to this erotic relationship.[60]

The reader encounters the dog-demons again in GE 7:

Later, when he [Andrew] approached the gate of Nicomedia, a dead man was being carried out of the city on a bier. His old father, supported by the hands of slaves, scarcely was able to pay for the funeral. His mother, bent over with age, hair unkempt, followed the corpse wailing: "Woe is me, for I have lived so long that I am spending for my son's funeral what I had saved for my own."

As they followed the corpse, screaming and mourning these and related misfortunes, the apostle of God arrived, and moved by the tears he said, "Please tell me what happened to this boy for him to have departed from this light."

They were afraid to answer, but from the servants the apostle heard this: "When this youth was alone in his bedroom, all of a sudden seven dogs rushed in and attacked him. He was savagely mangled by them, fell, and died."

Then the blessed apostle sighed, raised his eyes toward heaven, and spoke through his tears: "Lord, I know that the attack was the work of the demons that I expelled from Nicea. I now ask you, O gracious Jesus, to revive him."

Jesus did, and the youth's grateful parents permitted Andrew to take the boy along with him.

This lad is a counter-Actaeon, famous hunter and dog trainer, whose myth was one of the most popular in antiquity.[61] One day in the wild, Actaeon came upon Artemis bathing nude. To punish her peeping admirer, the goddess transformed him into a stag and his own hounds, deceived by his new appearance, ripped him to shreds. Apollodorus, an early witness to the story, says the dogs numbered fifty, but he names only seven.[62] Artistic representations of Actaeon usually depict him being attacked by five to nine dogs, often by seven. When Actaeon's parents, Autonoe and Aristaeus, discovered what had happened, they were inconsolable. The following portrayal of their grief comes from the epic poem *Dionysiaca* by Nonnos of Panopolis (fifth century C.E.).

> His mother in her passionate love, unshod, unveiled, was scourged with grief. She tore her hair, she rent all her smock, she scored her cheeks with her nails in sorrow till they were red with blood; baring her bosom, she reddened the lifegiving round of the breasts which had nursed her children, in memory of her son; over her sorrowing face the tears ran in a ceaseless flood and drenched her robes.[63]

The parallels between the Actaeon myth and GE 6–7 can hardly be attributed to accident. Actaeon transforms into a stag while the demons in GE 6 transform into dogs, but the result of both transformations is a lethal attack caused by supernatural evil—Artemis or demons. Both stories also emphasize the unrelenting grief of the parents. In *The Acts of Andrew* the Christian God raises the dead, unlike the demonic Artemis who slew Actaeon. The selection of Nicea and Nicomedia as the locations for GE 6 and 7 may be due to their sharing of the Greek root νικ-, 'victory'.[64]

Storms, Pirates, and Sailors (GE 8–10)

Gregory radically abbreviated the next three episodes and did not retain the name of a single character, rendering the task of detecting possible Homeric hypertextuality nearly impossible. For example, GE 8 narrates an entire voyage in three sentences. Having left Nicomedia, Andrew boarded a ship and sailed the Propontis,[65] headed for Byzantium. "A storm arose on the sea, a strong wind pressed down on them, and the ship foundered. At last, just when everyone was expecting to perish, the blessed Andrew prayed to the Lord, commanded the wind, and was silent. The raging waves of the sea became placid, and there was calm" (GE 8). Even in this obviously truncated version there are possible traces of *The Odyssey*. Odysseus himself endured many a gale at sea, saved from Davy Jones's Locker by divine intervention.[66] Of course, such calmings of the sea also occur in the Gospels,[67] but there is no evangelical equivalent to the story that follows it in Gregory:

Having been saved from the immediate crisis, they reached Byzantium.[68] Proceeding from there in order to go to Thrace, they saw a multitude of men a long way off with swords drawn and brandishing spears as though they intended to attack them. When the apostle Andrew saw them, he made the sign of the cross against them and said, "I pray, O Lord, that their father [the devil] who incited them to do this may fall. May they be thrown into disorder by divine power, so that they cannot harm those who hope in you."

As he said this, an angel of the Lord passed by with great splendor and touched their swords. They fell sprawling on the ground. The blessed apostle passed by with his entourage unscathed, for the entire gang threw away their swords and adored him. (GE 9)[69]

No Odyssean hypertext would be complete without such savages. Odysseus himself, once on land, was vulnerable to various sorts of violent natives, such as the Laestrygonians, who

came thronging from all sides, a host past counting, not like men but like the Giants. They hurled at us from the cliffs with rocks huge as a man could lift, and at once there rose throughout the ships a dreadful din, alike from men that were dying and from ships that were being crushed. And spearing them like fishes they bore them home, a loathly meal.[70]

Whenever he landed on a strange shore, Odysseus quite appropriately asked himself, "[T]o the land of what mortals am I now come? Are they cruel, and wild, and unjust? or do they love strangers and fear the gods in their thoughts?"[71]

Travelers washed ashore in Odyssean imitations generally are weak, unarmed, broke, broken, and easy prey to robbers or savages or merciless opportunists.[72] It is possible that the author of *The Acts of Andrew* had in mind some particular mythological identification of the Thracian horde, perhaps even the Laestrygonians, but Gregory's stripped-down version, without names or other distinguishing peculiarities, thwarts further specificity.[73]

Gregory abbreviated the next chapter even more drastically:

The holy apostle arrived at Perinthus, a Thracian coastal city, and there found a boat about to leave for Macedonia. Again, an angel of the Lord appeared to him and commanded him to board the boat. As he preached the word of God on board, a sailor and all who were with him believed in the Lord Jesus Christ, and the holy apostle glorified God that even on the sea there was someone to hear his preaching and to believe in the son of God Almighty. (GE 10)

The original *Acts* probably named the sailor and given the content of Andrew's preaching.[74] One of the sailors converted at sea may have been Anthimus (GE 21), a hypertextual alternative to the Thracian Orpheus, famed singer and an Argonaut. One therefore might well suspect that Gregory's reference to "a sailor and all who were with him" here in GE 10 refers to Jason and the Argonauts.

The Double Wedding (The Wedding at Sparta, GE 11)

GE 11 begins with the following festivities at Philippi:

> There were two brothers at Philippi, one of whom had two sons, the other
> two daughters. Both brothers were rich; they were great nobles. One said to
> the other, "Look, we both have vast wealth, and there is no one in the city
> worthy of breeding with our clan; therefore, let's merge our families into one.
> Let my sons marry your daughters, so that we might more easily consolidate
> our wealth." This speech pleased his brother, and once the pact was made,
> they secured the deal with an earnest sent by the boys' father.

> On the wedding day, the word of the Lord came to them saying, "Do not
> marry your children until my servant Andrew comes. . . ." The nuptial
> chamber already had been prepared, the guests called, and all the wedding
> arrangements were held in readiness. (GE 11)

In Book 4 of *The Odyssey*, Telemachus arrived in Sparta, at the home of the
fabulously wealthy Menelaus and Helen, who just then were throwing a wedding
feast for their two children. Menelaus had pledged his daughter Hermione to
Achilles' son, and had acquired the daughter of Alector for Megapenthes, his son
by a slave woman. "So they were feasting in the great high-roofed hall, the
neighbours and kinfolk of glorious Menelaus, and making merry."[75] As in GE,
Homer here sends a stranger to a wedding celebration for two couples whose
marriages had been arranged by rich parents. The very presence of arranged
marriages in Gregory suggests a throwback to an archaic Greek custom.

When Andrew finally arrived, the families of those to be married "were
jubilant, ran to him with wreaths, fell at his feet, and said, 'O servant of God,
having been apprised of you, we await you, that you might come and tell us what
we should do. We got word to receive you, and were told that our children
should not be united before you arrived.'" Similarly, when Telemachus and his
friend arrived chez Menelaus, they were shown lavish hospitality. Maidservants
bathed, anointed, and dressed them, and "placed before them platters of all
manner of meats, and set by them golden goblets."[76]

As one might now expect, Andrew could put a damper on a good time,
especially on a wedding feast. The apostle addressed them:

> [R]epent, for you have sinned against the Lord inasmuch as you want to unite
> blood relatives in marriage. We do not forbid or shun weddings—from the
> beginning God commanded the male and the female to be joined together—but
> we do condemn incest. . . . Keep uncontaminated what you hear, so that God
> may be with you, and so that you may receive interest from your wealth—that
> is, everlasting life which never ends.

Andrew's denunciation of wealth here in GE 11 probably corresponds with the
perspective of the ancient *Acts* itself, but surely not his rejection merely of

incest.[77] Another text, *The Ps.-Titus Letter on Virginity*, alludes to this story and gives the lie to Gregory: "At last, when Andrew arrived at a wedding, he too, to demonstrate God's glory, disjoined men and women whose marriages had been arranged and taught them to continue being holy as singles."[78] Like GE and Homer, the passage tells of a wedding for "men and women whose marriages had been arranged," but here marriage itself, not merely incest, falls under apostolic condemnation. The author of *The Acts of Andrew* apparently saw in the double wedding feast in Book 4 of *The Odyssey* an ideal setting for Andrew's ascetic message, where he could get two brides with one scold.

Exochus (Melampus, GE 12)

Gregory next tells this story:

> At Thessalonica there was a young man, exceedingly noble and rich, named Exochus. Without his parents' knowledge, he came to the apostle. . . . The holy apostle indeed preached to him the Lord Jesus Christ. The youth believed and attached himself to the holy apostle, forgetting about his parents and altogether disregarding his financial affairs.
>
> When his parents inquired about him, they learned that he was staying with the apostle in Philippi. They brought gifts with them and begged the lad to abandon him, but he refused. (GE 12)

Exochus (Ἔξοχος, 'preeminent')[79] is a counter-Melampus, whom Homer called "a rich man and one that had a very excellent house (ἔξοχα δώματα)."[80] Melampus fled his fatherland (πατρίδα) because of his tyrannical uncle, Neleus.[81] For a full year Neleus maliciously retained his nephew's wealth until Melampus acquired it again and moved to another location where he built "a high-roofed house."[82] Exochus also appears in a tall house:

> The holy apostle descended from the third story and preached to them the word of God. When they did not listen, he went back to the boy and shut the doors of the house. They assembled an armed band and came to set fire to the house where the youth was, saying, "Let the lad perish who forsook his parents and native land (*patriam*)." They brought out bundles of stakes, reeds, and torches and began to ignite the house.[83]
>
> As the fire rose, the youth grabbed a small flask of water and said [a prayer]. . . . When he had said this, he sprinkled the water from the small flask, and immediately the entire fire was controlled so that it was as though it had never burned.

According to post-Homeric tradition, Melampus, too, performed miracles. Some considered him the first mortal gifted with clairvoyance and prophecy.

One tradition stated that he spent a year in prison, where "he heard the worms in the hidden part of the roof, one of them asking how much of the beam had been already gnawed through, and others answering that very little of it was left."[84] Melampus told his jailer he wished to be moved to another cell. When the roof of his former cell fell in, his jailer released him "perceiving that he was an excellent soothsayer."[85] To return to GE 12: "When the boy's parents saw this [the extinguishing of the fire], they said, 'Look, our son already has been turned into a sorcerer.' They brought out a ladder and intended to scale up to the third story to slay them [Exochus and Andrew] by sword, but the Lord blinded them so they could not see the ladder's ascent." A citizen of Philippi named Lysimachus (Λυσίμαχος, 'ending of warfare', 'peacemaker') warned the crowd not to fight against God.[86] His parents returned home and gave Exochus's inheritance to the public treasury. Fifty days later they died. The authorities then gave Exochus his entire patrimony, which he in turn donated to the poor as he traveled with the apostle.

Both Exochus and Melampus are miracle-working plutocrats residing in tall houses, who left their homelands and oppressive relatives. Both are held hostage in structures that witness to their supernatural powers. Ultimately both men escape confinement and recover the wealth their relatives had withheld from them. Melampus uses his money to build a mansion; Exochus his to feed the poor.

The next story in GE 13 takes Andrew and Exochus to a theater in Thessalonica where the youth preaches, a task performed by no one other than Andrew in the entire *Acts*. Unfortunately, Gregory fails to provide the content of the speech, but he does say that the crowd "was amazed at the boy's insight," and pleaded with him to heal a lad who lay seriously ill. Exochus's profundity and miraculous powers befit a counter-characterization of Melampus the prophet and magician.[87]

Carpianus and Adimantus (Zeus and Sarpedon, GE 13)

GE 13 and 14 narrate two healings at a theater in Thessalonica where Exochus and Andrew preached. In the first, the crowd asked them to "save the son of Carpianus, our fellow-citizen, for he is gravely ill." Andrew consented, so Carpianus

> went to his house and said to the boy, "Today you will be healed, my beloved Adimantus," for this was the boy's name.

> "My dream has indeed come true," he told his father, "for in a vision I saw this man restoring me to health." When he had said this, he clothed himself, rose from his cot, and proceeded to the theater so quickly that his parents could not follow him. Falling at the blessed apostle's feet, he gave thanks for his restored health. (GE 13)

Gregory here retains two personal names. Carpianus (Καρπίανος), the name of the father, means 'fruitful' and may allude to Zeus's epithets Carpius (Κάρπιος) and Epicarpius (Ἐπικάρπιος). Carpianus is a resident of Thessalonica, where, on a clear day, one can see "Macedonian Olympus." Adimantus (Ἀδείμαντος) means 'fearless', an adjective appropriate for Sarpedon, Zeus's son. According to *The Iliad*, Sarpedon led the Lycian army to join the Trojan side of the war and, after Hector, was the most valiant Trojan. Sarpedon's fearless abandon inspired his comrades to break down the Achaeans' mighty wall.[88] Homer states that in courage Sarpedon was preeminent.[89] The Stoic philosopher Epictetus used Sarpedon as an example of daring in the face of death;[90] the emperor Julian valued his courage and irrational recklessness.[91]

While slaying a Greek in single combat, Sarpedon sustained a fatal blow, but his father Zeus brought him back to life.[92] He was not so lucky the next time, for fate dictated that he would be slain by the hero Patroclus. Zeus himself was helpless: "'Ah, woe is me, for that it is fated that Sarpedon, dearest of men to me, be slain by Patroclus, son of Menoetius.' . . . [H]e shed bloody rain-drops on the earth, shewing honour to his dear son.'[93] When Sarpedon died, one of his own comrades lamented that "a man far the noblest hath perished, even Sarpedon, the son of Zeus; and he succoureth not his own child."[94]

This incident became a whipping boy for Homer's critics, such as Plato's Socrates, who took exception to Zeus's undignified weeping at Sarpedon's death.[95] Christian authors chimed in. Athenagoras, like Plato, quoted *Iliad* 16.433–34 and 522 to ridicule Zeus's lamentation and inability to raise his own son back to life: "Zeus does not defend his son."[96] Clement of Alexandria observed that "the will of Zeus has been overcome, and your supreme god, defeated, is lamenting for Sarpedon's sake."[97] Minucius Felix mocked Zeus because "he bewailed in showers of blood his son Sarpedon, because he could not save him from death."[98]

There is a significant disparity between the stories of Sarpedon and Adimantus, which might seem to argue against relating the two characters. Sarpedon died; Adimantus was merely sick. But perhaps the author needed to keep his counter-Sarpedon alive in order to provide one additional clue. Adimantus had a dream of Andrew restoring his health, and the dream came true. Sarpedon received no revelations in *The Iliad*, but he received more than his share in post-Homeric mythology. The *daemon* of Sarpedon inspired oracles throughout the East. The Church father Tertullian knew of a Sarpedonian oracle in the Troad,[99] and Cilicia boasted two of them—the Sarpedonian Artemis and the Sarpedonian Apollo.[100] A fifth-century text now known as *The Life and Miracles of St. Thecla* documents the popularity of an oracle of Sarpedon in Seleucia, Isauria, on the southern coast of Asia Minor: "No one is ignorant of this Sarpedon, for we have known that the legend is ancient from histories and books."[101] In addition to granting oracles, Sarpedon healed, until Thecla herself appeared at the shrine, silenced it, and replaced its healing powers with her own.[102]

Although it is possible that the author of *The Acts of Andrew* intended to oppose the cult of Sarpedon by making his hypertextual Sarpedon helpless and dependent on the healing of Andrew's God, it is more likely that he wanted to criticize Sarpedon's father. Whereas Zeus stood by helpless at the death of his son, in a similar situation Andrew raised a boy back to life. This interpretation is entirely consistent with the uses of this passage by Athenagoras, Ps.-Justin, and Clement of Alexandria, and makes sense of the affirmation of the crowd: "No one equals Andrew's God!"

The Dead Youth (Hector, GE 14)

GE 14 also takes place in Thessalonica:

> One of the citizens whose son had an impure spirit asked the blessed apostle: "Please heal my son, man of God, for he is deeply disturbed by a demon." Foreseeing his impending expulsion, the demon led the boy to a secluded room and strangled him, wringing out his life with a noose.

> When the boy's father found him dead he wept profusely and said to his friends, "Take the carcass to the theater, for I am sure that the stranger who proclaims the true God can revive him." (GE 14)

GE 14 contains few clues concerning the identity of the characters; Gregory named neither the father nor the son. Even so, the dead youth probably represents Hector. Both in Homer and in later Greek authors, the two Trojan champions, Sarpedon and Hector, frequently shared the same stage.[103] Four details of the story itself also point in this direction: the demon who killed him, the noose that strangled him, the father that wept for him, and the nightfall that saw his return home.

Achilles slew Hector with the unfair assistance of Athena,[104] and for the author of the *Acts*, of course, Athena was merely a demon. Achilles then lashed Hector's corpse to his chariot and dragged him feet first around Patroclus's grave.[105] The demon in GE 14 killed the lad by "wringing out his life with a noose," which could be a faint allusion to the rope Achilles used to drag Hector about. GE's statement "When the boy's father found him dead, he wept profusely, and said to his friends, 'Take the carcass to the theater'" calls to mind Hector's father, Priam, whose grief Homer never tired of emphasizing and whose efforts to recover the carcass of his son caps off the entire *Iliad*:

> She [Iris, messenger of the gods] came to the house of Priam, and found therein clamour and wailing. His sons sat about their father within the court sullying their garments with their tears, and in their midst was the old king close-wrapped in his mantle; and upon the old man's head and neck was filth in abundance, which he had gathered in his hands as he grovelled on the earth. And his daughters and his son's wives were wailing throughout the house.[106]

In spite of the great dangers of his mission, Priam set out with a wagon at night to fetch Hector's body from Achilles.[107] The Trojan king told the Greek hero: "[F]or never yet have mine eyes closed beneath mine eyelids since at thy hands my son lost his life, but ever do I wail and brood over my countless sorrows, grovelling in the filth in the closed spaces of the court."[108] Achilles released the corpse and invited Priam to spend the night. While the Greeks slept, Hermes warned Priam to escape with the body in the middle of the night, lest he perish there amid the ships of the Myrmidons.[109] When they arrived at Troy at daybreak, Cassandra, Priam's daughter, first spotted the returning wagon and announced its arrival:

> [N]or was any man left there within the city, neither any woman, for upon all had come grief that might not be borne; and hard by the gates they met Priam, as he bare home the dead. First Hector's dear wife and queenly mother flung themselves upon the light-running waggon, and clasping his head the while, wailed and tore their hair; and the folk thronged about and wept. And now the whole day long until set of sun had they made lament for Hector with shedding tears there without the gates, had not the old man spoken amid the folk from out the car: "Make me way for the mules to pass through; thereafter shall ye take your fill of wailing, when I have brought him to the house."[110]

Take their fill of wailing they did, until the end of the epic, nearly one hundred more lines or ten more days.

The crowds in GE 14, however, did not break into dirges but into paeans of joy, because Andrew had raised the lad back to life: "'All of us now believe in the God you preach.' They led him out to the house with torches and lamps—it was already past nightfall—and brought him inside his house." Among all the healing stories in *The Acts of Andrew* only here do events take place at night, and they do so here in order to call attention to their similarities to Priam's rescue of the corpse. Athena had helped Achilles kill Hector and brought grief on old Priam, but Andrew's God gave life and produced joy.

Medias and Philomedes (Zeus and Hephaestus, GE 15)

According to GE 15, a man named Medias entreated Andrew to heal his severely crippled son. The apostle agreed and went with him to Philippi.

> When he entered the city gate, an old man ran to him pleading for his children, whom Medias had forced into confinement for unspeakable immorality and who festered with sores.

> The holy apostle turned to Medias and said, "Listen, sir, you beg for your son to be healed, yet at your own home people are detained in shackles with rotting flesh. If you want your prayers to come before God, first release the

chains of those who suffer so that your son too may be freed of his disability. I see that your cruelty impedes my prayers."

Medias fell at his feet, kissed him, and said, "I will free these two and seven others unknown to you, so that my son may be healed." He ordered them arrayed before the blessed apostle, who laid hands on them, washed their wounds for three days, restored their health, and gave them freedom.

The next day Andrew said to the boy, "Rise up in the name of the Lord Jesus Christ who sent me to cure your infirmity." He took his hand, lifted him, and immediately the lad straightened up and walked, magnifying God. The name of the lad who had been crippled for twenty-two years was Philomedes.

The names Medias (Μειδίας) means 'laughter'; Philomedes (Φιλομμειδής) means 'laughter-loving'. There is nothing funny about this story in GE, but there is in its Homeric antecedent.

While Odysseus feasted at Alcinous's palace, the blind bard, Demodocus, broke into a song that told this story. Lame Hephaestus, son of Zeus, discovered that his wife, Aphrodite, was sleeping with Ares. The master smith forged a trap to place around his bed, "fine as spiders' webs, so that no one even of the blessed gods could see them, so exceeding craftily were they fashioned."[111] "So they two went to the couch, and lay them down to sleep, and about them clung the cunning bonds of the wise Hephaestus, nor could they in any wise stir their limbs or raise them up."[112] Then Hephaestus called on all the gods to

"see a laughable matter and a monstrous, even how Aphrodite, daughter of Zeus, scorns me for that I am lame and loves destructive Ares because he is comely and strong of limb, whereas I was born misshapen. . . ." [T]he gods, the givers of good things, stood in the gateway; and unquenchable laughter arose among the blessed gods as they saw the craft of wise Hephaestus.[113]

All laughed but Poseidon, who asked that the couple be released from their chains. Reluctantly, the chthonian blacksmith relented. Ares left for Thrace, but "laughter-loving Aphrodite (φιλομμειδὴς Ἀφροδίτη)" went to Cyprus, where "the Graces bathed her and anointed her with immortal oil."[114]

It would appear that the author of The Acts of Andrew rewrote this story, making Zeus and Hephaestus into Medias ('laughter') and Philomedes ('laughter-loving') as hypertextual clues. Like Hephaestus, Philomedes was lame. Although Gregory's account does not say whether the son or the father was responsible for the confinement of the two siblings, it is quite possible that in the original this was the work of the son, which again would parallel the song of Demodocus. The crime of the siblings that Gregory calls an "unspeakable immorality" is probably incest.[115] Ares and Aphrodite were both children of Zeus. When Medias claimed to have had seven others in confinement as well, the author may be suggesting the freeing of seven of Zeus's many captives, such as Prometheus and Phineas. Andrew, like Poseidon, required that the captives be released, and, like the Graces, washed their wounds and healed them. This done, Andrew healed the cripple.

This recasting of the song of Demodocus conforms with early Christian objections to the lameness of Hephaestus and the adultery of Ares and Aphrodite. Apologists parroted Plato's contempt for Homer's Zeus who threw Hephaestus down to earth, crippling him.[116] More frequent was the complaint that lame gods are not gods at all.[117] But perhaps no story more thoroughly tarnished Homer's reputation than Hephaestus's ensnaring Ares and Aphrodite in flagrante. Plato's Socrates would not tolerate such a depiction of the gods in his ideal city.[118] Later authors added their objections.[119]

Allegorical ingenuity, however, exculpated the culprits. For example, an allegorist of the first century C.E. saw here a narrative expression of Empedoclean physics: Ares, the god of war, stood for strife; Aphrodite stood for love; and their post-Homeric daughter, Harmonia, represented the necessary tension between the two. The gods laughed at the sight because they rejoiced that at last the two primordially separated principles combined into their dynamic symbiosis.[120] Others took the union of the gods to be the conjunction of the planets Mars and Venus.[121] Neoplatonists and Neopythagoreans took Aphrodite as the soul, Ares as the body, and Hephaestus's bonds as the durable liaison between soul and body.[122]

Christian readers remained unimpressed: the song of Demodocus was a dirty story pure and simple. Tatian, Theophilus, Ps.-Justin, Athenagoras, Aristides, Minucius Felix, Athanasius, Prudentius, and *The Ps.-Clementine Recognitions* all debunked it,[123] but it was Clement of Alexandria who got the most mileage out of it, mentioning it three times in his *Protrepticus*.[124] Here are excerpts from one of them:

> Further, the marriages of gods, their acts of child-begetting and child-bearing which are on men's lips, their adulteries which are sung by bards, their feastings which are a theme of comedy, and the bursts of laughter which occur over their cups, these exhort me to cry aloud, even if I would fain keep silence,—Alas for such atheism! . . . [F]or the true worship of God you have substituted a travesty, the fear of daemons.[125]

Referring to the bard Demodocus, Clement quotes *Odyssey* 8.266:

> Then to the harp's sweet strains a beautiful song he opened;

Sing to us that beautiful strain, Homer,

> Telling the love of Ares and Aphrodite fair-girdled,
> How at the first they met in the halls of Hephaestus in secret;
> Many the gifts he gave, and the bed and the couch of Hephaestus
> Sullied with shame. (*Odyssey* 8.267–70)

Cease the song, Homer. There is no beauty in that; it teaches adultery. We have declined to lend even our ears to fornication. . . .

But most men are not of this mind. Casting off shame and fear, they have their homes decorated with pictures representing the unnatural lust of the daemons. In the lewdness to which their thoughts are given, they adorn their chambers with painted tablets hung on high like votive offerings, regarding licentiousness as piety and when lying upon the bed, while still in the midst of their own embraces, they fix their gaze upon that naked Aphrodite, who lies bound in her adultery.[126]

The author of The Acts of Andrew added his voice to Clement's by replacing the song of Demodocus with the story of Medias and his crippled son, Philomedes. Andrew first ordered the release of the incestuous children and healed their wounds. Then he healed Philomedes. Whereas Zeus crippled his own son and either was unable or unwilling to heal him, Andrew's God makes the lame dance.

Nicolaus (Menelaus, GE 16)

According to GE 16,

Later, a citizen named Nicolaus displayed a gilded carriage with four white mules and four white horses and offered them to the blessed apostle saying, "Take these, servant of God, for I found none of my possessions dearer than these, only let my daughter, plagued by extreme torment, be healed."

The blessed apostle smiled and said to him, "I do indeed receive your gifts, Nicolaus, but not these visible ones. For if you offer for your daughter the most precious things in your home, how much more would you owe for your soul? Here is what I long to receive from you: that your inner self recognize the true God, its maker and the creator of all; that it reject the earthly and crave the eternal; that it neglect the fleeting and love the everlasting; that it deny what is seen and, by contemplation, cast spiritual glances at what is not seen. When you have become alert to these things by means of trained perception, you will merit attaining eternal life and your daughter's restored health, and still more that you may enjoy in her the delights of eternity."

By saying this, he persuaded everyone to forsake idols and to believe in the true God. He healed Nicolaus's daughter of her illness.

Two characters in The Acts of Andrew bear the name Nicolaus (Νικόλαος) and both transvalue Homer's Menelaus (Μενέλαος). GE 28, which takes place in Menelaus's Sparta, takes aim at this obsession for Helen, but here in GE 16 the issue is his legendary wealth.

Like Nicolaus, Menelaus had a beloved daughter (Hermione) and gave lavish gifts. When Telemachus left Sparta to return to Ithaca, Menelaus offered him "splendid gifts, three horses and a well-polished car."[127] Telemachus refused the gifts; what would he do with a carriage on rocky Ithaca?[128] Menelaus then increased his generosity: "Of all the gifts that lie stored as treasures in my house, I will give thee that one which is fairest and costliest. I will give thee a well-wrought mixing bowl."[129] Telemachus takes: Ithaca cannot use a carriage, but it can always use another wine crater. Compare the following:

Odyssey 4.589–91 and 613	GE 16
"Then will I send thee forth with honour and give thee splendid gifts, **three horses** **and a well-polished car.** . . .	Nicolaus displayed **a gilded carriage with four white** **mules and four white horses** and offered them to the blessed apostle saying, "Take these, servant of God, for I found
Of all the gifts that lie stored **as treasures in my house,** I will give thee **that one** **which is fairest and costliest.**"	**none of my possessions dearer** **than these.**" [Andrew:] "[I]f you offer **the most precious things in your** **home** for your daughter. . . ."

Telemachus wanted the wine crater; Andrew wanted Nicolaus's spiritual perspicuity.[130]

Andrew's statement that Nicolaus will enjoy in his daughter "the delights of eternity" again may point to Menelaus, whose eternal state was to be eternal bliss. Because he had married Helen, daughter of Zeus, he would spend an afterlife on "the Elysian plain . . . , where life is easiest for men."[131] Both men enjoy endless bliss because of women: Menelaus's wife, Nicolaus's daughter.

The Young Demoniac (Apollo, GE 17)

Andrew is still in Macedonia in GE 17:

On the following day, while Andrew was teaching, a young man cried out in a loud voice: "What do you have to do with us, Andrew, God's servant? Have you come here to chase us from our haunts?"

Then the blessed apostle called the youth to himself and said, "Tell me, contriver of crime, what is your work?"

"I have inhabited this boy from his youth," he said, "thinking I would never leave him. But three days ago I heard his father telling a friend, 'I will go to Andrew, God's servant, and he will heal my son.' Now I have come in order to desert him in your presence, for I fear the tortures you inflict on us."

Insofar as Gregory names none of these characters and supplies no distinguishing characteristics, it is impossible to relate the story to Greek mythology with confidence. On the other hand, the story takes place in Macedonia, probably Thessalonica, which is the venue for several stories about the Olympians. Insofar as *The Acts of Andrew* repeatedly identifies the Olympians as demons, one should perhaps look among the gods for the Homeric equivalent to this demoniac. The only hope of finding a mythological antecedent for this story lies in its unusual ending: "God displayed his grace through the holy apostle such that everyone voluntarily came to hear the word of salvation and said, 'Tell us, man of god, who is the true God in whose name you cure our sick?' Even philosophers would come and debate with him, and no one could oppose his teaching." This ending seems to relate the character to healing—"who is the true God in whose name you cure our sick?"—and to philosophy—"philosophers would come and debate with him." Not until the passion does one find another reference to philosophers, so their appearance here encourages hypertextual suspicions.

The Greek deity most commonly associated with healing and philosophy is Apollo.[132] Furthermore, he was characteristically depicted as a youth—even though his son Asclepius is usually bearded.[133] Apollo also is the god of prophecy, whose oracles attracted anxious tourists throughout the ancient world, especially at Delphi, where the Sibyl spoke on behalf of Pythian Apollo. The demon in GE 17 similarly predicts his torture at Andrew's hands. The depiction of the lad as demon-possessed would correspond with Apollo's association with prophetic madness and with early Christian claims that the Delphic oracle was inspired by demons.[134] Due to the scarcity of evidence in GE 17, however, the identification of the demoniac with Apollo must remain uncertain.

Varianus and Aristobula (Zeus and Hera, GE 18a)

GE 18 begins:

[A]n opponent of apostolic preaching arose and went to the proconsul Varianus saying, "A troublemaker has arisen in Thessalonica, preaching that the temples of the gods should be destroyed, the rites rejected, and all decrees of ancient law struck down. He also preaches that only one God should be worshiped, whose servant he declares himself to be."

When the proconsul heard this, he sent infantry and cavalry to make Andrew appear before him. When they came to the gate, they determined in which house the apostle resided. But on entering and seeing his face shining brilliantly, they fell at his feet terrified.[135] Then the blessed apostle told his audience what the proconsul had ordered for him. The crowd came with swords and clubs wanting to kill the soldiers, but the holy apostle restrained them.

Gregory goes on to say that one of the soldiers, a demoniac, died when Andrew exorcised him. Andrew then restored the boy's life.

On the surface, the text seems quite straightforward, but a fourth-century Coptic fragment suggests that these few lines represent a narrative much longer in the original. *Papyrus Coptic Utrecht 1* begins where the excerpt from Gregory ends, with the soldiers attempting to arrest the apostle:

> When Andrew, the apostle of Christ, heard that they had arrested those who were in the city because of him, he rose up, went out into the middle of the street, and said to the brethren that there was no cause for concealing who they were.
>
> While the apostle spoke these words, there was a young man among the four soldiers in whose body a demon was hidden. When that young man came before the apostle Andrew, he cried out, "O Varianus (ογαριανε), what have I done to you that you should send me against this religious man?" When the youth had said this, the demon threw him down and caused him to froth at the mouth.

This passage retains the more original name of the proconsul, Varianus, and states that he sent only four soldiers after Andrew, not Gregory's inflated "infantry and cavalry." More intriguing is what is missing from *Papyrus Coptic Utrecht 1.* The document calls itself "The Act of Andrew." The use of the singular "Act" suggests that it told of a single episode from *The Acts of Andrew.*[136] The fragment begins on page nine; the first eight pages are missing. It would appear that these eight pages narrated the same story that now occupies only seven lines in Gregory's Latin version.

Later in his epitome, Gregory himself hints that he had indeed omitted a crucial episode relevant to Andrew's confrontation with the proconsul. The apostle and his entourage traveled to a woman's farm, where a young boy lay dead, smitten by a serpent. "[T]he apostle said to the proconsul's wife, 'Go and revive the boy.' Without hesitation, she went to the corpse and said, 'Lad, in the name of my God Jesus Christ rise up unscathed.' He arose at once." Surely this unnamed, miracle-working woman played a significant role in the original. Presumably she had converted to Christ and no longer cavorted with Varianus. The conflict between the proconsul and the apostle may not have involved inactivity in pagan temples, as in Gregory, but inactivity in the bedroom. Many such vindictive, jilted husbands stalk the pages of the apocryphal Acts searching for their newly converted, no longer cooperative wives.

The suspicion that Gregory omitted this woman's conversion finds confirmation in two ancient hymns written by Manichaeans, eastern Gnostics who accepted as Scripture several Christian apocrypha, including Andrew's *Acts.* These hymns name seven women whose chastity resulted in domestic violence against them, and all appear in the extant texts of the apocryphal Acts. For example, *The Psalms of Sarakoton* mentions Thecla, the heroine of *The Acts of Paul*, and Drusiana, who repulsed the sexual advances of her husband according to *The Acts of John.*[137] The last line reads: "Maximilla and Aristobula (ⲀⲢⲒⲤⲦⲞⲂⲞⲨⲖⲀ)—they inflicted great torture on them." Maximilla is the heroine at the end of *The Acts of Andrew*, who refuses to satisfy the libido of Aegeates, her husband. Aristobula appears again in connection with Maximilla in *The Psalms of Heracleides*: "A despiser of the body is Thecla, the lover of God. / A shamer of the serpent is Maximilla the faithful. / Another receiver of good news is Iphidama her sister, / imprisoned in the prisons." Iphidama is one of Maximilla's servants in *The Acts of Andrew*. Next one reads of Aristobula: "An athlete in the contest is Aristobula (ⲀⲢⲒⲤⲦⲞⲂⲞⲨⲖⲀ) the steadfast." The phrase "athlete in the contest" was Christian shorthand for anyone who renounced sexual intercourse. The next heroine, Eubula, comes from *The Acts of Peter*. Then one finds Drusiana from *The Acts of John*, and finally Mygdonia, who refused to go to bed with her husband according to *The Acts of Thomas.*[138]

Insofar as Thecla, Maximilla, Iphidama, Eubula, Drusiana, and Mygdonia all appear in the apocryphal Acts, Aristobula surely did, too. Her identification with Maximilla and Iphidama would suggest that she played some role in *The Acts of Andrew*, but most scholars have argued rather that she appeared in *The Acts of John*. In *Acts of John* 59 one reads of an Aristobula whose husband, Tertullus, died while she was traveling with the apostle. There can be little doubt that John's *Acts* once contained a story about Tertullus and Aristobula in which she may have resisted sex with him at the cost of persecution.[139] Two arguments, however, favor the association of the Aristobula in the Manichaean hymns rather with *The Acts of Andrew*. In the first place, in both hymns, Aristobula is linked directly with heroines of Andrew's *Acts*, Maximilla and Iphidama. Even though a heroine of *The Acts of John*, Drusiana, also appears in both hymns, she is never associated with Aristobula. Secondly, if Aristobula were the name of Varianus's wife in *The Acts of Andrew*, it would be a valuable and entirely consistent hypertextual clue pointing to Homeric epic, as will soon become clear.

From these texts one might tentatively reconstruct the following story. While Andrew was in Thessalonica, Aristobula converted and became an athlete in the contest for celibacy. The proconsul Varianus then "inflicted great torture on" her. Somehow Aristobula survived and accompanied Andrew to a farm, where she raised the dead youth back to life. The surviving manuscripts permit no further reconstruction of the missing episode.

One can, however, deduce additional hints concerning the Homeric hypertextuality of the original by investigating the names Varianus and Aristobula. Much of the narrative takes place in Macedonia because of Macedonian Olympus, the home of the Greek gods. Insofar as Varianus is the most powerful person in Macedonia, he ought to play the part of Zeus, the father of the Olympians. The name Varianus derives from the Latin participle *varians* and means 'changeable' or 'unstable'. The English words 'variant' and 'variation' come from this root. One might translate Varianus into Old English as Sir Vacillates-a-lot, into French as Monsieur Caprice, into German as Herr Wankelmut, or into English as Mr. Fickle. Mr. Fickle is indeed an apt name for Zeus.

Christians enjoyed reminding their pagan readers that Zeus frequently transformed himself into other shapes when on the prowl for mortal lovers. For example:

> [S]ome mortals he [Zeus] violated after having transformed himself, like a magician. He corrupted Antiope . . . by turning into a satyr, . . . Alcmene when he changed into her husband, . . . Aegina when changed into an eagle, . . . Mantea . . . when changed into a bear, . . . Danaë . . . when changed into gold, . . . Europa when changed into a bull, Eurymedusa . . . when changed into an ant, . . . Thelia . . . when changed into a vulture, . . . Imandra . . . when changed into a rain shower, Cassiopeia when changed into her husband, . . . Leda . . . when changed into a swan, . . . and again when changed into a star, . . . Lamia when changed into a lapwing bird, Mnemosyne when changed into a shepherd, . . . Nemesis when changed into a goose, Semele . . . when changed into fire. . . . He sired from Demeter, his own daughter, Persephone, whom he also corrupted when he changed into a serpent.[140]

Aristides, Tatian, Athanasius, and Clement of Alexandria voiced the same objections.[141] To these early Christians, Zeus might indeed have been known as Mr. Fickle.

If Varianus represents Zeus, Aristobula should be his wife, Hera. Aristobula's name derives from ἄριστος 'excellent' or 'best' and βούλη meaning 'plan', 'counsel', or 'idea'. One might translate her name as Frau Gutbegriff, Madame Bonne Idée, or Ms. Best Plan. The name points to one of the most scandalous of all of Homer's episodes, Hera's seduction of Zeus on Mount Ida in *Iliad* Book 14.

While Zeus looked on, the Trojans were trouncing the Achaeans, so Hera devised a plan that would distract her husband's attention from the battlefield and permit the Greeks to gain the upper hand:

> [O]ne strategy struck her mind as best:
> she would dress in all her glory and go to Ida—
> perhaps the old desire would overwhelm the king
> to lie by her naked body and make immortal love
> and she might drift an oblivious, soft warm sleep
> across his eyes and numb that seething brain.[142]

One might translate the first line more literally: "In her soul it seemed that this was the best plan." The Greek words rendered here "best plan" are ἀρίστη βούλη, the same words that form the name Aristobula. The following necessarily lengthy excerpts tell how Hera executed her superlative design.

Hera cleansed her enticing body
of any blemish, then she applied a deep olive rub.
. . . .
Then round her shoulders she swirled the wondrous robes
that Athena wove her, brushed out to a high gloss
and worked into the weft an elegant rose brocade.
She pinned them across her breasts with a golden brooch
then sashed her waist with a waistband
floating a hundred tassels, and into her earlobes,
neatly pierced, she quickly looped her earrings,
ripe mulberry-clusters dangling in triple drops
and the silver glints they cast could catch the heart.
. . . .
Now, dazzling in all her rich regalia, head to foot,
out of her rooms she strode and beckoned Aphrodite
away from the other gods and whispered. . . .
. . . .
"Give me Love, give me Longing now, the powers
you use to overwhelm all gods and mortal men!"
. . . .
Aphrodite, smiling her everlasting smile, replied,
"Impossible—worse, it's wrong to deny your warm request,
since you are the one who lies in the arms of mighty Zeus."
With that she loosed from her breasts the breastband,
pierced and alluring, with every kind of enchantment
woven through it . . . There is the heat of Love,
the pulsing rush of Longing, the lover's whisper,
irresistible—magic to make the sanest man go mad.
. . . .
Hera broke into smiles now, her eyes wide—
with a smile she tucked the band between her breasts.[143]

Zeus didn't have a chance:

[Q]uick on her feet [Hera] scaled Gargaron peak,
the highest crest of Ida. And Zeus spotted her now
Zeus who gathers the breasting clouds. And at one glance
the lust came swirling over him, making his heart race,
fast as the first time—all unknown to their parents—
they rolled in bed, they locked and surged in love.
He rose before her now, he savored her name:
"Hera—where are you rushing?
. . . .

Now—
come, let's go to bed, let's lose ourselves in love!
Never has such a lust for goddess or mortal woman
flooded by pounding heart and overwhelmed me so.
Not even then, when I made love to Ixion's wife

. . . .

not when I loved Acrisius' daughter Danaë—marvelous ankles—

. . . .

not when I stormed Europa

. . . .

not even Semele, not even Alcmena queen of Thebes

. . . .

not when I loved Demeter, queen of the lustrous braids—
not when I bedded Leto ripe for glory—
    Not even you!
That was nothing to how I hunger for you now—
irresistible longing lays me low!"
Teeming with treachery noble Hera led him on:
"Dread majesty, son of Cronus, what are you saying?
You are eager for bed now, burning to make love,
here on Ida's heights for all the world to see?

. . . .

[T]hink of the shocking scandal there would be!
But if you're on fire, overflowing with passion,
there's always your own bedroom.

. . . .

There we can go to bed at once—since love is now your pleasure!"
And Zeus who gathers the breasting clouds assured her,
"Hera—nothing to fear, no god or man will see us—
I will wrap us round in a golden cloud so dense
not even the sun's rays, the sharpest eyes in the world,
will pierce the mist and glimpse us making love!"
With that the son of Cronus caught his wife in his arms
and under them now the holy earth burst with fresh green grass,
crocus and hyacinth, clover soaked with dew, so thick and soft
it lifted their bodies off the hard, packed ground . . .
Folded deep in that bed they lay and round them wrapped
a marvelous cloud of gold, and glistening showers of dew
rained down around them both. And so, deep in peace,
the Father slept on Gargaron peak, conquered by Sleep
and strong assaults of Love, his wife locked in his arms.[144]

As Zeus slept, the Achaeans turned the battle in their favor. When Zeus finally awoke and saw the carnage, he raged and promised Hera that the Greeks would suffer even more now because of her deception.

Many intellectuals considered this story an outrage. Plato's Socrates faulted Homer for having depicted Zeus neglecting his intentions for the Trojans, "because of the excitement of his passions, and [he] was so overcome by the sight of Hera that he is not even willing to go to their chamber, but wants to lie with her there on the ground."[145] Another ancient critic used the story to prove Homer a liar. How could he have known about Hera's seduction of Zeus on top of Mount Ida, especially since they were shrouded in a cloud of gold?[146]

Ancient Victorians insisted that a careful reading of the epics would show that Homer actually criticized the immorality of the gods. Because he had given into his lust, Zeus failed to accomplish his intentions for Troy.[147] Another moralist, Plutarch, pointed out that Hera, too, failed to get her way. After all, Zeus rebuked Hera the morning after and promised to punish the Achaeans even more severely.[148]

Other ancients recognized that even though such moralistic interpretations vindicated Homer, they did so at the expense of the gods, who had become examples of how mortals ought *not* conduct themselves. More draconian measures were required in order to excuse the gods of sexual impropriety. An Alexandrian grammarian named Aristophanes proposed that Zeus's list of infidelities was a later interpolation: "[T]he eleven lines are spurious . . . because the recounting of names is untimely." That is, Zeus wanted to sleep with Hera, so he surely would not have risked offending her by listing liaisons. The grammarian also pointed out that in general Zeus's hormones were immune to his wife. He would never have slept with her on Mount Ida had she not worn Aphrodite's irresistible garment.[149] The girdle made him do it.

Philosophers, however, preferred another solution: allegory. Physical philosophers thought Zeus stood for ether at the most rarefied periphery of the universe. Hera stood for air, the realm of humidity symbolized by the cloud of gold. "Hera's beautifying of herself for Zeus's eyes, and the charms connected with the girdle . . . are a sort of purification of the air [Hera] as it draws near the fiery element [Zeus]."[150] This conjunction of air and ether took place during the spring. Hera anointed herself with oil to symbolize the fecundity of the earth after the winter; her perfume represents spring flowers. She fixed her hair with ornaments like trees growing new leaves. Aphrodite's girdle is simply the spring air so accommodating to young lovers. Thus, when Hera and Zeus slept together, the whole world bloomed, a cipher for springtime.[151]

According to Platonists, the story disclosed the mysteries of the relationship between the physical world and the divine, between the phenomenal, sensate world and the world perceptible only to intelligence. Zeus represents the great demiurge; Hera is his creative power from whom the inferior world of matter derived. Human beings, children of the divine couple, reside in the material world but may ascend to god by adorning themselves with virtue, symbolized by Hera beautifying herself with jewelry and fine clothing.[152] Aphrodite's irresistible girdle stands for spiritual beauty, which summons the soul to seek the divine. Zeus refuses to make love in his bedroom because it stands for the material world. His union with Hera is nothing other than the reunification of the highest god with his powers of creation, a union which could only take place in the rarefied intellectual realm, symbolized by the highest peak on Mount Ida. Hera lies on the ground to symbolize the inferiority of the sensate world. Zeus takes her in his arms in order to depict the divine embrace of all his emanations. When they unite, the grass and flowers flourish, portraying the generative power of the world of ideas.[153]

Early Christians were unimpressed by such allegorical sleights of hand. Episodes like Hera's seduction of Zeus demonstrated that Greek gods were merely immoral demons. Apologists loved to cite Zeus's catalog of lovers in *Iliad* 14 as evidence of pagan decadence.[154] Clement of Alexandria told his pagan readers:

> Now listen to the loves of these gods of yours; to the extraordinary tales of their incontinence. . . . Listen, too, to their revels, their embraces. . . . So completely was he (Zeus) given over to lust, that every woman not only excited his desire, but became a victim of it. . . . [I]f you but let him catch a glimpse of a woman's girdle, even Zeus is exposed and his locks are put to shame.[155]

Tertullian's *Apology* mocks Homer for having represented Zeus carousing with Hera "in the most disgraceful way, advocating his incestuous passion for her by a description and enumeration of his various amours."[156] The Latin apologist Minucius Felix faulted Zeus who, "enticed by the girdle of Venus [Aphrodite], . . . lay more eagerly with his wife . . . than he was accustomed to do with his adulterous loves."[157]

It would appear that the author of *The Acts of Andrew* wished to rewrite the tale of Hera's "best plan" in *Iliad* 14 and to transform Hera the vamp into Aristobula the chaste. The story takes place in Thessalonica because of its proximity to Macedonian Olympus. The name of the proconsul, Varianus, calls to mind Zeus's infamous infidelities in disguise. Aristobula received her name from Hera's ἀρίστη βουλή in *Iliad* 14.161. When Andrew arrived, Aristobula converted, refused to sleep with her lustful husband, and endured his tortures.[158] Later she reappears in the narrative as a miracle worker.

The Magician and the Virgin (Simon Magus and Helen, *PCU 1*)

The next story now appears only in *Papyrus Coptic Utrecht 1*. Gregory omitted it entirely. One of Varianus's soldiers was possessed of a demon and fell into convulsions before the apostle. Andrew asked the demon why he had possessed the lad; here is the demon's explanation:

> This young man whose body is convulsed has a virgin sister who is a great

devotee of asceticism. I tell you truly that she is near to God because of her purity, her prayers, and her love. Now, to tell it without elaboration, there was someone living next door to her house who was a great magician (ⲘⲀⲅⲟⲥ). Here is what happened: One evening the virgin went up on her roof to pray, the young magician (ⲘⲀⲅⲟⲥ) saw her at prayer, and Semmath entered into him to fight with this great ascetic. The young magician (ⲘⲀⲅⲟⲥ) said to himself, "Even though I have spent twenty years under my teacher before acquiring this ability, this now is the beginning of my career (ⲧⲉⲬⲚⲎ). If I do not over-power this virgin, I will not be able to do anything." So the young magician (ⲘⲀⲅⲟⲥ) conjured up some great supernatural forces (ⲀⲨⲚⲀⲘⲓⲥ) against the virgin and sent them after her. When the demons left to tempt her or to win her over, they acted like her brother and knocked at the door. She got up and went downstairs to open up, supposing it was her brother. But first she prayed fervently, with the result that the demons became like [. . .] <they> fell down and flew away [. . .] <the young> man [. . .].

The manuscript breaks off here for two pages; when it resumes it would appear that the magician had sent the demon to possess the virgin's weaker sibling, the soldier. The virgin went to see a powerfully spiritual woman named Eirousia (from ῥύσια, 'rescue'?), who promised to send the youth to Andrew for healing.

This story, too, has a Homeric background, but indirectly, via traditions about Simon Magus and his consort, Helen, a putative reincarnation of Helen of Troy, the most beautiful of all Greek women and a widely distributed sexual commodity. Later I will investigate traditions about Helen in connection with GE 28, but for now I focus on what Justin Martyr had to say about Simon Magus.

[A]fter Christ's ascent into heaven the demons put forward various men who said that they were gods. . . . One was a certain Simon, a Samaritan from the village of Gitta, who in the time of Claudius Caesar, through the arts (τέχνης) of the demons who worked in him, did mighty works of magic (δυνάμεις . . . μαγικάς). . . . Almost all the Samaritans . . . confess this man as their first god and worship him as such, and a woman named Helena, who traveled around with him (συμπερινοστήσασαν αὐτῷ) in those days, and had formerly been a public prostitute, they say was the first Concept (ἔννοια) produced from him. . . . I have compiled and have on hand a treatise against all the heresies which have arisen, which I will give you if you would like to consult it.[159]

Despite Justin's invitation to Emperor Antoninus Pius to consult his *Syntagma of All Heresies*, one can no longer do so; it no longer exists. Several scholars have tried to reconstruct this work from later writings, especially from Irenaeus's *Adversus haereses* and Hippolytus's *Refutatio*, but these reconstructions have met with little agreement. Even so, there can be little doubt that Irenaeus obtained his impressive information about Simon Magus from Justin.[160] The following outline of Simonianism comes mostly from Hippolytus's *Refutatio*, but in nearly every case parallels exist in Irenaeus.

Although Simon claimed to be a God, he was merely adept at "the craft (τέχνη) of Thrasymedes," viz. magic. He taught that his first thought (Epinoia) created the physical world and its ruling powers, who then captured their cerebral mother, continually trapping her in material bodies in order to prevent her escape to the realm of the divine. "She was the lost sheep." One of her manifestations was as Helen of Troy, who proved her divinity by punishing the epic poet Stesichorus after her death. Stesichorus, who reviled her in his *Helen*, lost his sight, but regained it by exculpating her in another epic, *The Palinodes*.[161] As her last manifestation, Simon's Epinoia took the form of a whore, conveniently named Helen, "standing on a roof (ἐπὶ τέγους . . . στῆναι) in Tyre, a city of Phoenicia. Once he had brought her down, he discovered her. He claimed that it was for the purpose of seeking out this first [thought] that he appeared [on earth]—namely, to rescue (ῥύσηται) her from bondage."[162] Simon claimed that by redeeming Helen, he provided salvation to humankind.[163] His followers practiced sexual promiscuity and issued aphrodisiacs, love-charms, demonic dream-inducers, and guardian spirits.[164]

Justin's comments on Simon and Helen have too much in common with the story of the magician and the virgin to be happenstance. Both in Justin and in *The Acts of Andrew*, a young magician (μάγος) sees a woman on a roof and intends to seduce her as the initial demonstration of his craft (τέχνη). Whereas Simon's Helen is a whore advertising her services on the roof, the young woman in *The Acts of Andrew* is a virgin who has gone up on the roof to pray. The young magician sent demons to seduce her, like Justin's Simonians who employed aphrodisiacs, love-charms, and demonic envoys. Simon had his way with Helen, but the young man never saw the virgin's bed because of her prayers. There also may be wordplay between the name of the virgin's counselor, Eirousia ('Ρυσία), and Simon's claim to have liberated Helen (ῥύσηται αὐτήν). One might schematize these similarities like this:

Justin's *Syntagma* (in Irenaeus and Hippolytus)	PCU 1 (= *Acts of Andrew*)
1. Σίμων ὁ μάγος	1. Young ⲙⲁⲅⲟⲥ
2. Whore on a roof (to prey)	2. Virgin of a roof (to pray)
3. Magus "redeems" Helen as his first miracle ("the τέχνη of Thrasymedes")	3. Magician tries to seduce virgin as the beginning of his craft (ⲧⲉⲭⲛⲏ)
4. Simonians use demonic seducers	4. Magus sends demonic seducer
5. Whore comes down from roof, sleeps with Simon	5. Virgin comes down from roof, rebuffs demons
6. Simon rescues (ῥύσηται) her	6. Eirousia (ⲉⲓⲣⲟⲩⲥⲓⲁ) rescues the virgin

Apparently the author of the *Acts*, familiar with Justin's depiction of Simon and Helen in his *Syntagma*,[165] transvalued Helen's prostitution into the virgin's resolve to celibacy.

The Deserter (Ares, *PCU 1* and GE 18b)

The soldier whose resident demon narrated the story in *PCU 1* also appears in GE 18. When taken together, these two accounts reveal a character who trades one kind of military service for another, service for Rome for service for Christ. His virgin sister proved to be stronger than he, for she thwarted the demonic assault when he could not. Thus Andrew praises virgins as "warriors" who "have not acquired weapons and shields or endured warfare in vain." The exorcism of the young man consisted not merely in his return to sanity, but also in his "arming himself for the palace," that is, the replacement of earthly weapons with heavenly ones.[166] Andrew told the demon: "It is now time for you to come out of this young man, so that he may arm himself for the heavenly palace." The demon left. Immediately the soldier stripped off his uniform, threw it before the apostle, and spoke:

> "O man of God, I spent twenty coins to obtain these items of this temporary uniform, but now I want to give all that I own to obtain these items of the uniform of your God."

> "O you unfortunate child!" his fellow-soldiers told him. "If you deny the uniform of the king, they will punish you."

> The young man said to them, "I am indeed unfortunate because of my previous sins. Would that my punishment were only for denying the uniform of this king and not for despising the uniform of the king of the ages! You fools, do you not see what sort of man this is? There is no sword in his hand nor any instrument of war, and yet these great acts of power issue from his hand."

The Coptic fragment ends here, leaving the reader to assume that Varianus would punish the soldier for desertion, just as the soldiers had warned: "If you deny the uniform of the king, they will punish you." The predictable punishment was death.[167] Gregory's epitome omits any trace of the demoniac's rejection of military service, but does state that the soldier was slain—not at Varianus's arrival but at the demon's departure. If one prefers the cause of death anticipated in the Coptic fragment, the story would have told of Varianus executing the deserter.[168] Andrew then raised him back to life.

Neither *PCU 1* nor Gregory names the young soldier, but he seems to be none other than Ares, the god of war, who characteristically appears in the visual arts with full armor. The exorcism takes place in Macedonia, where the author of the *Acts* placed his transvaluative stories about the residents of Macedonian Olympus. Ares is not only the Greek god most closely associated with warfare but also a half-brother to Helen, which would conform with the familial arrangement between the young man and the counter-Helen in *PCU 1*. More significantly, Ares is repeatedly associated with madness, the madness of war.

Ares' mania appears in *Odyssey* 11.537 and *Iliad* 5.717 and 830–31. Athena addressed "furious Ares" thus: "Thou madman, distraught of wit, thou art beside thyself! Verily it is for naught that thou hast ears for hearing, and thine understanding and sense of right are gone from thee."[169] Hera too called Ares "crazed."[170] An allegorical scholion on *Iliad* 20.67 (attributed to Theagenes of Rhegium) took Homeric references to Ares as a cipher for irrationality. The apologist Athenagoras objected to *Iliad* 15.605 and 5.31: "'He [Hector] raged (μαίνετο) as when Ares with his spear'—be silent, Homer, a god does not rage (μαίνεται)! Yet you tell me of a god who is bloodthirsty and a bane of men— 'Ares, Ares, bane of men, bloodthirsty one.'"[171] *The Acts of Andrew* apparently has transformed Helen into a virgin and her brother Ares into a military martyr. Like Hera and Athena at the end of *Iliad* Book 5, the author "made Ares, the bane of mortals, to cease from man-slaying."[172] In Andrew's *Acts*, the counter-Ares discards his weapons when he recognizes the power of God: "There is no sword in his hand nor any instrument of war, and yet these great acts of power issue from his hand."

Andrew and the Beasts (Heracles, GE 18c)

When Andrew raised the disarmed soldier from the dead, Varianus

> sent wild beasts into the stadium and ordered the blessed apostle dragged and flung into it. They seized him, dragged him by the hair, beat him with clubs, threw him into the arena, and dispatched a ferocious, horrible boar. The boar circled God's saint three times and did him no harm. When the crowd saw this, they gave glory to God.

> The proconsul again gave orders, this time that a bull be released, led in by thirty soldiers and provoked by two beast-fighting gladiators [a Greek fragment reads: "chief-hunters"]. It did not touch Andrew, but wantonly dismembered the gladiators, gave a roar, and fell dead. Immediately the people shouted: "Christ is the true God!"[173]

This story and the next transvalue the Heracles saga. Among the famous Labors of Heracles are his encounters with the Erymanthian boar and the Cretan bull. Heracles conquered them with physical might, Andrew by divine power.[174]

Like Heracles, Andrew also encountered a wild cat: "Seething with rage, the proconsul at last ordered a fierce leopard sent in. When dispatched, the leopard ignored the people,[175] leaped onto the proconsul's throne, seized his son, and strangled him. The proconsul was so overtaken by insanity that he felt no pain and said nothing whatever about these events." This leopard is a stand-in for the Nemean lion; Varianus's son probably is Zeus's son, a hypertextual Heracles. This identification allows one to explain the curious behavior of the cat, who strangled his prey (*suffocavit eum*). One might have expected the leopard to have clawed him to death, or bitten his throat, or mangled his limbs, or carried out some other disgusting but normal leopardly act. Leopards do not choke.

The reader is to see here feline revenge on Heracles' strangling of the Nemean lion. This beast, invincible to iron, bronze, or stone, could only be subdued by hand-to-claw combat. Heracles therefore trapped it, "and putting his arm around its neck held it tight till he had choked it (ἔπνιξε)."[176] Another version reads: "and winding his arms about its neck choked it (ἀπέπνιξε)."[177] Ancient artists graced many a vase with Heracles strangling the lion.

In *The Acts of Andrew* the apostle accomplished three Herculean feats by divine power alone: overcoming the violence of a ferocious boar, bull, and wild cat. The Thessalonian leopard paid Heracles back for having choked the Nemean lion, but Andrew raised the lad back to life: "For a long time he prayed, stretched out on the ground, then, taking the corpse's hand, he awakened him. When the people saw this they magnified God and would have killed Varianus, but the apostle would not allow it. Varianus left befuddled for his praetorium." The next chapter in GE transvalues yet another of the Labors of Heracles, his slaying of the dragon guarding the golden apples of the Hesperides.

The Snake at the Oak (The Dragon at the Golden Tree, GE 19)

GE 19 begins:

> After this, a young man who already had been with the apostle told his mother what had happened and brought her to meet the saint. When she came, she fell at his feet and asked to hear the word of God. Her request granted, she asked him to come to her farm, where a snake of astonishing size was devastating the entire region.

Gregory names neither the young apostolic companion nor his mother, but one can deduce their identities from the unusual allusion to the woman's garden, which Gregory here calls an *ager*, 'field', and later a *praedium*, 'farm'. Greek mythology knows of only one garden owned by a woman and vexed by a viper. For Hera's wedding gift, Gaia (Mother Earth) gave her a tree that bore golden apples. The newlywed planted it in her own garden and entrusted it to the Hesperides. When Hera discovered that these daughters of Atlas had pilfered its precious fruit, she placed Ladon, the sleepless dragon, in the garden to protect it. The eleventh Labor of Heracles sent him off to steal these golden apples from Ladon. According to one version of the myth (Apollonius Rhodius's), Heracles slew the dragon with arrows poisoned by the gall of the hydra: "[the serpent] lay fallen by the trunk of the apple-tree; only the tip of his tail was still writhing; but from his head down his dark spine he lay lifeless; and where the arrows had left in his blood the bitter gall of the Lernaean hydra, flies withered and died over the festering wounds."[178] It therefore would appear that the land-owning woman is another hypertextual Hera.[179] Andrew takes on the role of the dragon-slaying Heracles, smiting the snake with a rebuke instead of an arrow or a club:

> As the apostle approached, the serpent hissed loudly, raised its head, and advanced to meet him. It was fifty cubits long, and everyone there was gripped by terror and fell to the earth.

> "Murderer!" said God's saint. "Hide the head you raised at the beginning for the destruction of humankind! Submit yourself to the servants of God and die!"[180]

> The snake immediately gave a deep roar, slithered around a mighty oak nearby, tied itself around it, vomited a stream of venom and blood, and perished.

Gregory states that the tree was an oak. This detail may point to the serpent of Colchis, who guarded not golden apples but also the golden fleece nailed to a mighty oak. Heracles and the rest of the Argonauts set out on their famous voyage in quest of the fleece in order to satisfy the command of the wicked King Pelias. The best-known telling of the story, that in Apollonius Rhodius's *Argonautica*, retained Heracles as one of the Argonauts, but made him disembark long before the ship anchored at Colchis. In Apollonius, Medea the sorceress sedated the snake with magic. Jason and Medea

> came to the sacred grove, seeking the huge oak tree on which was hung the fleece. . . . [A]t that time did that monster roll his countless coils covered with dry scales. And as he writhed, the maiden came before his eyes, with sweet voice calling to her aid Sleep, highest of gods, to charm the monster. . . . And Aeson's son followed in fear, but the serpent, already charmed by her song, was relaxing the long ridge of his giant spine, and lengthening out his myriad coils . . . ; but still he raised aloft his grisly head, eager to enclose them both in his murderous jaws. But she with a newly cut spray of juniper, dipping and drawing untempered charms from her mystic brew, sprinkled his eyes, while she chanted her song; and all around the potent scent of the charm cast sleep; and on the very spot he let his jaw sink down; and far behind through the wood with its many trees were those countless coils stretched out.

> Thereupon Jason snatched the golden fleece from the oak.[181]

Some versions of the story place Heracles himself at the scene, as in the depiction of the hero on a fourth-century B.C.E. wine crater, where Heracles is ready to club a dragon coiled around an oak that is draped by the golden fleece.[182] Greeks familiar with the Heracles cycle should have recognized in *The Acts of Andrew* similarities between these serpents and the roaring, poisonous, bloody, serpentine foe of Andrew who dies knotted around an oak.

GE 19 continues:

> The holy apostle traveled to the woman's farm, where a young boy smitten by the snake lay dead. When Andrew saw his parents weeping he said to them, "Our God, who wants you to be saved, sent me here so that you might believe in him. Go now and see that your son's murderer is dead."

> "We will not grieve our son's death," they said, "if we see revenge on his enemy."

> When they departed, the apostle said to the proconsul's wife, "Go and revive the boy."

> Without hesitation, she went to the corpse and said, "Lad, in the name of my God Jesus Christ rise up unscathed." He arose at once.

> His parents returned jubilant at seeing the dead snake, and when they found their son alive they fell at the apostle's feet and gave thanks.

The proconsul's wife is, of course, Aristobula, hypertextual Hera. In the Heracles cycle, Hera consistently persecutes the hero because he was Zeus's bastard son by Alcmene, one of Hera's many mortal rivals. In *The Acts of Andrew*, however, the counter-Hera does not oppose the counter-Heracles but raises him back to life.[183] Jealous violence turns into compassionate healing.[184]

GE 18 and 19 transformed the Heracles saga into the Labors of Andrew against a boar, a bull, and a leopard that avenged the Nemean lion by strangling Varianus's son (≈ Heracles son of Zeus).[185] The gigantic serpent Ladon also seems to have gotten his revenge by slaying a Heraclean youth in a woman's garden, where a Christianized Hera (Aristobula) raised him back to life. *The Acts of Andrew* thus contributed to the controversies over Heracles in the early church.

The careers of Heracles and Christ display tantalizing parallels.[186] Both heroes had divine fathers (Zeus/God) and mortal mothers (Alcmene/Mary), whose actual husbands (Amphitryon/Joseph) were from royal stock and accepted the boys as their own sons. Villains (Hera/Herod) tried to slay the babies in their cradles (by serpents/by swords), but both were spared (by precocious strength/by precautious flight). Early in life both youths traveled to a desolate place to be tempted with a choice between easy vice and arduous virtue; both chose virtue.[187] The careers of both heroes consisted largely of extraordinary ordeals that they overcame through supernatural means. Having acceded to the wills of their divine fathers, both died violent deaths, the bodies of neither could be found, both became gods, both appeared to mortals after their deaths, and both ascended to heaven in a cloud. Just as Heracles had conquered wild beasts, including the hound Cerberus, whom he fetched from Hades, Jesus conquered demons and preached in hell.[188] Greek philosophical schools transformed Heracles the giant brute into a paragon of virtue because he had endured his trials stoically.[189] Indeed, some intellectuals considered him "the savior of the earth and of humankind."[190] So many additional details exist between the two heroes that one probably should relate both Heracles and Christ to a common 'heroicology'.[191]

Ancient pagans and Christians alike recognized the parallels between Heracles and Christ, but they assessed them differently. The pagan critic Celsus asked why Christians rejected the divination of Greek heroes like Heracles, but accepted identical claims about Jesus.[192] Justin Martyr turned the argument around: Why did pagans believe the divine conceptions, resurrections, and ascensions of their heroes but deny such claims about Jesus? "In saying that the Word, who is the first offspring of God, was born for us without sexual union, as Jesus Christ our Teacher, and that he was crucified and died and after rising again ascended into heaven we introduce nothing new beyond [what you say of] those whom you call sons of Zeus."[193] Justin had in mind Heracles along with Hermes, Asclepius, Dionysus, the Dioscuri, Perseus, and Bellerophon. The similarities between the heroes and Christ were due to diabolical imitations generated from a perverse reading of scripture: "And when they say that Heracles was strong and wandered about all over the earth, and was begotten by Zeus from Alcmene, and when he died ascended to heaven, should I not suppose that the scripture which speaks similarly of Christ has been imitated: 'strong like a giant to run his race'?"[194]

In their battle to elevate Christ over Heracles and other sons of Zeus, Christians focused on Heracles' notorious vices. Lactantius was representative:

> Hercules, who because of his strength is regarded as the most famous and as a sort of Africanus among the gods, has befouled with outrages, adulteries, and lusts (has he not?) the whole earth which he is said to have passed through and cleansed. This is not surprising, since he was born of the adultery of Alcmena. What traces of divine nature could there have been in one who, himself enslaved by his own vices, marred males and female alike with infamy,[195] corruption, and disregard of all laws? Certainly the deeds which he performed should not be judged great and marvelous, so that they would seem to be attributed to divine powers. . . .

> No one has denied the point that Hercules was a servant, not only of Eurystheus, a king, which many see honorable to a certain extent, but also to an unchaste women, Omphala, who used to bid him set at her feet, clothed in her garments, performing appointed tasks. . . .[196] Excited by rage and madness, this same figure slew his wife together with his children—and men think him a god![197]

In chapter 5 I will show how GE 27 objected to Heracles' pederastic affair with young Hylas and how GE 29 transvalued his slaying of wife and children. In chapter 6 I will tell how, in Passion 2–5, Andrew cured an ersatz-Heracles of his divinely inflicted madness. Here in GE 18 and 19, however, the author set his sights on four of Heracles' twelve Labors: the boar of Erymanthus, the bull of

Crete, the lion of Nemea, and the dragon of the Hesperides. Andrew overcomes these beasts by spiritual, not physical, strength. Indeed, two Heraclean characters, the son of Varianus and the lad on the farm, are slain by a leopard and a serpent but are raised by Andrew's revivifying power.

Andrew's Cross (Odysseus's Oar, GE 20)

According to GE 20,

> The following night the blessed apostle saw a vision which he narrated to the other brethren: "My good friends, listen to my dream. I saw a great mountain raised on high with nothing earthly on it, and it so radiated with light that it seemed to illumine the world. And there, standing with me, were my beloved brothers, the apostles Peter and John. Extending his hand to the apostle Peter, John raised him to the mountain's summit, turned, and asked me to ascend after Peter saying, 'Andrew, you will drink Peter's cup.'[198] With his hands outstretched he said, 'Come to me and stretch out your hands to join my hands, and let your head touch mine.' When I did so, I found myself shorter than John. 'Would you like to know,' he then asked, 'to what this symbol you see refers, or who it is who speaks with you?'
>
> "'I long to know these things,' I said.
>
> "'I am the word of the cross,' he said, 'on which you soon will hang for the name of the one you proclaim.' He also told me many other things about which I can say nothing now, but which will become apparent when I approach this sacrifice."

This story obviously owes a great deal to the transfiguration of Jesus,[199] but it also relies on Odysseus's speech to the Phaeacians about his visit with Tiresias in the netherworld, where the blind savant told him how he was to die:

> Take a well-shaped oar and go
> until you reach men who do not know the sea
> and who eat food that is not mixed with salt:
> they know neither of red-cheeked ships
> nor of well-shaped oars, which are wings of ships.
> I'll tell you a very clear sign (σῆμα), and you won't miss it:
> when you come across another man on the road
> who says that you have a chaff-wrecker on your shining shoulder,
> then plant (πήξας) the well-shaped oar in the earth
> and perform a fine sacrifice to lord Poseidon. . . .
> . . . .
> A very gentle death

will come to you away from the sea and slay you
in a comfortable old age. And the people around you
will be prosperous. This is the truth that I tell you.[200]

Behind this passage is a folktale told among sailors to this very day, according to which a sailor, weary of rowing and the dangers of the sea, carries an oar inland until someone mistakes it for a board or a farm implement. There the sailor plants his oar, or builds a house, or settles down to a life of ease, as in this English example:

> It is said that an English seaman once became so weary at heart from the dangerous uneasiness of his profession that when he returned to his home port he put an oar on his shoulder and wandered inland in search of people who did not know the wild sea. He went from place to place with his burden and lingered nowhere until he came to a village where they asked him what kind of strange implement he was carrying; there he settle down. The parable is found here and there in old sea stories, where shipwrecked persons narrate it to their companions as a consolation, and tormented and discouraged seafolk swear to one another to follow its example if they should ever touch foot again on English soil.[201]

Here is an American version: "'I'm gonna put this goddam oar over my shoulder,' a weary seine hauler snorts, 'and head west, and the first sonofabitch asks me what it is, that's where I stick it in the ground and settle.'"[202]
Greek sailors tell the same story of the prophet Elijah in order to explain why his shrines always sit atop mountains:

> St. Elias was once a seaman. On account of his endless rowing, the man got tired (rowing while eating, that's the way they had it in those days). He put his oar on his shoulder and left to go to find a place where they didn't even know the name of it.[203] He walks to the village, he asks, "What is this called?" "An oar," they say. He walks to another village, he asks, "What is this called?" "An oar." What the devil! He became desperate. Keeping on with his inquiry he finally asks at one village situated at the very top of the mountain, "What is this called?" "A piece of wood." Thank God! He sets the oar straight up, builds a hut, and resolves to remain there for the rest of his life. For this reason they always put St. Elias on mountaintops.[204]

Another version of the tale even brings in the apostles:

> "Ah well," says Giorgis, "tis a poor trade this, as the holy Elias found." "What was that?" I asked. "The prophet Elias," quoth he, "was a fisherman; he had bad weather, terrific storms, so that he became afraid of the sea. Well, so he left his nets and his boat on the shore, and put an oar over his shoulder, and took to the hills. On the way, who[m] should he see but a man. "A good hour to you," says he. "Welcome," says the man. "What's this, can you tell

me?" says St. Elias. "That?" says the man. "Why that's an oar." Eh, on he goes till me meets another man. "A good hour to you," says St. Elias. "You are welcome," says the man. "What's this?" says St. Elias. "Why, that's an oar, to be sure," says the man. On he goes again, until he comes to the very top of the mountain, and there he sees another man. "Can you tell me what this is?" asks St. Elias. "That?" says the man. "Why that's a stick." "Good!" says St. Elias. "This is the place for me, here I abide." He plants the oar in the ground, and that is why his chapels are all built on the hill tops." "Well, well, I didn't know the prophet Elias followed the sea; of course the holy apostles did, we all know that." "Aye, and so they did. You know why they left it, sire, don't you?" "Why?" "Well, you see, Christ and the Apostles went a-fishing. The Apostles fished all day, and caught nothing. Christ took the nets, and turned them upside down, so that the corks sank and the lead floated; and they caught a great haul—a masterpiece! (ἀριστούργημα). At this the Apostles were frightened. What! said they, we are fishers, and understand that craft, and we catch nothing; Christ knows nothing about it, yet he catches a great haul ᴡith the nets upside down. We will have no more to do with this uncanny trade; so they left their nets and boats, and ceased to be fishers."[205]

The point of these tales of the planted oar is to contrast the dangers and hardships of the sea or the caprices of fishing with the safety and comforts of terra firma.

Homer apparently knew this same tradition. At the beginning of the *nekyia*, the soul of Elpenor asks Odysseus to return to Circe's island to bury his body under a planted oar: "[B]urn me with my armour, all that is mine, and heap up a mound for me on the shore of the grey sea, in memory (σῆμα, lit. 'a sign') of an unhappy man, that men yet to be may learn of me. Fulfil this my prayer, and fix upon the mound my oar wherewith I rowed in life when I was among my comrades."[206] As soon as Odysseus returned to Aeaea, at the edge of the sea, he burned Elpenor's corpse. "But when the dead man was burned, and the armour of the dead, we heaped up a mound and dragged on to it a pillar, and on the top of the mound we planted his shapely oar."[207]

In the case of Odysseus's own death, Homer adapted the folktale to conform with the epic at large. In the first place, Homer does not narrate Odysseus's actual planting of the oar or his death, so the tale appears only as Tiresias's prophecy, which the hero narrated to the Phaeacians and later to Penelope.[208] Furthermore, Odysseus's home was little sea-bound Ithaca, where everyone knew what an oar was. Instead of having Odysseus settle far from the sea, Homer sent him far inland to placate the sea-god Poseidon, whose son, Polyphemus, Odysseus had blinded. Once propitiated, Poseidon would let Odysseus die in peace.[209]

In order to understand the relationship of this episode to *The Acts of Andrew* one must jump ahead to the Passion, where the apostle preaches on his way to the edge of the sea, where he will die. He ends his speech with these words: "This is the end of my speech, for I think that while we were speaking, we arrived at the designated place. The planted cross (πεπηγὼς σταυρός) is a sign (σημεῖον) to me designating the spot" (Passion 53). Odysseus would know where to plant his oar because of the sign (σῆμα) of the ignorant landlubber. The "planted cross" itself serves Andrew as a sign (σημεῖον), presumably because on the radiant mountain John had told him about it in GE 20: "He also told me many other things . . . which will become apparent when I approach this sacrifice." The participle πεπηγώς, 'planted', comes from the same Greek verb Tiresias used when he commanded Odysseus to plant (πήξας) his oar. These correspondences can hardly be accidental.

In light of the tradition of the planted oar one might expect Andrew's seaside cross to represent relief from the dangers and weariness of life. This is precisely Andrew's own interpretation in his address to the cross:

> He left everyone, approached the cross, and spoke to it out loud: "Greetings, O cross! Greetings indeed! I know well that, though you have been weary (κεκμηκότα) for a long time, you too at last are at rest (ἀναπαυόμενον), planted (πεπηγμένον) and awaiting me. I come to you, whom I have comprehended. I recognize your secret (μυστήριον) for which you were planted (πέπηγας). So then . . . receive me, I who have been weary (κεκμηκότα) for so long." (Passion 54)

Andrew recognized the secret or mystery of the cross from its having been "planted" in the earth to symbolize its rest from labor. It had retired from the galley. In order to help the reader recognize the secret too, the author provided three instances of the verb πήγνυμι (πεπηγώς, πεπηγμένον, πέπηγας; cf. *Odyssey* 11.129: πήξας).

Nowhere else in early Christian literature does one find an exhausted cross; exhaustion better befits an oar. The weariness of rowing was proverbial in the ancient world, and often was expressed with cognates of the word used of the cross in *The Acts of Andrew*: κάμνειν, 'to weary'. For example, Odysseus collapses in weariness (κεκμηῶτα) after rowing for ten days.[210] Likewise *The Iliad* speaks of sailors who "have grown weary (κάμωσιν) of beating the sea with polished oars of fir, and with weariness (καμάτῳ) are their limbs fordone."[211] The weariness of the cross for such a long time (ἐκ πολλοῦ κεκμηκότα) represents the apostle's own weariness at the end of life's long voyage (τὸν πολλὰ κεκμηκότα). Both of them will rest at last. According to Andrew's Passion, the cross is also Andrew's mast for speeding him effortlessly homeward to heaven on his true *nostos*. This imagery befits Andrew, the old fisherman who had left his boat and nets to angle for *anthropoi*.[212]

It would therefore seem reasonable to assume that among the "many other things" that John told Andrew on the mountain in GE 20 was the meaning of the planted cross at the edge of the sea. It symbolized the weariness of life and the rest that death offers. One also might identify other possible points of contact between Andrew's vision and Odysseus's visit with Tiresias. Both heroes tell of their encounters with the dead in the first person singular. Odysseus claimed that he traveled to the dark land of the Cimmerians, "wrapped in mist and cloud. Never does the sun look down on them with his rays."[213] Andrew, on the other hand, ascended a brilliantly luminous mountain. Odysseus called forth the dead, including his own mother; Andrew met his deceased "beloved brothers, the apostles Peter and John." After Odysseus's speech, the Phaeacians were silent and spellbound.[214] "When the brethren heard these things [from Andrew], they wept effusively, slapped their faces, and shrieked."

Those who heard the speeches of Odysseus and Andrew prophesying their deaths then sent them on their way. In both cases the hero plans to leave and prays for his hosts' safety, the audience responds favorably, ritual offerings are made, and the heroes depart for Achaea.

Odyssey 13	GE 20
"**Lord Alcinous**, renowned above all men, pour libations now, and **send ye me on my way** in peace (lit. 'unscathed'); and yourselves too—Farewell! For now all that my heart desired has been brought to pass: a convoy, and gifts of friendship.	"**Dear friends,** you should know that **I will be leaving you,** but I trust in Jesus, whose word I preach, that he will **keep you from evil. . . ."**
	After this, his hand outstretched, he prayed to the Lord:
May the gods of heaven bless them to me, and on my return may I find in my home my peerless wife with those I love **unscathed;** and may you again, remaining here, make glad your wedded wives and children; and may the gods grant you prosperity of every sort, and **may no evil come upon your people."** So he spoke, **and they all praised his words,** and bade send the stranger on his way, **since he had spoken fittingly.** (41–48)	"**O Lord,** please guard this flock which already knows your salvation, **so that the wicked one will not prevail,** and that it may be entitled to guard forever **unharmed** what it received at your command and by my guidance."
	When he had said this, all present responded, "Amen!"
So he spoke, and Pontonous **mixed the honey-hearted wine and served out to all**, coming up to each in turn; and they poured libations to the blessed **gods.** (53–55)	He took bread, gave thanks, broke it, **and gave it to all**, saying, "Receive the grace which Christ the Lord our **God** gives your through me his servant."
So the goodly Odysseus spake and passed over the threshold. And with him the mighty Alcinous sent	And when he had kissed everyone and commended them to the Lord,

forth a herald to **lead him to the swift ship and the shore of the sea**. (63–65)	**he went on to Thessalonica.**

Odysseus sailed off "to his own native land (ἐς πατρίδα γαῖαν)."[215] Andrew returned to Thessalonica for two days and then sailed to Patras (Πάτραι), a short channel hop from Ithaca. The parallels between GE and Odysseus's voyage back to Ithaca continue into chapter 21.

Anthimus (Orpheus, GE 21)

According to GE 21,

> Many of the faithful from Macedonia went with him in two boats. All sought to board the boat carrying the apostle, longing to hear him talk, so that not even while sailing would they be without the word of God. The apostle said to them, "I know your desire, beloved, but this boat is small. Therefore, let the young men and baggage board the larger ship, and you travel with us in this smaller one." He gave them Anthimus to soothe them, and commanded them to board the other boat, which he ordered always to be nearby so that they too might see him and hear the word of God. While he napped . . .

Several unusual details in this text cry out for explanation. In the first place, this is the only place in the *Acts* where Andrew sails with a large retinue, so large that they must travel in two boats. Second, the apostle takes the smaller of the two boats and puts "the young men and the baggage" in the larger. One would have expected him to have taken the larger ship, which could have accommodated more auditors. Third, Anthimus appears in the story entirely unannounced. Fourth, Andrew ordered the larger ship to stay nearby so the young men, too, could hear him preach, but immediately he takes a nap.

These peculiarities once again point to dependence on Greek mythology. The Phaeacians sent Odysseus home in one of their own ships, manned by their own young men. No sooner had the oars cut the sea than "sweet sleep fell upon his eyelids, an unwaking sleep, most sweet, and most like unto death."[216] He slept so soundly that he was oblivious when the Phaeacians deposited him at the Ithacan shore.[217] Such an identification explains why the apostle travels with a large entourage and falls asleep on his way to Patras.

The larger of the vessels, the one containing the young men and the baggage, probably is the most famous of all ancient ships, the *Argo*, which boasted fifty-four oars and was the first vessel fit to sail the open seas. The young men, then, would be the Argonauts. Anthimus, whom Andrew put on board "to soothe (*consolaret*) them," is Orpheus. The name Anthimus derives from the root ανθ-, which denotes flowers (as in anthology, 'a gathering of flowers'). Compounds with ανθ- often appear in Orphic contexts. According to Clement of Alexandria,

Orphics used the word ἄνθιον, 'flowery', to designate spring and the return of Dionysus.[218]   Dionysus himself was named Anthius.[219]   The Anthesteria designated the great three-day Athenian festival for the god of wine held every spring during the month Anthesterion. The name Anthimus (Ἄνθιμος) also might have evoked the image of a clean-shaven, even effeminate youth (ἄνθος means 'youthful bloom'), which is how ancient artists usually depicted Orpheus. Apt translations of the name might be Narcissus, Rosebud, or Mr. Tulips.   I prefer Blossoms.

Orpheus was an unlikely Argonaut. Some ancient interpreters denied that such a wimp as Orpheus could have sailed with virile heroes such as Heracles.[220] According to the most famous and influential telling of the Argo tale, *The Argonautica* by Apollonius Rhodius, Orpheus's primary function was to soothe heroic emotions at sea: "Orpheus lifted his lyre in his left hand and made essay to sing."[221] He sang primordial myths, and then he "stayed his lyre and divine voice. But though he had ceased they still bent forward with eagerness all hushed to quiet, with ears intent on the enchanting strain; such a charm of song had he left behind in their hearts."[222]   When the Argonauts sped past the Sirens they avoided shipwreck not by stuffing their ears with wax but by stuffing them with Orpheus's beguiling melodies:

> And they were already about to cast from the ship the hawsers to the shore [of the Sirens' island], had not Thracian Orpheus, son of Oeagrus, stringing in his hands his Bistonian lyre, rung forth the hasty snatch of a rippling melody so that their ears might be filled with the sound of his twanging; and the lyre overcame the maidens' voice.[223]

Orpheus's enchantment worked on all but Butes, who leapt into the sea and swam to the island, "his soul melted by the clear ringing voice of the Sirens." Aphrodite came to his rescue by fishing him out of the brine and taking him off to be her lover.[224]

> Like Orpheus, Anthimus, too, failed to keep all his passengers out of the drink.

> While he [Andrew] napped, someone [a youth in the larger boat] was jarred by a moderate wind and fell into the sea. Anthimus wakened him saying, "Good teacher, help! One of your servants perishes!"

> The apostle awoke and rebuked the wind. It was silent and the sea once again became calm. The person who had fallen in was carried to the ship with the help of the waves. Anthimus took his hand, lifted him on board, and all were amazed at the power of the apostle, for even the sea obeyed him. After twelve days, they landed at Patras, a city in Achaea, left the ship, and stayed at some inn.[225]

Whereas Aphrodite rescued Butes from Sirens only to take him away as her pet, Andrew's God restored the lad to his ship.[226]   Another tradition claimed that

Orpheus assisted the Argonauts by calming the sea with his singing,[227] the very feat Andrew accomplished with his rebuke.

Scholars long have debated the significance of Orpheus's surprising appearance in early Christian wall decorations. The Thracian poet characteristically sits in a bucolic setting, wearing a Phrygian cap, playing a lyre, and surrounded by docile wild animals. The scene calls to mind David the shepherd boy or Christ the good shepherd, except for the wild animals. These Christian Orpheuses seem to be metaphors for Christ, whose song brings harmony and peace to the universe.[228] Clement of Alexandria denounced "Thracian Orpheus" who "outraged human life, being influenced by demons,"[229] but he also saw in Orpheus an analogy to Christ, who tamed the most violent beast of all, the human, and whose song "tuned into concert the discord of the elements, that the whole universe might be in harmony with it."[230] Eusebius concurred:

> [T]he Greek tale relates that Orpheus charmed all sorts of wild beasts and tamed the wrath of savages with his singing. . . . So in this way the all-wise Logos of God that makes everything harmonious, providing all sorts of remedies for the manifold evils to which the souls of mankind were subjected, took in hand a musical instrument, the product of His own skill, man. On this He began to play songs, not for wild beasts but for rational animals, healing with the remedies of divine instruction every violent habit and wild and savage passion of the soul, of Greek or barbarian.[231]

Of all Greek mythological characters Orpheus/Anthimus was the best suited to soothe sailors at sea as Andrew sailed back to Achaea.[232]

Gregory abruptly introduced Anthimus here in chapter 21 without having prepared the reader for his appearance. In the original *Acts*, Anthimus may have appeared earlier, when Andrew sailed from Thrace, Orpheus's exotic and savage *patria*. While the ship sailed for Macedonia, the apostle converted "a sailor and all who were with him" (GE 10). This sailor and crew might have represented Jason and the Argonauts, including Orpheus, presumably the same group of "young men" now manning the large ship sailing from Macedonia to Patras.

Conclusion

This chapter analyzed GE 2–21 and parallels, Andrew's return trip or *nostos* from Myrmidonia to Achaea. The first three tales, which took place in Amasia, concerned characters that Odysseus saw in the netherworld. The apostle restored sight to the blind clairvoyant (≈ Tiresias, GE 2), raised Demetrius's "Egyptian boy" back to life (≈ Achilles' lover, Patroclus, GE 3), and rescued Sostratus (≈ Oedipus) from his incestuous mother (≈ Jocasta, GE 4). In Sinope, at the home of Gratinus (≈ Nestor of Gerenius), he exorcised a lad whom a demon had attacked in a woman's bath (≈ Telemachus bathed by Polycaste, GE 5). He rid Nicea of its plague of demons by turning them into dogs, who later, in

Nicomedia, savaged a youth (≈ Actaeon) until he died; Andrew raised him back to life (GE 6–7). On his way from Asia Minor to Macedonia, Andrew endured a storm, escaped Thracian pirates, and converted a shipful of sailors (≈ the Argonauts, GE 8–10).

GE 11–20 took place in Macedonia, the region of Macedonian Olympus, the home of the gods. Andrew first broke up a double wedding at Philippi (cf. the double wedding at Menelaus's Spartan palace, GE 11), rescued Exochus from his angry relatives (≈ Melampus, GE 12), and in Thessalonica raised back to life two dead youths—Carpianus's son, Adimantus (≈ Zeus's son, Sarpedon, GE 13) and an unnamed strangled demoniac (≈ Hector, GE 14). The apostle then healed lame Philomedes (Hephaestus) when his father Medias (≈ Zeus) agreed to release two young people shackled in his home (≈ Ares and Aphrodite, GE 15). Then Andrew healed the daughter of Nicolaus (≈ Hermione of Menelaus, GE 16), exorcised a clairvoyant demoniac (≈ Apollo, GE 17), and converted Aristobula (≈ Hera) so that she no longer would sleep with her lustful husband, the proconsul Varianus (≈ Zeus, GE 18a). A young soldier sent to arrest Andrew was possessed of a demon, who told the apostle of a magician (≈ Simon Magus) who had tried in vain to seduce a Christian virgin whom he had seen on a roof (≈ Helen, *PCU 1*). When exorcised, the soldier (≈ Ares) abandoned his weapons and uniform. Varianus executed him, but Andrew restored him to life (GE 18b). Varianus then threw Andrew into an arena to fight a boar, a bull, and a leopard. Unlike Heracles, who defeated such animals with his strength, Andrew did so by divine power. The leopard avoided the apostle, but strangled Varianus's son (≈ Heracles), making amends for the Nemean lion (GE 18c). Andrew then went to a woman's farm (≈ Hera's garden) where a dragon (≈ Ladon, the serpent guarding the apples of the Hesperides) bedeviled the area. Like Heracles but without a club, the apostle slew the serpent; it then coiled around the oak, like the dragon that guarded the golden fleece (GE 19). Andrew then received a vision warning him that he would be crucified, like his brother Peter. The apostle told him secrets about his death, which were to become known when Andrew "approached" his sacrifice (GE 20). In the Passion, Andrew "approaches" his cross and greets it as though it were his oar, planted, waiting for the old, weary sailor of Christ. Behind this imagery is the prophecy of Tiresias that Odysseus would at last find rest from the sea if he would plant his oar into the ground so far inland that the locals would mistake it for a winnowing shovel. In GE 21 Andrew finally sails from Macedonia for Patras, and falls asleep in the smaller of the two ships, like Odysseus sailing back to Ithaca with the Phaeacians. The young men and the baggage travel in the larger of the two ships (≈ the Argo), and Andrew gives them Anthimus (≈ Orpheus) to console them. One of the crew falls into the sea (≈ Butes), but Andrew commands the sea to return him to the ship, and the lad is spared.

Insofar as this section of *The Acts of Andrew* survives almost exclusively in Gregory's brutalized epitome, some of the above identifications are tenuous, especially where Gregory has failed to record the names of the characters or left out other hypertextual details. Even so, the general pattern is clear: every episode calls to mind a Greek myth, often from Homeric epic. The same pattern holds for GE 22–33, Andrew's ministry back in Achaea.

Notes

1. It is not clear why the author selected Amasia to represent the netherworld. Perhaps he saw in its location far inland on the river Iris resonance with a tradition that placed one entrance to Hades at rivers along the north shore of Anatolia. See Xenophon *Anabasis* 6.2.2 and Apollonius *Argonautica* 2.726–51. I suspect rather a wordplay between Ἀμασία and ἀμαθία, 'ignorance'. In Homer's netherworld, only Tiresias retained intelligence (*Odyssey* 10.490–95).

2. E.g., Pausanius 9.30.9.3, Strabo *Geography* 7, frags. 14 and 15 ("Olympus belongs to Macedonia") and 13.1.53, scholion to *Iliad* 14.226, and frequently in Eustathius's commentaries.

3. *Odyssey* 10.490–95 and the scholia, including Eustathius *Ad Homeri Odysseam* 1665 (on 10.492). See especially Apollodorus *Library* 3.6.7 (and Frazer's superb notes in the Loeb edition), Hesiod *Melampodia* 2–3, Lucian *Dialogues of the Dead* 9 (445–47), Ovid *Metamorphoses* 3.316–38, and Hyginus *Fabulae* 75. Other ancients claimed that Athena blinded Tiresias for peeping at her as she bathed (Callimachus *The Bathing of Pallas*).

4. E.g., Aeschylus *Seven Against Thebes*, Sophocles *Antigone*, Euripides *Bacchae* and *Phoenician Women*.

5. *Odyssey* 10.490–95. In his denunciation of the *nekyia*, Plato took issue with Homer's claim that after death only Tiresias retained his intellect (*Republic* 3.386d).

6. Cf. Porphyry *On the Styx* (*apud* Stobaeus 1.424.7–24 [Wachsmuth and Hense]).

7. *Protrepticus* 12.119.3.

8. Ibid., 4.49.1–3.

9. *Contra gentes* 9. See also Justin Martyr *First Apology* 29, Athenagoras *Legatio* 30.2, Hegesippus (*apud* Eusebius *Historia ecclesiastica* 4.8), Tertullian *Adversus Marcionem* 1.18.4, Tatian *Oratio ad graecos* 10.2, *Sibylline Oracles* 8.57, and Prudentius *Contra orationem Symmachi* 1.271–77. The pagan author Celsus argued that the honor Christians gave to Jesus was "no different from that paid to Hadrian's favorite" (*Contra Celsum* 3.36 [Chadwick]).

10. Homer identifies Patroclus as Achilles' slave in *Iliad* 23.89; cf. Lucian *Parasite* 47.

11. *Odyssey* 11.485 and 491.

12. In Homeric allegories, Demeter often stands for chthonic powers. See Pépin, *Mythe et allégorie*, 565.

13. *Iliad* 18.22–27. See also 18.70–77, 235, and 316–23, 19.4–6, 23.58–61, 136–37,

and 222–25, and 24.3–12 and 122–30.

14. Plato's Socrates took Achilles' grief to be entirely unacceptable of a hero, for it would never inspire the courage needed for good warriors:

> we shall request Homer and the other poets not to portray Achilles, the son of a goddess, as
>
> > Lying now on his side, and then again on his back,
> > Again on his face [*Iliad* 24.10–12],
>
> and then rising up and
>
> > Drifting distraught on the shore of the vast unharvested ocean [*Iliad* 24.12],
> > nor as clutching with both hands the sooty dust and strewing it over his head [*Iliad* 18.23–24], nor as weeping and lamenting in the measure and manner attributed to him by the poet. (*Republic* 3.388a–b)

15. *Odyssey* 11.465–70.

16. Ibid., 24.73–77. See also *Iliad* 23.83–84, where the ghost of Patroclus says: "Lay not my bones apart from thine, Achilles, but let them lie together."

17. Sophocles *Philoctetes* 434, Hyginus *Fabulae* 257, Ovid *Tristia* 5.4.25, and Lucian *Toxaris, or Friendship* 10.

18. Plato *Symposium* 179e–180a. See also Chariton *Chaereas and Callirhoe* 1.5 and Lucian *Amores* 54 and *True Story* 2.19.

19. In *The Iliad* the body of Patroclus was not raised back to life, but it was protected from decay thanks to the goddess Thetis, Achilles' mother, who placed ambrosia and nectar in his nostrils (19.37–39).

20. Theophilus *Ad Autolycum* 3.6, Justin Martyr *First Apology* 5, 21, and 25, *Second Apology* 12, Tatian *Oratio ad graecos* 8, 10, and 34, *Ps.-Clementine Recognitions* 10.28, 38, and 42, Clement of Alexandria *Protrepticus* 2.31, 33, and 4.43, Ps.-Justin *Cohortatio ad gentiles* 2, and Prudentius *Contra orationem Symmachi* 1.59–71.

21. Gen. 39:6b–20.

22. E.g., *Iliad* 6.155–97.

23. E.g., Apollodorus *Epitome* 1.18–19. Similar tales appear in Apuleius *Metamorphoses* 10.2–12, Xenophon of Ephesus *Ephesiaca* 3.5–6 and 12, and Heliodorus *Aethiopica* 1.9–18.

24. The story was already traditional and popular prior to Homer. See Sophocles *Oedipus the King* and *Oedipus at Colonus*, Apollodorus *Library* 3.5.7, Seneca *Oedipus*, Euripides *The Phoenician Women*, Hyginus *Fabulae* 66 and 67, and a myriad of allusions.

25. Although the text does not explicitly say she is a widow, the same story retold in *The Acts of John by Prochorus* does (Zahn, 135–50). Her widowhood would explain both her motivation (no sexual partner) and opportunity (no one else in the house).

26. *Odyssey* 11.271–80.

27. Cicero *Pro Sex. Roscio Amerino* 25, Quintilian *Institutio oratoria* 7.8.6, Juvenal *Satire* 8.214, and Seneca *De clementia* 1.15.

28. Cicero *Epistula ad Q. Fratrem* 1.2.2.

29. Apuleius tells a story remarkably similar to GE 4. A wicked stepmother tries to bed her unwilling stepson and then denounces him before the authorities for incest. Here, too, the lad is punished by *culleum* (*Metamorphoses* 10.2–12, esp. 8).

30. *Legatio* 3.1.

31. Ibid., 32.1 (Schoedel); cf. 34.2.

32. Ibid., 34.3 (Schoedel).

33. *First Apology* 26–27.

34. Ps.-Justin *Ad graecos* 3.

35. *Apud* Eusebius *Historia ecclesiastica* 5.1.14.

36. *Octavius* 31, probably referring to Sophocles' *Oedipus the King* and *Oedipus at Colonus*.

37. *Iliad* 2.335 and 601, 4.317, 7.170 and 181, 8.112 and 151, 9.162 and 179, 10.102, 128, 138, 143, 157, 168, 203, and 543, 11.516 and 655, and 14.42 (cf. 7.78–125, 8.105–15, 132, and 156–57, 9.52, 10.543–54, 11.511–20, 680–81 and 720, and 23.301–48), *Odyssey* 3.102, 210, 253, 386, 397, 405, 417, and 474 and 4.161.

38. *Odyssey* 3.436 and 444.

39. Prieur, *Acta Andreae*, 578, n. 2.

40. It is also possible that Gratinus plays on another favorite Homeric predicate for Nestor: γέρων (genitive: γέροντος), 'old man'.

41. *Odyssey* 3.475–78 and 481–85. Earlier Athena had told Nestor: "[B]ut do thou send this man on his way with a chariot and with thy son, since he has come to thy house, and give him horses, the fleetest thou hast in running and the best in strength" (3.368–70; cf. 324–26). For Nestor as a horseman see also Tatian *Oratio ad graecos* 32.

42. *Odyssey* 24.366.

43. Ibid., 4.48–49 and 17.87–88.

44. Ibid., 6.221–22.

45. Ibid., 4.252, 5.264, 6.216, 7.296, 8.449–454, 10.361–64, and 19.320.

46. Ibid., 3.464–68. Apuleius may have had Telemachus and Polycaste in mind when writing of Lucius's affair with Photis (*Metamorphoses* 1.23–24).

47. Scholion on *Odyssey* 3.464.

48. Scholion on *Odyssey* 6.215. Helen says she bathed Odysseus in 4.252.

49. Scholion on *Odyssey* 6.221.

50. Scholion on *Odyssey* 3.464.

51. Scholion on *Odyssey* 3.467. See also Eustathius *Ad Homeri Odysseam* 1477 and 1796 and Stanford, *Ulysses Theme*, 120.

52. *Catalogues of Women and Eoiae* 12. See also the scholia on *Odyssey* 16.118.

53. *Palatine Anthology* 14.102.

54. According to GE, their maladies resulted from Gratinus's seeking out a prostitute and his wife's extramarital affairs, but these causes seem to be Gregory's creation. *The Acts of Andrew* is rigorously ascetic; marital sex itself was sin. Not so for Gregory, who consistently altered the requirement of celibacy in his source into denunciations of incest, prostitution, or adultery (e.g., GE 11 and 18). In the original *Acts*, then, Gratinus and his

wife might have been punished merely for their shared bed. If so, one might suspect that the author took offense at *Odyssey* 3.402–3: "[Nestor] himself slept in the inmost chamber of the lofty house, and beside him lay the lady his wife, who had strewn the couch."

55. *Odyssey* 3.479–80: "And the housewife placed in the car bread and wine and dainties [for Telemachus], such as kings, fostered of Zeus, are wont to eat"; cf. 3.346–50 and 387–89.

56. *Iliad* 20.232–35.

57. E.g., *Homeric Hymn* 5 [*To Aphrodite*] (Ganymedes was carried off "because of his beauty [διὰ κάλλος]"), Apollodorus *Library* 3.12.2, Lucian *Dialogues of the Gods* 10 (4), Philo *On Providence* (*apud* Eusebius *Praeparatio evangelica* 8.14), and Oenomaus (*apud* Eusebius *Praeparatio evangelica* 5.34); cf. Ps.-Lucian *Carmidemus* 7.5.

58. Hyginus *Fabulae* 271.

59. E.g., Justin Martyr *First Apology* 21 and 25, Ps.-Justin *Ad graecos* 2, Aristides *Apology* 9, Tatian *Oratio ad graecos* 10, Clement of Alexandria *Protrepticus* 2.33.5 and 4.49.1 and *Stromateis* 1.21.137.1, *Ps.-Clementine Homilies* 4.16 and 5.15 and 17, Minucius Felix *Octavius* 24, Eusebius *De laudibus Constantini* 7.4.8, and Athanasius *Contra gentes* 11.

60. A ninth-century Byzantine monk named Epiphanius wrote a life of Andrew in which he mentioned a character named Callistus, not in Nicea but in nearby Chalcedon who "was smitten by a demon and died. Andrew raised him up by prayer and publicly exposed the artifices of the ruler of demons" (E 240C [= *L* 22]). It is extremely difficult to correlate Epiphanius's account with Gregory's, but if the two Callistuses are the same character, one might imagine that the demon who smote him was a hypertextual Zeus, "the ruler of the demons." Given the tawdry condition of the textual witnesses, all one ought to say is that Callistus seems to be a counter-Ganymedes.

61. Actaeon was a favorite topic not just of mythographers but of artists as well. Many Greek vases depict him being torn apart by four to seven dogs. Other objects present his mother, Autonoe, holding his body and grieving. See "Actaeon" and "Autonoe" in *LIMC*. See also Lucian *Dialogues of the Gods* 18 (245).

A particularly informative parallel to GE 7 appears in the use of the Actaeon myth in Apuleius's *Metamorphoses*, where the protagonist, a picaresque Odysseus, admires a statue of Artemis flanked by dogs, "their eyes threatened, their ears stiffened, their nostrils flared, and their mouths opened savagely" (2.4). Behind the image of Artemis, "the image of Actaeon could be seen, both in stone and in the spring's reflection, leaning towards the goddess with an inquisitive stare, in the very act of changing into a stag and waiting for Diana (= Artemis) to step into the bath." This passage is not a gratuitous ecphrasis but a strategic foreshadowing of later events in which Lucius himself, transformed into an ass, must put up with savage mastiffs. For example, "all the villages . . . called their dogs and sicked them on me from every side, provoking them to attack me in their furious rage and tear me to shreds. At that point, then, I was beyond doubt at death's door" (4.3; cf. 8.17 and 9.36–37). In another tale, a robber disguised himself in a bear skin only to be killed by a pack of hunting dogs (4.19–20).

62. The dogs named are Lynceus, Balias, Amarynthus, Spartus, Omargus, Bores, and

Arcana (*Library* 3.4.4).

63. *Dionysiaca* 5.373–80. On the sorrow of Actaeon's parents see also Diodorus Siculus 4.81.4, Euripides *Bacchae* 337–40, and Statius *Thebaid* 4.562.

64. Epiphanius the monk, in his account of Andrew's victory over demons at a shrine of Artemis—investigated briefly in chapter 3 in connection with Artemis Taurica and Andrew's visit to the city of the barbarians—explicitly relates the name Nicea with νίκη:

> And when they returned [to Nicea] they found a large rock along the road where there was a statue of Artemis in which lived many spirits granting visions and seeking sacrifices. From the ninth hour to the third they permitted no one to come along that road. Andrew came with his disciples and stayed there. The demons fled like crows crying, "O power from Jesus the Galilean! His disciples pursue us everywhere!" Andrew ripped down the statue and set up a cross. The rock and the area was purified of demons. The region was quite appropriately named Nicea ['victory']. (232B–C; cf. *L* 18–19a)

It is exceedingly difficult to know how much of Epiphanius's account one can attribute to the ancient *Acts* or where to place his tales within Gregory's framework. Perhaps the correspondence between Artemis here and the counter-Actaeon in GE 7 is mere coincidence, but it is possible also that Artemis once appeared in *The Acts of Andrew* in connection with the dog-demons.

65. Gregory actually reads "Hellespont," which is at the far end of the sea of Marmara, or the Propontis, from both Nicomedia and Byzantium. Although this geographical error may have been in Gregory's source, it is more likely that he created it himself. Throughout his epitome Gregory shows little discomfort with awkward, roundabout itineraries.

66. E.g., *Odyssey* 5.333–50.

67. Mark 4:35–41, Matt. 8:23–27, and Luke 8:22–35.

68. GE says nothing about Andrew's exploits in Byzantium. In the seventh or eighth century, when Byzantium was desperate for apostolic credentials in its struggles against the church in Rome, it occurred to someone that Andrew, Peter's brother, the Protocletos ('first-called'), was a prime candidate for promotion to the founder of the church in that city. Thus, a list of apostolic activities written under the pseudonym Epiphanius of Salamis recorded that "Stachys, whom Paul also mentions in the same Epistle [Romans 16:9] was instituted first Bishop of Byzantium by Andrew the Apostle" (Dvornik, *Apostolicity*, 175). Byzantine lives of Andrew routinely repeated this claim in their accounts of Andrew's visit to the city (*Narratio* 8, E 244C, *L* 32).

69. Thrace was notorious for savagery and bandits. See, for example, Clement of Alexandria: "the most barbaric of the Thracians" (*Protrepticus* 2.13.2); cf. *Iliad* 4.532–33, 10.433–45, and 471–73.

70. *Odyssey* 10.118–24.

71. Ibid., 13.200–202; cf. 6.119–21 and 19.175–76.

72. For example, the Trojan romance of Ps.-Dictys, who demythologized Odysseus's monsters into natural wonders or venal humans, says that Odysseus "had lost most of his ships and men to Scylla and Charybdis, that savage, whirling pool that sucks down

everything within its reach. Then he and the survivors had come into the hands of Phoenician pirates" (6.5 [Frazer]). The Argonauts, after narrowly escaping the crashing rocks, were terrified "to set foot on the mainland. For on every side there are unkindly men" (Apollonius Rhodius *Argonautica* 2.630). Apollonius modeled his battle between Jason's crew and the rock-throwing savages on the shores of the Propontis directly on Homer's encounter with the Laestrygonians (1.936–1011). Heliodorus's *Aethiopica* begins with a young couple sitting among the dead passengers of their ship, stranded on a foreign shore. Pirates picking over the booty discover and kidnap them. These events are likened to "a return from Troy" (2.21). Two of Heliodorus's characters learn in a dream that they are to suffer afflictions like Odysseus's, "and encounter enemies both by sea and land." Indeed, they board ship, run into gales, their vessel nearly sinks, and then is overrun by pirates (5.22–27). In the novel of Achilles Tatius, a violent storm fills the sea with corpses and casts survivors on a beach "wholly infested by robbers" (3.5). According to Xenophon's *Ephesiaca*, after "a mighty gale" threw a young man into the sea, he swam to an unfamiliar coast and himself became a robber in order to survive (3.2). Again: "I have recovered you after my long wandering over land and sea. I have escaped the threats of brigands, and plots of pirates" (5.14 [Hadas]). Apuleius parodied this topos by having a charlatan, playing the role of Odysseus, retell a tale of adventures at sea:

> I wish all our foes and enemies would encounter such a dreadful, really Odyssean voyage. First, the ship we were sailing on was battered by storm blasts from every direction, lost both its rudders, and was with difficulty beached on the farther shore, where it sank to the bottom. We lost all our belongings and managed to swim ashore. Whatever we then collected out of the stranger's pity or friends' kindness was all stolen by a band of robbers, and Arignotus, my only brother, who was trying to put up a defence against their bold attack, had his throat slit before my eyes, poor wretch. (*Metamorphoses* 2.14)

73. Thrace was the traditional location of the Gigantomachy, or the Battle of the Giants (e.g., Pausanius 8.29.1–2). The stories that follow in *The Acts of Andrew* repeatedly depict the apostle as a new Heracles, the great hero of the Gigantomachy. Thus it is possible that these pirates were those giants of old.

74. In *Acts of Peter* (*AV*) 5, Peter converses with a Captain Theon and converts him while sailing for Rome. This story may have inspired GE 10.

75. *Odyssey* 4.15–17.

76. Ibid., 4.57–58.

77. *The Odyssey*, too, has a multiple marriage of relatives. When Odysseus arrived at the island home of Aeolus, he came upon a feast celebrating the wedding of Aeolus's six sons to his six daughters (*Odyssey* 10.1–12); cf. Ovid *Heroides* 11, Hyginus *Fabulae* 238, Diodorus Siculus 5.8, and Pausanias 10.38.2. It is perhaps worth noting that Menelaus and Agamemnon also married sisters, Helen and Clytemnestra.

78. *Ps.-Titus Letter on Virginity* 488–92.

79. Homer uses the adjective ἔξοχος to describe, for example, the bard Demodocus, "praised above all men for his singing" (8.487). Later tradition called Homer himself the

poet *par excellence* (κατ' ἐξοχήν).

80. *Odyssey* 15.227.

81. Ibid., 15.228.

82. Ibid., 15.230–41.

83. *The Manichaean Psalm-Book* also refers to this story. In a list of apostolic sufferings one learns of Andrew that "they set fire to the house beneath him" (142.20 [Allberry]).

84. Lucian mentions a character who "had ears sharper than Melampus" (*Essays in Portraiture Defended* 20).

85. Apollodorus *Library* 1.9.12.

86. Perhaps it is not happenstance that Melampus had a granddaughter named Lysimache—the feminine form of Lysimachus—who had a son named Parthenopaeus, 'praise of virginity' (Apollodorus *Library* 1.9.13).

87. Melampus healed the lad Iphiclus (Apollodorus *Library* 1.9.12). Clement of Alexandria blamed Melampus for initiating the festivals of Demeter (*Protrepticus* 2.13.5).

88. *Iliad* 12.290–308; cf. 397–99.

89. Ibid., 12.101–4.

90. *Dissertationes* (Arrian) 1.27.8.

91. *Oration* 2.73b.

92. *Iliad* 5.655–98.

93. Ibid., 16.433–34 and 459–60; cf. Lucian *True Story* 1.17.

94. *Iliad* 16.521–22.

95. *Republic* 3.388c–d. Socrates' denunciation of Zeus's tears over Sarpedon's death were intended for the ears of Plato's brother Adimantus: "[F]or if, dear Adeimantus, our young men should seriously incline to listen to such tales," they would lack courage (*Republic* 3.388c–d). The names Sarpedon and Adimantus are separated by eleven words, by one line. It is possible that the author of *The Acts of Andrew* named the lad Adimantus in order to point to this well-known Platonic passage, but it is safer to attribute the name instead to its meaning 'fearless'.

96. *Legatio* 21. See also Ps.-Justin *Cohortatio ad gentiles* 2.

97. *Protrepticus* 4.55.3–4, with reference to *Iliad* 16.433–34.

98. *Octavius* 22. See also Firmicus Maternus *Error of Pagan Religions* 12.8.

99. *De anima* 46.

100. Strabo *Geography* 14.676c and Diodorus Siculus 32.10.2.

101. Miracle 1 (Dagron).

102. Miracles 1, 11, 18, 27, and 40.

103. E.g., Plato *Republic* 3.388c–d. Julian: "the bravest . . . of the Trojan army [were] Hector and Sarpedon" (*Oration* 2.55b).

104. *Iliad* 22.238–47 and 297–301.

105. Ibid., 22.395–404 and 24.12–21.

106. Ibid., 24.160–66; cf. 22.408 and 426–28. This very passage may have inspired *AAMt* 32. See chapter 2, 58.

107. See *Iliad* 24.351, 362–63, and 509–12.

108. Ibid., 24.637–40.

109. Ibid., 24.677–88.

110. Ibid., 24.707–17.

111. *Odyssey* 8.280–81.

112. Ibid., 8.296–98.

113. Ibid., 8.307–10 and 325–27.

114. Ibid., 8.362 and 364–65. See also Ovid *Metamorphoses* 4.167–89. The epithet φιλομμειδής also appears in *Iliad* 4.10, 5.375, and 14.211. Clement of Alexandria prefers Hesiod's explanation of the epithet: φιλομηδέα ('testicle-loving'): "because she was born from the μηδέα, those lustful members that were cut off from Uranus and after the separation did violence to the wave" (*Protrepticus* 2.14.2; cf. Hesiod *Theogony* 200). Apuleius plays on Aphrodite's laughter in *Metamorphoses* 6.9.13 and 16.

115. Theophilus likewise accused the gods of "unspeakable unions (ἀρρήτοις μίξεις)" (*Ad Autolycum* 3.3). In addition to keeping the couple, Medias claims he kept seven other people shackled in his home—nine altogether. Gregory provides no clues concerning their identity. In Pythagorean allegorical calculus, Hephaestus symbolized the number nine (*Theologumena arithmeticae* 58).

116. *Republic* 2.378d. See Clement of Alexandria *Protrepticus* 2.29 (cf. 7.76.1) and Athanasius *Contra gentes* 12. Heraclitus the allegorist explained the story as a physical allegory about fire in order to vindicate Zeus of maiming his own child (*Quaestiones Homericae* 26–27).

117. Aristides *Apology* 8 and 10: "It cannot be that a god should be . . . lame" (ANF); cf. Athenagoras *Legatio* 21.3, Ps.-Justin *Ad graecos* 3, Tatian *Oratio ad graecos* 8, and Theophilus *Ad Autolycum* 3.3.

118. *Republic* 3.390c–d. Plato also cited the song of Demodocus to ridicule Homer's depiction of the gods laughing (3.389a).

119. See Buffière, *Mythes d'Homère*, 72, 168–72, 330, 464–66, and 548.

120. Heraclitus *Quaestiones Homericae* 69; cf. Ps.-Plutarch *De vita et poesi Homeri* 101 and Cornutus *Epidrome* 19. Proclus took a similar position; see Lamberton, *Homer the Theologian*, 227–29.

121. Plutarch rejected this allegory (*How the Young Man Should Study Poetry* 19e–20b); cf. Plotinus *Enneads* 2.3.6. See Jean Pépin, "Plotin et les mythes," *RPL* 53 (1955): 26–27.

122. Aristides Quintilianus *De musica* 2.17. See also Plutarch *How the Young Man Should Study Poetry* 19f–20b and Buffière, *Mythes d'Homère*, 464–68.

123. Tatian *Oratio ad graecos* 34, Theophilus *Ad Autolycum* 3.3, Ps.-Justin *Ad graecos* 3, Athenagoras *Legatio* 21, Aristides *Apology* 10, Minucius Felix *Octavius* 22.5, Athansius *Contra gentes* 12, Prudentius *Contra orationem Symmachi* 1.625–26, and *Ps.-Clementine Recognitions* 10.

124. *Protrepticus* 2.33.8, 2.36.4, and 4.58.4.

125. Ibid., 4.58.4.

126. Ibid., 4.59. Xenophon of Ephesus describes similar erotic art that depicts the affair of Ares and Aphrodite (*Ephesiaca* 8). The song of Demodocus was danced (Lucian

The Dance 63) and targeted in satire (Lucian *The Cock* 3 and *The Dialogues of the Gods* 17 [242–45] and Ps.-Lucian *Patriot* 6).

127. *Odyssey* 4.589–91.

128. Ibid., 4.601–8.

129. Ibid., 4.613–14.

130. Andrew's speech to Nicolaus also may point to Menelaus. When Telemachus arrived at Sparta, he did not immediately disclose his identity, but Menelaus and Helen recognized him at once from his visual resemblance to his father (*Odyssey* 4.113–19 and 138–54). Andrew wants Nicolaus to recognize the true God. More significant perhaps is the apostle's desire that Nicolaus set his sights beyond his wealth to things divine. In *Odyssey* Book 4, Telemachus compares Menelaus's home with "the court of Olympian Zeus within, such untold wealth is here" (4.74–75). The king of Sparta, however, knew that Zeus's wealth far exceeded his, adding: "I have no joy in being lord of this wealth; and you may well have heard of this. . . , for full much did I suffer. . . . Would that I dwelt in my halls with but a third part of the wealth, and that those men were safe who then perished in the broad land of Troy" (4.93–99). Menelaus despised his wealth in light of the great human suffering caused by his insistence to rescue Helen; Andrew tells Nicolaus to despise his wealth in favor of "spiritual glances at what is not seen."

131. *Odyssey* 4.563–65. See also the discussion of GE 28 in chapter 5, 190–93.

132. Apollo appears as a healer, for example, in Tatian *Oratio ad graecos* 8, Lucian *Dialogues of the Gods* 3 (274), 15 (238), and 18 (244). He also sired the healing god, Asclepius. For Apollo's role in philosophy, see Plato *Apology* 20e, Lucian *Zeus Rants* 26, *How to Write History* 16, and *Hermotimus* 15. Ancient tradition had it that Apollo was Plato's actual father.

133. Lucian *Zeus Rants* 26, *On Sacrifices* 11, and *Syrian Goddess* 35.

134. E.g., Origen *Contra Celsum* 7.3; cf. 3.2529. *The Sibylline Oracles* quote the prophet herself denouncing the putative source of her inspiration: "I am not an oracle-monger of false Phoebus, whom vain men called a god, and falsely described as a seer" (*Sibylline Oracles* 4.4–6 [Collins]); cf. Clement of Alexandria *Protrepticus* 4.50.

135. This reference to the terrifying brilliance of Andrew's face may have been inspired by the shining visage of Achilles, which struck fear among the Trojan ranks (*Iliad* 18.205–6 and 225–27). Cf. GE 26.

136. The singular "Act" designates such single episodes in *The Acts of Thomas*, *The Acts of Philip*, and "The Act of Peter."

137. *Manichaean Psalm-Book* 143.4–16 (Allberry):

Thecla, the lover of God whom they lifted onto the fire,
She received the sign of the cross. She burned in the fire rejoicing.
Though naked in the midst of the crowd, she was not ashamed.
They threw her to the bears. They released lions against her.
They lashed her to the bulls. They released seals against her.
She suffered all these things yet was not intimidated,
    she did not [. . .] them.

Her affection was for a wreath. Her fight was for purity.
The blessed Drusiana too—she also suffered the same things,
    imprisoned fourteen days like her teacher, her apostle.
Maximilla and Aristobula—they inflicted great torture on them.   (Translation mine)

138. *Manichaean Psalm-Book* 192.25–193.5 (Allberry):

A despiser of the body is Thecla, the lover of God.
A shamer of the serpent is Maximilla the faithful.
Another receiver of good news is Iphidama her sister,
    imprisoned in the prisons.
An athlete in the contest is Aristobula the steadfast.
An illuminator is Eubula the aristocrat,
    who moved the heart of the prefect.
A [. . .] who loves her teacher is Drusiana, the lover of God, shut
[up for fourteen] days and longing for her apostle.
[A . . .] whom they found is Mygdonia in the land
[of] India.   (Translation mine)

139. Junod and Kaestli, *Acta Iohannis*, 94–95.

140. *Ps.-Clementine Recognitions* 10.22 (ANF); cf. *Ps.-Clementine Homilies* 5.12–14. The parallels between the *Recognitions* and the *Homilies* are so close that some such list of Zeus's amours must one have appeared in the so-called Basic Writing.

141. Aristides *Apology* 9.7: "Zeus is introduced, and they say that he was king of their gods, and that he changed himself into animals that he might debauch mortal women. For they allege that he transformed himself into a bull for Europa, and into a swan for Leda, and into a satyr for Antiope, and into a thunderbolt for Semele" (ANF). Tatian *Oratio ad graecos* 10: "There are legends of human transformations, but with you even the gods are transformed. Rhea becomes a tree, Zeus a serpent. . . . Tell me: does a god become a swan? or take the form of an eagle? or boast of his passion for boys because Ganymedes is his cup-bearer?" (Whittaker). Athansius *Contra gentes* 11: "One can see him [Zeus] overcome by pleasures, the slave of women and on their account venturing to appear in the form of irrational animals, beasts, and birds" (Thomson); cf. Clement of Alexandria *Protrepticus* 2.31–32 and *Stromateis* 5.14.111.3–6. The objection is as old as Plato: "Do you think that God is a wizard and capable of manifesting himself by design now in one aspect, now in another, at one time himself changing and altering his shape in many transformations?" (*Republic* 2.380d; cf. 2.381b–d). See also Ovid *Metamorphoses* 6.103–14 and Apuleius *Metamorphoses* 6.22, where Venus (= Aphrodite) blames Cupid for having tarnished her reputation through Zeus's "scandalous adulteries by vile transformations . . . into snakes, flames, beasts, birds, and herd-cattle."

142. *Iliad* 14.161–65; Fagles 14.198–203.

143. Ibid., 14.170–223; Fagles 14.209–69, with many omissions.

144. Ibid., 14.292–98 and 313–53; Fagles 14.353–59 and 375–421, with minor omissions.

145. Plato *Republic* 3.390b–c.

146. Dio Chrysostom *Discourse* 11, *Troiana*.

147. "Homer . . . declares that even the highest gods are in no wise protected by their own power, but receive the greatest injuries if they are misled by pleasure. For all the plans that Zeus made for the Trojans as he lay awake were upset when day came because he was overmastered by pleasure" (Athenaeus *Deipnosophists* 12.511a).

148. "[Homer] has shown excellently well how the favour that women win by philters and enchantments and the attendant deceit in their relations with their husbands, not only is transitory and soon sated and unsure, but changes also to anger and enmity, so soon as the pleasurable excitement has faded away" (*How the Young Man Should Study Poetry* 20b).

149. Scholion on *Iliad* 14.317. Aristophanes' solution was adopted by other grammarians, including the famous Aristarchus.

150. Plutarch *How the Young Man Should Study Poetry* 19.

151. See Heraclitus *Quaestiones Homericae* 39.

152. Her earrings stand for the highest of divine emanations, her sandals the basest, her one hundred tassels the many souls ascending to the divinity. She uses ambrosia and oil in order to depict god's powers of preservation.

153. The reconstruction of this allegorical interpretation, preserved primarily in the writings of the Neoplatonist Proclus, relies on Buffière, *Mythes d'Homère*, 544–48.

154. Athenagoras *Legatio* 21.5, Ps.-Justin *Cohortatio ad gentiles* 2, Aristides *Apology* 9, Athanasius *Contra gentes* 11, and *The Ps.-Clementine Recognitions* 10.20–23. Athanasius also complains that Zeus was the object of plots (ἐπιβουλευόμενον) by Hera and others (*Contra gentes* 11).

155. *Protrepticus* 2.27.

156. *Apology* 14.3 (FC); cf. *Ad nationes* 1.10.39.

157. *Octavius* 22 (ANF).

158. Our sources provide no indication whatsoever concerning the type of torture Aristobula endured, but if her punishment was consistent with her role as a Christianized Hera, the most fitting punishment would be hanging from a height with anvils attached to her feet. Zeus once used this form of punishment against Hera, and he reminded her of it just after he woke from sleeping with her on Mount Ida: "Dost thou not remember that thou wast hung from on high, and from thy feet I suspended two anvils, and about thy wrists cast a band of gold that might not be broken?" (*Iliad* 15.17–20). Ancient critics knew this episode as "Hera's punishment (κόλασις Ἥρας)" and were disturbed by its violence. Some critics expunged lines 18–31; others allegorized it (e.g., Cornutus *Epidrome* 17.26–1727 and Heraclitus *Quaestiones Homericae* 40). See Cedric H. Whitman, "Hera's Anvils," *HSCP* 74 (1970): 37–38.

159. *First Apology* 26 (Richardson). Justin here does not directly relate Simon's Helen to Helen of Troy, although he seems to suggest the parallel by the use of two unusual expressions. The first is the exceedingly rare συμπεριvοστέω, a compound related to the

famous Homeric word νόστος, 'return'. Just as Menelaus made a successful *nostos*, bringing Helen back to Sparta, so Simon, too, used to wander about on his return with his Helen.

The second expression is the phrase loosely translated here "had formerly been a public prostitute," literally "had formerly stood on a roof (πρότερον ἐπὶ τέγους σταθεῖσαν)." Scholars usually consider this expression metonymy for prostitution; indeed, τέγος of itself can mean 'brothel'. It is also possible, however, that Justin (and perhaps Simon before him) was comparing Simon's Helen with the famous scene in *Iliad* Book 3, where Helen, atop the walls of Troy, identifies the Achaean heroes for her captors.

160. Irenaeus's statements concerning Simon almost certainly derived from Acts 8 and some antecedent heresiological account. Irenaeus apparently had no personal encounters with Simonians, and, unlike Hippolytus, who had access to the (Simonian?) *Apophasis Megale*, he seems to have known no Simonian writing. On the other hand, Justin, like Simon, came from Samaria and undoubtedly knew of Simonianism first hand, as one can detect from *First Apology* 26, quoted above. Furthermore, the *Syntagma* surely gave considerable space to Simon; otherwise, Justin would not have invited the emperor to consult the work if he wished to know about this heresy in more detail. Several correspondences exist between *First Apology* 26 and Irenaeus's discussion, correspondences best explained by assuming that Irenaeus had read Justin's discussion concerning Simon in the *Syntagma*, which contained points of contact with what Justin later abbreviated in *First Apology* 26. Finally, Irenaeus acknowledges his dependence on Justin's *Treatise Against Marcion* (*Adversus haereses* 4.6.2), which perhaps increases the chances of his knowing Justin's *Syntagma* as well.

161. This reference to the poems of Stesichorus by Simon (or by Justin or by Irenaeus) probably derived from Plato's *Phaedrus* (243a); the epics had vanished long before the first century C.E.

162. *Refutatio* 6.19.3–4.

163. Ibid., 6.19.5–6.

164. Ibid., 6.20.1. Hippolytus also states that Simon allegorized Homeric epic, including Helen's carrying a lamp, the Trojan horse, and "very many other accounts" (6.19). According to Epiphanius, Simon took the episode of Helen's signaling the Achaeans with her lamp to represent his Helen's role as a revealer. The Trojan horse was ignorance, which people receive to their own destruction (*Panarion* 21.3). For the philosophical background to Simon's Helen see Marcel Detienne, "La Légende pythagoricienne d'Hélène," *RHR* 152 (1957): 129–52.

165. For a defense of the hypothesis that *The Acts of Andrew* relied directly on Justin's *Syntagma*, see Dennis R. MacDonald, "Intertextuality in Simon's 'Redemption' of Helen the Whore: Homer, Heresiologists, and *The Acts of Andrew*," in *Society of Biblical Literature 1990 Seminar Papers*, ed. David J. Lull (Atlanta: Scholars Press, 1990), 336–43.

166. This is the point also of *The Vision of Dorotheus* (*Bodmer Papyrus 29*). See earlier discussion, 25–26.

167. See, for example, *The Acts of Paul* 11 (Martyrdom 2), *The Martyrdom of*

Marinus, The Acts of Maximilian, The Acts of Marcellus, The Martyrdom of Julius the Veteran, The Martyrdom of Dasius, and the Coptic *Martyrdom of Abadious.* The doffing of a military uniform was a topos in martyrological texts. See also Tertullian *On Idolatry* 19:1–3 and *On the Crown* 1, Basil *Letter* 106, Prudentius *Crowns of Martyrdom* 1.34 and 61, Council of Nicea, canon 12, Council of Toledo, canon 8, Paulinus *Letter* 18.7, Pope Damascus *Epigram* 8.4–7, and Pope Siricius *Letter* 5.2 (canon 3).

168. Varianus arrived at the scene "in a fit of rage, and even though he stood next to the holy apostle, he was unable to see him. Andrew said, 'I am the one you seek, proconsul.' Immediately his eyes were opened." Varianus's momentary blindness may be another hypertextual clue to Zeus, whom Ate ('rash impulse') temporarily blinded at the birth of Heracles (*Iliad* 19.91–131).

169. *Iliad* 15.128–29. See also 5.30–35, 16.245, 15.605 (μαίνετο δ' ὡς ὅτ' Ἄρης, "he was raging like Ares"), and 17.210–12.

170. Ibid., 5.761.

171. *Legatio* 21.3; cf. Clement of Alexandria *Protrepticus* 2.29.2 (citing *Iliad* 5.31 or 455), Aristides *Apology* 10, and Athanasius *Contra gentes* 26.

172. *Iliad* 5.909.

173. It would appear that this episode was informed by the Thecla section of *The Acts of Paul,* where a Roman official casts her into an arena to fight beasts—a lioness, a bear, a lion, seals, and bulls. Andrew's ordeal ends with the death of Varianus's son; Thecla's with the death of Tryphaena, her patron. Furthermore, both Thecla and Andrew face the beasts because a woman rejected the sexual advances of a Roman official: Thecla rebuffed Alexander; Aristobula rebuffed Varianus. See Dennis R. MacDonald, "From Audita to Legenda: Oral and Written Miracle Stories," *Forum* 2.4 (1986): 15–26.

174. Andrew's beating "with clubs (*fustibus*)" might call to mind Heracles' favorite weapon.

175. Or perhaps: "the apostle."

176. Apollodorus *Library* 2.5.1; cf. Euripides *The Madness of Hercules* 153–54.

177. Diodorus Siculus 4.2.4.

178. *Argonautica* 4.1401–5; cf. Diodorus Siculus 4.26.2–4 and Apollodorus *Library* 2.5.11.

179. Her son, "who already had been with the apostle," may be Hephaestus, the Philomedes of GE 15. The garden is in Macedonia but some distance from Thessalonica. This setting is apt of Philippi, Philomedes' hometown.

180. Andrew's rebuke refers, of course, to the serpent in Gen. 3.

181. *Argonautica* 4.123–63.

182. *LIMC* 2.2.432, s.v. "Argonautai." See also Apollodorus *Library* 1.9.19 (referring to Demaratus).

183. For Christian references to Heracles and the golden apples see Ps.-Justin *Ad graecos* 3 and Tatian *Oratio ad graecos* 10.2. Athanasius wrote: "Heracles was worshipped as a god by the Greeks because he fought with men equal to himself and killed wild beasts by trickery. What was that compared to what was accomplished by the Word, who banished illnesses and demons and death itself?" (*De incarnatione* 49 [Thomson]).

184. This reading of the story would suggest that the parents correspond to Alcmene and Zeus, but nothing said about them allows a more certain identification.

185. The Labors of Heracles probably informed *The Testaments of the Twelve Patriarchs*, Judah 2.2–7, where the patriarch claims to have chased down a deer and a gazelle and to have slain a lion, a bear, a boar, an ox, and a leopard.

186. Several scholars have succumbed to overinterpreting these parallels. More measured treatments include the following: Arnold J. Toynbee, *A Study of History*, vol. 6 (London: Oxford University Press, 1939), 465–76; Wilfred L. Knox, "The 'Divine Hero' Christology in the New Testament," *HTR* 41 (1948): 229–49; Marcel Simon, *Hercule et le christianisme* (Paris: Belles Lettres, 1955); and especially Abraham J. Malherbe, "Herakles," *RAC* 14.568–73, and David E. Aune, "Heracles and Christ: Heracles Imagery in the Christology of Early Christianity," in *Greeks, Romans, and Christians: Essays in Honor of Abraham J. Malherbe*, ed. David L. Balch, et al. (Minneapolis: Fortress Press, 1990), 3–19.

187. Prodicus claimed that virtue and vice, in the form of two women, each enticed Heracles to choose her over her rival (*apud* Xenophon *Memorabilia* 2.1.21–34 and Dio Chrysostom *Discourse* 1.69–84).

188. These parallels are adaptations of those presented by Toynbee (*Study of History*, 6.469–76).

189. For discussions of Heracles the philosopher see Hoïstad, *Cynic Hero*, 22–73, and G. Karl Galinsky, *The Herakles Theme: The Adaptations of the Hero in Literature from Homer to the Twentieth Century* (Totowa: Rowman and Littlefield, 1972), 101–83.

190. Dio Chrysostom *Discourse* 1.84; cf. Julian *Oration* 7.220a.

191. See especially the similarities cited in Malherbe, "Herakles," 568–73. Parallels among the narrations of heroic careers has also generated attention from folklorists. See: Johann Georg von Hahn, *Sagwissenschaftliche Studien* (Jena: Friedrich Mauke, 1876), esp. 340–41; Lord Raglan, *The Hero: A Study in Tradition, Myth, and Drama* (London: Methuen, 1936); Otto Rank, "The Myth of the Birth of the Hero," in *Myth of the Birth of the Hero, and Other Writings*, ed. Philip Freund (New York: Vintage Books, 1959); and Jan De Vries, *Heroic Song and Heroic Legend*, trans. B. J. Timmer (London: Oxford University Press, 1963), esp. 210–26. For the application of a hero tale-type to biblical heroes see David K. Jaeger, *The Initiatory Trial Theme of the Hero in Hebrew Bible Narrative* (Ann Arbor: University Microfilms, 1992).

192. Origen *Contra Celsum* 3.22; cf. 7.53.

193. *First Apology* 21.1 (Richardson); cf. Theophilus *Ad Autolycum* 1.13.

194. *Dialogue with Trypho* 69.3, quoting Ps. 19:5 (LXX 18.5).

195. On Heracles' pederasty see discussion of GE 27, 187-88. Apologists especially objected to his deflowering of fifty virgins in a single night: Tatian *Oratio ad graecos* 21, Clement of Alexandria *Protrepticus* 2.33.4, and Arnobius *Adversus nationes* 4.26.

196. Tertullian excoriated Heracles as a transvestite (*De pallio* 4); cf. Clement of Alexandria *Protrepticus* 2.35.1, Origen *Contra Celsum* 3.22 and 7.54, and Athanasius *Contra gentes* 12.

197. *Divine Institutes* 1.9 (FC); cf. 5.10.

198. Cf. Mark 10:38–39, Matt. 20:22–23, and John 21:18–19. From John's statement that Andrew's death will resemble Peter's, it would appear that the author assumed that readers would have known how Peter died, from the prophecy of his death in John 21:18, from common Christian tradition, or from *The Acts of Peter*. Later it will become apparent that the author of the *Acts* almost certainly modeled the execution of Andrew after that of Peter in *The Acts of Peter*.

199. Mark 9:2–8, Matt. 17:1–8, and Luke 9:28–36. Jesus ascended a mountain, "and his face shone like the sun, and his garments became white as light" (Matt. 17:2). Andrew ascended a mountain full of light. Instead of seeing Moses and Elijah, Andrew saw Peter and John. In Luke's version of the transfiguration, the content of the discussion on the mountain was Jesus' death. Andrew is told that he, like Jesus and Peter, will die on a cross. Jesus' transfiguration took place in Caesarea Philippi. Andrew's vision probably came to him in Philippi.

200. *Odyssey* 11.119–30 and 134–36. The translation comes from William F. Hansen, "Odysseus and the Oar: A Folkloric Approach," in *Approaches to Greek Myth*, ed. Lowell Edmunds (Baltimore: Johns Hopkins University Press, 1990), 246 and 255. Oars planted over the burial mounds of sailors appear also in *Odyssey* 12.13–15 and *Aeneid* 6.232–35.

201. Hansen, "Odysseus and the Oar," 243–44, translating a story told in Karl Reinhardt in his *Von Werken und Formen: Vorträge und Aufsätze* (Godesberg: Helmut Küpper, 1948), 505–6, n. 30.

202. Robert Hughes, "Something Fishy in the Hamptons" (review of Peter Matthiessen, *Men's Lives: The Surfmen and Baymen of the South Fork*), *New York Review of Books* 33 (October 23, 1986): 21, cited by Hansen, "Odysseus and the Oar," 244.

203. According to yet another version, "St. Elias was a seaman and got so tired of the seaman's life—at that time they did not have engines and sails, only an oar—that he put his oar on his shoulder and said, 'I'm not coming back to the sea'" (Hansen, "Odysseus and the Oar," 243).

204. Ibid., translating a story told in Nikolaos G. Polites, Μελέται περὶ τοῦ βίου καὶ τῆς γλώσσης τοῦ ἑλλενικοῦ λαοῦ, vol. 1: Παραδόσεις (Athens: P. D. Sakellarios, 1904), 2.801–2. Odysseus, too, founded shrines at the tops of mountains (Hansen, "Odysseus and the Oar," 249).

205. W. H. D. Rouse, "A Greek Skipper," *The Cambridge Review* 27 (1906): 414–15.

206. *Odyssey* 11.74–78.

207. Ibid., 12.12–15.

208. Cf. *Odyssey* 23.266–84. See also Hansen, "Odysseus and the Oar," 246–47.

209. Hansen writes,

Odysseus's demon takes the form not of the sea but rather of the Sea, personalized as Poseidon, Lord of the Sea. This subtle shift from dangerous sea to hostile sea god is the principal difference between the Odyssean form of the story and the ordinary tradition. . . .

Having placated the Lord of the Sea, Odysseus need never again fear the sea wherever he may settle. Like Elias and the rest, Odysseus achieves permanent relief from the threats of the sea, but unlike them he is not bound to his inland sanctuary. Reconciled to the god of sea and storm, Odysseus is free to return home. ("Odysseus and the Oar," 248–49)

210. *Odyssey* 10.28–33. See also 5.457, 472, and 493, 7.325, 8.2, 9.75, 10.31, 143, and 363, 13.282, and 14.318.

211. *Iliad* 7.4–6. Apollonius Rhodius speaks of "tireless (ἀκαμάτῃσιν) oars" (*Argonautica* 2.661).

212. Mark 1:17, Matt. 4:19, and Luke 5:10.

213. *Odyssey* 11.15–17.

214. Ibid., 13.1–2.

215. Ibid., 13.51–52.

216. Ibid., 13.79–80.

217. This story also influenced the account of Andrew's sleepy disembarkation at Myrmidonia in *AAMt* 16 and 17.

218. *Stromateis* 5.8 (49.3–4 = Orphic frag. 33).

219. Pausanius 7.21.6.

220. Carol Wendel, ed. *Scholia Apollonium Rhodium vetera*, 2d edition (Berlin: Weidmann, 1958), 8–9.

221. *Argonautica* 1.494–95.

222. Ibid., 1.512–15.

223. Ibid., 4.903–9.

224. Ibid., 4.911–20. The tale of Butes also appears in Apollodorus *Library* 1.9.25 and Hyginus *Fabulae* 14 and 260.

225. *The Acts of John by Prochorus* contains a story almost certainly inspired by this episode in the ancient *Acts*:

[O]ne of the soldiers, a youth, ran off to the prow of the ship, and was thrown into the sea. Then the ten soldiers (?) came to the place where John and I were detained and said to him, "Sir, look how all of us grieve over our great misfortune, and how you are unperturbed and without grief. In fact, after the catastrophe you are all the more cheerful."

"What do you want me to do?" asked John.

They said, "If you can somehow help, do so!"   (Translation mine)

When John asked the sailors what gods they worshiped, they mentioned Apollo, Zeus, Heracles, Asclepius, and Ephesian Artemis. John: "These gods of yours cannot help or restore the lad or relieve your sorrow."

He [John] stood at the top of the ship, knocked off his irons, moaned, wept bitterly, and said, "Sea, sea, thus says the Son of God who walked upon your expanses and for whose sake I, his servant, bear these irons: yield up the youth to us in good health!"

At John's word there was a bubbling up and a roar of the sea such that everyone on board was in peril. A wave broke over our starboard throwing the lad alive at John's feet. Everyone venerated him, saying, "Your God truly is the Lord of heaven, earth, and sea!" They came and freed him from the irons, and we enjoyed great boldness among them. When we arrived at a village named Habitation, we docked and everyone went out on land. (*AJPr* [Zahn 48.8–50.7])   (Translation mine)

226. Such divine rescues of capsized voyagers likewise appear in *The Odyssey* and its literary brood. Odysseus himself survives the wrecking of his raft thanks to the goddess Ino, who lent the hero her veil as a miraculous life preserver (5.333–50). In *The Aeneid*, Juno calls on Aeolus, king of the winds, to "Hurl fury into thy winds, sink and o'erwhelm the ships, or drive the man asunder and scatter their bodies o'er the deep" (1.68–70). Aeolus does so, and, had Neptune not calmed the sea, all of the Trojans with Aeneas would have perished in the tempest. Most sailors overboard were not so lucky, "whirled about by a gust and sucked under by the seething waves" (Petronius *Satyricon* 114 [Arrowsmith]).

227. Philostratus *Imagines* 2.15; cf. *The Orphic Argonautica.*

228. Christ and Orpheus are explicitly identified with each other on a third-century seal (W. K. C. Guthrie, *Orpheus and Greek Religion: A Study of the Orphic Movement* [London: Methuen, 1935], 265–66).

229. *Protrepticus* 1.3.1.

230. Ibid., 1.5.1. Clement also quoted an Orphic poem that promoted monotheism (ibid., 7.73–74; cf. Ps.-Justin *Cohortatio ad gentiles* 15, *De monarchia* 2, Athenagoras *Legatio* 18 and 20, and Tatian *Oratio ad graecos* 1.10). See the discussion and translations by Michael Lafargue in *Old Testament Pseudepigrapha*, vol. 2, *Expansion of the "Old Testament" and Legends, Wisdom and Philosophical Literature, Prayers, Psalms, and Odes, Fragments of Lost Judeo-Hellenistic Works*, ed. James H. Charlesworth (Garden City: Doubleday, 1985), 795–801.

231. *In Praise of Constantine* 14.5 (Drake).

232. For Christian attitudes toward Orpheus see: Dieterich, *Nekyia*; André Boulanger, *Orphée. Rapports de l'orphisme et du christianisme* (Paris: F. Rieder, 1925); R. Eisler, *Orphisch-dionysische Mysteriengedanken in der christlichen Antike* (Leipzig: B. G. Teubner, 1925); Vittorio D. Macchioro, *From Orpheus to Paul: A History of Orphism* (New York: Henry Holt, 1930); Guthrie, *Orpheus*; Eleanor Irwin, "The Song of Orpheus and the New Song of Christ," and Patricia Vicari, "*Sparagmos:* Orpheus Among the Christians," both in *Orpheus: The Metamorphoses of a Myth*, ed. John Warden (Toronto: University of Toronto Press, 1982), 51–83; and above all Robert A. Skeris, *XPΩMA ΘEOY: On the Origins and Theological Interpretation of the Musical Imagery Used by the Ecclesiastical Writers of the First Three Centuries, with Special Reference to the Image of Orpheus* (Altötting: Coppenrath, 1976), esp. 146–56 and 253–59.

5

Back in Achaea

From this point to the end of the *Acts*, Andrew never leaves Achaea. After a few episodes in Patras (GE 22–24) he travels to Corinth (GE 25–27), Sparta (GE 28), Megara (GE 29), and returns to Patras (GE 30–33), where he will die. *The Acts of Andrew* thus conforms with *Odyssey* Books 13–24, which pertain entirely to Achaea. Books 13 and 14 take place in Ithaca, Book 15 moves to Sparta in order to bring Telemachus home via Pylos, and from the end of Book 15 to the end of the epic, the action occurs entirely in Ithaca.

GE 22–33 survives primarily in Gregory's epitome, but there are a few fortunate exceptions. The story of Lesbius in GE 22 exists in two Greek versions (*M* and *L*), which are witness to a common prototype. The tales told in GE 30–33 also appear in two Greek versions (E and *L*). In each instance, the Greek recensions reproduce the tale from *The Acts of Andrew* more faithfully than the Frankish epitomizer, and thus the hypertextual ambitions of the *Acts* lie closer to the surface.[1]

Lesbius (Dionysus, GE 22)

Andrew's first activities after returning to Achaea involve the proconsul Lesbius, whose name points to the island of Lesbos, famous for its viticulture.[2] The very word λέσβιον came to represent a wine cup.[3] One therefore might translate the name Lesbius as Mr. Goblet. Lesbius is Dionysus, the god of wine.

Euripides tells how Dionysus forcibly introduced his cult to Thebes. King Pentheus had heard of the miracles performed by the foreign god, but attributed them to fraud and magic. He locked up some of the maniacal Maenads, who had roamed the mountains in violent ecstasy. Pentheus even arrested Dionysus himself, mistaking the "stranger" for a mere corybant, and sent soldiers to bring the divine impostor back to Thebes for execution. The god then produced a series of miracles to demonstrate his power: prison escapes, earthquakes, strategically accurate lightning bolts, and supernaturally powerful deeds by his Maenads. The god's power only perfected Pentheus's weakness; more determined than ever to fight force with force, the king went mad. When he cross-dressed as a Maenad in order to spy on the raging women, his own mother

177

mistook him for a lion cub, dismembered him, and carried his head on a thyrsus back to Thebes in victory. Thereafter no Theban dared oppose the rites sacred to the strange god.

This tale inspired the account of Andrew's return to Patras, but now the tables have turned. Andrew plays the role of Dionysus by introducing a "strange god" to Achaea, whereas Lesbius/Dionysus plays Pentheus by attributing Andrew's miracles to magic and by seeking to kill him:

> When he entered the city, a rumor spread that a stranger (ξένος) had entered the city,[4] reportedly naked,[5] destitute, and bringing with him for his journey nothing but the name of a certain person named Jesus through whom he performs signs and great wonders, eradicates diseases, casts out demons, raises the dead, cures lepers, and heals every kind of suffering.[6] When the proconsul Lesbius heard this,[7] he was disturbed and said, "He is a magician and charlatan.[8] We must not give him attention, but rather seek help from the gods." He wanted to arrest and destroy him.[9]

At night, while the Maenads conducted their mysteries, Dionysus demonstrated his power to Pentheus, but without securing his compliance. The angel sent to Lesbius was more persuasive:

> At night an angel of the Lord appeared to the proconsul Lesbius and with great manifestation (ἐμφανεία)[10] and an awesome threat said, "What have you suffered from this stranger (ξένου) Andrew such that you wickedly contrived to lay hands on him and defrauded the God he preaches? Now behold the hand of his Lord is on you, and you will be crazed (παραπλήξ) until you know the truth through him." The angel vanished from him and he was struck dumb.

The god who crazed others now is crazed.[11]

> Not much later, partially regaining his senses [literally: becoming sober again], he called his bodyguard and with tears said to them, "Take pity on me! Quickly search the city for a certain stranger (ξένον), a tramp called Andrew who preaches a foreign god (ξένον θεόν) through whom I will be able to learn the truth." They ardently sought out the blessed Andrew, and when they found him they brought him to the proconsul.

Unlike Pentheus, Lesbius recognized divine power when he saw it:

> Seeing him, the proconsul fell at his feet and begged him: "Man of God, stranger and connoisseur of a strange god (ξένε καὶ γνῶστα ξένου θεοῦ), take pity on one deceived, a stranger (ξένον) to the truth, one spotted with the stains of sins, one who knows many false gods but who is ignorant of the only true God. I beg the God in you, stretch out to me the hand of salvation, open to me the door of knowledge, shine on me the light of righteousness."

The blessed apostle, stunned and tearful at the words of the penitent, lifted up his eyes toward heaven, placed his right hand over his entire body, and said: "O my God Jesus Christ, unknown by the world but now revealed through us, . . . touch your servant and heal him, thereby perfecting your vessel (σκεῦος),[12] so that even he may be among your people, preaching your vigorous power." Immediately he grasped his right hand and raised him up.

After rising, he gave thanks to the Lord and said: "Stranger (ξένε), surely he is God who needs neither hours nor days nor seasons. Therefore, I devote myself and all my house to you. I believe in the one who sent you to us."

"Since you have believed so greatly in the one who sent me," Andrew told him, "you will be abundantly filled with knowledge."[13]

The entire city of Patras became devotees of Christ, just as Thebes had been persuaded to serve Dionysus:

Astonishment overtook all those living in the city, who shouted out, "Great is the power of the foreign God (ξένου θεοῦ)! Great is the God preached by the stranger (ξένου), Andrew! From today on let us destroy the statues of our idols, let us cut down their groves, let us crush their monuments, let us reject the polytheistic knowledge of vain demons. Let us recognize rather the only God, the one preached by Andrew. Great is the God of Andrew!"[14] Together they all rushed to the temples and burned up, pulverized, cut down, scorned, trampled on, and destroyed their gods saying, "Let Andrew's God alone be named." The proconsul Lesbius likewise rejoiced at the cry of the citizenry and exulted at the action of the crowd.

Lesbius accompanies Andrew during the next several episodes and continues to play the role of a Christianized Dionysus. In GE 24, he compensates a youth for wealth lost by shipwreck, and in GE 26 Andrew refuses a gift because Lesbius was able to satisfy all his material needs: "Had I desired money, I would have prevailed on the more opulent Lesbius, who could make me exceedingly wealthy." One of Dionysus's epithets was Plutodotes, 'wealth-giver'.

This transvaluation of Dionysus corresponds with other early Christian statements concerning the god of the vine. Clement of Alexandria encouraged his pagan readers to throw off their Bacchic wantonness and to take on Christian respectability. Here Clement refers to Euripides' Pentheus:

I would pity him in his drunkenness, and would appeal to him to return from this madness to sober salvation, seeing that the Lord also welcomes the repentance, and not the death, of a sinner. Come, thou frenzy-stricken one (παραπλήξ),[15] not resting on thy wand, not wreathed with ivy! Cast off thy headdress; cast off thy fawnskin; return to soberness![16]

If all that survived of this story were Gregory's version, the only hint of

Dionysus would be the name Lesbius. Gregory never refers to Andrew or his god as strangers to Patras; Lesbius does not attribute apostolic miracles to magic or seek to kill Andrew after he had arrived; the proconsul is not struck mad by an angel but is physically beaten by two demons. In other words, Gregory has removed nearly all evidence of the hypertextual strategies of the ancient *Acts*, and one must assume that he did the same with other stories as well.

Trophime and Callisto (Atalanta and Aphrodite, GE 23)

The next episode, preserved by Gregory alone, concerns Lesbius's wife, Callisto, and his former mistress, Trophime. The name Callisto (Καλλίστω), 'most beautiful', might refer to any number of women in Greek mythology, but the content of the story indicates that Lesbius's wife is a hypertextual Aphrodite, the goddess of love, the most beautiful of goddesses.[17] One of Aphrodite's many lovers was Dionysus,[18] played by Lesbius in *The Acts of Andrew*. Like Aphrodite, Callisto hungered for love. When Lesbius converted and renounced sex, she objected strenuously, but found amorous companionship with a pimp whom she used to meet at a bath. The pimp probably is the beautiful Adonis, notorious for his many admirers of both sexes and Aphrodite's special love pet. To early Christians Aphrodite personified promiscuity. Justin Martyr spoke for many when he complained that she had been "sex-crazed for Adonis."[19]

The name of Lesbius's former mistress, Trophime, means 'suckling' (Τροφίμη), and designates Atalanta, who, exposed by her parents, was suckled by a bear and raised in the wild. This *enfant sauvage* grew up determined to preserve her virginity, a decision that put her at cross-purposes with Aphrodite, the love goddess. She killed several centaurs who wanted to defile her. This tomboy also defeated Peleus in a wrestling bout.[20] When her father insisted that she marry, Atalanta agreed but on condition that her husband-to-be could outrace her. Suitors too slow were slain—until Aphrodite intervened by tricking her foe: "When many had already perished, Melanion came to run for love of her, bringing golden apples from Aphrodite, and being pursued he threw them down, and she, picking up the dropped fruit, was beaten in the race."[21] Ovid placed this tale on the lips of Aphrodite herself while she and Adonis necked, "pillowing her head against his breast and mingling kisses with her words."[22] The goddess ended the tale by telling her lover how she had turned Atalanta and Melanion into lions in order to punish them for ingratitude for her distracting apples.

Compare these traditions about Atalanta and Aphrodite with GE 23:

> Trophime, at one time the proconsul's mistress and the lover of yet another man, left her husband and devoted herself to apostolic teaching.[23] For this purpose she often visited the house of the proconsul where the apostle regularly taught. Her enraged husband came to her lady [Callisto] and said, "Trophime is resuming her former prostitution with my lord the proconsul, and now sleeps with him repeatedly."

Ablaze with bitterness, she said, "So that is why my husband deserted me and for the last six months has not made love with me: he prizes his maidservant!"

Callisto then ordered Trophime placed in a brothel. Here Trophime, like Atalanta, had to fight to preserve her chastity.

Trophime entered the brothel and prayed incessantly. Whenever men came to sleep with her, she would place the gospel which she had with her on her breast, and all the men would fail to approach her. A certain rogue came to abuse her, and when she resisted, he tore off her clothes, and the gospel fell to the ground. Trophime wept, stretched her hands toward heaven, and said, "Do not let me be defiled, O Lord, for whose name I choose chastity!"

Immediately an angel of the Lord appeared to the youth, and he fell at the angel's feet and died. When she had been comforted, she blessed and glorified the Lord who had not allowed her to be violated. Later she raised the lad in the name of Jesus Christ, and all the city ran to the sight.

This brothel scene is the Christian equivalent to Atalanta's wrestling match with Peleus.[24]

Trophime thus protected her honor. Callisto and her lover were not so lucky; instead of an angel they encountered a demon, who slew them in their love nest, a bath. Callisto's nurse then came to Andrew begging for mercy,[25] but Lesbius, irate that Callisto had cheated on him, preferred her dead. Andrew rebuked him: "for we should show mercy to those seeking it, so that we may obtain mercy from God."[26] Andrew raised her back to life.[27] Revived, Callisto said:

"Let me . . . make peace with Trophime on whom I have brought so much harm."

"Have no fear," said the holy apostle, "for Trophime does not hold these wicked acts against you nor does she seek revenge, but gives thanks to God for whatever happens to her." When Trophime was summoned, he reconciled her with Callisto, the proconsul's wife, who had been raised.

Thus ersatz-Atalanta and ersatz-Aphrodite made amends. "Atalanta" won the chastity she so desired; the goddess of love pursued continence. "Dionysus" became more manly: "Lesbius so progressed in the faith that one day he came to the apostle and confessed all his sins. The holy apostle told him, 'I thank God, my son, that you fear the coming judgment. Act like a man and be strong (*viriliter age et confortare*) in the Lord whom you trust.'"[28] Ps.-Justin too faulted effeminate Dionysus: "What reverence is due . . . a man decked out with cymbals, garlands, and women's clothing, who conducts orgies with a herd of women?"[29] "Teach Dionysus how to act like a man!"[30]

Philopater and Verus (Orestes and Pylades, GE 24)

In Gregory's next tale, Lesbius and Andrew sat on a beach near Patras,

> when a corpse that had rotted in the sea was thrown onto shore at the apostle's
> feet. Then the holy apostle rejoiced in the Lord and said, "This corpse should
> be resuscitated, so that we might learn what the enemy has done to him."
> After he had uttered a prayer, he grabbed the dead man's hand, lifted him up,
> and immediately he came to life and began to speak. Because the man was
> nude, Andrew gave him a tunic and said, "Explain to us in detail all that
> happened to you."
>
> "I will hide nothing from you, whoever you are," he said. "I am the son of
> Sostratus, a citizen of Macedonia, recently arrived from Italy. When I
> returned home I heard that a new teaching had arisen which no one had ever
> heard before, and that signs, portents, and many cures were done by a certain
> teacher who asserts that he is a disciple of the true God. When I heard these
> things, I hurried to see him, for I decided that there was no God other than the
> one who did such things. While I was sailing with my slaves and friends, a
> storm suddenly broke out, the sea was wild, and we were overcome by the
> turbulence." (GE 24)

This episode may have been influenced by Books 5 and 6 of *The Odyssey*.
According to Homer, Poseidon aroused a storm to throw Odysseus from his skiff
into the sea. Had Athena not calmed the tempest, he never could have won the
Phaeacian beach.[31] When the princess Nausicaa came to the shore to do her
laundry, Odysseus, though stark naked, introduced himself, told her how a
δαίμων had thrown him into the drink, and begged for clothing.[32] The maiden
complied and took him to her parents, to whom Odysseus revealed his identity
with words similar to those of the young man in GE 24.

Odyssey 9.16–21	GE 24
"First now **will I tell you may**	"**I will hide nothing from you**
name that ye, too, may know it. . . .	whoever you are.
I am Odysseus, son of Laertes. . . .	**I am the son of Sostratus,**
I dwell in clear-seen Ithaca."	**a citizen of** Macedonia."

Odysseus then regaled the Phaeacians with his fabulous adventures—which
occupy four entire Books of the epic (9–12)—including how his shipmates
perished at sea.[33] The young man in GE 24 likewise told Andrew how he had lost
his crew in a gale. In the end, Lesbius/Dionysus, 'the wealth-giver', compensated
the lad for his capsized treasure, just as the Phaeacians had compensated
Odysseus.[34]

In light of these parallels, one might naturally take the young man as a
hypertextual Odysseus, but the rest of GE 24 suggests another identification.
When the revived lad, named Philopater, asked that Andrew rescue the rest of his

crew, the apostle prayed, and "immediately thirty-nine corpses appeared on the shore, washed up by a cooperative wave." Andrew asked the youth which of the crew he would like to see raised first.

"Warus," he said, "my foster brother (conlactaneum)."

Then Andrew knelt to the ground, raised the palms of his hands to heaven, and prayed for a long time weeping, "Good Jesus, raise this dead man who was reared (nutritus est) with Philopater, that he may know your glory and that your name may be magnified among the people." Immediately the boy rose up, and all present were astonished.

Here again the names of the characters provide the best hypertextual clues. Philopater, 'father-lover', befits Odysseus, who indeed loved Laertes. On the other hand, Odysseus had no foster brother to correspond with Warus in GE 24. The name Warus probably is a corruption of the Latin *Verus*, 'true'. I suggest that Philopater and Verus are Orestes and his ever-faithful foster brother, Pylades, truer than a biological brother. When Agamemnon, Orestes' father, returned from Troy he fell to the treachery of his wife Clytemnestra and her lover Aegisthus. The infant Orestes was sent to king Strophius of Phocis,[35] where he was raised by Anaxibia, Agamemnon's sister and mother of Pylades. The two boys grew up together and became proverbially loyal friends.[36]

When he became a man, Orestes, along with his sister, Electra, and Pylades, risked death and the vengeance of the Erinnyes by killing his father's murderers. He thus achieved the status of a $\phi\iota\lambda o\pi\acute{\alpha}\tau\omega\rho$, 'father-lover'.[37] Homer's heroes held before young Telemachus the example of Orestes in order to encourage Odysseus's son to rid his father's house of the ruinous suitors.[38] The saga of Orestes commended itself to the tastes of tragedians. Euripides, for example, devoted three plays to Orestes (*Electra, Orestes,* and *Iphigenia at Tauris*), from which one learns that he was nurtured ($\tau\rho\acute{\epsilon}\phi\epsilon\iota\nu$ = *lactere*) at the home of Strophius with Pylades,[39] who became his faithful ($\pi\iota\sigma\tau\acute{o}\varsigma$),[40] sure ($\sigma\alpha\phi\acute{\eta}\varsigma$),[41] and best-loved ($\phi\acute{\iota}\lambda\tau\alpha\tau o\varsigma$) friend.[42] Repeatedly Orestes and Pylades offered to die for the other.[43] *Verus* would quite appropriately describe such a 'true' friend. Together the two youths sailed for Tauris in a fifty-oared ship,[44] whence they rescued Iphigenia from serving at the homicidal altar of Artemis. As they left, they nearly suffered shipwreck until Athena intervened.[45]

In GE 24, Andrew prays for the thirty-eight shipmates of Philopater and Verus:

"Lord Jesus, I ask that these who have been swept here from the depths of the sea also may rise again." Then he ordered each of the brothers to take a corpse and say, "Jesus Christ, the son of the living God, revives you." When this was done, the thirty-eight were aroused, and the spectators glorified God: "None is like you, O Lord."

Lesbius gave Philopater many gifts, saying, "Do not let the economic loss sadden you, and do not depart from the servant of God." So he was continuously with the apostle and gave ear to everything he said.

Calliope (Circe, GE 25)

According to GE 25, at Corinth lived "a woman named Calliope who had slept with a murderer and conceived out of wedlock. When the time for her delivery came, she had hard labor and was not able to deliver. She said to her sister, 'Please go and invoke our goddess Diana (Greek: Artemis) to take pity on me, for she is the deity of childbirthing.'" Calliope (Καλλιόπη) means 'gorgeous voice', from the Greek words κάλλος, 'beauty', and ὄψ, 'voice' (whence the word 'calliope'). Homer mentions several excellent sopranos: Calypso,[46] the Sirens,[47] and the Muses (one of whom was named Calliope),[48] but the Calliope in *The Acts of Andrew* probably imitates Circe.

When Odysseus's search party arrived at her gates, "within they heard Circe singing with sweet voice (ὀπὶ καλῇ)."[49] One of them said, "Friends, within someone goes to and fro before a great web, singing sweetly, so that all the floor echoes."[50] One of Homer's epithets for Circe, δεινὴ θεὸς αὐδήεσσα, was commonly understood as "dread-singing goddess."[51]

Like Calliope, Circe "had slept with a murderer and conceived out of wedlock," that is, with Odysseus. After he rescued his crew from her magical brew, the king of Ithaca spent a year with Circe and, according to post-Homeric tradition, sired the bastard Telegonus.[52] Odysseus not only killed many Trojans in the war and Penelope's suitors in Ithaca, he also instigated the treacherous murder of Palamedes and mercilessly slew the Trojan infant Astyanax.[53]

The tradition relating Artemis, the virgin goddess, to healthy childbirth was ancient and ubiquitous.[54] But according to *The Acts of Andrew*, Artemis possessed no such obstetric powers: "When the sister [of Calliope] did as she had been ordered [viz. invoked the statue of Artemis for help], the devil came to her at night and said, 'Why do you uselessly invoke me, since I am unable to help you? Instead, go to Andrew the apostle of God in Achaea, and he will take pity on your sister.'" The woman went to Achaea and brought him back to Corinth.

> When the blessed apostle saw the woman writhing from the tortures of hard labor, he said, "It is quite fitting that you suffer these pains! You endure intolerable torments because you married badly and conceived with a trickster. Furthermore, you consulted demons who cannot help anyone, not even themselves. Now believe in Jesus Christ, the son of God, and bring forth your infant, but the baby will be stillborn because you conceived it unworthily."

> The woman believed, and when everyone had left the room, she birthed a dead baby. Thus was she relieved of her suffering.

Andrew's depiction of Calliope's lover as a "trickster (*doloso*)" aptly describes wily Odysseus. Furthermore, according to Ovid, Circe's appetite for sex was voracious:

> [N]o one more than she
> Was ready to make love at any hour—
> Whether she had an innate liking for it,
> Or whether Venus, angry at Circe's father
> Because he had betrayed her love for Mars,
> Gave Circe more than ladylike desires.[55]

Apparently the author of *The Acts of Andrew* transformed the tale of Odysseus's amorous sojourn with Circe and her birthing of Telegonus in order to score three points. He criticized Odysseus for murder and deceit, Circe for lust, and Artemis for inability to help in childbirth, in spite of her reputation.[56]

Sostratus and Leontius (Agamemnon and Achilles, GE 26)

According to GE 26, "When the blessed apostle had done many signs and portents in Corinth, Sostratus, Philopater's father, was warned in a vision to visit the apostle." Insofar as Philopater is a hypertextual Orestes, Sostratus should be Agamemnon. Indeed, this identification works perfectly. Sostratus was an wealthy man; not only had he lavishly provisioned Philopater's ship, he traveled about with a slave, and in the end "offered the apostle many gifts" that would have made Andrew rich. Agamemnon's wealth was legendary and Homeric.[57] The name Sostratus also points to Agamemnon: 'one who has offered the σῶστρα', an offering of thanksgiving for rescue from danger.[58] Trouble in the house of Atreus caused the two sons of Plisthenes, Agamemnon and Menelaus, to flee Argos for fear of death. One version of the story has their nurse grabbing one baby under each arm and fleeing to Polypheides of Sicyon for protection.

The very fact that Sostratus received a vision to look for the apostle may point to the infamous dream of Zeus to Agamemnon in *Iliad* Book 2.[59] Zeus wanted to deceive the timid Greeks into taking the field in order to punish Agamemnon and the other Achaeans for having slighted Achilles. The dream promised certain triumph, but all along Zeus had planned to hand the victory to Trojans. By depicting the greatest of the gods intentionally deceiving mortals, Homer earned the contempt of many ancients, including Plato's Socrates and Christians.[60] Unlike Zeus's dream to Agamemnon, the dream of Sostratus was altogether trustworthy: "As Andrew was walking with Lesbius and others, Sostratus recognized him, for he looked just like he had in the dream."

Sostratus's slave was named Leontius, 'lionlike', which might at first remind one of Heracles, who often wore a lion head and skin for his helmet and cloak. But insofar as Heracles never appears in connection with Agamemnon, Leontius probably is Achilles, who served in the Trojan War under Agamemnon, and whom Homer depicted as a lion.

> But over against him came Achilles rearing like some lion
> out on a rampage, and a whole town of men has geared
> for the hunt to cut him down: but at first he lopes along,
> all contempt, till one of the fast young hunters spears him—
> then . . . crouched for attack, his jaws gaping, over his teeth
> the foam breaks out, deep in his chest the brave heart groans,
> he lashes his ribs, his flanks and hips with this tail,
> he whips himself into fighting-fury, eyes glaring,
> hurls himself head-on—kill one of the men or die,
> go down himself at the first lethal charge!
> So now magnificent pride and fury lashed Achilles
> to go against Aeneas the greathearted fighter.[61]
>   [Achilles was] like some lion
> going his own barbaric way, giving in to his power,
> his brute force and wild pride, as down he swoops
> on the flocks of men to seize his savage feast.
> Achilles has lost all pity![62]

Of course, Homer used such similes to describe several warriors in *The Iliad*, but Leontius's statement to Sostratus in GE 26 best makes sense when applied to Achilles: "Master, do you see how the man's face shines with light?" In *The Iliad* it was the face of Achilles that glowed in the dark:

> crowning his head the goddess [Athena] swept a golden cloud
> and from it she lit a fire to blaze across the field.
> . . . .
> [C]harioteers were struck dumb when they saw that fire,
> relentless, terrible, burst from proud-hearted Achilles' head,
> blazing as fiery-eyed Athena fueled the flames.[63]

Because of Andrew's radiance, Sostratus and Leontius decided to follow the apostle and to hear his teachings.

> On the next day, he [Sostratus] offered the apostle many gifts, but God's saint told him, "I cannot accept anything from you, but I would make you yourselves my prize by your believing in Jesus who sent me to evangelize in this place. Had I desired money, I would have prevailed on the more opulent Lesbius who could make me exceedingly wealthy. Offer me instead whatever promotes your salvation."

Sostratus/Agamemnon was wealthy, though not as wealthy as Lesbius/Dionysus, the 'wealth-giver' (Polydotes). The wealth Andrew sought was Sostratus's soul.

The Men at the Bath (Heracles and Hylas, GE 27)

According to GE 27,

> A few days later he ordered a bath prepared for him, and when he went there to bathe he saw an old man possessed of a demon trembling terribly. As he wondered at him, another, a young boy, came from the pool, fell at the apostle's feet, and said, "What do we have to do with you, Andrew? Have you come here to drive us from our dwellings?"

Whenever characters in *The Acts of Andrew* bathe together, they are also involved in sexual relations.[64] The same holds true here. Gregory names neither the pederast nor his beloved, but probably behind this tale lies the myth of the Argonautic lovers Heracles and Hylas. The story was popular ("Who has not told of the boy Hylas?" asked Virgil),[65] but its classical expression comes from Apollonius Rhodius. As the Argo put to shore,

> Hylas with pitcher of bronze in hand had gone apart from the throng, seeking the sacred flow of a fountain, that he might be quick in drawing water for the evening meal. . . . And quickly Hylas came to the spring which the people who dwell thereabouts call Pegae. And the dances of the nymphs were just now being held there; for it was the care of all the nymphs that haunted that lovely headland. . . . [A] water-nymph was just rising from the fair-flowing spring; and the boy she perceived close at hand with the rosy flush of his beauty and sweet grace. For the full moon beaming from the sky smote him. And Cypris [Aphrodite] made her heart faint, and in her confusion she could scarcely gather her spirit back to her. But as soon as he dipped the pitcher in the stream, leaning to one side, and the brimming water rang loud as it poured against the sounding bronze, straightway she laid her left arm about upon his neck yearning to kiss his tender mouth; and with her right hand she drew down his elbow, and plunged him into the midst of the eddy.[66]

Heracles went looking for his young lover in an inconsolable frenzy: "[S]weat in abundance poured down from his temples and the black blood boiled beneath his heart."[67] No one ever saw Hylas again.[68]

The tale of Heracles and Hylas might account for the homoeroticism at the pool between an old man and a youth, the depiction of the old man "trembling terribly,"[69] and the possession of the youth. Andrew exorcised the men and they "returned to their own homes," which suggests that they ceased from their amours. Andrew then decided to take a bath himself, now that the area had been sanitized, and preached against demons—not demons generally but water-demons in particular. "As the blessed apostle bathed, he told them, 'The enemy of humankind lies in ambush everywhere, whether in baths or in rivers. For that reason the name of the Lord should continually be invoked, so that he who wants to attack you will have no power.'" Behind this passage surely lurk the nymphs who stole Hylas. Andrew's speech resonates with the Christian author

Prudentius, who denounced "nymphs who swim and live in the water, dwelling at the bottom of a deep pool like frogs, a divine authority seated in common seaweed!"[70]

Clement of Alexandria referred to Hylas along with Hyacinthus, Pelops, Chrysippus, and Ganymedes in order to fault Olympian pederasty.[71] The Christian Prudentius wrote: "The passion of Heracles, who was notorious for his love of a girlish boy, raged even on the thwarts while Argo tossed on the waters, and he blushed not to cover his wickedness under the wild beast's skin of Nemea and to search of Hylas, when he disappeared, as if he had lost a wife."[72] The author of *The Acts of Andrew* apparently shared this contempt, and composed the tale of the two men in the bath to express it.

Nicolaus and the Whore (Menelaus and Helen, GE 28)

In GE 16 a wealthy man named Nicolaus (Νικόλαος) played the role of Menelaus (Μενέλαος) by offering Andrew extravagant gifts. Another Nicolaus appears in GE 28, a resident of Sparta, the hometown of Menelaus and Helen. This character, too, is a counter-Menelaus, but the issue here is not Menelaus's wealth but his womanizing.

> [A]n old man named Nicolaus came to the apostle wearing torn clothing and said, "Servant of God, I have lived for seventy-four years, and during this time I persisted in debauchery, prostitution, and fornication. Often I ran madly to the brothel and kept myself occupied with illicit sex, but three days ago I heard of the miracles you do and your teachings which are full of lifegiving words. I thought to myself that I would leave my debauchery and come to you, in order that you may show me a better course. But while I considered this, another feeling came over me, namely, that I should abandon and not do the good I had planned. Then, when my conscience was smitten, I took a gospel and prayed to the Lord to put these things behind me once and for all. A few days later, when my perverse thoughts were inflamed, I went again to a brothel unaware of the gospel I had on me. A whore saw me and said, 'Get away, get away, old man, for you are an angel of God! Do not touch me or approach this place, for I see in you a great mystery.' Stupefied, I considered what this mystery might be, and I remembered that I had a gospel with me. I left and came to you, servant of God, so that you may have pity on my vices."

The name Nicolaus and the setting in Sparta point unmistakably to Menelaus; the whore here is Helen, the most beautiful of all Greek women and lover to a host of heroes. She had been courted by the best of the Achaeans, including Odysseus, Diomedes, Ajax, Philoctetes, Teucer, Patroclus, and, of course, Menelaus, whom Helen chose for his immense wealth. Paris of Troy came to Sparta, enjoyed Menelaus's hospitality, and coaxed his wife into escaping with him. After Paris died, she married Deiphobus;[73] soon thereafter she returned to

Sparta with Menelaus. Others claimed that she later married Achilles.[74] Post-Homeric tradition claimed that Theseus kidnapped her even before she turned ten.[75] Although most authors supposed that when her brothers, Castor and Polydeuces, rescued her she had not been violated, Pausanius claims she had borne Theseus a daughter.[76]

Her beauty and host of lovers made her one of antiquity's most notorious sluts, "the Aegyan bitch."[77] In *The Iliad* Helen calls herself a bitch.[78] Euripides' Teucer spoke for many: "[T]he whole of Greece detests the daughter of Zeus."[79] When epic poet Stesichorus made a point of besmirching her already tarnished reputation, he lost his sight. In his *Palinodes*, however, he claimed that only her phantom had gone off with Paris. Propitiated, Helen healed him.[80] Her reputation was so tawdry that rhetoricians tried to exculpate her in order to hone their skills of persuasion.[81]

As one might expect, Odyssean hypertexts enjoyed toying with the myth of Menelaus and Helen. For example, in Lucian's *True Story* the narrator claims to have visited the Elysian fields, where he saw Helen still flirting, fleeing, and fornicating, and Menelaus still in hot, vindictive pursuit. When he overtook the lovers' ship, he bound Helen's lover and accomplices together by their penises "and sent them away to the place of the wicked."[82]

Christian authors, however, enjoyed reminding their pagan readers that Zeus's daughter could not countenance continence. According to Clement of Alexandria, Paris's "clothing, luxury, and good looks corrupted the Spartan woman; barbarian foppery proved Zeus's daughter to be a whore."[83] When Menelaus caught up with her, he should have slain her; but when he saw her breast, he dropped his sword in order to fondle her.[84] Tatian also reviled Helen the whore, "who forsook flaxen-haired Menelaus, and followed the turbaned and gold-adorned Paris. . . . Euripides has wisely represented this woman as put to death by Orestes."[85] In a Valentinian Gnostic text, Helen symbolizes the soul that likewise fell into the world and became a prostitute. Now the soul longs for home and husband, like Helen, who lamented her ten-year detention in Troy: "It is Aphrodite who deceived me and brought me out of my village. My only daughter [Hermione] I left behind me, and my good, understanding, handsome husband [Menelaus]."[86] We already have seen how Helen's harlotry became a theological opportunity for Simon Magus.

GE 28, however, does not focus on the ersatz-Helen but on Nicolaus, the ersatz-Menelaus, and his addiction to sex. Already in Homer, Menelaus had come under fire for woman-chasing. After all, Menelaus's determination to recover Helen from the arms of Paris was the Homeric motivation for the entire Trojan war, which some Achaeans and Trojans—not to mention nearly all readers of *The Iliad*—thought altogether ludicrous.[87] Later writers also mocked Menelaus's mania.[88] For example, Euripides makes Menelaus's brother, Agamemnon, chide him: "[B]ut one desire thou hast, / In thine arms to clasp a lovely women!—reason dost thou cast, / Yea, and honour to the winds!"[89] An address to Greeks transmitted under the name of Justin Martyr accused Helen's spouse of "extravagant lust . . . madness and unrestrained desire."[90] The author of *The Acts of Andrew* apparently shared this assessment and presented Andrew's preaching of celibacy as adequate for quenching even Menelaus's flame.

The continuation of the story in GE focuses less on Nicolaus's libido than on his stomach, and here again one detects traces of Menelaus. No character in Homeric epic knew better than Menelaus how to throw a soirée, as was the case when Telemachus first arrived in Sparta. "So saying he [Menelaus] took in his hands roast meat and set it before them, even the fat ox-chine which they had set before himself as a mess of honour. So they put forth their hands to the good cheer lying ready before them."[91] Just before Telemachus left for home, Menelaus suggested he have a snack for the road: "And the grave housewife brought and set before them bread, and therewith meats in abundance, granting freely of her store. And hard by the son of Boethoüs carved the meat, and divided the portions, and the son of glorious Menelaus poured the wine."[92]

No so in GE. A heavenly voice told Andrew that for Nicolaus "to be saved, he must fast until he is exhausted." The old man "gave all his possessions to the poor," and "was so tortured with guilt that for six months he drank only water and ate only dry bread. Having attained the proper penance, he passed from this world." This six-month anaphrodisiac of bread and water is quite a contrast with Menelaus's fabled table and bed.

GE continues with an epilogue unique in the stories contained in *The Acts of Andrew*. A heavenly voice said, "'Andrew, Nicolaus, for whom you interceded, has become mine.' He gave thanks, told the brethren that Nicolaus had departed from the body, and prayed that he might rest in peace." This divine assurance that Nicolaus had achieved eternal rest once again transvalues Menelaus, who was promised an afterlife of bliss at the "Champs Elysées" because he was the husband of Helen, daughter of Zeus:

> [I]t is not ordained that thou shouldst die and meet thy fate in horse-pasturing Argos, but to the Elysian plain and the bounds of the earth will the immortals convey thee, where dwells fair-haired Rhadamanthus, and where life is easiest for men . . . for thou hast Helen to wife, and art in their eyes husband of the daughter of Zeus.[93]

Nicolaus, too, gained eternal bliss, but in his case he did so by conquering his passion for the harlot of Sparta and by avoiding banquets.

Antiphanes (Heracles, GE 29a)

According to GE 29, "When he was staying at that place (Sparta) Antiphanes of Megara came to him and said, 'Blessed Andrew, if you have the kindness commanded by the savior whom you preach, show it now and free my house from the calamity threatening it, for it is exceedingly troubled.'" Megara, an Achaean city west of Athens, shares its name with the wife of Heracles. Moreover, the name Antiphanes may point to Heracles, though ironically; it means 'inconspicuous', 'undistinguished'. The home of Megara and Heracles, like that of Antiphanes, was "exceedingly troubled," as one learns best from *The Madness of Heracles* by Euripides.

In order to fetch Cerberus, the hound of Hades, Heracles left Thebes and his wife Megara with their three sons. His long journey to the netherworld made his family doubt his return, even though they desperately needed his help. The tyrant Lycus was about to kill them. At last Heracles returned and freed them from danger, but his persistent foe Hera struck him mad such that he slew his own wife and children. This tragic tale was popular quite independent of Euripides:[94] it was the subject of dances,[95] of an annual festival in Thebes,[96] of poems by Panyassis and Stesichorus,[97] and of Christian contempt. Athenagoras and Clement of Alexandria seem to refer to Euripides' depiction of Heracles' violent frenzy in *The Madness of Heracles*.[98] The apologist Aristides ridiculed pagans for claiming that "Herakles got drunk and went mad and cut the throats of his own children. . . . Now how should he be a god, who was drunk and a slayer of children?"[99]

This tale may also lie behind GE 29. When Andrew asked Antiphanes what had happened to his family, he got this reply:

> When I returned home from a trip, I passed through the entrance to my atrium and heard the voice of my doorkeeper crying bitterly. When I asked why, those present told me that he had been severely tortured by a demon, along with his wife and son. When I went upstairs, I saw other servants grinding their teeth, attacking me, and laughing hysterically. I went past them up to the third floor where my wife lay, having been badly battered by them. She was so disturbed, so weary with madness, hair falling in front of her eyes, that she could not see or recognize me.

At first glance, this brief narration of troubles chez Antiphanes seems to have little to do with Heracles. Nothing is said about Antiphanes' children, no one dies, and Antiphanes himself is not struck mad.

There are, however, several details that point to the Heracles tale. Antiphanes, too, seems to have been absent from home for a long time, long enough at least for his entire household to have become tormented by demons. One learns a great deal about Antiphanes' home in these few lines. It contained a *ianua*, 'entrance', to an atrium, where the *ianitor*, 'doorkeeper', kept watch. Other servants lived on the second floor, the family on the third. This is quite a distinguished residence for Mr. Undistinguished! When Euripides told the story of the slaying of Megara, he presented Heracles' palace with an elaborate entrance, lofty gates, pillars (most likely around an atrium), several floors, and a staff of slaves.[100] Both magnificent homes suffered catastrophes: Antiphanes prays: "[F]ree my house from the calamity threatening it, for it is exceedingly troubled"; Heracles says: "I knew that trouble on my house had fallen."[101] Compare the following:

Madness of Heracles 523–30	GE 29
"All hail, **mine house**, hail,	"When **I returned home** from a trip,
portals of mine hearth! . . .	I passed through the entrance to
Ha! what is this?—	**my atrium,**
my sons before the halls / In death's	and **I heard the voice**
attire and with head chapleted!— /	
And, mid a throng of men,	
my very wife!— /	
My father weeping over some	**of my doorkeeper crying** bitterly.
mischance! / Come, let me draw	
nigh these and question them. /	
Wife, **what strange stroke hath**	**When I asked why . . ."**
fallen on my house?"	

Antiphanes learned from other slaves what had happened to the porter, his wife, and son; Heracles learned what had happened to his family from Megara and his father Amphitryon, but at the end of the play it is a slave who narrates at length how the hero had slain his family.[102] Antiphanes' servants attacked him "laughing hysterically," like Heracles who slew "with a manic laugh."[103] According to Euripides, Hera struck Heracles with madness by sending Iris and Lyssa (Rainbow and Madness) against him, like the demons who bedeviled the house in Megara. Antiphanes claimed that his wife was unable to recognize him because "she was so disturbed, so weary with madness, hair falling in front of her eyes." Compare that with the madness of Heracles who, unable to recognize his wife and sons, slew them: "[H]e seemed no more the same, / But wholly marred, with rolling eyes distraught, / With bloodshot eye-roots starting from his head, / While dripped the slaver down his bearded cheek."[104]

When Amphitryon and the chorus discovered the horrors at Heracles' home, they wept profusely;[105] when Andrew heard of Antiphanes' story, he was "moved with compassion":

> Then, moved with compassion, the holy apostle said, "There is no respect of persons with God, who came in order to save all the lost."[106] He said, "Let us go to his house."

> He left Lacedaemon, came to Megara, and passed through the entrance to the house. Immediately all the demons cried out with the fury of a single voice, "Holy Andrew, why do you persecute us here? Why are you in a house not given to you? Occupy those houses which are yours, but do not in addition infiltrate those given to us."

> The holy apostle was astonished at them, and went upstairs to the bedroom where the woman lay. After he prayed, he took her hand and said, "May the Lord Jesus Christ heal you." Immediately the woman got up from the cot and blessed God. In the same manner, he laid hands on each one who had been

harassed by a demon, restored them to health, and accepted Antiphanes and his wife as exceptionally strong (*firmissimos*) assistants for preaching the word of God.[107]

In light of *The Madness of Heracles*, this passage seems to contrast Hera's destruction with Christ's healing. Even Euripides faulted the goddess for having stricken Heracles with his violent madness.[108]

One might fairly object that if the author had wanted to transvalue Heracles, he should have made Antiphanes himself go mad and slay his family. Andrew then could have performed an even more magnificent miracle, an exorcism in addition to the reviving of the family. In chapter 6 I discuss another character, Alcman, who plays the hypertextual, crazed Heracles. A demon strikes him mad, but Andrew exorcises him. The name Alcman (Ἀλκμάνης) points unmistakably to Heracles, the son of Zeus and Alcmene (Ἀλκμήνη). Apparently the author wished to employ Euripides' play twice: first here in GE 29, where Andrew purged the palace of demons, and again in Passion 2–5, where the apostle will exorcise a counter-Heracles.

Aegeates (Poseidon, GE 29b)

The stories in GE 29b–33 survive also in two related Greek recensions that are generally more reliable than Gregory in retaining the text of the ancient *Acts*. According to these recensions, when Andrew and the proconsul Lesbius returned to Patras, they discovered that the emperor had replaced Lesbius with the rogue Aegeates. Apart from *The Acts of Andrew* and documents derived from it, Αἰγεάτης never appears as a name; it is a geographical designation meaning 'one from Aegae'. The sixth-century ethnographer Stephen of Byzantium said that people who lived in any one of "the many Aegaes" were called either Αἰγαῖος or Αἰγεάτης.[109] *The Acts of Andrew* denominates this major character with an extremely rare, city-designating adjective in order to identify him with Odysseus's oceanic foe, Poseidon Aegeates.

> Thrice he [Poseidon] strode in his course, and with the fourth stride he reached his goal, even Aegae, where was his famous palace builded in the depths of the mere, golden and gleaming, imperishable for ever.[110]

> So saying, he lashed his fair-maned horses, and came to Aegae, where is his glorious palace.[111]

Allegories of *The Odyssey* routinely took Poseidon as a cipher for materiality. Stoics and other physical allegorists supposed that Poseidon was water.[112] In the psychological allegories of Pythagoreans and Neoplatonists he represents γένεσις, the soul's 'coming-into-being' in the material world.[113] Like Poseidon, Aegeates represents insensate materiality. He is akin to the sea (τῇ συγγενῇ σου θαλάσσῃ) troubled by waves, "decorated on all sides by his material veneer" so that he cannot comprehend transcendence.[114]

Aegeates not only plays Poseidon but he also absorbs Odysseus's vices: gluttony, deceit, and violence. Maximilla and Stratocles, Aegeates' wife and brother, are hypertextual Penelope and Telemachus, Odysseus's wife and son. When Aegeates returns from a long trip, like Odysseus, his family will not welcome him, unlike Penelope and Telemachus. Raging like a lion—and like Odysseus—Aegeates will destroy his principal rival for Maximilla's affections, the apostle. In chapter 6 I explore these recharacterizations at length.

Sosius and Iphidama (Eumaeus and Eurycleia, GE 30)

According to the Greek parallels to GE 30, when Andrew and disciples entered Patras they were entertained at the home of "a man named Sosius, whom Andrew healed of a terminal illness." The apostle then healed a paralytic.

> As reports of the healing circulated, Maximilla, the proconsul's wife, sent her faithful servant Iphidama, who was worthy to see, speak with, and hear Andrew. When Iphidama left, she met Sosius, Andrew's disciple, with whom he was staying as a guest (ἐξενίζετο). He instructed her in the word of God and in divine healing. When he brought her to Andrew, she fell at his feet and listened to his words. Then she told her lady.

Sosius and Iphidama represent Odysseus's servants Eumaeus and Eurycleia. When Odysseus returned to Ithaca, not far from Andrew's Patras, he stayed as an unrecognized guest in the hut of his loyal swineherd, Eumaeus. The swineherd's accommodations were crude; nevertheless, he entertained the stranger with exemplary hospitality. Odysseus blessed him for his generosity:

> "[M]ay Zeus and the other immortal gods grant thee what most thou desirest, since thou with a ready heart hast given me welcome."

> To him then, swineherd Eumaeus, didst thou make answer, and say: "Nay, stranger (Ξεῖν'), it were not right for me, even though one meaner than thou were to come, to slight a stranger (ξεῖνον): from Zeus are all strangers (ξεῖνοι).[115]

Odysseus made Eumaeus's shack his residence while he planned his assault against the suitors. Similarly, Andrew lodged with Sosius throughout his stay at Patras.[116]

Throughout the end of *The Acts of Andrew* Iphidama plays the role of Penelope's trustworthy servant, Eurycleia (Εὐρυκλεία, 'renowned far and wide'), whose most common Homeric epithet is "dear nurse."[117] She is also called "wise" and "true-hearted."[118] Above all of Odysseus's maidservants, she proved herself faithful throughout the twenty years of her master's absence. Long before Penelope, she discovered Odysseus's identity, by recognizing the scar on his leg while washing his feet. After the slaying of the suitors, the "old dame went up to the upper chamber, laughing aloud, to tell her mistress that her dear husband was in the house."[119] Similarly, Iphidama is described as faithful and "worthy to see, speak with, and hear Andrew."

Later, Maximilla took sick and sent Iphidama to summon the apostle.

"Holy Andrew," Iphidama said, "my mistress Maximilla, who is suffering from a high fever, asks you to come to her, for she eagerly desires to hear your teaching. Her husband the proconsul stands at the cot weeping and wielding a sword in his hand."

He and his disciples went with her and entered the bedroom where the unfortunate woman lay. He found the proconsul clasping a sword and awaiting his wife's demise, wishing to do away with himself so as to die with her. Andrew spoke to him softly, "Do yourself no harm. Put your sword back in its scabbard, child, for a time will come when it will be drawn against us." The ruler understood nothing, but allowed him to pass.

The author used the popular novelistic motif of a lover's suicide to dramatize Aegeates' great love for his wife.[120] (Odysseus, too, so loved Penelope that he sacrificed immortality with Calypso in order to return home.) "The apostle then went to the sick woman's cot and rebuked the fever saying, 'Fever, leave her alone!' He placed his hands on her, and immediately she broke into a sweat, and the fever left her."

The Beggar at the Portico (Irus the Beggar, GE 31)

The Greek recensions tell this tale, which parallels GE 31: "Leaving there, the blessed one, weary with old age (γήρως), was propped up by his own disciples, and he saw someone who had been paralyzed for a long time lying inside the portico begging. Many of the citizens used to give him a handout for his food." This scene transforms the fight of the beggars in *The Odyssey*. "Odysseus entered the palace in the likeness of a woeful and aged (γέροντι) beggar, leaning on a staff."[121] The hero begged in his own hall for handouts from the feasting suitors, until the beggar Irus decided that he was butting in on his territory: "Now there came up a public beggar who was wont to beg through the town of Ithaca, and was known for his greedy belly."[122] Irus insisted on entering the hall and told Odysseus to be gone. The prospect of a fight excited the perpetual banqueters, who goaded them on. Odysseus claimed that an old man (ἄνδρα γέροντα) like himself ought not fight a younger man like Irus,[123] but at last he consented.

Irus let drive at the right shoulder, but Odysseus smote him on the neck beneath the ear and crushed in the bones, and straightway the red blood ran forth from his mouth, and down he fell in the dust with a moan, and he gnashed his teeth, kicking the ground with his feet. . . . Then Odysseus seized him by the foot, and dragged him forth through the doorway until he came to the court and the gates of the portico.[124]

Both Odysseus and Andrew were old men, each needing assistance just to stand. Inside porticos beggars made their rounds to receive handouts. Here the similarities end. Whereas Odysseus debilitated Irus, Andrew rehabilitated the paralytic: "Andrew says to him, 'Jesus the Christ heals you!' He gave him his hand, and at once the man became well. He ran through the middle of the city showing himself off and glorifying God."

The Blind Family (Phineus, GE 32)

According to GE 32, "As he went on from there, he saw a man with his wife and son, all blind, and he said, 'Truly this is the work of the devil, for he has blinded them in mind and body.'" Andrew's statement here calls to mind GE 2, where he says of another blind man, "I know truly that this is not the voice of a human but of the devil, who does not allow that man to receive his sight." The man in GE 2 was a hypertextual Tiresias, who had been blinded by Hera but granted prophetic powers by Zeus. On the basis of this parallel, one probably should search Greek mythology for some other mortal whom a god punished with blindness. There is no shortage of such characters: Helen blinded Stesichorus, the Muses blinded Thamyris, Dionysus blinded Lycurgus, Zeus blinded Phineus, and Aphrodite blinded Anchises and Erymanthus. Unfortunately, there is no blind family in Greek mythology to correspond with the three characters here in GE 32. Furthermore, there are no proper nouns suggesting what myth, if any, might lie behind the tale. But of the options, one is more plausible than the others.

Apollonius Rhodius wrote that when the Argonauts came to Bithynia, they found

> Phineus who above all men endured most bitter woes because of the gift of prophecy which Leto's son [Apollo] had granted him aforetime. And he reverenced not a whit even Zeus himself, for he foretold unerringly to men his sacred will. Wherefore Zeus sent upon him a lingering old age, and took from his eyes the pleasant light, and suffered him not to have joy of the dainties untold that the dwellers around ever brought to his house, when they came to inquire the will of heaven. But on a sudden, swooping through the clouds, the Harpies with the crooked beaks incessantly snatched the food away from his mouth and hands.[125]

The Argonauts put the Harpies to flight and gave Phineus a long overdue feast. Then, like blind Tiresias in *The Odyssey*, Phineus told his visitors what perils they would have to endure on their voyage if they would gain the golden fleece at Colchis. In gratitude for this information, Jason prayed that some god might restore his sight,[126] to which Phineus replied, "[T]hat is past recall, nor is there any remedy hereafter, for blasted are my sightless eyes."[127] The blind man in GE 32 was more fortunate:

> To them he [Andrew] said, "In the name of my God, Jesus Christ, I restore to you the light of your physical eyes. He also deigns to unlock the darkness of your minds, so that you may be saved by recognizing the light which illumines everyone who comes into this world." He touched their eyes, and immediately they received their sight and kissed his feet, glorifying and thanking God.

The most problematic aspect of this identification of the blind man with Phineas pertains to the blind wife and son in GE 32. In this regard, however, one might mention another episode of the Phineus myth. His wife, Idaea, resented his two sons by an earlier marriage and accused them of treachery or lechery, for which Phineus had them blinded.[128] Traditions about Phineus were extremely fluid, but none of them speaks of the blindness of his wives and none attributes the blindness of his sons to divine activity, which the reference to the devil in GE 32 may imply. The author or the manuscript tradition has provided too few clues to guarantee an unambiguous mythological identification. Fortunately, the identification of the character in the next story is transparent.

The Leper at the Harbor (Philoctetes, GE 33)

The story told in GE 33 also survives in a reliable Greek recension:

> Some people came to him [Andrew] and asked him not to recoil from going also to the harbor, for they said that there, thrown (ἐρρῖφθαι) on a dung heap, was a certain man, one of the ancients, of noble pedigree and renown, who had become shriveled and hideous with leprosy and who reeked with stench (δυσωδίας πλείστης). "Passers-by throw scraps to him as to a dog, not daring to approach anyone so utterly ulcerated (ἡλκωμένῳ). Time and again all of Patras has offered to give handsome sums to physicians to heal him, because he was the son of one of their celebrated fleet commanders (ναυάρχου), but he was unable to get even the slightest relief from any of them."

> When Andrew heard this, he was moved to compassion and went to him. Many of those in the crowd went with him, inquisitive about what would happen, but because no one else could tolerate the efflux of stench (δυσώδους), only Andrew approached the man. "I have come to you," Andrew told him, "so that I might heal you through my physician."

This leper is a hypertextual Philoctetes, son of the Argonaut Poias and himself an admiral of seven Peloponnesian ships that sailed against Troy. Along the way, Philoctetes was bitten by a poisonous water snake. The resulting incurable wound emitted such a foul odor that none of the Achaeans could tolerate sharing

ships' quarters with him. At Agamemnon's command, Odysseus abandoned
Philoctetes on the island of Lemnos where he stayed for ten years in intolerable
pain. In the words of Sophocles' chorus: "[N]o sadder fate is known" than that
of Philoctetes.[129] According to an oracle, the Achaeans would never take Troy
without the bow of Heracles which had fallen to Philoctetes. Diomedes or, more
commonly, Odysseus, returned to Lemnos in order to get the bow, either by
persuasion, or by force, or by kidnapping the stinking archer bow and all. Then,
one of the sons of Asclepius (or the god himself) healed Philoctetes, so that he
could use his bow and unparalleled marksmanship for slaying Paris and helping to
win the Achaean cause.[130]

Homer himself knew of Philoctetes' hardships,[131] but it was tragedians who
gave him fame. Aeschylus, Euripides, Sophocles, and the Latin author Accius
each wrote a play entitled *Philoctetes*;[132] only Sophocles' survives. Three
Egyptian papyri bear witness to the use of Philoctetes as a rhetorical exercise in
Greek schools.[133] Dio Chrysostom composed a purely rhetorical discourse about
him,[134] and so did Philostratus the younger and Aelius Aristides.[135] Quintus
Smyrnaeus also told the story, describing the sailor's putrid wound luridly.[136]

Our witnesses to *The Acts of Andrew* do not name the leper, but other
statements point unmistakably to Philoctetes. He is "one of the ancients, of noble
pedigree and renown" and "the son of one of their celebrated fleet commanders."
Philoctetes was the son of an Argonaut and himself the commander of seven
ships. The invalid was abandoned at the shore of the harbor, like Philoctetes on
the beach of Lemnos.[137] The old man lay thrown (ἐρρῖφθαι) on a dung heap,
lying (κατέκειτο) on the ground, ulcerated (ἠλκωμένῳ), reeking with stench
(δυσωδίας) such that people threw scraps of food to him without approaching.

These descriptions appear repeatedly in connection with Philoctetes.
According to Homer, "Philoctetes lay (κεῖτο) suffering grievous pains in an
island, even in sacred Lemnos, where the sons of the Achaeans had left him in
anguish with an evil wound (ἕλκεϊ) from a deadly water-snake. There he lay
(κεῖτ᾽) suffering."[138] Sophocles described the wound with graphic and repulsive
detail. Philoctetes speaks of himself as

> that man, of whom thou mayst have heard,
> Heritor of the bow of Heracles,
> The son of Poeas, Philoctetes, whom
> The Atridae and the Cephallean prince
> Cast forth (ἔρριψαν) thus shamelessly, a derelict,
> Plague-stricken wasting slowly, marked for death
> By a man-slaying serpent's venomous fangs
> Thus plagued, my son, they left me here, what time
> Their fleet from sea-girt Chryse touched this shore.
> . . . .
> Flinging me as they went, some cast off rags,

A beggar's alms, and scraps of food.
. . . .
So here for ten long years I linger on
Consumed with hunger, dying inch by inch,
Only the worm that gnaws me dieth not.[139]

Apollodorus wrote: "[T]he sore (ἔλκους) did not heal and stank (δυσώδους γενομένου), the army could not endure the stench."[140] Philostratus the younger described an artistic representation of Philoctetes that presented him "with face haggard because of his malady and with clouded brow above lowered eyes, hollow eyes with sickly glare, showing hair that is full of filth and grime, his beard unkempt, shivering, himself clothed in rags. . . . [H]is foot dripping with devouring poison."[141] No one described the sufferings of Philoctetes in more detail or with images more instructive of this section of *The Acts of Andrew* than Quintus Smyrnaeus:

To hallowed Lemnos came those heroes twain
    [Odysseus and Diomedes];
They marked the rocky cave where lay (κεῖτο) the son
Of princely Poeas. Horror came on them
When they beheld the hero of their quest
Groaning with bitter pangs, on the hard earth
Lying.
. . .
Never his groaning ceased, for evermore
The ulcerous black wound (ἕλκος), eating to the bone,
Festered with thrills of agonizing pain.
. . . .
And from the ulcerous wound (ἕλκεος) aye streamed to earth
Fetid corruption fouling all the floor
Of that wide cave. . . .[142]

Odysseus and Diomedes brought him to the shore: "There washed they all his body and that foul wound (ἕλκος) / With sponges and with plenteous water bathed: / So was his soul refreshed."[143] From Lemnos they took him to Troy, where

                one drew near,
Podaleirius, godlike in his power to heal.
Swifter than thought he made him whole and sound;
For deftly on the wound (ἕλκος) he spread his salves,
Calling on his physician-father's name (Asclepius);
And soon the Achaeans shouted for joy,

All praising with one voice Asclepius' son.
Lovingly then they bathed him.

. . . .

And glad at heart were all that looked on him;
And from affliction he awoke to joy.

. . . .
                    it seemed
The work of hands immortal. And indeed
So was it verily, as their hearts divined.[144]

The healing of the leper at the harbor in *The Acts of Andrew* also was "the work of hands immortal." The invalid asked:

"Friend, is your physician divine or human? No human can heal me."

"I detect that you are truly being saved," Andrew told him, "for even now God is present with you to raise you up from here, for I have called to him with visible sounds. You will see in yourself the power of the sounds, for you will walk with me healed."[145]

The author narrates the actual healing of the leper with details as disgusting as those found in any version of the healing of Philoctetes:

When he had said this to the sick man, who was shocked by Andrew's promise, the apostle prayed, and after prayer he stripped the invalid of all the rags he was wearing, which were putrid and dripping with pus from the old man's many revolting sores (ἑλκῶν). As the rags dropped to the earth, many maggots filled the spot. There was a short distance between the ground where he was lying and the sea, and Andrew commanded him to get up and walk with him. By the Lord's power, he stood up without any assistance and went off with the apostle, as large quantities of pus dribbled from him and as his entire body oozed. So abundant was the flow of pus that wherever he walked there was a trail of slime clearly visible to everyone.

When they both got to the sea, the apostle again spoke to him: "Now I wash your body so that it might be made well. You yourself will wash your soul." He lifted him up, brought him into the sea, and brought him out. By the Lord's grace, the man immediately became whole, without a blemish on his body—no ulcer, no wound, no scar (μήτε ἕλκος μήτε τραῦμα μήτε οὐλήν)—but was vibrant and had a pure body.

As was the case with Philoctetes, the healing of the leper produced great joy among those who witnessed it:

Just when the apostle commanded him to be given clothes, the one who earlier had been neglected and weak was now so transported by joy that he did not want to take them but ran through the city naked and screaming, so that his prior acquaintances could contrast what they had known him to be with what he had become. He went to their agora and shouted: "I thank you, O God who sent your man to me! I thank you, you who had mercy on me! Everyone had given up hope for me, but you alone showed compassion. No one dared draw near to me, but now all draw near to your glory." While he was speaking many such things, stark naked, he still hesitated taking the clothes until the apostle arrived and scolded him to get dressed.[146] When he had taken the garments and dressed himself, he followed the apostle. Everyone saw that he had become well and they were astounded.

Some of the similarities between this story and those concerning Philoctetes are stock teratalogical motifs, but others are quite unusual. In both accounts the victim is the son of a sailor. Both accounts emphasize the pussy discharge, nauseating stench, and incurable sores. Both victims are washed in the sea and miraculously healed. One need not suppose that *The Acts of Andrew* borrowed from any particular narration of the Philoctetes story now known to us; the story was commonplace. Insofar as those who told the story frequently did so in order to fault Odysseus for having abandoned Philoctetes on Lemnos, it is possible that the author wished to present Andrew as an anti-Odysseus, as one who did not abandon the smelly outcast but who healed him.[147]

Conclusion

GE 22–33 narrates Andrew's ministry in Achaea, beginning in Patras, where the apostle introduced the new religion, converting Lesbius (≈ Dionysus, 22), Trophime and Callisto (≈ Atalanta and Aphrodite, 23), and Philopater and Verus (≈ Orestes and Pylades, 24). Andrew traveled from Patras to Corinth to rescue Calliope from hard labor (≈ Circe, 25) and where he converted Sostratus and Leontius (≈ Agamemnon and Achilles, 26) and exorcised the two men bathing (≈ Heracles and Hylas, 27). At Sparta he rescued Nicolaus (≈ Menelaus) from his addiction to a strumpet (≈ Helen, 28). At Megara he exorcised the home of Antiphanes (≈ Heracles) from the demons troubling it (29). Andrew returned to Patras in GE 30 and found Aegeates (≈ Poseidon and to some extent Odysseus) in the proconsulship instead of Lesbius. The proconsul's wife Maximilla (≈ Penelope) sent her faithful maidservant Iphidama (≈ Eurycleia) to speak with the apostle who was staying with Sosius (≈ Eumaeus). Andrew then healed Maximilla of a fever and prevented Aegeates from ending his life out of love for her. He healed a begging paralytic at a portico (≈ Irus, 31), a blind family (≈ the family of Phineus, 32?), and a stinking leper (≈ Philoctetes, 33). Granted some of these identifications are speculative, but most are nearly certain. It is reasonable to suppose that the author wrote each story with some intended hypertextual strategy in mind, even if the precise mythological antecedent is elusive in the derivative texts or to modern eyes.

The single most influential text lying behind these stories is Homer's *Odyssey*: Circe (GE 25), Odysseus, Penelope, Eumaeus, and Eurycleia (30), and Irus (31). *The Iliad* may have informed GE 16 (Agamemnon and Achilles) and 28 (Menelaus and Helen), but these tales were so well known that there is no need to posit direct literary dependence. This observation holds true as well for the possible reliance on *The Argonautica* of Apollonius Rhodius. Traditions concerning Heracles and Hylas (GE 27) and Phineus (32) could as easily have come from the myth-rich air as from a scroll. On the other hand, several of the stories betray possible textual contacts with tragedies, especially those of Euripides: *The Bacchae* (GE 22), *Orestes* or *Iphigenia in Tauris* (24), *The Madness of Heracles* (29), and either his lost *Philoctetes* or that of Sophocles. The heavy reliance on Homer and Euripides not only matches the pattern in *The Acts of Andrew* throughout but it also correlates with the statistical pattern in the uses of ancient literature generally. Catalogues of manuscripts found in Hellenistic and Imperial Egypt, Philo's quotations of Greek literary authors, and the citations of these authors in early Christian texts generally follow the same pattern. Homer, Euripides, Plato; win, place, show.

The preceding analysis of GE 22–33—and indeed, of GE 2–21 as well—has labored against the lamentable textual condition of this section of *The Acts of Andrew*. Even though the text of *The Acts of Andrew and Matthias in the City of the Cannibals* is comparatively secure, many scholars have doubted that it ever appeared as the beginning of the ancient *Acts*.[148] In other words, to this point my interpretation has necessarily relied on texts whose relationships to the original *Acts of Andrew* are suspect for one reason or another.

The same cannot be said of Andrew's Passion, which undoubtedly concluded the ancient *Acts*, and whose recent textual reconstruction is reliable. If one is to make a case for Homeric hypertextuality in *The Acts of Andrew*, one will have to account for the characterizations, tale-types, motifs, and theological strategies of this concluding section, where at last one can moor one's interpretive craft against solid textual piles.

Notes

1. In my edition I preferred GE to *M* and *L* at several points, but at the time I was unaware of Lesbius's relationship with Dionysus, which tilts the balance decisively in favor of the Greek recensions.

2. Athenaeus *Deipnosophists* 1.31a: "I will furnish the Lesbian [wine] . . . and nobody will have a headache." Aulus Gellius *Attic Nights* 13.5 (quoting Aristotle on his comparison of two wines): "Both are very good indeed, but the Lesbian is the sweeter

(ἡδίων ὁ Λέσβιος)"; cf. Virgil *Georgics* 2.90.

3. LSJ, λέσβιος II.2. Athenaeus *Deipnosophists* 11.486a–b: *"Lesbion*. That this is a kind of cup is indicated by Hedylus in his *Epigrams*, as follows: 'Callistion, she who could hold her own in the drinking contest with men—no sham miracle either—drank up six quarts on an empty stomach; it is her *lesbion*.'"

4. Euripides designated Dionysus a ξένος repeatedly in *The Bacchae*: e.g., lines 233, 353, 441, 453, 642, 800, 1063, 1068, and 1077.

5. Dionysus frequently is depicted nude in ancient art. See *LIMC* 3.2 s.v. Dionysus, nos. 102, 119a, 120c, 122–25, 316, 382, and Bacchus nos. 1–5.

6. Cf. *Bacchae* 449–50: πολλῶν . . . θαυμάτων.

7. Cf. *Bacchae* 215–25.

8. Cf. *Bacchae* 233–34: "Men say a stranger (ξένος) to the land hath come / A juggling sorcerer."

9. Cf. *Bacchae* 239–41, 352–57, and 781–86.

10. Cf. *Bacchae* 22: ἐμφανὴς δαίμων.

11. Cf. *Iliad* 6.132: "mad Dionysus (μαινομένοιο Διωνύσοιο)." Clement of Alexandria (*Protrepticus* 7.76.2) and Ps.-Justin (*De monarchia* 6) cite this Homeric line to denounce Dionysus as a maniac; cf. Theophilus *Ad Autolycum* 1.9.

12. The use of σκεῦος to designate Lesbius may be a play on his name, Mr. Goblet.

13. Mr. Goblet will be filled to the brim.

14. The last three sentences appear only in *M*; apparently they fell out of *L* by haplography due to the similarities between "Great is the God preached by the stranger, Andrew" and "Great is the God of Andrew." The twice-repeated phrase, "great God (μέγας ὁ θεός)" resonates with *Bacchae* 329 (μέγαν θεόν) and 1031 (θεὸς φαίνει μέγας), both used of Dionysus.

15. *M* and *L* use this same word for Lesbius's madness.

16. *Protrepticus* 12.118.5–119.1; cf. Justin Martyr *First Apology* 54, Athenagoras *Legatio* 22, and Origen *Contra Celsum* 2.34. *Christus patiens*, often ascribed to Gregory of Nazianzus, versified the crucifixion and took over several lines from *The Bacchae*. Mary's mourning the death of Jesus was modeled after Agave's mourning of her son, Pentheus. See Loeb edition of *The Bacchae*, 122–23.

17. The judgment of Paris decided the matter once and for all, even though Aphrodite bribed him with Helen's love so that he would choose her over Hera and Athena.

18. They are the putative parents of monstrous Priapus (Pausanius 9.31.2).

19. *First Apology* 25; cf. Ps.-Justin *Ad graecos* 4, Aristides *Apology* 11.3, Clement of Alexandria *Protrepticus* 2.33.9 and 2.39.2 and *Stromateis* 2.20.106.2–107.3, and Athanasius *Contra gentes* 26.

20. E.g., Apollodorus: "Grown to womanhood, Atalanta kept herself a virgin. . . . The centaurs Rhoecus and Hylaeus tried to force her, but were shot down and killed by her. She went moreover with the chiefs to hunt the Calydonian boar, and at the games held in honour of Pelias she wrestled with Peleus and won" (*Library* 3.9.2).

21. Apollodorus *Library* 3.9.2; cf. Hyginus *Fabulae* 185 and Clement of Alexandria *Stromateis* 4.19.

22. *Metamorphoses* 10.558–59.

23. Atalanta had relations not only with Melanion but also with Meleager, by whom she conceived the ironically named Parthenopaeus; cf. Tatian *Oratio ad graecos* 8.

24. Christian women actually were placed in brothels as a form of punishment: "Women who refuse to sacrifice are put into a brothel" (*Martyrdom of Pionius* 7 [Musurillo]); cf. Tertullian *Apology* 50, *On Monogamy* 15, and Eusebius *Historia ecclesiastica* 6.5. The most striking parallel to this passage in *The Acts of Andrew* appears in *The Martyrdom of Agape, Irene, and Chione* 5–6. The prefect Dulcitius:

> "I sentence you to be placed naked in the brothel with the help of the public notaries of this city and of Zosimus the executioner. . . ." After those who were put in charge had taken the girl off to the public brothel in accordance with the prefect's order, by the grace of the Holy Spirit which preserved and guarded her pure and inviolate for the God who is the lord of all things, no man dared to approach her, or so much as tried to insult her in speech. (Musurillo)

25. This nurse may be Dione, Aphrodite's mother according to Homer, who consoled and healed the beautiful goddess when she was wounded by Diomedes (*Iliad* 5.370–415). Christian apologists often cited the wounding of Ares and Aphrodite to demonstrate the weakness of Greek gods (e.g., Athenagoras *Legatio* 21, Theophilus *Ad Autolycum* 1.9, Clement of Alexandria *Protrepticus* 2.36.1, and Athanasius *Contra gentes* 12).

26. Andrew's rebuke of Lesbius's severity may have been directed at the cruelty of Dionysus in *The Bacchae*.

27. Gregory says nothing of the status of the dead pimp.

28. *M* and *L* say nothing about Lesbius's manliness:

> Because a great crowd was causing a disturbance, and because the word of the blessed Andrew and his preaching spread everywhere unresisted, the emperor sent a successor for Lesbius and terminated his rule. On receiving the imperial command, Lesbius went with joy to the blessed Andrew and said, "Now I will believe in the Lord even more, because I have shed vain glory, put off the pride of the world, and thrown aside the distraction of life. Therefore, O man of God, take me as your fellow traveler. Receive me as one faithful speaking faithfully and witnessing to all people concerning our common savior, Christ." Leaving the praetorium, he traveled with Andrew. [*L* adds: "touring all the territory of Achaea with the announcer of the divine preaching."]

29. *Oratio ad gentiles* 2; cf. Origen *Contra Celsum* 3.23.

30. *Oratio ad gentiles* 2.

31. *Odyssey* 5.291–453.

32. Ibid., 6.127–85.

33. Especially *Odyssey* 12.417–19.

34. Ibid., 13.1–15.

35. Phocis, like Philopater's Macedonia, was north of the Peloponnese.

36. See, e.g., Lucian *Toxaris, or Friendship*: "That is why we honour Orestes and

Pylades, because they practiced best what Scythians hold good, and excelled in friendship (φιλίᾳ), an achievement which we admire before all things else" (7).

37. The very word is used by Orestes himself in Euripides *Orestes* 1605.

38. *Odyssey* 3.305–28 and 4.512–47; cf. 1.28–41.

39. *Electra* 18. Cf. 917–21 and 709: συνεκτραφείς.

40. Ibid., 83, and *Orestes* 1015–16 and 1405.

41. *Orestes* 1155 and 1619 and *Iphigenia in Tauris* 919.

42. *Orestes* 725 and 732 and *Iphigenia in Tauris* 708; cf. *Orestes* 732–33 and 802–6.

43. *Orestes* 1069–73 and 1084–99, and *Iphigenia in Tauris* 597–608, 674–86, and 716–17.

44. *Iphigenia in Tauris* 1124 and 1347.

45. Ibid., 1379–1474. The friendship of Orestes and Pylades generated the following praise written at about the same time as *The Acts of Andrew*:

Phocis united Orestes to Pylades right from their infancy. Taking the love-god as the mediator of their emotions for each other, they sailed together as it were on the same vessel of life. Both did away with Clytemnestra as though both were sons of Agamemnon, by both of them was Aegisthus slain. Pylades it was who suffered the more from the Avengers who hounded Orestes, and he stood trial along with him in court. Nor did they restrict their affectionate friendship to the limits of Hellas, but sailed to Scythia at the very ends of the earth, one of them afflicted, the other ministering to him. (Ps.-Lucian *Amores* 47)

46. *Odyssey* 5.61: "singing with a sweet voice (ὀπὶ καλῇ)."

47. Ibid., 12.192.

48. *Iliad* 1.604: the Muses "sing sweetly (ὀπὶ καλῇ)"; cf. *Odyssey* 24.60.

49. *Odyssey* 10.221.

50. Ibid., 10.226–27; cf. 254.

51. Ibid., 10.136, 11.8, and 12.150; cf. Ovid *Metamorphoses* 14.20 and especially Virgil: "Songs can even draw the moon from heaven; / by songs Circe changed the comrades of Ulysses" (*Eclogue* 8.69–70) and "Closely they skirt the shores of Circe's land, where the rich daughter of the Sun thrills her untrodden groves with ceaseless song" (*Aeneid* 7.10–12).

52. See, e.g., Apollodorus *Epitome* 7.16 and Hyginus *Fabulae* 125. Telegonus was the protagonist of the no longer extant *Telegonia* by Eugammon of Cyrene.

53. See also his lying and cruelty to Dolon in *Iliad* Book 10.

Calliope's sister in *The Acts of Andrew*, who went to implore Artemis to help, may be Circe's sister and Minos's wife Pasiphae, who had her own obstetric difficulties. She mated with a bull and birthed the monstrous minotaur.

Neither Circe nor Pasiphae had connections with Corinth. This geographical allusion may signal nothing hypertextually, but it might point to Circe indirectly through her niece Medea, whom Jason divorced once he arrived at Corinth. See, for example, Apollodorus *Library* 1.9.28 and Euripides *Medea*.

54. One of Artemis's epithets was Εἰλείθυια, 'goddess who helps in childbirth'. See

Odyssey 20.60–78, *Iliad* 21.482–84, Plato *Theaetetus* 149b–c, Lucian *Dialogues of the Gods* 18 (245) and 25 (287), and Apuleius *Metamorphoses* 11.2: "Phoebus' sister, who brought forth populous multitudes by relieving the delivery of offspring." In the *Hymn to Artemis* by Callimachus, the goddess boasts this special gift:

> On the mountains will I dwell and the cities of men I will visit only when women vexed by the sharp pangs of childbirth call me to their aid—even in the hour when I was born the Fates ordained that I should be their helper, forasmuch as my mother suffered no pain either when she gave me birth or when she carried me in her womb, but without travail put me from her body. (Callimachus *Hymns* 3.20–25)

55. *Metamorphoses* 14.25–27 (Gregory).

56. The hypertextuality of the story might also find support in the absence of the father from the scene. Odysseus had been long gone when Telegonus was born. There also might be a wordplay on the name Telegonus, 'born from afar', so named because Odysseus was long gone by the time of his birth. It is possible—but farfetched, alas—that the author of the *Acts* took the name to mean 'far from birth' (τελε-γονος), i.e., stillborn.

57. E.g., *Iliad* 2.107–8 and 569–80.

58. *The Acts of Andrew* had named another character Sostratus, the young man wrongly accused of incest in GE 4, the counter-Oedipus.

59. This same story informed *AAMt* 24, where the devil gave evil advice to the Myrmidons (see chapter 2, 52–53).

60. E.g., Plato *Republic* 2.383a, Justin Martyr *First Apology* 25, Tatian *Oratio ad graecos* 21, and Irenaeus *Adversus haereses* 1.12.

61. *Iliad* 20.164–75 (Fagles 20.194–205).

62. Ibid., 24.41–44 (Fagles 24.48–52); cf. 572 and 18.316–23.

63. Ibid., 18.205–6 and 225–27 (Fagles 18.238–39 and 260–62); cf. 22.25–32:

> Him [Achilles] the old man Priam was first to behold with his eyes, as he sped all-gleaming over the plain, like to the star that cometh forth at harvest-time, and brightly do his rays shine amid the host of stars in the darkness of the night, the star that men call by name the Dog of Orion. . . . Even in such wise did the bronze gleam upon the breast of Achilles as he ran.

See also *Iliad* 20.28 and 45–46, 22.317–20, and 24.630.

64. Cf. GE 5 and 23.

65. *Georgics* 3.6.

66. *Argonautica* 1.1207–39.

67. Ibid., 1.1261–62.

68. See also Apollodorus *Library* 1.9.19, Theocritus *Idyll* 13, Propertius 1.20.17–50, and Valerius Flaccus *Argonautica* 3.535–97.

69. Theocritus, too, described Heracles' madness over the loss of Hylas:

> When a fawn cries in the hills, some ravening lion will speed from his lair to get him a meal so ready; and even so went Heracles wildly to and fro amid the pathless brake,

and covered much country because of his longing for the child. . . . But he alas! was running whithersoever his feet might carry him, in a frenzy (μαινόμενος), the god did rend so cruelly the heart within him. (*Idyll* 13)

Valerius Flaccus wrote: "[T]hen turns he [Heracles] pale indeed, and black sweat pours down, and dumb frenzy holds him" (*Argonautica* 3.576–77).

70. *Peristephanon* 10.241–45.

71. *Protrepticus* 2.33.5. See also *Ps.-Clementine Homilies* 5.15.

72. *Contra orationem Symmachi* 1.116–19. See also Lactantius *Divine Institutes* 5.10, Arnobius *Adversus nationes* 4.26, and Firmicus Maternus *Error of Pagan Religions* 12.2.

73. E.g., Lycophron *Alexandra* 168; cf. *Odyssey* 8.517 and Quintus Smyrnaeus *Posthomerica* 13.355.

74. E.g., Pausanius 3.19.11–13 and Philostratus *Heroicus* 211–13.

75. Apollodorus *Library* 3.10.7 and *Epitome* 1.23, Diodorus Siculus 4.63, Hyginus *Fabulae* 79, and Ps.-Lucian *Charidemus* 16.

76. E.g., Pausanius 2.22.6, who cites earlier authorities; cf. Plato *Republic* 3.391c–d.

77. Lycophron *Alexandra* 850.

78. *Iliad* 6.344–45; cf. 3.404 and 414, 6.356, 19.325, and 24.775.

79. *Helen* 81.

80. Plato *Phaedrus* 243a and Pausanius 3.19.13.

81. Gorgias vindicated her in his *Helen* but admitted in the end that he was merely spoofing. Isocrates' exoneration of her in *Helen* is merely a pretentious school exercise.

82. *True History* 2.25–26. Lucian also ridicules Helen of her amours in *The Judgments of the Goddesses* 13–15.

83. *Paidagogos* 3.2.13.1–2; cf. *Protrepticus* 2.35.2.

84. *Stromateis* 2.20.106–7.1, quoting Euripides *Andromache* 629. Vaseware frequently depicts Menelaus chasing Helen and dropping his sword as he does so (*LIMC* s.v. Helen, nos. 260, 262, 264, 265, 266, 269, 270, 271, 272, 272bis, 274, 275, and 277; cf. nos. 290–360, where Helen is led away by various men). See also Quintus Smyrnaeus *Posthomerica* 13.385–405. Nicolaus in Andrew's *Acts* had no sword to drop; he dropped his Gospel instead.

85. *Oratio ad graecos* 10.3 (ANF). Tatian surely has in mind Orestes' attempt in *Orestes* 1105–1473, but he either misunderstood the text or intentionally distorted it. Orestes wanted to kill Helen and nearly did so, but just as he was about to plunge his sword into her neck, Apollo snatched her away. As a matter of fact, among ancient authors Euripides was unusually sympathetic to Helen.

86. *Exegesis on the Soul* (*NHL* II.6.37.2–5), quoting *Odyssey* 4.261–64.

87. Achilles in particular complained of Menelaus's obsession (*Iliad* 9.337–45; cf. 2.161–62, 177–78, and 590, 3.156–60, and 7.348–53).

88. For an extended treatment of Menelaus's wanderings in search of Helen, see Lycophron *Alexandra* 820–76.

89. *Iphigenia at Aulis* 385–87. Aristotle is said to have vindicated Menelaus's character by noting that Homer never gave him a concubine, unlike his brother

Agamemnon, whose field hut was full of women taken in battle (Athenaeus *Deipnosophists* 13.556d–e, citing *Iliad* 2.226–28).

90. *Oratio ad graecos* 1.

91. *Odyssey* 4.65–67.

92. Ibid., 15.135–41.

93. Ibid., 4.561–69; cf. Euripides *Helen* 1676–79 and Apollodorus *Epitome* 6.29.

94. For variations of this story see: Apollodorus (*Library* 2.4.12), Diodorus Siculus (4.11 and 55), and Hyginus (*Fabulae* 31–32); cf. Lucian *Dialogue of the Gods* 15 (237).

95. Lucian *The Dance* 41.

96. Pindar *Isthmian Odes* 4.61–68. Thebans proudly showed visitors the tomb of Heracles' children (Pausanius 9.11.2).

97. Pausanius 9.11.2.

98. Athenagoras *Legatio* 29.1 and Clement of Alexandria *Protrepticus* 7.76.5. Clement quotes from *The Madness of Heracles* in *Stromateis* 5.11.75.2. See also Lactantius *Divine Institutes* 1.9.

99. *Apology* 10 (ANF).

100. *Madness of Heracles* 523, 1030, and 1037–38.

101. Ibid., 597; cf. 890, 893, 905, and 919–21.

102. Ibid., 922–1015.

103. Ibid., 935.

104. Ibid., 931–34; cf. 990.

105. Ibid., 1017–68.

106. This sentence suggests that Antiphanes was somehow unworthy to receive special consideration, but there is nothing in Gregory otherwise to suggest what his vices might have been.

107. An exorcism of a house appears in Lucian *The Lover of Lies* 30–31.

108. *Madness of Heracles* 1303–10; cf. 830–32.

109. *Ethnica* (Meineke), s.v. Αἰγαὶ πολλαί. Thus, an author of a poetic epigram called himself Ἰσίδωρος Αἰγεάτης, Isidore of Aegae (*Anthologia graeca* 7.280).

110. *Iliad* 13.20–22.

111. *Odyssey* 5.380–81. See also *Iliad* 8.203, Homeric Hymn 3 (to Poseidon), Pindar *Nemean Odes* 5.37, Strabo *Geography* 8.7.4 and 9.2.13, Philostratus the elder *Imagines* 1.8, Stephen of Byzantium *Ethnica*, s.v. Αἰγαὶ πολλαί, and Homeric scholia.

112. E.g., Porphyry (citing Theagenes of Rhegium) *Quaestiones Homericarum* 1.240: τὸ δὲ ὕδωρ Ποσειδῶνα; and Ps.-Plutarch *De vita et poesi Homeri* 97: Ποσειδῶν δὲ τὴν τοῦ ὕδατος οὐσίαν. Cf. Maximus of Tyre 32, Diogenes Laertius 7.147–48, and Fulgentius *Mythologicae* 1.4. See Buffière, *Mythes d'Homère*, 117–22.

113. According to Proclus, Poseidon in Homer stands for γενεσιουργά (*In Platonis rem publicam comm.* 2.239). Cf. *In Platonis Cratylum comm.* 151: ἡ θάλασσα τῇ γενέσει ἀναλογεῖ; and 152: Ποσειδῶν ἐστιν θεὸς νοερὸς δημιουργικὸς καὶ τὰς ψυχὰς κατιούσας εἰς τὴν γένεσιν ὑποδεχόμενος, Ἅδης δὲ θεὸς νοερὸς δημιουργικὸς τὰς λύων ἀπὸ τῆς γενέσεως; cf. 158. See also Buffière, *Mythes d'Homère*, 414–17.

114. Passion 62.

115. *Odyssey* 14.53–58; cf. 15.304–45.

116. The name Sosius (Σώσιος) may simply symbolize his cure (σωτηρία) from a serious illness through apostolic power, but a somewhat more satisfactory solution might be to contrast Sosius's status as Mr. Rescued with the tragedy of Eumaeus's enslavement. He was born free into a wealthy family (Εὔμαιος = 'well-nursed'), but while still an infant was kidnapped by pirates in a series of tragic events that led finally to his sale to Laertes, Odysseus's father. Eumaeus tells his own tale in *Odyssey* 15.403–92.

117. φίλη τροφός, *Odyssey* 2.361, 4.742, 19.21, 22.419, 480, 485, and 492, and 23.25, 39, 69, and 289; μαῖα φίλη, 19.500, 20.129, and 23.11, 35, 59, and 81.

118. Ibid., 1.428, 19.357, 20.134, and 21.381.

119. Ibid., 23.1–2.

120. See Parthenius's *Love Romances* 4, 5, 10, 11, 17, 27, 28, 31, and 36.

121. *Odyssey* 17.336–38.

122. Ibid., 18.1–2.

123. Ibid., 18.53.

124. Ibid., 18.95–102.

125. *Argonautica* 2.178–89.

126. Ibid., 2.438–42.

127. Ibid., 2.444–45. Compare Apollonius's version of Phineus with Apollodorus *Library* 1.9.21 and Hyginus *Fabulae* 19. Aeschylus and Sophocles both penned tragedies, now lost, bearing the title *Phineus*.

128. Apollodorus *Library* 1.9.21, Hyginus *Fabulae* 19, and Sophocles *Antigone* 968–76. Diodorus Siculus gives his own rationalistic account of Phineus's sons, but must admit "that certain writers of myths say that the sons of Phineus were blinded by their father and that Phineus suffered the like fate at the hands of Boreas" (4.44.4). One tradition claimed that Asclepius restored sight to the two lads (Phylarchus *apud* Sextus Empiricus *Adversus mathematicos* 1.262).

129. *Philoctetes* 682. Philoctetes' pain was proverbial. See, for example, Cicero *Tusculan Disputations* 2.7.19, 2.14.33, and 2.19.44: "[W]hat if the pain be as severe as that of Philoctetes?"

130. Compare the accounts in Sophocles *Philoctetes*, Apollodorus *Epitome* 3.27 and 5.8, Aelius Aristides 38.10, Quintus Smyrnaeus *Posthomerica* 9–10, and Hyginus *Fabulae* 102. See also Philostratus *Heroicus* 5.

131. *Iliad* 2.718–25 and *Odyssey* 3.190. The lost epic *Cypria* apparently told a much fuller version of the sufferings of Philoctetes.

132. According to Plutarch, the comic playwright Aristophon offered his audience sadistic pleasure in his depiction of Philoctetes' sufferings, even though audiences generally recoiled from "a diseased and ulcerous person as an unpleasant sight" (*How the Young Man Should Study Poetry* 18c).

133. See Pack, *Literary Texts*, nos. 2454, 2455, and 2723.

134. *Discourse* 59.

135. See also Ovid *Metamorphoses* 13.

136. *Posthomerica* 9.334–546.

137. There also might be a wordplay between Lemnos (Λῆμνος) and the word used for "harbor" in *The Acts of Andrew*, λιμήν, genitive λιμένος.

138. *Iliad* 2.721–24.

139. *Philoctetes* 261–70, 274–75, and 311–13.

140. *Epitome* 3.27.

141. *Imagines* 17.

142. *Posthomerica* 9.353–57, 375–77, and 389–90.

143. Ibid., 9.428–30.

144. Ibid., 9.461–67, 469–70, and 481–82.

145. This curious reference to "visible sounds" may reflect an exegetical tradition on the Septuagintal rendition of Exod. 20:18. Philo wrote:

Then from the midst of the fire that streamed from heaven there sounded forth to their utter amazement a voice, for the flame became articulate speech in the language familiar to the audience, and so clearly and distinctly were the words formed by it that they seemed to see rather than hear them. What I say is vouched for by the law in which it is written, "All the people saw the voice (ἑώρα τὴν φωνήν)," a phrase fraught with much meaning, for it is the case that the voice of men is audible, but the voice of God truly visible. Why so? Because whatever God says is not words but deeds, which are judged by the eyes rather than the ears. (*Decalogue* 46–47; cf. *On the Migration of Abraham* 47 and *Moses* 2.213)

146. Depictions of Philoctetes in ancient art often show him nude.

147. Cf. Tatian *Oratio ad graecos* 32.

148. For discussions of this hotly debated matter see MacDonald, *Acts of Andrew*, 3–47, and the conclusion to this volume, 316–18.

6

Recognitions

The third and final section of *The Acts of Andrew* narrates events leading up to the apostle's death at the hands of Aegeates. The text of this section—conventionally but somewhat inaccurately called the Passion—survives nearly intact, thanks in large measure to the transformation of the martyrdoms of the apocryphal Acts into hagiographies for liturgical use. In this chapter I analyze Passion 1–50, Andrew's preaching in Patras. In chapter 7 I discuss Passion 51–64, Andrew's execution.

Even before the curtain lifts on Passion 1, the reader has seen the mise-en-scène. Andrew resides with Sosius in Patras, the Greek city closest to Odysseus's Ithaca and the location for all of the action until the end of the *Acts*. The proconsul Aegeates will play the role of Odysseus by slaying Andrew, his rival for the heart of Maximilla, a hypertextual Penelope. Maximilla's servant, Iphidama, calls to mind Penelope's faithful servant, Eurycleia, and Aegeates' brother, Stratocles, represents Telemachus, son of Penelope and Odysseus. Much of the narrative takes place in the praetorium of Aristocles ('superlative renown'), with its upstairs bedrooms, lavish banquets, vicious dogs, and treacherous servants. As such, it corresponds with the magnificent palace of Odysseus, whose Homeric renown (κλέος) as one of the "best (ἄριστοι) of the Achaeans" was surpassed only by Achilles. Throughout the Passion Andrew can be seen to have absorbed some of Odysseus's traits, but more often than not he appears as a Christianized Socrates.

The barefoot philosopher has appeared frequently in the analysis already. The author agreed with many of Socrates' objections to Homer's deities and heroes, such as Zeus's deceitful dream,[1] the bribery of gods through sacrifices,[2] Achilles' murder of the twelve Trojan warriors, his dragging of Hector's corpse,[3] Zeus's grief at the death of Sarpedon,[4] his crippling of his own son, Hephaestus,[5] his lust for Hera on Mount Ida,[6] and the adultery of Ares and Aphrodite.[7] In his writing of the Myrmidons' visit to hell, the author adapted Socrates' myth of Er at the end of *The Republic* in order to transvaluate Homer's *nekyia* in *Odyssey* Book 11.[8] When Andrew left the Myrmidons he entrusted them to Bishop Plato, just as Socrates had given way to his star pupil, Plato. Had more of these earlier sections of the *Acts* survived, especially the speeches, one might have found even more evidence of Socrates.

211

In Passion 1–50, the concern of this chapter, one detects Socratic influence especially on Andrew's pedagogy, which imitates Socratic interrogation. The next chapter looks at Passion 51–64, where Andrew's martyrdom imitates Socrates' execution as told in Plato's *Phaedo*. Throughout both chapters, the combination of characterizations from *The Odyssey* (Maximilla, Aegeates, and Stratocles) with Andrew's role as a new Socrates creates confusion unless the reader keeps in mind the apologetic strategies of the entire work; namely, that the Platonizing Christian author has construed the apostle as a Christianized Socrates in order to transform Homeric (and post-Homeric) gods and heroes into exemplary followers of Jesus Christ. No ancient character was more capable than Socrates of ridding the Greek landscape of venal gods and heroes, as Justin Martyr knew:

> Socrates . . . was accused of the very same crimes as ourselves. For they said that he was introducing new divinities, and did not consider those to be gods whom the state recognised. But he cast out from the state both Homer and the rest of the poets, and taught men to reject the wicked demons and those who did the things which the poets related.[9]

Throughout *The Acts of Andrew*, the apostle, befitting a Christianized Socrates, opposes demons who represent Homeric gods, and in the end he, too, will die for having introduced a new religion.

With respect to *The Odyssey*, Passion 1–50 corresponds to Books 14–21, the so-called "recognitions."[10] The dog Argo, Telemachus, Eurycleia, and Eumaeus gradually come to recognize that the old beggar in their midst is none other than the returned king of Ithaca. The word γνωρίζειν, 'to recognize', recurs in the Passion nineteen times. Believers are those who recognize the devil for what he is (3 and 49), who recognize the soul's ascent to immateriality (37), who recognize God (38), and who are recognized by God (33 and 55). At the very end of the *Acts*, Andrew recognizes his cross (54) and glories in having been "recognized by the relative," that is, recognized by God (62).

The most important recognitions in *The Acts of Andrew*, however, are self-recognitions induced by the apostle's preaching and Socratic questioning. Andrew thus succeeds in assisting others to satisfy the Delphic imperative so important to Socrates: γνῶθι σαυτόν, "know thyself." The self-recognitions of Maximilla and Stratocles require them radically to alter the behavior of their Homeric antecedents, Penelope and Telemachus. Andrew, the Christian Socrates, corrects Homer's moral errors and, like Socrates, will die unjustly for his trouble.

The Arrival of Stratocles (Telemachus, Passion 1)

The Passion of Andrew begins with Aegeates away from home: "At the same time that his wife was healed, the proconsul Aegeates took leave for Rome, to the emperor Nero" (Passion 1). Aegeates' absence, though brief, will function much like Odysseus's absence at Troy and at sea. When Aegeates returns, he will find his household troubled by Andrew and will attempt to slay him, as Odysseus did Penelope's suitors. The text next introduces Aegeates' brother, Stratocles, "who had petitioned Caesar not to serve in the army but to pursue philosophy, arrived in Patras from Italy at that very moment" (Passion 13). In Greek there is an obvious and ironic wordplay between the name Stratocles 'renowned in battle' (Στρατοκλῆς) and his decision no longer to fight (μὴ στρατεύεσθαι). By the end of the *Acts*, Stratocles will have renounced violence altogether and will have returned to childlike innocence. By so doing, he reverses the direction of development of Telemachus, Odysseus's son.

When his father left to fight in Troy, Telemachus was a mere infant and therefore grew up without a father's tutelage. Odysseus's son first appears in the epic as a cowering, sulking wimp in his early twenties. Out of pity, Athene pledges to "set courage in his heart" and to guide him to Sparta and Pylos "to inquire concerning the return (νόστον) of his dear father, should he perhaps hear of it, that noble renown (κλέος ἐσθλόν) may be his among humankind."[11] This speech establishes expectations for the entire epic: Telemachus will learn by asking the Achaean heroes how to oust those who are squandering his estate, and in the end he will indeed acquire "noble renown" by joining his father in slaying the suitors.[12] Although in the battle itself Telemachus sustains a minor wound and makes a nearly fatal mistake—like all children, forgetting to close a door behind him—he fights gloriously with sword and spear and "gleaming bronze"; he slays four. It is his baptism by carnage that initiates him into manhood and awards him κλέος. Odysseus addresses his son: "Telemachus, now shalt thou learn this—having thyself come to the place of battle, where the best warriors are put to the trial—to bring no disgrace upon the house of thy fathers, for we have ever excelled in strength and in valour over all the earth."[13] Indeed, the name Telemachus, like Stratocles, is military: 'fighter from afar' (τηλε-μαχος), either because he grew up while his father was fighting far off in Troy,[14] or more likely because he was adept with his ever-present spear,[15] which, along with his dogs, was his most distinctive signature in artistic representations.[16] Telemachus's name, therefore, anticipates his development into a hero through warfare. Some scholars contend that the maturation of Telemachus governs the structure of the epic as a whole.[17] Whatever the case may be, few characters in ancient fiction have undergone a more thorough transformation than Telemachus's from rattle to spear.[18]

This depiction of ideal masculinity in violent Telemachus apparently offended the author of *The Acts of Andrew*, who presented Stratocles as a military dropout searching for the true philosophy and who would, in the end, become as harmless as a child. The name Stratocles, which incorporates the Homeric κλέος, does not represent the goal of his development, 'battle-praise', but his lamentable starting point.

The arrival of Stratocles caused quite a commotion: "Excitement overtook the entire praetorium of Aristocles, because he [Stratocles] had not come to visit

Aegeates for a long time. Maximilla too left the bedroom delighted to greet him, and when she had welcomed him, she entered with him." Whenever Penelope greeted someone in *The Odyssey* she had to descend from her upstairs bedroom, where no men except her son and later, of course, her husband were allowed. Maximilla's bedroom too plays an important role in *The Acts of Andrew*; she invites nearly everyone to her bedroom *except* her husband.[19]

Passion 1 also calls to mind Telemachus's return from Pylos. Without telling his mother, the youth had left Ithaca to consult Nestor and Menelaus about his plight. When Penelope learned that he had left, she was inconsolable with fear that the suitors would kill him on his return. Thus, when he did at last come back safely, Eurycleia and Penelope were ecstatic. Compare the following.

Odyssey 17.32–39	Passion 1
With a burst of tears she [Eurycleia] came straight toward him, and round about them gathered the other maids of Odysseus of the steadfast heart, and they kissed his head and shoulders in loving welcome.	Excitement overtook the entire praetorium of Aristocles, because he [Stratocles] had not come to visit Aegeates for a long time.
Then forth from her chamber came wise Penelope, . . . and bursting into tears **she flung her arms about her dear son,** and kissed his head and both his beautiful eyes.	**Maximilla, too, left the bedroom** **delighted to greet him,** **and when she had welcomed him,** she entered with him.

Passion 1 continues: "At daybreak, she [Maximilla] was alone while Stratocles fulfilled his social obligation to his friends, comporting himself graciously to everyone and greeting them all appropriately and measuredly." No character in the apocryphal Acts has better manners than Stratocles, and this is due to his Homeric hypertextuality. Telemachus was a paradigm of probity. For example, when he first returned to the palace, he told his mother to return to her bedroom, while he himself would show hospitality to a friend.[20] Homer's epithets for Telemachus enhance his noblesse oblige: "prudent," "high-minded," and "great-hearted."[21] Later interpreters appealed to Telemachus and his education by Mentor (Athena in disguise), Nestor, and Menelaus in order to instruct young boys in etiquette.[22]

The Healing of Alcman (Heracles, Passion 2–5)

While Stratocles was greeting his friends, "one of the boys under the supervision of Aristocles and whom he loved dearly was stricken by a demon and lay in feces out of his mind" (Passion 2). Stratocles was desperate about this situation until Maximilla emerged from her bedroom—like a Penelope—to tell him about

Andrew's powers of healing. Stratocles' servant is a hypertextual Heracles; the hypotext again is *The Madness of Heracles* by Euripides.

GE 29 told the story of Antiphanes of Megara, who returned to his home only to find it infested with demons. Antiphanes, 'inconspicuous', stood for Heracles, who killed his children in a fit of rage, the subject of Euripides' play. Curiously enough, in GE 29 Antiphanes himself was not crazed, which one might have expected in a hypertextual rendition. Apparently the author of the *Acts* decided to place his version of Heracles' madness later, here in Passion 2–5.

The lad's name was Alcman ('Aλκμάνης), 'violent madness'. Of itself this translation might be sufficient to think of Heracles, but even more significant is the relationship of Alcman to the name of Heracles' mother, Alcmene ('Aλκμήνη).[23] By now it should come as no surprise that when the *Acts* states someone "was stricken by a demon . . . out of his mind (παραπλήξ)," the demon probably stands for an Olympian: Heracles' madness was the work of Hera.[24] Euripides even uses expressions later found in *The Acts of Andrew* to describe this divine mania.[25] When Stratocles discovered what had happened to his servant, he lamented as the chorus did for Heracles.[26] Andrew's arrival at the praetorium also might point to the play: "On entering the gate he said, 'Some force is fighting inside; hurry brothers!' He asked questions of no one but burst inside to the place where Stratocles' lad was foaming at the mouth, entirely contorted" (Passion 3). Euripides placed his chorus, other characters, and most of the action outside the palace, while Heracles slew his family inside. Sounds of terror issued from within, alerting the actors and the audience that a horrible fight was taking place there. They, like Andrew, detected that "some force is fighting inside."

In the play, a servant emerges from the palace to give an eyewitness account of the violence.[27] The doors then open for everyone to behold the bloody work and Heracles asleep, lashed to a pillar lest he do more harm.[28] The description of Heracles' madness resembles Alcman's:

Madness of Heracles 931–34	Passion 3
"[Heracles] seemed no more the same, / But wholly marred, with rolling eyes distraught, / With bloodshot eye-roots starting from his head, / While dripped the **slaver** (ἀφρόν) down his **bearded cheek** [cf. 867: "eyes **contorted** (διαστρόφους)"].	[Alcman] was **foaming at the mouth** (ἤφριζεν) entirely **contorted** (διάστροφος).

When the apostle entered the palace, people there abused him, mistaking him for a beggar:

> Those who came dashing because of Stratocles' ruckus had no idea who Andrew was when they saw him smiling (μειδιῶντα). . . . Those who already had met and approved of Andrew gave ground, fearing him like some god.[29] Stratocles' servants, on the other hand, viewed him as a shabby tramp and tried

to beat him up. When the rest saw them humiliating (ἐνυβρίζοντας) him, they rebuked those who did not know (ἀγνοοῦσιν) what they were doing. (Passion 3)

The residents of Patras can hardly be blamed for having mistaken Andrew for a beggar. When he arrived in Patras, he was "naked, destitute, and carrying with him for the journey nothing but the name of a certain person named Jesus" (GE 22).

The abuse of Andrew as a beggar in Passion 3 calls to mind not Euripides but Homer's depiction of Odysseus among the suitors. Athena told the hero,

> Now, for a while,
> I shall transform you; not a soul will know you (ἄγνωστον),
> the clear skin of your arms and legs shriveled,
> your chestnut hair all gone, your body dressed
> in sacking that a man would gag to see,
> and the two eyes, that were so brilliant, dirtied—
> contemptible, you shall seem to your enemies.[30]

Thus, when Odysseus appeared to the suitors, they treated the apparent beggar with disdain and blows. The suitors themselves narrate how Eumaeus the swineherd "brought his master, clad in mean raiment, in the likeness of a woeful and aged beggar, leaning on a staff, and miserable was the raiment that he wore about his body; and not one of us could know (γνῶναι) that it was he ... but we assailed him with evil words and with missiles."[31] In spite of this humiliation, Odysseus smiled (μείδησε) in crafty self-confidence.[32] Eumaeus and Telemachus, recognizing the beggar's true identity, rebuked the suitors for their hubris. If any one word is associated with the suitors in *The Odyssey* it is ὕβρις and its cognates, which apply seventeen times to the suitors for their arrogant treatment of Odysseus and his estate.[33]

Greek intellectuals frequently saw in Odysseus's rags a metaphor for the philosophical life. Cynics, who themselves often looked like tramps and begged for their livelihoods, identified with Odysseus, who, according to a fragment of Epictetus, "was no less pre-eminent in his rags than in his rich and purple cloak."[34] Dio Chrysostom's accolades for Diogenes the Cynic included likening him to Odysseus, "a king and lord, who in the guise of a beggar moved among his slaves and menials while they caroused in ignorance of his identity," enduring their "riotous conduct and ὕβρις."[35]

It would therefore appear that Andrew's peculiar reception at the praetorium derives from *The Odyssey*. He enters as a smiling beggar confident that he will overcome Alcman's demon. Some beat him up, ignorant (ἀγνοοῦσιν) of his true identity, while others who recognize him fear him as a god and rebuke the others for their hubris (ἐνυβρίζοντας).[36]

Andrew then exorcised the youth, again calling to mind *The Madness of*

Heracles. "When the demon had left, Alcman got up from the ground, Andrew extended his hand to him, and the lad walked with him, self-composed, steady on his feet, conducting coherent conversation, affectionately looking at Andrew and his master, and inquiring about the cause for the crowd inside." So, too, in Euripides: when Heracles awakes he is in full control of his faculties but oblivious to the horrors he had wrought.[37] The next section of the play contains nineteen interrogative sentences placed on the lips of Heracles, who wants to learn what had happened. For example, he asks why his father is weeping, why he is bound to the pillar, why bloody corpses lie strewn around him, and who killed them.[38] Amphitryon tries to avoid telling the hero the entire dreadful truth;[39] similarly, Andrew told inquisitive Alcman: "There is no need for you to learn about anything alien to you. It is enough for us to see in you what we have seen" (Passion 5).

Apparently the author of *The Acts of Andrew* crafted Alcman as an exorcised Heracles. Like the son of Alcmene, Alcman frothed at the mouth, writhed, and, when exorcised, asked what had happened to him. Transvaluative moral of the story: whereas the goddess Hera struck Heracles with mania, the God of the Christians restores demoniacs to their senses.[40]

The Bedroom of Maximilla (Penelope, Passion 6)

According to Passion 6, "Maximilla took Andrew and Stratocles by the hand and entered her bedroom along with any of the brethren who were there. Once seated, they looked at the blessed Andrew so that he might speak" (Passion 6). Maximilla's bedroom already has appeared twice in the *Acts*, but now, her husband away, she opens it up to "the brethren." In no other apocryphal Acts, in no other early Christian narrative for that matter, can one find references to women's bedrooms as brash, suggestive, and potentially scandalous as this. Even the word selected for bedroom suggests sex. The author might have used the more archaic and poetic θάλαμος, 'boudoir', as in Homer, or the discreet δωμάτιον, 'chamber', but instead he chose κοιτών, 'bedroom', the room for the κοίτη or 'bed', metaphorically, 'intercourse'.

The author emphasized Maximilla's open-door policy in order to contrast her with Penelope. "[M]y mother . . . does not often appear before the wooers," states Telemachus, "but apart from them weaves at her loom in an upper chamber."[41] No suitor is allowed on the upper floor, and only Penelope's servants, Telemachus, and Odysseus are allowed in her bedroom. Moreover, only one maidservant and, apart from Odysseus, no man—not even Telemachus—has seen her bed.[42] When she does show herself to the suitors partying in the hall below, she remains a picture of veiled purity.[43] Her business with the suitors completed, she returns to her quarters to weep on her "bed of tears."[44] For most of the narrative, the reader is to assume that she is in her bolted bedroom weeping alone,[45] or with her maidservants.[46] Homer uses Penelope's deliberate choreography between her chamber and the hall to dramatize her chastity. How differently *The Odyssey* would read if Penelope, like Maximilla, took the suitors by the hand and led them to her bedroom!

The Birth Pangs of Stratocles (Theaetetus, Passion 7–12)

In Maximilla's bedroom Andrew addresses Stratocles and establishes the goal the youth will attain by the end of the *Acts*: the birthing of his spiritual fetus. In the context of the Passion as a whole, this development of the onetime soldier into an infant reverses Telemachus's maturation through violence, but behind this particular section of the Passion is not Homer's *Odyssey* but Plato's *Theaetetus*.[47]

When Socrates expressed his desire to find a young man displaying unusual promise for philosophy, his interlocutor mentioned a certain Theaetetus of impeccable character and intelligence.[48] In order to determine whether or not the youth was indeed exceptional, Socrates began questioning him, socratically of course. Theaetetus answered well for a while, but when confronted with questions he could not field, he confessed confusion and consternation.

> Soc. Yes, you are suffering the pangs of labour (ὠδίνεις), because you are not empty, but pregnant.
>
> Theaet. I do not know, Socrates; I merely tell you what I feel (πέπονθα).
>
> Soc. Have you then not heard, you absurd boy, that I am the son of noble and burly midwife (μαίας)?[49]

Socrates claimed to have learned maieutics, midwifery, from his mother, but his vocation differed from hers, he said, "in being practised upon men, not women, and in tending their souls in labour (τικτούσας), not their bodies. But the greatest thing about my art is this, that it can test in every way whether the mind of the young man is bringing forth (ἀποτίκτει) a mere image, an imposture, or a real and genuine offspring."[50] Socrates does not teach; he merely elicits, so help him god:

> I am, then, not at all a wise person myself, nor have I any wise invention, the offspring born of my own soul; but those who associate with me, . . . all of them to whom the god is gracious make wonderful progress. . . . And it is clear that they do this, not because they have ever learned anything from me, but because they have found in themselves many fair things and have brought them forth. But the delivery is due to the god and me.[51]

Furthermore, Socrates claimed that just as midwives could intuit who was pregnant and who not, he could, too: when he asked his vexing questions the truly wise would be thrown into labor pains. Socrates saw it as his duty to induce such pains, "to cause people disorientation."[52] This phrase translates ἀπορεῖν, 'to produce ἀπορία', literally 'the state of having no exit', apposite both for a fetus during labor and for a brainchild struggling for expression.[53] As Socrates explains it:

> Now those who associate with me are in this matter also like women in childbirth (τικτούσαις); they are in pain (ὠδίνουσι) and are full of trouble (ἀπορίας) night and day (νύκτας τε καὶ ἡμέρας), much more than are the women. . . .
>
> Now I have said all this to you at such length, my dear boy, because I suspect that you, as you yourself believe, are in pain (ὠδίνειν) because you are pregnant (κυοῦντα) with something within you.[54]

Similarly, Andrew recognizes that Stratocles, the would-be philosopher, is pregnant with his inner self, and tells him so in Maximilla's bedroom:

> I must bring out into the open the person now latent within you. Your total bewilderment (διαπορεῖν) and pondering of the source and cause of what has happened are the greatest proofs that the soul within you is troubled (τεταραγμένης),[55] and the perplexity (ἀπορία), hesitation, and astonishment in you please me. Bring to birth (ἀποκύησον) the child you are carrying and do not give yourself over to labor pains (ὠδῖσιν) alone. I am no novice at midwifery (μαιευτικῆς) or divination (μαντικῆς). (Passion 7)[56]

The author's dependence on Plato is transparent, not merely because he uses the technical word "maieutics," but also because Andrew boasts of his clairvoyance. Like Socrates, he knows from Stratocles' perplexity that he is pregnant. The speech continues:

> I desire what you are birthing (ἀποτίκτεις). I love what you are stifling. I will suckle what is within you. I know the one who is silent. I know the one who aspires. Already your new self speaks to me. Already I encounter those things he has suffered (πέπονθε) for so long. He is ashamed of his former religion; he mourns his former public conduct; he considers all his former worship vacuous; he has no idea (διαπορεῖ) what true religion is; he tacitly reproaches the useless gods of his past; having become a vagabond (ἀλήτης),[57] he suffers (πάσχει) in order to become educated (παιδείας). Whatever his former philosophy, he now knows that it was hollow. He sees that it is destitute and worthless. Now he learns that it promises nothing essential. Now he admits that it pledges nothing useful. Right? Does the person inside you not say these things, Stratocles? (Passion 7)

Andrew's speeches to Stratocles, including this one, often take the form of Socratic questions. Later Andrew will claim that Christ did not send him to teach anything, but merely "to remind (ὑπομνῆσαι) everyone akin to these words that all people pass their time among ephemeral evils" (Passion 47). Andrew's pedagogy, like that of Socrates, is not didactic but mimetic, not declarative but evocative, not impregnating but obstetric—and painful. "After a loud groan (στενάξαι), Stratocles answered as follows: 'Most prophetic (μαντικώτατε) man, truly a messenger of the living God, I too will not separate from you until I recognize myself (ἐμαυτὸν γνωρίζω)'" (Passion 8).

This is the first of several theological recognitions in the Passion. Insofar as Stratocles represents Telemachus in the *Acts*, his self-recognition may be the author's alternative to Telemachus's recognition of his father. When Odysseus finally revealed his identity to his son, he said, "I am thy father, for whose sake thou hast with groaning (στεναχίζων) endured many griefs," but the lad was reluctant to believe him lest he "weep and groan (στεναχίζω) yet more."[58] Once he was convinced that the tramp was his sire, he cried profusely.[59] In *The Acts of Andrew* such weeping occurs in the process of Stratocles' learning to recognize himself.

More significantly, this self-recognition (ἐμαυτὸν γνωρίζω) calls to mind the famous inscription of the Apollo temple at Delphi warning all who entered: "know thyself (γνῶθι σαυτόν)."[60] From Socrates on, Greek thinkers pondered the meaning of this enigmatic imperative.[61] For many Neoplatonists and Christian Gnostics, as well as for the author of *The Acts of Andrew*, to know or to recognize oneself was to understand that one's soul is eternal, immaterial, and akin (συγγενής) to the divine.[62] Cognates of συγγενής, 'akin', and συγγένεια, 'kindred', appear throughout the Passion to refer to the soul's kinship with God or with other souls of like faith.[63] Unbelievers, on the other hand, are akin to the demonic, the material, and the base.[64] Like the good Platonist he was, the author portrayed self-recognition as the understanding of one's inner self and its affinities with the spiritual.[65] Maximilla will come to recognize her soul as her inner husband; Stratocles will recognize his soul as his spiritual infant, with Andrew as its midwife.

Stratocles stayed

> with the apostle night and day (νυκτὸς καὶ ἡμέρας) and never left him, sometimes examining, learning from, and interrupting him, and other times remaining silent. . . .[66] [W]hile the rest of the believers were doing something else, he questioned (ἐπυνθάνετο) him in private. When the others fell asleep, he would lie awake and by his enthusiastic interruptions would not let Andrew sleep. (Passion 8)

Telemachus, too, spent nights awake,[67] much of his time pressing to learn of his father's fate, to "gain knowledge (πυνθάνομαι) by hearing the words of others."[68] The word πυνθάνεσθαι, 'to learn' or 'inquire', and its cognates are associated with Telemachus throughout *The Odyssey* and with Stratocles throughout *The Acts of Andrew*.[69]

Andrew revealed Stratocles' inquiries (πεύσεις) to the other believers and told him not merely to ask him questions (ἀναπυνθανόμενος) in private,[70] but also to hear the apostle's public speeches, insofar as he must not conceal his labor pains (ὠδῖνας) from his peers (Passion 9). Once again, Andrew employs midwives as metaphors:

> Take the example of a woman in labor (ὠδίνουσα): When the labor pains overcome her and the fetus is pressured by some power to come forth—not to stay within but to be squeezed outside—the fetus becomes clear and noticeable to the attending women who take part in such mysteries (the fetus itself cried out when the mother had cried out earlier). Then, postpartum, they at last provide for the infant whatever care these initiates might know, whatever their life-giving technique might be. Likewise, Stratocles, my child, we too must not be passive but bring your embryos (κυήματα) into the open, so that they may be registered and be brought to the donative of saving words by many kindred (συγγενῶν), whose associate I found you to be.[71] (Passion 9)

Andrew's preaching accomplished its intent: "Stratocles, full of gratitude, Maximilla, Iphidama, Alcman, along with many of the other brethren, were deemed worthy of the Lord's seal (σφραγῖδος)" (Passion 10). Scholars disagree about the meaning of the "Lord's seal";[72] here it seems to refer to some rite guaranteeing the welfare of the soul against the onslaught of demonic powers. By referring to the seal here, immediately after Andrew's Socratic discourse to Stratocles, the author can play hypertextually one last time with Plato's *Theaetetus*.

In order to present his explanation of true and false opinions, Socrates proposed to Theaetetus that "in our souls is a block of wax" on which the senses make imprints (ἀποτυποῦσθαι) or impressions (ἐνσημαινομένους).[73] Once Socrates called these impressions a "seal (σφραγῖδα)."[74] False opinions arise when these impressions become confused with each other, as when one impression overstrikes another. One therefore must "hold the two imprints each under its proper perception";[75] in other circumstances, one must put "the proper imprints and seals (ἀποτυπώματα καὶ τύπους) fairly and squarely upon one another,"[76] that is, to match sense perception perfectly with the impressions already made on the soul. Not all souls, however, possess qualities that allow for perfect impressions. "When the wax in the soul . . . is deep and abundant and smooth and properly kneaded, the images that come through the perceptions are imprinted (ἐνσημαινόμενα) upon this heart of the soul." Such people hold true opinions. But when the soul "is unclean or of impure wax . . . infected with earth or dung which is mixed in it," the impressions are indistinct and produce false opinions.[77]

In *The Acts of Andrew*, immediately after one reads that those in Maximilla's bedroom "were deemed worthy of the Lord's seal (σφραγῖδα)," the apostle exhorts them to keep their impressions distinct, for reasons not epistemological but soteriological:

> My children, if you keep this impression (τύπον) unconfused by other seals (σφραγίδων) that imprint (ἐτυπουσῶν) different designs, God will command you and receive you into his domain.[78] Because such a radiant image appears

in your souls which are essentially set loose from your bodies, the punishing powers, evil authorities, fearsome rulers, fiery angels, hideous demons, and foul forces—who cannot endure being forsaken by you, since they have nothing to do with the symbol of the seal (σφραγῖδος) since it is kindred (συγγενοῦς) to light—run aground and sink during their flight to their kindred (συγγενές): darkness, fire, gloom, and whatever other impending punishment one might imagine. (Passion 11)

According to Socrates, the disadvantage of dirty wax in one's soul was false opinion, but the damage of soul dirt in Andrew's speech is demonic doom:

But if you pollute the brilliance of the grace given you, those awful powers will taunt you and toy with you by dancing here and there. Like an impostor or a tyrant, each will demand its own. Then it will do you no good to call on the God of your seal (σφραγῖδος) which you defiled by apostasizing from him. So, my children, let us guard the deposit entrusted to us. Let us return the deposit spotless to the one who entrusted it to us. (Passion 11–12)

This unusual treatment of the impressions on the soul, following as it does Andrew's Socratic maieutics, is best explained as a hypertextual treatment of the *Theaetetus*.

The Return of Aegeates (Odysseus, Passion 13–14a)

In Passion 13, the author again puts his hand to rewriting *The Odyssey*, in particular, Odysseus's return to Ithaca to find his wife trapped in her bedroom and his halls infested with her suitors. When Aegeates returns from Rome, he, too, finds rivals *chez lui*, not in the hall but in the bedroom:

There was great joy among the brethren as they gathered together night and day at the praetorium with Maximilla. On the Lord's day, when the brethren were assembled in Aegeates' bedroom listening to Andrew, the proconsul arrived. When her husband's arrival was announced to Maximilla, she panicked, anticipating the outcome, that he would apprehend so many people inside.

When Andrew saw her perplexity, he said to the Lord, "Do not permit Aegeates to enter this bedroom, Lord Jesus, until your servants can leave here without fear, for they have come together for your sake, and Maximilla constantly pleads with us to meet and take our rest here. Inasmuch as you have judged her worthy to deserve your kingdom, may she be especially emboldened, and Stratocles too. Save us all by repelling that savage lion armed to attack us." (Passion 13)

Odyssey Books 4 and 17 contain identical similes prophesying that when Odysseus returned he would rage like the king of beasts: "Even as when in the thicket-lair of a mighty lion a hind has laid to sleep her new-born suckling fawns, and roams over the mountain slopes and grassy vales seeking pasture, and then the lion comes to his lair upon the two lets loose a cruel doom, so will Odysseus let loose a cruel doom upon these men."[79] Indeed, when Eurycleia opened the doors of the hall after he and Telemachus had completed their slaughter, "she found Odysseus amid the bodies of the slain, all befouled with blood and filth, like a lion that comes from feeding on an ox of the farmstead, and all his breast and his cheeks on either side are stained with blood, and he is terrible to look upon; even so was Odysseus befouled."[80]

Unlike Odysseus, however, Aegeates could do no harm:

> As the proconsul Aegeates came in, he got an urge for a bowel movement, asked for a chamber pot, and spent a long time sitting, attending to himself. He did not notice all the brethren exit in front of him. For Andrew laid his hand on each one and said, "Jesus will screen your appearance from Aegeates, in order to secure your invisibility before him." Last of all, Andrew sealed himself and left. (Passion 13)

This peculiar—and hilarious—punishment is particularly apt for a hypertextual Odysseus, whom ancient readers frequently criticized for gluttony.[81] Particularly offensive was his claim that a well-stocked table was the summum bonum.[82] Aegeates, too, could eat "like a wild beast" (Passion 46), but here in Passion 13 he paid for his gluttony with a difficult stool: "When this grace of the Lord was completed, Stratocles, because he had been away from his brother for a long time, went out and embraced Aegeates, with a smile on his face but with no joy in his soul. The rest of his servants and freedmen greeted him in the same manner" (Passion 14a). These lukewarm greetings contrast starkly with the demonstrative greetings Odysseus received on his return from Troy.[83] In *The Acts of Andrew* such demonstrations of affection apply not to Aegeates but to Andrew in his role of helping others to recognize their true kinship.

The Empowerment of Maximilla (Penelope, Passion 14b–16)

The next several chapters of the Passion focus on Maximilla and are best understood in light of Penelope's role as the ideal wife. Even though Homer's Penelope was manipulative, suspicious, and pathologically fretful, the great bard also presented her as "full of every virtue," excelling all women in beauty and greatness.[84] One ancient reader went so far as to claim that Homer framed the entire epic to extol "the glory of Penelope, and the whole scene is set to display her chastity alone. Toils by land and sea, ten years of war, ten years of wandering, all do but illustrate the fidelity of a wife."[85] This is poetic hyperbole, not ancient literary criticism at its best; even so, Homer obviously shaped the narrative from beginning to end to portray Penelope as the epitome of wifely virtues.[86] Her counterpart is Clytemnestra, the conniving, adulterous wife of

Agamemnon, who sent him to his grave when he returned from the Troad.[87] From Hades, Agamemnon's bitter shade speaks for Homer when he predicts that "the fame of [Penelope's] virtue shall never perish, but the immortals shall make among men on earth a pleasant song in honor of constant Penelope."[88]

Homer was right: "Penelope is praised by nearly everyone for her love for her husband."[89] "Do you not see that Penelope's faithfulness retains its renown through the ages and that her reputation never wanes?"[90] "Penelope's reputation for chastity is legendary."[91] These accolades from an emperor, a poet, and an anonymous novelist show with what regard the ancients thought of Odysseus's wife.[92] To be sure, others maligned her as the paragon of fornication for sharing her bed with her suitors,[93] but this is merely a burlesque of her reputation for chastity.[94]

At no time was this veneration of Ithaca's queen more widespread than during the second and third centuries C.E., which produced Levantine, Anatolian, Peloponnesian, and Sicilian inscriptions as well as Roman sarcophagi extolling women for their chastity by comparing them with Penelope.[95] These archaeological objects are surviving samples of a larger class of such "new Penelope" adulations. She had become "the glory of the female sex,"[96] an ideal nearly unattainable for real women, as Aristophanes already had lamented: "[Y]ou won't discover any Penelope alive to-day."[97]

Of Penelope's virtues, authors of this period most frequently praised her σωφροσύνη, a noun intractable of English translation, nearly equivalent to the French *sagesse*. Perhaps the English word that comes closest is 'discretion', especially sexual discretion, even chastity. In *The Odyssey*, σωφροσύνη and σώφρων, 'discreet', appear only three times, never of Penelope. Instead, her Homeric epithets are ἐχέφρων, 'prudence', and περίφρων, 'circumspect'. Insofar as ἐχέφρων became increasingly rare in post-Homeric Greek, and περίφρων came to mean 'arrogant', the -φρων adjective most apposite of Penelope in the Hellenistic and Imperial periods was σώφρων.[98]

Many considered her "altogether lovely and σώφρων."[99] According to Dio Chrysostom, Penelope "was regarded as an extremely discreet woman (σφόδρα σώφρονος . . . γυναικός)."[100] Demetrius Poliorcetes reportedly boasted that any whore in his camp was "more discreet (σωφρονέστερον) than any Penelope" in his opponent's.[101] One of Lucian's prostitutes complains to her favorite client that she had been devoted to him "as discreetly as Penelope (ὥσπερ ἡ Πηνελόπη ἐσωφρόνουν)."[102] Julian recognized that Homer found little to praise in Penelope apart from her σωφροσύνη.[103] In the opinion of the great Byzantine Homerist Eustathius, "the primary point of this poem [viz. *The Odyssey*] was σωφροσύνη," with Penelope as it primary exemplar.[104] Clement of Alexandria held Penelope to be an example of chastity worthy even of Christian women. He quoted lines about Penelope from Euripides' *Orestes* as proof of her virtue: "Odysseus's wife Telemachus / Slew not; she took no spouse while lived her lord, / But pure her couch abideth in her halls." Clement added: "By reproaching wanton adultery, he [Euripides] depicted love of one's husband as a fitting image of σωφροσύνη."[105]

But even the σωφροσύνη of a Penelope fell short of the expectations placed on women in the communities that produced the apocryphal Acts, whose heroines, such as Thecla in *The Acts of Paul*, Mygdonia and Tertia in *The Acts of Thomas*, and Agrippina, Nicaria, Euphemia, and Doris in *The Acts of Peter*, crown their conversions with uncompromising continence.[106] The story of Aristobula and Varianus in *The Acts of Andrew* probably advocated the same behavior. Whereas Penelope guarded her chastity against the suitors in order to be faithful to Odysseus, these women guarded their chastity against all comers, *including* husbands, in order to be faithful to the Christ announced by the apostles. "Of all possible guests at a society wedding, an apocryphal Apostle was the worst."[107]

Maximilla, too, is independent, continent, and resolute; but in her case, more than with any other apocryphal heroine, the transvaluation of Penelope is pointed and complete. The *Acts* redefines the ideal woman by having Maximilla absorb and intensify the traits in Penelope the author admired and by transforming those he disliked. Like Penelope, Maximilla is chaste and wise, but she is not one to remain cooped up in her bedroom alone weaving, weeping, and waiting patiently for her husband. Her development in the narrative consists in her self-liberation from the constraints of domestic, conjugal life in order to pursue holiness and philosophical detachment, even if it required inviting Andrew and "the brethren" to meet in her bedroom. The author skillfully depicts Maximilla as a critique of the submissive, passive wife of which Penelope had become a cliché.

In order to accomplish this characterization of Maximilla, the author could not afford to make Andrew resemble Homer's Odysseus, who slew the suitors for love of his wife, so he attributed these characteristics instead to Aegeates. Odysseus's weakness for romance and his strength against the suitors typify the proconsul, who longs for his wife's embrace, threatens to exterminate all rivals for her affection, and does indeed, in the end, eliminate the spoiler of his home. Expressed otherwise, in order to empty Andrew of any association with Odysseus's violence and eroticism, the author siphoned them off onto Aegeates. Like Odysseus, the proconsul is "a cheat, a destroyer, . . . a murderer, an insolent egotist, a flatterer . . . terrible, petulant, unmerciful" (Passion 62).

Burdened with such a husband, Maximilla would have to be quite a woman to stand up to him. She is. Her very name suggests strength, insofar as Maximilla is a borrowing of a Latin name derived from *maximus* and meaning 'greatest'. Iphidama ('Ιφιδάμα), the name of her servant—a name not otherwise attested in the Hellenistic or Imperial periods—is a compound of the archaic adverb ἶφι, 'by force', and the root of the verb δαμάζειν, 'to subdue'. Homer himself combines the two words to express "vanquishing by force."[108] Both primary female characters in the Passion, therefore, have virile names whose impact on the ancient Greek reader must have been similar to Mack and Butch, quite a contrast with ancient etymologies of Penelope: 'weaver' or 'duck'.[109]

Furthermore, the Passion repeatedly deploys military metaphors when

speaking of Aegeates' sexual advances and Maximilla's repulsions.[110] By the
end of the Passion, Andrew addresses her as "wise man (φρονίμου ἀνδρός),"
whose mind is to "stand firm." This is the author's answer to Homer's favorite
epithet for Penelope, "wise Penelope (περίφρων Πηνελόπεια)."

In Passion 14, after Aegeates' long journey to Rome, he attempts to make love
with his wife, and thereby plays the role of Odysseus trying to win Penelope's
affections after returning from Troy:

> But Aegeates, out of passion for Maximilla, rushed into the bedroom
> assuming she was still asleep. She was at prayer. When she saw him, she
> looked away toward the ground.

> "First give me your right hand," he told her. "I will kiss the woman I will
> call no longer 'wife' but 'queen' (δέσποιναν), so that I may find relief in your
> chastity (σωφροσύνη) and love for me."

Here Aegeates, defining σωφροσύνη as sexual fidelity to him alone, pledges to
elevate Maximilla to the status of queen (δέσποινα), used repeatedly in *The
Odyssey* for Penelope.[111]   In her prayer, however, Maximilla redefined
σωφροσύνη as absolute continence: "Rescue me at last from Aegeates' filthy
intercourse and keep me pure and chaste (σώφρονα), giving service only to you,
my God."[112] This subtle contrast of two definitions of σωφροσύνη corresponds
with the transformation of the word from its classical to its Christian
associations.[113]

When Penelope finally recognized her husband, she "flung her arms about the
neck of Odysseus and kissed his head," and then "the two had their fill of the joy
of love."[114] Aegeates had no such luck:

> When he approached her mouth intending to kiss it, she pushed him back and
> said, "Aegeates, after prayer a woman's mouth should never touch a man's."

> Taken back by the sternness of her face,[115] the proconsul left her. Because
> he had just completed a long journey, he put off his traveling clothes, relaxed,
> and lay down to sleep.

While Aegeates slept, Maximilla sneaked the apostle into her bedroom, where
Andrew prayed that God would empower her to withstand her husband's assaults.
Notice the military imagery:

> May your word and power be mighty in her, and may the spirit in her struggle
> even against Aegeates, that insolent and hostile snake. O Lord, may her soul
> remain forever pure. . . . In particular, protect her, O Master, from this
> disgusting pollution. With respect to our savage and ever boorish enemy,
> cause her to sleep apart from her visible husband and wed her to her inner
> husband, whom you above all recognize (γνωρίζεις). (Passion 16)[116]

The Deception of Euclia (Melantho, Passion 17–22)

Maximilla's strategy for eluding Aegeates' embrace was not exactly what Andrew had in mind.

> Maximilla then planned the following. She summoned a shapely, exceedingly wanton servant-girl named Euclia and told her what she delighted in and desired. "You will have me as a benefactor of all your needs, providing you scheme with me and carry out what I advise." Because she wanted to live chastely from that time on, Maximilla told Euclia what she wanted and got her word agreeing to it, and so for some time she employed the following subterfuge. Just as a woman customarily adorns herself to look like her rival, Maximilla groomed Euclia in just such finery and put her forward to sleep with Aegeates in her stead. Having used her as his lover, he let her get up and go to her own bedroom, just as Maximilla used to. By so doing, Maximilla escaped detection for some time, and thereby got relief, rejoiced in the Lord, and never left Andrew. (Passion 17)[117]

Euclia (Εὔκλια, 'she-of-good-repute') maintained the ruse for eight months and continually blackmailed her mistress for more money, jewelry, clothing, and manumission. She even flaunted her deception before the other servants and stationed (ἐπέστησεν) two of them at his head (πρὸς τῇ κεφαλῇ αὐτοῦ) to witness the act (Passion 18).[118] Maximilla agreed to these terms so that she could spend "her nights resting with Andrew along with Stratocles and all the other brethren" (19).

In order to keep the affair under raps, Maximilla bribed her servants with one thousand denarii each. It was not enough:

> [T]hey went to their master immediately, money in hand, and told him the whole story, including how their own fellow servant submitted to the plan Maximilla devised because she no longer wanted to sleep with Aegeates, repulsed by sex with him as a heinous and despicable act. . . . (Passion 21)

> The proconsul, furious at her [Euclia] for boasting to her fellow servants and for saying these things in order to defame her mistress—he wanted the matter hushed up since he was still affectionate for his spouse—cut out Euclia's tongue, mutilated her, and ordered her thrown outside. She stayed there without food for several days before she became food for the dogs. The rest of the servants who had told their story to him—there were three of them—he crucified. (Passion 22)

This gruesome episode so uncharacteristic of early Christian narrative derives from Homer's depiction of Odysseus's treacherous and lustful maidservant Melantho. When Odysseus returned to Ithaca, he learned that twelve of his fifty maidservants, Melantho especially, had slept with the suitors. Odysseus threatened to expose Melantho's conduct to Telemachus "that on the spot he may cut thee limb from limb."[119]   After slaying the suitors, Telemachus, with Odysseus's encouragement, punished the unfaithful maidservants, including Melantho: "[T]he women held their heads in a row, and round the neck of all nooses were laid, that they might die most piteously. And they writhed a little while with their feet, but not long."[120] Melanthius, Odysseus's turncoat goatherd, was even less fortunate; they "cut off his nostrils and his ears with the pitiless bronze, and drew out his vitals for the dogs to eat raw, and cut off his hands and his feet in their furious wrath."[121] The similarities between these passages and Aegeates' vengeance against his servants are undeniable; both mention fornicating and greedy domestics, tattling fellow servants, enraged masters, hangings, defacings, dismemberments, and anthropophagous dogs.

The Arrest of Andrew (Passion 23–28a)

Convinced that Maximilla was having an affair, Aegeates promised to forgive her if she would return to his bed. His entreaties call to mind Odysseus's memorable encounter with Nausicaa on the beach of the island of the Phaeacians. He awoke famished from a long sleep after having suffered shipwreck and saw the maiden with her entourage. He debated whether he "should grab her knees" in entreaty for hospitality or "stand apart . . . lest the maiden's heart should be wroth with him if he clasped her knees."[122] Standing aloof, Odysseus says,

> I beseech thee, O queen,—a goddess art thou (θεός νύ τις), or art thou mortal? If thou art a goddess (τις θεός), one of these who hold broad heaven, to Artemis, the daughter of the great Zeus, do I liken thee most nearly in comeliness and in stature and in form.[123] But if thou art one of the mortals who dwell upon the earth, thrice-blessed then are thy father and thy honored mother, and thrice-blessed thy brethren.[124]

Odysseus continues: "I marvel at thee, and greatly fear to touch thy knees (γούνων ἄψασθαι); but sore grief has come upon me."[125]

Similarly, in the *Acts*, Aegeates spent a sleepless night "and ate nothing at all . . . because of anguish" at what Maximilla had done. After imploring his gods,

> he went to his spouse, fell at her feet weeping, and said, "I, your husband, cling to your feet (ἅπτομαί σου τῶν ποδῶν), I who have been your mate now for twelve years, who always revered you as a goddess (τινὰ θεάν) and still do because of your σωφροσύνη and generally discreet character, even though it might have been tarnished somewhat—even you are mortal." (Passion 23)

The two passages share too much to be unrelated. Each tells how an anguished, hungry man begs obsequiously for assistance from a woman whom he likens to a goddess. Odysseus considers clinging to Nausicaa's feet;[126] Aegeates does so in fact to Maximilla.

Maximilla rebuffed Aegeates' requests because she loved another:

> I am in love, Aegeates. I am in love, and my beloved is not of this world and therefore is imperceptible to you. Night and day it kindles and enflames me with love for it. You cannot see it for it is difficult to see, and you cannot separate me from it, for that is impossible. Let me have intercourse and take my rest with it alone. (Passion 23)

Maximilla's consistent use of the neuter here instead of the masculine signals to the reader that her lover is impersonal. Aegeates, incapable of understanding that she meant "her inner husband," assumed she loved the apostle.

Aegeates' confusion concerning Maximilla's lover intensified when one of his slaves told him that Maximilla

> has so given way to desire for him [Andrew] that she loves no one more than him, including you I would say. Not only has she become intimately involved with the man, but she has tied up your brother Stratocles with the same passion for him that has tied her up. They confess but one God, the one that man disclosed to them, denying the existence of every other on earth. But listen to what your brother did that was craziest of all. Even though he is of noble stock, the most honored man in Achaea, addressed as brother of the proconsul Aegeates, he carries his own little oil flask to the gymnasium. Even though he owns many slaves, he appears in public doing his own chores—buying his own vegetables, bread, and other necessities and carrying them on foot through the center of the city—making himself look simply repulsive to everyone. (Passion 25)

In Book 1 of *The Odyssey*, Telemachus sulks powerlessly, longing to establish himself as "lord of our own house and of the slaves."[127] Indeed, by the end of the epic he uses an iron glove to punish those servants who had cooperated with the suitors.[128] Stratocles, on the other hand, renounces his economic and honorific advantages and takes care of his own menial tasks, like a slave:

> He [Aegeates' servant] told this to his master who was taking a stroll, staring at the ground (εἰς γῆν ὁρᾶν)[129] for a long time, and then the youth spotted Andrew from a distance and shouted out loud: "Look, master! There is the man responsible for the present disruption of your household." The entire crowd turned to see the cause of his outburst. Without another word, the youth—who was as fearsome as Aegeates, as though he were his brother and not really his slave—ran from the proconsul, seized Andrew, and forcibly brought him to Aegeates, wrapping around his neck the towel that the blessed one used to wear over his shoulder (περιβαλὼν αὐτοῦ τῷ αὐχένι ᾧ ἐχρῆτο ἐπὶ τοῦ ὤμου ὁ μακάριος σαβάνιον).[130] (Passion 26)

This passage, too, echoes *The Odyssey*, where one reads that Odysseus once sneaked into Troy by disguising himself as a beggar, "casting around his shoulders wretched wraps (σπεῖρα κάκ' ἀμφ' βαλών)."[131] Both Odysseus's rags (σπεῖρα) and Andrew's towel (σαβάνιον) were not proper garments but lengths of cloth draped on a shoulder, which made both men look like tramps.[132]

Aegeates appealed to Andrew, "Teach me too the nature of your fame or what sort of power you have such that, even though you appear in this manner like an old tramp, you have lovers who are rich and poor, including infants" (Passion 26). Such scenes demonstrate the author's daring in recruiting the power of eroticism to serve continence, in transforming the fidelity of a Penelope into uxorial defiance for the sake of a more worthy suitor, her true self. The proconsul arrested the apostle with the words: "Corrupter! You will see my rewards (εὐχαρίστους) to you for your benefactions (εὐεργεσίας) to Maximilla."[133]

Aegeates then went to Maximilla and Iphidama to inform them that Andrew was now in prison and would suffer miserably. "He left smiling (μειδιῶν), leaving her to eat" (Passion 27). Maximilla then sent Iphidama to go to the garrison to see the apostle. "Iphidama changed out of (μεταμφιασθεῖσα) her usual garb and dutifully rushed off" (Passion 28).[134]

Iphidama in Prison (Socrates' Friends, Passion 28b–29a)

Throughout the Passion, Andrew's speeches recast passages from Plato's *Phaedo*, the philosopher's account of the death of Socrates and one of the most famous texts of Greek antiquity. Socrates, in jail, tells his friends about the nature of the soul, namely that it is alien to the body and akin (συγγενής) to the divine;[135] therefore, there is no reason for him to fear death. Like the barefoot philosopher, Andrew entertains his friends in his prison cell and speaks to them of the kinship of the soul and why he does not fear his execution. Passion 28b–29a describes Iphidama's first visit with the apostle in prison and uses language borrowed directly from the beginning of Plato's *Phaedo*. Phaedo, Plato's narrator, tells how he and his comrades went to see Socrates in prison.

Phaedo 59d–60a
We used to meet at daybreak in the court where the trial took place, for it was near **the prison** (δεσμωτήριον); and every day **used to wait about** talking with each other until **the prison was opened** (ἀνοιχθείη τὸ δεσμωτήριον). [And again later: the jailer ... told us **to wait** and not go in until he told us. ... So after **a little delay**, he came and told us to go in.]

Passion 28b–29a
Once she discovered where **the prison** (δεσμωτήριον) was. ... When the faithful Iphidama **had stood for an hour**, she saw the gate of **the prison opened**

No one detected her as

We **went in** then **and found Socrates just released** (εἰσελθόντες οὖν κατελαμβάνομεν τὸν μὲν Σωκράτη ἄρτι λελυμένον) and Xanthippe—you know her—with his little son in her arms, sitting beside him. Now when Xanthippe **saw** (εἶδεν) us, she cried out **and said** (εἶπεν)... [Socrates sent Xanthippe away].	**she entered and found the apostle speaking** (εἰσῆλθε καὶ κατέλαβε τὸν ἀπόστολον ὁμιλοῦντα) with his fellow inmates. ... When he turned and **saw** (εἶδεν) Iphidama, **his soul was elated and he said** (εἶπεν)... **Andrew dismissed her.**

Notice that in *The Acts of Andrew* Iphidama's delay "for an hour" is entirely unexplained, whereas in the *Phaedo* the two delays are well motivated. In the first, Socrates' friends arrived before the visiting hours; in the second, the friends had "a little delay" because Socrates was getting final instructions about hemlock etiquette.[136] Once again, the thematic and verbal parallels between *The Acts of Andrew* and Plato are too striking to be attributed to chance or to generic literary interests.

The Invisibility of the Women (Odysseus's Mist, Passion 29b–34)

Already in Passion 13 Andrew had promised his followers, "Jesus will screen (περισκεπάσει) your appearance from Aegeates, in order to secure your invisibility." Consequently, Aegeates "did not notice all the brethren exit in front of him." In Passion 28, Iphidama had sneaked into Andrew's prison cell undetected. Homer, too, frequently refers to such divinely provided invisibility shields,[137] and the passage most illuminating of Passion 29b–34 is Odysseus's invisibility in *Odyssey* Book 7.

When Odysseus was washed up on the shore of the island of the Phaeacians, Athena promised to shroud him in a mist to make him invisible until he arrived at the palace of Alcinous and Arete where he could plead for mercy. In *The Acts of Andrew*, the apostle prays that a similar cover be provided for Iphidama and Maximilla so that they may come to him in prison without detection.

Odyssey 7.14–17 Athene, with kindly purpose, **cast about** (ἀμφί) **him a thick mist,** **that no one** (μή τις) **of the great-hearted Phaeacians,** meeting him, should speak mockingly to him. ...	Passion 29 **"Shield her with your covering** (περισκέπασον ... τῇ σῇ περιβολῇ) both now as she leaves and this evening when she returns with her mistress, so that they will be visible **to none** (μή τινι) **of their enemies."**

Iphidama then left the prison, again undetected, and told Maximilla what had happened. Her mistress rejoiced and insisted that no one would be able to sequester her in her bedroom in order to keep her from seeing Andrew: "Glory be to you, O Lord, for I am about to see your apostle again without fear. Even if an entire legion kept me locked up under key, it would not be strong enough to prevent me from seeing your apostle" (Passion 30).

In order to keep her in her room like an obedient Penelope, Aegeates posted four soldiers to stand guard outside her door and another four to join the jailer to insure no one would open the gate of the prison. The soldiers proved useless because of the women's invisibility, just as the Phaeacians were unable to see Odysseus shrouded in Athena's mist. As Odysseus approached the palace, he met Athena disguised as a young woman; as Maximilla and Iphidama approached the prison, they met Christ disguised as a young boy.

Odyssey 7.18–20, 27–30, and 37–38	Passion 32
But **when he was about to enter the lovely city**, then the goddess, flashing-eyed Athene, met him in the guise of **a young maiden** carrying a pitcher, and she **stood (στῆ) before him**. . . .[138]	**When she arrived at the prison gate**, she found **a beautiful young boy standing (ἑστῶτα) before opened doors,**
Then the goddess . . . **answered him,** "Then verily, Sir stranger, I will shew thee that palace as thou didst bid me. . . . Only **go thou** quietly, and I will lead the way." . . . So speaking, **Pallas Athene led the way quickly**, and he followed the footsteps of the goddess.[139]	**who told them,** "**Both of you go**. . . ." **Running ahead of them, he went** to Andrew.

The Greek text for the next section contains a sizable gap, the content of which can partially be recovered from a passage of the Latin father Evodius of Uzala, who stated that after the beautiful lad brought the women to Andrew, he "went on to Aegeates' praetorium, entered the women's bedroom, and mimicked a woman's voice to sound like Maximilla grumbling over the sufferings of the female sex and Iphidama responding. When Aegeates heard this conversation, he thought they were there and went away."[140] The women, however, stayed with the apostle in prison and heard him preach. So also in *The Odyssey*, before Odysseus arrived at the palace of the Phaeacians, Athena left him and went to "the well-built house of Erectheus."[141] Immediately, however, the action reverts to Odysseus in the palace. This shift in locations precisely at the same point in the narratives of both texts surely is no accident but hypertextual resonance.

Andrew preached in prison encouraging the women to rejoice in spite of his calamity, and he did so by listing the benefits of being faithful to Christ.[142] Three times Andrew uses the key word γνωρίζειν, 'to recognize':

> We are not cast to the ground [viz. earthly], for we have been recognized (γνωρισθέντες) by such a height. We do not belong to time, so as to be dissolved by time. We are not the product of motion, which disappears of its own accord, nor the cause of coming-to-be (γενέσεως αἰτία).[143] . . . [We belong] to the savior, through whom we have recognized (ἐγνωρίσαμεν) the destroyer; to the light, through whom we have cast off the darkness; to the one, through whom we have turned from the many; to the heavenly, through whom we have learned about the earthly; to the enduring, through whom we see things that do not endure. . . . [W]e have been recognized (γνωρισθῆναι) by him. (Passion 33)

For Platonists, the word γένεσις, translated here as "coming-to-be," meant the binding of the soul to the body, its 'becoming' (γενόμενος) in the material world. In other contexts γένεσις represents the material world itself, especially in its role of compromising the welfare of the soul. Passion 12 contains a speech in which Andrew gave hope to those who "desire a life not subject to γένεσις." Here in Passion 33, Andrew claims that those who have been recognized (γνωρισθῆναι) by God are above time, motion, the many, the earthly, the ephemeral, that is, above γένεσις.[144]

After this speech, the women leave, but only temporarily. "Every day they were strengthened in the hope of the Lord; they convened fearlessly at the prison and were incessantly with Maximilla and Iphidama and the others, because they were screened by the covering (περισκεπόμενοι τῇ περιβολῇ) and grace of the Lord" (Passion 34).

Maximilla Becomes Male (Passion 35–41)

The women continued to visit Andrew in prison until Aegeates gave Maximilla an ultimatum: either resume sexual relations with him at once and see Andrew released, or persist in her chastity and watch the apostle's torturous death (Passion 36). Maximilla again went to the apostle. "Putting his hands on her eyes and then bringing them to her mouth, she kissed them and began to seek his advice about every aspect of Aegeates' ultimatum" (Passion 37).[145] Andrew once again urged her to protect herself militantly against intercourse.[146] She will be saved by her "recognizing (γνωριζούσῃ) that [her soul] is being raised up" and by rejecting sex (Passion 37). In this way she can reverse the fall of the mind, which "was brought down" and "slipped away from itself" into the material world when Eve, through ignorance, disobeyed and ate of the forbidden fruit, viz. sexual intercourse.[147] Together, Maximilla and Andrew represent a spiritual couple who, by sexual abstinence, must undo the fall of the first couple. "What Eve disobeyed, you obeyed; what Adam agreed to, I flee; the things that tripped them up, we have recognized (ἐγνωρίσαμεν)" (Passion 37).

In addition to Genesis, the author has in mind Plato's notion of the soul. Andrew says,

> Well done, O human who learns what is not yours and speeds on to what is yours. . . . I recognize (γνωρίζω) that you are more powerful than those who presume to dominate you. . . . O human being, if you understand all these things in yourself—that you are immaterial, holy, light, akin (συγγενής) to the unbegotten, intellectual, heavenly, transparent, pure, beyond the flesh, beyond the world, beyond the powers, beyond the authorities over whom you really are, if you comprehend yourself in your condition, if you perceive with the mind through which you excel, if you see your face in your essence,[148] having broken every shackle (I mean not only those shackles acquired by γένεσις but also those beyond the realm of γένεσις, whose magnificent names we have present to you)—then desire to see him who was revealed to you without coming into being (γενόμενον), whom you alone soon will recognize (γνωρίσῃ), if you take courage. (Passion 38)

Like Socrates in the *Phaedo*, Andrew is not afraid to die: "Let him [Aegeates] destroy this body as he will, for it is only one body and it is akin (συγγενοῦς) to him" (Passion 39).

Once again he tells Maximilla to wage her war against her husband: "[D]o not yield yourself to Aegeates. Stand up against his ambushes. . . . If I am driven from here, perhaps I can help others of my kindred (συγγενεῖς) because of you" (Passion 40). As if this virile imagery were not sufficiently clear, Andrew then addresses her as a man:

> I beg you, wise man (φρονίμου ἀνδρός), that your clearsighted mind stand firm. I beg you, mind unseen, that you may be protected. I entreat you, love Jesus. Do not be overcome by the inferior. You whom I entreat as a man, assist me in my becoming perfect. Help me too, so that you may recognize (γνωρίσῃς) your true nature. Suffer with my suffering, so that you may recognize (γνωρίσῃς) what I suffer and escape suffering. (Passion 41)

Maximilla, the hypertextual Penelope, has become male in order to repel her husband's advances.[149] Now Stratocles, the onetime soldier and hypertextual Telemachus, finally gives birth to his inner self.

Stratocles Gives Birth (Theaetetus, Passion 42–46)

While Andrew was instructing Maximilla in these arts of self-defense, Stratocles suffered from spiritual labor pains. Andrew asked him,

> Why are you afflicted with many tears and why do you groan out loud? Why do you despair? Why your great grief and great sorrow? You recognize (γνωρίζεις) what has been said, so why do I beg you, child, to live accordingly? Do you know to whom I have said these things? Has each

engaged your mind? Has it reached your intellectual faculty? Do I still have the one who listened to me? Do I find myself in you? (Passion 42)

These nine questions are the first of fifty-three; indeed, Andrew's entire speech in Passion 42 consists of questions, except for the last sentence where he answers his own questions on behalf of Stratocles' inner self "who weeps once again." The hypertextual reason for these questions obviously is to portray Andrew as a new Socrates, whose midwifery requires such labor-inducing questions. The speech produced its goal: at last Stratocles gave birth.

> Then Stratocles approached Andrew weeping and wailing. Andrew took Stratocles' hand and said, "I have the one I sought. I have found the one I desired. I hold the one I loved. I rest because of the one I have waited for. The very fact that you are still groaning louder and are weeping uncontrollably symbolizes for me that I have already achieved rest, because not in vain have I spoken to you the words which are akin (συγγενεῖς) to me." (Passion 43)

Stratocles responded that his weeping in part was due to the apostle's imminent death. The "seeds of the words of salvation" had just now been sown; who will nurture them? Similarly, Socrates' friends asked him where they would be able to find a singing nurse once their teacher had been executed. Compare:

Phaedo 77e–78a	Passion 44
	"For you yourself may leave. . . .
"Where (πόθεν) then, Socrates,"	But after this, **where (ποῦ)** and in whom
he said, "**shall we find**	**will I seek and find**
a good singer of charms,	your care and love?"
since you are leaving us?"	

Socrates told his friends to look to each other for comfort; Andrew told Stratocles to look to himself (Passion 45).

While Andrew thus addressed Stratocles, Maximilla ran off to inform Aegeates of her decision never to return to his bed (Passion 46). The proconsul decided to have the apostle crucified at once, but Maximilla returned to the prison to hear the apostle preach yet again.

Andrew's Last Will and Testament (Passion 47–50)

Although Andrew will preach from his cross later in the Passion, this final sermon in prison is the last time he addresses "the brethren" and serves as his last will and testament. The speech divides clearly into two sections: in chapters 47–48 Andrew interprets his career; in chapters 49–50 he explains why he must die and encourages others to follow his soul on its ascent to God.

In the first section, Andrew recalls Christ's commissioning him—not to teach, but, like Socrates, to remind:[150]

> Brethren, the Lord sent me as an apostle to these regions . . . not to teach anyone but to remind everyone akin (συγγενῆ) to these words that all people pass their time among ephemeral evils reveling in their destructive fantasies, which I have continually encouraged you to shun. I have urged you to pursue (ἐπείγεσθαι) things that are stable, and to flee (φυγήν ποιήσασθαι) from all that undulates. Look, not one of you stands firm, but everything—including human conventions—is in flux. (Passion 47)

Like Odysseus, believers must flee from the sea of γένεσις and seek that which stands firm—heaven, one's true home. If they do so, the God of mercy will receive them and give them eternal rest (ἀναπεπαυμένους).[151] Such maritime imagery recurs repeatedly in Andrew's speeches from the cross.

The second section of this speech (49–50) turns the reader's attention from Andrew's ministry to his imminent death, which all believers must be prepared to share:

> Do not let what is about to happen to me trouble you as though it were some strange marvel,[152] namely that God's servant, by whom God himself provided many things through acts and words, will be violently driven from this passing life by a wicked man. This violence will not come upon me only, but also on all who have loved, believed, and confessed. (Passion 49)

Andrew then reveals the devil's game whereby he attacks souls too weak "to recognize themselves (γνωρίζεσθαι)" and who forgot "to recognize (γνωρίζεσθαι)" the devil for who he was.[153] Because Christ has exposed the devil's nature, believers must speed away from wickedness toward their divine homeland:

> Let us not be vexed or agitated by the storm, and let us not transport on our souls traces of the devil which are not ours. But since we have been entirely buoyed up by the whole word, let us all eagerly anticipate the goal and let us take flight from him, so that at last he may be exposed for what he is by nature, as we fly off to those things which are ours. (Passion 50)

Conclusion

In this chapter I have argued for the author's indebtedness to Plato; indeed, some passages reflect a direct knowledge of the Socratic discourses. The *Theaetetus* seems to lie behind Andrew's maieutic speeches to Stratocles (Passion 7–9 and 42–43) and his discussion of the "Lord's seal" (11–12). Iphidama's visit with Andrew in prison (28b–29a) and Stratocles' inquiries about spiritual progress after the apostle's death call to mind Plato's *Phaedo*. *The Madness of Heracles* by Euripides seems to have informed the healing of Alcman (2–5).

But once again the primary hypotext behind this section of *The Acts of Andrew* is Homer's *Odyssey*, especially Books 17–23, where Telemachus, Eumaeus,

Eurycleia, and Penelope recognize that the stranger in rags is the king of Ithaca. The Passion transforms these recognitions into recognitions of the characters' true selves, of their kinship with the divine.

In order to accomplish this transformation, the author radically altered the characterizations of Odysseus, Telemachus, and Penelope. Although Andrew himself at times imitates Odysseus (e.g., his appearance as a beggar, his abuse by servants, and his knowing smile), Aegeates takes on Odysseus's role as a jealous husband returned from a long trip who raged like a lion in order to destroy his rivals and who viciously punished his unfaithful servants.

The most dramatic recharacterizations, however, pertain to Telemachus and Penelope. Whereas Telemachus ('fighter from afar') became a man through warfare, Stratocles ('battle-praise') left the army to study philosophy and, thanks to Andrew's midwifery, gave birth to his spiritual fetus. At the end of *The Odyssey*, Telemachus became a bloodied warrior, heir to the estate, and stern master of his servants. Stratocles, by contrast, will renounce violence, reject his brother's wealth, and look after his own domestic needs.

For her part, Maximilla transvalues passive, bedroom-bound Penelope. During Aegeates' absence, she invited Stratocles and "the brethren" into her boudoir to hear Andrew preach. When her husband learned of these meetings, she bribed Euclia (≈ Melantho) to sleep with him in her place. For the author of *The Acts of Andrew* Penelope had compromised her fabled σωφροσύνη by sleeping with Aegeates, so he extended Maximilla's σωφροσύνη even to her conjugal bed. To the end, Maximilla will reject Aegeates' offer to become his queen (δέσποινα), thus refusing to play the role of a Penelope.

One need not be a Jungian to appreciate the reversal of gender expectations in the rhetoric of Passion 1–50. Andrew urges Maximilla to fight against her husband's advances and to abandon her bedroom and home. Stratocles, on the other hand, is to bring his true self to birth, to mother his own essence. It is he, not Maximilla, who weeps constantly until his true nature breaks forth. Perhaps here, more than in any other early Christian text, one finds a conscious articulation of gender transformation, one bordering on gender reversal.[154] The soldier becomes a mother and the wife wages war with her husband.

In one crucial respect, however, Penelope and Maximilla are alike: both are philosophers. Forty-six times Homer speaks of "wise Penelope (περίφρων Πηνελόπεια)," seven times of "prudent Penelope (ἐχέφρων Πηνελόπεια)." Furthermore, he makes it clear that no woman was her equal in mental capacities. She eclipsed all in mind and sage advice,[155] in cunning, noble heart, and intelligence.[156] A Homeric scholiast was merely paraphrasing Homer by observing that "in beauty and mental qualities Penelope outshines all women."[157] Such exceptional wisdom was not merely a personal quality; it was a divine gift: "Athena has endowed her above other women with knowledge of fair handiwork and an understanding heart."[158] Thus, Eustathius asks: "How is it that 'wise Penelope' had thoughts known by no other heroine?" "Penelope is a philosopher," he answers, because "the gods had given her the mind she had."[159]

Homeric allegorists took Penelope as a cipher for philosophy itself. Psychological allegorists deciphered Odysseus as the soul lost in the material world, seeking its heavenly *patria*. Calypso, who wanted to keep Odysseus on her lush island Ogygia, represents the allurement of embodiment that veils (καλύπτειν) the true self. In spite of Calypso's beauty, Odysseus longs for Penelope, that is, philosophy and its preoccupation with the intelligible world.[160]

In addition to symbolizing philosophy, Penelope was "the weaving philosopher."[161] A pun on the word ἀναλύσις, which can mean either 'unraveling' or 'solution', prompted readers to see in Penelope's web, which she wove during the day and unraveled at night,[162] an allegory of a sophisticated weaving together of syllogistic propositions and their 'analysis'. Had one of Penelope's own maidservants not tattled on her, the thick-headed suitors would never have figured out what she was doing, because such philosophical activity is "truly divine."[163]

Maximilla, however, is not a philosopher trained in syllogistic manipulation. She is a philosopher more like Porphyry's wife, Marcella. The philosopher's famous letter to her provides a close analogy to Andrew's instructions to Maximilla and forms a fitting conclusion to this chapter.

Government duty sent Porphyry abroad for an extended period just ten months after he had married Marcella, a former widow and mother of seven. While away, Porphyry wrote her a letter whose content leaves little doubt that Andrew's goal, like Porphyry's, was a woman's education in philosophy. Porphyry claimed he had married Marcella because he recognized her "natural aptitude for the right philosophy" and wanted to help her "retain her hold on philosophy."[164] Insofar as "the gods commanded purity through abstinence from food and intercourse,"[165] the couple had forsworn sex in order to enjoy a more profound eroticism. Even though her husband was absent, he would be "united" with her "night and day in a pure and most beautiful intercourse," if she took care to "ascend" into herself in preparation for ascending to the gods.[166]

Porphyry, like the author of *The Acts of Andrew*, laments "the nature and extent of the soul's fall into γένεσις" as into a foreign land[167] and compares the soul's return to its transcendent condition with Odysseus's return to Ithaca: it is incumbent "for those of us who intend to keep in mind our νόστος away from our descent into this foreign realm to make an ascent past pleasure (ἡδονῆς) and ease as though we were traveling through a region flat enough for a chariot."[168] Those "who have fallen into γένεσις" must make the difficult ascent by means of "discipline and remembrance of the fall."[169] "Virtue alone draws the soul upward and to its kindred (τὸ συγγενές)."[170] Because the goal of philosophy is nothing other than the soul's "ascent to the gods,"[171] Porphyry can write,

> do not be overly concerned about whether your body is male or female; do not regard yourself as a woman, Marcella, for I did not devote myself to you as such. Flee from every effeminate element of the soul as if you are clothed in a male body. For the most blessed offspring come from virginal soul and unmated intelligence.[172]

Marcella, therefore, was a philosopher in so far as she had trained herself through contemplation and ascetic discipline to liberate the mind from its material captivity, to "flee from the body."[173]

The parallels between Porphyry and *The Acts of Andrew* suggest that it was just such an interpretation of Platonism that informed his depiction of Maximilla. Like Marcella, she must become like a man by nurturing her soul to transcend γένεσις and to pursue her kindred, her true homeland. It is just such a journey that best explains Andrew's understanding of his death, the topic of the following chapter.

Notes

1. Plato *Republic* 2.383a and *AAMt* 24.
2. Plato *Republic* 2.364d and *AAMt* 26.
3. Plato *Republic* 3.391b–c and *AAMt* 22–31.
4. Plato *Republic* 3.388c–d and GE 13.
5. Plato *Republic* 2.378d and GE 15.
6. Plato *Republic* 3.390b–c and GE 18.
7. Plato *Republic* 3.390c–d and GE 15.
8. See chapter 3, 85–100.
9. *Second Apology* 10 (ANF).
10. In Aristotle's view, *The Odyssey* was "loaded with recognition (ἀναγνώρισις)" (*Poetics* 24.3). On the importance of these recognition scenes in ancient readings of *The Odyssey* see especially N. J. Richardson, "Recognition Scenes in the *Odyssey* and Ancient Literary Criticism," *Papers of the Liverpool Latin Seminar* 4 (1983): 219–35.
11. *Odyssey* 1.83–95.
12. See Jaeger, *Paideia* 1.29–30. According to the moral allegorizing of Ps.-Plutarch, Telemachus represents τιμή (*De vita et poesi Homeri* 185).
13. *Odyssey* 24.506–9.
14. According to Eustathius: ἐπειδὴ τῆλε μαχομένου τοῦ πατρὸς ἐτράφη (*A d Homeri Odysseam* 1479; cf. 1394).
15. Lucian *Lexiphanes* 12.
16. On the name Telemachus see "Telemachus," P-W, 2d series, 5.325–26.
17. See Édouard Delebecque, *Télémaque et la structure de l'Odyssée*, Centre d'étude et de recherches helléniques de la Faculté des lettres d'Aix, Publication des annales de la Faculté des lettres, Aix-en-Provence, n.s. 21 (Gap: Éditions Ophrys, 1958). At least one ancient author agreed: "Throughout all the events, the epic records the progressive

nurturing of intelligence in Telemachus" (Heraclitus *Quaestiones Homericae* 63.9).

18. C. M. H. Millar and J. W. S. Carmichael go too far by saying that Telemachus "is, perhaps, the only character in Greek literature who shows any development" ("The Growth of Telemachus," *G&R* 1 [1954]: 58), but their discussion is helpful for monitoring the development of Telemachus in the epic.

19. Maximilla's bedroom was also featured in GE 30, where Andrew cured her fever.

20. *Odyssey* 17.52–56: "I will go to the place of assembly that I may bid to our house a stranger who followed me from Pylos on my way hither. Him I sent forward with my godlike comrades, and I bade Peiraeus take him home and give him kindly welcome, and show him honour until I should come."

21. Homer highlights Telemachus's social savoir-faire also in *Odyssey* 1.118–24 and 309–13, 15.279–81, 513–15, and 542–46, 16.42–48 and 78–97, 17.84–100, and 20.255–95.

22. E.g., Athenaeus *Deipnosophists* 5.181e–192 and Heraclitus *Quaestiones Homericae* 61–63.

23. Notice also that Alcman was "under the supervision of Aristocles" ('superlative renown'), perhaps another reason for identifying him with the most renowned of all Greeks heroes.

24. See especially *Madness of Heracles* 822–42 and 1307–21.

25. Ibid., 935: παραπεπληγμένῳ; 1105: πέπληγμαι; 1189: μαινομένῳ πιτύλῳ πλαγχθείς. Compare also "he lay in feces (ἐν κοπρῶνι ἔκειτο)" (Passion 2) with "he lay on the pavement (ἔκειτο κρηπίδων ἔπι)" (1009).

26. *Madness of Heracles* 874–75, 890, and 901–3.

27. Ibid., 908–1016.

28. Ibid., 1029–30.

29. When Odysseus revealed himself to Telemachus and Penelope, he, too, looked like a god (*Odyssey* 16.183 and 23.163).

30. *Odyssey* 13.397–402 (Fitzgerald); cf. 4.244–48 and 13.429–38.

31. Ibid., 24.156–61.

32. Ibid., 20.301; cf. 23.111.

33. Maximus of Tyre made the suitors the personification of ὕβρις (32.9d).

34. Epictetus, fragment 11.

35. Dio Chrysostom 9.9; cf. 14.22.

36. Andrew launches into an extended denunciation of so-called physicians and magicians who were unable to help Alcman because they were kindred to the very demon who possessed the lad. This denunciation of physicians kindred to the demonic may relate them to traditions about the god Asclepius, the god of healing.

37. *Madness of Heracles* 1089–1108.

38. Ibid., 1111–14, 1124, 1130–32, and 1134.

39. Ibid., 1125.

40. Cf. Athenagoras *Legatio* 29 and especially Clement of Alexandria, who ridiculed Euripides for having depicted "Heracles in a state of madness" (*Protrepticus* 7.76.5).

41. *Odyssey* 15.515–17.

42. Ibid., 23.226–30.

43. The following is typical: "She went down the high stairway from her chamber, not alone, for two handmaids attended her. Now when the fair lady had come to the wooers, she stood by the doorpost of the well-built hall, holding before her face her shining veil; and a faithful handmaid stood on either side of her" (*Odyssey* 1.330–35); cf. 16.409–16, 18.182–84 and 206–11, and 21.63–65.

44. E.g., *Odyssey* 17.101–3; cf. 1.360–64, 4.758–60, 16.449–50, 18.302–3, 19.600–603, and 21.354–57.

45. Ibid., 4.799–802, 19.512–17 and 594–97, and 20.56–60; cf. 4.787–90, 11.181–83, 16.36–39, 17.6–8, 18.174–75 and 202–4, 19.262–64, and 21.56–57.

46. Ibid., 7.718–20, 21.354–58, and 23.32–35.

47. So also Prieur, *Acta Andreae*, 184–85.

48. *Theaetetus* 143e–144b.

49. Ibid., 148e–149a.

50. Ibid., 150b–c.

51. Ibid., 150c–d.

52. Ibid., 149a–c.

53. Cf. *Theaetetus* 190e–191a and *Republic* 7.515d.

54. *Theaetetus* 151a–b

55. Cf. *Theaetetus* 168a, where Socrates says that philosophical questions should cause confusion (ταραχῆς). The notion that spiritual development required a troubled soul was common among early Christians. See, for example, *Gospel of Thomas* 2 (= Oxyrhynchus papyrus 654) cited also by Clement of Alexandria (*Stromateis* 2.45.5 and 5.14.96). See also Prieur, *Acta Andreae*, 182.

56. At the beginning of *Theaetetus* the narrator shows respect for Socrates' prophetic abilities (μαντικῶς) in having properly divined the youth's outcome (142c). Cf. *Odyssey* 2.170, where Nestor too claims he is not inexperienced in divination (οὐ γὰρ ἀπείρητος μαντεύομαι).

57. Homer uses ἀλήτης repeatedly of Odysseus the beggar who suffered abuse at the hands of the suitors (*Odyssey* 17.501, 576, and 578, 18.18–19, and 21.400).

58. Ibid., 16.188–89 and 195.

59. Ibid., 16.213–19. Telemachus's tears moisten many pages of the epic; e.g., 1.241–44, 2.80–81, and 4.13–19, where Menelaus and Helen recognized from his weeping at the mention of Odysseus that he was the hero's son. As Athenaeus noted, Telemachus was "recognized (γνωριζομένους) by tears" (*Deipnosophists* 5.182a). Cf. Maximus of Tyre on Alcinous's recognizing Odysseus from his tears: γνωρίσας δακρύει (16.7). Andrew recognized from Stratocles' tears that he was spiritually pregnant.

60. So also Prieur, *Acta Andreae*, 186.

61. E.g., Plato *Philebus* 48c and *Charmides* 164e–165a. The most authoritative treatment of "know thyself" and its ancient interpreters is that of Pierre Courcelle, *Connais-toi toi-même. De Socrate à Saint Bernard*, 3 vols. (Paris: Études augustiniennes, 1974–1975). For discussions most relevant to this study see 1.69–111.

62. Ibid., 69–96.

63. Cf. Justin Martyr *Dialogue with Trypho* 4.

64. In Passion 4 and 5, Andrew explained that physicians were unable to exorcise Alcman because they themselves were kindred (συγγενεῖς) to the demons. Cf. Passion 42: "kindred (συγγενής) of the snake."

65. Édouard Des Places made an exhaustive study of συγγένεια in his *Syngeneia. La Parenté de l'homme avec Dieu d'Homère à la patristique*, Études et commentaires 51 (Paris: C. Klincksieck, 1964); see especially his discussion of Christian uses of the term (183–212). Particularly relevant to *The Acts of Andrew* are his observations concerning συγγένεια and Socrates' interrogative pedagogy: the philosopher asked questions in order to put the answerer in touch with the natural kinship of her or his soul (100–102).

66. According to Plutarch, Pythagoreans appealed to Odysseus's silencing of Telemachus (*Odyssey* 19.40–43) in order to support their notion of "firm silence (ἐκσίγησις)," the ability to refrain from "indiscriminate questions about the gods" (fragment 207). See also Stobaeus 33.17 and Ps.-Plutarch *De vita et poesi Homeri* 149.

67. *Odyssey* 1.443–44 and 15.6–8.

68. Ibid., 2.314–15.

69. E.g., *Odyssey* 1.94, 2.215, 264, 314, and 360, and 13.415. In *The Acts of Andrew* see Passion 52 and 55.

70. Similarly, Socrates encouraged Theaetetus to ask questions: "[O]r if you prefer the method of questions, ask questions; for an intelligent person ought not to reject this method; on the contrary, he should choose it before all others" (*Theaetetus* 167d).

71. Cf. *Theaetetus* 160e–161a, where Socrates refers to the practice of the midwife presenting the newborn to the family for acceptance.

72. Prieur discusses in detail the possible meanings of the seal (*Acta Andreae* 190–92).

73. *Theaetetus* 191c–d.

74. Ibid., 192a.

75. Ibid., 194a.

76. Ibid., 194b.

77. Ibid., 194e–195a.

78. Cf. *2 Clement* 7.6.

79. *Odyssey* 4.335–40 = 17.126–31.

80. Ibid., 22.401–6; cf. 4.724 and 814 and 6.130.

81. Odysseus's table transgressions are discussed in the following: Plato *Republic* 3.390b, Athenaeus *Deipnosophists* 10.412 and 12.513, Lucian *The Parasite* 10 and *Podagra* 261–62, and Eustathius *Ad Homeri Odysseam* 1837. E. D. Phillips collected evidence for the ridiculing of Odysseus in classical Greek comedies, some of which faulted him for gluttony ("The Comic Odysseus," *G&R* n.s. 6 [1959]: 58–67).

82. *Odyssey* 9.5–11:

I myself declare that there is no greater fulfilment of delight than when joy possesses a whole people, and banqueters in the halls listen to a minstrel as they sit in order due, and by them tables are laden with bread and meat, and the cup-bearer draws wine from the bowl and bears it round and pours it into the cups. This seems to my mind the fairest thing there is.

Cf. 6.217–50, 7.177–80 and 215–19, and 14.109–14.

83. For example, Telemachus,

> flinging his arms about his noble father, wept and shed tears, and in the hearts of both arose a longing for lamentation. And they wailed aloud more vehemently than birds, sea-eagles, or vultures with crooked talons, whose young the country-folk have taken from their nest before they were fledged; even so piteously did they let tears fall from beneath their brows. (*Odyssey* 16.213–19)

Eurycleia saw Odysseus's scar: "Then upon her soul came joy and grief in one moment, and both her eyes were filled with tears and the flow of her voice was checked" (19.471–73). His two most faithful manservants "flung their arms about wise Odysseus, and wept; and they kissed his head and shoulders in loving welcome. And even in like manner Odysseus kissed their heads and hands" (21.223–25). His faithful maidservants "thronged about Odysseus and embraced him, and clasped and kissed his head and shoulders and his hands in loving welcome" (22.498–500).

84. *Odyssey* 2.193 and 18.248–49.

85. Claudian *Shorter Poems* 30.25–28. Cf. Ovid *Tristia* 2.375–76: "What is the *Odyssey* except the story of one woman wooed in her husband's absence for love's sake by many suitors?" This same judgment has been expressed more recently by Joseph Courtois, "L'Odyssée, poème de fidélité," *ÉtClass* 25 (1957): 65–73.

86. This assessment holds even when one grants to Marylin A. Katz her contention that Penelope's role in the epic is ambiguous and complex (*Penelope's Renown: Meaning and Indeterminacy in the "Odyssey"* [Princeton: Princeton University Press, 1991]).

87. Homer contrasts Penelope and Clytemnestra in *Odyssey* 11.440–46.

88. Ibid., 24.196–99.

89. Julian *Epistles* 42 (to Callixeine, 388c).

90. Ovid *Tristia* 5.14.35–36; cf. 1.6.21–30 and 5.5.45, *The Art of Love* 1.477 and 3.15, and *Metamorphoses* 13.301.

91. Ps.-Dictys *Journal of the Trojan War* 6.6.

92. See also Iamblicus *De vita Pythagorica* 57, Propertius *Elegies* 3.12.37 and 13.24, Horace *Satire* 2.5.76–83 and *Odes* 3.10.11; cf. Euripides *Orestes* 590 and Hyginus *Fabulae* 256.

93. E.g., Pausanius 8.12.5–6, Apollodorus *Epitome* 7.38–39, and Nonnos Abbas in Gregory of Nazianzus *Oratio contra Iulianum* 1 (*PG* 36.1008); cf. Seneca *Epistula* 88. Even Penelope's chastity was seen as a seductive ruse: "Penelope, your every thought was in your cunt. You remained chaste (*casta*) in order to look over the dinner guests and to fill your house with fuckers" (*Priapea* 68.27–30). Servius knew another tradition:

> [W]hen he [Odysseus] returned home to Ithaca after his wanderings, it is said that he found among his household gods Pan, who was reported to have been born from Penelope and all the suitors, as the name itself Pan seems to indicate; although others report that he was born from Hermes, who transformed himself into a goat and slept with Penelope. But after Odysseus saw the deformed child, it is said that he fled

[again] to his wanderings. (Commentary on *The Aeneid* 2.44, translation from Katz, *Penelope's Renown*, 77)

94. According to Polybius, teachers of rhetoric regularly assigned students to compose eulogies of Thersites, Homer's despicable rogue, and denunciations of Penelope (*Histories* 12.26.5). The purpose of the assignment, of course, was to find something praiseworthy in Thersites or blameworthy in Penelope, even though her moral character was nearly unassailable.

95. Marie-Madeleine Mactoux writes: "Comme à l'époque hellénistique, mais d'une manière plus fréquente, Pénélope est choisie comme élément de comparaison dans des épitaphes ou des inscriptions honorifiques qui se multiplient au IIe et IIIe siècles" (*Pénélope. Légende et mythe*, Annales littéraires de l'université de Besançon 175, Centre de recherches d'histoire ancienne 16 [Paris: Belles Lettres, 1975], 167).

96. Ps.-Virgil *Culex* 265.

97. *Thesmophoriazusae* 549.

98. Euripides *Troades* 422: σώφρονος . . . γυναικός; Aristophanes *Thesmophoria-zusae* 547: γυνὴ σώφρων; Achilles Tatius 1.8: Πηνελόπης . . . τῆς σώρφρονος; Heraclitus *Quaestiones Homericae* 78.3: σώφρων Πηνελόπη; Libanius *Declamationes* 6.59: γυναικὸς . . . σώφρονος; cf. Theognis *Elegies* 1126, Heliodorus *Aethiopica* 5.22, Maximus of Tyre 40.3, Clement of Alexandria *Paedogogos* 2.10:97.2, and Eustathius 1435 (passim). Lucian uses both περίφρων and σώφρων of Penelope in *Essays in Portraiture* 20. Isaac Porphyrogenitus claimed Penelope was ἔμφρονός τε καὶ σώφρονος (*Praefatio in Homerum* 41; Jan Fredrik Kindstrand, *Isaac Porphyrogenitus: Praefatio in Homerum*, Acta Universitatis Upsaliensis, Studia Graeca Upsaliensia 14 [Uppsala: University of Uppsala, 1979], 31). For Latin authors on Penelope's *pudicitia* see: Seneca *Epistula* 88, Ovid *Tristia* 5.5.45, Horace *Satire* 2.5.77, Claudian *Shorter Poems* 30.20–28, and Martial *Epigrams* 1.62.6, 2.7.5, and 2.104.15–16. Helen North notes: "although Homer never uses the word sophrosyne in this connection [viz. as a woman's virtue], it is regularly so used in the classical period, when Penelope by reason of her faithfulness becomes the most prominent exemplar of the virtue" (*Sophrosyne: Self-Knowledge and Self-Restraint in Greek Literature* [Ithaca: Cornell University Press, 1966], 21; see also 248–49).

99. Nonnus Abbas in Gregory of Nazianzus *Oratio contra Iulianum* 1 (*PG* 36.1008).

100. Dio Chrysostom 15.4.

101. Athenaeus *Deipnosophists* 14.614e. See also Plutarch *Life of Demetrios* 25.

102. *Dialogues of the Courtesans* 12.1. See also *True Story* 2.36.

103. *Panegyric in Honor of Eusebeia* 127c and 128d.

104. *Ad Homeri Odysseam* 1380. Cf. Isaac Porphyrogenitus *Praefatio in Homerum* 41 and Ps.-Plutarch *De vita et poesi Homeri* 185.

105. *Paidagogos* 3.8.41.5, quoting *Orestes* 588–90.

106. For discussions of these heroines see: G. Bardy, "Apocryphes à tendance encratite," *DS* 1.752–65; Stevan L. Davies, *The Revolt of the Widows: The Social World of the Apocryphal Acts* (Carbondale: Southern Illinois University Press, 1980); Dennis R. MacDonald, *The Legend and the Apostle: The Battle for Paul in Story and Canon*

(Philadelphia: Westminster Press, 1983); Virginia Burrus, *Chastity as Autonomy*; and Jean-Daniel Kaestli's response to Burrus (*Semeia 38: The Apocryphal Acts of Apostles*, ed. Dennis R. MacDonald [Decatur: Scholars Press, 1986], 119–31). See also Ross Kraemer, "The Conversion of Women to Ascetic Forms of Christianity," *Signs* 6 (1980–81): 298–307. But see the caveats of Jean-Daniel Kaestli, "Fiction littéraire et réalité sociale: Que peut-on savoir de la place des femmes dans le milieu de la production des Actes apocryphes des apôtres?" *Apocrypha: Le Champ des apocryphes*, vol. 1: *La Fable apocryphe*, ed. Pierre Geoltrain et al. (Turnhout: Brepols, 1990), 279–302.

107. Robin Lane Fox, *Pagans and Christians* (New York: Alfred A. Knopf, 1987), 357.

108. *Iliad* 19.417 and *Odyssey* 18.156: ἶφι δαμῆναι. Several Homeric characters have names with ἶφι prefixes: Iphianassa, Iphiclus, Iphinous, Iphitus, Iphition, Iphimedeia, Iphicles, and even Iphidamas. One thinks also of the tragic Iphigenia, not mentioned by Homer, but an important character in the larger story of the Trojan war. According to Apollodorus, among Penelope's suitors was an Iphidamas (*Epitome* 7.27).

109. See "Penelope," P-W 19.461–63.

110. Military imagery was used also in Passion 13, where Andrew prayed that God would strengthen (ἐπιστηριχθήτω) Maximilla against Aegeates.

111. *Odyssey* 14.9, 127, and 451, 15.374 and 377, 19.83, and 23.2. δέσποινα also is used for Maximilla in Passion 18, 22, 36, and 64.

112. In two related and late Greek passions Maximilla says, "I would sooner die than forsake my σωφροσύνη" (E 249B and *L* 44).

113. In her study of the development of σωφροσύνη in Greek literature, Helen North observed the following:

> During the long period of transition [from pagan to Christian civilization] each of the Platonic virtues suffered radical alteration. For sophrosyne the gravest danger lay in the tendency of many Christian moralists to overemphasize its relation to chastity. They adopted the connotation that was most popular throughout the Greek world in the first century of our era—sophrosyne interpreted as control of the appetites—and still further intensified this concept, claiming sophrosyne (chastity, purity) as a specifically Christian virtue, which distinguished the Christian from his pagan neighbor. (*Sophrosyne*, 312)

Much of North's discussion of σωφροσύνη in patristic literature is relevant background to *The Acts of Andrew* (see esp. 319–53).

114. *Odyssey* 23.207–8 and 300.

115. The austerity of Maximilla's face probably is a play on the notorious hardness of Penelope's heart just prior to her recognition of Odysseus. Telemachus says: "[T]hy heart is ever harder than stone" (23.103). Odysseus says: "No other woman would harden her heart as thou dost. . . . [T]he heart in her breast is of iron" (23.168 and 172; cf. 230).

116. Cf. *Acts of Thomas* 14 and 88. See also the excellent discussion of spiritual marriages in Prieur, *Acta Andreae*, 193–96.

117. Jean-Daniel Kaestli identified parallels in Greek romances to these substituted

bed partners ("Fiction littéraire," 295–97). He singled out Aristides of Miletus *Milesiaca*, Apuleius *Metamorphoses*, and Parthenius *Lover Romances* (see 16 and 17), but the motif ultimately is folkloristic. The examples in Parthenius differ from the story of Euclia in that women substitute themselves for other women in order to sleep with the desired men rather than to avoid such unions.

118. Four times in *The Odyssey* characters "stand over the head" of someone sleeping in bed, and in each instance Homer uses the identical expression: στῆ ... ὑπὲρ κεφαλῆς. The phantom of Iphthime "stands over the head" of the bed of Penelope (4.803), Athene at the bed of Nausicaa (6.21) and again at the bed of Odysseus (20.32), and Eurycleia at the bed of Penelope (23.4; cf. 20.94). Cf. *Iliad* 23.68, where Homer uses the same expression for the appearance of Patroclus's ghost to Achilles.

119. *Odyssey* 18.339.

120. Ibid., 22.471–73.

121. Ibid., 22.475–77.

122. Ibid., 6.141–47.

123. Penelope, too, is likened to a goddess (ibid., 19.53–54; cf. 4.120–22, 6.15–16 and 7.71, and 8.467).

124. Ibid., 6.149–55.

125. Ibid., 6.168–69.

126. Cf. *Odyssey* 6.310–11, 7.142, 10.323, and 13.231.

127. Ibid., 1.397–98.

128. Ibid., 16.304–7 and 22.462–64.

129. Cf. *Odyssey* 23.90–91, where Odysseus was "looking down (κάτω ὁρόων)" as he waited for Penelope to recognize him.

130. The rare word σαβάνιον refers to a rough linen rag used for wiping the body after bathing. Clement of Alexandria states that when Jesus washed the feet of his disciples he wore this simple towel (σαβάνῳ περιζωσάμενος; *Paidagogos* 2.3.38).

131. *Odyssey* 4.245 (my translation).

132. In this connection it is worth noting that in Greek art Odysseus often appears naked except for a chlamys draping a shoulder.

133. Compare this with the proverb cited in *Odyssey* 22.319: "[T]here is no gratitude (χάρις) in aftertime for good deeds (εὐεργέων) done." See also Athena's comment in 22.234–35: "that thou mayest know what manner of man Mentor, son of Alcimus, is to repay kindness (εὐεργεσίας) in the midst of the foe." Penelope's suitors had given her many gifts but in the end were killed, an injustice that several ancient authors held against her. See *Odyssey* 18.281–83 and 290–303.

134. Similarly, when Odysseus was about to reveal his identity to Penelope he smiled (μείδησεν) (*Odyssey* 23.111) and told Telemachus and the servants to change clothes: "First bathe yourselves, and put on (ἀμφιέσασθε) your tunics, and bid the handmaids in the halls to take their raiment" (23.131–32). Cf. 23.142–43: "First they bathed and put on (ἀμφιέσαντο) their tunics, and the women arrayed themselves."

135. E.g., *Phaedo* 79c: "[T]o which class do you think the soul has greater likeness and kinship (ξυγγενέστερον)?" "[T]he soul is like the divine." Cf. 79b: "Now to which

class should we say the body is more similar and more closely akin (ξυγγενέστερον)?"

136. Ibid., 59d.

137. For example, "Aphrodite snatched him [Paris] up, full easily as a goddess may, and shrouded him in a thick mist" (*Iliad* 3.380–81). Nearly identical wording describes Poseidon saving the Moliones (*Iliad* 11.752), Apollo saving Hector (20.444) and Agenor (21.597), and Apollo hiding himself in a cloud (16.789–90 and 21.549). Athena "enwrapped herself in a lurid cloud" (17.551) and Hera "shed thick mist" over her horses (5.776). When Odysseus returned to Ithaca, "about him the goddess . . . shed a mist, even Pallas Athene, daughter of Zeus, that she might render him unknown, and tell him all things, so that his wife would not know him, nor his townsfolk, nor his friends, until the wooers had paid the full price of all their transgressions" (*Odyssey* 13.189–93).

138. Cf. *Odyssey* 10.278 and 13.221–22.

139. See also 7.39–42: "And as he went through the city in the midst of them, the Phaeacians . . . took no heed of him, for . . . Athene . . . shed about him a wondrous mist, for her heart was kindly toward him"; and 139–40: "But the much-enduring Odysseus went through the hall, wrapped in the thick mist which Athene had shed about him."

140. *De fide contra Manichaeos* 38.

141. *Odyssey* 7.78–81.

142. For an analysis of this discourse see Prieur, *Acta Andreae*, 196–99. Cf. Plato's *Phaedo* 79d–80b, where Socrates, discussing the kinship of the soul, likewise advances a list of contrasts between the soul and the body.

143. Cf. *Phaedo* 95e: "[T]he cause of coming-to-be (περὶ γενέσεως . . . τὴν αἰτίαν) . . . must be thoroughly discussed."

144. On "the cause of γένεσις" see: Plato *Philebus* 27a–b, *Timaeus* 28a, 29d, and 44c, *Phaedo* 95e, and especially *Laws* 10.891e. See also Prieur, *Acta Andreae*, 207–12, who cites a relevant and fascinating parallel in *Acts of Peter* 38.

145. These gestures may have something to do with the strange kisses of hands after characters recognize Odysseus: "[T]hey kissed his head and shoulders in loving welcome. And even in like manner Odysseus kissed their heads and hands" (*Odyssey* 21.224–25); and "They thronged about Odysseus and embraced him, and clasped and kissed his head and shoulders and his hands in loving welcome" (22.498–500). Before she was certain of Odysseus's identity, Penelope debated if she should "clasp and kiss his head and hands" (23.87; cf. 208 and 19.417). When Telemachus returned from Pylos, Eumaeus "kissed his head and both his beautiful eyes and his two hands" (16.15–16). Cf. 17.35 and 39, and especially Achilles Tatius 5.27: "[S]he loosed my bonds and kissed my hands, and placed them, first on her eyes and then upon her heart, saying . . ."

146. Passion 37 says: "Do not commit this act. Do not submit to Aegeates' threat. Do not be moved by his speech. Do not fear his disgusting schemes. Do not be conquered by his artful flatteries. Do not consent to yield yourself to his filthy acts of wizardry. Endure each of his tortures." In Passion 29, in the context of praying for Iphidama's empowering, Andrew addresses Jesus as the one "who instills courage (εὐθαρσίαν . . . δίδως)."

147. See Prieur, *Acta Andreae*, 205 and 207, as well as Peter Nagel, "Die Wieder-

gewinnung des Paradieses durch Askese," *FF* 34 (1960): 375–77.

148. Cf. Plato *Alcibiades* 132e.

149. Prieur discusses in detail the motif of becoming male (*Acta Andreae*, 212–14). See also James Lagrand, "How Was the Virgin Mary like a Man (*'yk gbr'*)? A Note on Mt. 1:18b and Related Syriac Christian Texts," *NovT* 22 (1980): 97–107, and my *There Is No Male and Female: The Fate of a Dominical Saying in Paul and Gnosticism*, Harvard Dissertations in Religion 20 (Philadelphia: Fortress Press, 1987), 92–102.

150. One can find a similar attitude toward learning in *Phaedo* 72e: "[O]ur learning is nothing else than recollection."

151. The word ἀνάπαυσις and cognates appear repeatedly in the passion and derive from a distinctive philosophical conceptuality. See: Philipp Vielhauer, "'Ανάπαυσις, zum gnostischen Hintergrund des Thomas-Evangeliums," in *Apophoreta: Festschrift für Ernst Haenchen*, BZNW 30, ed. W. Eltester and F. H. Kettler (Berlin: Alfred Töpelmann, 1964), 281–99; and Jacques E. Ménard, "Le Repos, salut du gnostique," *RevScRel* 51 (1977): 71–88.

152. Cf. *Phaedo* 62a.

153. The subtle devices of the devil treated in Passion 50 might be compared with Socrates' discussion of the subtle temptations of pleasure against the soul (*Phaedo* 83d).

154. Such a gender reversal may also be found in the treatise on education by the philosopher Musonius Rufus, who insisted that girls ought to learn ἀνδρεία and boys σωφροσύνη. See Discourse 4 in Hense's edition as well as Discourse 3 on women learning philosophy.

155. *Odyssey* 19.326: νόον and ἐπίφρονα μῆτιν.

156. Ibid., 2.117–18 and 121: κέρδεα, φρένας, and νοήματα; cf. 11.445–46 and 18.248–49.

157. Philostephanus's scholion on *Odyssey* 15.16.

158. *Odyssey* 2.116–17.

159. Eustathius *Ad Homeri Odysseam* 1437.

160. Ibid., 1389. See Mactoux, *Pénélope*, 169–70.

161. Eustathius *Ad Homeri Odysseam* 1437: τῇ φιλοσόφῳ . . . ὑφαντικῇ.

162. *Odyssey* 2.105 and 24.140.

163. See Buffière, *Mythes d'Homère*, 463–64; and Mactoux, *Pénélope*, 168–72.

164. *Ad Marcellam* 3.37–38 and 5.79–80 (Wicker).

165. Ibid., 28.439–40.

166. Ibid., 10.176–80.

167. Ibid., 5.74–75.

168. Ibid., 6.100–103.

169. Ibid., 6.108–113.

170. Ibid., 16.284–85.

171. Ibid., 6.105.

172. Ibid., 33.511–15 (Wicker, slightly altered).

173. Ibid., 10.176.

7

Slaying the Suitor

Ancient readers knew Book 22 of *The Odyssey* as the *mnesterophonia*, 'the slaying of the suitors', in which Odysseus finally revealed his identity to his rivals and slew them with the help of Telemachus and his faithful servants. Chapters 51–64 of the Andrean Passion roughly correspond to the *mnesterophonia* insofar as Maximilla, Stratocles, and Aegeates continue to play out their roles as transvalued Penelope, Telemachus, and Odysseus. But unlike in *The Odyssey*, here the protagonist is the victim, not the victor. Like most other apostles in the apocryphal Acts and their Lord, Andrew suffers martyrdom; indeed at points one detects the influence of *The Acts of Peter*, which narrates the crucifixion of Andrew's brother.[1] But the most obvious hypotext behind Passion 51–64 is Plato's *Phaedo*, the death of Socrates, evidence of which appeared in the previous chapter in connection with the prison visits of Iphidama, Maximilla, and Stratocles.

By modeling the apostle's death after the *Phaedo*, the author developed far more completely than any of his contemporaries that aspect of the Socratic tradition most resonant with the experience of early Christians: his unjust execution for having corrupted the youth and for having introduced new deities to replace the gods sanctioned by the state. Furthermore, during the last day of Socrates' life, as narrated in the *Phaedo*, the philosopher instructed his friends concerning the immortality of the soul and the postmortem rewards of the righteous. Because of his firm conviction that he thus would be vindicated in the next world, Socrates drank his poison joyfully. The parallels between the *Phaedo* and the death of Jesus repeatedly impressed Christians as providential.[2]

When Justin Martyr argued that all who lived by the *Logos* prior to Jesus were Christians without the name, the first name that occurred to him was Socrates, who (along with Heraclitus, Abraham, Ananiah, Azariah, Mishael, and Elijah) suffered for religious ideals.[3] Justin equated the Athenians' hostility toward Socrates with pagan attitudes toward Christians,[4] and even likened Socrates to Jesus:

When Socrates tried by true reason and with due inquiry to make these things clear and to draw men away from the demons, they, working through men who delighted in wickedness, managed to have him put to death as godless and

249

impious, saying that he was bringing in new divinities. And now they do the same kind of thing to us. For these errors were not only condemned among the Greeks by reason, through Socrates, but among the barbarians, by Reason himself, who took form and became man and was called Jesus Christ.[5]

Justin Martyr probably identified his own persecution with that of Socrates (it was after all by dint of the sword that Justin won his last name); he was fully aware that he too might fall under the penalty of death and was willing to join his voice to that of Socrates, "If this is pleasing to God [Plato: the gods], so be it."[6]

Among early Christian apologists, Tertullian distinguished himself as the most obsessed with the barefoot philosopher, both positively and negatively. On the positive side, he, like Justin, admired Socrates' railing against Greek superstition and his facing death with good-humored courage.[7] In his *Ad nationes* Tertullian wrote,

> Socrates was condemned on that side (of his wisdom) in which he came nearest in his search to the truth, by destroying your gods. Although the name of Christian was not at that time in the world, yet truth was always suffering condemnation. Now you will not deny that he was a wise man, to whom your own Pythian (god) had borne witness. Socrates, he said, was the wisest of men. Truth overbore Apollo, and made him pronounce even against himself; since he acknowledged that he was no god, when he affirmed that that was the wisest man who was denying the gods.[8]

But Tertullian's attitude toward Socrates could also be critical. At the beginning of his *De anima*, or *On the Soul*, he contrasted his own discussion of the soul with that of Socrates in Plato's *Phaedo*. He complained, for instance, that on the day of Socrates' death he could hardly have had sufficient equanimity to speak coherently about the soul. After all, he was in prison, his wife Xanthippe was hysterical, and he had to say farewell to his tender-aged, soon-to-be orphaned children. Socrates' apparent self-composure and even joy was a sham intended to deprive his accusers of sadistic pleasure at his death. His teaching on the soul issued not from divine revelation or cool reason but from his boyhood *daemon*, "the worst kind of teacher surely."[9] Even though Socrates had spoken against Greek religious superstitions, he lost his stomach for rationality in the end when he told his comrade to sacrifice a cock to Asclepius.[10] Furthermore, divine wisdom, Tertullian insisted, does not corrupt youth:

> [I]t stands condemned not merely in one city but in all the world.... [I]t does not die by emptying the cup in convivial fashion, but it perishes on the cross, by being burned alive, or by whatever other horror human ingenuity can devise.... And so, where there is a question of examining the soul here in the dungeon of this world (far darker than the prison where Socrates met with Cebes and Phaedo), let us study the question in accordance with the teachings of God.[11]

One can find the same ambivalence toward Socrates in Origen. On the one hand, the great Alexandrian theologian agreed with a tradition concerning heroes of the "best life," such as Heracles, Odysseus, and Socrates.[12] He also admired Socrates' ability to make his companions

advance so far in philosophy that Phaedo was adjudged by Plato as worthy to expound Socrates' discourse on immortality and to describe his courage in prison, when he gave no thought to the hemlock but fearlessly and with complete calm in his soul talked of important and profound questions, which even people who are quite ordered in mind and are undisturbed by any difficult circumstance are scarcely able to follow.[13]

But like Tertullian, Origen listed Socrates among "those who taught such profound philosophy about the soul and the future course of the soul that has lived a good life, [but who] abandon the great truths that God revealed to them to attend to mean and trivial things and give a cock to Asclepius."[14] In both texts, Origen has in mind the account of Socrates' death in Plato's *Phaedo*, just as Tertullian had at the beginning of *De anima*.[15]

Plato's Socrates also influenced Christian martyrological literature.[16] The martyr Pionius claimed that his punishment was even worse than what Socrates suffered.[17] When Phileas was commanded to sacrifice, he responded: "I will not. I am concerned for my soul. Christians are not the only ones who are concerned for their souls; pagans are, too. Take Socrates for example. When he was being led to his death, even with his wife and children present, he did not turn back, but eagerly embraced death."[18] The martyr apparently had in mind the *Phaedo*. Late in the second century or early in the third, a certain Mara bar Sarapion, writing to his son in Syriac from a jail near the Euphrates, likened his unjust imprisonment to those of Pythagoras, Socrates, and Jesus.[19]

Even pagans identified the fate of Christian martyrs with Socrates. According to Celsus, Christians "teach their doctrines in secret . . . to escape the death penalty. He [Celsus] compares the danger to the risks encountered for the sake of philosophy by Socrates."[20] The great humorist Lucian, contemptuous yet fascinated by a philosophical charlatan named Peregrinus, states that at one point in his career the sham *sophos* joined ranks with the Christians, became a biblical interpreter, and for his efforts landed in jail—a calamity that so expanded his reputation that they called him "the new Socrates."[21]

The analogy between Christian martyrs and Socrates finds its most expansive treatment—apart from *The Acts of Andrew*— in *The Martyrdom of Apollonius*. The martyr argued that his refusal to sacrifice to the emperor was in the spirit of Socrates, who snubbed the gods of Athens,[22] and that Christians generally, like the philosopher, may be counted on to believe

that the soul is immortal, to be convinced that there will be a judgement after death, and that there will be a reward given by God after the resurrection, to those who have lived a good life, for their labours on behalf of virtue.[23]

After teaching us this doctrine vigorously and persuading us with many arguments, he himself [Jesus Christ] attained a great reputation for virtue. Still was he despised by the ignorant, like the philosophers and just men who lived before him. For the wicked have no use for the righteous.[24]

The author had in mind Socrates as foremost among these suffering philosophers: "The Athenian informers convinced the people and then unjustly condemned Socrates; so too our Saviour and teacher was condemned by a few malefactors after they had him bound."[25] The text invites the reader to view Apollonius's own death as an *imitatio Socratis* as well as an *imitatio Christi*.

Material evidence also survives as a testament to the identification of Socrates with Jesus. A Syrian mosaic depicting Socrates teaching six of his disciples—three on either side of him with the philosopher elevated in the middle—resembles Christian representations of Jesus in the same posture, teaching six disciples, three to a side. After a detailed analysis of the evidence, one authority concluded:

At some time during the third century, some Christian artist, whose views on Socrates may have resembled those of Justin, adopted the composition portraying Socrates and his disciples and thus established a type for the portrayal of Christ as the Teacher of Truth, a type that was to evolve into some of the most majestic compositions of Early Christian art.[26]

Passion 51–64 of *The Acts of Andrew* borrows from the Socratic tradition more persistently than any other early Christian text. The parallels include the charges against Andrew, his laughter in spite of his execution, his teachings on the immortality of the soul, his refusal to escape from his fate, and the weeping of his friends because of being deprived of him. Consistent with the hypertextual strategies examined thus far, the similarities include shared vocabulary, otherwise inexplicable details, and corresponding order of presentation. In one important respect, however, the apostle retained his role as a Christianized Odysseus: Aegeates ordered him lashed to his cross at the edge of the sea, like Odysseus at his mast sailing past the Sirens on his way home.

Directly adjacent to the Syrian mosaic of Socrates mentioned above is another that depicts Odysseus returning home to the arms of Penelope while several female servants look on. The juxtaposition of these two mosaics can hardly be accidental; presumably these two heroes were selected as examples of great sages.[27] Taken together, the mosaics provide a visual metaphor for the Passion of Andrew, which oscillates between Odysseus and Socrates in its depiction of Andrew, the Christian sage. During the sixth century the building was expanded into a Christian church, with the mosaics left in place.

The Accusation Against Andrew (Socrates, Passion 51)

The *Phaedo* begins with Phaedo's first-person narration of Socrates' last day of life. Early in the morning his friends arrived at the prison (δεσμωτήριον, 59d–e) and found his executioners instructing him concerning the drinking of the hemlock. The formal charge against him was this: "Socrates is a wrongdoer (ἀδικεῖν) for corrupting (διαφθείροντα) the youth and for not believing in the gods the city believes in, but in new spiritual beings" (*Apology* 24b). The situation and charges against Andrew were similar:

> Early the next morning, Aegeates summoned Andrew from prison (δεσμωτηρίου) and said to him, "The time to complete my judgment against you has arrived,[28] you stranger, alien to this present life, enemy of my home, and corrupter of my entire house. Why did you decide to burst into places alien to you and corrupt (ὑποδιαφθεῖραι) a wife who used to please me in every way and never slept with another man? She has convinced me that she now rejoices in you and in your god." (Passion 51)[29]

As was the case with Socrates, early in the morning just prior to his execution Andrew is in prison, accused of corrupting someone and of promoting a new god. In his charge that the apostle had corrupted his wife "who had never slept with another man," Aegeates seems still to suppose that Andrew had been sleeping with Maximilla. Many ancient authors took the Athenian accusation against Socrates of having corrupted the youth as an objection to his notorious pederasty. This is precisely how Tertullian understood it: "Socrates . . . was proclaimed the corrupter of young boys. A Christian [male] makes no perversion even of the female sex."[30]

Aegeates then gave orders, which outraged people far and wide:

> He commanded that Andrew be flogged with seven whips. Then he sent him off to be crucified (ἀνασκολοπισθῆναι) and commanded the executioners not to impale him with nails but to stretch him out tied up with ropes, and to leave his knees uncut, supposing that by so doing he would punish Andrew even more cruelly.

> This matter became known to everyone, for it was rumored throughout Patras that the stranger, the righteous one, the man who possessed God, was being crucified (ἀνασκολοπίζεται) by the impious Aegeates, even though he had done nothing improper. All alike were outraged. (Passion 51)

In this text and throughout the passion, the author used the unusual verb ἀνασκολοπίζειν, 'to fix to a stake', instead of the more common σταυροῦν, 'to fix to a cross'.[31] The selection of this verb points to a fascinating use of Plato in ancient Christian apologetics.

In *The Republic*, Glaucon played devil's advocate by suggesting that more important than actual righteousness was a reputation for being righteous, for without such a reputation even "the just man (ὁ δίκαιος) will have to endure the lash (μαστιγώσεται), the rack, chains (δεδήσεται), the branding-iron in his eyes, and finally, after every extremity of suffering, he will be crucified (ἀνασχινδυλευθήσεται)."[32] For his part, Socrates insisted that even though the righteous may suffer unjustly in this life, one must remember that in the afterlife all will stand before unerring judges who will reward the just and punish the wicked. Plato's readers naturally interpreted this passage concerning the execution of the innocent in light of Socrates' own unjust death.[33]

Early Christians, however, interpreted the passage as a foreshadowing of the sufferings of Christ.[34] For example, Clement of Alexandria supposed that Plato had adumbrated the death of Christ in this passage, and he quoted it in its entirety.[35] Eusebius, who quoted *verbatim et in extenso* Clement's interpretation of the same passage,[36] extended Plato's meaning to embrace not only Christ but also the Hebrew prophets, the apostles, and all Christian martyrs:

> [E]ven now, the noble witnesses of our savior throughout the region of human habitation—who practice "not only seeming to be, but actually being" just (δίκαιοι) and pious—have suffered the very things Plato listed, for they have been whipped (ἐμαστιγώθησαν), have endured bonds (δεσμά) and racks, and even had their eyes gouged out, and finally, having suffered every torment, have been crucified (ἀνεσκινδυλεύθησαν). If you should look among the Greeks, you would not find any their peer, so that one might aptly say that the philosopher [Plato] did nothing other than prophesy through these words concerning those among us who excel in piety and true righteousness (δικαιοσύνῃ).[37]

In *The Martyrdom of Apollonius*, the martyr interpreted the same Platonic text to refer to Christ. In this case, however, the author substituted the verb ἀνασκολοπίζειν for Plato's ἀνασχινδυλεύειν. The two verbs are in fact synonyms; ἀνασκολοπίζειν all but replaced ἀνασχινδυλεύειν in the Hellenistic period.[38] This alteration is significant for the argument insofar as this is the word that appears repeatedly in *The Acts of Andrew* when speaking of the apostle's crucifixion. Compare the version of the Platonic passage as quoted by *The Martyrdom of Apollonius* with Passion 51:

The Martyrdom of Apollonius 40 (citing Plato *Republic* 2.631e–632a)	Passion 51
"'**The just man** (ὁ δὲ δίκαιος),' he [Plato] says, 'will **be whipped** (μαστιγωθήσεται),	He commanded that Andrew **be whipped** (μαστιχθῆναι) with seven **whips** (μάστιξιν). Then he sent him off **to be crucified** (ἀνασκολοπισθῆναι), and commanded the executioners not to impale him with nails but to stretch him out **tied up** (δεθέντα) with ropes. . . .
tortured, **bound** (δεθήσεται), his eyes gouged out,[39] and after suffering	[F]or it was rumored throughout Patras

finally all sorts of penalties will	that the stranger, **the righteous one** (ὁ δίκαιος), the man who possessed
finally **be impaled**	God, was being **crucified**
(ἀνασκολοπισθήσεται).'"	(ἀνασκολοπίζεται) by the impious
(Musurillo)	Aegeates, even though he had done nothing improper.

The author of *The Martyrdom of Apollonius* undoubtedly interpreted *Republic* 2.361e–362a in light of the execution of Socrates, for he mentions Socrates immediately after citing this passage (41).

The density of similarities and the use of distinctive vocabulary strongly imply that the author of *The Acts of Andrew*, like Clement, Eusebius, and the author of *The Martyrdom of Apollonius*, saw in Plato's hypothetical "just one" a foreshadowing of Christian persecutions and modeled Passion 51 such that the reader would further associate Andrew's execution with the death of Socrates.

The Vengeance of Stratocles (Telemachus, Passion 52–53a)

The executioners took Andrew off but ran into Stratocles, the former soldier, who had not yet forgotten how to fight:

> Stratocles did not spare any of them but gave each a beating, ripped their clothing from top to bottom, tore Andrew away, and told them, "Thank the blessed one for educating me and teaching me to check my violent temper. Otherwise, I would have demonstrated for you what Stratocles and Aegeates the rogue are capable of. For we (believers) have learned to endure our afflictions." He grabbed the apostle's hand and went away with him to the seaside location where he was to be hung up. (Passion 52)

Here again Stratocles reverses the development of Telemachus, who had learned from Nestor and Menelaus that he should slay the suitors, as he did, of course, in the *mnesterophonia* at the side of Odysseus. Stratocles, on the other hand, had learned not to inflict violence but to endure it, in spite of this momentary relapse. "Stratocles walked with the apostle to the designated spot, but he was perturbed, furious with Aegeates, now and then railing against him in silence." This passage too might call to mind Telemachus, who "nursed in his heart great grief for the smiting [of Odysseus by a suitor] . . . ; but he shook his head in silence, pondering evil in the deep of his heart."[40] Andrew then warned Stratocles not to give way to his baser instincts but to curb his impulsiveness.[41]

The Simile of the Eagle (Socrates' Chariot, Passion 53b)

The Armenian version of the Passion retains a speech at this point that is missing in all Greek versions but that undoubtedly appeared in the ancient *Acts*.[42] As

Andrew and Stratocles walk to the cross at the edge of the sea, the apostle
compares the soul to an eagle longing to soar to heaven. Behind this speech lies
Plato's *Phaedrus* and the famous simile of the soul as a chariot pulled by two
winged horses.[43] Socrates used this image for explaining the struggle between
the soul's desire to ascend to the intelligible world and its lamentable pull toward
the material. One of the horses strives for the heights, the other drags it
downward, so the charioteer must manage his unruly team if he would rise to
heavenly beauty:

Phaedrus 246b–c	Passion 53
"We will **liken the soul** to the composite nature of a pair of winged horses and a charioteer. . . ."	"For it seems to me that **it** [the soul] **is like** the regal bird, the eagle, that flies from earth on high and is adorned with the rays of sunlight **by nature high-flying,**
[Cf. 246d: "**The natural function** of the wing is **to soar upwards** and carry that which is heavy up to the place where dwells the race of gods."] "Soul . . . transverses the whole heaven . . . it **mounts upward** and governs **the whole world**; but the soul which has	If he, **soaring** with light wings, flies around **the earth** having left the usual traveling orbit of those living in the light, he is corrupted by the earth,
lost its wings is borne along until it gets hold of something solid, when it **settles down**, taking upon itself an **earthly** body."	and **his wings grow heavy.** And the eagle is indeed transfigured, for although his nature is appropriate to **the earth**, nesting is unbecoming to his wings.
[Cf. 247b: "the horse of evil nature **weighs the chariot down,** making **it heavy and pulling it toward the earth**."][44]	**While being drawn to earth,** he appears ridiculous to those who see him."

According to Andrew, the soul desires to fly to heaven and for this reason grows
"spiritual wings." Socrates too insisted that when one contemplates heavenly
beauty, "he feels his wings growing, and longs to stretch them for an upward
flight, but cannot do so, and,

Phaedrus 249c	Passion 53
"**like a bird gazes upward** and neglects the things below."[45]	"**Like the eagle**, as the soul **makes its upward ascent** to heaven on high, so also shall we ascend to the heights and not be **weighed down**."

The ultimate goal of the philosophical life, according to Socrates, is the soul's shedding of the body, like an old garment. Andrew agreed:

Phaedrus 256d	Passion 53
"And at last, **when they** [the righteous] **depart the body,** they are not winged, to be sure, but their wings have begun to grow. . . . [They] **shall live a happy life** in the light as they journey together, and because of their love shall be alive in their plumage when they receive their wings."[46]	"[W]hen he [the perfectly just] **will put off the earthly body, and the** next time arise clothed in heavenly glory, and then **into coveted paradise will they enter rejoicing** with the angels in the infinite **joy** of God."

Apparently the author of *The Acts of Andrew* adapted this passage from the *Phaedrus* in order to express his own understanding of the soul's soaring off to God away from the material world.[47] "When I die, hallelujah, by and by, I'll fly away."

The Mystery of the Cross (Odysseus's Mast, Passion 54–55a)

This next section of the Passion has already been analyzed in chapter four in connection with GE 20. In a dream, Andrew was taken to a radiant mountain, where the apostle John told him that he would "drink Peter's cup"; he too would be crucified: "He [John] also told me many other things about which I can say nothing now, but which will become apparent when I approach this sacrifice. . . . For I am already being untied from the body, and I go to that promise he saw fit to promise me" (GE 20). Among the "many other things" John revealed to Andrew must have been something about a planted cross that would serve him as a sign, for immediately after the peripatetic address about the eagle, he says: "This is the end of my speech, for I think that while we were speaking we arrived at the designated place; the planted (πεπηγώς) cross is a sign (σημεῖον) to me indicating the spot" (Passion 53b). This passage and its anticipation in GE 20 seem to be hypertextual appropriations of Tiresias's prophecy in *Odyssey* Book 11 that Odysseus would die in peace if he took his oar inland until he was given the sign (σῆμα) of someone asking him about the farm implement on his shoulder. There he must "plant (πήξας)" his oar and sacrifice to Poseidon.[48]

Andrew, too, was given "a sign," a "planted cross" at the edge of the sea: "He left everyone, approached the cross, and spoke to it in a loud voice." The content of this address shows that Andrew knew perfectly well why it had been planted: John had told him that it would symbolize his rest from the weariness of rowing through the sea of life.

Greetings, O cross! Greetings indeed! I know well that, though you have been weary for a long time planted (πεπηγμένον) and awaiting me, you too will rest at last. I come to you, whom I have known. I recognize (γνωρίζω) your mystery (μυστήριον), why you have been planted (πέπηγας). So then, cross that is pure, radiant, full of life and light, receive me, I who have been weary for so long. (Passion 54)

But Odysseus's oar does not exhaust the mystery of Andrew's cross, for it cannot explain the unusual means of Andrew's attachment to it: he was tied upon the cross while he became "untied from the body":

> The blessed one said these things standing on the ground looking intently at the cross. When he came to it, he commanded the brethren to summon the executioners who were standing far away to carry out their orders. When they came, they tied up only his feet and armpits, without nailing up his hands or feet nor severing his knees because of what the proconsul had commanded them.
>
> When the brethren standing around, so many they were nearly innumerable, saw that the executioners had withdrawn and had carried out against the blessed one none of the usual procedures suffered by those who are hung up, they expected to hear something more from him. (Passion 54–55a)

Aegeates tied Andrew to the cross to prolong his agony, but the author tied him to the cross to shorten the reader's confusion concerning the mystery of the cross. As with other apocryphal Acts, the means of execution carries heavy semiotic freight.

For example, one might compare this section of the Passion with the description of Peter's death in *The Acts of Peter*, from which the author of *The Acts of Andrew* almost certainly borrowed. After all, John had told Andrew that he would "drink Peter's cup." The two martyrdom accounts do indeed share a great deal. Both apostles convert the wives or mistresses of Roman officials,[49] who rage like beasts, and determine to execute the apostles in order to win back their partners. Both apostles are arrested and, without trials, are condemned to crucifixions. Like Andrew, when Peter approaches his cross he addresses it and promises to disclose its mystery: "Approaching and standing before the cross, he began to say, 'O name of the cross, cryptic mystery (μυστήριον). . . . I will make clear to you what you are. I will no longer suppress the hidden mystery (μυστήριον) of the cross that for so long has been shut up in my soul.'"[50]

Peter does not disclose the meaning of the cross in his address to it; rather, he asks to be hanged upside down so that the manner of his crucifixion might symbolize its mystery. He tells the crowd: "You must know the mystery (μυστήριον) of all nature, and the beginning of all things, how it came about. For the first man, whose likeness I have in my appearance, in falling head-downwards showed a manner of birth that was not so before."[51] Peter goes on to explain that he is returning to his Lord in the same way Adam had fallen into the world, topsy-turvy.[52]

Andrew, too, is crucified in an unusual manner: he is not nailed to his cross but lashed to it by his feet and armpits. Whereas Peter's speech from the cross interpreted his inverted cross as an imitation of Adam's head-first descent, Andrew's speeches interpret his lashing to a cross at the brink of the sea as an imitation of Odysseus's lashing to the mast while he sailed home past the Sirens.[53] The identification of the cross of Christ with the mast of Odysseus was metaphorical cliché, and it merits an extended treatment here. If any image would have shaken the reader awake to the hypertextual intentions of the *Acts*, it would have been his lashing to a cross on a beach next to a turbulent sea.

The single-masted square-rigging of ancient ships, crossbeams rigidly fixed at right-angles to the mast, left ships looking very much as though they were bearing crosses, and not just to Christian eyes. Even Artemidorus, a pagan contemporary of the authors of *The Acts of Andrew*, saw crosses on ships. To dream of "Being crucified is auspicious for all seafarers. For the cross, like a ship, is made of wood and nails, and the ship's mast resembles a cross."[54]

Speaking for his Christian contemporaries, Minucius Felix claimed that "we quite naturally see the sign of the cross on a ship driven by swollen sails."[55] Justin Martyr's list of indispensable cross-shaped objects leads off with the mast: "No prow can split the sea unless this trophy called a sail remains intact on the ship."[56] When Clement of Alexandria recommends symbols suitable for signet rings, nautical images dominate: a fish, a fisherman, an anchor, and "a ship running with a strong wind," viz. with billowed sail.[57] Hippolytus viewed the life of the church as a voyage:

> The sea is the world in which the church like a ship at high sea endures tempests but does not wreck. She brings Christ with her, the seasoned pilot, and carries amidships her trophy over death, for she bears with her the cross of the Lord, and the ladder ascending to the yardarm crossbar stands for Christ's Passion, which draws the faithful up to an ascent to heaven.[58]

In the end, the ship and her cargo will "come to rest (ἀναπαυόμεναι) in Christ's kingdom." The popularity of the mast metaphor can be seen from its uses by Tertullian,[59] Athanasius,[60] Gregory of Nyssa,[61] Ambrose,[62] Proclus,[63] and Venantius Fortunatus.[64]

More than any other mast, it was Odysseus's that early Christians saw in Christ's cross.[65] Hippolytus, for example, insisted that when his readers encounter the enticements of Gnostic teachers they should either seal up their ears or lash themselves to the cross:

> The Sirens would deceive voyagers by singing clearly and harmoniously, convincing those who listened to their melodious voice to come near. They say that when Odysseus learned of this, he stopped up the ears of his shipmates with wax, and lashing himself (προσδήσαντα) to the wood, he sailed safely

past the Sirens, listening to their song. My advice to my readers is to do the same: either, out of weakness, to wax up their ears to sail right through the teachings of the heretics without hearing any one of their slick enticements to pleasure (ἡδονήν), like the Sirens' luscious lays, or faithfully to lash oneself (προσδήσαντα) to Christ's wood, so that even though one hears, he or she will not be distracted, standing erect, relying on that to which one is securely strapped.[66]

According to Augustine, God has "set up a mast by which we might traverse the sea, for no one is able to traverse the sea of this world unless carried by the cross of Christ." All those who "embrace this cross" will "arrive at the homeland" (*ad patriam*).[67] In another sermon traditionally attributed to Augustine, an unknown preacher says that if one would successfully sail "this great and spacious sea," one should "cling to the cross and not abandon it until he or she arrives at the port of salvation."[68] The cross is likened to Odysseus's mast also by Clement of Alexandria,[69] Ambrose,[70] Paulinus of Nola,[71] Peter Chrysologus,[72] and Maximus of Turin.[73]

Uses of such scenes from *The Odyssey* as moral allegories applied to the voyage of life was by no means a Christian innovation. Platonic tradition already had allegorized Odysseus as a cipher for the soul returning to its immaterial homeland.[74] This imagery accounts for the popularity of Odysseus and *The Odyssey* among Christian Gnostics and later Christian Neoplatonists. Irenaeus and Hippolytus are not simply mudslinging when they aver that Valentinians and Naassenes treat Homer as their prophet.[75] The Nag Hammadi tractate calling itself *The Exegesis on the Soul*, and properly assigned to the circle of Valentinus, likens Odysseus's weeping on Calypso's Ogygia, longing to return to distant Ithaca, with the soul's longing to return to its preincarnate home.[76] Hippolytus outlines an elaborate Naassene allegory of Hermes leading the souls of the slain suitors into the netherworld in *Odyssey* 24, here reinterpreted as Christ, the new Hermes, guiding souls back into the Pleroma.[77] On the basis of this passage, scholars have identified frescoes at Porte Majeure and nearby Viale Manzoni as Gnostic. One fresco depicts Christ with a golden wand, like Hermes in *The Odyssey*, as a psychopomp for Naassene souls. Another depicts Odysseus longing for Ithaca as a cipher for the soul's longing for its primordial and eschatological home.[78]

Several sarcophagi of the third and fourth centuries portray Odysseus at the mast with alluring Sirens. Scholars have variously assessed the meaning of these representations, but it would appear that they express the Neoplatonic notion of the soul's ascent to the intelligible world, a notion picked up also by Christians.[79] Several of the sarcophagi in question were in fact found in a Christian cemetery from the end of the third century, which suggests either that they were originally Christian, or, more likely, that these sarcophagi represent stock pagan funerary motifs taken over by Christians to image the soul's *nostos* to its *patria*.[80] Even more relevant to the depiction of Andrew in *The Acts of Andrew* is a passage from Clement of Alexandria, in which he challenges his pagan readers to abandon their traditions, like Odysseus fleeing his monstrous, singing foes:

> Let us then flee [pagan] custom, let us flee it as one would a dangerous headland, or the peril of Charybdis, or the mythical Sirens. Custom strangles, diverts from the truth, and carries its victim away from life. It is a trap, a chasm, a pit, and a voracious evil. "From this smoke and surf keep the ship well away."[81] Let us flee, O crew, let us flee this wave. It vomits fire, it is a wicked island heaped high with bones and corpses, and pleasure (ἡδονή) sings there, a slut in her prime who delights in music déclassé. "Come hither, as thou farest, renowned Odysseus, great glory of the Achaeans; stay thy ship that thou mayest listen to the voice of the gods."[82] She praises you, sailor, and calls you much-famed in song. The whore tries to take for herself the glory of the Greeks. A heavenly wind helps you, so leave her to roam among the dead. Pass by pleasure (ἡδονήν). She deludes. "Do not let a flaunting woman coax and cozen and deceive you: she is after your barn."[83] Sail past the song, it causes death. You need but will it, and you have conquered ruin.[84]

They will avoid shipwreck by binding themselves with the bond that guarantees freedom: "If you are tied up (προσδεδεμένος) to the wood (of the cross), you will be untied (λελυμένος) from corruption. The word of God will steer you, and the holy wind (τὸ πνεῦμα τὸ ἅγιον) will bring you to anchor in the harbors of heaven."[85] His readers, therefore, are superior to "the old man of Ithaca," who longed only for the smoke from his own hearth instead of longing "for truth and for the heavenly homeland (πατρίδος)."[86] The allegory of Odysseus and the Sirens "is probably the most noteworthy example of a Greek myth for which the Christians were able, at the beginning, to make use of Platonic exegesis, and yet to reach finally a result in which the myth seems made expressly to receive a Christian meaning."[87]

This rich legacy of combining Homeric myth with Platonism explains the mystery of Andrew's seaside cross to which he is lashed. In his speeches from the cross, Andrew depicts his death as his voyage home using images and vocabulary drawn from Socrates' statements concerning his own death in the *Phaedo*. Andrew's death is his "exit" (Passion 63 and 64) and his "departure" (56). By means of the cross he will "flee" (61), "abandon" (56), and "release" himself (57) from γένεσις (33 and 38), from "all that is earthly" (61), and "undulating" (61), so that he may "leave" (62), "fly up" (50), "flee toward," and "speed away" (ἐπείγεσθαι, 37, 57, and 62) to his Lord and to "things that are stable" (47). Andrew's lashing to the cross (ἀπέδησαν αὐτοῦ τοὺς πόδας καὶ τὰς μασχάλας; Passion 54) allows him to travel to his heavenly harbor just as Odysseus's lashing to the mast (ἔδησαν ὁμοῦ χεῖράς τε πόδας τε; *Odyssey* 12.178) allowed him to reach Ithaca.

Frequently in the speeches Andrew works a sophisticated wordplay on the verbs λύειν, 'to loosen', and δεῖν, 'to tie'. Plato's Socrates repeatedly spoke of the philosopher's quest to loosen the soul from the body in order for it to ascend to its kindred, intellectual realm. As long as the soul remained tied to the body, it would be tainted by the constraints of the material world. Death, then, was the ultimate untying of the soul. Homer used the same verbs in *The Odyssey* for Odysseus's lashing to and being untied from the mast. The combination of Socrates and Odysseus in Andrew creates the magnificent paradox that as long as Andrew remained tied to his cross/mast, he was untying his soul from his body; if he were to be untied from the cross/mast, he would tie himself ever more tightly to the body and matter. Like Socrates, Andrew so longed for release from the body that he gladly endured his attachment to the cross.

The Laughter from the Cross (Socrates' Laughter, Passion 55)

Chapters 55–63 once again borrow extensively from Plato's account of Socrates' death. Relevant to Passion 55 is the motif of laughter, which recurs throughout the *Phaedo* in order to underscore Socrates' courage in facing his execution.[88] For example, when Crito asked, "How shall we bury you?" he replied:

> "However you please, . . . if you can catch me and I do not get away from you." And he laughed (γελάσας) gently, and looking towards us, said: "I cannot persuade (πείθω) Crito, my friends, that the Socrates who is now conversing and arranging the details of his argument is really I; he thinks I am the one whom he will presently see as a corpse, and he asks how to bury me."[89]

Similarly in Passion 55, while Andrew was hanging on the cross, "he shook his head and smiled (μειδιῶν)."[90] Stratocles objected: "Why do you smile (μειδιᾷς), Andrew, servant of God? Should your laughter (γέλως) not make us mourn and weep (κλαίειν) because we are being deprived (στερισκόμεθα) of you?" Twice in the *Phaedo* one finds similar sentiments expressed at the hero's departure:

> [W]e felt that he was like a father to us and that when bereft (στερηθέντες) of him we should pass the rest of our lives as orphans.[91]

> I wrapped my face in my cloak and wept (ἀπέκλαιον) for myself; for it was not for him that I wept, but for my own misfortune in being deprived (ἐστερημένος) of such a friend.[92]

Andrew explained to Stratocles that he was laughing because Aegeates still could not comprehend that slaying his body would have no effect on his soul, his spiritual essence. Andrew's answer is tantalizingly similar to another text in the *Phaedo* where Socrates again laughed at his friends' inability to understand that his death was no tragedy but the ultimate release of his soul:

Phaedo 84d–e
[H]e **laughed** (ἐγέλασεν) gently and said, "Ah, **Simmias!**

I should have hard work to
persuade (πείσαιμι)
other people **that** I do not regard
my present situation as a misfortune,
when I **cannot** even **make you**
believe (πείθειν) it."

Passion 55
Andrew **answered**, "Shall I not **laugh** (γελάσω), **Stratocles** my child? . . .

He [Aegeates] has not yet been
persuaded (πέπεισται)
that we are alien to him
and his designs.
He is **not able to hear**, since if we were
able, he would have heard that the person
who belongs to Jesus and who has been
recognized (γνωρισθείς) by him
in the end cannot be punished."

The *Phaedo* and Passion 55 both present their heroes, just prior to their executions, laughing (γελᾶν) because they cannot persuade (πειθεῖν) others that their souls will outlive their bodies. While they laugh, their friends weep (ἀποκλαίειν/κλαίειν) because they are being deprived of (στερεῖσθαι/στερίσκεσθαι) their spiritual guides. In light of the other points of contact between the deaths of the two heroes, one must attribute these similarities to strategic hypertextual dependence.

The Immortality of the Soul (Socrates' Psyche, Passion 56–58)

While hanging on the cross Andrew addressed the crowds standing nearby and instructed them on the nature of the soul and of death, namely that death does not represent the end of existence but the beginning of a life for the soul far better than its life in the body. This is the very topic, of course, that Socrates discussed with his friends the day of his death. The parallels with Plato's *Phaedo* are striking, not only in their general sentiments, but even in their vocabulary and order of treatment.[93] Both martyrs begin their speeches with a statement concerning the immortality of the soul, then turn to the pleasures of eating, then sex, then possessions, and finally the concern for the body instead of the soul. This order and the vocabulary must point to literary dependence:

Phaedo 64c–e
"We **believe** (ἡγούμεθα), do we not,
that death is the **separation**
(ἀπαλλαγήν) of the soul from the
body, and that **the state of being**
dead (τὸ τεθνάναι) is the state in
which the body is
separated (ἀπαλλαγέν) by itself,

Passion 56
"If you **suppose** (ἡγεῖσθε) that
the state of being dead (τὸ τεθνάναι)
is the end (τέλος) of an
ephemeral life,[94]

behold, I am **leaving** (ἀπαλλάσσω) this

and the soul (ψυχήν)

is **separated** (ἀπαλλαγεῖσαν)
from **the body** (σώματος)
and **exists** alone by itself?"
[Cf. 70a: "They fear that when
the soul leaves (ἀπαλλαγῇ) **the
body** it **no longer exists** anywhere."]
"Is death anything other than this?"
"No, it is this," said he [Simmias].
"Now, my friend, see if you agree
with me; for, if you do, I think we
shall get more light on our subject.
Do you think a philosopher would
be likely to **care much about
the so-called pleasures** (ἡδονάς),

such as **eating and drinking**?"
"By no means, Socrates,"
said Simmias.

"How about **the pleasures
of love**?"
"Certainly not."
"Well, do you think such a man
would think much of the other
cares of the body—I mean such as
the **possession** (κτήσεις) of fine
clothes and shoes and other personal
adornments? Do you think he
would care about them or despise
them . . . ?" "I think the true
philosopher would despise them,"
he replied.

"Altogether, then, you think such a
man would not

life.[95] If you understand the conjunction
of **the soul** (ψυχῆς) with a **body**
(σῶμα) to be **the soul** (ψυχήν) itself,
so that after the **separation**
(χωρισμόν)[96]
nothing at all **exists**,

you possess the intelligence of animals
and one would have to list you among
ferocious beasts.

And if you **love
immediate pleasures** (ἡδέα)
and pursue them above all, in order
to **enjoy their fruits** exclusively,
you are like thieves.
And if you suppose that you are merely
that which can be seen and nothing more,
you are slaves of folly and ignorance.[97]
And if you perceive that only this
nocturnal light exists and nothing
in addition to it, you are kindred
(συγγενεῖς) to this night. . . .[98]
And if you suppose that you are happy
because you have a healthy body,
you actually are miserable. And if your
external prosperity makes you happy,
you truly are most wretched.
And if **the pleasure and intercourse**
of marriage please you,
and if the corruption which is from them,
full of pain, makes you sad, . . .
it will upset you.
And if the rest of your
possessions (κτήματα) draw you
to themselves
as though you belonged to them,

may their impermanence reproach you.
What benefit is there for you who
gain (κεκτημένοις) for yourselves
external goods but do not gain
your very selves? . . . Or why
all the rest of

devote himself to the body, but would, so far as he was able, turn away from **the body** and **concern himself with the soul?"**	**the concern for externals,** while you yourselves **neglect what you actually are?"**

The first ellipsis in the right-hand column above represents a peculiar passage concerning "bodily bulk." Behind this enigmatic statement lies a passage from the *Phaedo* in which Socrates claims that he once assumed that what one ate determined one's bodily mass. Later he came to think that such characteristics were due instead to the abstractions of smallness and greatness. Compare the following:

Phaedo 96c	Passion 56
"For I had **thought** previously that it was plain to everyone **that man grows through eating** and drinking, for when from the food **he eats** . . . then the small **bulk** (ὄγκον) **becomes greater** and the small man large. . . ."	"And if you **think that your earthly food** is capable of **creating bodily bulk** (ὄγκον) and the blood's constitutive power, you yourselves are earthly."

The passage in Passion 56 makes little sense except in the context of Socrates' argument.

Andrew then bids his hearers to join him in leaving this life:

> I entreat you who have come here together for my sake, abandon this entire life and hasten to overtake my soul, which speeds (ἐπειγομένην) toward things beyond time, beyond law, beyond speech, beyond body, beyond bitter and lawless pleasures (ἡδονάς) full of every pain. Observe now, even you, with the eyes of your soul (τοῖς τῆς ψυχῆς ὀφθαλμοῖς), those things about which I speak. (Passion 57)

Plato, too, spoke of "the eyes of the soul" as an image of spiritual insight: "[I]f we are ever to know anything, we must be free (ἀπαλλακτέον) from the body, we must behold the actual realities with the eyes of the soul alone."[99]

The verb ἐπείγεσθαι, 'to speed', applied above to Andrew's soul, is rare in Christian texts, but it appears eighteen times in *The Odyssey* to describe the hero's *nostos* back to Ithaca.[100] The author apparently wanted to compare the journey of Andrew's soul to the divine realm not only with the journey of Socrates' soul to the divine but also with Odysseus's journey home. Like Odysseus who sailed past the Sirens, Andrew is speeding past pleasures.

Andrew then encourages those surrounding his cross to "participate in another fellowship (κοινωνίαν κοινωνήσατε) for yourselves" (Passion 57); that is, to replace one fellowship or association with another. At first glance one might be tempted to relate this usage of κοινωνία to one of its many appearances in the New Testament, but it is wiser again to look at the *Phaedo*. According to the dying Socrates, the philosopher is one who "separates the soul from communion (κοινωνίας) with the body."[101] At death, the soul "takes leave of the body, and avoiding, so far as it can, all association (κοινωνοῦσα) or contacts with the body, reaches out toward the reality."[102] Later Socrates says, "And while we live, we shall, I think, be nearest to knowledge when we avoid, so far as possible, intercourse and communion (κοινωνῶμεν) with the body, except what is absolutely necessary, and are not filled with its nature, but keep ourselves pure from it until God himself sets us free."[103] Andrew could not have said it better.

After the apostle exhorted his listeners to seek another fellowship, he added imperatives that point unmistakably to Odysseus lashed to his mast while his crew rowed with wax in their ears: "Wrap yourselves with my lashes, and wipe your ears to hear what I say. Flee (πεφεύγεσθε) with me from everything merely temporal. Even now speed away (ἐπείχθητε) with me" (Passion 57).[104] In this context, this passage surely means that his followers are similarly to bind themselves to the cross/mast and to wipe their ears of wax as they abandon this physical life for a voyage to the hereafter.[105]

One might object, however, that this interpretation confuses the imagery: Andrew appears both as Odysseus and as the Siren whose song those at the foot of his cross are to hear. This apparent confusion in Andrew's role issues from the author's awareness that the Sirens were not entirely malevolent. Even though Homer depicts them as destructive, they do indeed impart knowledge "of all things that come to pass upon the fruitful earth."[106] Anyone who hears their song indeed "goes his way a wiser man,"[107] as Cicero was quick to point out.[108] Odysseus is far superior to his companions for having heard their song. For Neopythagoreans (and for Plato in the myth of Er), the Sirens personified the harmony of the spheres. Odysseus's companions failed to hear this divine music and remained ignorant of things divine because of their "fleshly obstructions and passions."[109]

Early Christian authors at times contrasted the Sirens' deadly knowledge, with the knowledge of God. Methodius of Olympus (ca. 300) began his treatise on free will by telling his readers that when listening to "the choir of prophets" there is no need to take Odyssean precautions, whether wax or ropes:

> [O]ne need not stop up the ears of companions, nor wrap oneself up with a bond (δεσμῷ περιβάλλειν) out of fear of the consequences of listening. . . . We do not have the Sirens off the shore of Sicily, nor the ropes of Odysseus, nor wax melting into people's ears, but a complete relaxing of bonds (δεσμῶν), and unobstructed hearing for everyone who comes near.[110]

After apologizing to his audience for appealing to Homer for sermonic illustration, Ambrose nevertheless urged them to imitate Odysseus, who for a merely earthly home remained unmoved by the pleasures offered him by the Lotus-eaters, by the gardens of Alcinous, and by the Sirens:

Therefore, we should not stop up our ears but unobstructed them so that Christ's voice might be heard, for whoever comprehends it will not fear shipwreck. No one should lash him or herself to the mast with physical straps like Odysseus but should bind the soul to the wood of the cross with spiritual bonds, so as to be unattracted to the lures of lust and undeterred from following his or her natural course into the dangerous waters of desire.[111]

Andrew's instruction that his hearers wipe their ears to hear his voice obviously conforms with uses of Odyssean imagery as found in these texts.

In the section that follows, the author interpreted Andrew's death not only in terms of the voyage of Odysseus but also in light of the journey of Socrates' soul.

Phaedo 67b–c	Passion 58
	"For this reason men quietly
"I **have great hopes** that	**take courage** (θαρροῦσιν)
	in the knowledge of God.[112]
when I reach the place to which	On the one hand
I am going, I shall there, if	**I am leaving** (ἄπειμι)[113]
anywhere, attain fully to that which	
has been my chief object in my	
past life, so that **the journey** which	**to prepare routes** there
is now imposed upon me is begun	
with good hope; and the like hope	
exists **for everyman who** thinks	**for those who** align themselves with me
that his mind has been **purified**	and **are prepared** with a **pure**
(κεκαθαρμένην) and **made ready.**"	(καθαρᾷ) faith and with love for him."

A similar passage appears also in *Phaedo* 80d–81a:

But the soul, the invisible, which **departs into another place** which is, like itself, noble and **pure** (καθαρόν) and invisible, to the realm of the god of the other world in truth, to the good and wise god, whither, if god will, **my soul is soon to go,**—is this soul . . . destroyed when it departs from the body . . . ? [The soul will not be destroyed] if it **departs pure** (καθαρὰ ἀπαλλάττηται), dragging with it nothing of the body, because it never willingly associated (κοινωνοῦσα) with the body in life. . . .

Then if it is in such a condition, **it goes away** into that which is like itself, into the invisible, divine, immortal, and wise, and when it arrives there is it happy, freed from error and folly and fear and fierce loves and all the other human ills, and as the initiated say, lives in truth through all after time with the gods.[114]

Socrates also spoke of the fate of defiled souls, which parallels Andrew's discussion of the punishments of the wicked in Passion 58:

Phaedo 81a–b
"But, I think,
if when it departs (ἀπαλλάττηται)
from the body it is defiled and
impure, because it was always with
the body and cared for it and loved
it and was fascinated with its desires
and **pleasures** (ἡδονῶν), so that

it thought nothing
(μηδὲν ἄλλο δοκεῖν) **was true**
except the corporeal. . . —do you
think a soul in this condition will
depart (ἀπαλλάξεσθαι) pure
and uncontaminated?"

Passion 58
"On the other hand,
with respect to those who have come here
not out of love for God
but out of hypocrisy and because of
unfruitful

pleasures (ἡδονῶν), who have
submitted themselves to superstition,
disbelief, and every other ignorance,
and **who suppose nothing else exists**
(μηδὲν εἶναι ἕτερον . . . ὑπειληφόσιν)
after one's release from here, all these
monsters fly out. . . ."

For Plato, such a soul will not leave the body "pure and uncontaminated" and so "is dragged back into the visible world" and reincarnated "into the bodies of asses and other beasts of that sort" or "into the bodies of wolves and hawks and kites" or "of bees or of wasps or ants, or into the human race again."[115] The author of *The Acts of Andrew* probably did not believe in reincarnation, but he did believe in demonic creatures who inhabited the regions between the earth and heaven. When the unrighteous die, their souls escape their bodies, but then,

> all these monsters fly out, become agitated, rush forth, take wing, ravage, fight, conquer, rule, wreak vengeance, enflame, rage, afflict, punish, and attack. They blaze, exercise violence, and do not withdraw or relent, but rejoice, exult, smile, mock, and take their rest and delight in all who are similar to them, possessing those who succumbed to them by not believing in my God. (Passion 58)[116]

Although many of the parallels between the *Phaedo* and Passion 56–58 are inexact, the density of common motifs, vocabulary, and concerns surely point to literary dependence. The order of the parallels is also instructive. Of the Platonic texts discussed above that are most similar to Passion 56–58 only one occurs in a different order from the presentation in *The Acts of Andrew*:

The separation of soul from body	*Phaedo* 64c
The pleasures of eating	*Phaedo* 64d
[On food and bodily bulk	*Phaedo* 96c]
The pleasures of sex	*Phaedo* 64d
Possessions	*Phaedo* 64d
Care for externals instead of care for the soul	*Phaedo* 64e
Fellowship (κοινωνία) with the body	*Phaedo* 67a
The soul of the teacher leaving ahead of the others	*Phaedo* 67b–c

The fate of pure souls   *Phaedo* 80d–81a
The fate of impure souls   *Phaedo* 81a–b

The Attempted Escape (Crito's Plan, Passion 59–60)

Andrew preached from the cross "for three days and nights," and none of the crowd left the spot. They were as impressed by Andrew as the Athenian executioner had been of Socrates:

Phaedo 116c	Passion 59
"I have **found you** **in all this time** in every way **the noblest** (γενναιότατον) and gentlest and best man who has ever come here,	**On the fourth day,** when they **observed his nobility** (γενναῖον), the adamance of his thought, the sheer abundance of his words, the value of his exhortation, the stability of his soul, the prudence of his spirit, the firmness of his mind,
and now I know your **anger** is directed against others, not against me, for you know who are to blame."[118]	and the precision of his reasoning,[117] they were **furious** with Aegeates and together ran off to the tribunal.

The crowds appealed to the proconsul to release the apostle to reverse his unjust decision. This passage calls to mind Plato's *Crito* and the attempt of Crito and others to snatch Socrates away from his prison by bribing the guards.[119] The philosopher refused.[120] Compare the following:

Crito 50c	Passion 59
"Or should we tell them [the judges],	As he [Aegeates] sat there they [the crowd] cried out, "What is this **judgment** (κρίσις) of yours, O proconsul! **You have**
'**The city has done us an injustice** (ἠδίκει . . . ἡ πόλις) and **has not made its decision rightly** (οὐκ ὀρθῶς τὴν δίκην ἔκρινεν).'"	**judged wickedly** (κακῶς ἐδίκασας)! You have **made an unjust decision** (ἀδίκως ἔκρινας)! . . . **The city** (ἡ πόλις) is in an uproar! You are **wronging us** all (ἡμᾶς ἀδικεῖς)!"

Thus the residents of Patras promised: "Bring the man down and we will all become philosophers (φιλοσοφήσομεν)" (Passion 59). The conversion of the crowds to Andrew's God implies their espousal of the philosophical life, the very goal Socrates sought for his friends in prison.

 Aegeates decided against risking a revolution at the hands of two thousand infuriated subjects: "He rose from the tribunal and went off with them, promising to release (ἀπολύειν) the blessed Andrew. . . . The crowd was jubilant because the blessed Andrew was about to be untied (λύεσθαι)" (Passion 60).

This passage sets up a wordplay on 'untying' critical for understanding the presentation of Andrew's death. The verb λύειν figures prominently both in *The Odyssey* and in the *Phaedo*. Odysseus sails home past the Sirens unscathed because he is bound (δεῖσθαι) to the mast. If he were to be untied (λύεσθαι) from the mast he would perish. In the *Phaedo*, on the other hand, the philosopher longs to have his soul untied (λύεσθαι) from his body so that it can rise to the divine. In *The Acts of Andrew* these competing uses of the metaphor of 'untying' play off against each other and create a paradox. Because Andrew's body is tied to his cross, his soul is able to escape and to be bound to its Lord; but if his body were to be untied from the cross, his soul would remain tied to the body. This paradox pervades Andrew's last speech from the cross in Passion 61–62, where he, like Socrates, prefers death.

The Refusal to be Untied (Socrates' Resolve, Passion 61–62)

Even though his friends had arranged for his escape, Socrates refused to leave. In the *Crito* he argued that to do so would be to undermine the authority of the state merely to suit one's own welfare, but in the *Phaedo* he states that the philosopher actually should long for death as the untying (λύσις) of the soul from the body. The following dialogue between Socrates and Simmias seems to be what the author of *The Acts of Andrew* had in mind when composing Passion 61–62.

"Well, then, this is what we call death, is it not, a release and separation (λύσις καὶ χωρισμός) of the soul from the body?"

"Exactly so," said he [Simmias].

"But, as we hold, the true philosophers and they alone are always most eager to release (λύειν) the soul, and just this—the release and separation (λύσις καὶ χωρισμός) of the soul from body—is their study, is it not?"[121]

"Obviously."

"Then, as I said in the beginning, it would be absurd if a man who had been all his life fitting himself to live as nearly in a state of death as he could, should then be disturbed when death came to him. Would it not be absurd?"

"Of course."

"In fact, then, Simmias," said he, "the true philosophers practise dying, and death is less terrible to them than to any other men. Consider it in this way. They are in every way hostile to the body and they desire to have the soul apart by itself alone. Would it not be very foolish if they should be frightened and troubled when this very thing happens, and if they should not be glad to go to the place where there is hope of attaining what they longed for all through life—and they longed for wisdom—and of escaping (ἀπηλλάχθαι) from the companionship of that which they hated?"[122]

Similarly in *The Acts of Andrew*, when the apostle learned that Aegeates was coming to release him from his cross, he upbraided his followers for their attachment to this world and for assuming that he wanted to be freed:

Why this excessive fondness for the flesh? Why this great complicity with it? Do you again encourage me to put back among things in flux? If you understood that I have been loosened (ἐλύθην) from ropes (δεσμῶν) but tied up (ἐδέθην) to myself, you yourselves would have been eager to be loosened (λυθῆναι) from the many and to be tied up (δεθῆναι) to the one.[123] What should I say? I know well that what I am saying will happen, for your yourselves will I tie up (δήσω) with me, and after liberating myself, I will release (ἀπολύσω) myself from all things and become united with the one who came into being for all and who exists beyond all. (Passion 61)

Thus, when Aegeates himself arrives at the cross, Andrew refuses to be untied:

Would you untie (λύσεις) the one who is tied up (δεθέντα), proconsul? Would you untie (λύσεις) the one who has fled? Would you untie (λύσεις) the one who was liberated? Would you untie (λύσεις) the one recognized by his kindred (τὸν γνωρισθέντα ὑπὸ τοῦ συγγενοῦς)? . . . I possess the one with whom I will always be. I possess the one with whom I will be a compatriot for countless ages. It is to him that I go (ἄπειμι). It is to him that I speed on (ἐπείγομαι). . . . In as much as I recognized you through your turning to me, I am released (ἀπαλλάσσομαι) from you. Proconsul, I know well that you bewail and mourn because of what I am saying to you as I flee off to the one beyond you. You will weep, beat your breast, gnash your teeth, grieve, despair, lament, anguish, and comport yourself like your relative (συγγενίδι) the sea, which you now see furiously troubled by waves because I am leaving (ἀπήλλαγμαι) all of you. . . . My kindred and I speed on to things our own (οἱ ἐμοὶ συγγενεῖς ἐπὶ τὰ ἡμῶν ἐπειγόμεθα). (Passion 62)

In addition to hypertextual play with Plato's *Phaedo*, this text also plays with Homer's *Odyssey*. Aegeates is like his "relative the sea," an allusion to his name 'one from Aegae', home of Poseidon. Aegeates thus symbolizes the sea, which in turn symbolizes the material world, which the apostle desires to leave. The author also twice uses the Homeric verb ἐπείγεσθαι to refer to Andrew's journey to his heavenly home. It would appear that the author wished to contrast the apostle's desire to remain bound to his cross/mast with Odysseus, who, after hearing the Sirens, begged his shipmates to free him (λῦσαι) from his bonds.[124] Instead, they wrapped him up to the mast with even more straps (δεσμοῖσι).[125]

The Release of Andrew's Soul (Socrates' Death, Passion 63)

Despite Andrew's protestations, the proconsul "attempted to approach the wood to untie (λῦσαι) Andrew." Then the apostle uttered his last:

> O Master,[126] do not permit Andrew, the one tied (δεθέντα) to your wood to be untied (λυθῆναι) again. O Jesus, do not give me to the shameless devil, I who am attached to your mystery. O Father, do not let your opponent untie (λυέτω) me, I who am hanging upon your grace. May that runt no longer humiliate the one who has known your greatness. But you yourself, O Christ, you whom I desired, whom I loved, whom I know, whom I possess, whom I cherish, whose I am, receive me, so that by my departure (ἔξοδος) to you there may be a coming together (σύνοδος) of my many kindred (συγγενῶν), those who rest (ἀναπαυομένων) in your majesty.[127] (Passion 63)

Socrates said much the same just before he died: "[T]he soul . . . departs into the realm of the pure, the everlasting and the changeless, and being akin (συγγενής) to these it dwells always with them whenever it is by itself and is not hindered, and it has rest (πέπαυται) from its wanderings."[128]

After his prayer, Andrew at last attains the untying of his soul from his body and leaves for his eternal home: "When he had said these things and further glorified the Lord, he handed over his spirit, so that we wept (κλαιόντων) and everyone grieved his separation" (Passion 63). Here again the author likens Andrew to Socrates. Just prior to taking the cup of poison, Socrates said, "I may and must pray to the gods that my departure hence be a fortunate one; so I offer this prayer, and may it be granted."[129]

Notice also the curious intrusion of the first person plural "we wept." At the end of the *Phaedo*, Phaedo describes the sorrow of Socrates' friends, and uses the first person plural to do so:

> [W]hen we watched him drinking and saw that he had drunk the poison, we could do so [hold back their tears] no longer, but in spite of myself my tears rolled down in floods, so that I wrapped my face in my cloak and wept (ἀπέκλαιον) for myself. . . . Crito . . . could not restrain his tears. But Apollodorus, who had been weeping (κλαίων) all the time before, then wailed and made us all break down.[130]

By using "we wept" the author again alerts the reader to see Andrew's death as the death of a Christian Socrates.

The Burial of Andrew's Body (Socrates' Corpse, Passion 64a)

The author of the *Acts* describes the burial of Andrew's body as follows: "After the departure (ἔξοδον) of the blessed apostle, Maximilla, accompanied by Stratocles, completely disregarding those standing around her, came forward, untied the corpse of the blessed one, and having provided it with the necessary attention, buried it at nightfall" (Passion 64a). So also in the *Phaedo*, women were assigned the task of burying the body of Socrates.[131] The author of the *Acts* is careful to avoid saying that Maximilla buried Andrew, she buried only his corpse; the apostle already had made his exit (ἔξοδος). This conforms with Socrates' request that no one "say at the funeral that he is laying out Socrates. . . . No, you must be of good courage, and say that you bury my body,—and bury it as you think best and seems most fitting."[132]

The Denouement (Penelope and Telemachus, Passion 64b)

Passion 64 continues:

> She [Maximilla] separated from Aegeates because of his beastly soul and lawless public life. Thereafter, though he shammed good behavior, she had nothing whatever to do with him. Choosing instead a life holy and quiet, provided for by the love of Christ, she spent her time happily with the brethren. Even though Aegeates often importuned her and offered her the opportunity to manage his affairs, he was not able to persuade her.

To the end, Maximilla plays out her role as a counter-Penelope, refusing to bed with her husband and to be the queen (δέσποινα) of his house, choosing rather to live "with the brethren." Her refusal drove him mad. "One night, undetected by anyone in his household, he threw himself from a great height and died."[133]

The end of the story concerns Stratocles:

> Stratocles, Aegeates' brother according to the flesh, did not want so much as to touch the property Aegeates left—the wretch died childless. He said, "May your possessions go with you, Aegeates! May Jesus be my friend and I his! Casting from me the entire lot of external and internal evils and entrusting to that one everything I own, I thrust aside everything averse to him."[134]

This renunciation of wealth completes Stratocles' transvaluation of Telemachus's three symbols of manhood: the warrior's spear, the master's whip, and the heir's purse. By abandoning his rightful inheritance, Stratocles again reverses the development of Telemachus, who began the narrative impoverished by the greedy suitors,[135] but in the end enjoyed immense wealth. Not only had he brought back from Sparta Menelaus's marvelous gift but he also was the only heir of the suitors' gifts to Penelope and of the Phaeacians' gifts to Odysseus, "gifts past telling, stores of bronze and gold and woven raiment, more than Odysseus would ever have won for himself from Troy, if he had returned unscathed with his due share of the spoil."[136]

Telemachus's development into manhood involved slaying the suitors, punishing the slaves, and becoming heir to a fortune. Stratocles, however, renounced violence in favor of gentleness, eschewed his role as a slave owner in favor of performing his own menial tasks, and turned his back on wealth in order to secure the friendship of Jesus.

Conclusion

Passion 51–64 narrate Andrew's imprisonment and execution, which, in the context of the Homeric hypertextuality of the *Acts* as a whole, correspond to the *mnesterophonia*, 'the slaying of the suitors'. The primary characterizations still derive from Homer: Maximilla ≈ Penelope, Stratocles ≈ Telemachus, Iphidama ≈ Eurycleia, and Aegeates ≈ Poseidon and Odysseus's vices. Andrew, of course, is the suitor slain. The depiction of Andrew shares some qualities with Odysseus—his eloquence, his lashing to the mast, his endurance—and others with the dying Socrates, especially as depicted in Plato's *Phaedo*.

The parallels between Andrew and Socrates simply cannot have been accidental, as the following comparison make clear. Several of the parallels with the *Phaedo* follow an identical order:

	Plato	Andrew's Passion
Visitors at the prison	*Phaedo* 59d–60a	28b–29a
The sentence for corrupting youths and bring new gods	*Apology* 24b	51
The righteous one flogged and crucified	*Republic* 2.361e–362a	51
The simile of the soul	*Phaedrus* 246a–256d	53b
The laughing martyr	*Phaedo* 84d–e	55
The immortality of soul	*Phaedo* 64–81	56–58
separation of soul and body	*Phaedo* 64c	56
pleasures of eating	*Phaedo* 64d	56
food and bodily bulk	*Phaedo* 96c	56
pleasures of sex	*Phaedo* 64d	56
possessions	*Phaedo* 64d	56–57
care for externals	*Phaedo* 64e	57
fellowship with the body	*Phaedo* 67a	57
teacher going ahead to afterlife	*Phaedo* 67b–c	57
fate of pure souls	*Phaedo* 80d–81a	58
fate of impure souls	*Phaedo* 81a–b	58
The attempt to release the martyr, martyr's refusal	*Crito*, passim	59–60
The philosopher longs for release	*Phaedo* 67d–68a	61–62
The hero's death, "we wept"	*Phaedo* 117c–d	63

The author's reliance on the *Phaedo* may also illumine the choice of Andrew to be the protagonist of the *Acts*. Socrates discusses at some length the importance of courage (ἀνδρεία) at one's death: "Then is it not . . . a sufficient indication, when you see a man troubled because he is going to die, that he was not a lover of wisdom but a lover of the body? . . . [I]s not that which is called courage (ἀνδρεία) especially characteristic of philosophers?"[137] The philosopher alone is brave because only wisdom can vanquish fear.[138] Socrates and Andrew both exemplify ἀνδρεία insofar as both face their deaths knowing that death is but a transition to a better life.[139]

This ends the narrative section of *The Acts of Andrew*; the only task left is to analyze the author's postscript. Here the author provided one final clue concerning how he wished his readers to receive the book.

Notes

1. On the relationships between *The Acts of Peter* and *The Acts of Andrew* see Prieur, *Acta Andreae*, 400–403.

2. The parallels may have been less providential than literary. The author of the Gospel of Mark may have shaped his account of Jesus' trial and execution after Plato's *Apology* and *Phaedo*. See especially David Lawrence Barr, "Toward a Definition of the Gospel Genre: A Generic Analysis and Comparison of the Synoptic Gospels and the Socratic Dialogues by Means of Aristotle's Theory of Tragedy," Ph.D. diss., Florida State University, 1974.

The status of Socrates in early Christianity has been the subject of several scholarly investigations. In addition to the works cited in later notes, see: Adolf von Harnack, *Sokrates und die alte Kirche* (Giessen: Alfred Töpelmann, 1901); Johannes Geffcken, *Sokrates und alte Christentum* (Heidelberg: C. Winter, 1908); and Daniel Jackson, "Socrates and Christianity," *CF* 31 (1977): 189–206. I have profited greatly from an unpublished paper by Willy Rordorf, "Socrate dans la littérature chrétienne des premiers siècles." With respect to the influence of Plato generally on the second century see Phillip De Lacy, "Plato and the Intellectual Life of the Second Century A.D.," in *Approaches to the Second Sophistic*, ed. G. W. Bowersock (University Park: American Philological Society, 1974), 4–10.

3. *First Apology* 46.

4. *Second Apology* 10. Elsewhere Justin claimed that Socrates and Homer both anticipated the Christian understanding of the immortality of the soul (*First Apology* 18). See also *Second Apology* 7 and Athenagoras *Legatio* 31.

5. *First Apology* 5 (Richardson). See also Ps.-Justin *Cohortatio ad gentiles* 36, where the author argues that Socrates was the wisest of all men insofar as he knew that he did not know. For this Christian author, Socrates was correct; it was impossible for him to know anything prior to the revelation of Jesus Christ. Incidentally, this perspective is altogether incompatible with Justin's *logos spermatikos*, and his claim that Socrates knew enough to

merit divine approval.

6. *First Apology* 68, quoting Plato *Crito* 43d. Cf. Clement of Alexandria *Stromateis* 11.80.4–5, quoting Plato *Apology* 30c–d.

7. *Apology* 14.7.

8. *Ad nationes* 1.4 (ANF).

9. Clement of Alexandria was more positive about Socrates' demon (*Stromateis* 1.17.83.4, 5.14.91.5, and 6.6.53.2–3). See also 1.22.150.4: "What is Plato but Moses speaking Attic Greek?"

10. According to the *Phaedo*, Socrates wished to sacrifice to Asclepius, the god of healing, because he viewed his death as a healing of the disease called life. See also Prudentius *Apotheosis* 200–211.

11. *De anima* 1 (FC).

12. *Contra Celsum* 3.66 (Chadwick).

13. Ibid., 3.67 (Chadwick).

14. Ibid., 6.4 (Chadwick).

15. See also *Contra Celsum* 4.67, 5.20, 7.56, and 8.8. For Socrates in later Christian authors see, among other works, the following: Basil *To Young men, on How They Might Derive Benefit from Greek Literature* 7 and 10–11 and Augustine *City of God* 8.3.

16. See Klaus Döring, "Das Beispiel des Sokrates bei den frühchristlichen Märtyrern und Apologeten," in *Exemplum Socratis. Studien zur Sokratesnachwirkung in der kynisch-stoischen Popularphilosophie der frühen Kaiserzeit und im frühen Christentum*, Hermes. Zeitschrift für klassische Philologie 42 (Wiesbaden: Franz Steiner Verlag, 1979), 143–61.

17. *Martyrdom of Pionius* 17.

18. *Acts of Phileas* 4 (Latin recension; Musurillo).

19. George M. A. Hanfmann, "Socrates and Christ," *HSCP* 60 (1951): 216–17. Christian Gnilka claims that Cyprian's last act of ordering his friends to pay his executioner twenty-five pieces of gold was inspired by Socrates' ordering a cock sacrificed to Asclepius ("Ultima verba," *JAC* 22 [1979]: 5–21). On Socrates' death as a model for Christians see also Gregory of Nazianzus *Epistula* 32 (*PG* 37.72B). Gregory of Nyssa quite obviously narrated the death of his sister Macrina with Plato's *Phaedo* in mind (*Life of Macrina* 22–26).

20. *Apud* Origen *Contra Celsum* 1.3 (Chadwick). Epictetus and Marcus Aurelius, however, contrasted the deaths of philosophers with those of Christian martyrs (Epictetus *Dissertationes* [Arrian] 4.7.6 and Marcus Aurelius *Meditations* 11.3).

21. *Passing of Peregrinus* 12. Lucian's depiction of Peregrinus shows that he had in mind the *Phaedo* and Socrates' spiritual lessons in prison. "From the very break of day aged widows and orphan children could be seen waiting near the prison, while their officials even slept inside with him. . . . Then elaborate meals were brought in, and sacred books of theirs were read aloud." Like Socrates, Christians "have convinced themselves, first and foremost, that they are going to be immortal and live for all time, in consequence of which they despise death and even willingly give themselves into custody" (13).

22. *Martyrdom of Apollonius* 19.

23. In the *Phaedo* Socrates argues at length for the immortality of the soul and the

rewards of the righteous after death.

24. *Martyrdom of Apollonius* 37–38.

25. Ibid., 41 (Musurillo).

26. Hanfmann, "Socrates and Christ," 217.

27. Jean C. Balty writes: "Ulysse n'était-il pas, pour le poète [Homer] et toute l'antiquité classique, païenne et chrétienne, un autre type de sage [*un autre type* of Socrates]? Le rapprochement des deux thèmes ne peut être fortuit" ("Nouvelles mosaïques païennes et groupe épiscopal dit 'cathédrale de l'est' à Apamée de Syrie," *Comptes rendus des séances de l'académie des inscriptions et belles-letters* 1 [1972]: 109).

28. Cf. *Phaedo* 59e.

29. For other instances of the verb διαφθείρειν, 'corrupt', in the context of the charges against Socrates see *Euthyphro* 2c–3a and *Apology* 23d, 24b–27a, and 33c–34b.

30. *Apology* 46 (FC). See also: Lucian *The Eunuch* 9, *Dialogues of the Dead* 6 (20), *True Story* 2.17, and Ps.-Lucian *Amores* 48–49 and 54. See also Döring, *Exemplum Socratis*, 157. Notice also that in Passion 26 Aegeates had asked the apostle how it was that he had so many lovers (ἐραστάς), "rich and poor, including infants."

31. E.g., Passion 45 and 46.

32. *Republic* 2.361e–362a.

33. Ernst Benz discusses at length the possibility that Plato wrote the passage in light of his own conviction that Socrates was the paradigmatic suffering righteous one ("Der gekreuzigte Gerechte bei Plato, im Neuen Testament und in der alten Kirche," *Abhandlungen der Geistes- und Sozialwissenschaftlichen Klasse* 12 [1950]: 1037–43).

34. See Ernst Benz, "Gekreuzigte Gerechte," 1059–74, and "Christus und Socrates in der alten Kirche," *ZNW* 43 (1950–51): 195–224; and Édouard Des Places, "Un Thème platonicien dans la tradition patristique: Le Juste crucifié (Platon, *République*, 361e4–362a2)," in *Studia Patristica* 9, TU 94, ed. F. L. Cross (Berlin: Akademie-Verlag, 1966), 30–40.

35. *Stromateis* 5.14.108.4; cf. 4.7.52.1–2 and 4.11.78.2.

36. *Praeparatio evangelica* 13.13.35.6. See also *Historia ecclesiastica* 8.8:

[O]thers with good courage stretched forth their heads to them that cut them off [like Paul in *The Acts of Paul*], . . . and others again were crucified (ἀνασκολοπισθέντες), as malefactors usually are [like Andrew in *The Acts of Andrew*], and some, even more brutally were nailed in the opposite manner, head-downwards [like Peter in *The Acts of Peter*], and kept alive until they should perish of hunger on the gibbet.

In spite of the ancient historian's contempt for the apocryphal Acts, his information here seems to be derived from the Acts devoted to Paul, Andrew, and Peter.

37. *Praeparatio evangelica* 12.10.7.1–11.

38. Des Places, "Thème platonicien," 32–33.

39. It is worth noting that the Myrmidons had gouged out Matthias's eyes in *AAMt* 2.

40. *Odyssey* 17.489–91; cf. 20.184.

41. Similarly, Odysseus told Telemachus that even if he should see the suitors dragging him by the feet, he must restrain himself (16.277; cf. 20.311). Plutarch was

impressed by this speech insofar as it suggested that boys, like Telemachus, should "keep quiet and be restrained" (*How the Young Man Should Study Poetry* 31c–d).

42. *The Acts of Philip*, Act 3 contains a similar discourse which almost certainly was modeled after this speech in *The Acts of Andrew*. See also Prieur, *Acta Andreae*, 227–31.

43. See also Prieur: "Le texte de la *Passion arménienne* a pourtant de profondes ressemblances avec le text platonicien, et mérite d'en être rapproché" (*Acta Andreae*, 235).

44. Cf. *Phaedrus* 248c: "filled with forgetfulness and evil and grows heavy, and when it has grown heavy, loses its wings and falls to the earth."

45. On the growth of spiritual wings and feathers see also *Phaedrus* 251b–c.

46. Cf. *Phaedo* 109e, *Republic* 7.517b–d, and *Timaeus* 81d.

47. Cf. Gregory of Nyssa *Life of Moses* 307: "For he who elevates his life beyond earthly things through such ascents never fails to become even loftier than he was until, as I think, like an eagle in all things in his life may be seen above and beyond the cloud whirling around the ether of spiritual ascent" (Malherbe and Ferguson; this text looks suspiciously similar to Philo *On the Creation* 70). Clement of Alexandria was particularly fond of Socrates' chariot as a metaphor for the soul or mind: *Stromateis* 3.2.14.1: "heaven takes pleasure in two charioteers"; 7.7.40.1: "raising the soul aloft, winged with longing for better things, we compel it to advance to the region of holiness, magnanimously despising the chain of the flesh" (ANF); 5.13.83.1: "yet it is not without eminent grace that the soul is winged, and soars, and is raised above the higher spheres laying aside all that is heavy, and surrendering itself to its kindred element (συγγενεῖ)" (ANF); 5.8.53.1: "Plato, in his book *On the Soul* says that the charioteer and the horse that ran off—the irrational part, which is divided in two, into anger and concupiscence—fall down" (ANF); and especially 5.2.14.1–2, where Clement refers to the *Phaedrus* explicitly and uses it to express the soul's hope for heaven. Cf. *Paidagogos* 3.11.53.2 and *Protrepticus* 10.106.3: "Perchance the Lord will grant you wings." See also *Corpus Hermeticum* 11.19 and Plotinus *Enneads* 7.7.22. On the soul's flight from the body like an eagle, see *The Teachings of Silvanus NHL* 114.17–19.

The choice of the eagle in *The Acts of Andrew* in lieu of the chariot may have been due to the importance of bird omens in Homer epic. When Telemachus threatened the suitors with divine punishment, Zeus "sent forth two eagles, flying from on high" who tore at each other viciously (*Odyssey* 2.146–54). At Menelaus's palace, "Even as he [Telemachus] spoke a bird flew by on the right, an eagle, bearing in his talons a great, white goose," an omen of Odysseus's vengeance against the suitors (15.160–78). On his way home, Telemachus again was interrupted by a flying, fortune-telling fowl. "Even as he spoke a bird flew forth upon the right, a hawk, a swift messenger of Apollo. In his hands he held a dove" (15.525–26). Penelope dreamed of a violent eagle (19.536–50). As the suitors plotted the death of Telemachus, "there came to them a bird of their left, an eagle of lofty flight clutching a timid dove" (20.242–43). See also *Iliad* 8.245–52, 12.201, 13.821–23, 17.674–78, and 24.292–321.

48. See the discussion on 150–55.

49. Peter converts a prefect's concubines and an imperial confidant's wife. Andrew converts the wife of a proconsul.

50. *Acts of Peter* 37 (8).

51. Ibid., 38 (9).

52. In the Greek version of *The Acts of Thomas*, the apostle dies when speared by four soldiers. The apostle interpreted this means of death to symbolize the composition of his body from four elements (165). When Paul was beheaded in *The Acts of Paul*, out of his severed neck spilled milk, symbolic of his nutritious teaching and example. John is not martyred at the end of his *Acts*, which corresponds with traditions that the apostle died at a ripe old age of natural causes.

53. Those familiar with the tradition of Andrew's saltire or X-shaped cross (from which derive *inter alia* the Union Jack and the epistolary symbol for a kiss) might well be taken back by this explanation of the cross as a mast, but Andrew's saltire is relatively recent. Louis Réau, an authority on Christian iconography, dated the symbol to the tenth century, although it was not dominant in Andrew's art until the fifteenth (*Iconographie de l'art chrétien* [Paris: Presses universitaires de France, 1958], 3.1:78–80). See also Emile Mâle, "Histoire et légende de l'apôtre saint André dans l'art," *RDM* 5 (1951): 412–20. Some manuscripts of Isidore of Seville's *Etymologiae* claim the saltire was an ancient tradition (*vetus traditio sit*) already by his time (early seventh century), but these texts seem to have been written much later, and the section on the letter "X" is without doubt an interpolation (*Etymologiae* 1.3 [*PL* 80.77]). The basilica of Hagios Andreas in Patras, Greece, sells a credulous, propagandistic, but informative booklet on Orthodox traditions concerning the apostle's cross (Nikodemus Vallendra, Ὀ σταυρὸς τοῦ μαρτυρίου τοῦ ἀποστόλου Ἀνδρέου [Athens, 1980]), and displays encased fragments of his X-shaped cross—immediately behind a reliquary containing his alleged head.

The origin of the saltire is unknown, but it most likely derives from a desire to provide Andrew with an iconographic signature that would distinguish his cross from Christ's Roman cross and Peter's upside-down cross (so Réau, *Iconographie*, 3.1:80). Wilhelm Bousset proposes a relationship between the interpretation of Andrew's cross as a unification of cosmic cardinal points and the X-shaped sutures on the world-soul in Plato's *Timaeus* 36b ("Platons Weltseele und des Kreuz Christi," *ZNW* 14 [1913]: 273–85, esp. 280–81).

54. *Oneirocritica* 2.53 (White).

55. *Octavius* 29. Hugo Rahner's discussion of the mast/cross metaphor in early Christianity remains useful, in spite of his romantic notions concerning Christian attitudes toward Homer (*Greek Myths and Christian Mystery*, trans. Brian Battershaw [London: Burns and Oates, 1963; ET of the 1957 German edition], 328–86). See also his "Das Schiff aus Holz," *ZKT* 67 (1943): 1–21.

56. *First Apology* 55.

57. *Paidagogos* 3.11. For discussion of ships in early Christian art see Georg Stuhlfauth, "Das Schiff als Symbol der altchristlichen Kunst," *RivAC* 19 (1942): 111–41.

58. *Antichrist* 59. Cf. Ps.-Macarius *Spiritual Homilies* 44.6 (*PG* 34.781D): life is a voyage ending "at the heavenly harbor of rest (ἀναπαύσεως)." For an excellent discussion of harbor images in ancient religion and philosophy see Campbell Bonner, "Desired Haven," *HTR* 34 (1941): 49–67.

Here in Hippolytus, as in Justin, the cross suffers from an apparent mixed metaphor: mast/trophy. See also Methodius of Olympus: the cross is "a trophy against material spirits (or winds), a release from death, footing for an ascent to a true day and a ships' ladder for those who are hastening (ἐπειγομένων) to enjoy the light there" (*Against Porphyry* 1.7–10 [*PG* 18.400c]). The 'trophy' was a makeshift military monument erected at the τροπή or place of 'turning back' of an enemy's assault. Often it consisted of an upright wooden timber or timbers supporting a crossbeam on which were attached captured weapons. One sometimes finds the cross called a trophy with this primary military, nonnautical association (e.g., Justin Martyr *First Apology* 55, Minucius Felix *Octavius* 29, and Tertullian *Apology* 16.7 and *Ad nationes* 1.12), but just as often it is merged with the image of the mast. In spite of scholarly conjecture, there is no evidence that masts were called trophies in antiquity (see Cyril C. Richardson, *Early Christian Fathers* [New York: Macmillan, 1970], 278, n. 58). This mixed metaphor—mast/trophy—seems to be a distinctively Christian concoction.

The cross also is called a trophy in three sources dependent on *The Acts of Andrew*. Two related Greek recensions include among Andrew's words to the cross, "O cross, trophy of Christ's victory over enemies" (*M* 14 and *L* 46b). According to one Latin Passion, Andrew tells his executioner he has no fear because of "the trophy of the cross" (*AAA* 2.1:22). Neither of these readings seems to have been original to the ancient *Acts*.

59. *Against Marcion* 3.18.

60. In a sermon on Matt. 20:1, according to a Coptic manuscript in the British Museum. See W. E. Crum, *Catalogue of the Coptic Manuscripts in the British Museum* (London: Longmans, 1905), 62. Athanasius also claims "the ship of salvation" has two oars, viz. the two testaments, Christ is its pilot, the bishop its rudder, God's power its sail, and the heavenly Jerusalem its harbor.

61. *In Christi resurrectionem 1* (*PG* 46.624D–625A). According to Gregory, when Jesus spoke of the "iota" and the "serif" that will never pass away (Matt. 5:18), he was referring to the cross. The "I" is the upright and the κεραία or "serif" is the crossbeam. This interpretation derives from a pun on the word κεραία, whose primary definition was 'horn', but which came to mean both 'serif', the scribal hook to a letter, and a mast's yardarm, "as we know from sailors." Cf. *Life of Moses* 2.151 (*PG* 44.371).

62. *On Virginity* 18.118 (*PL* 16.297) and *Commentary on the Psalms* 47.13 (CSEL 64.355). See also Ps.-Ambrose *Sermo* 46.4.10 (*PL* 17.697A–B).

63. *Oratio* 27.5 (*PG* 65.813B–C). This passage is loaded with Homeric vocabulary:

High rise the waves, but the helmsman is from heaven. Raging the tempests blow, but the ship has the cross amidships. The storms battle furiously against one another, but the keel of the ship is divinely secure. The waters can never reach to heaven. The evil spirit of the wind is powerless against the Holy Spirit. (Rahner, *Greek Myths*, 374)

64. *Miscellanea* 8.6 (*PL* 88.276C): "O Christ, steer our souls through these stormy waves by the cross which is our mast and our sail-bearing yard-arm, until thy strong hand, after all the storms of the age, lets us ride at anchor in the port of eternal life" (Rahner, *Greek Myths*, 373).

65. Rahner, *Greek Myths*, 328–86, and Pépin, "Christian Ulysses," 9–14.

66. *Refutatio* 7.1. Cf. Ps.-Basil *Commentary on Isaiah* 276 (*PG* 30.604C) and Jerome: "We are sailing with all speed back to our homeland, and so we must turn deaf ears to the death-bringing songs of the Sirens as we pass them on our way" (*Capitulationes libri Iosue, praefatio* [*PL* 28.506B]). Siegfried Walter de Rachewiltz provides a helpful survey of the Sirens in Christian sources in "De Sirenibus: An Inquiry into Sirens from Homer to Shakespeare" (Ph.D. diss., Harvard University, 1983), 64–120. See also Georg Weicker, *Der Seelenvogel in der alten Literatur und Kunst. Eine mythologisch- archaeologische Untersuchung* (Leipzig: B. G. Teubner, 1902), and H.-I. Marrou, "Sirène" s.v. *DACL*.

67. *Tract. in Ioh.* 2.2 (on John 1:6; CCSL 36.12–13).

68. Ps.-Augustine *Sermo* 247.7 (*PL* 39.2204A).

69. *Protrepticus* 12.18.1–4.

70. *Expositio in Lucam* 4.2 (CCSL 14.106); cf. *De fide* 3.4 (497; *PG* 16.590).

71. *Epistulae* 30 (CSEL 29.186).

72. *Sermo* 8 (*PL* 52.208B).

73. *Homily* 49 (CCSL 23.145): "For the mast, which is the cross, enables him who is bound to it, to reach his homeland (*patriae*) in safety" (Rahner, *Greek Myths*, 383). See also Fulgentius *Mythologiae* 2.8.

74. Eustathius *Ad Homeri Odysseam* 1389: "According to Platonists the true homeland (πατρίς) of the soul is the intelligible world." Calypso represents the body that detains the soul, and Penelope, for whom Odysseus longs, is philosophy. According to Porphyry, Numenius and his circle (second century C.E.) were quite correct in seeing in Homer's Odysseus one who sails

through the successive states of γένεσις and so being restored to his place among those beyond all wave crash and "ignorant of the sea"

until you reach men who do not know the sea and put no salt on their food [*Odyssey* 11.122–23].

"Open sea" (θάλασσα) and "wavecrash" (κλύδων) are expressions which likewise in Plato refer to the material universe. (*De antro nympharum* 34 [Lamberton, 39])

Demophilus the Pythagorean (Mullach, 1.486): "[O]ne who longs to see virtue like a homeland (πατρίς) must pass by pleasures (ἡδονάς) as though there were sirens." See also Buffière's treatment of Numenius and of water as a symbol for γένεσις (*Mythes d'Homère*, 413–17). Cf. Proclus, *In Platonis Timaeum comm.* 1.179, and Julian, *In matrem deorum* 169e: "For what could be more blessed, what more joyful than a soul which has escaped from limitlessness and generation (γένεσιν) and inward storm, and has been translated to the very gods?"

Plotinus, too, was fond of Odyssean imagery to express the ascent of the soul.

"Let us flee to our own land (ἐς πατρίδα)" (*Iliad* 2.140, 9.27), one might better urge. What is this flight and how shall we be borne away? Just as Odysseus says he was delivered from a witch like Circe or Calypso, claiming—and I believe he hints at some further meaning—that it did not please him to stay, though there he enjoyed visual delights (ἡδονάς) and was in the presence of enormous beauty on the level of the senses. Our land (πατρίς) is that place from which we came and our father is there. (*Enneads* 1.6.8 [trans. Lamberton, *Homer the Theologian*, 107])

Cf. *Enneads* 5.9.1, Ps.-Plutarch *De vita et poesi Homeri* 126, and Proclus *In Platonis Cratylum comm.* 158 (403d): the three Sirens represent heaven, netherworld, and Poseidon's watery kingdom. Souls must sail past them on their voyage to God through γένεσις, the sea here below. Cf. Hermias, *In Platonis Phaedrum schol.* 259a (Courveur, 214), and Maximus of Tyre 11.10 (Hobein). See also Buffière, *Mythes d'Homère*, 395–97 and 417–18. The most complete and systematic allegorization of the Sirens appears in Eustathius *Ad Homeri Odysseam* 1707–09, where the Sirens represent ἡδονή and Odysseus is the philosopher, strapped "upright" with the thongs of philosophy. The "sweet wax" in the ears of his shipmates likewise is philosophy, which filters the songs of the Sirens into pleasant and harmless education (Buffière, *Mythes d'Homère* 380–83).

75. Irenaeus *Adversus haereses* 4.33.3 and Hippolytus *Refutatio* 5.8.1.

76. *Exegesis on the Soul* (*NHL* II.6) 136.25–36, quoting *Odyssey* 1.48–59. The same document goes on to quote 4.260–64, interpreting Helen's languishing far from home with the soul's longing to return to her "perfect husband" (136.36–137.11). Maddalena Scopello suggests that the author drew from a Homeric florilegium and not directly from *The Odyssey* ("Les Citations d'Homère dans le traité de l'exégèse de l'âme," in *Gnosis and Gnosticism*, Nag Hammadi Studies 8, ed. Martin Krause [Leiden: E. J. Brill, 1977]), 3–12.

77. *Refutatio* 5.7. Jean Daniélou says of this passage, "No other document exhibits such a mixture of authentic Christian typology and Homeric allegorisation, all transmuted into Gnostic symbolism" (*History*, 2.88).

78. Jérôme Carcopino, *De Pythagore aux apôtres. Études sur la conversion du monde romain* (Paris: Flammarion, 1956), esp. 175–88, and Marcel Detienne, "Ulysse sur le stuc central de la Basilique de la Porta Maggiore," *Latomus* 17 (1958): 270–86. See also Daniélou, *History*, 2.88.

79. See Pierre Courcelle, "Quelques symboles funéraires du néo-platonisme latin," *REA* 46 (1944): 73–93. "Ulysse représente, sur nos sarcophages, l'âme du défunt en route vers la patrie céleste et l'apothéose; . . . les Sirènes représentent un obstacle qu'il doit surmonter" (80).

80. See the cautions of Theodor Klauser, "Studien zur Entstehungsgeschichte der christlichen Kunst VI. 15. Das Sirenabenteuer des Odysseus—ein Motiv der christlichen Grabskunst?" *JAC* 6 (1963): 71–100.

81. *Odyssey* 12.219–20.

82. Ibid., 12.184–85.

83. Hesiod *Works and Days* 373–74.

84. *Protrepticus* 12.118.1–4; translation mine, except for the poetic quotations which conform, whenever possible, with Loeb.

85. Ibid. This same imagery appears in the preceding chapter of Clement's *Protrepticus*, in a discussion of Adam's fall because of pleasure, the evil Siren.

Thus did pleasure (ἡδονή) prevail. The man [i.e., Adam] who, because of innocence, had been unbound (λελυμένος) was found to be bound (δεδεμένος) by sins. The Lord chose to release him from his ropes (δεσμῶν) once again, so he wrapped himself up (ἐνδεθείς) in flesh (this is a divine mystery [μυστήριον]), he overpowered the serpent and enslaved the tyrant death. Even more remarkably, because of his outstretched hands he presented unbound (λελυμένον) that very man who had been led astray by pleasure (ἡδονῇ), bound up (δεδεμένον) in corruption. (11.111.1–2)

The μυστήριον here quite likely is the resemblance between Odysseus and Christ, as in *The Acts of Andrew*. Cf. Eustathius *Ad Homeri Odysseam* 1389: Calypso "detained Odysseus the philosopher like a person tied up (ἐνδεδεμένον) to flesh." The Pythagorean Euxitheus similarly spoke of the soul's being "wrapped up in the body (ἐνδεδέσθαι τῷ σώματι)" (Athenaeus *Deipnosophists* 4.157c). Cf. Plutarch: ἐδεδεμένη τῷ σώματι (*On Flight* in Stobaeus 3.40.5 [Wachsmuth and Hense]).

86. *Protrepticus* 9.86.2, apparently inspired by *Odyssey* 1.57–58.

87. Pépin, "Christian Ulysses," 18.

88. Phaedo expressed the wide swing in emotions he and his associates experienced as "sometimes laughing (γελῶντες) and sometimes weeping" (*Phaedo* 59a). Socrates told a joke that made Simmias laugh (γελάσας), and say, "I don't feel much like laughing (γελασείοντα) just now, but you made me laugh (γελάσαι)" (64a). Cebes, too, laughs (62a, 77e, and 101b), but no one laughs or cracks jokes more often than Socrates himself.

89. Ibid., 115c.

90. Cf. *Odyssey* 20.300–302: "Odysseus avoided it with a quick turn of his head, and in his heart he smiled (μείδησε) a right grim and bitter smile."

91. *Phaedo* 116a.

92. Ibid., 117d.

93. On the general subject of the *Phaedo* and early Christian attitudes toward the soul, see Jean Coman, "L'Immortalité de l'âme dans le Phédon et la résurrection des morts dans la littérature chrétienne des deux premiers siècles," *Helikon* 3 (1963): 17–40.

94. In *Phaedo* 77b Socrates refutes "the common fear . . . that when a man dies the soul (ψυχή) is dispersed and this is the end (τέλος) of his existence." See also 84b.

95. For this last phrase I am following the Armenian version, which seems to be supported by one important Greek recension.

96. In the *Phaedo* Plato too uses χωρισμός to speak of the separation of the soul from the body. For example, 67d: χωρισμὸς ψυχῆς ἀπὸ σώματος (cf. 66e: ἡ ψυχὴ ἔσται χωρὶς τοῦ σώματος, and 67c: χωρίζειν . . . ἀπὸ τοῦ σώματος τὴν ψυχήν); cf. Clement of Alexandria *Stromateis* 7.12.71.3.

97. Cf. *Phaedo* 66d, on being enslaved (δουλεύοντες) to the care of the body.

98. Cf. Plato *Timaeus* 45d.

99. Cf. *Republic* 533d: τὸ τῆς ψυχῆς ὄμμα; *Sophist* 254a: τὰ . . . τῆς . . . ψυχῆς ὄμματα.

100. E.g., *Odyssey* 12.167, 13.115, and 15.297; cf. 23.235. For the same verb in nautical contexts see Sophocles *Philoctetes* 499 and 1451, Euripides *Iphigenia at Tauris*

1393, Thucydides 3.49, and Ps.-Nonnus of Panopolis on John 6:16. See especially Clement of Alexandria *Stromateis* 7.10.57.5, where he describes the nature of the true Gnostic, whose soul "hastens (ἐπείγεται) through the holy Septenniad to the ancestral court at the Lord's own mansion."

101. *Phaedo* 65a.

102. Ibid., 65c; cf. 66a: κοινωνῇ.

103. Ibid., 67a.

104. This passage is reconstructed from several damaged readings in the manuscripts. The Greek manuscript conventionally known as *Ann Arbor 36* reads: καὶ ὑπερβάλλετε ἑαυτοῖς ἐμαῖς ἠνοίαις, "and submit yourselves to my" something or other; ἠνοίαις is corrupt. This sentence is also preserved by the Armenian passion, which reads "wrap yourselves in my afflictions," which seems to be a translation of περιβάλλετε instead of ὑπερβάλλετε and ἀνίαις instead of ἠνοίαις. The prefixes περι- and ὑπερ- are occasionally mistaken for each other, especially when written in ligatures. My edition restores the text by preferring περιβάλλετε from the Armenian, and by omitting the omicron from ἠνοίαις in *Ann Arbor 36* to read ἡνίαις, 'lashes' or 'reins'. The sentence then reads: περιβάλλετε ἑαυτοῖς ἐμαῖς ἡνίαις, "Wrap yourselves with my lashes," that is, bind yourselves to the cross as I am bound.

105. See also Passion 50, where Andrew tells his listeners, "Let us not be vexed or agitated by the storm. Let us not transport on our souls traces of the devil which are not ours. But since we have been entirely buoyed up, let us all eagerly anticipate the goal, and let us take flight from him . . . as we fly off to those things which are ours."

106. *Odyssey* 12.191.

107. Ibid., 12.188.

108. *De finibus* 5.18 (49): "Apparently it was not the sweetness of their voices nor the novelty and diversity of their songs, but their professions of knowledge that used to attract the passing voyagers; it was the passion for learning that kept men rooted to the Sirens' rocky shores."

109. E.g., Plutarch *Quaestiones convivales* 9.14.6.2. For a nuanced interpretation of the Sirens, see Eustathius *Ad Homeri Odysseam* 1707–09. See also Delatte, *Littérature pythagoricienne* 133.

110. *De autexusio* 1.1–3. The use here of περιβάλλειν supports the conjectural reading of *The Acts of Andrew* presented above: περιβάλλετε ἑαυτοῖς ἐμαῖς ἡνίαις.

111. *Expositio in Lucam* 4.2 (CCSL 14.106).

112. Socrates often uses the verb θαρρεῖν, 'to be courageous', to express the proper attitude toward death for people know death to be nothing more than the separation of the soul from the body (e.g., *Phaedo* 63e, 87e, 88b, 95c, and 114d).

113. Cf. *Phaedo* 61c, where Socrates says: "I am leaving (ἄπειμι) today."

114. So also in *The Acts of Andrew*, the apostle's soul leaves to prepare routes for other souls in the divine realm, and fights against the enemies of the soul who, like the monsters in *The Odyssey*, might threaten it. "I am stifling the fire, banishing the shadows, extinguishing the furnace, killing the worm, eradicating the threat, gagging the demons, muzzling and destroying the ruling powers, dominating the authorities, throwing down the

devil, casting out Satan, and punishing wickedness" (Passion 58); cf. *The Teachings of Silvanus, NHL* 114.5–10 and 117.13–17.

115. *Phaedo* 81e–82b.

116. Souls are also harassed after death in *Testament of Asher* 6:5.

117. The list of virtues in Passion 59 are particularly apt for an orator. The author therefore may have had in mind not Socrates as much as Odysseus, to whom Homer awarded preeminence in speech: "[W]henso he uttered his great voice from his chest, and words like snowflakes on a winter's day, then could no mortal man beside vie with Odysseus" (*Iliad* 3.221–23). Homer allowed Odysseus himself to narrate Books 9–12 of *The Odyssey*, and when he finished, the Phaeacians "were all hushed in silence, and were spellbound" (13.1–2). Homer's praises of Odysseus's powerful speeches did not escape later authors who generally recognized that he had "made the farthest advance in the practice of oratory" (Aelius Aristides *Orationes* 2.96), "was the most awesome of the Greeks in wordcraft" (Epictetus *Dissertationes* [Arrian] 2.24.26), and possessed "the supreme gift of eloquence" (Quintilian *Institutio oratoria* 12.10.64). Many saw in Odysseus's epithet πολύτροπος—often translated as 'shifty', or 'full of tricks', or 'much traveled'—another instance of Homer's praise of his elocution: 'rich in tropes'. On Odysseus's oratory see also Strabo *Geography* 1.2.5, Cicero *Brutus* 40, Aulus Gellius *Attic Nights* 1.15.3 and 6.14.7, Lucian *Dialogues of the Dead* 19 (363) and *The Wisdom of Nigrinus* 37–38, and Ps.-Lucian *In Praise of Emosthenes* 5. For a discussion of this matter see Detienne, *Homère*, 52–55.

118. Cf. *Phaedo* 89a.

119. *Crito* 44e–45c.

120. Clement of Alexandria referred to Socrates in the *Crito* as an example of someone "who prefers a good life and death to life itself [because he] thinks that we have hope of another life after death" (*Stromateis* 5.2.14.1 [ANF]).

121. Cf. *Phaedo* 67a, 83a, and 84a on the soul's release (λύειν).

122. Ibid., 67d–68a (Loeb, slightly altered). Clement of Alexandria probably had this text in mind when writing *Stromateis* 4.3.12.5 and 7.12.71.3; cf. 5.11.67.1–2.

123. The Armenian Passion reads instead:

If you knew one rope among the many, you, the many, would be free by releasing the one. If you should cry about your bonds, you would feel immediately the release of them. If you saw the one, which was not himself tied, you would release yourself, for you are tied to him. If you know his bonds, you can untie yourself, that you might be tied to him.

124. *Odyssey* 12.193.

125. Ibid., 12.196.

126. The Greek word here translated "master" is δέσποτα. Cf. *Phaedo* 63c: "I am going to gods who are good masters (δεσπότας)."

127. Cf. *Phaedo* 63e: "I think a man who had really spent his life in philosophy is naturally of good courage when he is to die, and has strong hopes that when he is dead he will attain the greatest blessings in that other land." See also 67b–c: "I have great hopes

that when I reach the place to which I am going, I shall there, if anywhere, attain fully to that which has been my chief object in my past life, so that the journey which is now imposed upon me is begun with good hope" (Clement of Alexandria quotes this text positively in *Stromateis* 4.22.144.2–3); 67e: philosophers "hope of going to the place where there is hope of attaining what they longed for all through life"; 68a and 69e (on finding friends on the other side of the grave); 95b–c (on faring better in the next life); 115a: the wise man "awaits his departure to the other world, ready to go when fate calls him"; and 115e: "after I drink the poison, I shall no longer be with you, but shall go away to the joys of the blessed."

128. *Phaedo* 79c–d. Cf. 84b: the soul "believes it must live, while life endures, and then at death pass on to that which is akin (ξυγγενές) to itself and of like nature, and be free (ἀπηλλάχθαι) from human ills." See slso 86a–b.

129. Ibid., 117c.

130. Ibid., 117c–d.

131. Ibid., 115a.

132. Ibid., 115e–116a.

133. Some interpreters think, on the basis of Passion 62, that Aegeates threw himself into the sea: "You will weep, beat your breast, gnash your teeth, grieve, despair, lament, anguish, and comport yourself like your relative the sea, which you now see furiously troubled by waves." If this interpretation holds, it would confirm the identification of Aegeates not only with Odysseus but also with Poseidon Aegeates ('of Aegae'). By throwing himself into the sea, Aegeates returns to the realm of the Lord of the Sea.

134. Cf. Passion 8: "he declared that he would bid adieu to all his possessions."

135. E.g., *Odyssey* 1.90–92 and 386–87, 2.55–79, 123–25, 141–43, and 203–4, 4.318–22, and 14.95–108.

136. Ibid., 13.135–38. See also 5.38–40, 8.435–40, 13.7–15, 14.80–108, 16.229–32, 18.290–303, and 23.338–41.

137. *Phaedo* 68b–c; cf. 79d–e, 83e, and 115a. Clement of Alexandria seems to have been thinking of *Phaedo* 68b–d when he wrote of Gnostic ἀνδρεία in the face of death (*Stromateis* 7.11.4–67.1).

138. Lucian parodied Socrates' courage. Cerberus, the hound of Hades, speaks:

When he [Socrates] was at a distance [from the entrance to Hades], Menippus, his face seemed completely impassive as he approached, and he appeared to have not the slightest fear of death, and he wanted to impress this on those who stood outside the entrance, but when he had peeped into the chasm, and seen the darkness, and I had bitten him and dragged him by the foot, because he was still slowed down by the hemlock, he shrieked like an infant, and cried for his children and went frantic. (*Dialogues of the Dead* 4 [21])

139. Socrates himself cited Odysseus as example of endurance (*Phaedo* 94d quoting *Odyssey* 22.17–18).

8

Postscript

Unlike all other apocryphal Acts, *The Acts of Andrew* concludes with a postscript written by the author himself.

> Hereabouts I should make an end of the blessed tales, acts, and mysteries difficult—or should I say impossible—to express. Let this stroke of the pen end it. I will pray first for myself, that I heard the things that were said just as they had been said (ἀκοῦσαι τῶν εἰρημένων ὡς εἴρηται), both the obvious and also the obscure, comprehensible only to the intellect. Then I will pray for all who are convinced by what was said (τῶν εἰρημένων), that they may have fellowship with each other, as God opens the ears of the listeners, in order to make comprehensible all his gifts in Christ Jesus our Lord, to whom, together with the Father, be glory, honor, and power with the all-holy and good and life-giving Spirit, now and always, forever and ever, amen.

Before discussing what this postscript may disclose about the *Acts* itself, I should address the apparent disagreement between its elocution in the first person singular and external testimony to multiple authorship.

Authorship

Philaster of Brescia (d. ca. 397), who apparently had access to *The Acts of Andrew*, claimed it was written by "the disciples who followed the apostle."[1] More detailed testimony to multiple authorship comes from Philaster's younger contemporary, Pope Innocent I (d. ca. 417), who warned a Spanish bishop to shun a book bearing the name Andrew and written "by the philosophers Xenocharides and Leonidas."[2] The book in question was *The Acts of Andrew*.[3] Innocent surely did not concoct his information regarding the authorship of Andrew's *Acts*. He would never have called the authors philosophers voluntarily; to him they were heretics. Furthermore, the sophisticated content of the *Acts* suggests that it was indeed the work of one or more Christian Platonists like those active in Alexandria at the end of the second century.[4] It is possible, of course, that readers fond of the *Acts* later attributed it to these philosophers, but the names Xenocharides and Leonidas, otherwise unattested in documentation from the early church, make this hypothesis improbable as well. It is difficult to imagine what might have been gained by foisting the work onto two traditional nobodies. One probably should assume that the names appeared in the original.

These witnesses to multiple authorship would seem incompatible with the first-person-singular postscript, but a closer investigation suggests a solution. The author of the postscript does not claim to have been an eyewitness to the events recorded. His prayer was not that he had seen what had actually taken place but merely that he had "heard the things that were said just as they had been said." The author could have meant "the things that were said" in Andrew's own discourses, but this would account for only a fraction of the content; it would exclude, for example, Andrew's miracles and martyrdom. Instead, the author seems to be locating himself as a transcriber at the end of a chain of oral transmission. That is why he prays that he had recorded accurately "the things that were said just as they had been said"—said by his informants. At the beginning of the *Acts*, now lost, the author may have identified these informants, whom Philaster understood to be Andrew's "disciples" and whom Innocent referred to as "the philosophers Xenocharides and Leonidas."[5] Unfortunately, one can no longer determine if the names in any way referred to Andrew's frequently mentioned but never named disciples or to the unnamed philosophers who converted in Philippi (GE 17). Insofar as neither name is a likely pseudonym,[6] one might conclude that one name designated an oral informant, the other the author himself. Be that as it may, appeals to channels of oral transmission occur repeatedly in early Christian literature.[7]

In this regard, it is worth noting that four documents related to *The Acts of Andrew* contain statements regarding the fictive circumstances of their composition. According to *P* (the unpublished Greek manuscript so important for reconstructing Andrew's return to Myrmidonia), Bishop Plato wrote down all that had happened in the city of the cannibals.[8] *The Acts of John by Prochorus*, likewise dependent on *The Acts of Andrew*, states that the lottery in Jerusalem determined that Prochorus, one of the Seventy, would accompany the apostle John to Asia: "Sometime after the ascension into heaven of our Lord Jesus Christ, all the apostles were gathered at Gethsemane. . . . [John drew Asia.] And an assistant from the Seventy was assigned to each one [of the apostles], and I, Prochorus, drew [the lot to go] with John. Having left Jerusalem, we went to Joppa. . . ."[9]

Ps.-Prochorus sustains the first-person narration to the end of the book. A Latin Passion of Andrew written in the sixth century apparently relied on the ancient *Acts* for much of its content. Here again one finds a first-person introduction, this time in the plural: "All of us presbyters and deacons of the churches in Achaea are writing the passion of the holy apostle Andrew, which we all saw with our own eyes. . . . [T]he holy Andrew, whose passion we were able to view personally and are accordingly able to disclose."[10] The beginning of the *AAMt* surely inspired the beginning of *The Acts of Thomas*:

AAMt 1
At that time
(κατ' ἐκεῖνον τὸν καιρόν)
all of the apostles were
(ἦσαν πάντες οἱ ἀπόστολοι)
gathered together
and divided the regions among
themselves by casting lots,
so that each would leave for
his allotted share.

The lot fell
(κατὰ κλῆρον οὖν ἔλαχεν)
on Matthias to go to the city
called Myrmidonia.

Acts of Thomas 1
At that time
(κατ' ἐκεῖνον τὸν καιρόν)
all we apostles were
(ἦμεν πάντες οἱ ἀπόστολοι)
in Jerusalem. . . .
[A]nd we **divided the regions**
of the inhabited world
so that each of us **might go to**
his allotted area and to the
people to which the Lord sent him.
The lot fell
(κατὰ κλῆρον οὖν ἔλαχεν)
on India to be for
Judas Thomas, even Didymus.

One major difference between the two is the first person plural in *The Acts of Thomas*. From this curious "we" one might expect an extended first person narration; instead, the narrator turns immediately to the more common omniscient third.

It is quite possible, of course, that no relationship whatever exists between the lost beginning of *The Acts of Andrew* and the appeals to eyewitness testimony in *P*, *The Acts of John by Prochorus*, the Latin Passion, and *The Acts of Thomas*; such appeals to tradition were commonplace. But if *The Acts of Andrew* began with a statement concerning the author and his informants, it might help to explain the frequency of these notices in later texts derived from it, and, more importantly, such an introduction would have prepared the reader for the anonymous first-person-singular postscript.

Allegorical Readings

More relevant to the general hypothesis of this study, however, is the distinction the author draws between the two levels of meaning in the text:

> I will pray first for myself, that I heard what was actually said, both the obvious (συμφανές) and also the obscure (ἀφανῶν), comprehensible only to the intellect (διανοίᾳ). Then I will pray for all who are convinced by what was said, that they may have fellowship with each other, as God opens the ears of the listeners, in order to make comprehensible all his gifts.[11]

The vocabulary here belongs to allegory. Philo used similar expressions at the beginning of his allegorization of the decalogue, where he promised to explain its allegorical meanings in order to disclose its richer truths: "For knowledge loves to learn and advance to full understanding (διάνοιαν) and its way is to seek the hidden meaning (τὰ ἀφανῆ) rather than the obvious (τῶν ἐμφανῶν)."[12]

Similarly, the author of the *Acts* wished the reader to seek out the deeper levels of meaning, "the obscure, comprehensible only to the intellect." These deeper meanings may be nothing more than its spiritual or philosophical truths, as in Philonic allegories; I would suggest rather that the author hereby is alerting the reader to divine its hypertextual intentions. The "obvious (συμφανές)" has to do with the surface reading, the "obscure (ἀφανῶν)" refers to its transvaluation of Greek mythology and philosophy. Only when "God opens the ears of the listeners" will they receive "*all* his gifts."[13]

Nonallegorical Readings

From what now can be known concerning later readings of *The Acts of Andrew*, it would appear that the author's prayer went unanswered. Only two ancient readers seem to have recognized—partially at best—its indebtedness to classical literature. The first is Dorotheus, "son of Quintus the poet," discussed earlier in chapter 1. *The Vision of Dorotheus* consists of 343 lines in dactylic hexameters heavy with distinctively Homeric vocabulary. During his heavenly transport, Dorotheus selected the name Andrew because he lacked ἀνδρεία, 'courage'.[14] Unfortunately, one can no longer discover if Dorotheus had been inspired by *The Acts of Andrew*. One can only say that the two earliest writings devoted to the apostle Andrew are Homeric hypertexts, and both replace the violence of Homer's heroes with the nonresistance of Christian martyrs.

The second reader was the Manichaean Agapius, who may have seen similarities between the now nonexistent visit of the Myrmidons to the netherworld and Plato's myth of Er. At least Photius, the sole surviving witness to Agapius, claims that he used both *The Acts of Andrew* and Plato to support his belief in reincarnation.[15] There is no reason to suspect, however, that Agapius had detected the relationship of the *Acts* to Homer or Greek mythology.

With the possible exceptions of Dorotheus and Agapius, no one else seems to have recognized the *Acts'* interests in ancient Greek literature. The various recastings of it by Gregory of Tours, Epiphanius the Monk, Nicetas the Paphlagonian, and the authors of *Narratio* or the several derivative Andrean passions reveal no awareness of its distinctive hypertextuality. *The Acts of Andrew* influenced a brood of later apocrypha, and here again one finds nearly nothing to suggest attention to Homer, Plato, or Greek myths.[16] Had ancient readers of the *Acts* recognized its transvaluative agenda, they might have treated it with more respect, for its revisions of ancient literature and mythology correspond with the perspectives of venerated apologists such as Justin Martyr and Clement of Alexandria.

One should hardly be surprised that later readers failed to detect its more "obscure" layer of meaning "comprehensible only to the intellect." In the first place, few other early Christian texts display this same hypertextual playfulness, so readers of the *Acts* would not have been prepared to see it here. Secondly, the textual transmission of the *Acts* gradually but consistently obscured its classical antecedents. By the end of the fourth century, the story of Andrew among the Myrmidons circulated independently. Soon thereafter, the name Myrmidonia fell out of all Greek texts of the *AAMt* (apart from *P*) as well as from its translations into Syriac, Coptic, Ethiopic, Armenian, and all Slavonic versions. When detached from the rest of the *Acts* and when denuded of every reference to Myrmidonia, the *AAMt* lacked important clues concerning its Homeric heritage. Although some variant of Myrmidonia persisted in the Latin and Anglo-Saxon versions, Homer's epics were unavailable in western Europe until 1488.[17]

During the fourth and fifth centuries, Latin authors also rewrote Andrew's Passion and they, too, obscured its dependence on Greek classics. For example, one Passion, *Conversante et docente*, omitted every reference to Maximilla's rejection of Aegeates' bed, to Stratocles' conversion to pacifism, and to Andrew's Platonizing speeches. That is, Maximilla, Stratocles, and Andrew no longer represent Christian alternatives to Penelope, Telemachus, and Socrates. Much the same can be said for the putative *Letter of the Presbyters and Deacons of Patras.*

By the late sixth century, the entire *Acts* had been translated into Latin, and it was in this form that it fell into the hands of Gregory of Tours. Gregory knew no Greek and probably little Homer, so the hypertextual significance of the names and tales in his source escaped him. By narrating "the miracles only, omitting all that bred disgust," he also omitted much that might have bred suspicions of its hypertextual targets.[18] From the sixth century on, the shape of Andrew's memory in the West derived almost totally from the Latin *AAMt*, Gregory's epitome, or from information ultimately derived from them (e.g., Ps.-Abdias). In these sources little remains to suggest Greek mythology, literature, or philosophy.

Even in the Greek-speaking East, *The Acts of Andrew* suffered from misunderstandings and textual tampering. Some ecclesiastics thought Manichaeans had interpolated the work and therefore took it upon themselves to purge it of such "distortions."[19] The most obvious victim was the visit to the netherworld, which, except for traces, has disappeared.[20]

Far more determinative for Andrew's fate was his usefulness to the See of Byzantium.[21] The increasing tensions between Rome and Byzantium put the latter in need of a legitimating apostle, someone to rival Peter of the Roman church. None of the Twelve was better suited for this role than Andrew, who, according to the Gospel of John, was the first disciple Jesus had called. Only after responding to Jesus himself did Andrew bring his brother Peter to his Lord. Furthermore, *The Acts of Andrew* had placed the apostle in Byzantium (GE 8), and in the mid-fourth century, during the reign of Constantius, a certain military official named Artemius transferred Andrew's relics from Patras to the Church of the Holy Apostles at Constantinople.[22] The ancient *Acts* apparently narrated no apostolic work at the capital, but what tradition lacked, ecclesiastical expediency supplied. An eighth-century rewriting of *The Acts of Andrew* states that

after having sailed down through the same *Pontus Euxinus* [Black Sea] which flows toward Byzantium, [he] landed on the right bank, and after arriving at a place called Argyropolis, and having constructed there a church, he ordained one of the seventy disciples called Stachys whom also Paul the Apostle, the mouthpiece of Christ, the vessel of election, mentions in the Epistle to the Romans [16:9] as beloved [by him], Bishop of Byzantium, and left him to preach the word of salvation. He, because of the pagan godlessness that prevailed in that region, and the cruelty of the tyrant Zeuxippus, a worshiper of idols who held sway there, turned toward western parts, illuminating with his divine teaching the darkness of the West.[23]

Later Greek rewritings of *The Acts of Andrew* included similar notes concerning the Protocletos, 'first-called', to justify the apostolicity of Byzantium.[24]

Had Andrew not been so useful to the eastern See, fewer textual witnesses to his *Acts* would have survived, but this tradition concerning Stachys also guaranteed that the apostle had permanently evolved from a playful, literary alternative to Odysseus and Socrates into a historical datum. The ninth-century monk Epiphanius knew of traditions that took Myrmidonia to be Sinope. The local residents proudly showed the monk Andrew's prison, the fig trees where the escaped had hidden, and the beach where the apostle baptized them. There was also a magnificent statue of the apostle allegedly erected while the apostle was still alive.[25] Epiphanius's travels also exposed him to traditions that the apostle had evangelized the Scythians, the Sogdians, the Gorsini, the Iberi, the Sousi, the Phousti, and the Alani. Installing bishops along the way, he had visited Amisus, Trapezunta, Iberia, Phrygia, Ephesus, Bithynia, Laodicea, Mysia, Odyssopolis, Olympus, Nicea, Nicomedia, Chalcedon, Heraclea, Amastra, Zalichus, Neocaesarea, Sebastopolis Magna (Colchis), and Zecchia, as well as Byzantium, Argyropolis, Macedonia, and Achaea. As another ninth-century author put it: Andrew "was allotted . . . every region and city along the north and south shores of the Black Sea."[26] Russian Orthodox tradition went so far as to claim that Andrew had anticipated the founding of churches in Ukrainian Kiev.[27] Visitors today may admire Kiev's Church of St. Andrew, perched high on a bluff overlooking the Dniepr River. One will find fragments of Andrew's cross and his skull beautifully encased in silver at his magnificent basilica in Patras, Greece.

This development of the apostle from fiction to fact illustrates how later tradition read Andrean texts against the backdrop not of epic but of expedient 'history'. The textual transmission of *The Acts of Andrew* bears many scars from wounds inflicted by this tendency toward objectification and its consequent obfuscation of fictional playfulness.

Even the development of Andrew's depiction in art disguised his role as an alternative to Greek myth. All depictions of Andrew's cross prior to the tenth century placed him on an upright cross, which would allow an identification with Odysseus's mast. First in the tenth century and characteristically after the fifteenth, the Roman cross was replaced by the saltire or X-shaped cross in Andrean iconography. It is this cross that graces the Scottish flag, the Union

Jack, and the Confederate flag. In this form, the visual similarities between Andrew's cross and Odysseus's mast were destroyed.

Andrew's Own Epic

The apostle's past as fisherman, his victory against cannibals, his courageous death, and especially the assonance of his name with ἀνδρεία fostered a tradition that came to regard him as an apostolic superman, but without any of the transvaluative ironies of *The Acts of Andrew*.[28] A Coptic homily claimed that "Andrew was the most fiery of the apostles. If a city received not his preaching, he was wroth (and wished) that a fire from heaven might burn it. Hence another apostle was sent with him to remind him of the Lord's command to preach to all nations."[29] Sometime in the sixth or seventh century, a Latin author recast the story of Andrew among the Myrmidons into a heroic poem that depicted him as the "manly apostle," "amazing disciple, powerful hero," who "preached courageously."[30] The apostle appears here as a fearless hero with indomitable powers for vanquishing Christ's foes.

The Byzantine author Nicetas the Paphlagonian (early tenth century) recast the life of Andrew by Epiphanius the monk and in so doing portrayed the apostle as quintessential virility:

> Let him be extolled as attainable for us, Andrew, Christ's general (στρατηγέτης), whose very name indicates manliness (ἀνδρείας), mighty in deed and word, who was appointed for battle against enemies seen and unseen and who seized the victory over both. Let him be applauded with words of power, he who donned unconquerable strength with the mighty panoply of the almighty spirit, who girded his loins with truth and courage (ἀνδρεία) and shod his feet with preparation of the gospel of peace, through which he snatched the nations from the gullet of the tyrannous enemy, safely took them captive, and presented them to the Savior, obedient in faith. Let him be glorified with paeans, illustrious Andrew, the stele of eponymous courage (ἀνδρείας).[31]

Elsewhere the same author called the apostle "the paradigm of true manliness (ἀνδρεία), the diamond of strong endurance, the statue (ἀνδριάς) of perseverance, the rock after the rock, the unbroken foundation of the Church."[32] Nicetas even provided a physical description of him as virile: "[H]e was no runt in size but was quite tall, slightly stooped, with a long nose and heavy eyebrows."[33]

For the most part, Nicetas attributed Andrew's miraculous power to divine assistance, but in other cases, he praised his native physical strength. For instance, an immense dragon was terrorizing an area near Nicea.

> [W]hen appropriately named 'manliness' (ἀνδρείας) learned of the dragon, he took along two disciples and courageously (ἐν ἀνδρικῷ) and confidently went

to it, holding in his hand an iron rod in the shape of the life-giving cross with which he always supported himself. When he approached the place, the dragon sensed their arrival and went out against them, but having a calling adequate to the task, Andrew courageously (ἀνδρίως) took the iron rod and planted it in the eye of the destructive dragon and drove it all the way through the other eye. The dragon died then and there.[34]

But the zenith of Andrew's inflation into a Christian warrior had already occurred in England prior to Nicetas with the composition of *Andreas*. An unknown Anglo-Saxon author recast *The Acts of Andrew and Matthias* (known probably from a faithful Latin translation) into an epic poem reminiscent of *Beowulf*.[35] No longer a poor itinerating holy man, the apostle now sails off as a mighty knight in the service of Christ his liege, making war on the infidel. The values promoted here have more in common with the code of warriors in Homer than with *The Acts of Andrew*.[36] The author wastes no time in establishing its heroic tenor:

> Listen! We have heard in the old days
> of twelve under the stars, glorious heroes,
> Lord's thanes. Their might did not fail
> in warfare when banners clashed together
> after they separated as the Lord himself,
> highking of the heaven, taught them their lot.
>   Those were famous men upon the earth,
> ready generals and bold in battle,
> strong fighters when shield and hand
> defended helmet on the battlefield.[37]

But none of these warrior-apostles could match Andrew in valor: "the noble one . . . nor was his heart timid, / but he was resolute for the work of renown, / hard and bold, by no means a coward, / ready, eager for battle, for God's campaign."[38] He is called "holy campaigner," "blessed warrior," "bold in battle," "protector of warriors," "prince," "champion of Christ," "battle-bold hero," "joy of princes," "victory-bold," "glory-hard earl," and "quick warrior." Andrew's disciples no longer are fearful companions but "thanes / chosen for battle." In the *AAMt* the disciples had decided to sail off with Andrew because they were helpless without him, but in *Andreas* these "battle-bold warriors" went to "Mermedonia" because they sought military glory.[39]

The "Mermedonians" here have become a mighty army under the Devil's strategic command, marching with shields, spears, steeds, and swords.[40] The conflict between Andrew and the cannibals thus is fought as a war between good and evil. Christ told Andrew:

> "Battle is certain for you;
> your body shall be divided by wounds

of hard sword strokes; blood shall flood
like water.

. . . . .

Bear that pain;
do not let the glory of the heathens, the grim spear-struggle,
turn you away to forsake God,
your Lord. Be always eager for glory."

. . . .

   Then the battle-hard man remembered,
was patient, went quickly into the city,
the resolute warrior, pushed on by courage;
the champion bold in mind trusted in the Lord.[41]

Such military imagery pervades these 1722 lines and promotes the notion that "the living God will never forsake / an earl upon the earth if his courage endures."[42]

Christological monikers further betray the author's prejudices in favor of Anglo-Saxon royalty, the divine right of kings, and feudal militarism. Christ is "renown of kings," "lord of armies," "defender of princes," "ruler of warriors," "chief of warriors," "ruler of armies," "powerful Lord . . . the faithful king," "ruler of nations," "lord of troops," "king of victories," "lord of lords," "prince, king of everyone alive," "victory-lord," "king of all kings," "guardian of victories," "shield against the enemies' weapons," "glory of kings, creation's mighty lord," and "glory of heroes." The author of *Andreas* uses regal and military imagery to describe Christ: "He made known . . . / that he was rightful king / over middle-earth, strengthened by might, / ruler and worker of glory."[43]

Andreas thus is a heroic hypertext of the first story in *The Acts of Andrew*, which in turn was a hypertextual alternative to the heroic values of Homer's *Iliad*. By recasting the story of Andrew and the cannibals into an epic poem, the author of *Andreas* unwittingly reinstalled a heroic world view. The rarefied intellectual atmosphere of late second-century Alexandria that produced Andrew's *Acts* became polluted with the heavy clouds of medieval feudalism, noisy with the clashing of arms and the shouting of armies.

In spite of the poem's near reversal of the ethics of *The Acts of Andrew*, it witnesses the epic potential of the Myrmidon story. The author of the *Acts* retained echoes of Homer's depictions of savagery, courageous suffering, and the intervention of supernatural powers. An unknown Anglo-Saxon apparently saw in these residual epic elements inspiration for dressing Andrew in chainmail and sending him off to fight the infidel.

Conclusion

The postscript to *The Acts of Andrew*, unique among the apocryphal acts, urged the reader to understand not only its obvious but also its obscure meanings, to penetrate beyond the surface story to its deeper significance. The author thereby alerted the reader to view the book as an allegory of sorts (which is how many of his contemporaries understood both the Bible and Homer), an allegory whose legends would replace the Greek myths discernible at the deeper level. Few if any readers caught on. Indeed, by the mid-tenth century the story of the Myrmidons was recast as an epic poem by an Anglo-Saxon Homer.

Notes

1. *Diversarum hereseon liber* 61 (CSEL 38).

2. *Epistle* 6.7 (Wurm, 77–78).

3. Earlier in the same sentence, Innocent lashed out against writings bearing the names Peter and John, "written by a certain Leucius"—undoubtedly *The Acts of Peter* and *The Acts of John*. Innocent also complained about writings related to Thomas, probably *The Acts of Thomas*.

4. The theology of the *Acts* conforms closely to that described by Roelof Van den Broek in his excellent discussion of Christian Platonism at Alexandria ("The *Authentikos Logos:* A New Document of Christian Platonism," *VC* 33 [1979]: 260–86). Notice that by altering a single letter, Leonidas becomes Leonides, the name of Origen's educated father. For a fuller discussion of authorship, see MacDonald, *Acts of Andrew*, 47–51.

5. In this regard it is worth noting that at the beginning of Plato's *Phaedo* Echecrates asks Phaedo the philosopher if he was with Socrates on the day of his death or if he heard "about it from someone else" (57a). Phaedo claimed that he was there and would be willing to tell Echecrates everything: "It is always my greatest pleasure to be reminded of Socrates whether by speaking of him myself or by listening to someone else" (58d). Echecrates then asked him to "tell us everything as accurately as you can."

6. Other characters in the *Acts* are more probable pseudonymous authors, especially Stratocles, who indeed plays this role in the Armenian Passion.

7. For example, the author of the Gospel of Luke attempted to bolster the reliability of his account by appealing to "eyewitnesses and servants of the word" (Luke 1:2). Papias of Hierapolis in Phrygia began his *Explanation of the Sayings of the Lord* by citing authoritative tradents:

I shall not hesitate to append to the interpretations all that I ever learnt well from the presbyters and remember well, for of their truth I am confident. . . . [I]f ever anyone came who had followed the presbyters, I inquired into the words of the presbyters, what Andrew or Peter or Philip or Thomas or James or John or Matthew, or any other of the Lord's disciples had said. . . . For I did not suppose that information from books would help me so much as the word of a living and surviving voice." (*apud* Eusebius *Historia ecclesiastica* 3.39.3–4)

Irenaeus, a contemporary of the author of *The Acts of Andrew*, wrote a Roman presbyter named Florinus, warning him to avoid teachings contrary to what had been handed down by "those who were presbyters before us, they who accompanied the apostles" (*apud* Eusebius *Historia ecclesiastica* 5.20.4). To defend his position, Irenaeus reminded Florinus that the two of them in their youth had spent time in the home of Polycarp,

so that I can speak even of the place in which the blessed Polycarp sat and disputed, how he came in and went out, the character of his life, the appearance of his body, the discourses that he made to the people, how he reported his intercourse with John and with the others who had seen the Lord, how he remembered their words, and what were the things concerning the Lord which he had heard (ἀκηκόει) from them, and about their miracles, and about their teaching, and how Polycarp had received them from the eyewitnesses of the word of life, and reported all things in agreement with the Scriptures. I listened (ἤκουον) eagerly even then to these things through the mercy of God that was given me, and made notes of them, not on paper but in my heart. (Ibid., 5.20.5–7)

Clement of Alexandria, too, at the beginning of his *Stromateis*, insisted that he was profoundly dependent on traditions he had heard:

Now this work of mine in writing is not artfully constructed for display; but my memoranda are stored up against old age, as a remedy against forgetfulness, truly an image and outline of those vigorous and animated discourses which I was privileged to hear (ἐπακοῦσαι), and of blessed and truly remarkable men. . . . Well, they preserving the tradition of the blessed doctrine derived directly from the holy apostles, Peter, James, John, and Paul, the sons receiving it from the father . . . , came by God's will to us also to deposit those ancestral and apostolic seeds. . . . The writing of these memoranda of mine, I well know, is weak when compared with that spirit, full of grace, which I was privileged to hear (ὑπακοῦσαι). . . . And we profess not to explain secret things sufficiently—far from it—but only to recall them to memory. (*Stromateis* 1.1.11.1–14.1 [ANF])

See M. Hornschuh, "The Apostles as Bearers of the Tradition," *NTApoc* 2.74–87.

8. *Paris graecus 1313*: ὁ Πλάτων ἔγραψεν ταῦτα ἀπ' ἀρχῆς ἕως τέλους (141b).

9. *Acts of John by Prochorus* 1 and 7 (Zahn) (translation mine).

10. *Passio sancti Andreae apostoli* 1 (*AAA* 2.1:1–3).

11. Plato and many of his ancient admirers were convinced that the nature of things divine was comprehensible only to the intellect (see especially Plato *Republic* 529d: διανοίᾳ ληπτά). Cf. Eusebius *Praeparatio evangelica* 11.7.9.6.

12. *Decalogue* 1.1.

13. This image may have been inspired by the stuffed up ears of Odysseus's shipmates, which seems to lie behind Passion 57: "[W]ipe your ears to hear what I say."

14. Pages 25–26.

15. See pages 94–95.

16. These texts include *The Acts of Thomas, The Acts of Philip, The Acts of John by Prochorus, The Acts of Mark, The Acts of Peter and Andrew, The Martyrdom of Matthew,* several Ethiopic apocrypha, and probably *The Acts of Xanthippe and Polyxena.* In *The Acts of Mark,* Mark teaches an Egyptian about Christ by referring to the prophets. The man responds: "I never heard about the writings of which you speak, only *The Iliad* and *The Odyssey* and whatever other literature Egyptian boys study." The apostle then made it clear to him that "the wisdom of this world is foolishness with respect to God" (*PG* 115.165). Unfortunately, there is nothing in this text to suggest that the author's reference to the Homeric epics derived from an alert reading of *The Acts of Andrew.*

17. Furthermore, few readers in the West would have known enough Greek to have identified Myrmidonia with μύρμηκες, 'ants'.

18. Gregory had personal reasons too for writing the *Liber de miraculis*: his own birthday fell on Andrew's feast day.

19. See John of Thessalonica *Discourse on the Dormition of the Holy Virgin* (*PO* 19.377.8–10) and Turibius of Astorga *Epistula ad Idacium et Ceponium* 5 (*PL* 54.694). These texts are discussed in more detail on page 95.

20. The visit to the netherworld may already have been scotched from the Latin translation that Gregory epitomized.

21. See Dvornik, *Apostolicity*, and Chrysostome Konstantinidis, "La Fête de l'apôtre saint André dans l'église de Constantinople à l'époque byzantine et aux temps modernes," in *Melanges en l'honneur de Monseigneur Michel Andrieu*, Revue des sciences religieuses, volume hors séries (Strasbourg: Palais Universitaire, 1956), 243–61.

22. See Dvornik, *Apostolicity*, 227–31.

23. *Narratio* 8. The translation comes from Dvornik (ibid., 172), who claims that the author of *Narratio* took this information from Ps.-Epiphanius (175).

24. Epiphanius the Monk 244c and *Laudatio* 32; cf. Ps.-Dorotheus, s.v. Andrew.

25. Behind this claim may be Andrew's erection of a church where the water-spewing statue once stood (*AAMt* 30 and 32).

26. Nicetas the Paphlagonian *Oration IV, In Praise of St. Andrew* (*PG* 105.64C).

27. For these traditions see especially: Dvornik, *Apostolicity*; Felix Haase, *Apostel und Evangelisten in den orientalischen Überlieferungen*, NTAbh 9 (Münster: Aschendorff, 1922), 249–52; Michael Murjanoff, "Andreas der Erstberufene im mittelalterlichen Europa," *Sacris Erudiri* 17 (1966): 411–27; and Bohdan Georg Mytytiuk, *Die ukrainischen Andreasbräuche und verwandtes Brauchtum*, Veröffentlichungen des Osteuropa-Institutes München: Reihe Geschichte 47 (Wiesbaden: Harrassowitz, 1979).

28. A sermon about the apostle wrongly attributed to Athansius spoke of him as "aptly named for apostolic manliness (ἀνδρείας)" (*PG* 28.1104). *The Acts of Peter and Andrew*

dubbed him "the good competitor (ἀγωνιστής)" (2), and *The Manichaean Psalm-Book* declared: "A mind strong in how much is Andrew" (*Manichaean Psalm-Book* 192.6 [Allberry], restoring the text to read ϩчнаϣт, 'strong'). A Syriac text translated the name Andrew as "Mighty One" or "Conqueror" (E. A. W. Budge, ed. and trans. *The Contendings of the Apostles* [London: Oxford University Press, 1935], 585).

29. British Museum Coptic 259 (in older catalogue, Or. 3581 A[85]), according to Crum, *Coptic Manuscripts*, 116.

30. *Rec. Vaticana*: *virilem apostolum* (121v), *virilis robuste* (127r), *viriliter* (122r).

31. *Laudatio* 1. Other examples of the pun on ἀνδρεία appear in *Laudatio* 3, 5, 8, 16, 17, 18, 19, 26, 29, 30, 46, 48, and 52. See also Theophanes Cerameus (*PG* 132.899 and 905).

32. *Oratio* 4 (*PG* 105.64B–C).

33. *Laudatio* 12. This description corresponds with artistic representations of the apostle, especially in the East, where he characteristically appears as a tall, bearded old man, with a pointed nose and bushy eyebrows. In order to pick Andrew out of a crowd, one should look especially for disheveled hair, as though the apostle had just disembarked and had lost his comb at sea.

34. Ibid., 16.

35. On the Andrean source behind *Andreas* see Brooks, *Andreas*, xv–xviii. Much of the scholarship on *Andreas* has focused on its relationship to *Beowulf*. See Brooks, *Andreas*, xxii–xxvii, and Robert Boenig, *Saint and Hero: "Andreas" and Medieval Doctrine* (Lewisburg: Bucknell University Press, 1991), 11–23.

36. For a discussion of heroic vocabulary in *Andreas* see Claes Schaar, *Critical Studies in the Cynewulf Group* (New York: Haskell House, 1967), 310–18.

37. *Andreas* 1–10. For the most part, the translations come from Robert Boenig, *The Acts of Andrew in the Country of the Cannibals: Translations from the Greek, Latin, and Old English*, Garland Library of Medieval Literature, series B, 70 (New York: Garland, 1991).

38. *Andreas* 231–34.

39. Ibid., 408–14:

"We will be hateful in every land,
despised by the peoples, when the sons of men,
eager for glory, sit in counsel
over which of them always best supported
their lord in battle when hand and shield,
ground by swords, sharply suffered
on the battle plain in the war play."

40. For example:

Then from far and wide the troops gathered,
the folk's chief spears. The faithless host came

with weapons to the fort. (Ibid., 1067–69)
The battle-bold of the army leapt up with a shout,
and the warriors pierced to the wall's gates
keen under banners, in a great crowd
to the battle, with spears and swords. (1202–1205)

41. Ibid., 951–54, 956–59, and 981–84.
42. Ibid., 459–60.
43. Ibid., 699–702. This brashly regal and military imagery renders Christ nearly indistinguishable from God, "king of heaven," "God of armies," "king of kings," and "lord of lords."

Conclusion

The driving concern of *The Acts of Andrew* was the transvaluation of Greek mythology. The author composed the *Acts* as an *Odyssey* of sorts, with Andrew, 'Mr. Manliness', the old fisherman, as the protagonist. The narrative begins with the apostle in Achaea, whence he is called to rescue Matthias from the Myrmidons, Achilles' ferocious troops in *The Iliad*. The story of the Myrmidons combined motifs from the Circe tale in *The Odyssey* and filled it with characterizations drawn from the great war with Troy, especially as depicted in Homer's *Iliad*. A no longer extant ministry in "the city of the barbarians" probably consisted of a confrontation with the Taurian shrine to Artemis. The missing tour of hell may have provided an alternative to Homer's *nekyia*, shaped in part by Plato's myth of Er. From Myrmidonia, Andrew gradually returned to Achaea in a *nostos* modeled after *The Odyssey*, traveling by way of northern Anatolia, Thrace, and Macedonia, encountering along the way characters reminiscent of several Greek heroes. Events in Macedonia for the most part concern the deities resident on Macedonian Olympus. Andrew's voyage from Macedonia to Achaea shares details with the voyage of the Argo and Odysseus's final voyage to Ithaca. Once in Patras, Andrew converted the proconsul and toured the Peloponnese, where he encountered counterparts to many of the best of the Achaeans. The apostle returned to Patras, where he performed more miracles and converted Maximilla and Stratocles, wife and brother of Aegeates, the new proconsul. Maximilla transvalued Penelope, Stratocles reversed the development of Telemachus, and Aegeates absorbed Odysseus's traits as a lovesick murderer. Sometimes Andrew, too, reminds one of Odysseus—for example, when he is tied to the cross like Odysseus at the mast—but for the most part he represents a Christianized Socrates, unjustly slain for corrupting the youth by promoting a new god. Throughout the *Acts*, the author sided with Plato's Socrates against the immorality of Homer's immortals, so the reader is hardly surprised to find the apostle sharing Socrates' fate at the end.

To this point I have cited evidence for the transvaluative hypertextuality of *The Acts of Andrew*, but have not tested the evidence against criteria for establishing intertextual dependence. After doing so, I will suggest what insights this reading of the *Acts* provides for the study of early Christianity.

Criteria for Literary Dependence

I will test the hypothesis against five criteria: (1) density and order, (2) explanatory value, (3) accessibility, (4) analogy, and (5) motivation. It will be seen that *The Acts of Andrew* satisfies each criterion brilliantly.

Density and order pertains to the parallels between two documents; the more one finds, the stronger the case for literary connection between them. Conversely, the fewer the parallels, the weaker the case. One ought also to ask if the alleged parallels between the two texts follow a similar or radically different order of presentation. Sometimes, for example, one may find loose similarities between two texts—shared vocabulary, tale-types, motifs, or characterizations—but the mere presence of these similarities does not require literary influence. On the other hand, when similarities appear in the same order, the case for literary dependence strengthens, especially in cases where there seems no other explanation for the order of these items in the hypertext.

By *explanatory value* I mean the ability of alleged parallels between hypotext and hypertext to account for otherwise inexplicable difficulties in the latter. Stated otherwise, if one can understand a text perfectly well without appeal to its dependence on an antecedent, the case for that dependence diminishes; the more difficulties in the text the hypotext explains, the surer the case for influence.

One may find striking parallels between two texts, but they carry little weight if the author of the hypertext could not have had access to its alleged target, and this is what I mean by *accessibility*. Thus, the more widespread the circulation of the alleged hypotext, the more plausible the case that it might have influenced the hypertext.

The case for the influence of one text on another gains credibility if one can demonstrate that the same hypotext influenced other texts as well. On the other hand, if there are no other examples of such influence, one might well be suspicious of influence in the case at hand. It is this issue that I examine under the criterion of *analogy*.

When authors rewrite texts, they have some reason for doing so. The project may be friendly to the hypotext: a commentary, a translation, or an imitation; it may also be transgressive: a parody, a travesty, or a transvaluation. Whatever the reason, the author apparently thinks that the desired task would be accomplished best by recomposing. Therefore, when one argues for the influence of one text on another, one ought to be able to explain why the author went to the trouble, that is, his or her *motivation*.

Density and Order

Virtually every episode in the *Acts* shows evidence of hypertextual playfulness and conforms to a consistent, if complex, apologetic project. Nearly every major Greek mythological character gets attention. For example, the author transvalued or otherwise recast each of the twelve Olympians. Zeus appears variously as the devil,[1] as Carpianus ('fruitful'),[2] as Medias ('laughter'),[3] and most notably as the wicked proconsul Varianus ('fickle').[4] Each of the last three characters resides in Macedonia, the district of Mount Olympus. Hera is Varianus's wife, Aristobula ('good plan');[5] Hephaestus has become the lame Philomedes ('laughter-loving');[6] Aphrodite is the lustful Callisto ('most-beautiful');[7] Apollo is the unnamed friend of philosophers whom Andrew exorcised;[8] Ares is the unnamed, demon-possessed soldier, who, when exorcised, threw off his uniform;[9] Poseidon of Aegae is the vindictive Aegeates;[10] Dionysus is the wealthy proconsul Lesbius ('goblet');[11] Heracles is Varianus's unnamed son, who was strangled by the wild cat,[12] the youth slain by the serpent,[13] the old man with the young lover,[14] Antiphanes ('inconspicuous'), whose house was troubled by demons,[15] and the demon-possessed Alcman.[16] Artemis appears as herself.[17] Sometimes the roles of the gods are played by demons. The author of the *Acts* transvalued neither Hermes nor Athena; instead, he borrowed motifs from their Homeric depictions and applied them sympathetically to Jesus.[18]

In addition to the Olympians, scores of lesser deities, heroes, and supporting characters also find counterparts in *The Acts of Andrew*. From the period of Greek mythological time prior to the Trojan War (where one would also date Heracles) one might mention Oedipus and Jocasta (Sostratus and his lustful mother),[19] Ganymedes (Callistus ['most-beautiful']),[20] Actaeon (the boy ripped by dogs),[21] and Melampus (the seer Exochus ['preeminent']).[22] Argonauts, too, are transvalued: Atalanta is the chaste Trophime ('suckled'),[23] Hylas is the young bathing lover,[24] Orpheus is Anthimus ('blossoms'), and Butes is the man fished from the brine.[25] Phineus, whom the Argonauts rescued from Zeus's punishment, probably is the blind man with a blind wife and son.[26]

Many characters transvalue players in the Trojan War: Agamemnon now appears as the old man who sacrificed his children in the *AAMt* and as the wealthy Sostratus.[27] Menelaus is gift-giving Nicolaus of Philippi,[28] womanizing Nicolaus of Sparta,[29] and one of the two wealthy brothers who married their children to each other.[30] Helen appears in the guise of the whore of Sparta,[31] Nestor of Gerenios as Gratinus the horseman,[32] Philoctetes as the leper at the harbor,[33] Hector as the youth revived at night,[34] and Sarpedon as Adimantus ('fearless'), son of Carpianus (Zeus).[35] The greatest of Homer's Achaeans, Achilles, appears as Leontius ('lionlike'),[36] and as Demetrius ('of Demeter', goddess of the nether gloom), lover of an "Egyptian boy" (Patroclus). The author of *The Acts of Andrew* applied several of Achilles' traits to the Myrmidons as a whole. For example, Homer states that Achilles was thirsty for blood and eager to eat Hector's flesh raw, sacrificed twelve Trojans on Patroclus's huge pyre, dragged Hector's body behind his chariot to mutilate it, and fought the mighty river Scamander. In the *AAMt*, all of the Myrmidons were cannibals; they daily slew victims at their huge outdoor oven; together they dragged Andrew's body through their streets; they all fell prey to the deluge produced from the statue.

A few characters in the *Acts* find correlates in the tragic house of Atreus. The children nearly sacrificed to save their father's hide represent Orestes and

Iphigenia, Agamemnon's children. Philopater ('father-lover'), and Verus ('faithful'), seem to be Orestes and his loyal friend, Pylades.[37]

The Odyssey provided *The Acts of Andrew* its richest store of narrative inspiration. Indeed, the *Acts* as a whole derived its general design from the tale of Odysseus, including a *nostos* ('return'), a *nekyia* ('visit to the netherworld'), several *anagnoriseis* ('recognitions'), and a *mnesterophonia* ('suitor-slaying'). The following delineation involves only the most obvious parallels between the *Acts* and *Odyssey* 1–9. Observe how frequently the parallels in Andrew's *Acts* follow Homer's order.

Odyssey	*Acts of Andrew*
2.265–92: Athena consoles Telemachus.	AAMt 3: Jesus consoles Matthias.
2.407–19: Athena sails in disguise.	AAMt 5–7: Jesus sails in disguise.
3.464–69: Polycaste bathes Telemachus.	GE 5: Woman bathes a youth who then is stricken by a demon.
4.1–18: Double wedding at Sparta.	GE 11: Double wedding at Philippi.
4.589–619: Menelaus's lavish gift to Telemachus.	GE 16: Nicolaus's lavish gift to Andrew.
5.270–80: Odysseus's skillful sailing.	AAMt 8–9: Jesus' skillful sailing.
5.291–450: Storm at sea.	AAMt 8: Storm at sea.
5.451–53: Zeus calms the sea.	AAMt 9: Jesus calms the sea.
7.14–42: Odysseus shrouded in a mist to make him invisible.	Passion 29: Iphidama shrouded in a mist to make her invisible.
8.266–366: Lame Hephaestus traps Ares and Aphrodite.	GE 15: Lame Philomedes had trapped a couple at his home.
8.548–86: Alcinous asks Odysseus to tell his story.	AAMt 10–11: Captain Jesus asks Andrew to tell his story.
9.1–11: Odysseus extols the joys of listening to a bard.	AAMt 11: Captain Jesus rejoices at Andrew's account of Jesus' wonders.

The Acts of Andrew gives special attention to *Odyssey* Book 10 and Homer's Circe, the singing goddess. GE 25 represents her as Calliope ('beautiful voice') "who had slept with a murderer and conceived out of wedlock." This rogue of a mate was Odysseus himself, father of the bastard Telegonus by Circe. More significantly, the author of the *Acts* modeled the frame of the Myrmidon story after Homer's Circe in *Odyssey* Book 10. Here is a breakdown of their shared motifs, in precisely the same order:

Odyssey	*Acts of Andrew*
10.206–9: Odysseus's crew cast lots.	AAMt 1: Apostles cast lots.
10.233–43: Circe's drug turns people into beasts.	AAMt 2: Cannibals' drug turns people into beasts.
10.277–301: Hermes appears to Odysseus as a young man warning him about Circe.	AAMt 18: Jesus appears to Andrew as a young man warning him about the Myrmidons.

10.302–14: Hermes leaves and Odysseus enters Circe's abode.	*AAMt* 18–19: Jesus leaves and Andrew enters Myrmidonia.
10:382–99: Circe restores the crew to their former condition.	*AAMt* 21: Andrew restores the prisoners to their former condition.
10.467–11.3: Odysseus leaves Circe's island for the netherworld.	*AAMt* 33: Andrew leaves Myrmidonia, perhaps for the netherworld.

The Acts of Andrew also targeted *Odyssey* Book 11, the famous *nekyia*. Four separate and sizable units of text looked to the *nekyia* for inspiration: (1) the journey of the sphinx to summon the dead patriarchs, (2) the Myrmidonian tour of hell, (3) three episodes at Amasia narrated in GE 2–4 (Tiresias, Achilles and Patroclus, Oedipus and Jocasta), and (4) Andrew's dream concerning his planted cross. (In the parallels listed below, none is given from the Myrmidonian tour of hell since the text of this tour has not survived.)

Odyssey	*Acts of Andrew*
11.23–36: Odysseus digs a pit and fills it with blood.	*AAMt* 22 (cf. 31): The Myrmidons had built a pit into which ran the blood of their victims.
11.36–50: The dead gather at the pit, so many that Odysseus forces them to stand back.	*AAMt* 15: The twelve patriarchs come forth from their tombs; the sphinx sends back all but three.
11.90–96: The soul of blind Tiresias comes and recognizes Odysseus.	GE 2: A blind man comes and recognizes Andrew.
11.100–137: Tiresias tells Odysseus what will happen back in Ithaca advises him to plant his oar in the ground in order to die in peace.	*AAMt* 20 (cf. Passion 53–54): John tells Andrew what will happen in Patras and and advises him to look for the planted cross; there he will die.
11.271–80: Odysseus sees the soul of Jocasta, mother of Oedipus, who killed herself on learning of her crime.	GE 4: Andrew confronts the lustful mother of Sostratus, who accused her son of seeking sex with her. The authorities punished Sostratus as a parricide. God saved him but slew his mother.
11.467–503: Odysseus sees Achilles with his loving comrade, Patroclus.	GE 3: Andrew meets Demetrius, whose "Egyptian boy" had died. Andrew raises him.

The sole parallel to *Odyssey* Book 12 involves Odysseus's strapping himself to his mast and sailing past the Sirens. Similarly, Andrew was tied to his cross as his soul sped on to its true homeland (Passion 54).

When Odysseus ceased telling his long tale to the Phaeacians, he took his leave of them, prayed for them, shared a drink, and left for Ithaca (13.41–65). A strikingly similar scene appears in GE 20: after Andrew revealed his dream to his converts in Thessalonica, he prayed for them, celebrated the Eucharist, and left for Patras. Compare also the voyage of Odysseus to Ithaca with that of Andrew to Myrmidonia. The order of presentation is identical.

Odyssey	*Acts of Andrew*
13.75–80: Odysseus falls asleep on a ship.	*AAMt* 16: Andrew falls asleep on a ship.
13.116–25: The sailors deposit Odysseus, still asleep, on the shore.	*AAMt* 16–17: The angelic crew deposit Andrew and his disciples, still asleep, at Myrmidonia.
13.187–97: Odysseus awakes on shore of Ithaca and looks around.	*AAMt* 17: Andrew awakes at the gate of Myrmidonia and looks around.
13.221–36: Athena appears to Odysseus in the form of a young man to explain the situation.	*AAMt* 18: Jesus appears to Andrew in the form of a young man to explain the situation.

In *Odyssey* Book 15 Homer embeds a short narrative about the ancient seer Melampus, who owned an excellent house (ἔξοχα δώματα) and was persecuted by his own kin (225–41). Melampus appears in the *Acts* as young Exochus with the huge house and wicked parents (GE 12).

The interplay between *Odyssey* 17–22 and Andrew's passion is so intricate that a list of comparisons can hardly do them justice. Suffice it to say that Maximilla transvalues Penelope by inviting Andrew and company into her bedroom and by refusing sex with her own husband. Stratocles reverses the development of Telemachus by first appearing as a soldier, then seeking education, and finally becoming like an infant.[38] The proconsul Aegeates represents Odysseus insofar as he returns from a long journey, finds a crowd of men in his wife's bedroom, and, raging "like a lion," tries to kill them (Passion 13). Later, he does indeed kill his primary rival, the apostle.

Even minor characters in the passion call to mind residents of Ithaca. Andrew's host, Sosius, and Maximilla's servants, Iphidama and Euclia, display resemblances to Odysseus's servant, Eumaeus, and Penelope's servants, Eurycleia and Melantho.[39] The punishment of Euclia in Passion 22 points to the punishment of Melanthius in *Odyssey* 22.475–77. Throughout Passion 1–50 Andrew encourages his auditors to recognize their true nature. These self-recognitions transform the recognitions of Odysseus that dominate the second half of *The Odyssey*.

Interwoven with these characterizations drawn from *The Odyssey* is Andrew's depiction as a Christianized Socrates modeled after Plato's Socratic dialogues. Like Socrates, Andrew saw it as his task to ask penetrating questions of the young in order to trouble their souls into enlightenment. Thus Andrew, no "novice to midwifery [maieutics] or divination" (Passion 7), repeatedly questioned the young Stratocles about his inner self in order to produce labor pains. The parallels to Plato's *Theaetetus*, where the philosopher most fully presents Socrates' midwifery, jump out at the reader in Passion 7–9 and 42–43. The proconsul's accusation that the apostle had corrupted his wife by preaching this new god was modeled after a similar charge against Socrates.[40] When Aegeates ordered

Andrew crucified, he used the unusual verb ἀνασκολοπίζειν, 'to impale', which harks back to Plato's discussion of the suffering of the righteous in *Republic* 2.361e–362a (Passion 51). On the way to his cross, Andrew preached about the soul's flight to god by using the simile of an eagle, apparently inspired by Socrates' simile of the chariot in *Phaedrus* 246a–256d (Passion 53a). The most obvious parallels between Andrew's passion and Socrates pertain to Plato's *Phaedo*. Compare the following and notice the relatively few deviations in order.

	Plato's *Phaedo*	Andrew's Passion
Visitors at the prison	59d–60a	28b–29a
The immortality of soul	64–81	56–58
Separation of soul and body	64c	56
Pleasures of eating	64d	56
Pleasures of sex	64d	56
Possessions	64d	56–57
Care for externals	64e	57
Fellowship with body	67a	57
Teacher going ahead to afterlife	67b–c	57
The philosopher longs for release	67d–68a	61–62
Fate of pure souls	80d–81a	58
Fate of impure souls	81a–b	58
The laughing martyr	84d–e	55
Food and bodily bulk	96c	56
The hero's death, "we wept"	117c–d	63[41]

Of course, some of the points of hypertextual contact presented here are stronger than others. When identifications are uncertain, they almost always appear in passages retained only by Gregory's drastic epitome or in passages missing entirely. The more secure the text, as in the *AAMt* and the Passion, the more obvious its classical antecedents.

Even if one were to disqualify three-fourths of the evidence argued for here, the remaining quarter would demonstrate more investment in transforming Greek mythology than one can find in all previous Christian narrative combined. What is more, the appropriation of Greek myth is consistent. Andrew overpowers the vices of gods and heroes or converts them into Christian virtues: Myrmidons become vegetarians, Oedipus refuses his mother, Menelaus stops chasing women, Aphrodite becomes chaste, Ares abandons his weapons. Mythological characters with physical ailments find healing from Christ, like lame Hephaestus, blind Tiresias, and fetid Philoctetes. Heroes slain now revive, such as Actaeon, Patroclus, Hector, and Sarpedon. The author intensified the virtues of mythological characters and applied them to the apostle or other of Christ's faithful: Orpheus ≈ Anthimus, Penelope ≈ Maximilla, Atalanta ≈ Trophime. In each case, the author accomplished these transformations through recharacterization and plot manipulation.

The author also consistently employed certain devices to alert the reader to the

Acts' hypotextual target. The most common device was proper nouns (e.g., Myrmidonia ≈ Myrmidons, Nicolaus ≈ Menelaus, Varianus ≈ Zeus, Aristobula ≈ Hera, Anthimus ≈ Orpheus, Lesbius ≈ Dionysus, Stratocles ≈ Telemachus). In some instances, the geographical setting provides the clues (Amasia for the netherworld, Macedonia for the Olympians, Achaea for Greek heroes, Patras for residents of Odysseus's Ithaca). If one tests the hypothesis for hypertextuality against the criterion of density and order, it passes with flying colors.

Explanatory Value

One might agree that the *Acts* satisfies the first criterion but nevertheless rightly complain that critics often have exaggerated the interpretive utility of literary influence. As long as one can account for a text as its stands on its own, one should avoid appealing to sources or prototypes. True enough, but *The Acts of Andrew* simply does not make reasonable sense when read in isolation. In fact, it was the very incomprehensibility of a surface reading that teased me to look for a richer perspective in the first place.

Why, for example, does the *Acts* begin by sending Andrew to Achaea and almost immediately fetch him to rescue Matthias from Myrmidonia? Andrew's brief, uneventful stint in Greece appears to be entirely gratuitous; Jesus could have appeared to the apostle while he was still in Jerusalem, just as he did to Peter in *The Acts of Peter*. Furthermore, Myrmidonia never was a historical place, and efforts to identify it with Scythian Myrmekion force the proverbial square peg into a round hole.

Why, then, did the author narrate his first story in cannibalistic Never Land? And why does the apostle die in Patras, a city with no visible anterior connections with Andrew, no proconsul, and no Christian community until more than a century later? Why the high density of Greek names in the *Acts*, proportionately larger than those in the other apocryphal Acts? Even the names of the Roman proconsuls Lesbius and Aegeates are Greek. And why does the author sometimes invent names, like Gratinus and Aegeates? Why does Andrew spend so much time in Macedonia, which occupies most of his energies on his return journey? And why does Andrew take a short tour of the Peloponnese after arriving in Patras? Why does Aegeates insist on tying Andrew to his seaside cross? These and scores of other peculiarities have no obvious solution if one reads the text in isolation or against probable historical circumstances. Whatever its liabilities, the hypothesis for transvaluative hypertextuality as advanced here provides a consistent and plausible answer to each of these difficulties.

I would never suggest that this hypothesis accounts for every aspect of the text, nor would I doggedly defend every mythological identification suggested in this volume. But I would insist that a surface reading of the *Acts* presents the reader with difficult interpretive challenges, challenges best met by reading the text against Euripides, Plato, and, above all, Homer.

Accessibility

When one asserts that one text recast another, one must be willing to test that assertion against evidence concerning the physical distribution of the earlier, targeted text. The wider the distribution, the more copies in circulation, and the greater its role in cultural institutions, the more plausible the case for its influence on later literature. Conversely, a case for the influence of an obscure text must be considered less likely.

As reasonable as this criterion might seem at first, satisfying it is no easy matter; manuscript distribution in the ancient world remains largely invisible. Even though fragments survive of hundreds of manuscripts whose content one can correlate with allusions to texts in later writings, both types of evidence— physical and literary—present the interpreter with difficulties. Physical evidence survives from relatively few areas of the Mediterranean, most abundantly from Egypt, and may reflect the accident of manuscript survival rather than the popularity of their contents. Likewise, literary allusions are not always what they seem at first, for they may not derive directly from their apparent source but from any number of intervening media, such as memory, tradition, handbooks of quotations, partial copies, scholia, or commentaries. For good reason, then, scholars of ancient literature exercise caution when attempting to map intertextual influence. The reader of the present volume may suspect that I have tossed all such caution to the wind, recklessly drawing parallels and claiming literary dependence with little regard to the complexities of the physical distribution of books in the ancient world or the various media that might explain the relationship of one text to another. Let me here defend myself.

If any literature other than the Bible satisfies the criterion of accessibility it is Homeric epic. The physical evidence, the density of citations, and the privileged status of the epics in Greek education guarantee the plausibility of its influence. This said, one must acknowledge that even copies of Homer were not easy to come by. Moreover, materially, the epics are not two works but forty-eight; each book or "song" occupied a separate scroll, and individual scrolls often circulated independently. Some copies of the poems, therefore, may have been incomplete. More important, parallels between Homer and later literature could result not only from direct imitation but also from memory or other means.

Many of the parallels argued for in this volume may be attributed to the author's memory or to the general knowledge of the epics in Greek-speaking civilizations; in such cases one need not assume the author had consulted a text. In several instances, however, the points of contact are so complex, so literary, and so subtle that the author either knew the epics nearly by heart or, more likely, had access to manuscripts of several books. With respect to *The Iliad*, the author probably consulted a copy of Book 21, Achilles' fight with the Scamander, and perhaps Books 22 and 23, the dragging of Hector's corpse. The author's use of *The Odyssey* was far more extensive, and he probably had access to Books 2, 5, 8–11, 13, 17–22, and perhaps 3, 4, 7, 12, and 15—thirteen to eighteen of the twenty-four books. Lest this appear to be an implausibly high number, one might note that the writings of Clement of Alexandria demonstrate an intimacy with even more of the forty-eight Homeric Books than I have argued for here.

I have also argued for access to books other than Homer's epics, including several plays by Euripides—*The Bacchae* and *The Madness of Heracles*, and perhaps also *Iphigenia at Aulis, Iphigenia in Tauris*, and his lost *Philoctetes* (or that of Sophocles). Even though Euripides' plays never rivaled Homer's epics in popularity, more fragments of his plays survive than of any other Greek playwright. Once again Clement provides evidence that he knew each of these plays, including the *Philoctetes*.

I have also insisted that the author knew and consciously used the following of Plato's Socratic dialogues: *Theaetetus, Phaedrus, Phaedo*, and perhaps *The Republic* and *Crito*. Several of Plato's dialogues virtually disappeared from scholarly discussions during the early Roman empire, even among Platonists. There is not much evidence for the *Crito*, for example, but the other four dialogues mentioned here (together with the *Timaeus*) formed a veritable canon of Platonism. Had the Christian Platonist who wrote *The Acts of Andrew* known any of Plato's dialogues, these are the ones; Clement unquestionably knew them.

Frequently I cited parallels between the *Acts* and the tale of the Argonauts, which found its most famous expression in *The Argonautica* by Apollonius of Rhodes. The author may have consulted *The Argonautica* (copies circulated widely) but one need not insist on such direct contact in order to explain the overlapping episodes and characterizations that display no striking lexical or sequential affinities.

To be sure, few Christian authors of the late second century had access to the kind of library argued for here. On the other hand, none of these works was obscure; each found its place of privilege in what one might call the Great Books curriculum for Greek education in the Roman empire. Each could have been as accessible to the author of Andrew's *Acts* as they were to Clement.

Analogy

More than any other book of the ancient world, *The Odyssey* has been the favorite target for hypertextual rewritings.[42] It almost certainly inspired three lost *Nostoi*, as well as the epics *Margites* and *Telegonia*. Its influence on Apollonius's *Argonautica*, Virgil's *Aeneid*, Ovid's *Metamorphoses*, and Ps.-Dictys' diary of the Trojan War is transparent. The very origins of the Greek historical novel may be traced to Homer's Odyssean epic.[43]

Three ancient novels provide the closest analogies to the kind of fiction we encounter in *The Acts of Andrew* insofar as each of them not only imitates *The Odyssey* but stakes its success, in part at least, on its readers' ability to interpret its Homeric hypertextuality. Each of them used proper nouns for their primary indicators of their indebtedness to Homer. All three novels were composed within approximately one hundred years prior to the *Acts*: Petronius's *Satyricon*, Lucian's *True Story*, and Apuleius's *Metamorphoses*.

Petronius, a bon vivant of the late first century C.E. satirized—one might better say satyrized—Odysseus's adamantine endurance and Penelope's chastity in order to lampoon the hypocritical pomposity of Roman high society. Petronius narrated the amorous misadventures of a young rhetorician named Encolpius ('Crotch') and his male lover, Giton. Their escapades send them through the bedrooms of Pannychis ('all-night-long'), Oenothea ('goddess-of-wine'), Tryphaena ('licentiousness'), and a vixen named Circe. They also meet opposition from Trimalchio ('trebly-rich'), Lichas (called a Cyclops), an incompetent, would-be epic poet named Eumolpus ('sweet-singer'), and professors of rhetoric named Agamemnon and Menelaus. A Penelope figure, renowned for chastity, is easily seduced. Giton, in order to avoid detection by a jealous lover, hooked his hands and feet into the webbing under a bed, "just as Odysseus once escaped the searching fingers of the Cyclops by clinging to the ram's belly."[44]

Much of *The Satyricon* is a parody of the consequences of Odysseus's offending Poseidon by blinding his son, Polyphemus. It tells how Encolpius offended Priapus, the god of the phallus, by killing his sacred goose. Priapus punished Encolpius with flaccidity in the only organ Encolpius seems to have cared about, and which he spent much of his energy—and many pages—to stiffen. Just as Odysseus had tasted Poseidon's "bitterness and rage," Encolpius lamented, so "now upon me too, Priapus's restless hatred falls, hounding me on, over land and sea, on and on, relentlessly on."[45] Only when he repented and gave homage to Priapus did his starch return, a burlesque of Odysseus's obligatory sacrifice to Poseidon in order to die in peace. One also reads of cannibalism, shipwreck, pirates, and magic.

For the most part, the romances, including the *Satyricon*, located their adventures in actual regions of the *oikoumene*, in unusual but generally plausible circumstances, among realistic buffoons, lushes, vamps, rakes, and pirates. Other novelists, however, imagined worlds as unimaginable as Odysseus's.[46] Perhaps the best exemplar of this genre is Lucian's *True Story* (second century C.E.), which parodies the novels of Ctesias and Iambulus,[47] and probably that of Antonius Diogenes, too.[48] In addition to these authors,

[m]any others, with the same intent, have written about imaginary travels and journeys of theirs, telling of huge beasts, cruel men and strange ways of living. Their guide and instructor in this sort of charlatanry is Homer's Odysseus, who tells Alcinous and his court about winds in bondage, one-eyed men, cannibals and savages; also about animals with many heads, and transformations of his comrades wrought with drugs [viz. by Circe]. This stuff, and much more like it, is what our friend humbugged the illiterate Phaeacians with![49]

Not to be outdone by Homer or his novelistic copycats, Lucian set out to lie more than any of them, pressing the genre to its limits and thereby supplying hilarious testimony concerning what ancient authors thought constituted imitations of *The Odyssey*: gales, shipwrecks, cannibals, fabulous creatures, visits to the netherworld, and successful homecomings.[50]

The closest pagan analogy to *The Acts of Andrew* came from the pen of another Platonist. Apuleius of Madauros in north Africa, like the author of the *Acts*, dubbed himself a philosopher and chose to write a novel in order to express religious and philosophical sentiments. Apuleius probably penned the *Metamorphoses* between 178 and 190 C.E., just a few years prior to *The Acts of Andrew*. Although composed in Latin, the book purports to be "a Grecian tale."[51] Indeed, Apuleius drastically modified a Greek story, originally written by Lucian, concerning a certain Lucius whose curiosity for magic led to his transformation into an ass. In Apuleius's version, Lucius remained in this condition until the end of the novel, when Isis took mercy on him and returned him into his original state.

Apuleius borrowed tales-types, characterizations, and entire episodes not only from Lucian's novel but from a wide variety of other Greek sources, including *The Odyssey*.[52] Indeed, Lucius relates his own sufferings to those of the king of Ithaca.[53] Like the author of *The Acts of Andrew*, Apuleius loved loading proper nouns with significance. He named a seductress Pamphile ('lover of all'), a banker Chryseros ('lover of gold'), a charlatan soothsayer Diophanes ('Zeus-revealing'), a salesman Cerdo ('profit'), a coward Thelyphron ('female-minded'), a sponsor of gladiatorial games Demochares ('crowd-pleaser'), a robber nursed on human blood Haemus ('blood'), a licentious priest with a preference for young boys Philebus ('youth-lover'), a rake Philesitherus ('fond of woman-chasing'), and a reliable but stupid slave Myrmex ('ant').[54]

At least once he used a name as a hypertextual indicator that a tale was a rewriting of a story from *The Odyssey*. Odysseus told Alcinous the following episode concerning a tragedy that took place just as he was about the set out for the netherworld.

> There was one, Elpenor, the youngest of all, not over valiant (ἄλκιμος) in war nor sound of understanding, who had laid him down apart from his comrades in the sacred house of Circe, seeking the cool air, for he was heavy with wine. He heard the noise and the bustle of his comrades as they moved about, and suddenly sprang up, and forgot to go to the long ladder that he might come down again, but fell headlong from the roof, and his neck was broken away from the spine, and his spirit went down to the house of Hades.[55]

When Odysseus conjured up the dead, the first soul to meet him was "unfortunate" Elpenor's, who begged the hero to return to Circe's island to give him a proper burial.

Apuleius tells a tale about another hapless youth, named Alcimus, the very word that Homer had used in describing Elpenor as "not valiant (ἄλκιμος)." In the middle of the night, Alcimus sneaked into the home of an old woman and right into her upstairs bedroom. Out of the window and to his comrades below he threw all of her belongings, and then in his greed rolled the woman out of her cot so he could throw it out too. The old woman tricked him to look out the window, and then pushed him out to his death. His comrades gave him no burial, but cast his body into the sea. Thus Alcimus, like Elpenor, "could not attract the approving nod of Fortune."[56] Apuleius's rewriting of Homer's story of Elpenor is a similar type of hypertextual activity that characterizes *The Acts of Andrew*. One also finds evidence in *The Metamorphoses* of the influence of Calypso,[57] Nestor and Polycaste,[58] Circe,[59] and Polyphemus.[60]

Furthermore, Apuleius, like the author of *The Acts of Andrew*, used fiction, including allegory, to express his distinctive version of religious Platonism.[61] The center of the novel consists of a magnificent Platonic allegory of the soul in the guise of Psyche ('soul') and Cupid (= Eros, 'love').[62] The allegory anticipates Lucius's salvation by Isis that dominates the end of the novel. A character named Socrates is a rogue whose only concerns are bodily comforts.[63] At other points the novelist seems to have had in mind the depiction of Socrates' death in the *Phaedo*.[64]

Like their pagan contemporaries, Jews and Christians, too, imitated Homeric epic, especially *The Odyssey*. Little survives from the dactylic hexameters of the Jews Theodotus, Philo Epicus, and Sosates, but what does survive shows unmistakable influence of Homer. Soon I hope to publish a description of the role *The Odyssey* played in the composition of the Book of Tobit, the Gospel of Mark, and the Acts of Luke. In the second century, Christians began writing centones on Christian topics by pasting together Homeric lines into an original creation. The late third-century *Vision of Dorotheus*, the earliest of all Christian hexametric poems, betrays reliance on Homer in nearly every line. The rewriting of Homer became a popular literary practice among Christians of the fourth and fifth centuries. Examples include Apollinarius of Laodicea's twenty-four books on the hexateuch, Gregory of Nazianzus's poetry, Ps.-Nonnos's recasting of the Gospel of John into hexameters, Eudocia's poems on various Christian themes, and Musaeus's hexametric allegory on the soul's ascent to God. The claim that *The Acts of Andrew* is a Christian *Odyssey* places it within one of the most vibrant literary traditions of the Roman empire and thus satisfies the criterion of analogy.

Furthermore, by replacing the virility, violence, and wealth of Homer's Odysseus with Andrew's celibacy, gentleness, and penury, *The Acts of Andrew* distinguishes itself from other ancient hypertexts of *The Odyssey*, none of which transvalued it so completely. The author of *The Telegonia*, Virgil, and Ps.-Dictys criticized Homer's Odysseus not to advance a set of ideals different from those of the heroic age but simply to show that Odysseus had not lived up to them. *The Argonautica* and the Hellenistic romances, whose characters often embody un-Homeric virtues, did not intentionally devalue or transvalue the likes of Odysseus and Penelope. They are rather thematic—and, in the case of *The Argonautica*, also poetic—imitations that quite naturally and unpolemically groomed their characters for a more romantic, less heroic readership. Even Petronius, whose characters' lax moral values had little in common with Homer's, did not challenge the ethics of *The Odyssey*. He contrasted his own licentious characters with Homer's not to promote hedonism as an answer to the rigorous morality of Greek epic but rather to mock the flabby and flatulent hypocrisy of his contemporaries by drawing sham comparisons with truly heroic greatness.[65] Even this interpretation may be too moralistic; Petronius wrote for a belly roar, not for a change of heart. The goal of *The Acts of Andrew* was more radical by far: the author rewrote *The Odyssey* in order to transvalue all of classical mythology.

Motivation

This criterion concerns the ability of the interpreter to answer the question: Why did the author go to the trouble of rewriting the alleged hypotext? By now the answer to this question should be obvious: the author wanted to claim the best of classical Greek antiquity for the Christian cause, and to distance it from the worse.

Among both pagan and Christian authors of the second and third centuries, no mythological figure—with the possible exception of Heracles—enjoyed greater popularity than Odysseus, and no philosopher inspired greater admiration than Socrates. To Stoics Odysseus was the champion of resolute fortitude against pleasures and passions; to Cynics he was the philosopher in rags; to rhetoricians he was the pinnacle of eloquence, the "man of many tropes"; to Neoplatonists he was a cipher for the soul afloat in γένεσις, longing to return to its true, noumenal *patria*. Christians, too, admired him, and drew parallels between his being tied to the mast and Christ nailed to the cross.

They also perceived analogies between the crucifixion of Jesus, their own persecutions, and the death of Socrates. Like the barefoot philosopher, the followers of Christ had attacked the Olympians for their immorality, had suffered abuse for allegedly corrupting the young, and had even died for their convictions, emboldened to do so by their confidence in the immortality of the soul. By portraying Andrew, the former fisherman, as a Christian Odysseus and Socrates, the author of the *Acts* filled him with content derived from classical Greek literature that was most congenial to the new religious movement. The author's adoption of ancient Greek worthies did not stop with Odysseus and Socrates. Andrew absorbs attributes also from Heracles. The suffering prophet Melampus now is the eloquent preacher Exochus; the great musician Orpheus comforts the brethren in the guise of Anthimus; Penelope, the great model of σωφροσύνη, finds her virtues intensified in Maximilla.

The author of the *Acts* also rewrote Greek classical literature in order to answer pagan accusations of Christian cannibalism and Oedipal sex, accusations that occupied the attention of second- and third-century apologists. The story of the Myrmidons depicts Homer's heroes themselves as cannibals. The mission to "the city of the barbarians" may have included an apostolic confrontation with the homicidal altar of Artemis at Tauris. Christians were not cannibals; pagans were. Several Christian apologists scoffed at Artemis of Tauris in order to make the same point.[66] Similarly, the story of the young Sostratus and his incestuous mother, a transformation of the myth of Oedipus and Jocasta, suggests that Christians rejected out of hand such unnatural unions.[67]

Most episodes of the *Acts*, however, seek neither to absorb the positive aspects of classical Greek tradition nor to shed pagan accusations of cannibalism and incest but rather to attack Greek myths as monuments to immorality. In many cases, the targets of these attacks are the same ones shot at by Plato's Socrates and Christian apologists. One might group the author's primary objections to Greek mythology into three categories: (1) physical disfigurement or death, (2) sex, and (3) violence.

In several episodes Andrew heals, exorcises, or raises back to life characters who had suffered in Greek mythology. Andrew restores sight to a blind man, old Tiresias, whom Hera had blinded. He revives Achilles' lover Patroclus; Actaeon, slain by Artemis and his own dogs; Sarpedon, the son of grieving but helpless Zeus; and Hector, victim of Athena's deceit. He heals lame Hephaestus, crippled by his own Olympian father, blind Phineas (another of Zeus's victims), and ulcerous Philoctetes. Characters notorious for madness now are liberated of their demons: raging Ares, crazed Dionysus, and mad Heracles.

The author's most persistent complaint against Greek gods and heroes pertains to their mating habits. One instance, already mentioned, involves Oedipus and Jocasta. Polycaste's scandalous bathing of Telemachus results in the lad's demon-possession until Andrew vanquishes the demon. In the guise of Aristobula, Hera no longer seeks to seduce her husband. Helen now is a virgin; Aphrodite stops her affairs; Circe suffers for having conceived illegitimate Telegonus; Menelaus finally bridles his womanizing; Penelope's chastity becomes heightened such that she forswears sex even with her husband. The *Acts* also rejects homoeroticism. The clearest example is that of Heracles and Hylas. The author also seems to have transformed the story of Achilles and his lover, Patroclus, whom the apostle raised back to life.

Finally, the author of the *Acts* also opposed Homer's depictions of warring gods and savage warriors. By portraying the Myrmidons as cannibals who slew their victims at a huge furnace and who dragged Andrew's body about for three days, the author scoffed at the violent barbarism of *The Iliad*. Homer's Achilles, the leader of the Myrmidons, wanted to eat Hector's flesh raw, slew twelve Trojans like cattle at the great pyre for Patroclus, and dragged Hector's corpse about for days. Agamemnon slew his own daughter in order to advance the Achaean cause, but in the *Acts*, Andrew's god forbids such slaughter of children and shows a counter-Agamemnon the horrors of Hell reserved for such pedicides. At "the city of the cannibals" Andrew may have halted human sacrifices to Artemis. Several victims of the savagery of the Trojan War win back their lives: Patroclus, Hector, and Sarpedon. Andrew exorcised a young soldier writhing in possession, a stand-in for Ares. On regaining his wits, he immediately abandoned his arms. Whereas Homer's Telemachus develops from an infant into a warrior who bagged his quota of suitors, Stratocles develops from a soldier into a spiritual infant through Andrew's midwifery. In the end, Stratocles renounces wealth, office, and violence.

For many of these episodes, one can find Plato or Christian apologists articulating the same objections to Homer's gods and heroes that I am arguing for here. There can be little doubt, then, that the author of *The Acts of Andrew* had a plausible and compelling motivation for such a thorough rewriting of classical Greek literature. He urged the reader to compare the worst of traditional pagan religion with the best of Christianity and to choose the later over the former. Ought one worship gods who blind, maim, fornicate, and murder, or the God of Andrew, who heals and revives? Ought one chose a life of violence and wanton sex, or a life of peace and chastity?

The hypothesis of this book satisfies all five criteria that one might apply to any claim of the influence of one text on another. Perhaps now at last one can assess the import of this reading of *The Acts of Andrew* for an understanding of early Christian life and literature.

Implications

Several important implications follow from this assessment of the literary strategies of the *Acts*.

The Acts of Andrew and Matthias in the City of the Cannibals

Jean-Marc Prieur concludes his discussion of the relationship between the *AAMt* and the rest of *The Acts of Andrew* with this statement: "Pour toutes ces raisons, nous estimons que le récit de la délivrance de Matthias par André n'a jamais fait partie des *AA*. Il a vu le jour en grec, comme un texte indépendant, celui des *AAMt*, qui faisait partie d'un groupe particulier d'apocryphes."[68] Earlier interpreters favored including the *AAMt* in their reconstructions of Andrew's *Acts*, in large part because Gregory presented a drastically shrunken version of it as the first story in his epitome. But Joseph Flamion's landmark study in 1911 convinced most specialists, including Prieur, that Gregory (or the Latin translation he epitomized) artificially combined two separate Andrean texts. According to Flamion, the original *Acts of Andrew* sent the apostle from Jerusalem west through Asia Minor to Achaea, that is, from GE 2, the healing of the blind man in Amasia, up to and including the apostle's burial in Patras. Centuries later, an Egyptian monk familiar with Andrew's associations with Achaea, created the story of his leaving Achaea in order to deliver Matthias from cannibals. *The Acts of Andrew and Matthias*, therefore, belongs not at the beginning of *The Acts of Andrew* but to a set of later apostolic apocrypha, which Flamion dubbed "the Egyptian Cycle" (viz. *The Acts of Peter and Andrew*, *The Martyrdom of Matthew*, the Old Slavonic *Act of Peter*, and so-called *Acts of Thomas–B*).

The introduction to my edition advanced detailed arguments against Flamion and Prieur; to rehearse them here would unnecessarily prolong this discussion. Suffice it to say that my emphasis there was on external witnesses that included the Myrmidon story at the beginning of the *Acts*. Gregory was by no means the only person to have known of this combination; so did the authors of the Greek Andrean passions known as *Narratio* and *Martyrium prius*, the homilist behind a fifth-century encomium to Andrew, as well as Epiphanius the Monk, Nicetas the Paphlagonian, Photius, and several later Byzantine historians. I further argued that one can find traces of *The Acts of Andrew*, including the *AAMt*, in *The Acts of Thomas*, *The Acts of Philip*, and *The Acts of John by Prochorus*.[69]

To this evidence I now would add what I consider the most conclusive argument of all. If one takes only the undisputed content of the *Acts*, GE 2 to the end of the Passion, one finds ample indications of the author's transvaluation of *The Odyssey* and other classical Greek literature. This hypertextual strategy distinguishes *The Acts of Andrew* from most early Christian books. Furthermore, the strategy is so consistent in the *Acts* that any additional content attributed to it must contribute to the same hypertextual project. The story of the Myrmidons not only contributes to a rewriting of Homer and shares the distinctive transformative techniques found in undisputed sections of the *Acts* but it also forms a necessary introduction to the entire enterprise. Without it, there would be no *nostos*, for Andrew would never have been in Achaea prior to GE 22. Furthermore, there would be no parallels to Achilles and his Myrmidons, to Agamemnon and Iphigenia, to the dragging of Hector's corpse, or to Achilles' fight with the River. There also would be no evidence pointing to a lost *nekyia*. Indeed, the *AAMt* is the Christianized *Iliad* one should expect to have preceded the Christianized *Odyssey* that characterizes the rest of the *Acts*. One might even say that had Gregory and others never attested to the inclusion of the Myrmidon story at the beginning of the *Acts*, literary considerations alone would provide sufficient reason for combining them.

To these arguments I would add one more. Charges and countercharges of cannibalism between pagans and Christians belong to the controversies of the second and third centuries, not to the fourth and fifth, when Flamion and Prieur would date their independent *AAMt*. From Athenagoras and Justin to Tertullian and Minucius Felix, Christian apologists felt obligated to address accusations of anthropophagy and quickly pointed out that more evidence existed for cannibalism among pagans than among Christians. The *AAMt* addresses this matter as though it were a current and vital concern; by the beginning of the fourth century it was passé.

The Apocryphal Acts

"The five earliest apocryphal acts, the Acts of Paul, Thomas, Peter, Andrew, and John, were composed anonymously between A.D. 175 and 225, and are examples of *popular* literature written by and for lower-class Christians."[70] David E. Aune is not alone in his characterization of the apocryphal Acts as literature of the Great Unwashed. Other scholars have also devalued the literary value of these books, either through negative comparisons with the canonical Acts or by appealing to pejorative assessments of Greek historical novels in general. In the case of *The Acts of Andrew*, this caricature will no longer do. According to external testimony, it was the work of philosophers, and its content leaves little doubt that its primary author was an intellectual with exceptional knowledge of Greek classics. Furthermore, the text targeted readers capable of discerning, at its deeper levels, subtle transformations of mythology. Although Andrew's *Acts* may be an exception to the rule of apocryphal proletarian composition and consumption, it is an exception that might cause one to reassess the rule itself. Indeed, *The Acts of John*, too, is more sophisticated than Aune's casual assertion would indicate. Be that as it may, the hypothesis concerning *The Acts of Andrew* demonstrates once again the danger of generalizing about the apocryphal Acts. Each Acts is a case unto itself.

Christianizing Homer and Christian Theology

Several questions suggest themselves when one looks at Homer in Byzantium. One is why, for thousands of years, a profoundly Christian society learnt to read with understanding from a poem that was not only couched in an archaic and difficult *Kunstsprache* but was also thoroughly pagan in atmosphere and filled with divine interventions, epiphanies, quarrels between gods, and the like. . . . Homer's *Iliad* and *Odyssey* never lost their place as the school texts par excellence.

Another strategy would have been to Christianize Homer, as Epictetus was Christianized. Systematic allegorical interpretation would have sanitised the venerable pagan poem. Some hesitant steps were taken in that direction, but there was never a Christian Homer as there was an *Ovide moralisé* in the West. Indeed, it would be quite hard for the most single-minded allegoriser to elicit an unambiguous Christian message from the *Iliad*. The *Odyssey* is another matter; it could easily be turned into a kind of *Pilgrim's Progress*.[71]

Robert Browning's explanation for the persistence of epic in Greek education combines "the inertia of the educational tradition" with Homer's role in providing "a kind of shorthand of cultural and ethnic identity."[72]

From the perspective of second-century apologists, however, the immorality of the epics provided an identity solely of shame, and they found in Plato's Socrates ample ammunition for their attacks. In order to refute Homer, they composed philosophical treatises exposing his poems as tissues of fabricated fictions.

Although the author of *The Acts of Andrew* agreed with the apologists in their moral outrage at epic poetry, he recognized the power of narrative and wrote his own epic of sorts in order to supplant Homer's naughty myths with edifying legends. In other words, the author did not begrudge the epics their status as fiction, as apologists did, nor demythologize them into physical or psychological truths, as pagan allegorists did; rather, he *trans*mythologized them. Here one finds the Christianized Homer that Browning claimed never existed. The author's allusions to *The Iliad* are predominantly negative, just as Browning might have guessed, judging from his pessimism about the difficulty of eliciting "an unambiguously Christian message" from it. On the other hand, the parallels with *The Odyssey* are generally positive; it was indeed "turned into a kind of *Pilgrim's Progress*."

In his transmythologizing, the author unabashedly composed fiction and abandoned every pretense of historicity. One reads of cannibals, a tour of hell, the slaying of an monstrous dragon, shipwrecks, demons, and pirates. He expected his readers to enjoy the *Acts* as edifying fiction, not as a documented chronicle of Andrew's career and execution. Its truthfulness pertains not to the accuracy of its historical information but to the ethical vision of its fictional presentation.

Furthermore, the author did not recoil from that aspect of fiction so potentially scandalous to religion—humor. Andrew's favorite meeting place in Patras was Maximilla's bedroom. When Aegeates learned about these boudoir Bible studies, he sprang into the bedroom, sword drawn, in order to slay everyone. Then he "got an urge for a bowel movement, asked for a chamber pot, and spent a long time sitting, attending to himself. He did not notice all the brethren exit in front of him" (GE 13). Maximilla decided she could no longer sleep with Aegeates, so she substituted her maid Euclia in her place. Obviously the author did not condone such bed-swapping. He included this widespread folkloric motif because he considered it entertaining.

I suspect that much of what Gregory found so disgusting in *The Acts of Andrew* was its humor. Not a trace of it survives in his grave epitome. Photius, the killjoy of Byzantium, wrote of the *Acts*: "It is stuffed with foolishness. . . . [T]his book contains innumerable childish, improbable, ill-conceived, false, foolish, self-contradictory, profane and godless things."[73] That is, one finds artistic creativity everywhere.

Unlike Photius, one might well admire the author's playful literary license, but one ought not elevate him into a baptized Lucian of Samosata or Apuleius of Madauros. As a narrator, his skills fall short of genius; his Andrew is moralistic, flat, and predictable, clearly no challenge to Homer's Odysseus in complexity or charm. Furthermore, the *Acts* never displaced Homer from his honorable place in Greek παιδεία, not even among Christians. Apart from Manichaeans and a few other groups considered heretical by ecclesiastical authorities, Christian intellectuals assailed *The Acts of Andrew* as ludicrous, heterodox, even diabolical. To the extent that Andrew's *Acts* found respect in the Church, it did so as a textual Osiris, as dismembered flotsam, fragments now and then popping to the surface, much of it now collected, but whole sections apparently lost forever.

But for all its weaknesses, *The Acts of Andrew* is a stunning achievement of theological artistry. It demonstrates that one way to transform culture is to transmythologize it through the reality of fiction, through the gravity of laughter, through the truth of myth.

Notes

1. The devil took the guise of an old man in order to urge the Myrmidons to seek out Andrew and kill him (*AAMt* 24). This episode trades on Zeus's lying dream to Agamemnon in the guise of old Nestor in *Iliad* Book 2.

2. His son Adimantus ('fearless'), had taken sick and would have died had the apostle not intervened (GE 13). Adimantus is the brave Trojan hero Sarpedon, whose death at the hands of Patroclus produced grief in the heart of his divine but helpless father.

3. Medias's son, Philomedes, was lame and he represents the lame god, Hephaestus, whose limping gait aroused sardonic laughter among the gods.

4. GE 18. The name Varianus refers to Zeus's infamous changing of shapes in order to seduce mortal lovers, a practice that won him the contempt of many pagans and Christians alike.

5. Ibid., 18 and 19. The name Aristobula derives from *Iliad* 14.161, where Homer introduces Hera's "good plan" to seduce Zeus so that Achaeans might trounce Trojans. Unlike Hera, Aristobula refuses sex with her husband, Varianus, and suffers for it (GE 18). Somehow (the relevant text does not survive) Andrew rescued Aristobula from her torture.

Myths about Hera lie behind other episodes as well. In GE 2 Andrew heals a man whom the devil had blinded. The blind man probably represents Tiresias, whom Hera had handicapped. GE 29 and Passion 2–5 both narrate exorcisms that trade on Heracles' madness as presented by Euripides in *The Madness of Heracles*. It was Hera who caused Heracles' dementia.

6. GE 15. Hephaestus was married to "laughter-loving Aphrodite (φιλομμειδὴς Ἀφροδίτη)."

7. Ibid., 23.

8. Ibid., 17.

9. Ibid., 18, and *PCU 1*.

10. Passion, passim.

11. GE 22–23.

12. Ibid., 18.

13. Ibid., 19.

14. Ibid., 27.

15. Ibid., 29.

16. Passion 2–5.

17. In GE 25 and perhaps also in the missing episode concerning "the city of the barbarians." Artemis is less visible in GE 7, where Andrew resuscitates a lad slain by seven dogs who were actually demons. Behind this episode is the story of Actaeon, who was ripped to bits by his own hounds as punishment for having peeped at Artemis bathing in the forest.

18. *AAMt* 4–11, 18, and 32. In each instance Jesus reveals himself as a youth, like Hermes and Athena had done in *The Odyssey*.

19. GE 5.

20. Ibid., 6.

21. Ibid., 7.

22. Ibid., 12.

23. Ibid., 23.

24. Ibid., 27.

25. Ibid., 21.

26. Ibid., 32.

27. Ibid., 26.

28. Ibid., 16.

29. Ibid., 28.

30. Ibid., 11.

31. Ibid., 28; see also *PCU 1* (the episode concerning Simon Magus).

32. GE 5.

33. Ibid., 33.

34. GE 14; cf. the dragging of Andrew's body in the *AAMt*.

35. GE 13.

36. Ibid., 3 and 26.

37. Ibid., 24.

38. Cf. especially Passion 1 and *Odyssey* 17.32–39.

39. Cf. also the beggar at the portico in GE 31 and Irus the beggar.

40. Plato *Apology* 24b.

41. This list differs from the one on page 274 insofar as this list follows the order of presentation in the *Phaedo* and ignores other Platonic dialogues.

42. So Genette, *Palimpsestes*, 201.

43. In Chariton's novel (the earliest Greek novel to survive complete, probably first century B.C.E.) suitors plot the dissolution of the marriage between Callirhoe and Chaereas, and a band of pirates steal Callirhoe from Syracuse and sell her to a lecherous slave master. In the end she again finds her husband and returns to Sicily. Throughout the novel, the reader finds similes, allusions, and quotations drawn from Homer. Callirhoe is "more beautiful than the Homeric goddess 'of the white arms and the fair ankles'" (Blake), lovelier than Helen, her wedding "much like that of Thetis," and her adventures far from home like those of Odysseus. She asks her master to play the role of Alcinous, who sent Odysseus home. Chaereas is friend to Polycharmus "just as Patroclus was to Achilles," and they are prepared to fight together "like Homer's heroes." King Artaxerxes convenes

such an "august tribunal one might well say with Homer, 'Now the gods sat by Zeus and held assembly.'" In spite of her grief at his departure, Chaereas' mother conveniently recites a Homeric couplet. According to B. P. Reardon, Chariton "quotes Homer over two dozen times" (*The Form of the Greek Romance* [Princeton: Princeton University Press, 1991], 74, n. 50). See also C. W. Müller, "Chariton von Aphrodisias und die Theorie des Romans in der Antike," *Antike und Abendland* 22 (1976): 115–36.

No less dependent on *The Odyssey* was the romance of Achilles Tatius (ca. 200 C.E.), which sent Clitiphon and Leucippe around the Mediterranean suffering robbers, pirates, cannibals, and shipwrecks before they returned to Byzantium in triumph. Here one finds references to Sirens (1.8.2, 3.10.3, and 6.10.4), Penelope (1.8.6), Odysseus (2.23.3), and Homer himself (2.1.1 and 3.20.4), as well as direct quotations from the epics (1.8.7, 2.15.3, and 36.3). Theagenes and Charicleia, the romantic protagonists of Heliodorus's huge *Aethiopica* (third or fourth century C.E.), outlast robbers, shipwrecks, slavery, pyres, wars, wooers, and human sacrifices at which they themselves were to be gifts to the gods. Heliodorus adopted some of these themes from earlier romances (especially from Achilles Tatius), but he also revealed his hypertextual direct dependence on *The Odyssey* by comparing his characters with Odysseus and Penelope. For example, Theagenes' father, Calasiris, claimed that Odysseus appeared to him in a dream, still recognizable from the scar on his once mighty thigh, warning him: "You will experience afflictions like mine, and encounter enemies by sea and land. But the girl you carry with you [Charicleia] salute in the name of my wife, Penelope, who says she is pleased with her because she values chastity above all else" (Hadas, 129). See also Introduction, 6–7.

44. *Satyricon* (Arrowsmith, 102).

45. Ibid. (Arrowsmith, 161).

46. Ctesias of Cnidos (ca. 400 B.C.E.) wrote a book on India, presenting it as a land of monstrous beasts: unicorn-asses, Greek-speaking birds, huge dogs that fought like lions, and the human-faced, lion-sized "martichora," which threw poisonous darts from its scorpionlike tail. Ctesias translated "martichora" as ἀνθρωποφάγον ('cannibal') because the beast, though not particularly finicky, adored *homo sapiens*. Ferocious griffins guarded vast mountains of gold and silver from which the most daring Indians chipped chunks of fortune. A river flowed with honey. Some trees attracted gold, silver, and gems to their roots, others bore amber, others oozed perfumes. The land was home to barking κυνοκέφαλοι ('dog-heads'), long-haired pygmies who tended miniature cattle, irenic primitives who lived to be two hundred, and savages with eight fingers on each hand.

Iambulus (ca. 100 B.C.E.) wrote of his capture by robbers, a brief sojourn in Ethiopia, and a voyage to a distant utopian island where fruit ripened year round, and which he, quoting from *The Odyssey*, likened to Scheria, the utopian island of the Phaeacians. People there lived to be 150, had flaps covering their large ears, and used their split tongues to conduct two conversations at once.

The Marvels Beyond Thule by Antonius Diogenes (ca. 100 C.E.) was an enormous work of twenty-four books (like *The Iliad* and *The Odyssey*), but now is known only from an epitome (Photius *Bibliotheca* codex 166). Dinias and his son, Demochares, traveled beyond distant Scythia, to the land where the sun rises, to the north pole, and even to the moon, observing along the way Homer's Cimmerians, a Siren's tomb, people blind during the day but sighted at night, and women who fought battles while their husbands kept house. Dinias miraculously returned to Tyre, transported there in his sleep, like Odysseus, who woke up to find himself back on the shores of Ithaca.

Philostratus claimed that during Apollonius's journeys he saw griffins, ferocious ants guarding gold, and Ethiopian tribes called Pygmies, Shadow-feet, and Man-eaters (Ἀνδροφάγοι) (*Life of Apollonius of Tyana* 6.1 and 25). *The Alexander Romance* (ca. 300 C.E.) contains a letter from Alexander the Great to Aristotle telling of gigantic scorpions, bats, wolves, lions, and wild boars, "men with six hands and twisted feet, dog-partridges, and other beastly creatures" (*Alexander Romance* 3.17.20 [Kroll, p. 109]). Lovers in the lost *Babylonica* of Iamblicus (ca. 170–200) lived happily ever after—after escaping crucifixion, ghosts, witches, and a robber fond of human steaks. Only fragments remain of Lollianus's novel *Phoinikika*—just enough to depict barbarians roasting their supper of captured traveler (Albert Henrichs, *Die Phoinikika des Lollianos. Fragmente eines griechischen Romans*, PTA 14 [Bonn: R. Halbelt, 1972]).

47. By his own admission (*True Story* 1.3).

48. According to Photius *Bibliotheca* codex 166.

49. *True Story* 1.3.

50. Lucian sailed past the Pillars of Hercules in quest of "the end of the ocean," but a gale lifted his ship and sent him off to the planets. He saw a war between creatures of the moon and the sun, floating islands, an inhabited ocean in the bowels of a whale, and even the Isle of the Blessed and the Isle of the Wicked. He witnessed a river of wine; a sea of milk with an island of cheese; people with heads of dogs, lobsters, fish, or bulls; women with grapevine arms or with donkey feet; and men with cork feet for walking on the water, or with prodigious endowments useful as masts when they floated on their backs. He observed warriors flying on vultures, sailing on dolphins, riding on ants two hundred feet long or on fleas "as large as twelve elephants." There were uniquely equipped soldiers— garlic-hurlers, millet-shooters, radish-tossing sky-dancers, pirates in pumpkins and nut-sailors in half-shells—gigantic spiders, flying frogs, candle-fish, lamp-people, and, of course, cannibals.

51. *Metamorphoses* 1.1.

52. On Apuleius's Greek sources see H. J. Mason, "Fabula Graecanica: Apuleius and his Greek Sources," in *Aspects of Apuleius' Golden Ass*, ed. B. L. Hijmans, Jr., and R. Th. van der Paardt (Groningen: Bouma's Boekhuis, 1978), 1–15.

53. *Metamorphoses* 9.13 (alluding to *Odyssey* 1.3):

Nowhere was there any consolation for my tortured curiosity, since everyone now took little account of my presence [as an ass] and freely did and said whatever they wished. That divine inventor of ancient poetry among the Greeks [viz. Homer], desiring to portray a hero of the highest intelligence, was quite right to sing of a man who acquired the highest excellence by visiting man cities and learning to know various peoples.

54. For a discussion of names in Apuleius and in Greek literature see B. L. Hijmans, Jr., "Significant Names and Their Function in Apuleius' *Metamorphoses*," in Hijmans and

van der Paardt, *Aspects*, 107–22 .

55. *Odyssey* 10.552–60.

56. *Metamorphoses* 4.12. A. G. Westerbrink discusses Apuleius's playful hypertextuality in "Some Parodies in Apuleius' Metamorphoses," in Hijmans and van der
Paardt, *Aspects*, 63–73.

57. *Metamorphoses* 1.12.

58. Ibid., 1.23–24.

59. Ibid., 2.5.

60. Ibid., 8.12–13. See also the recasting of Actaeon in 2.5, 4.3, and 20.

61. See James Tatum, *Apuleius and The Golden Ass* (Ithaca: Cornell University Press,
1979), esp. 105–34. Frank Regen discusses the fine points of Apuleius's Platonism in
*Apuleius philosophus Platonicus. Untersuchungen zur Apologie (De magia) und zu De
mundo.* Untersuchungen zur antiken Literatur und Geschichte 10 (Berlin: Walter de
Gruyter, 1971). For a treatment of allegory in *The Metamorphoses* see R. Heine,
"Picaresque Novel Versus Allegory," in Hijmans and van der Paardt, *Aspects*, 25–42.

62. *Metamorphoses* 4.28–6.24. This embedded story includes a descent into the
netherworld (6.16–19).

63. Ibid., 1.8–19.

64. Ibid., 1.6–7 and 10.33. Apuleius knew the *Phaedo* intimately: he had translated it
into Latin.

65. William Arrowsmith, *The Satyricon* (New York: New American Library, 1959),
x–xii.

66. E.g., Athenagoras *Legatio* 26.2, Clement of Alexandria *Protrepticus* 3.42.3,
Tertullian *Apology* 9, Minucius Felix *Octavius* 30, Origen *Contra Celsum* 5.27, and
Athanasius *Contra gentes* 25.

67. Incest also played a role in the tale of the double wedding at Philippi (GE 11),
where two brothers were about to marry their children to each other until Andrew came to
talk them out of it.

68. Prieur concludes: "For all these reasons, we suppose that the account of the
deliverance of Matthias by Andrew never formed part of *The Acts of Andrew*. It first saw
light of day in Greek as an independent text, namely the *AAMt*, which formed part of a
particular collection of apocrypha" (*Acta Andreae*, 35).

69. MacDonald, *Acts of Andrew*, 22–47.

70. David E. Aune, *The New Testament in Its Literary Environment*, Library of Early
Christianity (Philadelphia: Westminster, 1987), 141.

71. Browning, "Byzantines and Homer," 146.

72. Ibid., 146–47.

73. *Bibliotheca* codex 114.

Appendix: Andrew's Speech to the Cross

Most scholars have assumed that the mystery of the cross had nothing to do with *The Odyssey* but with a continuation of the speech to the cross in two Greek recensions:

> You have been planted in the world to stabilize the unstable. One of your timbers extends into heaven so that you might symbolize the heavenly word. Your crossbeam spreads to the right and left so that you might put to flight the jealous and opposing power and gather the world into a unity. Your base has been planted into the earth so that you might unite with things in heaven all that is upon the earth and beneath it.[1]

Two considerations, however, make it highly unlikely that this explanation originally appeared in *The Acts of Andrew*. First, it appears in only one strand of a rich manuscript tradition,[2] and there is no apparent reason why the other versions would have omitted such a beautiful and theologically acceptable elucidation.

Second, and more important, the Armenian Passion, which parallels much of this speech, issues from a more primitive textual stratum.[3] In place of the discursive interpretation of the cross's mystery in the Greek version printed above, the Armenian contains enigmas:

> I am learning to recognize your appearance, insofar as you hold yourself erect. I have seen something in you for it is also in me. I describe what is yours, since you are that which I understand, that which I love as I see it, that which I comprehend and perceive of you. What is your shape, O cross? What is your crossbeam? Where is the center? What is invisible in you? What is apparent? To what extent are you hidden? To what extent are you revealed through the cry of your companion?[4]

Of the two versions, the Armenian almost certainly is the earlier. Whereas the Armenian speech asks, "What is your shape?" the Greek provides an answer: "One of your timbers extends into heaven so that you might symbolize the heavenly word." "What is your crossbeam?" in the Armenian becomes "Your crossbeam spreads to the right and left so that you might put to flight the jealous and opposing power and gather the world into a unity." The Armenian question "Where is the center?" seems to find a Greek answer in "Your base has been planted into the earth so that you might unite with things in heaven all that is upon the earth and beneath it." The Greek version also repeatedly dissolves paradox into orthodox commonplace.[5] Conversely, if the Greek continuation of the speech were the more primitive, one would have to assume that the copyist responsible for the text behind the Armenian version, for reasons now invisible, objected to the explanation of the cross's mystery given in his or her source and intentionally obfuscated it. Manuscript replication usually moves in the opposite direction—from opacity to lucidity.

The different versions of this speech seem to have evolved as follows: The original speech did not explicate the mystery of the cross. It probably ended with Andrew's appeal to the cross to receive him. The continuation of the speech in the Armenian may have derived from the pen of a copyist who intensified the mystery of the cross by expanding the speech to include rhetorical questions, paradoxes, and riddles, as if to create a semiotic maelstrom. Still later, someone else copying this expanded version was troubled by an apparent absence of an explanation for the mystery of the cross and answered the rhetorical questions, resolved the paradoxes, and elucidated the riddles by interpreting the cross as a symbol for linking earth and heaven by means of reason, for dispersing evil, and for drawing the extremities into a unity.[6] This explanation of the cross, therefore, derives not from the earliest stage of textual development but from its respectable middle age.[7] The author of *The Acts of Andrew*, however, had expected the reader to see in Andrew's address to the cross a hypertext of Odysseus's planted oar and mast, to which he was lashed. These later scribes failed to see it.

Notes

1. This translation is based on *Martyrium prius*.

2. The two recensions in which this speech appears, *Martyrium prius* and *Laudatio*, do not attest to it independently but both borrow from a common source. This continuation of the speech is entirely unattested in *Martyrium alterum*, *SH*, *Ann Arbor 36*, Epiphanius the Monk, *Conversante et docente*, and the three versions of *Passio*.

3. *Narratio* likewise contains two possible echoes of the hymn to the cross, but they are too faint to demonstrate any genetic relationship.

4. Translated from Leloir's French translation (*Écrits apocryphes*, 1.242–43).

5. The Armenian version includes *inter alia* the following paradoxes, none of which is retained as a paradox in the Greek versions:

Well done, intelligent form,
    born of an intelligent word. . . .
Well done, vision of violence

Well done, vision of violence
>   that continually and violently treats violence with violence.

Well done, shape of understanding, who shaped the shapeless.

Well done, unbounded bond, that bound up the first one to be unbounded.

Well done, for the tortures of the invisible, previously invisible and
>   incomprehensible.

Well done, giver of correction, who corrects the one who needs no correction.

The paradox, "Well done, shape of wisdom that was shaped to be without shape," becomes in the Greek version, "Well done, shape of understanding, for you have given the shapeless your own shape." The Armenian "Well done, corrector of him who needs no correction" becomes "Well done, invisible correction, for you corrected harshly the basis of polytheistic knowledge."

6. See Prieur's superb treatment of the Greek versions of this speech (*Acta Andreae*, 246–55).

7. Gregory of Nyssa provides an intriguing parallel to this explanation. The name at which "every knee should bow, in heaven, and on earth and under the earth" (Phil. 2:10) is "cross." Its pinnacle represents the "hypercosmic," its middle the worldly, and its base the chthonic (*In Christi resurrectionem 1* [*PG* 46.624D]). The cross of Christ thus "pervades all things, binds together whatever exists, and pulls together into itself the extremities of the world" (ibid.).

Bibliography

Editions and Translations

Quotations from *The Acts of Andrew* conform to those accompanying my edition except where I changed my mind with respect to the selection of textual variants or when rewording enhanced comparisons between the *Acts* and other texts. For biblical texts I have followed the New Revised Standard Version. For other ancient texts I use translations from the Loeb Classical Library whenever possible insofar as they are readily accessible to most readers. When translations appear without explicit attribution, they derived from these translations or they are my own.

Other translations also inform this work, and when they do, acknowledgments are provided either by abbreviations (for which see the abbreviations page) or by the name of the translator indicated in parentheses. Section numbers of some ancient works deviate from edition to edition; in the case of fragments and inscriptions, there often is no standardized enumeration. In such cases I provide, in parentheses, the series (see abbreviations page) or the name of the editor whose edition I have used.

Allberry   Allberry, C. R. C. *A Manichaean Psalm-Book.* Manichaean Manuscripts in the Chester Beatty Collections 2. Stuttgart: W. Kohlhammer, 1938.

Arrowsmith   Arrowsmith, William, trans. *The Satyricon.* New York: New American Library, 1959.

Betz   Betz, Hans Dieter, trans. *The Magical Papyri in Translation.* Chicago: University of Chicago Press, 1985.

Blake   Blake, Warren E., trans. *Chariton's Chaereas and Callirhoe.* Ann Arbor: University of Michigan Press, 1939.

Boenig   Boenig, Robert. *The Acts of Andrew in the Country of the Cannibals: Translations from the Greek, Latin, and Old English.* Garland Library of Medieval Literature, Series B 70. New York: Garland, 1991.

Budge   Budge, E. A. W., ed. and trans. *The Contendings of the Apostles.* London: Oxford University Press, 1935.

Chadwick   Chadwick, Henry, trans. *Origen: Contra Celsum.* Cambridge: Cambridge University Press, 1965.

Collins   Collins, John J., trans. "Sibylline Oracles." *The Old Testament Pseudepigrapha.* Vol. 1, *Apocalyptic Literature and Testaments.* Ed. James H. Charlesworth. Garden City: Doubleday, 1983.

Connolly   Connolly, R. Hugh, ed. *Didascalia Apostolorum.* Oxford: Oxford University Press, 1929.

Couvreur   Couvreur, P., ed. *Hermeias von Alexandrien. In Platonis Phaedrum scholia.* Hildesheim: Georg Olms, 1971. Reprint of the 1901 edition.

Dagron   Dagron, Gilbert, ed. *Vie et miracles de sainte Thècle. Texte grec, traduction et commentaire.* Subsidia hagiographica 62. Brussels: Société des Bollandistes, 1978.

Drake   Drake, H. A., trans. *In Praise of Constantine: A Historical Study and New Translation of Eusebius's Tricennial Orations.* Berkeley: University of California Press, 1976.

Fagles   Fagles, Robert, trans. *The Iliad.* New York: Viking, 1990.

Fitzgerald   Fitzgerald, Robert, trans. *The Odyssey.* New York: Doubleday, 1961.

Frazer   Frazer, Richard McIlwaine, trans. *The Trojan War. The Chronicles of Dictys of Crete and Dares the Phrygian.* Indiana University Greek and Latin Classics. Bloomington: Indiana University Press, 1966.

Graesse   Graesse, J. G. Th., ed. *Jacobus a Voragine, Legenda Aurea.* 2d edition. Leipzig: Impensis librariae Arnoldianae, 1850.

Grant   Grant, Robert M., ed. and trans. *Theophilus of Antioch. Ad Autolycum.* Oxford Early Christian Texts. Oxford: Oxford University Press, 1970.

Gregory   Gregory, Horace, trans. *Ovid. The Metamorphoses.* New York: New American Library, 1960.

Hadas   Hadas, Moses, trans. *Heliodorus. An Ethiopian Romance.* Ann Arbor: University of Michigan Press, 1957.

    Hadas, Moses, trans. *Three Greek Romances.* Indianapolis and New York: Bobbs-Merrill, 1953.

Hense   Hense, Otto, ed. *C. Musonii Rufi reliquiae.* Bibliotheca scriptorum Graecorum et Romanorum Teubneriana. Leipzig: B. G. Teubner, 1990. Reprint of the 1905 edition.

Hobein   Hobein, Hermann. *Maximi Tyrii philosophumena.* Bibliotheca scriptorum Graecorum et Romanorum Teubneriana. Leipzig: B. G. Teubner, 1910.

Kroll   Kroll, William. *Historia Alexandri Magni (Pseudo-Callisthenes).* Berlin: Weidmann, 1926.

Lamberton   Lamberton, Robert, trans. *The Cave of the Nymphs.* Barrytown: Station Hill Press, 1983.

Malherbe and Ferguson   Malherbe, Abraham, and Everett Ferguson, trans. *Gregory of Nyssa. The Life of Moses.* New York: Paulist Press, 1978.

Marcovich   Marcovich, Miroslav, ed. *Hippolytus. Refutatio omnium haeresium.* Patristische Texte und Studien 25. Berlin: Walter de Gruyter, 1986.

Meineke   Meineke, August, ed. *Stephan von Byzanz. Ethnika.* Graz: Akademische Druck- und Verlagsanstalt, 1958.

Mullach   Mullach, Friedrich Wilhelm August, ed. *Fragmenta philosophorum graecorum.* 3 vols. Paris: Firmin-Didot, 1860–81.

Musurillo   Musurillo, Herbert, ed. and trans. *The Acts of the Christian Martyrs.* Oxford Early Christian Texts. Oxford: Oxford University Press, 1972.

Richardson   Richardson, Cyril C. *Early Christian Fathers.* New York: Macmillan, 1970.

Schermann   Schermann, Theodorus, ed. *Prophetarum vitae fabulosae indices apostolorum discipulorumque domini Dorotheo, Epiphanio, Hippolyto, aliisque vindicata.* Leipzig: B. G. Teubner, 1907.

Schoedel	Schoedel, William R., ed. and trans. *Athenagoras. Legatio and De Resurrectione.* Oxford Early Christian Texts. Oxford: Oxford University Press, 1972.
Thomson	Thomson, Robert W., ed. and trans. *Athanasius. Contra Gentes and De Incarnatione.* Oxford Early Christian Texts. Oxford: Oxford University Press, 1971.
Wachsmuth and Hense	Wachsmuth, Curtius, and Otto Hense. *Ioannis Stobaei anthologium.* 5 vols. Berlin: Weidmann, 1958. Reprint of 1884–1912 edition.
Wendel	Wendel, Carol, ed. *Scholia Apollonium Rhodium vetera.* 2d edition. Berlin: Weidmann, 1958.
White	White, Robert J., trans. *The Interpretation of Dreams = Oneirocritica* by Artemidorus Daldianus. Noyes Classical Studies. Park Ridge: Noyes Press, 1975.
Whittaker	Whittaker, Molly, ed. and trans. *Tatian. Oratio ad Graecos and Fragments.* Oxford Early Christian Texts. Oxford: Oxford University Press, 1982.
Wicker	Wicker, Kathleen O'Brien, ed. and trans. *Porphyry the Philosopher. To Marcella.* Texts and Translations 28, Graeco-Roman Religions 10. Atlanta: Scholars Press, 1987.
Wurm	Wurm, H., ed. "Decretals selectae ex antiquissimis Romanorum Pontificium epistulis decretalibus." *Apollinaris* 12 (1939): 46–78.
Zahn	Zahn, Theodor, ed. *Acta Joannis.* Hildesheim: H. A. Gerstenberg, 1975. Reprint of the 1880 edition.

Modern Works Cited

Anderson, Graham. *Eros Sophistes: Ancient Novelists at Play.* American Classical Studies 9. Chico: Scholars Press, 1982.

Arrowsmith, William. *The Satyricon.* New York: New American Library, 1959.

Attridge, Harold W. "The Original Language of the Acts of Thomas." In *Of Scribes and Scrolls: Studies on the Hebrew Bible, Intertestamental Judaism, and Christian Origins.* College Theology Society Resources in Religion 5. Festscrift John Strugnell. Ed. Harold W. Attridge et al., 241–50. Landham: University Press of America, 1990.

Aune, David E. "Heracles and Christ: Heracles Imagery in the Christology of Early Christianity." In *Greeks, Romans, and Christians: Essays in Honor of Abraham J. Malherbe.* Ed. David L. Balch et al., 3–19. Minneapolis: Fortress Press, 1990.

_____. *The New Testament in Its Literary Environment.* Library of Early Christianity. Philadelphia: Westminster, 1987.

Baker, Alfred T. "The Passion of Saint Andrew." *Modern Language Review* 11 (1916): 420–49.

Balty, Jean C. "Nouvelles mosaïques païennes et group épiscopal dit 'cathédrale de l'est' à Apamée de Syrie." *Comptes rendus des séances de l'académie des inscriptions et belles-lettres* 1 (1972): 103–27.

Bardy, G. "Apocryphes à tendance encratite." *Dictionnaire de spiritualité*, 1.752–65. Ed. Marcel Viller et al. Paris: Gabriel Beauchesne, 1937– .

Barr, David Lawrence. "Toward a Definition of the Gospel Genre: A Generic Analysis and Comparison of the Synoptic Gospels and the Socratic Dialogues by Means of Aristotle's Theory of Tragedy." Ph.D. diss., Florida State University, 1974.

Bauckham, Richard J. "The Apocalypse of Peter: An Account of Research." *Aufstieg und Niedergang der römischen Welt* 2.25.6.4713–50. Ed. Wolfgang Haase. Berlin: Walter de Gruyter, 1988.

Benz, Ernst. "Christus und Socrates in der alten Kirche." *Zeitschrift für die neutestamentliche Wissenschaft* 43 (1950–51): 195–224.

_____. "Der gekreuzigte Gerechte bei Plato, im Neuen Testament und in der alten Kirche." *Abhandlungen der Geistes- und Sozialwissenschaftlichen Klasse* 12 (1950): 1031–74.

Binder, G. "Eine Polemik des Porphyrios gegen die allegorische Auslegung des Alten Testaments durch die Christen." *Zeitschrift für Papyrologie und Epigraphik* 3 (1968): 81–95.

Blatt, Franz. *Die lateinischen Bearbeitungen der Acta Andreae et Matthiae apud Anthropophagos.* Beihefte zur Zeitschrift für die neutestamentliche Wissenschaft 12. Giessen: Alfred Töpelmann, 1930.

Boenig, Robert. *The Acts of Andrew in the Country of the Cannibals: Translations from the Greek, Latin, and Old English.* Garland Library of Medieval Literature, series B, 70. New York: Garland, 1991.

_____. *Saint and Hero: "Andreas" and Medieval Doctrine.* Lewisburg: Bucknell Univeristy Press, 1991.

Bonner, Campbell. "Desired Haven." *Harvard Theological Review* 34 (1941): 49–67.

Bonnet, Maximilian, ed. *Acta Andreae cum laudatione contexta et Martyrium Andreae graece: Passio Andreae Latine.* Supplementum codicis apocryphi 2. Paris: C. Klincksieck, 1895. Reprint of Analecta Bollandiana 13 (1894): 309–78.

_____, ed. "Gregorii episcopi turonensis liber de miraculis beati Andreae apostoli." In *Gregorii episcopi turonensis miracula et opera minora.* Monumenta Germaniae historica. Scriptores rerum Merovingicarum 1,2. Ed. Bruno Krusch, 821–46. Hanover: Hahn, 1885.

Bornkamm, Günther. *Mythos und Legende in der apokryphen Thomas-Akten.* Forschungen zur Religion und Literatur des Alten und Neuen Testaments n.s. 31. Göttingen: Vandenhoeck & Ruprecht, 1933.

Boulanger, André. *Orphée. Rapports de l'orphisme et du christianisme.* Paris: F. Rieder, 1925.

Boulenger, Fernand. *Saint Basil. Aux Jeunes Gens sur la manière de tirer profit des lettres helléniques.* Paris: Belles Lettres, 1935.

Bousset, Wilhelm. "Platons Weltseele und des Kreuz Christi." *Zeitschrift für die neutestamentliche Wissenschaft* 14 (1913): 273–85.

Bouvier, Bertand, and François Bovon. "Actes de Philippe. I d'après un manuscrit in-édit." In *Oecumenica et Patristica: Festschrift für Wilhelm Schneemelcher zum 75. Geburtstag.* Ed. Damaskinos Papandreou, 367–94. Stuttgart: Kohlhammer, 1989.

Bovon, François, ed. *Les Actes apocryphes des apôtres. Christianisme et monde païen.* Publications de la Faculté de Théologie de l'Université de Genève 4. Geneva: Labor et Fides, 1981.

Brooks, Kenneth R. *Andreas and the Fates of the Apostles.* Oxford: Oxford University Press, 1961.

Browning, Robert. "The Byzantines and Homer." In *Homer's Ancient Readers: The Hermeneutic of Greek Epic's Earliest Exegetes.* Magie Classical Publications. Ed. Robert Lamberton and John J. Keaney, 134–48. Princeton: Princeton University Press, 1992.

Bruce, Frederick Fyvie. *Commentary on the Book of Acts.* New International Commentary on the New Testament. Grand Rapids: Eerdmans, 1954.

Buchholz, Dennis D. *Your Eyes Will Be Opened: A Study of the Greek (Ethiopic) Apocalypse of Peter.* Society of Biblical Literature Dissertation Series 97. Atlanta: Scholars Press, 1988.

Budge, E. A. W., ed. and trans. *The Contendings of the Apostles.* London: Oxford University Press, 1935.

Buffière, Félix. *Les Mythes d'Homère et la pensée grecque.* Collection Budé. Paris: Belles Lettres, 1956.

Burrus, Virginia. *Chastity as Autonomy: Women in the Stories of Apocryphal Acts.* Studies in Women and Religion 23. Lewiston: Edwin Mellen, 1987.

Camelot, P. "Les Idées de Clément d'Alexandrie sur l'utilisation des sciences et de la littérature profane." *Revue des sciences religieuses* 21 (1931): 38–66.

Carcopino, Jérôme. *De Pythagore aux apôtres. Études sur la conversion du monde romain.* Paris: Flammarion, 1956.

Charlesworth, James H. *The Old Testament Pseudepigrapha.* 2 vols. Garden City: Doubleday, 1983 and 1985.

Clark, Raymond J. *Catabasis: Vergil and the Wisdom Tradition.* Amsterdam: B. R. Grüner, 1979.

Clarke, Howard. *Homer's Readers: A Historical Introduction to the "Iliad" and the "Odyssey."* Newark: University of Delaware Press, 1980.

Cohen, Shaye J. D. "Sosates the Jewish Homer." *Harvard Theological Review* 74 (1981): 391–96.

Coman, Jean. "L'Immortalité de l'âme dans le Phédon et la résurrection des morts dans la littérature chrétienne des deux premiers siècles." *Helikon* 3 (1963): 17–40.

Courcelle, Pierre. *Connais-toi toi-même. De Socrate à Saint Bernard.* 3 vols. Paris: Études augustiniennes, 1974–75.

_____. "Quelques symboles funéraires du néo-platonisme latin." *Revue des études anciennes* 46 (1944): 73–93.

Courtois, Joseph, "L'Odyssée, poème de fidélité." *Les Études classiques* 25 (1957): 65–73.

Crum, W. E. *Catalogue of the Coptic Manuscripts in the British Museum.* London: Longmans, 1905.

Daniélou, Jean. *A History of Early Christian Doctrine Before the Council of Nicaea*. Vol. 2. *Gospel Message and Hellenistic Culture*. Trans. J. A. Baker. Philadelphia: Westminster Press, 1973.

Davies, Stevan L. *The Revolt of the Widows: The Social World of the Apocryphal Acts*. Carbondale: Southern Illinois University Press, 1980.

Dawson, David. *Allegorical Readers and Cultural Revision in Ancient Alexandria*. Berkeley: University of California Press, 1992.

De Lacy, Phillip. "Plato and the Intellectual Life of the Second Century A.D." In *Approaches to the Second Sophistic*. Ed. G. W. Bowersock, 4–10. University Park: American Philological Society, 1974.

Delatte, Armand. *Études sur la littérature pythagoricienne*. Paris: Édouard Champion, 1915.

Delebecque, Édouard. *Télémaque et la structure de l'Odyssée*. Centre d'étude et de recherches helléniques de la Faculté des lettres d'Aix. Publication des annales de la Faculté des lettres, Aix-en-Provence, n.s. 21. Gap: Éditions Ophrys, 1958.

Des Places, Édouard. *Syngeneia. La Parenté de l'homme avec Dieu, d'Homère à la patristique*. Études et commentaires 51. Paris: C. Klincksieck, 1964.

_____. "Un Thème platonicien dans la tradition patristique: Le Juste crucifié (Platon, *République*, 361e4–362a2)." In *Studia Patristica* 9. Texte und Untersuchungen zur Geschichte der altchristlichen Literatur 94. Ed. F. L. Cross, 30–40. Berlin: Akademie-Verlag, 1966.

Detienne, Marcel. *Homère, Hésiode et Pythagore: Poésie et philosophie dans le pythagorisme ancien*. Collection Latomus 57. Brussels-Berchem: Latomus, 1962.

_____. "La Légende pythagoricienne d'Hélène." *Revue de l'histoire des religions* 152 (1957): 129–52.

_____. "Ulysse sur le stuc central de la Basilique de la Porta Maggiore." *Latomus* 17 (1958): 270–86.

De Vries. *Heroic Song and Heroic Legend*. Trans. B. J. Timmer. London: Oxford University Press, 1963.

Dieterich, Albrecht. *Nekyia: Beiträge zur Erklärung der neuentdeckten Petrusapokalypse*. 2d edition. Annotated by R. Wünsch. Leipzig: B. G. Teubner, 1913. Reprint of 1893 edition.

Dihle, Albrecht. "Neues zur Thomas-Tradition." *Jahrbuch für Antike und Christentum* 6 (1963): 54–70.

Döring, Klaus. *Exemplum Socratis. Studien zur Sokratesnachwirkung in der kynisch-stoischen Popularphilosophie der frühen Kaiserzeit und im frühen Christentum*. Hermes. Zeitschrift für klassische Philologie 42. Wiesbaden: Franz Steiner Verlag, 1979.

Dreyer, Oskar. Review of Glockmann, *Homer. Göttingische gelehrte Anzeigen* 222 (1970): 227–42.

Droge, Arthur J. *Homer or Moses? Early Christian Interpretations of the History of Culture*. Hermeneutische Untersuchungen zur Theologie 26. Tübingen: J. C. B. Mohr (Siebeck), 1989.

Dvornik, Francis. *The Idea of Apostolicity in Byzantium and the Legend of the Apostle Andrew.* Dumbarton Oaks Studies 4. Cambridge: Harvard University Press, 1958.

Eisler, Robert. *Orphisch-dionysische Mysteriengedanken in der christlichen Antike.* Leipzig: B. G. Teubner, 1925.

Ellsworth, J. D. "Ovid's 'Odyssey,' *Met.* 13.623-14.608." *Mnemosyne* 41 (1988): 333-40.

Finley, M. I. *The World of Odysseus.* 2d edition. New York: Penguin Books, 1978.

Flagg, Isaac. *Euripides. Iphigenia Among the Taurians.* Boston: Ginn, 1891.

Flamion, Joseph. *Les Actes apocryphes de l'apôtre André. Les Actes d'André et de Mathias, de Pierre et d'André et les textes apparentés.* Recueil de travaux d'histoire et de philologie 33. Louvain: Bureaux de Recueil, 1911.

Foerster, Werner. "Δαίμων, δαιμόνιον." *Theological Dictionary of the New Testament,* 2.1–20. Ed. Gerhard Kittel. Trans. Geoffrey W. Bromiley. Grand Rapids: W. B. Eerdmans, 1985.

Fortin, Ernest L. "Christianity and Hellenism in Basil the Great's Address *Ad Adulescentes.*" In *Neoplatonism and Early Christian Thought.* Ed. H. J. Blumenthal and R. A. Marcus, 189–203. London: Variorum Publications, 1981.

Fox, Robin Lane. *Pagans and Christians.* New York: Alfred A. Knopf, 1987.

Fusillo, Massimo. "Textual Patterns and Narrative Situations in the Greek Novel." In *Groningen Colloquia on the Novel.* Vol. 1. Ed. H. Hofmann, 17–31. Groningen: Egbert Forsten, 1988.

Galinsky, G. Karl. *The Herakles Theme: The Adaptations of the Hero in Literature from Homer to the Twentieth Century.* Totowa: Rowman and Littlefield, 1972.

Geffcken, Johannes. *Sokrates und alte Christentum.* Heidelberg: C. Winter, 1908.

Genette, Gérard. *Palimpsestes. La Littérature au second degré.* Paris: Éditions du Seuil, 1982.

Glockmann, Günther. *Homer in der frühchristlichen Literatur bis Justinus.* Texte und Untersuchungen zur Geschichte der altchristlichen Literatur 105. Berlin: Akademie-Verlag, 1968.

Gnilka, Christian. "Ultima verba." *Jahrbuch für Antike und Christentum* 22 (1979): 5–21.

Groag, Edmund. *Die römischen Reichsbeamten von Achaia bis auf Diokletian.* Akademie der Wissenschaft in Wien. Schriften der Balkankommission, Antiquarische Abteilung 9. Vienna: Hölder-Pichler-Tempsky, 1939.

Guthrie, W. K. C. *Orpheus and Greek Religion: A Study of the Orphic Movement.* London: Methuen, 1935.

Haase, Felix. *Apostel und Evangelisten in der orientalischen Überlieferungen.* Neutestamentliche Abhandlungen 9. Münster: Aschendorff, 1922.

Hägg, Tomas. *The Novel in Antiquity.* Berkeley: University of California Press, 1983.

Hanfmann, George M. A. "Socrates and Christ." *Harvard Studies in Classical Philology* 60 (1951): 205–33.

Hansen, William F. "Odysseus and the Oar: A Folkloric Approach." In *Approaches to Greek Myth.* Ed. Lowell Edmunds, 239–72. Baltimore: Johns Hopkins University Press, 1990.

Harnack, Adolf von. *Sokrates und die alte Kirche*. Giessen: Alfred Töpelmann, 1901.

Haspels, Caroline H. E. *Highlands of Phrygia: Sites and Monuments*. Princeton: Princeton University Press, 1971.

Hegel, Georg Wilhelm Friedrich. *Vorlesungen über die Philosophie der Weltgeschichte*. Ed. Georg Lasson. Leipzig: F. Meiner, 1923.

Heine, R. "Picaresque Novel Versus Allegory." In *Aspects of Apuleius' Golden Ass*. Ed. B. L. Hijmans, Jr., and R. Th. van der Paardt, 25–42. Groningen: Bouma's Boekhuis, 1978.

Hennecke, Edgar. *Handbuch zu den neutestamentlichen Apokryphen*. Tübingen: J. C. B. Mohr, 1904.

Hennecke, Edgar, and Wilhelm Schneemelcher, eds. *New Testament Apocrypha*. ET edition. Robert McL. Wilson. 2 vols. Philadelphia: Westminster Press, 1965.

Henrichs, Albert. "Pagan Ritual and the Alleged Crimes of the Early Christians: A Reconsideration." In *Kyriakon: Festschrift Johannes Quasten*. Vol. 1. Ed. Patrick Granfield and Josef A. Jungmann, 18–35. Münster: Aschendorff, 1970.

—————. *Die Phoinikika des Lollianos. Fragmente eines griechischen Romans*. Papyrologische Texte und Abhandlungen 14. Bonn: R. Halbelt, 1972.

Herington, C. J. "Homer: A Byzantine Perspective." *Arion* 8 (1969): 432–34.

Hijmans, B. L., Jr. Significant Names and Their Function in Apuleius' *Metamorphoses*." In *Aspects of Apuleius' Golden Ass*. Ed. B. L. Hijmans, Jr., and R. Th. van der Paardt, 107–22. Groningen: Bouma's Boekhuis, 1978.

Hijmans, B. L., Jr., and R. Th. van der Paardt, eds. *Aspects of Apuleius' Golden Ass*. Groningen: Bouma's Boekhuis, 1978.

Himmelfarb, Martha. *Tours of Hell: An Apocalyptic Form in Jewish and Christian Literature*. Philadelphia: University of Pennsylvania Press, 1983.

Höistad, Ragnar. *Cynic Hero and Cynic King. Studies in the Cynic Conception of Man*. Uppsala: Carl Bloms Boktryckeri A.-B., 1948.

Hubbard, Benjamin J. *The Matthean Redaction of a Primitive Apostolic Commissioning: An Exegesis of Matthew 28:16–20*. Society of Biblical Literature Dissertation Series 19. Missoula: Society of Biblical Literature, 1974.

Hughes, Robert. "Something Fishy in the Hamptons" (review of Peter Matthiessen, *Men's Lives: The Surfmen and Baymen of the South Fork*). *New York Review of Books* 33 (October 23, 1986): 21–24.

Hurst, André, Olivier Reverdin, and Jean Rudhardt. *Papyrus Bodmer XXIX: Vision de Dorothéos*. Cologne: Fondation Martin Bodmer, 1984.

Huxley, George Leonard. *Greek Epic Poetry from Eumelos to Panyassis*. Cambridge: Harvard University Press, 1969.

Irwin, Eleanor. "The Song of Orpheus and the New Song of Christ." In *Orpheus: The Metamorphoses of a Myth*. Ed. John Warden, 51–62. Toronto: University of Toronto Press, 1982.

Jackson, Daniel. "Socrates and Christianity." *Classical Folia* 31 (1977): 189–206.

Jaeger, David K. *The Initiatory Trial Theme of the Hero in Hebrew Bible Narrative*. Ann Arbor: University Microfilms, 1992.

Jaeger, Werner. *Paideia: The Ideals of Greek Culture.* 2d edition. 3 vols. Trans. Gilbert Highet. New York: Oxford University Press, 1945.

James, Montague Rhodes. *The Apocryphal New Testament.* Oxford: Oxford University Press, 1924.

_____. "The Rainer Fragment of the Apocalypse of Peter." *Journal of Theological Studies* 32 (1931): 270–79.

Jebb, Richard Claverhouse. *Homer: An Introduction to the "Iliad" and the "Odyssey."* 5th edition. Boston: Ginn, 1894.

Junod, Eric. "Créations romanesques et traditions ecclésiastiques dan les Actes apocryphes des apôtres. L'Alternative Fiction romanesque—vérité historique: une impasse." *Augustinianum* 23 (1983): 271–85.

_____. "Origène, Eusèbe et la tradition sur la répartition des champs de mission des apôtres (Eusèbe, HE III,1,1–3)." In *Les Actes apocryphes des apôtres. Christianisme et monde païen.* Publications de la Faculté de Théologie de l'Université de Genève 4. Ed. François Bovon, 233–48. Geneva: Labor et Fides, 1981.

Junod, Eric, and Jean-Daniel Kaestli. *Acta Iohannis.* 2 vols. Corpus Christianorum, Series Apocryphorum 1–2. Turnhout: Brepols, 1983.

_____. *L'Histoire des Actes apocryphes des apôtres du IIIe au IXe siècle: Le Cas des Actes de Jean.* Cahiers de la Revue de Théologie et de Philosophie 7. Geneva, 1982.

Kaestli, Jean-Daniel. "Fiction littéraire et réalité sociale: Que peut-on savoir de la place des emmes dans le milieu de la production des Actes apocryphes des apôtres?" In *Apocrypha: Le Champ des apocryphes.* Vol. 1: *La Fable apocryphe.* Ed. Pierre Geoltrain et al., 279–302. Turnhout: Brepols, 1990.

_____. "Les Principales Orientations de la recherche sur les Actes apocryphes des apôtres." In *Les Actes apocryphes des apôtres. Christianisme et monde païen.* Publications de la Faculté de Théologie de l'Université de Genève 4. Ed. François Bovon, 49–67. Geneva: Labor et Fides, 1981.

_____. "Response." In *Semeia 38: The Apocryphal Acts of Apostles.* Ed. Dennis R. MacDonald, 119–31. Decatur: Scholars Press, 1986.

_____. "L'Utilisation des Actes apocryphes des apôtres dans le manichéisme." In *Gnosis and Gnosticism.* Nag Hammadi Studies 8. Ed. Martin Krause, 107–16. Leiden: E. J. Brill, 1977.

Katz, Marylin A. *Penelope's Renown: Meaning and Indeterminacy in the "Odyssey."* Princeton: Princeton University Press, 1991.

Kerenyi, Karl. *Die griechisch-orientalische Romanliteratur in religionsgeschichtlicher Beleuchtung.* Darmstadt: Wisenschaftliche Buchgesellschaft, 1962. Reprint of 1927 edition.

Kessels, A. H. M. and P. W. Van der Horst. "The Vision of Dorotheus (Pap. Bodmer 29)." *Vigiliae Christianae* 41 (1987): 313–59.

Kindstrand, Jan Fredrik. *Homer in der zweiten Sophistik.* Acta Universitatis Upsaliensis. Studia Graeca Upsaliensia 7. Uppsala: University of Uppsala, 1973.

_____. *Isaac Porphyrogenitus: Praefatio in Homerum.* Acta Universitatis Upsaliensis. Studia Graeca Upsaliensis 14. Uppsala: University of Uppsala, 1979.

Klauser, Theodor. "Studien zur Entstehungsgeschichte der christlichen Kunst VI. 15. Das Sirenabenteuer des Odysseus—ein Motiv der christlichen Grabskunst?" *Jahrbuch für Antike und Christentum* 6 (1963): 71–100.

Knox, Wilfred L. "The 'Divine Hero' Christology in the New Testament." *Harvard Theological Review* 41 (1948): 229–49.

Konstantinidis, Chrysostome. "La Fête de l'apôtre saint André dans l'église de Constantinople à l'époque byzantine et aux temps modernes." In *Melanges en l'honneur de Monseigneur Michel Andrieu*. Revue des sciences religieuses, volume hors séries, 243–61. Strasbourg: Palais Universitaire, 1956.

Kraemer, Ross. "The Conversion of Women to Ascetic Forms of Christianity." *Signs* 6 (1980–81): 298–307.

Krapp, George Philip. *Andreas and the Fates of the Apostles*. Boston: Ginn, 1906.

Krause, Wilhelm. *Die Stellung der frühchristlichen Autoren zur heidnischen Literatur*. Vienna: Herder, 1958.

Lagrand, James. "How Was the Virgin Mary 'Like a Man' (*'yk gbr'*)? A Note on Mt. 1:18b and Related Syriac Christian Texts." *Novum Testamentum* 22 (1980): 97–107.

Lamberton, Robert. *Homer the Theologian: Neoplatonist Allegorical Reading and the Growth of the Epic Tradition*. Transformation of the Classical Heritage 9. Berkeley: University of California Press, 1986.

_____, and John J. Keaney, eds. *Homer's Ancient Readers: The Hermeneutics of Greek Epic's Earliest Exegetes*. Magie Classical Publications. Princeton: Princeton University Press, 1992.

Lawton, William Cranston. *The Successors of Homer*. New York: Cooper Square, 1969. Reprint of the 1898 edition.

Leloir, Louis. *Écrits apocryphes sur les apôtres. Traduction de l'édition arménienne de Venise. I. Pierre, Paul, André, Jean*. Corpus Christianorum, Series Apocryphorum 3. Turnhout: Brepols, 1986.

Lipsius, Richard Adelbert. *Die apokryphen Apostelgeschichten und Apostellegenden*. Braunschweig: C. A. Schwetschke, 1883.

Lipsius, Richard Adelbert, and Maximillian Bonnet, eds. *Acta Apostolorum apocrypha*. Hildesheim: Georg Olms, 1959. Reprint of the 1891–1903 edition.

Livrea, E. Review of Hurst, Reverdin, and Rudhardt, *Papyrus Bodmer XXIX*. *Gnomon* 58 (1986): 687–711.

Macchioro, Vittorio D. *From Orpheus to Paul: A History of Orphism*. New York: Henry Holt, 1930.

MacDonald, Dennis R. *The Acts of Andrew and The Acts of Andrew and Matthias in the City of the Cannibals*. Texts and Translations 33, Christian Apocrypha 1. Atlanta: Scholars Press, 1990.

_____. "*The Acts of Andrew and Matthias* and *The Acts of Andrew*," and "Response." In *Semeia 38: Apocryphal Acts of Apostles*. Ed. Dennis R. MacDonald, 9–26 and 35–39. Decatur: Scholars Press, 1986.

_____. "From Audita to Legenda: Oral and Written Miracle Stories." *Forum* 2.4 (1986): 15–26.

_____. "Intertextuality in Simon's 'Redemption' of Helen the Whore: Homer, Heresiologists, and *The Acts of Andrew.*" In *Society of Bibilical Literature 1990 Seminar Papers*. Ed. David J. Lull, 336–43. Atlanta: Scholars Press, 1990.

_____. *The Legend and the Apostle: The Battle for Paul in Story and Canon.* Philadelphia: Westminster Press, 1983.

_____. *There Is No Male and Female: The Fate of a Dominical Saying in Paul and Gnosticism.* Harvard Dissertations in Religion 20. Philadelphia: Fortress Press, 1987.

MacGregor, Geddes. *Reincarnation in Christianity: A New Vision of the Role of Rebirth in Christian Thought.* Wheaton: Theosophical Publishing House, 1978.

Mactoux, Marie-Madeleine. *Pénélope. Légende et mythe.* Annales littéraires de l'université de Besançon 175. Centre de recherches d'histoire ancienne 16. Paris: Belles Lettres, 1975.

Mâle, Emile. "Histoire et légende de l'apôtre saint André dans l'art." *Revue des deux mondes* 5 (1951): 412–20.

Malherbe, Abraham J. "Herakles." *Reallexikon für Antike und Christentum* 14.559–83.

Marrou, H.-I. *A History of Education in Antiquity.* Trans. George Lamb. New York: Sheed and Ward, 1956.

_____. S.v. "Sirène." *Dictionnaire d'archéologie chrétienne et de liturgie,* 15.1494–98. Ed. Fernand Cabrol and Henri Leclercq. Paris: Letouzey et Ané, 1907–53.

Mason, H. J. "Fabula Graecanica: Apuleius and his Greek Sources." In *Aspects of Apuleius' Golden Ass.* Ed. B. L. Hijmans, Jr., and R. Th. van der Paardt, 1–15. Groningen: Bouma's Boekhuis, 1978.

McCurdy, G. H. "Platonic Orphism in the Testament of Abraham." *Journal of Biblical Literature* 61 (1942): 213–26.

Meehan, Denis Molaise. *St. Gregory of Nazianzus. Three Poems.* The Fathers of the Church 75. Washington: Catholic University of America Press, 1986.

Ménard, Jacques E. "Le Repos, salut du gnostique." *Revue des sciences religieuses* 51 (1977): 71–88.

Millar, C. M. H., and J. W. S. Carmichael. "The Growth of Telemachus." *Greece and Rome* 1 (1954): 58–64.

Müller, C. W. "Chariton von Aphrodisias und die Theorie des Romans in der Antike." *Antike und Abendland* 22 (1976): 115–36.

Mueller, Martin. *The Iliad.* London: George Allen and Unwin, 1984.

Murjanoff, Michael. "Andreas der Erstberufene im mittelalterlichen Europa." *Sacris Erudiri* 17 (1966): 411–27.

Murrin, Michael. *The Allegorical Epic: Essays in Its Rise and Decline.* Chicago: University of Chicago Press, 1980.

Mytytiuk, Bohdan Georg. *Die ukrainischen Andreasbräuche und verwandtes Brauchtum.* Veröffentlichungen des Osteuropa-Institutes München: Reihe Geschichte 47. Wiesbaden: Harrassowitz, 1979.

Nagel, Peter. "Die apokryphen Apostelakten des 2. und 3. Jahrhunderts in der manichäischen Literatur." In *Gnosis und Neues Testament.* Ed. Karl-Wolfgang Tröger, 149–82. Berlin: Evangelische Verlagsanstalt, 1973.

_____. "Die Wiedergewinnung des Paradieses durch Askese." *Forschungen und Fortschritte* 34 (1960): 375–77.

Nau, François N. S.v. "Actes coptes." *Dictionnarie d'histoire et de géographie ecclésiastique.* Ed. Alfred Baurillart et al. Paris: Letouzey et Ané, 1912– .

Norden, Eduard. *P. Vergilius Maro Aeneis Buch VI.* 8th edition. Darmstadt: Wissenschaftliche Buchgesellschaft, 1984.

North, Helen. *Sophrosyne: Self-Knowledge and Self-Restraint in Greek Literature.* Ithaca: Cornell University Press, 1966.

Pack, Roger A. *The Greek and Latin Literary Texts from Greco-Roman Egypt.* 2d edition. Ann Arbor: University of Michigan Press, 1965.

Pépin, Jean. *Mythe et allégorie: Les Origines grecques et les contestations judéo-chrétiennes.* 2d edition. Paris: Études augustiniennes, 1976.

_____. "The Platonic and Christian Ulysses." In *Neoplatonism and Christian Thought.* International Society for Neoplatonic Studies. Ed. Dominic J. O'Meara, 3–18. Albany: State University of New York, 1982.

_____. "Plotin et les mythes." *Revue philosophique de Louvain* 53 (1955): 5–27.

Perry, Ben Edwin. *The Ancient Romances: A Literary-Historical Account of Their Origins.* Berkeley: University of California Press, 1967.

Pervo, Richard I. *Profit with Delight: The Literary Genre of the Acts of the Apostles.* Philadelphia: Fortress Press, 1987.

Peterson, Erik. "Die Taufe im acherusischen See." *Vigiliae Christianae* 9 (1955): 1–20.

Peterson, Peter Megill. *Andrew, Brother of Simon Peter: His History and His Legends.* Novum Testamentum, Supplements 1. Leiden: E. J. Brill, 1958.

Phillips, E. D. "The Comic Odysseus." *Greece and Rome* n.s. 6 (1959): 58–67.

Polites, Nikolaos G. Μελέται περὶ τοῦ βίου καὶ τῆς γλώσσης τοῦ ἑλλενικοῦ λαοῦ. Vol. 1. Παραδόσεις. Athens: P. D. Sakellarios, 1904.

Prescott, Henry W. *The Development of Virgil's Art.* Chicago: University of Chicago Press, 1927.

Prieur, Jean-Marc. *Acta Andreae.* Corpus Christianorum. Series Apocryphorum 5 and 6. Turnhout: Brepols, 1989.

Rachewiltz, Siegfried Walter de. "De Sirenibus: An Inquiry into Sirens from Homer to Shakespeare." Ph.D. diss., Harvard University, 1983.

Radermacher, Ludwig. *Hippolytus und Thekla. Studien zur Geschichte von Legende und Kultus.* Kaiserliche Akademie der Wissenschaften in Wien. Philosophisch-historische Klasse. Sitzungsberichte 182,3. Vienna: Alfred Hölder, 1916.

Raglan, Lord. *The Hero: A Study in Tradition, Myth, and Drama.* London: Methuen, 1936.

Rahner, Hugo. *Greek Myths and Christian Mystery.* Trans. Brian Battershaw. London: Burns and Oates, 1963. ET of the 1957 German edition.

_____. "Das Schiff aus Holz." *Zeitschrift für katholische Theologie* 67 (1943): 1–21.

Rank, Otto. *The Myth of the Birth of the Hero, and Other Writings.* Ed. Philip Freund. New York: Vintage Books, 1959.

Reardon, B. P. *Courants littéraires grecs des IIe et IIIe siècles après J.-C.* Annales littéraires de l'Université de Nantes 5. Paris: Belles Lettres, 1971.

_____. *The Form of the Greek Romance.* Princeton: Princeton University Press, 1991.

Réau, Louis. *Iconographie de l'art chrétien.* Paris: Presses universitaires de France, 1958.

Regen, Frank. *Apuleius philosophus Platonicus. Untersuchungen zur Apologie (De magia) und zu De mundo.* Untersuchungen zur antiken Literatur und Geschichte 10. Berlin: Walter de Gruyter, 1971.

Reinhardt, Karl. *Von Werken und Formen: Vorträge und Aufsätze.* Godesberg: Helmut Küpper, 1948.

Rexine, John E. "Daimon in Classical Greek Literature." *Greek Orthodox Theological Review* 30 (1985): 335–61.

Richardson, Cyril C. *Early Christian Fathers.* New York: Macmillan, 1970.

Richardson, N. J. "Recognition Scenes in the *Odyssey* and Ancient Literary Criticism." *Papers of the Liverpool Latin Seminar* 4 (1983): 219–35.

Roberts, Michael. *Biblical Epic and Rhetorical Paraphrase in Late Antiquity.* ARCA Classical and Medieval Texts, Papers and Monographs 16. Liverpool: Francis Cairns, 1985.

Robinson, James M., ed. *The Nag Hammadi Library.* 2d edition. San Francisco: Harper & Row, 1988.

Root, Robert Kilburn. *Andreas: The Legend of St. Andrew.* Yale Studies in English 7. New York: Henry Holt, 1899.

Rordorf, Willy. "Socrate dans la littérature chrétienne des premiers siècles." Unpublished paper.

Rouse, W. H. D. "A Greek Skipper." *The Cambridge Review* 27 (1906): 414–15.

Schaar, Claes. *Critical Studies in the Cynewulf Group.* New York: Haskell House, 1967.

Schneider, G. *Die Apostelgeschichte,* 2 vols. Herders theologischer Kommentar zum Neuen Testament. Freiburg: Herder & Herder, 1980–82.

Scopello, Maddalena. "Les Citations d'Homère dans le traité de l'exégèse de l'âme." In *Gnosis and Gnosticism.* Nag Hammadi Studies 8. Ed. Martin Krause, 3–12. Leiden: E. J. Brill, 1977.

Scott, John A. *Homer and His Influence.* Boston: Marshall Jones, 1925.

Simon, Marcel. *Hercule et le christainisme.* Paris: Belles Lettres, 1955.

Skeris, Robert A. *ΧΡΩΜΑ ΘΕΟΥ: On the Origins and Theological Interpretation of the Musical Imagery Used by the Ecclesiastical Writers of the First Three Centuries, with Special Reference to the Image of Orpheus.* Altötting: Coppenrath, 1976.

Söder, Rosa. *Die apokryphen Apostelgeschichten und die romanhafte Literatur der Antike.* Würzburger Studien zur Altertumswissenschaft 3. Darmstadt: Wissenschaftliche Buchgesellschaft, 1969. Reprint of 1932 edition.

Stanford, William Bedell. *The Ulysses Theme: A Study in the Adaptability of a Traditional Hero.* 2d edition. Oxford: Blackwell, 1963.

Strasburger, Hermann. *Homer und die Geschichtsschreibung.* Sitzungsberichte der Heidelberger Akademie der Wissenschaften. Philosophisch-historische Klasse. Heidelberg: C. Winter, 1972.

Stuhlfauth, Georg. "Das Schiff als Symbol der altchristlichen Kunst." *Rivista di archeologia cristiana* 19 (1942): 111–41.

Tatum, James. *Apuleius and The Golden Ass.* Ithaca: Cornell University Press, 1979.

Toynbee, Arnold J. *A Study of History.* Vol. 6. London: Oxford University Press, 1939.

Trempela, N. Ὁ ἀπόστολος Ἀνδρέας. βίος, δράσις καὶ μαρτύριον αὐτοῦ ἐν Πάτραις. Patras: 1956.

Vallendra, Nikodemus. Ὁ σταυρὸς τοῦ μαρτυρίου τοῦ ἀποστόλου Ἀνδρέου. Athens, 1980.

Van den Broek, Roelof. "The *Authentikos Logos*: A New Document of Christian Platonism." *Vigiliae Christianae* 33 (1979): 260–86.

Vicari, Patricia. "*Sparagmos*: Orpheus Among the Christians." In *Orpheus: The Metamorphoses of a Myth.* Ed. John Warden, 63–83. Toronto: University of Toronto Press, 1982.

Vielhauer, Philipp. "Ἀνάπαυσις, zum gnostischen Hintergrund des Thomas-Evangeliums." In *Apophoreta. Festschrift für Ernst Haenchen.* Beihefte zur Zeitschrift für die neutestamentliche Wissenschaft 30. Ed. W. Eltester and F. H. Kettler, 281–99. Berlin: Alfred Töpelmann, 1964.

_____. *Geschichte der urchristliche Literatur.* Berlin: Walter de Gruyter, 1975.

von Dobschütz, Ernst. "Der Roman in der altchristlichen Literatur." *Deutsche Rundschau* 111 (1902): 87–106.

von Gutschmid, Alfred. "Die Königsnamen in den apokryphen Apostelgeschichten. Ein Beitrag zur Kenntnis des geschichtlichen Romans." *Rheinisches Museum für Philologie* n.s. 19 (1864): 161–83 and 380–401.

_____. *Kleine Schriften.* Ed. Franz Rühl. Leipzig: B. G. Teubner, 1890.

von Hahn, Johann Georg. *Sagwissenschaftliche Studien.* Jena: Friedrich Mauke, 1876.

Weicker, Georg. *Der Seelenvogel in der alten Literatur und Kunst. Eine mythologisch-archaeologische Untersuchung.* Leipzig: B. G. Teubner, 1902.

Weinstock, Stefan. "Die platonische Homerkritik und ihre Nachwirkung." *Philologus* 82, n.s. 36 (1927): 121–53.

Wendel, Carol, ed. *Scholia Apollonium Rhodium vetera.* 2d edition. Berlin: Weidmann, 1958.

Westerbrink, A. G. "Some Parodies in Apuleius' Metamorphoses." In *Aspects of Apuleius' Golden Ass.* Ed. B. L. Hijmans, Jr., and R. Th. van der Paardt, 63–73. Groningen: Bouma's Boekhuis, 1978.

Whitman, Cedric H. "Hera's Anvils." *Harvard Studies in Classical Philology* 74 (1970): 37–42.

Wilken, Robert L. *The Christians as the Romans Saw Them.* New Haven: Yale University Press, 1984.

_____. "The Homeric Cento in Irenaeus, *Adv. Haer.* 1,9,4." *Vigiliae Christianae* 21 (1967): 25–34.

Wüst, Ernst. S.v. "Penelope." Pauly-Wissowa. *Real-Encyclopädie der classischen Altertumswissenschaft*, 19.460–93.

Zeegers-Vander Vorst, Nicole. *Les Citations des poètes grecs chez les apologistes chrétiens du IIe siècle*. Recueil de travaux d'histoire et de philologie 4.47. Louvain: Bibliothèque de l'Université, 1972.

Index